T0212972

Lecture Notes in Computer Science   10496

Commenced Publication in 1973
Founding and Former Series Editors:
Gerhard Goos, Juris Hartmanis, and Jan van Leeuwen

More information about this series at http://www.springer.com/series/7412

Volker Roth · Thomas Vetter (Eds.)

Pattern Recognition

39th German Conference, GCPR 2017
Basel, Switzerland, September 12–15, 2017
Proceedings

 Springer

Editors
Volker Roth
University of Basel
Basel
Switzerland

Thomas Vetter
University of Basel
Basel
Switzerland

ISSN 0302-9743   ISSN 1611-3349   (electronic)
Lecture Notes in Computer Science
ISBN 978-3-319-66708-9   ISBN 978-3-319-66709-6   (eBook)
DOI 10.1007/978-3-319-66709-6

Library of Congress Control Number: 2017941496

LNCS Sublibrary: SL6 – Image Processing, Computer Vision, Pattern Recognition, and Graphics

Printed on acid-free paper

This Springer imprint is published by Springer Nature
The registered company is Springer International Publishing AG
The registered company address is: Gewerbestrasse 11, 6330 Cham, Switzerland

Preface

It was an honor and a pleasure to organize the 39th German Conference on Pattern Recognition (GCPR) in Basel during September 12–15, 2017. This year's call for papers resulted in 60 submissions. Each paper underwent a rigorous double-blind reviewing procedure by typically three Program Committee (PC) members. Afterwards, one of the involved PC members served as moderator for a discussion among the reviewers and prepared a consolidation report that was also forwarded to the authors in addition to the reviewers. The final decision was made during a PC meeting held in Basel based on all reviews, discussions, and, if necessary, additional reviewing. As a result of this reviewing procedure, 33 submissions were accepted. The organizers selected 16 papers for oral presentation in a single-track program and 17 for poster presentation. In accordance with the conference tradition, we organized a Young Researchers Forum to promote scientific interaction between outstanding young researchers and our community.

The accepted papers cover the entire spectrum of pattern recognition, machine learning, image processing, and computer vision. We thank all authors for their submissions to GCPR 2017 and all reviewers for their valuable assessment. In addition to the presentations from the technical program we were also happy to welcome three internationally renowned researchers as our invited speakers to give a keynote lecture at GCPR 2017: Marcello Pelillo (Ca' Foscari University of Venice, Italy), Pietro Perona (California Institute of Technology, Pasadena, USA), and Kilian Q. Weinberger (Cornell University, Ithaca, USA). The technical program was complemented by a workshop on New Challenges in Neural Computation and by two tutorial sessions: one on Interpretable Machine Learning and one on Medical Image Analysis.

The success of GCPR 2017 would not have been possible without the support of many institutions and people. We would like to thank MVTec Software GmbH, Adobe, the University of Basel, Kanton Basel-Stadt, and DAGM (Deutsche Arbeitsgemeinschaft für Mustererkennung e.V.) for their sponsorship. Special thanks go to the members of the Technical Support and the Local Organizing Committee. Finally, we are grateful to Springer for giving us the opportunity of continuing to publish GCPR proceedings in the LNCS series.

This year's conference city, Basel, is located where the Swiss, French, and German borders meet. Almost 40 museums make Basel the city with the highest density of museums in the country. Founded in 1460, the University of Basel is the oldest university in Switzerland and has a history of success going back over 550 years. As one of the most dynamic and productive economic regions in Europe, Basel is a key location for the life-sciences industry. However, Basel is also a very green city, with several parks, the botanical gardens, the banks of the Rhine, and its famous zoo.

July 2017

Volker Roth
Thomas Vetter

Organization

Conference Committee

Conference Chairs

Volker Roth   University of Basel, Switzerland
Thomas Vetter   University of Basel, Switzerland

Program Committee

Andreas Dengel   Technical University of Kaiserslautern, Germany
Andreas Geiger   MPI for Intelligent Systems, Germany
Andreas Maier   University of Erlangen-Nürnberg, Germany
Andres Bruhn   University of Stuttgart, Germany
Angela Yao   University of Bonn, Germany
Arjan Kuijper   Frauenhofer IGD, Germany
Bastian Leibe   RWTH Aachen University, Germany
Bastian Goldlücke   University of Konstanz, Germany
Bernhard Rinner   University of Klagenfurt, Austria
Bernt Schiele   MPI for Informatics, Germany
Björn Schuller   University of Passau, Germany
Björn Menze   Technical University of Munich, Germany
Björn Ommer   University of Heidelberg, Germany
Bodo Rosenhahn   University of Hanover, Germany
Boris Flach   Technical University of Prague, Czech Republic
Carsten Rother   Technical University of Dresden, Germany
Carsten Steger   MVTec Software GmbH, Germany
Christian Theobalt   MPI for Informatics Saarbrücken, Germany
Christian Riess   University of Erlangen-Nürnberg, Germany
Christian Bauckhage   Fraunhofer IAIS, Germany
Christian Heipke   University of Hanover, Germany
Christoph Schnörr   University of Heidelberg, Germany
Csaba Beleznai   Austrian Institute of Technology, Austria
Daniel Cremers   Technical University of Munich, Germany
Daniel Scharstein   Middlebury College, VT, USA
Dietrich Paulus   University of Koblenz-Landau, Germany
Fred Hamprecht   University of Heidelberg, Germany
Gerhard Rigoll   Technical University of Munich, Germany
Gernot Fink   Technical University of Dortmund, Germany
Hanno Scharr   Jülich Research Centre, Germany
Helmut Mayer   Bundeswehr University Munich, Germany
Horst Bischof   Graz University of Technology, Austria

Jan-Michael Frahm	University of North Carolina, USA
Joachim Buhmann	ETH Zurich, Switzerland
Joachim Denzler	University of Jena, Germany
Joachim Weickert	Saarland University, Germany
Josef Pauli	University of Duisburg-Essen, Germany
Julia Vogt	University of Konstanz, Germany
Jürgen Gall	University of Bonn, Germany
Justus Piater	University of Innsbruck, Austria
Karsten Borgwardt	ETH Zurich, Switzerland
Klaus Tönnies	University of Magdeburg, Germany
Konrad Schindler	ETH Zurich, Switzerland
Laura Leal-Taixé	Technical University of Munich, Germany
Lorenzo Rosasco	University of Genoa, Italy
Marcello Pelillo	University of Venice, Italy
Marco Loog	Delft University of Technology, The Netherlands
Margrit Gelautz	Technical University of Vienna, Austria
Mario Fritz	MPI for Informatics, Germany
Martin Welk	UMIT Hall, Austria
Matthias Hein	Saarland University, Germany
Michael Goesele	Technical University of Darmstadt, Germany
Monika Sester	University of Hanover, Germany
Olaf Ronneberger	University of Freiburg, Germany
Olaf Hellwich	Technical University of Berlin, Germany
Paolo Favaro	University of Bern, Switzerland
Peter Gehler	MPI Intelligent Systems, Germany
Philipp Hennig	MPI Intelligent Systems, Germany
Philippe Cattin	University of Basel, Switzerland
Rainer Stiefelhagen	Karlsruhe Institute of Technology, Germany
Reinhard Klette	Auckland University of Technology, New Zealand
Reinhard Koch	University of Kiel, Germany
Rudolf Mester	University of Frankfurt, Germany
Slobodan Iliic	Technical University of Munich, Germany
Stefan Roth	Technical University of Darmstadt, Germany
Stefan Steidl	University of Erlangen-Nürnberg, Germany
Thomas Pock	Graz University of Technology, Austria
Thomas Fuchs	Memorial Sloan Kettering Cancer Center, New York, USA
Thomas Brox	University of Freiburg, Germany
Ullrich Köthe	University of Heidelberg, Germany
Uwe Franke	Daimler AG, Germany
Vaclav Hlavac	Czech Technical University Prague, Czech Republic
Walter Kropatsch	Technical University of Vienna, Austria
Wilhelm Burger	University of Applied Sciences Upper Austria, Austria
Wolfang Förstner	University of Bonn, Germany
Xiaoyi Jiang	Münster University, Germany

Technical Support, Conference Management System

Bas Kin   University of Basel, Switzerland
Mario Wieser   University of Basel, Switzerland
Sebastian Keller   University of Basel, Switzerland

Local Organizing Committee

Ruth Steinmann   University of Basel, Switzerland
Antonia Bertschinger   University of Basel, Switzerland
Patricia Krattiger   University of Basel, Switzerland

Sponsoring Institutions

MVTec Software GmbH, Munich, Germany
Adobe, Switzerland
University of Basel, Switzerland
Kanton Basel-Stadt, Switzerland
DAGM Deutsche Arbeitsgemeinschaft für Mustererkennung e.V., Germany

Awards 2016

German Pattern Recognition Award

The **Deutscher Mustererkennungspreis 2016** was awarded to Sebastian Nowozin for his outstanding work on Inference in Structured Probabilistic Models with Applications to Computer Vision.

DAGM MVTec Award

The **DAGM MVTec Award 2016** was awarded to Christoph Vogel for his dissertation on Robust and Accurate 3D Motion Estimation under Adverse Conditions.

GCPR Awards 2016

The **GCPR Best Paper Award 2016** was awarded to David Hafner, Peter Ochs, Joachim Weickert, Martin Reißel, and Sven Grewenig for the paper FSI Schemes: Fast Semi-iterative Solvers for PDEs and Optimization Methods.

GCPR 2016 Honorable Mentions

Jonas Uhrig, Marius Cordts, Uwe Franke, and Thomas Brox: Pixel-Level Encoding and Depth Layering for Instance-Level Semantic Segmentation.
Manuel Ruder, Alexey Dosovitskiy and Thomas Brox: Artistic Style Transfer for Videos.

Contents

Machine Learning and Pattern Recognition

Tracking

Biomedical Image Processing
and Analysis

A Quantitative Assessment of Image Normalization for Classifying Histopathological Tissue of the Kidney

Michael Gadermayr[1]([✉]), Sean Steven Cooper[1], Barbara Klinkhammer[2], Peter Boor[2], and Dorit Merhof[1]

[1] Aachen Center for Biomedical Image Analysis, Visualization and Exploration (ACTIVE), Institute of Imaging and Computer Vision, RWTH Aachen University, Aachen, Germany
Michael.Gadermayr@lfb.rwth-aachen.de
[2] Institute of Pathology, University Hospital Aachen, RWTH Aachen University, Aachen, Germany

Abstract. The advancing pervasion of digital pathology in research and clinical practice results in a strong need for image analysis techniques in the field of histopathology. Due to diverse reasons, histopathological imaging generally exhibits a high degree of variability. As automated segmentation approaches are known to be vulnerable, especially to unseen variability, we investigate several stain normalization methods to compensate for variations between different whole slide images. In a large experimental study, we investigate all combinations of five image normalization (not only stain normalization) methods as well as five image representations with respect to the classification performance in two application scenarios in kidney histopathology. Finally, we also pose the question, if color normalization is sufficient to compensate for the changed properties between whole slide images in an application scenario with few training data.

1 Introduction

Digital pathology is an emerging field requiring automated methods for processing huge amounts of image data. From a medical point of view, manifold problems have been identified and addressed by the image processing community in the recent past. Especially, high effort has been directed towards detecting and segmenting certain regions of interest, such as cells [1], nuclei [2], gland [3], mitosis [4] as well as renal glomeruli [5]. Mostly, the results of a detection or a segmentation are furthermore utilized as markers for histopathological research or clinical practice.

However, variations, such as different staining intensity and thickness of the slices as well as pathological modifications lead to qualitative differences between whole slide images (Fig. 1), even if all images show kidneys stained with the same dye and originating from the same scanner. As these variations have effects on color, texture and morphology [6], they can reduce the generalization ability of

© Springer International Publishing AG 2017
V. Roth and T. Vetter (Eds.): GCPR 2017, LNCS 10496, pp. 3–13, 2017.
DOI: 10.1007/978-3-319-66709-6_1

a classifier trained on images showing characteristics varying from the characteristics of the image to be evaluated.

The compensation of variability in texture (e.g. due to pathologies) cannot be performed easily in the image domain (and is not considered throughout this work). If changes in tissue texture should be justified, a normalization on feature level is typically performed. For this purpose, domain adaptation approaches [7] can be applied.

The differences in staining intensities on the other hand can be corrected effectively by means of stain-normalization methods [8]. However, it is not clear, if normalization generating a perceptual similarity over slides is advantageous for computer-based classification, because texture feature extraction methods, for example, are often designed to be robust to illumination changes [9]. Nevertheless, image descriptors containing specific color information (color features) are expected to profit from a compensation of the variability. Another question is, if domain specific normalization methods (stain normalization approaches [8,10]) which are optimized with respect to perceptual similarity are more appropriate than general purpose normalization approaches [11].

In this work, the focus is on investigating different stain-normalization methods with respect to tissue classification approaches. Although many approaches for stain-normalization were proposed [8,10,12], there is a lack of a quantitative assessment with respect to automated image analysis systems. In [13], a study on the impact of stain normalization on the classification performance with focus on a specific application has been conducted. However, the focus of this work was on two similar, domain specific normalization methods only.

Here, we perform experimentation with five normalization methods, six feature extraction approaches, two differently stained histopathological data sets from renal pathology and two different experimental settings. We investigate (1) if normalization is generally advantageous for tissue classification, (2) which normalization method is most appropriate and (3) the interplay between the normalization method and the image representation. Finally, we also pose the question (4), whether stain normalization is sufficient in settings with few training samples covering a low variability.

The rest of this paper is organized as follows. In Sect. 2, the medical background is outlined. Section 3 provides details of the study design. The results are presenting in Sect. 4 and discussed in Sect. 5. Finally, Sect. 6 concludes this paper.

2   Medical Background

In this work, the aim is to classify tissue from mouse kidneys. Specifically, the focus is on determining if the tissue is extracted from renal glomeruli or from other renal tissue which is the most relevant differentiation in renal pathology.

In the mammalian kidney, a glomerulus is the first segment of a nephron, a functional unit of the kidney. It consists of a tuft of small blood vessels, where

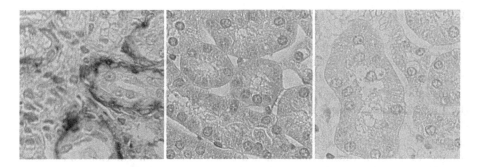

Fig. 1. Inter-slide variability between whole slide images stained with α-SMA

blood is filtered and urine is produced. Several kidney diseases affect and damage the glomeruli, which results in a loss of the vital filter function. The diagnosis, and thereby also the decision on adequate treatment is currently based on biopsies. There is a strong research focus on renal diseases and specifically on the analysis of glomerular damage. In research as well as clinical practice, the identification of the glomeruli is a mandatory first step in histopathological analysis. Since such manual assessment is extremely time consuming, a computer-aided detection would facilitate research and clinical practice.

We study the differentiation between glomerulus and non-glomerulus tissue in combination with the alpha smooth muscle actin (αSMA) staining as well as with the periodic acid schiff (PAS) staining (Fig. 2).

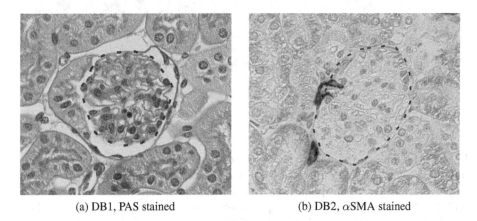

(a) DB1, PAS stained   (b) DB2, αSMA stained

Fig. 2. Example glomeruli in a whole slide image stained with αSMA and PAS. The dashed contours indicates the outline of the glomeruli.

3   Experimental Study

In this study, we investigate two similar classification scenarios from a pathologist's perspective. In both application scenarios, the aim is to classify tissue from mouse kidneys as outlined in Sect. 2.

In data set one (DS1), we study this differentiation in combination with the PAS staining, whereas in data set two (DS2), we study the αSMA staining (Fig. 3). Although from a pathologist's perspective the problem is quite similar, from an image processing perspective it is definitely not. Whereas the PAS stained data can be mostly distinguished based on color-information, in the case of αSMA, color information is less informative for discrimination of tissue and texture thereby becomes more relevant. The similarities considering the general application on the one hand and the dissimilarities from an image processing perspective on the other hand provide incentive for studying these two data sets in combination with different stain normalization methods as well as varying image representations.

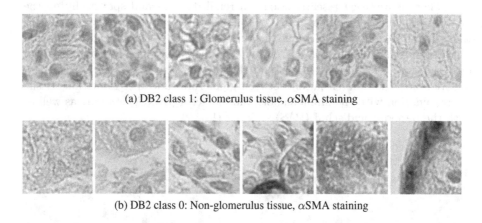

(a) DB2 class 1: Glomerulus tissue, αSMA staining

(b) DB2 class 0: Non-glomerulus tissue, αSMA staining

Fig. 3. Example patches of DS2, individually for the two classes.

3.1   Image Representations

In our experiments, the focus is on the traditional classification pipeline consisting of a separate image representation and a classification model. We consider this scenario only, as deep-learning based methods require large training data and, furthermore, training the deep models is computationally expensive. For this large study, we train 10,000 classification models (8 (whole slide images) × 50 (random splits) × 5 (image representations) × 5 (normalization methods)) and need to cope with limited training data. Additionally, by investigating diverse image representations with clear properties, more insight can be gained.

Specifically, the following five conceptually different feature extraction methods are investigated consisting of two texture features (1–2), two color features (3–4) and a convolutional neural network representation (5):

1. Fisher Vectors (FV) [14]: Improved Fisher vectors are utilized based on a dense SIFT [15] sampling at each second coordinate in the patches. As the classification task consists of two classes only, a Gaussian mixture model consisting of 16 components is trained [7].
2. Local Binary Patterns (LBP) [9]: A multi-resolution LBP version, with an eight sample neighborhood and a radius (distance between center point and neighboring points) of one and two pixels is deployed.
3. Lab-Color Histogram (HLAB) [16]: For this method, the image is converted to the CIELAB color space and for each channel, a histogram (binning: 16, linear space) is computed and finally these histograms are concatenated.
4. RGB-Color Histogram (HRGB) [5]: For this method, a histogram (binning: 16, linear space) is computed for each color channel in the RGB color space and finally these three histograms are concatenated building a 48-dimensional image representation.
5. Convolutional Neural Network (CNN) [17]: For this method, a convolutional neural network pre-trained on the ImageNet challenge data (http://www.image-net.org/challenges/LSVRC/), specifically the VGG-f net [17] is utilized. The images are fed through the CNN and the outputs of the first fully connected layer are extracted as feature vectors. We do not further train the net to avoid any bias due to the training data.

3.2 Stain Normalization Methods

We investigate five different methods to align the color properties of the whole slide images. Apart from typical methods developed for compensating stain variability in histopathology [8,10], we investigate methods not typically applied to whole slide images for stain normalization. Such methods are investigated because it is not clear if perceptual similarity or a perceptually high quality of whole slide images leads to high accuracies in classification. The following established normalization methods are investigated in this study:

- Stain-Normalization of Reinhard et al. (SR) [10]: This method relies on matching the color distribution of an image to that of a target image by using a linear transform in a certain perceptual colorspace, specifically the $l\alpha\beta$ color space. The aim is to adjust the mean values as well as the standard deviations of each channel in the two images in the this color space.
- Stain-Normalization of Marcenko et al. (SM) [8]: In this approach, the stains are separated first, by means of a so-called stain deconvolution, then normalized, separately for each stain and finally combined.
- Gray World (GW) [11]: Gray world is a simple general purpose normalization method assuming that the average of all pixel values is a neutral gray.
- Histogram Equalization (EQ): HE applies a monotonic mapping to each pixel (separately for each color channel) in a way that the obtained distribution becomes approximately evenly distributed.
- Histogram Normalization (NO): In case of HN, min-max-normalization is applied for each color channel to normalize the image.

Examples images for each normalization method including the original image (OR) are shown in Fig. 4.

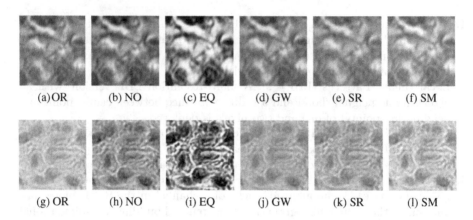

(a)OR   (b) NO   (c) EQ   (d) GW   (e) SR   (f) SM

(g) OR   (h) NO   (i) EQ   (j) GW   (k) SR   (l) SM

Fig. 4. Example PAS (a)–(f) (DS1) and αSMA patches (g)–(l) (DS2) processed with the normalization methods. Whereas the stain normalization approaches (SR, SM) provide a perceptually consistent normalization, especially the EQ method produces highly artificial images.

3.3   Evaluation Protocol

For evaluation purposes, we consider the classification of image patches extracted from whole slide images. The patch size was fixed to 128×128 pixels [5]. The patches are either extracted in regions completely showing tissue of a renal glomerulus or in regions showing exclusively other tissue. For the experiments, for each whole slide image, 200 patches for both classes are extracted. In case of αSMA, five whole slide images are considered and in case of PAS, three whole slide images are utilized showing typical variability. For each configuration considering a certain normalization, a certain image representation and a data set, we perform two experiments:

Experiment 1 (E1). We compute the accuracy for training with 80% of the patches (for each class) and evaluation with 20% of the image patches, all originating from the same whole slide image. Training and evaluation is repeated 50 times with random selections of the data for training and evaluation and finally only the mean is reported. This strategy is applied to each whole slide image and both data sets. Finally, the mean accuracy per staining is reported. This scenario is not practically relevant but required for studying the effects of normalization. Thereby, we obtain a measure if normalization destroys distinctive features in an idealistic scenario without stain-variability.

Experiment 2 (E2). In the second experiment, we perform a similar strategy with the same amount of training and evaluation data, but training and evaluation is performed on different whole slide images. Thereby, we obtain six combinations (i.e. results) in case of the PAS staining with three whole slide images, and 20 combinations in case of the αSMA data set. Again, 50 random splits are applied and finally, the mean over all splits and the combinations per staining are reported.

Evaluation Details. For classification, a linear support vector machine (LIB-LINEAR) is utilized as in previous work on renal tissue classification [5]. Due to the balanced setting for training and evaluation, the reported accuracies are balanced (i.e. guessing on average leads to an accuracy of 50%). To determine whether two settings are significantly different, the signed rank-sum test is applied with significance level $\alpha = 0.05$. All experiments are implemented in MATLAB 2016b. For image normalization, the stain normalization toolbox [18] is applied. For feature extraction, MatConvNet [19] and VLFeat [20] are utilized.

4   Results

In Fig. 5, the mean overall classification rates (accuracies) are shown individually for each combination of an image representation (horizontal axis) and an image normalization technique (vertical axis).

Figure 5(a) and (b) show the accuracies obtained by the intra-slide experiment E1 for the two data sets. CNN and LBP exhibit high accuracies independent of the underlying image normalization method. The features focusing on color (HRGB, HLAB) significantly lose distinctiveness with certain normalizations, such as NO and EQ, but also with the domain specific stain normalizations SM and SR. This effect is observed generally, but it is more distinct in case of DS1, that generally exhibits lower rates. EQ in combination with HRGB leads to the weakest accuracies, which is because EQ removes all information which is captured by the HRGB feature. Therefore, this combination is no longer considered in the following.

Considering the inter-slide experiment E2 (Fig. 5(c) and (d)), we notice that the accuracies are generally lower, as expected due to the shift in image properties. Not only color-based features, but in general all combinations lose distinctiveness (the accuracy differences are shown in Fig. 5(e) and (f)). We notice that there is not one single stain normalization method which leads to best rates in general. With LBP, FV (with both data sets), HLAB (with DS2) and CNN (with DS1), the best results are achieved in combination with EQ. In case of LBP, FV, HLAB (DS2) and CNN (DS2) the improvements compared to OR are statistically significant ($\alpha = 0.05$). Considering the different image representations, we notice that CNNs exhibit the best rates on average and are outperformed only in isolated cases.

The domain specific stain normalization methods (SM, SR) on average do not outperform the non-specific methods EQ and NO. Best outcomes with one of the specific techniques are obtained only once if combining SR with the HRGB feature.

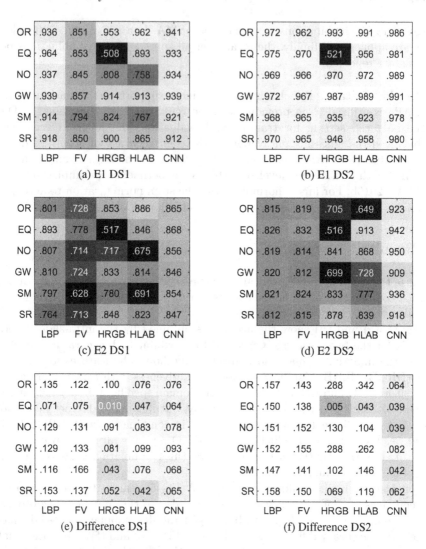

Fig. 5. This figure shows the mean overall classification rates, individually for each combination of an image representation (horizontal axis) and an image normalization technique (vertical axis). It can be differentiated between the two data sets (DS1, DS2) and the intra- (E1) and the inter-slide experiment (E2).

5   Discussion

In this work, we investigated the interplay between stain-normalization and automated tissue classification approaches in two histopathological applications.

Applying stain normalization in the experiment with similar staining properties (E1), we notice that especially color features strongly lose distinctiveness whereas other representations (LBP, CNN) are in general only marginally affected. For these representations (e.g. CNN), stain normalization methods at least do not destroy significant distinctive information which is an important criterion for real application scenarios. Interestingly, the non-specific normalization methods perform best in this setting. This scenario is specifically important because with increasing training data, showing staining characteristics similar to the evaluation data, the classification model can learn to tackle the variability. However, if the normalization method would remove discriminative information, this cannot be compensated.

Considering experiment E2, we observed that even in case of normalized color information, a distinct loss in accuracy occurs in each configuration. We notice that even domain specific normalization methods are in general unable to compensate for the change in image properties in the inter-slide experiment. Contrarily, the rather simple and non-domain-specific EQ technique leads to the best outcomes on average. Considering different image representations, we notice that CNN exhibits the highest rates independent of the normalization method.

Collecting the experimental results of E1 and E2, we summarize that CNN in combination with EQ and NO not only provides the best performances in the more realistic E2 setting. By considering the low loss of discriminative power (E1: EQ and NO compared to OR), indication is provided that in case of larger training corpi, these combinations still produce the best outcomes.

If looking at the accuracy-differences in case of image normalization (Fig. 5(e) and (f)), we need to highlight that the change in (distinctive) image properties between different whole slide images is obviously not limited to variations in color intensity. The benefit obtained with normalization is in most cases distinctly lower than the loss between the two experiments with normalization, providing evidence for further image specific changes between the whole slide images. Based on the high loss between the experiments with LBP, we assume that staining variability also leads to changes in micro-texture, which cannot be compensated by pixelwise color normalization. Finally, difficulties can arise due to inter-patient variability.

Based on this experimental evaluation, it can be observed that there is no strong correspondence between perceptual correctness and the classification performance as methods developed to provide perceptually "correct" images (SM, SR) do not show the best accuracies. In future, learning based methods, such as autoencoders, could be applied to obtain normalized images, optimized with respect to distinctiveness for classification or segmentation scenarios. By such methods the correction could furthermore be performed patch- instead of pixelwise to possibly facilitate a micro-texture correction and, furthermore, a normalization of patient specific properties.

6   Conclusion

Finally, we conclude that image normalization should be considered especially for applications with relatively small training data. In our experiments, domain-specific methods do not outperform other basic techniques. The best performances are obtained with the CNN feature and general purpose normalization techniques (NO, EQ) and even with increasing training data, it can be expected that these methods perform best. As the domain shift between slides cannot be compensated completely by means of the normalization methods, we suggest applying further approaches such as data augmentation and domain adaptation. Finally, image normalization could be performed in a domain specific way (e.g. by means of auto-encoders) to obtain a normalization which optimizes the distinctiveness of patches, instead of the visual similarity.

Acknowledgments. This work was supported by the German Research Foundation (DFG), grant no. ME3737/3-1.

References

1. Akram, S.U., Kannala, J., Eklund, L., Heikkilä, J.: Cell segmentation proposal network for microscopy image analysis. In: Carneiro, G., Mateus, D., Peter, L., Bradley, A., Tavares, J.M.R.S., Belagiannis, V., Papa, J.P., Nascimento, J.C., Loog, M., Lu, Z., Cardoso, J.S., Cornebise, J. (eds.) LABELS/DLMIA -2016. LNCS, vol. 10008, pp. 21–29. Springer, Cham (2016). doi:10.1007/978-3-319-46976-8_3
2. Wang, S., Yao, J., Xu, Z., Huang, J.: Subtype cell detection with an accelerated deep convolution neural network. In: Ourselin, S., Joskowicz, L., Sabuncu, M.R., Unal, G., Wells, W. (eds.) MICCAI 2016. LNCS, vol. 9901, pp. 640–648. Springer, Cham (2016). doi:10.1007/978-3-319-46723-8_74
3. BenTaieb, A., Hamarneh, G.: Topology aware fully convolutional networks for histology gland segmentation. In: Ourselin, S., Joskowicz, L., Sabuncu, M.R., Unal, G., Wells, W. (eds.) MICCAI 2016. LNCS, vol. 9901, pp. 460–468. Springer, Cham (2016). doi:10.1007/978-3-319-46723-8_53
4. Cireşan, D.C., Giusti, A., Gambardella, L.M., Schmidhuber, J.: Mitosis detection in breast cancer histology images with deep neural networks. In: Mori, K., Sakuma, I., Sato, Y., Barillot, C., Navab, N. (eds.) MICCAI 2013. LNCS, vol. 8150, pp. 411–418. Springer, Heidelberg (2013). doi:10.1007/978-3-642-40763-5_51
5. Gadermayr, M., Klinkhammer, B.M., Boor, P., Merhof, D.: Do we need large annotated training data for detection applications in biomedical imaging? A case study in Renal Glomeruli detection. In: Wang, L., Adeli, E., Wang, Q., Shi, Y., Suk, H.-I. (eds.) MLMI 2016. LNCS, vol. 10019, pp. 18–26. Springer, Cham (2016). doi:10. 1007/978-3-319-47157-0_3
6. Fioretto, P., Mauer, M.: Histopathology of diabetic nephropathy. Semin. Nephrol. **27**(2), 195–207 (2007)
7. Gadermayr, M., Strauch, M., Klinkhammer, B.M., Djudjaj, S., Boor, P., Merhof, D.: Domain adaptive classification for compensating variability in histopathological whole slide images. In: Campilho, A., Karray, F. (eds.) ICIAR 2016. LNCS, vol. 9730, pp. 616–622. Springer, Cham (2016). doi:10.1007/978-3-319-41501-7_69
8. Macenko, M., Niethammer, M., Marron, J.S., Borland, D., Woosley, J.T., Guan, X., Schmitt, C., Thomas, N.E.: A method for normalizing histology slides for quantitative analysis. In: Proceedings of the IEEE International Symposium on Biomedical Imaging: From Nano to Macro (ISBI 2009), pp. 1107–1110 (2009)
9. Ojala, T., Pietikäinen, M., Mäenpää, T.: Multiresolution gray-scale and rotation invariant texture classification with local binary patterns. IEEE Trans. Pattern Anal. Mach. Intell. (TPAMI) **24**(7), 971–987 (2002)

10. Reinhard, E., Ashikhmin, M., Gooch, B., Shirley, P.: Color transfer between images. IEEE Comput. Graph. Appl. **21**(5), 34–41 (2001)
11. Finlayson, G.D., Schiele, B., Crowley, J.L.: Comprehensive colour image normalization. In: Burkhardt, H., Neumann, B. (eds.) ECCV 1998. LNCS, vol. 1406, pp. 475–490. Springer, Heidelberg (1998). doi:10.1007/BFb0055685
12. McCann, M.T., Majumdar, J., Peng, C., Castro, C.A., Kovacevic, J.: Algorithm and benchmark dataset for stain separation in histology images. In: Proceedings of the IEEE International Conference on Image Processing (ICIP 2014), October 2014
13. Sethi, A., Sha, L., Vahadane, A., Deaton, R., Kumar, N., Macias, V., Gann, P.: Empirical comparison of color normalization methods for epithelial-stromal classification in h and e images. J. Pathol. Inform. **7**(1), 17 (2016)
14. Sánchez, J., Perronnin, F., Mensink, T., Verbeek, J.J.: Image classification with the fisher vector: theory and practice. Int. J. Comput. Vis. (IJCV 2013) **105**(3), 222–245 (2013)
15. Lowe, D.G.: Object recognition from local scale-invariant features. In: Proceedings of the Seventh IEEE International Conference on Computer Vision (CVPR 1999), vol. 2, pp. 1150–1157. IEEE (1999)
16. Herve, N., Servais, A., Thervet, E., Olivo-Marin, J.C., Meas-Yedid, V.: Statistical color texture descriptors for histological images analysis. In: Proceedings of the IEEE International Symposium on Biomedical Imaging: From Nano to Macro (ISBI 2011), pp. 724–727 (2011)
17. Chatfield, K., Simonyan, K., Vedaldi, A., Zisserman, A.: Return of the devil in the details: delving deep into convolutional nets. In: Proceedings of the British Machine Vision Conference (BMVC 2014) (2014)
18. Khan, A.M., Rajpoot, N., Treanor, D., Magee, D.: A nonlinear mapping approach to stain normalization in digital histopathology images using image-specific color deconvolution. IEEE Trans. Biomed. Eng. **61**(6), 1729–1738 (2014)
19. Vedaldi, A., Lenc, K.: Matconvnet - convolutional neural networks for matlab. In: Proceeding of the ACM International Conference on Multimedia (2015)
20. Vedaldi, A., Fulkerson, B.: VLFeat: an open and portable library of computer vision algorithms (2008). http://www.vlfeat.org/

Classification and Detection

Deep Learning for Vanishing Point Detection Using an Inverse Gnomonic Projection

Florian Kluger[1(✉)], Hanno Ackermann[1(✉)], Michael Ying Yang[2],
and Bodo Rosenhahn[1]

[1] Leibniz Universität Hannover, Hanover, Germany
{kluger,ackermann}@tnt.uni-hannover.de
[2] University of Twente, Enschede, The Netherlands

Abstract. We present a novel approach for vanishing point detection from uncalibrated monocular images. In contrast to state-of-the-art, we make no a priori assumptions about the observed scene. Our method is based on a convolutional neural network (CNN) which does not use natural images, but a Gaussian sphere representation arising from an inverse gnomonic projection of lines detected in an image. This allows us to rely on synthetic data for training, eliminating the need for labelled images. Our method achieves competitive performance on three horizon estimation benchmark datasets. We further highlight some additional use cases for which our vanishing point detection algorithm can be used.

1 Introduction

Vanishing points (VPs) are strong cognitive cues for the human visual perception, as they provide characteristic information about the geometry of a scene, and are used as a feature for relative depth and height estimation [23]. Their detection is a fundamental problem in the field of computer vision, because it underpins various higher-level tasks, including camera calibration [12,15,25], 3D metrology [8], 3D scene structure analysis [13], as well as many others. A vanishing point arises from a set of parallel lines as their point of intersection, at an infinite location initially, and is uniquely defined by the lines' direction. Under a projective transformation, parallel lines in space may be transformed to converging lines on an image plane, thus leading to a finite intersection point. The detection of VPs in perspective images is therefore a search for converging lines and their intersections, which is difficult in the presence of noise, spurious line segments, near-parallel imaged lines, and intersections of non-converging lines. These reasons make vanishing point detection a hard problem. Consequently, it has not been addressed often in the past years.

1.1 Related Work

Since the seminal work of Barnard [4], various methods designed to tackle this problem have been proposed. Some of them [15,20,22,25] rely on the Manhattan-world assumption [7], which means that only three mutually orthogonal vanishing directions exist in a scene, as is reasonably common in urban scenes where

© Springer International Publishing AG 2017
V. Roth and T. Vetter (Eds.): GCPR 2017, LNCS 10496, pp. 17–28, 2017.
DOI: 10.1007/978-3-319-66709-6_2

buildings are aligned on a rectangular grid. Others [3,18,21,27,28] rely on the less rigid Atlanta-world assumption [21], which allows multiple non-orthogonal vanishing directions that are connected by a common horizon line, and are all orthogonal to a single zenith. Few works [1,2,24] – including ours – make no such assumptions. Most methods are based on oriented elements – either line segments [15,18,20,25,27] or edges [3,21,22] – from which VPs are estimated, usually by grouping the oriented elements into clusters [15,18,22,25,27], or by fitting a more comprehensive model [2,3,24]. It is common to refine the thereby detected vanishing points in an iterative process, such as the Expectation Maximisation (EM) algorithm [15,22,25,27,28] which we are utilising as well.

Ever since the AlexNet by Krizhevsky et al. [16] succeeded in the 2012 ImageNet competition, convolutional neural networks (CNNs) [17] have become a popular tool for computer vision tasks, as they perform exceedingly well in a variety of settings. Borji [6] recently demonstrated a CNN based approach for vanishing point detection; however, it only detects up to one horizontal vanishing point. The approach of Zhai et al. [28] is much more comprehensive. It is based on a CNN which extracts prior information about the horizon line location from an image, and currently achieves the best state-of-the-art performance on horizon line detection benchmarks commonly used to evaluate vanishing point detection algorithms.

Unlike other methods, their approach begins by selecting horizon line candidates first, and then jointly scores horizon candidates and horizontal VP candidates, which are eventually refined in an EM-like process. As it is based on horizon lines, their approach is inherently limited to Atlanta-world scenes.

Contributions. In this work, we propose a more generalised approach using a CNN which does not operate on natural images, but on a more abstract presentation of the scene based on the Gaussian sphere representation of points and lines [4]. It is identical to an inverse gnomonic projection, which – very similar to an inverse stereographic projection – is a mapping that transforms the unbounded image plane onto a bounded space, thus making vanishing points far from the image centre easier to handle. While this necessitates an additional preprocessing step, it allows us to train the CNN solely using synthetic data, which we generate in a very straightforward manner, thus eliminating the need for labelled real-world data. The use of the CNN is motivated by the fact that spurious, yet significant VP candidates can occur (cf. Fig. 4), thus approaches based on voting are prone to fail. The advantage of using a CNN over, for instance, a support vector machine is that discriminative features are automatically learned. Our CNN is able to directly estimate VP candidates on the Gaussian sphere, which are then refined with an EM-like algorithm. We furthermore devised an improved line weighting scheme for the EM process, which imposes a spatial consistency prior over the line-to-vanishing-point associations in order to become more robust in the presence of noise and clutter. This is motivated by the fact that spurious lines, for instance caused by plants or shadows, are often spatially

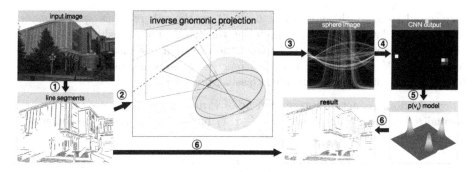

Fig. 1. Algorithm pipeline: (1) extract line segments; (2) map lines onto Gaussian sphere with inverse gnomonic projection (Sect. 2.1); (3) render image of half-sphere surface (Sect. 2.1); (4) compute CNN (Sect. 2.2) forward pass; (5) estimate a mixture of Gaussian distribution after CNN output (Sect. 2.4); (6) compute refined vanishing points and visualise line association (Sect. 2.4).

correlated. Combined with a line segment extractor as a preprocessing step, our method allows vanishing point estimation from real-world images with competitive accuracy.

2 Approach

Our approach consists of the following stages: First, line segments are extracted from the input image using the LSD line detector [11]. The lines are then mapped onto the Gaussian sphere, and its image is rendered (Sect. 2.1). This image is used as the input for a CNN (Sect. 2.2) which we trained solely on synthetic data (Sect. 2.3). This CNN then provides a coarse prediction of possible VP locations, which are ultimately refined in an Expectation Maximisation based process (Sect. 2.4).

2.1 Parametrisation

In order to deal with infinite vanishing points, it is reasonable to transform the unbounded image plane onto a bounded space, such as the Gaussian sphere representation, which based on an inverse gnomonic projection of homogeneous points $\mathbf{p} = (p_1, p_2, p_3)^T$ and lines in normal form $\mathbf{l} = (l_1, l_2, l_3)^T$, as described by Barnard [4]:

$$\frac{\mathbf{p}}{\|\mathbf{p}\|_2} = (\sin \alpha \cos \beta, \sin \beta, \cos \alpha \cos \beta)^T \qquad (1)$$

$$\beta(\alpha, \mathbf{l}) = \tan^{-1} \left(\frac{-l_1 \sin \alpha - l_3 \cos \alpha}{l_2} \right) \qquad (2)$$

The lines are projected from the image plane at a fixed distance onto the unit sphere at origin. A square image of the sphere's front half surface is rendered, so that the lines appear as opaque curves, and the image's x, y-coordinates correspond to azimuth and elevation (α, β) on the sphere. This *sphere image* (cf. Fig. 1) is later used as an input for the CNN. The vanishing points are likewise parametrised in the α, β-space, and are then quantised into bins on a regular $N \times N$ grid, so that the occurrence of a vanishing point within those bins can be treated as a multi-label classification task.

Normalisation: As actual images can be of various sizes, image coordinates are normalized to fit within a $(-1, 1) \times (-1, 1)$ border by applying the following, aspect ratio preserving, transformation:

$$\mathsf{H}_{norm} = \frac{1}{s} \begin{pmatrix} 2 & 0 & -w \\ 0 & 2 & -h \\ 0 & 0 & s \end{pmatrix} \tag{3}$$

with h and w being the image's height and width, respectively, and $s = \max(w, h)$.

2.2 Network Architecture

We used the popular AlexNet [16] as a basic architecture for our approach. This network consists of five convolutional layers – some of them extended by max pooling, local response normalisation, or ReLU layers – followed by three fully connected (FC) layers. Originally, its final layer has 1000 output nodes, to which a softmax function is applied, and a multinomial logistic loss function is used for training, as is common for *one-of-many* classification tasks.

While a regression approach may seem well suited for a task such as vanishing point detection from line segments, training CNNs for regression tasks is notoriously difficult. We therefore decided to reformulate it as a multi-label classification task by partitioning the surface of the Gaussian sphere into $N \times N$ patches, as described in Sect. 2.1, and assigning distinct class labels to each patch. In order to suit our task, we modified the last FC layer of the AlexNet to contain N^2 output nodes, and replaced the softmax with a sigmoid function. For training, we use a cross entropy loss function, which is well suited for multi-label classification tasks like this. The output of the network is a likelihood image of possible vanishing points in the given scene.

2.3 Training Data

Since suitable training data for vanishing point detection tasks is scarce, and compiling annotated data on our own would have been very laborious and time consuming, yet large amounts of training data are needed to obtain good results with deep learning, we decided to solely rely on a synthetically created dataset. Since our approach does not actually need natural images as an input, but relies on line segments only, we can create such synthetic data without much effort. To create a set of line segments as a piece of data for training, we proceed as follows: First, the number of vanishing directions $K_d \in [1, 6]$ is chosen. The first three (or less) directions are then chosen randomly, but with the condition that they

Fig. 2. Example from the synthetic training dataset (Sect. 2.3) with four vanishing directions. Different line colours denote different directions, with outlier lines shown in black. *Left:* 3D line segment plot. *Right:* 2D projection. (Color figure online)

must be mutually orthogonal. Additional directions are set as a linear combination of two randomly chosen, previously set directions, thus vanishing directions 4 to 6 do not form an orthogonal system. For each direction, a varying number of line clusters is placed in 3D space. Each cluster consists of a varying number of parallel or collinear line segments in close proximity. Additionally, some *outlier* line segments which are not aligned with any of the vanishing directions are interspersed. This 3D scene is then projected into 2D using a virtual pinhole camera with randomly chosen rotation, translation and focal length. Either uniform or Gaussian noise is added to the resulting 2D line segments, with its strength varying from example to example. These line segments are then finally cropped to fit within a $(-1, 1) \times (-1, 1)$ border. One example is shown in Fig. 2. Using this procedure, we create 96,000 examples for each number of vanishing directions, resulting in a dataset of 576,000 training examples. Each line segment is then converted into a line in normal form, and the true vanishing point for each vanishing direction is computed, so that every datum can be parametrised for CNN training as described in Sect. 2.1.

2.4 Vanishing Point Refinement

As the response of the CNN is rather coarse, a post-processing step is needed to determine the exact vanishing point locations. We decided to utilise a variant of the Expectation Maximisation (EM) algorithm, based on the method described by Košecká and Zhang [15] with additional modifications:

E-step: An affinity measure w_{ik} between a line segment l_i – or its corresponding homogeneous line $\mathbf{l}_i$ – and a vanishing point candidate $\mathbf{v}_k$ is calculated based on the posterior distribution:

$$w_{ik} \propto p(\mathbf{v}_k|\mathbf{l}_i) = \frac{p(\mathbf{l}_i|\mathbf{v}_k)\ p(\mathbf{v}_k)}{p(\mathbf{l}_i)} \tag{4}$$

with $p(\mathbf{l}_i) = \sum_k p(\mathbf{v}_k)p(\mathbf{l}_i|\mathbf{v}_k)$. We assume a likelihood modelled by:

$$p(\mathbf{l}_i|\mathbf{v}_k) \propto \exp\left(\frac{-d_{ik}^2}{2\sigma_k^2}\right) \tag{5}$$

with d_{ik} being a consistency measure between $\mathbf{l}_i$ and $\mathbf{v}_k$.

M-Step: New vanishing point estimates are obtained by solving the following least-squares problem:

$$J(\mathbf{v}_k) = \min_{\mathbf{v}_k} \sum_i w_{ik} d_{ik}^2. \tag{6}$$

Modifications. As in [15], we measure the distance $d_{ik}^{(1)} = \mathbf{l}_i^T \mathbf{v}_k$ on the Gaussian sphere to solve (6), but use an angle-based consistency measure, similar to the suggestions of [9,20], to compute (5), as this yields better accuracy. With $\mathbf{m}_i$ being the midpoint of $\mathbf{l}_i$ and $\mathbf{m}_i \times \mathbf{v}_k$ denoting a cross-product, we define:

$$d_{ik}^{(2)} = 1 - \cos(\angle(\mathbf{l}_i, \mathbf{m}_i \times \mathbf{v}_k)) \tag{7}$$

Departing from [15], we utilise the output of our CNN to estimate the prior $p(\mathbf{v}_k)$ and to initialise the VP candidates, and furthermore propose a modified affinity measure w_{ik} to consider the spatial structure of line segments.

Vanishing Point Prior: We treat the output of the CNN as an approximation of the true probability density distribution for $p(\mathbf{v}_k)$ in the (α, β)-space, which we model as a mixture of Gaussians with N^2 components of standard deviation σ_{prior}. Each component is located at the centre of the corresponding patch on the Gaussian sphere and weighted proportionally to its CNN response. This is illustrated in Fig. 1.

Initialisation: First, the K_{init} strongest local maxima of the CNN response are detected. Each of these corresponds to a patch on the Gaussian sphere image (cf. Fig. 1). Then, the global maximum within such a patch is detected and its position on the sphere converted back to euclidean coordinates, which yields an initial vanishing point candidate.

Affinity Measure: Originally, $w_{ik} = p(\mathbf{v}_k|\mathbf{l}_i)$ was used in [15] as an affinity measure. As it does not take the spatial structure of line segments into account, we devised a modified affinity measure based on the following assumptions: *1.* Line segments with similar orientation in close proximity likely belong to the same vanishing point. *2.* Line segments that lie within a neighbourhood of similarly oriented lines less likely originate from noise. Based on this intuition, we devised a similarity measure S_{ij} between two line segments $\mathbf{l}_i, \mathbf{l}_j$:

$$S_{ij} = \cos(\phi_{ij})\exp(\frac{-d_l(\mathbf{l}_i, \mathbf{l}_j)^2}{\sigma_l^2}) \tag{8}$$

with $\phi_{ij} = min\left(max\left(k_\phi \cdot \angle(\mathbf{l}_i, \mathbf{l}_j), -\frac{\pi}{2}\right), \frac{\pi}{2}\right)$, and $d_l(l_i, l_j)$ being the shortest distance between the two line segments. Using this similarity measure, we enforce a prior on w_{ik} in order to achieve higher spatial consistency between line segments w.r.t. their vanishing point associations. We further assign a higher relative weight to those line segments which, according to the similarity measure, appear to lie in a neighbourhood of other, similar line segments, assuming that this indicates a regular structure as opposed to noise.

Split and Merge: In some cases, a detection would occur at a spot within the image's borders which is not a true vanishing point, but merely a point of coincidental intersection of lines. In order to counteract this, we devised a *split-and-merge* technique which is applied once every f_s iterations of the EM process: First, a vanishing point within the image whose associated line segments have the highest standard deviation w.r.t. their angle is selected. Then, these line segments are split into two clusters based on their angle, from which two new vanishing points are calculated, replacing the old one. If one resulting vanishing point is too close to another, they will be merged together afterwards.

2.5 Horizon Line and Orthogonal Vanishing Point Estimation

As is customary, we used the horizon detection error metric to compare our approach to previous methods. We devised an algorithm that estimates three supposedly orthogonal vanishing points and a horizon line, given a set of previously determined vanishing points.

First, we select the N_{vp} most significant vanishing points – where significance is measured by the number of lines n_k associated with a vanishing point $\mathbf{v}_k$ – and consider every possible triplet $\mathcal{T}$. Any vanishing point with an elevation $|\beta_k| > \theta_z$ on the Gaussian sphere is considered as a zenith candidate $\mathbf{v}_z$. We then discard unreasonable solutions, e.g. those which would result in a horizon line slope $\phi_{hor} > \theta_{hor}$. We assume that the projection of the camera centre $\mathbf{c}$ coincides with the center of the image and calculate the angle $\phi_{hz,\mathcal{T}}$ between the tentative horizon line and the line $\mathbf{l}_{zc} = \mathbf{v}_z \times \mathbf{c}$, which ideally should be perpendicular [5]. Then we calculate a score value for each triplet:

$$s_\mathcal{T} = (1 - \cos(\phi_{hz,\mathcal{T}})) \cdot \sum_{i \in \mathcal{T}} n_i \qquad (9)$$

and select the triplet with the highest score. Finally, a horizon line $\mathbf{h}$ is calculated – under the condition that $\mathbf{h}$ and $\mathbf{l}_{zc}$ be perpendicular – by minimising:

$$J(\mathbf{h}) = \min_{\mathbf{h}} \sum_{i \in (\mathcal{T} \setminus zenith)} \frac{n_i}{\|\mathbf{v}_i - \mathbf{c}\|} (\mathbf{h}^T \mathbf{v}_i)^2 \qquad (10)$$

3 Experiments

We implemented and trained our CNN with the Caffe [14] framework and used an existing C++ library [11] for line detection. All other pre- and post-processing

Table 1. Parameters of our method used for all experiments.

Name	N		K_{init}	σ_{prior}	k_ϕ	N_{vp}	θ_z	θ_{hor}
Section	2.1 and 2.2	2.4	2.4	2.4	2.4	2.5	2.5	2.5
Value	20		25	$\frac{\pi}{1.282N}$	9	20	$\frac{\pi}{4}$	$\frac{\pi}{6}$

steps were implemented in Python, making use of the Numpy and Scikit-learn [19] packages. The parameters in Table 1 were used for all experiments. On an Intel Core i7-3770K CPU, our implementation takes 45 s on average to compute the result for a 640×480 pixel image. The majority of this time – almost 95% – is needed for the EM based refinement step.

3.1   Horizon Estimation

For a quantitative evaluation of our method, we computed the horizon detection error on two benchmark datasets that were commonly used to assess the performance of vanishing point detection in previous works [3,18,24,25,27,28], as well as a third, more recent dataset additionally used for evaluation in [28]. The horizon detection error is defined as the maximum distance between the detected and the true horizon line, relative to the image's height.

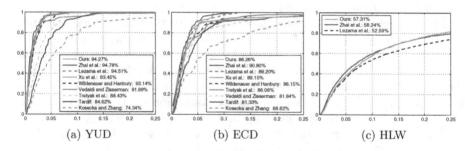

        (a) YUD   (b) ECD   (c) HLW

Fig. 3. Cumulative histograms of the horizon detection error. The horizon error is represented on the x-axis, while the y-axis represents the fraction of images with less than the corresponding error.

The *York Urban Dataset* (YUD) [9] contains 102 images of indoor and urban outdoor scenes, and three vanishing points corresponding to orthogonal directions are given as ground-truth for each scene. Generally, these scenes fulfil the Manhattan-world assumption, though our method does not take advantage of that. Figure 3a shows the cumulative horizon error histogram and the area under the curve (AUC) as a performance measure, comparing our approach to competing methods. We achieve a competitive AUC of 94.27%, compared to 94.78% of the current best state-of-the-art method [28]. In contrast to [28], in which only the horizon line estimation is evaluated, we are able to identify the three orthogonal vanishing directions with an accuracy of 99.13% within a margin of error of five degrees.

The *Eurasian Cities Dataset* (ECD) [3] contains 103 urban outdoor scenes which generally do not satisfy the Manhattan-world assumption, but often contain multiple groups of orthogonal directions, and are therefore more challenging compared to the YUD. The horizon line and a varying number of vanishing points are given as ground-truth for each scene. On this dataset, we achieve an AUC of 86.26%. Figure 3b gives a comparison to other state-of-the-art methods.

The *Horizon Lines in the Wild* (HLW) dataset [26] is a recent benchmark dataset which is significantly more challenging than both YUD and ECD, as many of its approximately 2000 test set images do not fulfil the Atlanta-world assumption. Here, our method achieves 57.31% AUC – slightly worse than [28] with 58.24%, but vastly better than [18] with 52.59%, see Fig. 3c.

Fig. 4. First 3 images show line segments associated with the three VPs used for horizon estimation (red, green, blue), estimated horizon (magenta) and ground truth horizon (cyan). Images 4–6 show the corresponding sphere images with most significant (green) and other detected (yellow) VPs, and ground truth (cyan). The 1st and 4th images show the best case example, the 2nd and 5th an average case example, the 3rd and 6th a failure case. (Color figure online)

Generally, our method appears to perform poorly when a large number of line segments near the horizon, large curved structures, or a very large number of noisy line segments are present. A representative failure case is shown by the 3rd and 6th images in Fig. 4.

3.2 Additional Applications

As camera systems are an essential source of data for autonomous vehicles and driver assistance systems upon which they base their actions, it is reasonable to extract as much useful information as possible from the images they capture. We want to illustrate that robustly estimated vanishing points are of great use for such applications.

In order to extract metrically correct measurements within a scene from camera images, knowledge of the cameras intrinsic parameters K is required. While they can be acquired by calibration before deploying the camera in a vehicle, shock and vibration may alter the camera's internal alignment over time, resulting in a need for recalibration. Such a recalibration is possible by way of determining the image of the absolute conic $\omega = K^{-T}K^{-1}$ from three orthogonal vanishing points if zero skew and square pixels are assumed. A method that facilitates this is outlined in [12], while a simplified version that assumes the camera's principle point to be known – but only needs two orthogonal vanishing points – is described in [25].

If the camera's intrinsic parameters are known, a homography $H = KRK^{-1}$, which is akin to a rotation of the camera with a 3D rotational matrix R, can be computed. This can be exploited to align one or two vanishing directions with the canonical x, y or z-axes in a way that results in a rectification of any plane which is aligned with said directions. Such a rectification can be used to extract relative measurements within a plane, e.g. for computing relative widths within a traffic lane (cf. Fig. 5a, b), or to project auxiliary information – such as street names or traffic signs – into a scene (cf. Fig. 5c) and display it to the driver, thus facilitating a form of visually appealing augmented reality without the need for explicit 3D reconstruction.

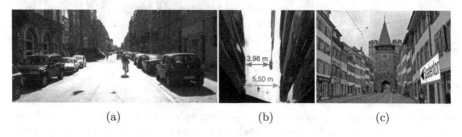

(a)   (b)   (c)

Fig. 5. (a) Image from the KITTI [10] dataset, with a detected vanishing point (red dot) arising from the central perspective. (b) Rectified version of *(a)* after aligning the vanishing direction with the y-axis. The relative amount of space next to the cyclist can be measured easily. (c) Image (Source: https://www.flickr.com/photos/david-perez/ 4493470850) of the *Spalentor* in Basel with a virtual sign projected onto a wall after estimating K from detected vanishing points and aligning the central vanishing point with the x-axis. (Color figure online)

4   Conclusion

We introduced a novel, deep learning based vanishing point detection method, which uses a CNN that operates on artificial images arising from a Gaussian sphere representation of lines and points using an inverse gnomonic projection. It is trained using synthetic data including noise and outliers exclusively, eliminating the need for labelled data. Despite not relying on either the Manhattan-world or Atlanta-world assumptions, which most related works do, it achieves competitive results on three benchmark datasets and good results in two further applications. Obviously, the capability of the trained CNN to handle different scenes depends on the training data. Since the proposed approach relies on synthetic data, it can be easily amended to represent different cases. The results on *Horizon Lines in the Wild* (HLW) demonstrates that the used training data is representative for difficult real images. Even more challenging scenarios, for instance no orthogonal VPs at all, can be approached by generating suitable training data and simply re-training the CNN.

References

1. Almansa, A., Desolneux, A., Vamech, S.: Vanishing point detection without any a priori information. IEEE Trans. Pattern Anal. Mach. Intell. **25**(4), 502–507 (2003)
2. Antunes, M., Barreto, J.P.: A global approach for the detection of vanishing points and mutually orthogonal vanishing directions. In: Proceedings of the IEEE Conference on Computer Vision and Pattern Recognition, pp. 1336–1343 (2013)
3. Barinova, O., Lempitsky, V., Tretiak, E., Kohli, P.: Geometric image parsing in man-made environments. In: Daniilidis, K., Maragos, P., Paragios, N. (eds.) ECCV 2010. LNCS, vol. 6312, pp. 57–70. Springer, Heidelberg (2010). doi:10.1007/978-3-642-15552-9_5
4. Barnard, S.T.: Interpreting perspective images. Artif. Intell. **21**(4), 435–462 (1983)
5. Beardsley, P., Murray, D.: Camera calibration using vanishing points. In: Hogg, D., Boyle, R. (eds.) BMVC92, pp. 416–425. Springer, London (1992)
6. Borji, A.: Vanishing point detection with convolutional neural networks. arXiv preprint arXiv:1609.00967 (2016)
7. Coughlan, J.M., Yuille, A.L.: Manhattan world: compass direction from a single image by Bayesian inference. In: The Proceedings of the Seventh IEEE International Conference on Computer Vision, vol. 2, pp. 941–947. IEEE (1999)
8. Criminisi, A., Reid, I., Zisserman, A.: Single view metrology. Int. J. Comput. Vis. **40**(2), 123–148 (2000)
9. Denis, P., Elder, J.H., Estrada, F.J.: Efficient edge-based methods for estimating manhattan frames in urban imagery. In: Forsyth, D., Torr, P., Zisserman, A. (eds.) ECCV 2008. LNCS, vol. 5303, pp. 197–210. Springer, Heidelberg (2008). doi:10.1007/978-3-540-88688-4_15
10. Geiger, A., Lenz, P., Stiller, C., Urtasun, R.: Vision meets robotics: the KITTI dataset. Int. J. Rob. Res. (IJRR) **32**, 1231–1237 (2013)
11. von Gioi, R.G., Jakubowicz, J., Morel, J.M., Randall, G.: LSD: a fast line segment detector with a false detection control. IEEE Trans. Pattern Anal. Mach. Intell. **32**(4), 722–732 (2010)
12. Hartley, R., Zisserman, A.: Multiple View Geometry in Computer Vision. Cambridge University Press, Cambridge (2003)
13. Hedau, V., Hoiem, D., Forsyth, D.: Recovering the spatial layout of cluttered rooms. In: 2009 IEEE 12th international conference on Computer Vision, pp. 1849–1856. IEEE (2009)
14. Jia, Y., Shelhamer, E., Donahue, J., Karayev, S., Long, J., Girshick, R., Guadarrama, S., Darrell, T.: Caffe: convolutional architecture for fast feature embedding. arXiv preprint arXiv:1408.5093 (2014)
15. Košecká, J., Zhang, W.: Video compass. In: Heyden, A., Sparr, G., Nielsen, M., Johansen, P. (eds.) ECCV 2002. LNCS, vol. 2353, pp. 476–490. Springer, Heidelberg (2002). doi:10.1007/3-540-47979-1_32
16. Krizhevsky, A., Sutskever, I., Hinton, G.E.: Imagenet classification with deep convolutional neural networks. In: Advances in Neural Information Processing Systems, pp. 1097–1105 (2012)

17. LeCun, Y., Bottou, L., Bengio, Y., Haffner, P.: Gradient-based learning applied to document recognition. Proc. IEEE **86**(11), 2278–2324 (1998)
18. Lezama, J., von Gioi, R.G., Randall, G., Morel, J.M.: Finding vanishing points via point alignments in image primal and dual domains. In: Proceedings of the IEEE Conference on Computer Vision and Pattern Recognition, pp. 509–515 (2014)
19. Pedregosa, F., Varoquaux, G., Gramfort, A., Michel, V., Thirion, B., Grisel, O., Blondel, M., Prettenhofer, P., Weiss, R., Dubourg, V., Vanderplas, J., Passos, A., Cournapeau, D., Brucher, M., Perrot, M., Duchesnay, E.: Scikit-learn: machine learning in python. J. Mach. Learn. Res. **12**, 2825–2830 (2011)
20. Rother, C.: A new approach to vanishing point detection in architectural environments. Image Vis. Comput. **20**(9), 647–655 (2002)
21. Schindler, G., Dellaert, F.: Atlanta world: an expectation maximization framework for simultaneous low-level edge grouping and camera calibration in complex manmade environments. In: Proceedings of the 2004 IEEE Computer Society Conference on Computer Vision and Pattern Recognition, CVPR 2004, vol. 1, p. I. IEEE (2004)
22. Tardif, J.P.: Non-iterative approach for fast and accurate vanishing point detection. In: 2009 IEEE 12th International Conference on Computer Vision, pp. 1250–1257. IEEE (2009)
23. Ueda, Y., Kamakura, Y., Saiki, J.: Eye movements converge on vanishing points during visual search. Jpn. Psychol. Res. **59**, 109–121 (2017)
24. Vedaldi, A., Zisserman, A.: Self-similar sketch. In: Fitzgibbon, A., Lazebnik, S., Perona, P., Sato, Y., Schmid, C. (eds.) ECCV 2012. LNCS, pp. 87–100. Springer, Heidelberg (2012). doi:10.1007/978-3-642-33709-3_7
25. Wildenauer, H., Hanbury, A.: Robust camera self-calibration from monocular images of Manhattan worlds. In: 2012 IEEE Conference on Computer Vision and Pattern Recognition (CVPR), pp. 2831–2838. IEEE (2012)
26. Workman, S., Zhai, M., Jacobs, N.: Horizon lines in the wild. arXiv preprint arXiv:1604.02129 (2016)
27. Xu, Y., Oh, S., Hoogs, A.: A minimum error vanishing point detection approach for uncalibrated monocular images of man-made environments. In: Proceedings of the IEEE Conference on Computer Vision and Pattern Recognition, pp. 1376–1383 (2013)
28. Zhai, M., Workman, S., Jacobs, N.: Detecting vanishing points using global image context in a non-manhattan world. In: Proceedings of the IEEE Conference on Computer Vision and Pattern Recognition, pp. 5657–5665 (2016)

Learning Where to Drive by Watching Others

Miguel A. Bautista$^{(\boxtimes)}$, Patrick Fuchs, and Björn Ommer

Heidelberg Collaboratory for Image Processing IWR,
Heidelberg University, Heidelberg, Germany
{miguel.bautista,patrick.fuchs,bjorn.ommer}@iwr.uni-heidelberg.de

Abstract. The most prominent approach for autonomous cars to learn what areas of a scene are drivable is to utilize tedious human supervision in the form of pixel-wise image labeling for training deep semantic segmentation algorithms. However, the underlying CNNs require vast amounts of this training information, rendering the expensive pixel-wise labeling of images a bottleneck. Thus, we propose a self-supervised approach that is able to utilize the myriad of easily available dashcam videos from YouTube or from autonomous vehicles to perform fully automatic training by simply watching others drive. We play training videos backwards in time and track patches that cars have driven over together with their spatio-temporal interrelations, which are a rich source of context information. Collecting large numbers of these local regions enables fully automatic self-supervision for training a CNN. The proposed method has the potential to extend and complement the popular supervised CNN learning of drivable pixels by using a rich, presently untapped source of unlabeled training data.

1 Introduction

The amount of video being recorded by dashboard cameras is increasing exponentially, thus becoming a potentially valuable source of training data for driver assistance and autonomous driving systems. However, the prevalent approach for many of these systems has been supervised learning of Convolutional Neural Networks (CNN) for semantic segmentation of traffic scenes [7,23,24]. A core sub-task of many of these systems is the detection of drivable surfaces (i.e. road detection to avoid lane departure or to plan driving trajectory), where tedious pixel-wise supervision of drivable areas needs to be collected in order to train a supervised model. While this supervision can improve the model performance on particular evaluation sub-sets [9,14], the statistics captured by these datasets may not be transferrable to other scenarios, e.g. a model trained on data collected in Germany [9] cannot be expected to perform equally in a UK based traffic scenario. Alternatively, scaling the labeling effort to the wide variety of traffic scenarios present all around the world is a futile undertaking.

Electronic supplementary material The online version of this chapter (doi:10. 1007/978-3-319-66709-6_3) contains supplementary material, which is available to authorized users.

Therefore, what we need is not simply more labelled data, as human annotators would always present a bottleneck to scale up learning. What we strive for is to enable learning algorithms to use the virtually unlimited number of dashcam videos available (YouTube, etc.), which are presently inaccessible for the current supervised learning methods since they are lacking labels altogether. For instance, the popular KITTI [14] and Cityscapes [9] datasets contain 290 and 25000 labeled training frames, respectively, compared to the potentially unlimited amount of unlabeled dashcam footage, which can be easily collected for all possible scenarios (i.e. different continents, countries, cities, weather conditions, etc.). Therefore, assuming that a supervised algorithm trained on datasets like [9,14] can be deployed in diverse real traffic scenarios is, at the very least, unrealistic. In addition, regardless of the amount of labeling effort and cost invested, the volume of unlabeled data will always be magnitudes larger.

A clear example are autonomous driving corporations like Tesla, Waymo, Uber, etc. where the competitive advantage is held by the corporation with more data collected. As an example, Tesla claims to have 1.3B miles of collected data, which to improve the autonomous capability of their cars has to be evaluated by experts and annotators. We hypothesize that a much more favorable situation would be to let an algorithm do the heavy-lifting and utilize the virtually infinite unlabeled dashcam footage collected every day. Moreover, the algorithm should not only learn from its own mistakes as in classical boosting but additionally from watching other cars drive. Moreover, large amounts of training data have become even more critical for the presently thriving deeper CNNs [19,31]. In recent years, there has thus been an increasing general interest in unsupervised training of CNNs on surrogate tasks [12,33] in order to exploit large amounts of unlabeled data that are infeasible to label. These unsupervised models can be then directly used as predictors [3,4] or further fine-tuned with only few labeled samples in order to compensate for the shift in both the task and data distribution [32].

The goal is then to learn a model for predicting drivable areas in an unsupervised manner, where we are only provided with unlabeled video sequences of a car interacting with other traffic partakers. Our hypothesis is the following: *can a CNN learn what areas are drivable by simply watching others?* The motivation has its roots in Experiential Learning inspired by Kurt Lewin and colleagues [22]. Here, the key paradigm is to learn through reflection on a human performing a particular task [5]. Human beings can learn by reflecting on experience [27] collected by watching other humans performing a particular task. For example, when walking over a frozen lake, a person will find a safe path to walk, by watching other persons on the ice and following their path. Furthermore, when analyzing how human beings learn to drive, we observe that a driving instructor is present only for a very limited initial period of time of only a few hours. However, after driving lessons we continuously improve our driving skills by watching others drive and reflecting on that experience. In addition, a human driver may have acquired their skills in particular country with small variation in conditions, but when travelling to another region can quickly learn to adapt by watching other traffic partakers and learning by reflection. In this sense, while the detection of drivable areas in a supervised manner is successfully tackled by current machine learning approaches, the adaptation and improvement that human drivers are capable by experiential reflection on other drivers remains an unexplored problem.

Motivated by this observation we propose to extract self-supervision of drivable surfaces from large video collections recorded only using inexpensive monocular dashboard cameras and no other more sophisticated and expensive sensor modalities such as RADAR [25], LIDAR [35], stereo cameras [8], etc., since they are far less likely to find on, for example, YouTube. To accomplish this task, we play the training videos backwards in time and track patches so as to find regions that cars have driven over (including the car that the camera is in). Similarly, we obtain patches that are unlikely to be drivable. All gathered patches are then used for discriminative training of a Fully Convolutional Network (FCN), following up on recent advances for self-supervised learning of CNNs [1,6,10,12,33]. Obviously, we only play backwards the unlabeled training videos for extracting self-supervision. During testing, the FCN predicts drivable areas in an image without using any extra information and by only computing a single forward pass. A visual example of the proposed pipeline is shown in Fig. 1.

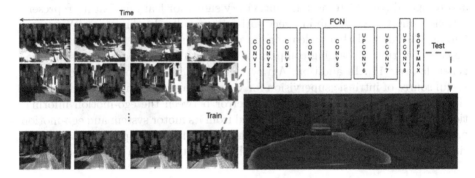

Fig. 1. Pipeline of the proposed approach for self-supervised learning of drivable surface. To obtain self-supervision, dashcam sequences are played back in time and patches that cars have driven over are marked as drivable and tracked. Using this self-supervision we propose to train an FCN that is able to effectively predict drivability of pixels without using any ground-truth labeled samples for training.

We evaluate our approach for unsupervised learning of drivable areas on the widely used KITTI [14] and Cityscapes [9] datasets, using only unlabeled video sequences provided with each dataset. In addition, we also gathered a collection of dashcam videos from YouTube and used them to train our model. The proposed approach shows how meaningful representations can be extracted from large volumes of unlabeled traffic footage. The goal is obviously not to completely replace supervised CNN training, but to open up the potential of adding a rich, presently untapped source of unlabeled training data.

2 Related Work

In this section, we review drivable surface detection methods both for the supervised and unsupervised settings. However, for a more extended survey of road detection methods, the readers may refer to a recent survey work [20].

A lot of attention has been paid to supervised classification models for drivable surface detection. Guo et al. [17] formulated the road detection problem in a maximum a posteriori (MAP) framework, and used a Markov random field to solve this problem. In latter work, they also incorporated semantic information and applied a graphical model to infer the road boundary [18]. Furthermore, following recent results of CNNs, Alvarez et al. [2] used a CNN to extract the appearance feature of a patch and classify a road scene into the sky, the vertical regions and the drivable regions. Furthermore, with the advent of CNNs approaches that trained FCNs on large labeled datasets have obtained successful results [7,23,24], at the cost of requiring tedious pixel-wise labeling. To circumvent the high cost of labeling images at the pixel level, virtual datasets have recently gained a lot of attention [15,28,29], while such datasets provide inexpensive labeling they fail to encode the variability of different traffic scenarios and lack the degree of realism provided by videos recorded in the physical world.

In the avenue of unsupervised learning recent works have exploited spatial and temporal context to obtain supervisory signal for learning feature representations using CNNs, obtaining very satisfying results. In this sense, Wang and Gupta [33], showed that video can be used as supervisory signal by tracking objects over time, obtaining comparable results to supervised methods on Imagenet dataset [11]. In addition, Agrawal et al. [1] showed that ego-motion is a useful source of intrinsic supervision for visual feature learning in mobile agents. However, this approach minimized the error between the ego-motion information (i.e. camera transformation) obtained from its motor system and ego-motion predicted using its visual inputs only. This is not directly applicable to our case since the ego-motion information from the car motor system is not available.

3 Unsupervised Learning of Drivable Surfaces

In this section we describe our approach for unsupervised learning of drivable areas. Our goal is to learn an FCN for prediction of drivable surfaces in a completely unsupervised manner. However, standard training of FCNs requires huge amounts of labeled training data, which is infeasible to collect for the many different driving scenarios in which these systems are deployed. In order to circumvent this problem, we propose to generate self-supervision by experiential reflection on unlabeled video sequences.

3.1 Self-supervision by Experiential Reflection

Video sequences recorded by dashboard cameras contain unparalleled numbers of traffic scenes in which a car drives around while interacting with other road

users, which cannot be utilized by supervised learning methods. A simple approach to exploit this tremendous source of untapped traffic information would
be to assume that a small fixed area in front of the car is drivable, generating self-supervision as the car moves during the video sequence. However, this
generated self-supervision will only model the statistics of a small fixed area in
front of the car bumper, neglecting the rich information provided by the scene
and other traffic partakers. In addition, such approach will fail to model drivable
areas far from the car, left and right turns or changes of drivable areas due to
environmental causes (i.e. changes in lighting, shadows, road marks, etc.). A
visual example of such self-supervision is shown in Fig. 2(a).

(a)

(b)   (c)

Fig. 2. (a) Self-supervision obtained by fixing a drivable area in front of the car. (b) Self-
supervision obtained using only the car that is recording the video sequence, where blue
and red patches correspond to drivable and non-drivable surfaces, respectively. (c) Self-
supervision computed using different traffic partakers, where blue patches correspond to
drivable surfaces of the egocentric point of view, green patches denote self-supervision
obtained from other cars and red patches correspond to non-drivable surfaces. (Color
figure online)

Interestingly, if such video sequences are played backwards in time, a human
observer can easily point what areas have been driven over by different traffic
partakers, and thus, can reflect on the experience (i.e. self-supervision) accumulated by watching such sequences to learn what makes an area drivable. Following
this observation, we propose to automatically obtain self-supervision by rewinding sequences back in time and keeping track of surfaces, i.e., image patches,
that different road users have driven over, reflecting on the experience obtained
by watching others to collect supervision.

Given a training video sequence $\mathcal{S} = \{\mathbf{I}_1, \ldots, \mathbf{I}_t\}$, we obtain self-supervision
by tracking patches that cars have driven over while playing the sequence back-
wards in time. To initialize the drivable patches to track, we can assume that
a small area in front of a moving car bumper is a drivable area composed of
several patches $\mathbf{P}_t^i \in \mathbb{R}^{h \times w \times 3}$, $\forall i \in \{1, \ldots, p\}$. For the point of view of the car
recording the sequence this is a trivial task, since the bumper position is fixed.

To extend this assumption to the rest of cars in the sequence we simply obtain object proposals using a car detector [16] and assume that the area directly below the detection is a drivable surface. When rewinding the sequence we track these patches using optical flow [26]. Flow is computed densely between pairs of consecutive frames $(\mathbf{I}_{t-1}, \mathbf{I}_t)$ and used to estimate a projective transformation with RANSAC [13]. This transformation compensates for the ego motion and is used to establish correspondences between a patch $\mathbf{P}_{t-1}^i$ and its successor $\mathbf{P}_t^i$, therefore being able to track patches that different cars have driven over (cf. supplementary material for sample video sequences).

To take account of tracking errors (e.g. patch drift) and of the movement of other road users, we compute the similarity between a patch $\mathbf{P}_{t-1}^i$ and its projected successor $\mathbf{P}_t^i$ to eliminate unreliable correspondences: since the projective transformation is estimated using consecutive frames, we can assume that the color histogram of a patch $\mathbf{P}_{t-1}^i$ and its projected successor $\mathbf{P}_t^i$ is highly similar. Let $\mathbf{h}(\mathbf{P}_t^i)$ denote the normalized color histogram of patch $\mathbf{P}_t^i$. Then, given the pairwise similarities between two consecutive patches:

$$s(\mathbf{P}_{t-1}^i, \mathbf{P}_t^i) = \mathbf{h}(\mathbf{P}_{t-1}^i)^\top \mathbf{h}(\mathbf{P}_t^i), \qquad (1)$$

We compute the distribution of distances and truncate it at the pivot point, thus effectively eliminating unreliable projected drivable patches (i.e. false positive patches which were projected to a highly dissimilar region) by stopping their tracks, while reliable tracks are computed until the similarity of two consecutive patches lies below the pivot point. Drivable patches are tracked for 63 frames on average with a maximum of 191 frames.

To obtain negatives, i.e., non-drivable patches, we randomly sample patches from image regions which were not driven over by any car and whose tracks consisted for more than ten frames (to avoid drifting patches or those occluded by other objects). In addition, we place negative patches inside the car bounding boxes computed in the previous step to include other cars in the negative training set. A visual example is shown in Fig. 2(b) where red and blue patches denote non-drivable and drivable surfaces, respectively. Furthermore, Fig. 2(c) also shows in green the self-supervision obtained by tracking patches that other road users drove over.

3.2   Learning Drivable Surfaces

CNNs are presently among the most powerful classification frameworks for Computer Vision [31]. Since our self-supervision strategy generates patches of drivable and non-drivable areas on an image, a natural choice would be to train a CNN to classify these image patches [21]. However, since our ultimate objective is to predict the drivability of individual pixels, such approach has two shortcomings: (i) estimating the drivability of a pixel using only local patch information is a hard task due to the lack of context information. (ii) testing is computationally prohibitive since all patches in an image need to be evaluated.

A more efficient approach is to cast the problem as pixel-wise labeling for each training image using the available self-supervision. All pixels contained in a drivable training patch are considered positive and all pixels contained in a non-drivable patch are negative. Then, a FCN architecture [7,23,24] is trained for predicting a pixel-wise label for each training image, where pixels which are not labeled as positive nor negative during the self-supervision step are not used during training. FCN architectures naturally incorporate context which is encoded by means of convolution and pooling operations, while being extremely efficient during testing due to their weight sharing scheme. However, a common problem of FCNs is to model long-range contextual interactions between pixels. In our particular case these long-range interactions encode extremely useful context that helps modelling what makes up a drivable area (e.g. drivable pixels on the correct side of a curb, road marks, etc.). Therefore, to include these long-range interactions we use dilated convolutions [34] through all our up-stream convolutional layers.

Once our FCN is trained, we compute a confidence map for each training image. However, thresholding these confidence maps to obtain predictions would not take into account the labeling of neighbor pixels. Therefore, we use GrabCut [30] to obtain a discrete labeling that aggregates local context at the pixel-wise label level, using this new self-supervised ground truth we further fine-tune our FCN and repeat this process for three iterations. Finally, we need discrete output prediction of drivability. Thus, provided the accuracy of the probability heat-maps yielded by our iterative approach, we simply threshold these confidence maps. Computing a confidence map for an image only requires a forward-pass, making it very effective for real-time deployment[1].

4   Experimental Results

In this section, we present both quantitative and qualitative results obtained by the proposed unsupervised learning approach on the main benchmarks for pixel-wise drivable surface detection, Cityscapes [9]. Our hypothesis is two fold: (i) Our self-supervised approach should perform well in zero-shot learning scenarios, where no labeled samples are provided for training. (ii) Self-supervised training should serve as a regularizer that helps to generalize when transferring between similar datasets. Extensive experimental results can be found in the supplementary material. All models, datasets and generated labels are publicly available at[2].

4.1   Datasets

Cityscapes. Cityscapes [9] is the biggest dataset available for semantic segmentation of traffic scenes. Cityscapes contains 25000 fully labeled images at

---

[1] Our approach runs at 15 FPS on a NVIDIA Titan X GPU.
[2] https://hcicloud.iwr.uni-heidelberg.de/index.php/s/tutGQ2J3XoUyqkU.

pixel-level. For evaluation purposes we only utilize the *road* category. Cityscapes [9] does not provide the video sequences of their vehicles driving around different cities, and only allowed us to use three sequences from a single city containing 30000 frames in total to utilize our self-supervised method.

YouTube Dashcam Dataset. To further evaluate the generality of our approach, we additionally acquired 13 dashcam sequences totalling 100000 frames that were recorded in the wild and uploaded to YouTube. These videos were all recorded in different cities from Germany and the United States showing varying weather conditions and seasons, therefore spanning a large variety of scenarios. Furthermore, we also collected two more sequences with difficult conditions: a dusty desert trail and a road covered in snow and mud, where each sequence contains 10000 frames.

4.2 Zero-Shot Learning

To assess the performance of our self-supervision method we tackle the problem of zero-shot learning of drivable areas on CityScapes [9]. That is, methods are provided with 0 ground-truth labeled training images. We compare state-of-the-art fully convolutional architectures with and without our self-supervision method trained on the unlabeled sequences of CityScapes (cf. Sect. 4.1). Table 1 summarizes the performance of two different architectures with and without our self-supervision method. We show results for our variant of FCN-8s [24] (with dilated upconvolutional layers), with and without Imagenet [11] pre-training. In addition, we also make use of the ResNet-101 model [19] pre-trained on Imagenet. In Table 1 we observe that our proposed approach for self-supervision drastically boosts the performance of zero-shot learning for all different architectures, where our self-supervision computed on the unlabeled sequences of Cityscapes is extremely helpful for both randomly initialized and pre-trained models. Note that a randomly initialized model with our self-supervision strategy is able to attain equivalent performance than the same model pre-trained on Imagenet [11]. Thus, being able to circumvent the use of the 1.2 M of Imagenet labeled samples. To the best of our knowledge, this is the first time that a

Table 1. Zero-shot results for Cityscapes benchmark.

Model	MaxF	IoU
FCN-8s Random Init.	49.5	32.9
FCN-8s Random Init. + Ours	82.6	70.4
FCN-8s Imgnet. Init.	51.3	34.7
FCN-8s Imgnet. Init. + Ours	81.9	69.4
ResNet-101 Imgnet. Init	52.5	34.9
ResNet-101 Imgnet. Init. + Ours	79.6	66.1

self-supervised method that performs equivalently in the absence of the widely adopted Imagenet pre-training strategy.

Finally, we show few score maps of drivable area yielded by our self-supervised approach Cityscapes [9] in Fig. 3. Note that our method does not use any ground-truth labeled image during training.

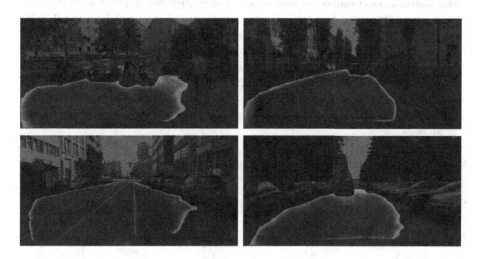

Fig. 3. Sample score maps for zero-shot learning on Cityscapes.

4.3 Transfer Learning

We now evaluate the ability of our approach to boost performance on a transfer learning task where a model is trained on one dataset and then transferred to another for evaluation. We employ the two most prominent datasets for esti-mating drivable areas, KITTI [14] and Cityscapes [9]. The underlying rationale is that if a model is performing well on KITTI it should also perform equiva-lently on Cityscapes. Therefore, we utilize the unlabeled sequences of Cityscapes (cf. Sect. 4.1) for pre-training the FCNs using our self-supervised strategy, before using the KITTI ground-truth labels to perform supervised learning. After train-ing this model is then evaluated on Cityscapes. We evaluate transfer learning based on two separate network architectures, FCN-8s [24] and ResNet-101 [19]. In Table 2 we show the MaxF and IoU scores on Cityscapes of the different models transferred from KITTI with and without our self-supervised pre-training (first two columns, denoted with KITTI-TF). We can see that our self-supervised pre-training is extremely useful when transferring models between datasets, boosting performance by at least 10%. This performance improvement is due to the reg-ularization properties of our self-supervision, which prevents the model from over-fitting to KITTI-like scenarios, thus improving the capability to generalize to previously unseen scenarios.

4.4 Self-supervision from the Wild: YouTube Dashcam Dataset

After providing results using the most prominent datasets for predicting drivable areas, we now study the problem of collecting self-supervision from the wild. We therefore utilize the YouTube Dashcam dataset described in Sect. 4.1, collecting self-supervision for 100000 frames of video data from different locations under different environmental conditions. For clarity, we follow the evaluation protocol for Cityscapes and evaluate the suitability of models trained with self-supervision from the wild for zero-shot learning. Table 2 reports the result of our self-supervised YouTube training (last two columns, denoted with YT-SS) where we show results for FCN-8s [24], with and without Imagenet [11] pre-training. In addition, we also make use of the ResNet-101 model [19] pre-trained on Imagenet. We can therefore observe how the self-supervision that we collected from video sequences from the wild is of tremendous power, boosting performance by 18% at least.

Table 2. Transfer learning results on Cityscapes when training using self-supervision from KITTI and from Youtube Dashcam dataset.

Model	MaxF/KITTI-TF	IoU/KITTI-TF	MaxF/YT-SS	IoU/YT-SS
FCN-8s Rand.	43.4	27.7	49.5	32.9
FCN-8s Rand. + Ours	55.1	38.0	70.6	54.5
FCN-8s Imgnet.	50.1	33.4	49.5	32.9
FCN-8s Imgnet. Init. + Ours	74.2	59.0		
ResNet-101 Imgnet.	72.5	56.8	49.5	32.9
ResNet-101 Imgnet. + Ours	82.0	69.5	75.8	61

5   Conclusions

In this paper we have presented a self-supervised approach for learning drivable regions from unlabeled dashcam videos. Based on experiential learning we aim to learn about drivable areas by watching others drive. Our simple, yet effective method makes large amounts of unlabeled training videos usable for training standard FCNs for pixel-wise predictions. Playing unlabeled dashcam sequences backwards in time and tracking patches the other cars have driven over allows us to gather large amounts of self-supervision which can be successfully leveraged by an FCN. For comparison and reproducibility, we train and evaluate on both KITTI and Cityscapes datasets obtaining competitive results for zero-shot learning tasks, where no ground-truth labeled image samples are provided for training. In addition, we introduce a novel dataset of dashcam sequences from YouTube where we collected self-supervision from 100000 frames and show that we can obtain valuable self-supervision from such an unconstrained source of video. The results obtained by the proposed approach show that powerful pixel-wise predictors of drivability can be learnt from large unlabeled video collections and demonstrate the potential of adding this rich, previously inaccessible resource to supervised FCN learning.

References

1. Agrawal, P., Carreira, J., Malik, J.: Learning to see by moving. In: Proceedings of the IEEE International Conference on Computer Vision, pp. 37–45 (2015)
2. Alvarez, J.M., Gevers, T., LeCun, Y., Lopez, A.M.: Road scene segmentation from a single image. In: Fitzgibbon, A., Lazebnik, S., Perona, P., Sato, Y., Schmid, C. (eds.) ECCV 2012. LNCS, vol. 7578, pp. 376–389. Springer, Heidelberg (2012). doi:10.1007/978-3-642-33786-4_28
3. Bautista, M.A., Sanakoyeu, A., Ommer, B.: Deep unsupervised similarity learning using partially ordered sets. In: Proceedings of IEEE Computer Vision and Pattern Recognition (2017)
4. Bautista, M.A., Sanakoyeu, A., Tikhoncheva, E., Ommer, B.: Cliquecnn: deep unsupervised exemplar learning. In: Advances In Neural Information Processing Systems, pp. 3846–3854 (2016)
5. Boyd, E.M., Fales, A.W.: Reflective learning key to learning from experience. J. Humanistic Psychol. **23**(2), 99–117 (1983)
6. Chan, F.-H., Chen, Y.-T., Xiang, Y., Sun, M.: Anticipating accidents in dashcam videos. In: Lai, S.-H., Lepetit, V., Nishino, K., Sato, Y. (eds.) ACCV 2016. LNCS, vol. 10114, pp. 136–153. Springer, Cham (2017). doi:10.1007/978-3-319-54190-7_9
7. Chen, L.C., Papandreou, G., Kokkinos, I., Murphy, K., Yuille, A.L.: DeepLab: semantic image segmentation with deep convolutional nets, atrous convolution, and fully connected CRFs. arXiv preprint arXiv:1606.00915 (2016)
8. Chen, X., Kundu, K., Zhu, Y., Berneshawi, A.G., Ma, H., Fidler, S., Urtasun, R.: 3D object proposals for accurate object class detection. In: Advances in NIPS, pp. 424–432 (2015)
9. Cordts, M., Omran, M., Ramos, S., Rehfeld, T., Enzweiler, M., Benenson, R., Franke, U., Roth, S., Schiele, B.: The cityscapes dataset for semantic urban scene understanding. In: Proceedings of the IEEE CVPR, pp. 3213–3223 (2016)
10. Dahlkamp, H., Kaehler, A., Stavens, D., Thrun, S., Bradski, G.R.: Self-supervised monocular road detection in desert terrain. In: Robotics: Science and Systems, vol. 38. Philadelphia (2006)
11. Deng, J., Dong, W., Socher, R., Li, L.J., Li, K., Fei-Fei, L.: Imagenet: A large-scale hierarchical image database. In: IEEE Conference on Computer Vision and Pattern Recognition, CVPR 2009, pp. 248–255. IEEE (2009)
12. Doersch, C., Gupta, A., Efros, A.A.: Unsupervised visual representation learning by context prediction. In: Proceedings of the IEEE International Conference on Computer Vision, pp. 1422–1430 (2015)
13. Fischler, M.A., Bolles, R.C.: Random sample consensus: a paradigm for model fitting with applications to image analysis and automated cartography. Commun. ACM **24**(6), 381–395 (1981)
14. Fritsch, J., Kuehnl, T., Geiger, A.: A new performance measure and evaluation benchmark for road detection algorithms. In: International Conference on Intelligent Transportation Systems (ITSC) (2013)
15. Gaidon, A., Wang, Q., Cabon, Y., Vig, E.: Virtual worlds as proxy for multi-object tracking analysis. CoRR abs/1605.06457 (2016). http://arxiv.org/abs/1605.06457
16. Girshick, R., Donahue, J., Darrell, T., Malik, J.: Rich feature hierarchies for accurate object detection and semantic segmentation. In: Proceedings of the IEEE CVPR, pp. 580–587 (2014)
17. Guo, C., Mita, S., McAllester, D.: MRF-based road detection with unsupervised learning for autonomous driving in changing environments. In: 2010 IEEE Intelligent Vehicles Symposium (IV), pp. 361–368. IEEE (2010)

18. Guo, C., Yamabe, T., Mita, S.: Robust road boundary estimation for intelligent vehicles in challenging scenarios based on a semantic graph. In: 2012 IEEE Intelligent Vehicles Symposium (IV), pp. 37–44. IEEE (2012)
19. He, K., Zhang, X., Ren, S., Sun, J.: Identity mappings in deep residual networks. In: Leibe, B., Matas, J., Sebe, N., Welling, M. (eds.) ECCV 2016. LNCS, vol. 9908, pp. 630–645. Springer, Cham (2016). doi:10.1007/978-3-319-46493-0_38
20. Hillel, A.B., Lerner, R., Levi, D., Raz, G.: Recent progress in road and lane detection: a survey. Mach. Vis. Appl. **25**(3), 727–745 (2014)
21. Jin, J., Fu, K., Zhang, C.: Traffic sign recognition with hinge loss trained convolutional neural networks. IEEE Transp. Intell. Trans. Syst. **15**(5), 1991–2000 (2014)
22. Kolb, D.A.: Experiential Learning: Experience as the Source of Learning and Development. FT Press, Upper Saddle River (2014)
23. Liu, W., Rabinovich, A., Berg, A.C.: Parsenet: looking wider to see better. arXiv preprint arXiv:1506.04579 (2015)
24. Long, J., Shelhamer, E., Darrell, T.: Fully convolutional networks for semantic segmentation. In: Proceedings of the IEEE Conference on Computer Vision and Pattern Recognition, pp. 3431–3440 (2015)
25. Lu, M., Wevers, K., Van Der Heijden, R.: Technical feasibility of advanced driver assistance systems (ADAS) for road traffic safety. Transp. Plan. Technol. **28**(3), 167–187 (2005)
26. Lucas, B.D., Kanade, T., et al.: An iterative image registration technique with an application to stereo vision. IJCAI **81**, 674–679 (1981)
27. Meltzoff, A.N., Brooks, R.: Self-experience as a mechanism for learning about others: a training study in social cognition. Dev. Psychol. **44**(5), 1257 (2008)
28. Richter, S.R., Vineet, V., Roth, S., Koltun, V.: Playing for data: ground truth from computer games. In: Leibe, B., Matas, J., Sebe, N., Welling, M. (eds.) ECCV 2016. LNCS, vol. 9906, pp. 102–118. Springer, Cham (2016). doi:10.1007/978-3-319-46475-6_7
29. Ros, G., Sellart, L., Materzynska, J., Vázquez, D., Lopez, A.M.: The SYNTHIA dataset: a large collection of synthetic images for semantic segmentation of urban scenes. In: 2016 IEEE Conference on Computer Vision and Pattern Recognition, CVPR 2016, Las Vegas, NV, USA, 27–30 June 2016, pp. 3234–3243 (2016)
30. Rother, C., Kolmogorov, V., Blake, A.: Grabcut: interactive foreground extraction using iterated graph cuts. ACM Trans. Graph. (TOG) **23**, 309–314 (2004)
31. Szegedy, C., Vanhoucke, V., Ioffe, S., Shlens, J., Wojna, Z.: Rethinking the inception architecture for computer vision. In: Proceedings of the IEEE CVPR, pp. 2818–2826 (2016)
32. Wang, X., Gupta, A.: Unsupervised learning of visual representations using videos. In: ICCV (2015)
33. Wang, X., Gupta, A.: Unsupervised learning of visual representations using videos. In: Proceedings of the IEEE International Conference on Computer Vision, pp. 2794–2802 (2015)
34. Yu, F., Koltun, V.: Multi-scale context aggregation by dilated convolutions. arXiv preprint arXiv:1511.07122 (2015)
35. Zhang, W.: Lidar-based road and road-edge detection. In: 2010 IEEE Intelligent Vehicles Symposium (IV), pp. 845–848. IEEE (2010)

Learning Dilation Factors for Semantic Segmentation of Street Scenes

Yang He[1(✉)], Margret Keuper[2], Bernt Schiele[1], and Mario Fritz[1]

[1] Max Planck Institute for Informatics, Saarbrücken, Germany
yang@mpi-inf.mpg.de
[2] University of Mannheim, Mannheim, Germany

Abstract. Contextual information is crucial for semantic segmentation. However, finding the optimal trade-off between keeping desired fine details and at the same time providing sufficiently large receptive fields is non trivial. This is even more so, when objects or classes present in an image significantly vary in size. Dilated convolutions have proven valuable for semantic segmentation, because they allow to increase the size of the receptive field without sacrificing image resolution. However, in current state-of-the-art methods, dilation parameters are hand-tuned and fixed. In this paper, we present an approach for learning dilation parameters adaptively per channel, consistently improving semantic segmentation results on street-scene datasets like Cityscapes and Camvid.

1 Introduction

Semantic segmentation is the task of predicting the semantic category for each pixel in an image, i.e. its class label from a given set of labels. It is considered a crucial step towards scene understanding and has a wide range of use-cases including autonomous driving and service robotics. The trade-off between local detail and global context is inherent in the task. The prediction of class labels requires sufficient contextual information, especially for semantic classes whose instances usually cover large portions of the image (e.g. *trucks*, *street*) or may lack local features (e.g. *sky*). At the same time, well localized detailed information is important for pixel-accurate prediction.

Recently, dilated convolutions have been proposed to improve semantic segmentation performance by providing larger receptive fields without sacrificing image resolution or adding network complexity [19]. While this principled idea has shown promise for recent architectures [3,20], the dilation parameters are not learned but hand-tuned and fixed. In contrast, we propose to learn the dilation parameters end-to-end thus generalizing the concept of dilated convolutions [19]. More specifically, we propose a fully trainable dilated convolution layer that allows to not only learn dilation parameters for each convolutional layer but for each channel individually. Thus, different features can be extracted and combined at different scales, rendering the network more flexible with respect to its receptive fields. We leverage the proposed layer to facilitate the learning of

© Springer International Publishing AG 2017
V. Roth and T. Vetter (Eds.): GCPR 2017, LNCS 10496, pp. 41–51, 2017.
DOI: 10.1007/978-3-319-66709-6_4

dilation parameters within three different network architectures for semantic segmentation, specifically Deeplab-LargeFOV [3], Deeplab-v2 [3] and PSPNet [20]. For the task of street scene segmentation, we show that the proposed method consistently improves results over the respective baselines.

Related Work: Several large-scale datasets have been released recently to research semantic segmentation. Autonomous driving scenarios are prominently represented for example with the Camvid [1] and Cityscapes [5] benchmark datasets. In this work, we focus on semantic segmentation in such street views, and build our model on recent successful architectures in this domain.

Dilated Convolutions for Semantic Segmentation. Contextual information plays a crucial role in semantic segmentation. Dilated convolutions [19] were introduced to aggregate context information without necessarily downsampling the resolution. With a defined dilation factor, convolution operations are performed by sampling discrete locations. Dilated convolution architectures are widely used in recent semantic segmentation methods for their ability to capture large context while preserving fine details. Chen *et al.* [3] propose to utilize a large dilation factor in the original Deeplab model [2] to provide large context, leading to better performance. However, local information is beneficial to recognize fine details. To leverage local and wide context information, Chen *et al.* [4] present the Deeplab-v2 model with atrous spatial pyramid pooling (ASPP), which combines multi-level dilated convolutions and report improved performance.

State-of-the-Art Architectures for Street Scenes. Recent state-of-the-arts are built on deep residual networks (ResNets) [7], which are powerful in various vision tasks. Pohlen *et al.* [14] propose a full-resolution residual network, which contains a two-stream architecture and achieves state-of-the-art performance on public benchmarks [5]. One stream performs on the full image resolution, capturing image details and precise image boundaries. The second stream undergoes a sequence of pooling operations to extract visual features for robust recognition. Zhao *et al.* [20] propose the pyramid scene parsing network (PSPNet), which provides multi-level global context information and achieve good performance in street view semantic segmentation.

Contributions: While dilation parameters for dilated convolutions are fixed and manually-tuned in previous work [3,19,20], we provide a method allowing to learn those parameters for each channel individually. Overall, the main contributions of this paper are: (1) We propose a learnable channel-based dilated convolution layer, whose dilation factors can be fractional numbers. The proposed layer is compatible with state-of-the-art CNN architectures and can be trained end-to-end without extra supervision; (2) We improve the recent state-of-the-art semantic segmentation networks PSPNet [20] and Deeplab-v2 [3] in various street view datasets [1,5] by replacing fixed dilated convolutions with the proposed layer. Our method achieves consistent improvement over baselines and yields visually more convincing predictions.

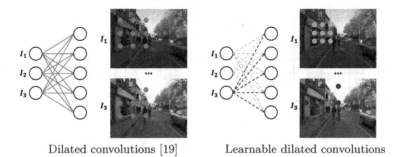

Dilated convolutions [19]   Learnable dilated convolutions

Fig. 1. Illustration of standard dilated convolutions (left) and the proposed channel based dilated convolutions (right). Standard dilated convolutions have a constant, manually set (solid lines) and integer valued dilation parameter for different channels. The proposed layer allows for channel-wise learning (dash lines) of dilation factors (encoded with different colors), which can take fractional values. (Color figure online)

2 Learning Dilation Factors for Convolutions

In this section, we describe the concept and formulation of the channel based fractional dilated convolution layer as illustrated in Fig. 1. Our proposed layer is a generalization of dilated convolutions as they were proposed in [19] (compare Fig. 1 (left)). Dilated convolutions provide a simple module facilitating to aggregate context information without pooling or downsampling the original image. It thus allows to preserve high spatial resolution. While previous dilated convolutions require manual tuning of an integer valued dilation parameter, the proposed method facilitates to learn dilation parameters from training data via back propagation. Thus, to allow for the definition of a gradient on the dilation parameter, these parameters can no longer be constrained to integer values but are relaxed to take a value in $\mathbb{R}^+$. To add further flexibility to the network w.r.t. the amount of context provided to each layer and each channel, we further allow for a channel-wise optimization of dilation parameters (compare Fig. 1 (right)).

For a learned, fractional dilation factor, the output feature map of the dilated convolutions is computed using bilinear interpolation – inspired by spatial transformer networks [9]. The proposed learnt dilated convolution layer is compatible with existing architectures, as it generalizes (and therefore can replace) convolutional and dilated convolutional layers in a given network architecture.

2.1 Forward Pass

We first give a brief recap on conventional dilated convolutions. With filter weights $\mathbf{W}$ and a bias term $\mathbf{b}$, the input feature $\mathbf{X}$ can be transformed to the output feature $\mathbf{Y}$ by

$$\mathbf{Y} = \mathbf{W} * \mathbf{X} + \mathbf{b}, \qquad or$$

$$y_{m,n} = \sum_c \sum_{i,j} w_{c,i,j} \cdot x_{c,m+i\cdot d,n+j\cdot d} + b, \qquad (1)$$

where d is the dilation factor, and must be an integer.

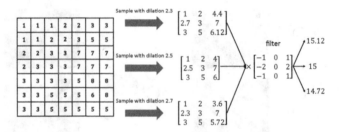

Fig. 2. An example of the proposed dilated convolutions with a fractional dilation factor. With different dilation factors (i.e., 2.3, 2.5 and 2.7 in this figure), we obtain different input features, and then get different output activations for the red location. Assuming the current dilation factor is 2.5, we will get an output 15. With a training signal, which expects the output activation increased or decreased, we can modify the current dilation factor along the direction to 2.3 or 2.7. (Color figure online)

We extend the dilated convolution by introducing a dilation vector $d_c \in \mathbb{R}^{c+}$ for different channels, which can take fractional values. The forward pass of the proposed dilated convolutions can be formulated as

$$y_{m,n} = \sum_c \sum_{i,j} w_{c,i,j} \cdot x_{c,m+i\cdot d_c,n+j\cdot d_c} + b. \tag{2}$$

$x_{c,m+i\cdot d_c,n+j\cdot d_c}$ cannot directly be sampled from the input feature $\mathbf{X}$ for most d_c. We obtain the value of a fractional position by employing bilinear interpolation on its four neighboring integer positions as shown in Fig. 2, specifically

$$x_{c,m+i\cdot d_c,n+j\cdot d_c} =$$
$$x_{c,\lfloor m+i\cdot d_c\rfloor,\lfloor n+j\cdot d_c\rfloor} \cdot (1-\Delta d)^2 + x_{c,\lfloor m+i\cdot d_c\rfloor,\lceil n+j\cdot d_c\rceil} \cdot (1-\Delta d)\cdot\Delta d \tag{3}$$
$$+ x_{c,\lceil m+i\cdot d_c\rceil,\lfloor n+j\cdot d_c\rfloor} \cdot \Delta d \cdot (1-\Delta d) + x_{c,\lceil m+i\cdot d_c\rceil,\lceil n+j\cdot d_c\rceil} \cdot (\Delta d)^2,$$

where $\Delta d = m + i \cdot d_c - \lfloor m + i \cdot d_c \rfloor = n + j \cdot d_c - \lfloor n + j \cdot d_c \rfloor$, is the decimal part of the dilation factor d_c.

2.2   Backward Pass

Chain rule and back propagation [16] are used to optimize a deep neural network model. For each layer, networks obtain the training signals (gradients) from the next connected layer, and use them to update the parameters in current layer. Then, the processed gradient is passed to the previous connected layer. Usually, those training signals are used to change the filter weights such that the output activation increases or decreases and the loss decreases. Besides changing filter weights, changing the dilation factor provides another way to optimize a convolution networks, as discussed in Fig. 2.

The proposed dilated convolution layer based on bilinear interpolation is differentiable to dilation factors. Therefore, it allows us to train a full model end-to-end without any additional training signal for dilation factors. Because Δd in Eq. (3) is the decimal part of c-th channel's dilation factor d_c, the gradient for updating d_c can be formulated as

$$
\begin{aligned}
\frac{\partial L}{\partial d_c} &= \frac{\partial L}{\partial y_{m,n}} \cdot \frac{\partial y_{m,n}}{\partial d_c} = \frac{\partial L}{\partial y_{m,n}} \cdot \frac{\partial y_{m,n}}{\partial \Delta d} \\
&= \sum_{i,j} \left(x_{c,\lfloor m+i\cdot d_c \rfloor, \lfloor n+j\cdot d_c \rfloor} \cdot (2 \cdot \Delta d - 2) + x_{c,\lfloor m+i\cdot d_c \rfloor, \lceil n+j\cdot d_c \rceil} \cdot (1 - 2 \cdot \Delta d) \right. \\
&\quad \left. + x_{c,\lceil m+i\cdot d_c \rceil, \lfloor n+j\cdot d_c \rfloor} \cdot (1 - 2 \cdot \Delta d) + x_{c,\lceil m+i\cdot d_c \rceil, \lceil n+j\cdot d_c \rceil} \cdot 2 \cdot \Delta d \right) \\
&\quad \cdot w_{c,i,j} \cdot \frac{\partial L}{\partial y_{m,n}}.
\end{aligned}
\tag{4}
$$

Besides the dilation factors, filter weights and bias term also require updating. The gradient for the filter weights $\mathbf{W}$ can be computed by

$$
\frac{\partial L}{\partial w_{c,i,j}} = \frac{\partial L}{\partial y_{m,n}} \cdot \frac{\partial y_{m,n}}{\partial w_{c,i,j}} = \frac{\partial L}{\partial y_{m,n}} \cdot x_{c,m+i\cdot d_c, n+j\cdot d_c},
\tag{5}
$$

where $x_{c,m+i\cdot d_c, n+j\cdot d_c}$ can be computed using Eq. (3). The gradient for the bias term $\mathbf{b}$ can be computed by

$$
\frac{\partial L}{\partial b} = \frac{\partial L}{\partial y_{m,n}}.
\tag{6}
$$

To employ back propagation for optimizing all the layers, the gradient for the input feature at location (p, q) can be computed as the sum of the gradients from all the locations of output side, who sample the location (p, q) in forward pass. The gradient at the output side $\frac{\partial L}{\partial y_{m,n}}$ will affect the gradients for all sampled input locations in bilinear interpolation. Specifically,

$$
\begin{aligned}
\frac{\partial L}{\partial x_{c,\lfloor m+i\cdot d_c \rfloor, \lfloor n+j\cdot d_c \rfloor}} &= \frac{\partial L}{\partial y_{m,n}} \cdot w_{c,i,j} \cdot (1 - \Delta d)^2, \\
\frac{\partial L}{\partial x_{c,\lfloor m+i\cdot d_c \rfloor, \lceil n+j\cdot d_c \rceil}} &= \frac{\partial L}{\partial y_{m,n}} \cdot w_{c,i,j} \cdot (1 - \Delta d) \cdot \Delta d, \\
\frac{\partial L}{\partial x_{c,\lceil m+i\cdot d_c \rceil, \lfloor n+j\cdot d_c \rfloor}} &= \frac{\partial L}{\partial y_{m,n}} \cdot w_{c,i,j} \cdot \Delta d \cdot (1 - \Delta d), \\
\frac{\partial L}{\partial x_{c,\lceil m+i\cdot d_c \rceil, \lceil n+j\cdot d_c \rceil}} &= \frac{\partial L}{\partial y_{m,n}} \cdot w_{c,i,j} \cdot (\Delta d)^2.
\end{aligned}
\tag{7}
$$

2.3   Network Architectures

We select a set of state-of-the-art methods which use fixed and manually set dilation parameters. We employ our method and make the dilation parameters in those models learnable. Next, we describe the baseline models [3, 20] in this paper and how we adopt them.

Deeplab-LargeFOV. [3] is a VGG [17] based semantic segmentation model. It replaces $conv5_1$, $conv5_2$ and $conv5_3$ in original VGG network with dilation 2. And it has a convolution layer $fc6$ with 512 input feature channels, 1024 output channels and dilation 12. We make $conv5_1$, $conv5_2$, $conv5_3$ and $fc6$ learnable, and set the range of them as $[1, 4]$, $[1, 4]$, $[1, 4]$ and $[4, 20]$.

Deeplab-v2. [3] uses ResNet-101 [7] to extract visual features. It modifies the original ResNet-101 with dilated convolutions. Before *res5c*, there are 23 layers with dilation 2, and 3 layers with dilation 4. There is an ASPP layer after *res5c*, which combines dilation 6, 12, 18 and 24 to recognize the class of each location. We set the range of the dilated convolution layer with dilation factor 2, 4, 6, 12, 18 and 24 to $[1, 4]$, $[1, 8]$, $[1, 11]$, $[7, 17]$, $[13, 23]$ and $[19, 29]$, respectively.

PSPNet. [20] has a similar architecture to *Deeplab-v2*, and achieves state-of-the-art performance on various datasets. There are 23 layers with dilation 2, and 3 layers with dilation 4. Similarly, we set the range of the dilated convolution layer with dilation factor 2 and 4 to $[1, 4]$ and $[1, 8]$. We show that our method can boost *PSPNet*, and achieve new state-of-the-art performance on the challenging street view dataset Cityscapes [5].

2.4   Implementation Details

We train our Deeplab-LargeFOV, Deeplab-v2 and PSPNet models with filter weights initialized from released, original models, which are trained on PASCAL VOC 2012 [6], MS-COCO [12] and Cityscapes [5], respectively. We initialize the dilation factors with the manually set value of the original dilated convolutions. We apply batch SGD with momentum to optimize the models. The batch size is set to 10, the momentum is 0.9 and the weight decay is 0.0005. We use the "poly" learning rate policy where the current learning rate is equal to the base learning rate multiplying $(1 - \frac{iter}{iter_{max}})^{power}$, and $power = 0.9$ for all the experiments. The other hyperparameters are presented in Table 1. We use the respective training code released from the authors. We implement our method using the *Caffe* [10] framework and the source code is available at https://github.com/SSAW14/ LearnableDilationNetwork. In our experiments, our models need 3% to 8% additional time in inference. Training Deeplab-LargeFOV, Deeplab-v2 and PSPNet need only additional 10%, 15% and 15% computational time compared to the base models, respectively.

Table 1. Hyperparameters in the experiments of this paper.

Datasets	Networks	Base learning rate	Iterations
Cityscapes	Deeplab-LargeFOV	1×10^{-3}	20,000
	Deeplab-v2	2.5×10^{-4}	20,000
	PSPNet	1×10^4	20,000
CamVid	Deeplab-v2	2.5×10^{-4}	15,000
	PSPNet	1×10^{-4}	10,000

3   Experiments

We evaluate the proposed method and baselines on the public benchmarks Cityscapes [5] and CamVid [1] using four evaluation metrics following previous work [8,13]: pixel accuracy (*Pixel Acc.*), mean class accuracy (*Cls Acc.*), region intersection over union (*Mean IoU*), and frequency weighted intersection over union (*f.w. IoU*).

3.1   Cityscapes

Cityscapes [5] is a recently released street scene dataset, which is collected from diverse cities in different seasons. The image resolution in Cityscapes is 1024×2048 and the image quality is very high. It defines 19 semantic classes covering traffic, stuff and objects. There are 2975, 500 and 1525 carefully annotated images for training, validation and testing. Besides, there are also 20,000 coarsely annotated images provided for additional training data. Following previous work [20], we leverage those coarse annotations during training to obtain state-of-the-art performance.

Ablation Study for Deeplab-LargeFOV. We first provide an ablation study on the Cityscapes validation set to show the effectiveness of learning dilation factors using the baseline model Deeplab-LargeFOV. We train models with different dilation configurations (see Table 2), varying fixed dilations in $conv5_1$ to $conv5_3$ from 1 to 4, and learning parameters for $conv5_1$ to $conv5_3$ and fc6.

The first row in Table 2 shows the performance of the baseline method without dilated convolutions, which is only 58.91% mean IoU. Fixed integer valued dilated convolution parameters can improve the performance to up to 62.51% for a factor of 4 in $conv5_1$ to $conv5_3$.

By replacing the fixed dilation parameters with our learnable dilated convolutions using the same dilation factors as initialization, we get a further improvement to up to 63.31% mean IoU. Besides, we also use uniform distribution for the initialization of dilated convolutions, obtaining 62.92% mean IoU, which is

Table 2. Ablation study on the Cityscapes validation set using the VGG based Deeplab-LargeFOV model. Black numbers for the convolutional layers indicate fixed dilation parameters, red numbers or ranges in our learnable dilated convolution layers indicate the initial values or distributions before training.

$conv5_1$	$conv5_2$	$conv5_3$	fc6	Pixel Acc.	Cls Acc.	f.w. IoU	Mean IoU	learned $conv5_{1-3}$	learned fc6
1	1	1	12	93.11	68.70	87.76	58.91		
2	2	2	12	93.49	71.76	88.36	61.44		
3	3	3	12	93.50	71.93	88.37	62.17		
4	4	4	12	93.49	72.35	88.38	62.51		
2.35	2.6	3.5	12	93.63	72.46	88.58	62.94		
2	2	2	12	93.50	73.25	88.41	62.31	✓	
2	2	2	12	93.65	72.64	88.61	62.86		✓
[1,4]	[1,4]	[1,4]	[4,20]	93.69	72.90	88.71	62.92	✓	✓
2	2	2	12	**93.72**	**73.38**	**88.77**	**63.31**	✓	✓

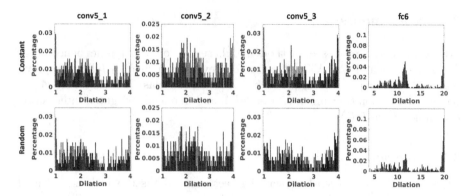

Fig. 3. The learned dilation distribution in the Deeplab-LargeFOV model on Cityscapes dataset. The first row shows the distribution using constant value initialization, and the second row shows the distribution using random noise as presented in Table 2.

comparable to constant value initialization, and better than the models with fixed dilation factors. We show the dilation distribution over input channels in Fig. 3. We observe that the learned dilation distributions of using constant value and random noise, are very similar, which is clearly shown the stability of optimization. We observe that our dilation covers most values in the range of $[1, 4]$ for conv5$_1$ to conv5$_3$, which allows us capture *local* details and *wide* context at the same time. The second observation is that there are some peaks in the distribution, which make the current layer capture more local information or capture a wider context. For a specific dilated convolution layer in a network, it is very difficult to know whether the current convolution should capture local or global information, which is why the proposed learning based model achieves better performance than all fixed dilation settings. To verify this point, we train a further model with fixed dilated convolutions with factors 2.35, 2.6 and 3.5 which are the average values of the learned dilation distribution over all channels. This model achieves better results than all the other fixed settings but is worse than the channel-wise learned setting.

Comparisons on Deeplab-v2 and PSPNet. We choose Deeplab-v2 and PSPNet as our baselines, which leverage the powerful ResNet [7] to build their models. We report the *Mean IoU* score. The comparison results on Cityscapes validation set can be found in Table 3. Compared our results to baselines, we observe that we got general improvement in most classes like "Fence", "Terrain", "Car" and "Bus". Particular, in some challenging and important (core role in traffic scenarios) classes like "Person" and "Rider", we got clearly improvements for Deeplab-v2 as well as PSPNet. Due to deformations and large appearance variances, "Person" and "Rider" are easily confused each other. By learning appropriate details and context, we boosted Deeplab-v2 and PSPNet to recognize "Person" (+0.6 percentage points (*pp*) for Deeplab-v2 and +1.3*pp* for PSPNet) and "Rider" (+0.8*pp* for Deeplab-v2 and +4.9*pp* for PSPNet).

Table 3. Comparison IoU scores on Cityscapes validation set.

Method	Road	Sidewalk	Building	Wall	Fence	Pole	Traf. Light	Traf. Sign	Vegetation	Terrain	Sky	Person	Rider
Deeplab-v2 [3]	97.2	78.7	90.2	49.3	48.8	52.5	**57.7**	69.7	90.8	59.4	92.7	76.6	53.3
Deeplab-v2 + ours	97.2	**79.1**	**90.5**	**52.2**	**49.9**	**53.2**	57.4	**70.1**	**90.9**	**59.6**	**92.9**	**77.2**	**54.6**
PSPNet [20]	98.3	86.4	**93.1**	**60.6**	65.9	**64.3**	72.0	81.1	92.6	64.7	94.9	82.5	61.5
PSPNet + ours	98.3	86.4	93.0	59.1	**66.4**	64.0	**72.7**	**81.3**	92.6	**65.6**	94.9	**83.3**	**66.4**

Method	Car	Truck	Bus	Train	Motorcycle	Bicycle	Mean IoU
Deeplab-v2 [3]	92.6	**66.8**	78.1	**61.3**	**60.4**	71.9	70.9
Deeplab-v2 + Ours	**92.8**	62.8	**79.9**	58.9	58.9	**72.2**	**71.1**
PSPNet [20]	95.3	81.4	89.7	**84.5**	62.8	78.7	79.4
PSPNet + Ours	**95.4**	**83.0**	**89.9**	80.6	**66.8**	**78.9**	**79.9**

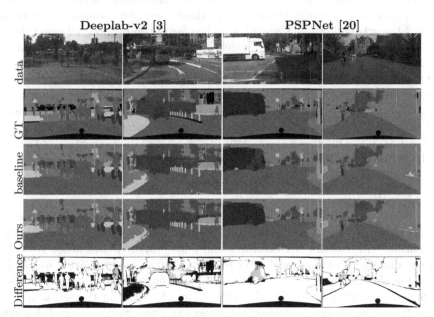

Fig. 4. Qualitative results on the Cityscapes validation set for Deeplab-v2 [3] (left) and PSPNet [20] (right). The first four rows show the raw images, ground truth, baselines' predictions and our predictions. The last row is a visual comparison of correctly classified pixels. In white areas, both predictions are correct, in *red* areas, only the baseline prediction is correct and in *cyan* colored areas, the proposed predictions are correct, while the baseline prediction is erroneous. (Color figure online)

Figure 4 shows some qualitative results from baselines and our models. In the left two columns, Deeplab-v2 baseline recognizes the rider and the middle section of the train to classes "person" and "bus", which are confusing to ground truth. In the right two columns, PSPNet baseline fails to recognize the font part of the truck and the rider, while our method shows improved predictions.

Table 4. Quantitative results on CamVid dataset. With the proposed dilated convolutions, our method achieves better performance than two baselines, and we present new state-of-the-art performance on the CamVid dataset.

Method	Building	Tree	Sky	Car	Sign	Road	Pedestrian	Fence	Pole	Sidewalk	Bicyclist	*mean IoU*
Dilation [19]	82.6	76.2	89.9	84.0	46.9	92.2	56.3	35.8	23.4	75.3	55.5	65.3
FSO [11]	84	77.2	91.3	85.6	49.9	92.5	59.1	37.6	16.9	76.0	57.2	66.1
Synthetic [15]	84.4	77.5	91.1	84.9	51.3	94.5	59	44.9	29.5	82	58.4	68.9
Deeplab-v2 [3]	83.8	**76.5**	90.9	**89.1**	46.0	**94.6**	57.0	28.4	19.6	**81.4**	50.1	65.2
Deeplab-v2 + ours	**84.1**	76.3	90.9	88.8	**47.5**	94.4	**58.1**	**32.4**	**20.0**	80.8	**54.0**	**66.1**
PSPNet [20]	87.8	**79.5**	**91.4**	91.4	57.7	96.5	66.7	58.6	**23.5**	87.8	66.9	73.4
PSPNet + ours	**88.0**	79.3	91.3	**91.7**	**58.8**	96.5	66.9	61.9	23.0	87.8	69.4	**73.9**

3.2 CamVid

CamVid is a smaller street view dataset captured from onboard camera. We not only compare our networks to baseline methods, but also compare to previous state-of-the-art methods on Camvid. For the ease of comparison, we utilized the training and test setup from [18], which has 11 semantic classes, 367 training, 100 validation and 233 test images. The image resolution in our experiments is 640×480. The quantitative results are summarized in Table 4. We improve over Deeplab-v2 and PSPNet for 0.9 *pp* and 0.5 *pp*, respectively. For most classes, we obtain comparable performance. Particularly, in the classes of "Sign", "Fence" and "Bicyclist", our method achieves clear improvements over Deeplab-v2 as well as PSPNet. This shows the benefit of our learned dilation: State-of-the art methods can be improved to recognize a range of classes better.

4   Conclusion

In this paper, we have presented learnable dilated convolutions, which is fully compatible with existing architectures and adds only little overhead. We have applied our novel convolutional layer to learn channel-based dilation factors in the semantic segmentation scenario. Thus, we were able to improve the performance of Deeplab-LargeFOV, Deeplab-v2 and PSPNet for the semantic segmentation of street scenes consistently across two datasets. We showed that our method is able to obtain visually more convincing results, and improved quantitative performance. Besides, a series of ablation studies shows that learning the dilation parameter is helpful to design better semantic segmentation models in practice.

References

1. Brostow, G.J., Shotton, J., Fauqueur, J., Cipolla, R.: Segmentation and recognition using structure from motion point clouds. In: Forsyth, D., Torr, P., Zisserman, A. (eds.) ECCV 2008. LNCS, vol. 5302, pp. 44–57. Springer, Heidelberg (2008). doi:10.1007/978-3-540-88682-2_5

2. Chen, L.C., Papandreou, G., Kokkinos, I., Murphy, K., Yuille, A.L.: Semantic image segmentation with deep convolutional nets and fully connected CRFs. In: ICLR (2014)
3. Chen, L.C., Papandreou, G., Kokkinos, I., Murphy, K., Yuille, A.L.: Deeplab: Semantic image segmentation with deep convolutional nets, atrous convolution, and fully connected CRFs. arXiv preprint arXiv:1606.00915 (2016)
4. Chen, L.C., Yang, Y., Wang, J., Xu, W., Yuille, A.L.: Attention to scale: scale-aware semantic image segmentation. In: CVPR (2016)
5. Cordts, M., Omran, M., Ramos, S., Rehfeld, T., Enzweiler, M., Benenson, R., Franke, U., Roth, S., Schiele, B.: The cityscapes dataset for semantic urban scene understanding. In: CVPR (2016)
6. Everingham, M., Van Gool, L., Williams, C.K., Winn, J., Zisserman, A.: The PASCAL visual object classes (VOC) challenge. IJCV **88**(2), 303–338 (2010)
7. He, K., Zhang, X., Ren, S., Sun, J.: Deep residual learning for image recognition. In: CVPR (2016)
8. He, Y., Chiu, W.C., Keuper, M., Fritz, M.: STD2P: RGBD semantic segmentation using spatio-temporal data-driven pooling. In: IEEE Conference on Computer Vision and Pattern Recognition (CVPR) (2017)
9. Jaderberg, M., Simonyan, K., Zisserman, A., et al.: Spatial transformer networks. In: NIPS (2015)
10. Jia, Y., Shelhamer, E., Donahue, J., Karayev, S., Long, J., Girshick, R., Guadarrama, S., Darrell, T.: Caffe: convolutional architecture for fast feature embedding. In: Proceedings of the ACM International Conference on Multimedia (2014)
11. Kundu, A., Vineet, V., Koltun, V.: Feature space optimization for semantic video segmentation. In: CVPR (2016)
12. Lin, T.-Y., Maire, M., Belongie, S., Hays, J., Perona, P., Ramanan, D., Dollár, P., Zitnick, C.L.: Microsoft COCO: common objects in context. In: Fleet, D., Pajdla, T., Schiele, B., Tuytelaars, T. (eds.) ECCV 2014. LNCS, vol. 8693, pp. 740–755. Springer, Cham (2014). doi:10.1007/978-3-319-10602-1_48
13. Long, J., Shelhamer, E., Darrell, T.: Fully convolutional networks for semantic segmentation. In: CVPR (2015)
14. Pohlen, T., Hermans, A., Mathias, M., Leibe, B.: Full-resolution residual networks for semantic segmentation in street scenes (2017)
15. Richter, S.R., Vineet, V., Roth, S., Koltun, V.: Playing for data: ground truth from computer games. In: Leibe, B., Matas, J., Sebe, N., Welling, M. (eds.) ECCV 2016. LNCS, vol. 9906, pp. 102–118. Springer, Cham (2016). doi:10.1007/978-3-319-46475-6_7
16. Rumelhart, D.E., Hinton, G.E., Williams, R.J.: Learning representations by back-propagating errors. Cogn. Model. **5**(3), 1 (1988)
17. Simonyan, K., Zisserman, A.: Very deep convolutional networks for large-scale image recognition. arXiv preprint arXiv:1409.1556 (2014)
18. Sturgess, P., Alahari, K., Ladicky, L., Torr, P.H.: Combining appearance and structure from motion features for road scene understanding. In: BMVC (2009)
19. Yu, F., Koltun, V.: Multi-scale context aggregation by dilated convolutions. In: ICLR (2016)
20. Zhao, H., Shi, J., Qi, X., Wang, X., Jia, J.: Pyramid scene parsing network. arXiv preprint arXiv:1612.01105 (2016)

Learning to Filter Object Detections

Sergey Prokudin[1]([✉]), Daniel Kappler[1], Sebastian Nowozin[2],
and Peter Gehler[1]

[1] Max Planck Institute for Intelligent Systems, Tübingen, Germany
{sergey.prokudin,daniel.kappler,peter.gehler}@tuebingen.mpg.de
[2] Microsoft Research, Cambridge, UK

Abstract. Most object detection systems consist of three stages. First, a set of individual hypotheses for object locations is generated using a proposal generating algorithm. Second, a classifier scores every generated hypothesis independently to obtain a multi-class prediction. Finally, all scored hypotheses are filtered via a non-differentiable and decoupled non-maximum suppression (NMS) post-processing step. In this paper, we propose a filtering network (FNet), a method which replaces NMS with a differentiable neural network that allows joint reasoning and re-scoring of the generated set of hypotheses per image. This formulation enables end-to-end training of the full object detection pipeline. First, we demonstrate that FNet, a feed-forward network architecture, is able to mimic NMS decisions, despite the sequential nature of NMS. We further analyze NMS failures and propose a loss formulation that is better aligned with the mean average precision (mAP) evaluation metric. We evaluate FNet on several standard detection datasets. Results surpass standard NMS on highly occluded settings of a synthetic overlapping MNIST dataset and show competitive behavior on PascalVOC2007 and KITTI detection benchmarks.

1 Introduction

Object detection is a fundamental structured prediction problem in computer vision. This problem is regularly approached with three main processing steps. In the first *region proposal* step a set of object hypotheses is generated using a proposal algorithm. Second, a multi-class classifier scores each hypothesis independent of all other hypotheses. We further refer to this as *proposal classification* step. In a final *filtering step* the redundant hypotheses are suppressed via non-maximum suppression (NMS).

The final filtering step is typically crucial in order to achieve good performance, e.g. on PascalVOC this step doubles the performance. Nevertheless, today NMS is still the main building block of current detection algorithms and is used frequently in most modern detection algorithms [13,14]. Greedy sequential NMS consists of the following heuristic steps: (i) sort proposals according to

---

S. Prokudin and D. Kappler—These authors are contributed equally to this work.

© Springer International Publishing AG 2017
V. Roth and T. Vetter (Eds.): GCPR 2017, LNCS 10496, pp. 52–62, 2017.
DOI: 10.1007/978-3-319-66709-6_5

(a) Highly occluded instances would be suppressed

(b) Parts of objects could be not suppressed

Fig. 1. Examples of NMS failures.

their classification scores, (ii) start from the highest scoring hypothesis remove all hypotheses with an overlap of a predefined threshold, (iii) repeat step (ii) until all hypotheses have been selected or removed.

Speed, ease and effectiveness are strong positive points but NMS also has some drawbacks:

- **non-adaptive:** The NMS decision rule is hard-coded using the proposal classification scores, overlap ratio between hypotheses and a single predefined threshold. Therefore, it does not allow to "reason-away" sets of bounding boxes, a feature that would entail more complex and flexible features.
- **non-differentiable:** NMS is a greedy, sequential, heuristic procedure applied separately of bounding box scoring. It prevents the former classification step from being jointly trained for the final loss function.

Figure 1 shows two common NMS failure cases: (a) suppressing nearby detections of highly occluded objects and (b) not suppressing hypotheses representing only parts of an object, i.e. the knee.

Recently, much progress has been made in improving the individual classification results [6,16] and fusing the proposal generation and classification steps [12–14,16]. Yet, only a few approaches have been proposed in order to replace the final sequential NMS step, e.g., by [8]. However, the latter approach is not differentiable since it uses NMS features and thus hinder end-to-end training of the entire detection pipeline.

In this paper we aim to take some steps to turn the NMS process into a differentiable building block that can be used in conjunction with any multi-class classifier. There are some features of NMS that make this a challenging task and we take some careful steps to not loose the performance of NMS while proposing

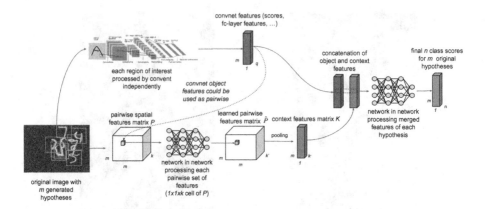

Fig. 2. FNet overview. Example on overlapping MNIST dataset, LeNet [10] is used for independent hypotheses classification.

a replacement that can be used in a wider context. We propose to replace the sequential NMS step with an additional feed-forward neural network that can be stacked on top of any existing classifier. For the remainder of this paper, we refer to this add-on as *filtering network*, or in short FNet. In contrast to the existing classifier, the proposed FNet processes the proposal hypotheses *jointly*, propagating errors to the individually processed hypotheses of the existing classifier.

Figure 2 depicts an overview of our proposed architecture, illustrated with LeNet [10] as the basic per hypothesis classifier. The main idea for the FNet structure is to use all information provided by all hypotheses in order to learn context features which allow to filter hypotheses based on global knowledge. The architecture is described in more detail in Sect. 4.

In order to verify ability of our approach to perform structured reasoning over a set of hypotheses, we replace NMS by learning an approximate NMS objective (Sect. 5.1). We demonstrate that FNet can reproduce NMS with high accuracy. Since FNet is composed of standard neural network components and has no sequential steps it achieves this performance while adding only a minor computational overhead to the detection pipeline. We further introduce a new loss function (net-loss), a sufficient objective to improve directly on the mean average precision (mAP) objective [5]. Results are reported on three datasets. Our experiments indicate that by leveraging features from the classifier networks, we are able to surpass NMS performance on a synthetic overlapping MNIST (oMNIST) dataset while being on par on KITTI and PascalVOC2007.

Thus, in summary the main contribution of this work is to replace NMS with a simple fully differentiable feed-forward network. FNet is is independent of the number of hypotheses, allows to make decisions over a set of hypotheses, and can be stacked on top of pre-trained object detection pipelines.

FNet is implemented in TensorFlow [1]. Just as traditional NMS postprocessing, it can be easily combined with any existing object detection model.

2   Related Work

There are two interconnected streams of research related to our approach in the literature: the first one aims to replace NMS with something more flexible, while the second one concentrates on building an end-to-end object detection pipeline.

Learning Non-maximum Suppression: The work of [15] analyzes the drawbacks of sequential NMS, and proposes to use an affinity propagation algorithm to pass information between hypotheses. While sharing the common high-level idea of using information between pairs of hypotheses to perform better filtering, this method differs from ours in the model used for describing hypotheses interactions and the loss function being optimized. Another promising approach is shown in [8]. There, all hypotheses are mapped to a spatial grid based on their center locations. The extracted pre-trained classification scores and intersections between hypotheses are then used as inputs for a convolutional network operating on this grid structure. Another aprroaches based on Hough transform were proposed in [2,9]. However, no end-to-end optimization was shown for these NMS replacements, leaving the approach detached from the underlying per hypotheses classifier networks.

End-to-end Learning of Object Detection Pipeline: Wan et al. [18] proposes a method to incorporate an object detector, deformable parts model and NMS in a fully differentiable pipeline. Nevertheless, the NMS step still remains a fixed transformation over a set of hypotheses, reformulated as a layer performing a particular operation. The same applies to Henderson and Ferrari [7], who propose a way to propagate gradients directly for the mean average precision (mAP) loss. There NMS is treated similar to a max-pooling step, where only the hypotheses representing a local-maximum propagate gradients. The problems illustrated in Fig. 1(a) therefore remain unchanged; hypotheses falling under the suppression condition will still be pruned out.

Finally, Stewart et al. [17] replace the NMS post-processing stage with LSTM cells in order to achieve better spatial reasoning for neighbouring hypotheses. However, this method requires the image to be divided into a regular grid of independent regions, e.g. 15×20, while predictions across regions are merged via a heuristic stitching step.

3   Problem Formulation

As mentioned before, the object detection pipeline is regularly a combination of three steps - searching for good hypotheses, generating independent predictions for each of them, and joint filtering of the final set. Our work focuses on the last step. Given a set of hypotheses for an image I, we assume the following information to be provided

$$H = \{[h_i, s(h_i), f(h_i)], i = 1, \ldots, m\}, \tag{1}$$

where $h_i \in \mathbb{R}^4$ are hypothesis bounding box coordinates (regularly represented as (x, y)-coordinates of upper left corner and width and height of a box). Scores are denoted by $s(h_i) \in \mathbb{R}^n$ for all n classes of interest. This is the output for every hypothesis from the proposal classification step. $f(h_i) \in \mathbb{R}^q$ is a feature vector per hypothesis (for example, CNN features). Here and below square brackets stand for concatenation of the vectors. The total number of hypotheses per image m can vary between images.

During training, ground truth hypotheses are denoted by G:

$$G = \{[g_i, c_i], i = 1, \ldots, d\}, \tag{2}$$

where $g_i \in \mathbb{R}^4$ - ground truth bounding box coordinates, $c_i \in \{1, \ldots, n\}$ - class label for the ground truth, d is the total number of ground truth objects on image. The proposed filtering step re-scores all class scores for every hypotheses $h_i \in H$ while considering all other hypotheses in H:

$$H \to H' = \{[h_i, s'(h_i, H), f(h_i)], i = 1, \ldots, m\}. \tag{3}$$

The classical NMS can be considered as copying the scores for unsuppressed hypotheses $s'(h_i) = s(h_i, H)$ and setting it to zero vector for suppressed ones $s'(h_j, H) = \hat{0}$. The new scores $s'(h_i, H)$ typically aim to minimize the mAP evaluation metric, described in [5] and discussed in Sect. 5.2.

4   Filtering Network Architecture

The focus of this work is on differentiable, thus, end-to-end learnable filtering of hypotheses for multi-class object detection. Our proposed *filtering network* FNet allows to optimize the underlying score generating network not only based on the scores but also its features in order to generate one matching hypothesis per ground truth bounding box labeling. The main idea of FNet is to utilize all the information (Eq. 1) provided by the earlier steps of a pipeline by building a pairwise matrix P (Eq. 5) in order to learn context features that will allow to filter hypotheses based on global knowledge. Thus, FNet is designed to directly solve the filtering step formalized in (Eq. 3):

$$s'(h_i, H) = FNet(h_i, H), i = 1, \ldots, m. \tag{4}$$

We start by building the pairwise matrix P

$$P_{i,j} = [f(h_i), f(h_j), h_i, h_j], \quad P \in \mathbb{R}^{m \times m \times k}, \tag{5}$$

consisting of two types of features, the feature vectors of the per-hypothesis network and the corresponding hypotheses locations. Based on P, we learn a new pairwise matrix $\hat{P}$

$$\hat{P}_{i,j} = \text{NiN}^{\text{pairwise}}(P_{i,j}), \quad \hat{P} \in \mathbb{R}^{m \times m \times k'}, \tag{6}$$

where NiN represents a network in network [11] which is convolved over the pairwise matrix P. The main idea behind the approach is that, given pairwise set of features $P_{i,j} \in \mathbb{R}^k$ (e.g. scores and features for both hypotheses under consideration plus ratio of overlap between corresponding bounding boxes), we learn a small network to abstract this data and produce a new feature vector $\hat{P}_{i,j} \in \mathbb{R}^{k'}$ that will represent learned relations between pair of hypotheses.

Since every image can have a different number of hypotheses m, we apply a reduction operator:

$$K = R(\hat{P}) : \mathbb{R}^{m \times m \times k'} \to \mathbb{R}^{m \times k'}, \tag{7}$$

which results in fixed sized context feature matrix K. Each i'th row of this matrix represents context features vectors for hypothesis i that we denote as $K_i = K(h_i)$. The original feature vector $f(h_i)$ is fused with its context feature vector $K(h_i)$ via another network in network, producing the final score $s'(h_i)$ for the given hypothesis

$$s'(h_i, H) = \text{NiN}^{\text{context}} (f(h_i), K(h_i)), \quad i = 1, \ldots, m. \tag{8}$$

Input Features. As discussed in the previous section, we generally consider two types of input features, network features $f(h_i)$ provided by earlier stages of the pipeline, and location coordinates h_i. Since there is usually problem specific knowledge present, in practice it is very helpful to add additional function of the input features

$$P_{i,j} = [f(h_i), f(h_j), f(h_i) - f(h_j), \text{sign}(f(h_i) - f(h_j)), \text{IoU}(h_i, h_j)], \tag{9}$$

where IoU stands for intersection over union between hypotheses areas, and sign returns an element-wise indication of the sign of a vector. Adding the difference between hypotheses and the sign provides a helpful signal to the network in order to decide whether or not there exists a better scored hypothesis. Using IoU as a feature provides further evidence of the relationship between two hypotheses besides their feature vectors and scores.

Reduction Operator. We select a combination of simple maximum and average pooling operations as the reduction operation of choice for all the considered experiments:

$$k_{it} = \left[\max_j \hat{P}_{i,j,t}, \frac{1}{m} \sum_j \hat{P}_{i,j,t} \right], t = 1, \ldots, k', K \in \mathbb{R}^{m \times k'} \tag{10}$$

5 Learning Objectives

We explore two possible learning objectives to optimize FNet. In order to verify the learning capacity of the proposed FNet architecture, we introduce a loss function that will force FNet to mimic decisions made by NMS. We hypothesize in Sect. 5.2 that a new loss function is required in order to improve over the previously presented NMS error cases. Henderson and Ferrari [7] show that mAP is a complex structured loss over thousands of hypotheses, thus, in this paper we propose to substitute the mAP with a proxy loss function (net-loss) that can be evaluated on a per image basis.

5.1 Approximate Non-maximum Suppression Objective

We can approximate the sequential NMS process with fixed IoU threshold a by decomposing decisions made for every hypothesis h_i with class score s_i into the following per-hypothesis labels:

$$l_z(h_i) = \begin{cases} 0, & \text{if } \exists h_j : \text{IoU}(h_i, h_j) > a \text{ and } s_z(h_j) > s_z(h_i); \\ 1, & \text{otherwise}; \end{cases} \tag{11}$$

where $z = 1, \ldots, n$, n is the number of classes and $s_z(h_i)$ is the score for class z and hypothesis i. Based on these labels, we can optimize a multi-class objective such as cross-entropy for the FNet score $s'(h_i, H)$ and the target labels of Eq. 11. In that case filtering scores $s'(h_i, H)$ cannot be used directly to represent class probabilities, since the network learns to mimic suppression. It is not aware of cases when a hypothesis is not suppressed by NMS. Since the hypothesis itself might have a low independent score itself, we obtain the final score per hypothesis h_i by multiplying the original score $s(h_i)$ with our filtering value $s'(h_i, H)$. This approach results in decreased scores for those of the hypotheses that have high suppression probabilities:

$$s''(h_i) = s(h_i) \cdot s'(h_i, H). \tag{12}$$

It is important to mention that there are cases when this non-sequential labeling will result in different selected set of hypotheses compared to the sequential NMS as shown in Fig. 3(a). For illustrative purposes, we assume that we have

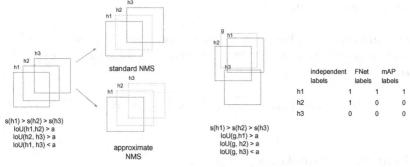

(a) Difference in behaviour of standard and approximate NMS procedures.

(b) Comparison of different hypothesis labelings used to train the network.

Fig. 3. Overview of learning objectives.

an ordered set of hypotheses with class scores $s(h_1) > s(h_2) > s(h_3)$. According to our labeling procedure, the lowest scoring hypothesis h_3 will have a zero label because of the high overlap with h_2 and the higher score. Whereas NMS will process all hypotheses sequentially starting from h_1, selecting it, then suppressing the highly overlapping h_2, and finally selecting h_3 because of absence of h_2 in the remaining set.

In the majority of cases, however, the selected sets behave very similar. For example, for proposals produced by FasterRCNN [14] on the PascalVOC2007 test set, decisions made by normal NMS and our approximate version agree on 98.1% of all hypotheses under consideration.

5.2   Network Detection Objective

The previously introduced labeling and loss for learning NMS only functions as a testbed showing the capabilities of our FNet architecture, capable of explaining away hypotheses in order to reproduce NMS results. Yet, this formulation will at best result in the approximate NMS solution in case of training convergence, thus, will not allow FNet to address the failure modes of sequential NMS. In the following we propose a new loss formulation which better approximates mAP. The mAP metric [5] has two significantly different properties compared to regularly used loss functions for end-to-end training. First, it penalizes the presence of multiple hypotheses corresponding to the same ground-truth region. Thus, a model intended to optimize for mAP should allow to explain away sets of hypotheses. Second, mAP is in fact structured over all hypotheses of all images in the test set, meaning that the change in the score obtained by hypothesis h_{ij} of the image I_i could result in different loss signal for hypothesis h_{pq} of image I_p. While there are works aiming to overcome this issue, e.g. [7], our work focuses on the hypotheses filtering. The ideas from [7] can be incorporated into our framework but is beyond the scope of this paper and therefore subject for future work.

Similar to the approximate NMS loss, we aim to generate per-hypothesis labels that will result in an improvement for mAP. In case of mAP, the aforementioned property of positive reinforcement of only the highest scoring hypothesis could be reformulated as the following per-hypothesis label:

$$l(h_i) = \begin{cases} 1, & \text{if } \exists g \in G : \text{IoU}(h_i, g) > a \text{ and } \nexists h_j, i \neq j : s_j > s_i, \text{IoU}(h_j, g) > a; \\ 0, & \text{otherwise.} \end{cases}$$

$$(13)$$

In other words, hypothesis h_i will get positive label if and only if there is some region g from the set of ground truth regions G that overlaps significantly with hypothesis under consideration, and hypothesis h_i has the maximum score of all hypotheses matching that ground truth region. The network is then trained to directly minimize cross-entropy between scores, output by FNet, and labels according to Eq. 13. The difference between regular independent per-hypothesis labeling and our network labeling is shown in Fig. 3(b). While both methods

Table 1. Results on oMNIST single digit canvas.

Digit	Network	Loss	Lenet-feature	mAP
1	LeNet + NMS			0.87
1	+ FNet	nms	score [s]	0.93
1	+ FNet	net	score [s] + fc	**0.97**
3	LeNet + NMS			0.87
3	+ FNet	nms	score [s]	0.90
3	+ FNet	net	score [s] + fc	**0.96**
6	LeNet + NMS			0.87
6	+ FNet	nms	score [s]	0.92
6	+ FNet	net	score [s] + fc	**0.96**

Table 2. Results on oMNIST multi-class digit canvas.

Network	Loss	Lenet-features	mAP
LeNet + NMS			**0.83**
+ FNet	nms	scores [s] + fc	0.81
+ FNet	net	scores [s] + fc	0.78

Table 3. Results on PascalVOC test

Method	Loss	mAP
FasterRCNN (no filtering)		0.270
+NMS		**0.680**
+FNet	net	0.675

penalize ill-located hypothesis h_3, the labeling induced by our method also force redundant hypothesis h_2 to be filtered - exactly in the same way it would be treated by mAP evaluation.

6   Experiments

For all considered experiments simple 2-layer neural network with the 512 hidden units and ReLU activations was used to represent both pairwise and context network in network (NiN).

Overlapping MNIST. We construct the dataset by randomly placing digits from the MNIST dataset on 128×96 black canvas with background Gaussian noise. In order to create a more realistic dataset we draw a number of digits per canvas uniformly from $[0, 24]$. For each digit, we draw a location uniformly at random from all valid coordinates of the canvas. An example of a generated image is shown in Fig. 2. We start with the setting when only one class of digits is placed on a canvas, resulting in images with highly overlapping instances of a single class. We experiment with three different digits being placed on a canvas ("1", "3", "6"). In all of the cases FNet shows a substantial performance gain over baseline NMS approach (Table 1). This suggests that the methods trained on real-world datasets with similar properties, i.e. a large number of overlapping instances of the same class (such as Caltech Pedestrian [4]), could potentially benefit from combining them with our architecture. The results for a multi-digit canvas are shown in Table 2. FNet still achieves comparable performance when trained for approximate NMS objective, while optimization for network loss gives notably worse performance. The issue, though, still could be addressed by proper hyperparameter tuning.

KITTI. Similar to the oMNIST experiment we use the scores and features from the last fully-connected layer of a pre-trained network as our per-hypothesis features vector $f(h_i)$, in this case MS-CNN [3]. The results for the per class

Table 4. Results on the KITTI benchmark validation set

Method	Loss	Car			Pedestrian		
		Easy	Mod	Hard	Easy	Mod	Hard
MS-CNN (no filtering)		0.722	0.669	0.540	0.540	0.494	0.442
+ NMS		**0.922**	**0.917**	0.813	**0.896**	**0.867**	0.744
+ FNet	nms	0.921	0.916	0.813	**0.896**	0.866	0.741
+ FNet	net	0.913	0.910	**0.865**	0.890	0.839	**0.746**

trained FNet on the classes 'Car' and 'Pedestrian' are shown in the Table 4. We omit the results for the class "Cyclist" since we were unable to reproduce the baseline network behaviour.

The FNet results in Table 4 indicate that our proposed approach is indeed expressive enough to be on par with the sequential NMS. Interestingly, using the net-loss discussed in Sect. 5.2 results in slightly worse performance on the 'Easy' and 'Moderate' data examples, though improvements can be observed in the harder cases of both classes. Notice, all results reported on MS-CNN have been trained as a replacement of sequential NMS on top of MS-CNN and not end-to-end.

PascalVOC2007. For the PascalVOC2007 dataset we use the hypotheses and features from a pre-trained FasterRCNN [3] as our baseline method. The feature vector $f(h_i)$ is again constructed from the scores and the last fully-connected layer of the pre-trained network. We train FNet using the proposed network based labeling (net-loss) with a single multi-class objective. The results in Table 3 show a small performance drop compared to the sequential NMS filtering step. Similar to the KITTI results, no end-to-end training was performed to achieve these results.

7   Conclusion

We have shown an architecture that allows to learn a filtering behaviour based on a potentially varying set of hypotheses per image, while being end-to-end differentiable. We have presented an approximate NMS labeling and shown in experiments on oMNIST and KITTI datasets that our FNet architecture can match the sequential NMS performance by fitting this proxy objective. Further, this network allows to directly optimize an objective that is better aligned with final evaluation metric. We have shown on the synthetic oMNIST example that in case of a large amount of highly overlapping objects of a same class a combination of a flexible filtering and proper loss can result in a notable performance gain.

Acknowledgments. The authors would like to thank the anonymous reviewers for their valuable comments and suggestions to improve the quality of the paper. This work was supported by Microsoft Research through its PhD Scholarship Programme.

References

1. Abadi, M., Agarwal, A., Barham, P., Brevdo, E., Chen, Z., Citro, C., Corrado, G.S., Davis, A., Dean, J., Devin, M., et al.: Tensorflow: large-scale machine learning on heterogeneous distributed systems. arXiv:1603.04467 (2016)
2. Barinova, O., Lempitsky, V., Kholi, P.: On detection of multiple object instances using hough transforms. IEEE Trans. Pattern Anal. Mach. Intell. **34**(9), 1773–1784 (2012)
3. Cai, Z., Fan, Q., Feris, R.S., Vasconcelos, N.: A unified multi-scale deep convolutional neural network for fast object detection. In: Leibe, B., Matas, J., Sebe, N., Welling, M. (eds.) ECCV 2016. LNCS, vol. 9908, pp. 354–370. Springer, Cham (2016). doi:10.1007/978-3-319-46493-0_22
4. Dollar, P., Wojek, C., Schiele, B., Perona, P.: Pedestrian detection: an evaluation of the state of the art. PAMI **34**, 743–761 (2012)
5. Everingham, M., Van Gool, L., Williams, C.K., Winn, J., Zisserman, A.: The pascal visual object classes (VOC) challenge. Int. J. Comput. Vis. **88**(2), 303–338 (2010)
6. He, K., Zhang, X., Ren, S., Sun, J.: Deep residual learning for image recognition. In: Proceedings of the IEEE Conference on Computer Vision and Pattern Recognition, pp. 770–778 (2016)
7. Henderson, P., Ferrari, V.: End-to-end training of object class detectors for mean average precision. arXiv:1607.03476 (2016)
8. Hosang, J., Benenson, R., Schiele, B.: A convnet for non-maximum suppression. In: Rosenhahn, B., Andres, B. (eds.) GCPR 2016. LNCS, vol. 9796, pp. 192–204. Springer, Cham (2016). doi:10.1007/978-3-319-45886-1_16
9. Kontschieder, P., Bulò, S.R., Donoser, M., Pelillo, M., Bischof, H.: Evolutionary hough games for coherent object detection. Comput. Vis. Image Underst. **116**(11), 1149–1158 (2012)
10. LeCun, Y., Bottou, L., Bengio, Y., Haffner, P.: Gradient-based learning applied to document recognition. Proc. IEEE **86**(11), 2278–2324 (1998)
11. Lin, M., Chen, Q., Yan, S.: Network in network. arXiv preprint arXiv:1312.4400 (2013)
12. Redmon, J., Divvala, S., Girshick, R., Farhadi, A.: You only look once: unified, real-time object detection. In: Proceedings of the IEEE Conference on Computer Vision and Pattern Recognition, pp. 779–788 (2016)
13. Redmon, J., Farhadi, A.: YOLO9000: better, faster, stronger. arXiv:1612.08242 (2016)
14. Ren, S., He, K., Girshick, R., Sun, J.: Faster R-CNN: towards real-time object detection with region proposal networks. In: Advances in Neural Information Processing Systems, pp. 91–99 (2015)
15. Rothe, R., Guillaumin, M., Gool, L.: Non-maximum suppression for object detection by passing messages between windows. In: Cremers, D., Reid, I., Saito, H., Yang, M.-H. (eds.) ACCV 2014. LNCS, vol. 9003, pp. 290–306. Springer, Cham (2015). doi:10.1007/978-3-319-16865-4_19
16. Simonyan, K., Zisserman, A.: Very deep convolutional networks for large-scale image recognition. arXiv:1409.1556 (2014)
17. Stewart, R., Andriluka, M., Ng, A.Y.: End-to-end people detection in crowded scenes. In: Proceedings of the IEEE Conference on Computer Vision and Pattern Recognition, pp. 2325–2333 (2016)
18. Wan, L., Eigen, D., Fergus, R.: End-to-end integration of a convolution network, deformable parts model and non-maximum suppression. In: Proceedings of the IEEE Conference on Computer Vision and Pattern Recognition, pp. 851–859 (2015)

Computational Photography

Motion Deblurring in the Wild

Mehdi Noroozi[(✉)], Paramanand Chandramouli, and Paolo Favaro

Institute for Informatics, University of Bern, Bern, Switzerland
{noroozi,chandra,paolo.favaro}@inf.unibe.ch

Abstract. We propose a deep learning approach to remove motion blur from a single image captured *in the wild*, *i.e.*, in an uncontrolled setting. Thus, we consider motion blur degradations that are due to both camera and object motion, and by occlusion and coming into view of objects. In this scenario, a model-based approach would require a very large set of parameters, whose fitting is a challenge on its own. Hence, we take a data-driven approach and design both a novel convolutional neural network architecture and a dataset for blurry images with ground truth. The network produces directly the sharp image as output and is built into three pyramid stages, which allow to remove blur gradually from a small amount, at the lowest scale, to the full amount, at the scale of the input image. To obtain corresponding blurry and sharp image pairs, we use videos from a high frame-rate video camera. For each small video clip we select the central frame as the sharp image and use the frame average as the corresponding blurred image. Finally, to ensure that the averaging process is a sufficient approximation to real blurry images we estimate optical flow and select frames with pixel displacements smaller than a pixel. We demonstrate state of the art performance on datasets with both synthetic and real images.

1 Introduction

This work is concerned with the removal of blur in real images. We consider the challenging case where objects move in an arbitrary way with respect to the camera, and might be occluded and/or come into view. Due to the complexity of this task, prior work has looked at specific cases, where blur is the same everywhere (the shift-invariant case), see *e.g.*, [26,35], or follows given models [20,34] and scenarios [15,28,38]. Other methods address the modeling complexity by exploiting multiple frames, as in, for example, [16]. Our objective, however, is to produce high-quality results as in [16] by using just a single frame (see Fig. 1). To achieve this goal we use a data-driven approach, where a convolutional neural network is trained on a large number of blurred-sharp image pairs. This approach entails addressing two main challenges: first, the design of a realistic dataset of blurred-sharp image pairs and second, the design of a suitable neural network that can learn from such dataset. We overcome the first challenge by using a commercial high frame-rate video camera (a GoPro Hero5 Black). Due to the high frame-rate, single frames in a video are sharp and motion between frames

© Springer International Publishing AG 2017
V. Roth and T. Vetter (Eds.): GCPR 2017, LNCS 10496, pp. 65–77, 2017.
DOI: 10.1007/978-3-319-66709-6_6

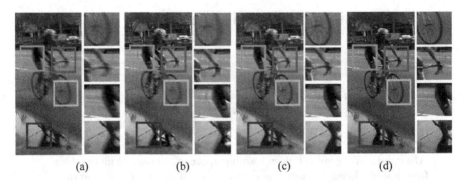

(a)   (b)   (c)   (d)

Fig. 1. (a) Blurry video frame. (b) Result of [34] on the *single* frame (a). (c) Result of the proposed method on the *single* frame (a). (d) Result of the multi-frame method [16].

is small. Then, we use the central frame as the sharp image and the average of all the frames in a video clip as the corresponding blurry image. To avoid averaging frames with too much motion, which would correspond to unrealistic motion blurs, we compute the optical flow between subsequent frames and use a simple thresholding strategy to discard frames with large displacements (more than 1 pixel). As we show in the Experiments section, a dataset built according to this procedure allows training a neural network and generalizes to images from other camera models and scenes. To address the second challenge, we build a neural network that replicates (scale-space) pyramid schemes used in classical deblurring methods. The pyramid exploits two main ideas: one is that it is easy to remove a small amount of blur, and the second is that downsampling can be used to quickly reduce the blur amount in a blurry image (within some approximation). The combination of these two contributions leads to a method achieving state of the art performance on the single image space-varying motion blur case.

1.1 Related Work

Camera Motion. With the success of the variational Bayesian approach of Fergus et al. [9], a large number of blind deconvolution algorithms have been developed for motion deblurring [2,5,25,26,29,35,41,44]. Although blind deconvolution algorithms consider blur to be uniform across the image, some of the methods are able to handle small variations due to camera shake [23]. Techniques based on blind deconvolution have been adapted to address blur variations due to camera rotations by defining the blur kernel on a higher dimensional space [11,12,38]. Another approach to handle camera shake induced space-varying blur is through region-wise blur kernel estimation [13,18]. In 3D scenes, motion blur at a pixel is also related to its corresponding depth. To address this dependency, Hu *et al.* and Xu and Jia [15,42] first estimate a depth map and then solve for the motion blur and the sharp image. In [45], motion blur due to forward or backward camera motion has been explicitly addressed. Notice that blur due to moving objects (see below) cannot be represented by the above camera motion models.

Dynamic Scenes. This category of blur is the most general one and includes motion blur due to camera or object motion. Some prior work [6,24] addresses this problem by assuming that the blurred image is composed of different regions within which blur is uniform. Techniques based on alpha matting have been applied to restore scenes with two layers [7,37]. Although these methods can handle moving objects, they require user interaction and cannot be used in general scenarios where blur varies due to camera motion and scene depth. The scheme of Kim *et al.* [19] incorporates alternating minimization to estimate blur kernels, latent image, and motion segments. Even with a general camera shake model for blurring, the algorithm fails in certain scenarios such as forward motion or depth variations [20]. In [20] Kim and Lee, propose a segmentation-free approach but assume a uniform motion model. The authors propose to simultaneously estimate motion flow and the latent image using a robust total variation (TV-L1) prior. Through a variational-Bayesian formulation, Schelten and Roth [30] recover both defocus as well as object motion blur kernels. Pan *et al.* [27] propose an efficient algorithm to jointly estimate object segmentation and camera motion by incorporating soft segmentation, but require user input. [4,10,33] address the problem of segmenting an image into different regions according to blur. Recent works that use multiple frames are able to handle space-varying blur quite well [16,39].

Deep Learning Methods. The methods in [32,43] address non-blind deconvolution wherein the sharp image is predicted using the blur estimated from other techniques. In [31], Schuler *et al.* develop an end-to-end system that learns to perform blind deconvolution. Their system consists of modules to extract features, estimate the blur and to perform deblurring. However, the performance of this approach degrades for large blurs. The network of Chakrabarti [3] learns the complex Fourier coefficients of a deconvolution filter for an input patch of the blurry image. Hradiš *et al.* [14] predict clean and sharp images from text documents that are corrupted by motion blur, defocus and noise through a convolutional network without an explicit blur estimation. This approach has been extended to license plates in [36]. [40] proposes to learn a multi-scale cascade of shrinkage fields model. This model however does not seem to generalize to natural images. Sun *et al.* [34] propose to address non-uniform motion blur represented in terms of motion vectors.

Our approach is based on deep learning and on a single input image. However, we directly output the sharp image, rather than the blur, do not require user input and work directly on real natural images in the dynamic scene case. Moreover, none of the above deep learning methods builds a dataset from a high frame-rate video camera. Finally, our proposed scheme achieves state of the art performance in the dynamic scene case.

2   Blurry Images in the Wild

One of the key ingredients in our method is to train our network with an, as much as possible, realistic dataset, so that it can generalize well on new data. As mentioned before, we use a high resolution high frame-rate video camera.

Fig. 2. A sample image pair from the WILD training set. Left: averaged image (the blurry image). Right: central frame (the sharp image).

We build blurred images by averaging a set of frames. Similar averaging of frames has been done in previous work to obtain data for evaluation [1,21], but not to build a training set. [21] used averaging to simulate blurry videos, and [1] used averaging to synthesize blurry images, coded exposure images and motion invariant photographs.

We use a handheld GoPro Hero5 Black camera, which captures 240 frames per second with a resolution of 1280×720 pixels. Our videos have been all shot outdoors. Firstly, we downsample all the frames in the videos by a factor of 3 in order to reduce the magnitude of relative motion across frames. Then, we select the number N_e of averaged frames by randomly picking an odd number between 7 and 23. Out of the N_e frames, the central frame is considered to be the sharp image. We assume that motion is smooth and, therefore, to avoid artifacts in the averaging process we consider only frames where optical flow is no more than 1 pixel. We evaluate optical flow using the recent FlowNet algorithm [8] and then apply a simple thresholding technique on the magnitude of the estimated flow. Figure 2 shows an example of the sharp and blurred image pair in our training dataset. In this scene, we find both the camera and objects to be moving. We also evaluate when the optical flow estimate is reliable by computing the frame matching error (L^2 norm on the grayscale domain). We found that no frames were discarded in this processing stage (after the previous selection step). We split our *WILD* dataset into training and test sets.

3   The Multiscale Convolutional Neural Network

In Fig. 3 we show our proposed convolutional neural network (CNN) architecture. The network is designed in a pyramid or multi-scale fashion. Inspired by the multi-scale processing of blind deconvolution algorithms [26,31], we introduce three subgraphs N_1, N_2, and N_3 in our network, where each subgraph includes several convolution/deconvolution (fractional stride convolution) layers. The task of each subgraph is to minimize the reconstruction error at a particular scale. There are two main differences with respect to conventional CNNs, which play a significant role in generating sharp images without artifacts. Firstly, the network includes a skip connection at the end of each subgraph. The idea behind this technique is to reduce the difficulty of the reconstruction task in the network by using the information already present in the blurry image.

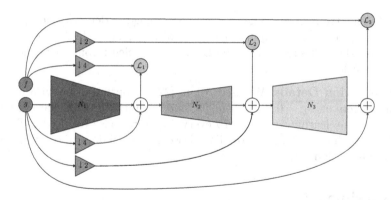

Fig. 3. The DeblurNet architecture. The multiscale scheme allows the network to handle large blurs. Skip connections (bottom links) facilitate the generation of details.

Table 1. The DeblurNet architecture. Batch normalization and ReLU layers inserted after every convolutional layer (except for the last layer of N_1) are not shown for simplicity. Downsampling ($\downarrow$) is achieved by using a stride greater than 1 in convolutional layers. A stride greater than 1 in deconvolutional ($\uparrow$) layers performs upsampling.

	N_1							N_2					N_3				
Type	conv	conv	conv	conv	conv	conv	conv	conv	conv	conv	conv	deconv	conv	conv	conv	conv	deconv
OutCh	96	256	384	384	256	256	3	256	256	256	256	3	256	256	256	256	3
Kernel	11	7	7	7	3	3	3	5	5	5	5	5	5	5	5	5	5
Stride	$\downarrow 2$	1	1	$\downarrow 2$	1	1	1	1	1	1	1	$\uparrow 2$	1	1	1	1	$\uparrow 2$

Each subgraph needs to only generate a *residual image*, which is then added to the input blurry image (after downsampling, if needed). We observe experimentally that the skip connection technique helps the network in generating more texture details. Secondly, because the extent of blur decreases with downsampling [26], the multi-scale formulation allows the network to deal with small amounts of blur in each subgraph. In particular, the task for the first subgraph N_1 is to generate a deblurred image residual at $1/4$ of the original scale. The task for the subgraph N_2 is to use the output of N_1 added to the downsampled input and generate a sharp image at $1/2$ of the original resolution. Finally, the task for the subgraph N_3 is to generate a sharp output at the original resolution by starting from the output of N_2 added to the input scaled by $1/2$. We call this architecture the *DeblurNet* and give a detailed description in Table 1.

Training. We minimize the reconstruction error of all the scales simultaneously. The loss function $\mathcal{L} = \mathcal{L}_1 + \mathcal{L}_2 + \mathcal{L}_3$ is defined through the following 3 losses

$$\mathcal{L}_1 = \sum_{(g,f)\in\mathscr{D}} \left| N_1(g) + D_{\frac{1}{4}}(g) - D_{\frac{1}{4}}(f) \right|^2$$

$$\mathcal{L}_2 = \sum_{(g,f)\in\mathscr{D}} \left| N_2\left(N_1(g) + D_{\frac{1}{4}}(g)\right) + D_{\frac{1}{2}}(g) - D_{\frac{1}{2}}(f) \right|^2 \quad (1)$$

$$\mathcal{L}_3 = \sum_{(g,f)\in\mathscr{D}} \left| N_3\left(N_2\left(N_1(g) + D_{\frac{1}{4}}(g)\right) + D_{\frac{1}{2}}(g)\right) + g - f \right|^2$$

where $\mathscr{D}$ is the training set, g denotes a blurry image, f denotes a sharp image, $D_{\frac{1}{k}}(x)$ denotes the downsampling operation of the image x by factor of k, and N_i indicates the i-th subgraph in the DeblurNet, which reconstructs the image at the i-th scale.

Implementation Details. We used Adam [22] for optimization with momentum parameters as $\beta_1 = 0.9$, $\beta_2 = 0.999$, and an initial learning rate of 0.001. We decrease the learning rate by .75 every 10^4 iterations. We used 2 Titan X for training with a batch size of 10. The network needs 5 days to converge using batch normalization [17].

4   Experiments

We tested DeblurNet on three different types of data: (a) the WILD test set (GoPro Hero5 Black), (b) real blurry images (Canon EOS 5D Mark II), and (c) data from prior work.

Synthetic vs Pseudo-Real Training. To verify the impact of using our proposed averaging to approximate space-varying blur, we trained another network with the same architecture as in Fig. 3. However, we used blurry-sharp image pairs, where the blurry image is obtained synthetically via a shift-invariant convolutional model. As in [3], we prepared a set of 10^5 different blurs. During training, we randomly pick one of these motion blurs and convolve it with a sharp image (from a mixture of $50K$ sharp frames from our WILD dataset and $100K$ cityscapes images[1]) to generate blurred data. We refer to this trained network as the *DeblurNet*^{SI}, where *SI* stands for shift-invariant blur. A second network is instead trained only on the blurry-sharp image pairs from our WILD dataset (a total of $50K$ image pairs obtained from the selection and averaging process on the GoPro Hero5 Black videos). This network is called *DeblurNet*^{WILD}, where *WILD* stands for the data from the WILD dataset. As will be seen later in the experiments, the *DeblurNet*^{WILD} network outperforms the *DeblurNet*^{SI} network despite the smaller training set and the fact that the same sharp frames from the WILD dataset have been used. Therefore, due to space limitations, often we will show only results of the *DeblurNet*^{WILD} network in the comparisons with other methods.

WILD Test Set Evaluation. The videos in the test set were captured at locations different from those where training data was captured. Also, incidentally, the weather conditions during the capture of the test set were significantly different from those of the training set. We randomly chose 15 images from the test-set and compared the performance of our method against the methods in [41], [34], the space-varying implementation of the method in [44], and *DeblurNet*^{WILD} trained network. An example image is shown in Fig. 4. As can be observed, blur variation due to either object motion or depth changes is the major cause of artifacts. Our *DeblurNet*^{WILD} network, however, produces

---

[1] www.cityscapes-dataset.com.

Fig. 4. An example from the WILD test set. (a) Blurry image, (b) sharp image (ground truth), (c) Xu and Jia [41], (d) Xu *et al.* [44], (e) Sun *et al.* [34], (f) *DeblurNet*^{WILD}.

artifact-free sharp images. While the example in Fig. 4 gives only a qualitative evaluation, in Table 2 we report quantitative results.

We measure the performance of all the above methods in terms of Peak Signal-to-Noise Ratio (PSNR) by using the reference sharp image as in standard image deblurring per-

Table 2. Average PSNR on our WILD test set.

[34]	[41]	[44]	*DeblurNet*^{SI}	*DeblurNet*^{WILD}
25.48	23.61	22.50	25.8	**28.1**

formance evaluations. We can see that the performance of the *DeblurNet*^{WILD} is better than that of the *DeblurNet*^{SI}. This is not surprising because the shift-invariant training set does not capture factors such as reflections/specularities, the space-varying blur, occlusions and coming into view of objects. Notice that the PSNR values are not comparable to those seen in shift-invariant deconvolution algorithms.

Qualitative Evaluation. On other available *dynamic scene blur* datasets the ground truth is not available. Therefore, we can only evaluate our proposed

Fig. 5. Test set from [20]. (a, e) Blurry image; (b, f) Kim and Lee [20]; (c, g) Sun *et al.* [34]; (d, h) *DeblurNet*^{WILD}.

network qualitatively. We consider 2 available datasets and images obtained from a Canon EOS 5D Mark II camera. While Figs. 5 and 7 show data from [20,34] respectively, Fig. 6 shows images from the Canon camera. In Fig. 6, we compare the methods of [41], [34] and [44] to both our *DeblurNet*^{SI} and *Deblur-Net*^{WILD} networks. In all datasets, we observe that our method is able to return sharper images with fine details. Furthermore, we observe that in Fig. 6 the *DeblurNet*^{WILD} network produces better results than the *DeblurNet*^{SI} network, which confirms once more our expectations.

Shift-Invariant Blur Evaluation. We provide a brief analysis on the differences between dynamic scene deblurring and shift-invariant motion deblurring. We use an example from the standard dataset of [23], where blur is due to camera shake (see Fig. 8). In the case of a shift-invariant blur, there are infinite {blur, sharp image} pairs that yield the same blurry image when convolved. More precisely, an unknown 2D translation (shift) in a sharp image f can be compensated by an opposite 2D translation in the blur kernel k, that is, $\forall \Delta$, $g(x) = \int f(y+\Delta)k(x-y-\Delta)dy$. Because of such ambiguity, current evaluations compute the PSNR for all possible 2D shifts of f and pick the highest PSNR. The analogous search is done for camera shake [23]. However, with a dynamic scene we have ambiguous shifts at every pixel (see Fig. 8) and such search is unfeasible (the image deformation is undefined). Therefore, all methods for dynamic scene blur would be at a disadvantage with the current shift-invariant blur evaluation methods, although their results might look qualitatively good.

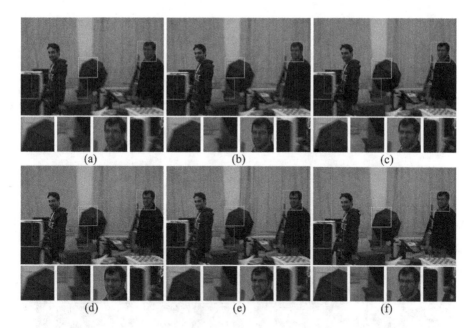

Fig. 6. Test set from the Canon camera. (a) Blurry image; (b) Xu *et al.* [44]; (c) Sun *et al.* [34]; (d) Xu and Jia [41]; (e) *DeblurNet*^SI; (f) *DeblurNet*^WILD.

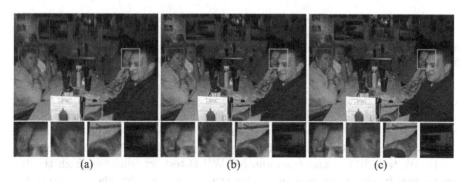

Fig. 7. Test dataset from [34]. (a) Blurry image, (b) Sun *et al.* [34], (c) *DeblurNet*^WILD.

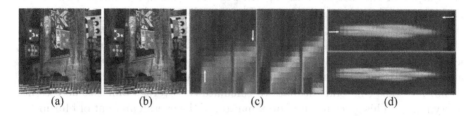

Fig. 8. Kohler dataset [23] (image 1, blur 4). (a) our result. (b) ground truth. (c, d) Zoomed-in patches. Local ambiguous shifts are marked with white arrows.

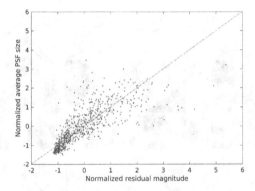

Fig. 9. Normalized average blur size versus normalized residual magnitude plot. Notice the high level of correlation between the blur size and the residual magnitude.

Fig. 10. The images with highest (first row) and lowest (second row) residual norm in the output layer. The image in the first column is the input, the second column shows the estimated residual (the network output), the third column is the deblurred image (first column + second column), and finally the forth column is the ground truth.

Analysis. Our network generates a residual image that when added to the blurry input yields the sharp image. Therefore, we expect the magnitude of the residual to be large for very blurry images, as more changes will be required. To validate this hypothesis we perform both quantitative and qualitative experiments. We take 700 images from another WILD test set (different from the 15 images used in the previous quantitative evaluation), provide them as input to the $DeblurNet^{WILD}$ network, and calculate the L^1 norm of the network residuals (the output of the last layer of N_3). In Fig. 10 we show two images, one with the highest and one with the lowest L^1 norm. We see that the residuals with the highest norms correspond to highly blurred images, and vice versa for the low norm residuals. We also show quantitatively that there is a clear correlation between the amount of blur and the residual L^1 norm. As mentioned earlier on, our WILD dataset also computes an estimate of the blurs by integrating the optical flow. We use this blur estimate to calculate the average blur size across the blurry image. This gives us an approximation of the overall amount of blur in an image. In Fig. 9 we show the plot of the L^1 norm of the residual versus the average estimated blur size for all 700 images. The residual magnitudes and blur sizes are normalized so that mean and standard deviation are 0 and 1 respectively.

5   Conclusions

We proposed DeblurNet, a novel CNN architecture that regresses a sharp image given a blurred one. DeblurNet is able to restore blurry images under challenging conditions, such as occlusions, motion parallax and camera rotations. The network consists of a chain of 3 subgraphs, which implement a multiscale strategy to break down the complexity of the deblurring task. Moreover, each subgraph outputs only a residual image that yields the sharp image when added to the input image. This allows the subgraph to focus on small details as confirmed experimentally. An important part of our solution is the design of a sufficiently realistic dataset. We find that simple frame averaging combined with a very high frame-rate video camera produces reasonable blurred-sharp image pairs for the training of our DeblurNet network. Indeed, both quantitative and qualitative results show state of the art performance when compared to prior dynamic scene deblurring work. We observe that our network does not generate artifacts, but may leave extreme blurs untouched.

Acknowledgements. Paolo Favaro acknowledges support from the Swiss National Science Foundation on project 200021_153324.

References

1. Agrawal, A., Raskar, R.: Optimal single image capture for motion deblurring. In: CVPR (2009)
2. Babacan, S.D., Molina, R., Do, M.N., Katsaggelos, A.K.: Bayesian blind deconvolution with general sparse image priors. In: Fitzgibbon, A., Lazebnik, S., Perona, P., Sato, Y., Schmid, C. (eds.) ECCV 2012. LNCS, vol. 7577, pp. 341–355. Springer, Heidelberg (2012). doi:10.1007/978-3-642-33783-3_25
3. Chakrabarti, A.: A neural approach to blind motion deblurring. In: Leibe, B., Matas, J., Sebe, N., Welling, M. (eds.) ECCV 2016. LNCS, vol. 9907, pp. 221–235. Springer, Cham (2016). doi:10.1007/978-3-319-46487-9_14
4. Chakrabarti, A., Zickler, T., Freeman, W.T.: Analyzing spatially-varying blur. In: CVPR (2010)
5. Cho, S., Lee, S.: Fast motion deblurring. ACM Trans. Graph. **28**(5), 1–8 (2009)
6. Couzinie-Devy, F., Sun, J., Alahari, K., Ponce, J.: Learning to estimate and remove non-uniform image blur. In: CVPR (2013)
7. Dai, S., Wu, Y.: Removing partial blur in a single image. In: CVPR (2009)
8. Dosovitskiy, A., Fischer, P., Ilg, E., Hausser, P., Hazirbas, C., Golkov, V., van der Smagt, P., Cremers, D., Brox, T.: Flownet: learning optical flow with convolutional networks. In: CVPR (2015)
9. Fergus, R., Singh, B., Hertzmann, A., Roweis, S.T., Freeman, W.T.: Removing camera shake from a single photograph. ACM Trans. Graph. **25**(3), 787–794 (2006)
10. Gast, J., Sellent, A., Roth, S.: Parametric object motion from blur. arXiv preprint arXiv:1604.05933 (2016)
11. Gupta, A., Joshi, N., Zitnick, C.L., Cohen, M., Curless, B.: Single image deblurring using motion density functions. In: Daniilidis, K., Maragos, P., Paragios, N. (eds.) ECCV 2010. LNCS, vol. 6311, pp. 171–184. Springer, Heidelberg (2010). doi:10.1007/978-3-642-15549-9_13

12. Hirsch, M., Sra, S., Schölkopf, B., Harmeling, S.: Efficient filter flow for space-variant multiframe blind deconvolution. In: CVPR (2010)
13. Hirsch, M., Schuler, C.J., Harmeling, S., Schölkopf, B.: Fast removal of non-uniform camera shake. In: ICCV (2011)
14. Hradiš, M., Kotera, J., Zemcík, P., Šroubek, F.: Convolutional neural networks for direct text deblurring. In: BMVC (2015)
15. Hu, Z., Xu, L., Yang, M.H.: Joint depth estimation and camera shake removal from single blurry image. In: CVPR (2014)
16. Hyun Kim, T., Mu Lee, K.: Generalized video deblurring for dynamic scenes. In: CVPR (2015)
17. Ioffe, S., Szegedy, C.: Batch normalization: accelerating deep network training by reducing internal covariate shift. arXiv preprint arXiv:1502.03167 (2015)
18. Ji, H., Wang, K.: A two-stage approach to blind spatially-varying motion deblurring. In: CVPR (2012)
19. Kim, T.H., Ahn, B., Lee, K.M.: Dynamic scene deblurring. In: ICCV (2013)
20. Kim, T.H., Lee, K.M.: Segmentation-free dynamic scene deblurring. In: CVPR (2014)
21. Kim, T.H., Nah, S., Lee, K.M.: Dynamic scene deblurring using a locally adaptive linear blur model. arXiv preprint arXiv:1603.04265 (2016)
22. Kingma, D., Ba, J.: Adam: a method for stochastic optimization. arXiv preprint arXiv:1412.6980 (2014)
23. Köhler, R., Hirsch, M., Mohler, B., Schölkopf, B., Harmeling, S.: Recording and playback of camera shake: benchmarking blind deconvolution with a real-world database. In: Fitzgibbon, A., Lazebnik, S., Perona, P., Sato, Y., Schmid, C. (eds.) ECCV 2012. LNCS, vol. 7578, pp. 27–40. Springer, Heidelberg (2012). doi:10.1007/978-3-642-33786-4_3
24. Levin, A.: Blind motion deblurring using image statistics. In: NIPS (2006)
25. Levin, A., Weiss, Y., Durand, F., Freeman, W.: Efficient marginal likelihood optimization in blind deconvolution. In: CVPR (2011)
26. Michaeli, T., Irani, M.: Blind deblurring using internal patch recurrence. In: Fleet, D., Pajdla, T., Schiele, B., Tuytelaars, T. (eds.) ECCV 2014. LNCS, vol. 8691, pp. 783–798. Springer, Cham (2014). doi:10.1007/978-3-319-10578-9_51
27. Pan, J., Hu, Z., Su, Z., Lee, H.Y., Yang, M.H.: Soft-segmentation guided object motion deblurring. In: CVPR (2016)
28. Paramanand, C., Rajagopalan, A.N.: Non-uniform motion deblurring for bilayer scenes. In: CVPR (2013)
29. Perrone, D., Favaro, P.: Total variation blind deconvolution: the devil is in the details. In: CVPR (2014)
30. Schelten, K., Roth, S.: Localized image blur removal through non-parametric kernel estimation. In: ICPR (2014)
31. Schuler, C.J., Hirsch, M., Harmeling, S., Schölkopf, B.: Learning to deblur. IEEE Trans. Pattern Anal. Mach. Intell. 38(7), 1439–1451 (2016)
32. Schuler, C.J., Christopher Burger, H., Harmeling, S., Scholkopf, B.: A machine learning approach for non-blind image deconvolution. In: CVPR (2013)
33. Shi, J., Xu, L., Jia, J.: Discriminative blur detection features. In: CVPR (2014)
34. Sun, J., Cao, W., Xu, Z., Ponce, J.: Learning a convolutional neural network for non-uniform motion blur removal. In: CVPR (2015)
35. Sun, L., Cho, S., Wang, J., Hays, J.: Edge-based blur kernel estimation using patch priors. In: ICCP (2013)
36. Svoboda, P., Hradiš, M., Maršík, L., Zemcík, P.: CNN for license plate motion deblurring. In: ICIP (2016)

37. Tai, Y.W., Kong, N., Lin, S., Shin, S.Y.: Coded exposure imaging for projective motion deblurring. In: CVPR (2010)

38. Whyte, O., Sivic, J., Zisserman, A., Ponce, J.: Non-uniform deblurring for shaken images. In: CVPR (2010)

39. Wieschollek, P., Schölkopf, B., Lensch, H.P.A., Hirsch, M.: End-to-end learning for image burst deblurring. In: Lai, S.-H., Lepetit, V., Nishino, K., Sato, Y. (eds.) ACCV 2016. LNCS, vol. 10114, pp. 35–51. Springer, Cham (2017). doi:10.1007/978-3-319-54190-7_3

40. Xiao, L., Wang, J., Heidrich, W., Hirsch, M.: Learning high-order filters for efficient blind deconvolution of document photographs. In: Leibe, B., Matas, J., Sebe, N., Welling, M. (eds.) ECCV 2016. LNCS, vol. 9907, pp. 734–749. Springer, Cham (2016). doi:10.1007/978-3-319-46487-9_45

41. Xu, L., Jia, J.: Two-phase kernel estimation for robust motion deblurring. In: Daniilidis, K., Maragos, P., Paragios, N. (eds.) ECCV 2010. LNCS, vol. 6311, pp. 157–170. Springer, Heidelberg (2010). doi:10.1007/978-3-642-15549-9_12

42. Xu, L., Jia, J.: Depth-aware motion deblurring. In: ICCP (2012)

43. Xu, L., Ren, J.S., Liu, C., Jia, J.: Deep convolutional neural network for image deconvolution. In: NIPS (2014)

44. Xu, L., Zheng, S., Jia, J.: Unnatural L0 sparse representation for natural image deblurring. In: CVPR (2013)

45. Zheng, S., Xu, L., Jia, J.: Forward motion deblurring. In: CVPR (2013)

Robust Multi-image HDR Reconstruction for the Modulo Camera

Florian Lang, Tobias Plötz$^{(\boxtimes)}$, and Stefan Roth

Department of Computer Science, TU Darmstadt, Darmstadt, Germany
`tobias.ploetz@visinf.tu-darmstadt.de`

Abstract. Photographing scenes with high dynamic range (HDR) poses great challenges to consumer cameras with their limited sensor bit depth. To address this, Zhao *et al.* recently proposed a novel sensor concept – the modulo camera – which captures the least significant bits of the recorded scene instead of going into saturation. Similar to conventional pipelines, HDR images can be reconstructed from multiple exposures, but significantly fewer images are needed than with a typical saturating sensor. While the concept is appealing, we show that the original reconstruction approach assumes noise-free measurements and quickly breaks down otherwise. To address this, we propose a novel reconstruction algorithm that is robust to image noise and produces significantly fewer artifacts. We theoretically analyze correctness as well as limitations, and show that our approach significantly outperforms the baseline on real data.

1 Introduction

Real world scenes often exhibit a significant dynamic range [17]. The intricate interplay between brightness and darkness, shadowy and sunny areas is often highly desirable from a photographer's standpoint. However, consumer cameras with image sensors that saturate when certain brightness levels are exceeded can only measure a significantly smaller dynamic range, *e.g.* 12 bits. When taking only a single image, the photographer faces the dilemma of losing detail either in the bright or in the dark parts of the scene; the whole scene cannot be captured in full detail. While various special sensors for HDR imaging have been developed, these are expensive [1], or sacrifice spatial [18] or intensity resolution [14].

Hence, various approaches aim to retain detail in the entire scene by reconstructing an HDR image from multiple captures, each with a different exposure time [4,9,10,17]. As conventional image sensors saturate at some brightness level, the bit depth in bright parts of the scene is necessarily limited and the reconstruction may lead to artifacts. The *modulo camera* concept of Zhao et al. [22] aims to mitigate this using a novel, practical sensor that, instead of saturating, resets pixels to zero as soon as their maximal value is reached during the exposure.

Electronic supplementary material The online version of this chapter (doi:10. 1007/978-3-319-66709-6_7) contains supplementary material, which is available to authorized users.

V. Roth and T. Vetter (Eds.): GCPR 2017, LNCS 10496, pp. 78–89, 2017.
DOI: 10.1007/978-3-319-66709-6_7

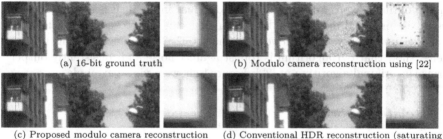

(a) 16-bit ground truth

(b) Modulo camera reconstruction using [22]

(c) Proposed modulo camera reconstruction

(d) Conventional HDR reconstruction (saturating sensor)

Fig. 1. Reconstruction of a 16-bit image from the Cityscapes dataset [3]. Multiple noisy 12-bit exposures of a modulo camera are simulated based on the ground truth in *(a)*. The approach of [22] produces visible outliers *(b)*. Our robust method *(c)* reconstructs the (noise-free) ground truth well. Reconstructing from the same number of exposures of a simulated conventional camera with saturation leads to much more noise *(d)*.

Hence, the least significant bits of the signal can be measured independently of its overall magnitude. This is in contrast to conventional cameras, which measure the signal correctly only up to the saturation level. To recover an HDR image from just a single modulo camera exposure, phase unwrapping techniques well-known in radar interferometry [8] or MRI [2] can be applied.

However, this requires the true image to be sufficiently smooth. For more complex and realistic scenes, [22] presents an approach for HDR reconstruction from multiple images. As in a conventional HDR pipeline, the exposure times of the captured images are chosen such that they measure different parts of the radiance range. The observed modulo values of each captured image are scaled by the exposure time and then iteratively combined into an estimate of the true HDR image. The benefit is that significantly fewer exposures are needed than with saturating sensors, making HDR imaging much more practical.

In this paper, we first consider the correctness of the reconstruction. As we will discuss, the original approach of Zhao *et al.* [22] provably works correctly, but only as long as there is no noise and exposure times can be set with perfect accuracy. Since the no-noise assumption is unrealistic, large areas of wrongly estimated pixels are produced when applied to images with typical noise levels. This is a significant impediment to the practical application of the modulo camera. To address this, we next introduce a novel, robust HDR reconstruction algorithm for modulo camera images. Analogous to the original approach, we calculate a simulated long exposure image and use its most significant bits. The crucial difference is that we additionally use the remainder of the simulated image and compare it to the actual values in the modulo capture. This way we can identify pixels for which the original algorithm would produce an incorrect reconstruction and correct these. Moreover, we make a number of theoretical contributions: First, we provide an analysis of correctness, showing that for a known noise distribution with certain properties, our algorithm reconstructs the true image even in the presence of noise. Moreover, we contribute explicit bounds on the optimal exposure times of the individual input images, which allow to assess the maximal measurable bit depth that can be recovered correctly with a chosen probability. Qualitative and quantitative experiments using realistic scenes show that our algorithm is robust against noise and consistently outperforms the original algorithm of [22]. Figure 1 shows a visual example.

2   Related Work

Capturing scenes with both bright and dark areas is challenging for consumer cameras, while the human visual system copes with such scenarios quite effortlessly. To address this gap, high dynamic range imaging aims to enable photographers to capture such scenes without loosing details. Significant research efforts have been dedicated to HDR imaging [17], resulting in techniques whose captured dynamic range even exceeds the capabilities of the human eye [12].

Multiple Exposures. The perhaps most widely used family of HDR techniques is based on capturing several images with different exposure times (some under-, some overexposed) and combining these. Multishot methods can even be used with photographic film [4]. In general, they proceed by estimating the inverse of the camera response function and weighted averaging of the different images [19]. Since conventional cameras saturate at a certain level, long exposures do not add details to saturated regions. Consequently, many images with different exposure times are needed [9] to avoid quantization effects and artifacts [22]. Stumpfel *et al.* [20] report that seven conventional images are needed to capture the dynamic range of real life scenes, even with an elaborate selection of exposure times [10] and calibration. On the other hand, the modulo camera allows for an HDR reconstruction that exceeds the dynamic range of typical scenes from three modulo images alone [22] (assuming noise-free images). Other multishot HDR approaches avoid having to recover the response function [16]. All multishot methods are challenged by dynamic scenes as well as noise. Moving objects or camera ego-motion lead to ghosting artifacts in the reconstruction. Multiple approaches for ghost-free reconstruction have been proposed [7,11,13]. Here we focus on static scenes without camera movement, and leave the dynamic setting for future work.

HDR Sensors. To increase the dynamic range without requiring multiple exposures, advanced sensors have been designed. They, for example, sacrifice spatial resolution for increased dynamic range using pixels of different size, effectively resulting in different exposures [18]. These have been realized in consumer cameras, *e.g.* the Fujifilm SuperCCD [6]. Using a high precision analog-digital converter can increase the dynamic range as well, while keeping the resolution. Another approach is to use thin-film on ASIC (TFA) sensors [1], which yield even more dynamic range. Adoption has been hindered by expensive production, and the sequential read-out for color images, requiring a three times longer exposure.

Special Sensors. In contrast to conventional saturating sensors with increased bit depth, it is also possible to change the camera response function.

Loose *et al.* [14] propose a sensor with a logarithmic response, which increases the dynamic range and allows for longer exposures without saturation. While the dynamic range increases, intensity resolution is reduced, especially for bright pixels. Another possibility is a sensor that measures gradients [21], which enables fine quantization and allows correcting saturated pixels. In contrast to these approaches, the modulo camera does not sacrifice spatial or intensity resolution. While the leading bits of the intensity values are lost, the details are preserved.

3   The Modulo Camera

Before introducing our approach, we formalize the properties of a conventional saturating sensor and review the modulo camera following [22]. For an ideal sensor with unbounded capacity, the observed image I arises from the scene radiance $R \in \mathbb{R}_0^+$ and the exposure time $\tau > 0$ as

$$I(\tau R) = \lfloor \lambda(\tau R + \epsilon(\tau R)) \rfloor, \tag{1}$$

where $\lfloor \cdot \rfloor$ denotes the floor operation and λ subsumes all multiplicative factors involved in the photon-to-digit conversion, *e.g.* the quantum efficiency, the analog amplification, and the analog-to-digital conversion factor. Inevitably, the observed image will be corrupted by noise ϵ, which arises from the Poisson arrival process of photons and from the electronics involved in the imaging process. Following the literature [5], we model ϵ as intensity-dependent Gaussian noise

$$\epsilon(\tau R) \sim \mathcal{N}(0, \sigma^2(\tau R)) \qquad \text{with} \qquad \sigma^2(\tau R) = \beta_1 \tau R + \beta_2. \tag{2}$$

For simplicity, we assume *w. l. o. g.* that $0 \leq R < 2^K$ and $\lambda = 1$. Hence, an exposure time $\tau = 1$ will result in a digital image with bit depth K. In practice, pixel elements have limited capacity. Hence, a saturating camera $S(\cdot)$ with bit depth $L < K$ will clip the recorded signal at a maximal value of $2^L - 1$:

$$S(\tau R) = \min(I(\tau R), 2^L - 1). \tag{3}$$

Due to the clipping all image structure in high-intensity areas will be lost. In contrast, a modulo camera $M(\cdot)$ [22] with bit depth L always retains the L least significant bits, as the sensing element is reset once it hits the maximal value:

$$M(\tau R) = I(\tau R) \bmod 2^L = I(\tau R) - k \cdot 2^L. \tag{4}$$

The true intensities can be reconstructed from the modulo image by estimating the number of rollovers k, *i.e.* how many times each pixel has been reset.

Multi-image Reconstruction. Given a series of exposure times $0 < \tau_1 < \ldots < \tau_n = 1$, we observe the corresponding modulo images $M_i = M(\tau_i R)$ with unknown rollover maps k_i. We iteratively reconstruct radiance maps $\tilde{R}_i, i = 1, \ldots, n$ approximating R, as well as rollover maps $\tilde{k}_i$ approximating k_i. We assume that $k_1 = 0$ for all pixels in M_1, *i.e.* the first image has no rollovers. This is equivalent to requiring that the first exposure time is sufficiently short with $\tau_1 \leq 2^{L-K}$. Hence, $\tilde{R}_1$ is obtained as the first modulo image M_1 divided by its exposure time

$$\tilde{R}_1 = \frac{M_1}{\tau_1}. \tag{5}$$

The original reconstruction algorithm of [22] now proceeds by recursively estimating the rollover map $\tilde{k}_i$ for the next exposure time and afterwards updating $\tilde{R}_i$. The rollover map for M_i can be estimated from $\tilde{R}_{i-1}$ by scaling with the new exposure time τ_i

$$\tilde{k}_i = \left\lfloor \frac{\tau_i \tilde{R}_{i-1}}{2^L} \right\rfloor. \tag{6}$$

Now we combine modulo image M_i and rollover map $\tilde{k}_i$ into a refined estimate

$$\tilde{R}_i = \frac{\tilde{k}_i 2^L + M_i}{\tau_i}. \tag{7}$$

Recalling that $\tau_n = 1$, a K-bit high dynamic range image is finally obtained as

$$\tilde{I} = \lfloor \tau_n \tilde{R}_n \rfloor = \tilde{R}_n. \tag{8}$$

Correctness. We show in the supplemental material that this reconstruction is provably exact, *i.e.* $\tilde{I} = I(\tau_n R)$, if the fraction $2^L \frac{\tau_{i-1}}{\tau_i}$ is a positive integer *and* if the recorded images are not corrupted by noise, *i.e.* $I(\tau_i R) = \lfloor \tau_i R \rfloor$, for all $i = 1, \ldots, n$. However, even miniscule amounts of noise can already cause the estimation of the rollovers $\tilde{k}_i$ from Eq. (6) to be incorrect, leading to visible artifacts, see Fig. 1b. A simple numerical example showing the limitations of the original approach is $R = 256$, $L = 8$ and $\tau_1 = 0.4$, $\tau_2 = 1$, for which it is easy to see that $\tilde{I} = 0 \neq I(\tau_2 R)$ even without noise.

Moreover, we note that image noise cannot be removed beforehand, since the modulo operation does not commute with image filtering in general. This is true even for linear filters with rational weights $\omega_i \in \mathbb{Q}$, *i.e.* there exist $x_i \in \mathbb{Z}$ such that

$$\left(\sum_i \omega_i x_i \right) \bmod n \neq \left(\sum_i \omega_i (x_i \bmod n) \right) \bmod n. \tag{9}$$

4   Robust HDR Reconstruction

Estimating the rollover image with the original reconstruction algorithm in Eq. (6) is susceptible to noise as $\tilde{k}_i$ may not match the true rollover map k_i that underlies the modulo observations M_i. We now present our algorithm that accounts for noise while reconstructing the scene radiance. In particular, we detect and correct for possible estimation errors Δ_i in $\tilde{k}_i$ such that

$$\hat{k}_i = \tilde{k}_i + \Delta_i, \qquad \Delta_i \in \mathbb{Z}. \tag{10}$$

Then we use $\hat{k}_i$ instead of $\tilde{k}_i$ for updating the radiance map as

$$\tilde{R}_i = \frac{\hat{k}_i 2^L + M_i}{\tau_i} = \frac{(\tilde{k}_i + \Delta_i) 2^L + M_i}{\tau_i}. \tag{11}$$

To find an optimal value for Δ_i, we want the simulated image $\tilde{I}_i = \lfloor \tau_i \tilde{R}_i \rfloor$ given the current radiance to be close to the simulated image $\bar{I}_i = \lfloor \tau_i \tilde{R}_{i-1} \rfloor$ based on the previous radiance estimate. Since the noise governing the non-rounded image intensities is assumed Gaussian, we formulate the following least-squares problem:

$$\min_{\Delta_i} \mathcal{L}(\Delta_i) \doteq \min_{\Delta_i} \| \lfloor \tau_i \tilde{R}_i \rfloor - \lfloor \tau_i \tilde{R}_{i-1} \rfloor \|^2 \tag{12}$$

$$= \min_{\Delta_i} \| \tau_i \tilde{R}_i - \lfloor \tau_i \tilde{R}_{i-1} \rfloor \|^2 \tag{13}$$

$$= \min_{\Delta_i} \| (\tilde{k}_i + \Delta_i) 2^L + M_i - \lfloor \tau_i \tilde{R}_{i-1} \rfloor \|^2, \tag{14}$$

which holds as $\tau_i \tilde{R}_i \in \mathbb{Z}$ and we plugged in Eq. (11). Using Eq. (6), we have

$$\mathcal{L}(\Delta_i) = \left\| \Delta_i 2^L + M_i - \underbrace{\left(\lfloor \tau_i \tilde{R}_{i-1} \rfloor - \left\lfloor \frac{\tau_i \tilde{R}_{i-1}}{2^L} \right\rfloor 2^L \right)}_{\doteq D_i} \right\|^2. \tag{15}$$

Since M_i and D_i are modulo values, it holds that

$$-2^L < M_i - D_i < 2^L, \tag{16}$$

which implies that $\mathcal{L}(\Delta_i) > \mathcal{L}(0)$ for $|\Delta_i| \geq 2$. Thus, the cost $\mathcal{L}$ is minimized for $\Delta_i \in \{-1, 0, 1\}$. We can now read off the optimal value as

$$\Delta_i = \underset{\Delta}{\operatorname{argmin}} \| \Delta 2^L + M_i - D_i \|^2 = \begin{cases} +1, \ M_i - D_i < -2^{L-1} \\ -1, \ M_i - D_i > +2^{L-1} \\ 0, \quad \text{else.} \end{cases} \tag{17}$$

This ensures that the reconstructed $\tilde{I}_i$ lies in the interval $[\bar{I}_i - 2^{L-1}, \bar{I}_i + 2^{L-1}]$.

Optimality. We now establish optimality conditions and show that our novel algorithm is indeed more robust than the original approach of [22]. To simplify notation, we write $I_i = I(\tau_i R)$ for the ideal image taken with an unbounded sensor. We then consider the compound noise between two images

$$e_i \doteq I_i - \frac{\tau_i}{\tau_{i-1}} I_{i-1} \tag{18}$$

$$= \epsilon(\tau_i R) - r(\tau_i R + \epsilon(\tau_i R)) - \frac{\tau_i}{\tau_{i-1}} \epsilon(\tau_{i-1} R) + \frac{\tau_i}{\tau_{i-1}} r(\tau_{i-1} R + \epsilon(\tau_{i-1} R)), \tag{19}$$

where $r(x) \doteq x - \lfloor x \rfloor$ is the rounding error with $0 \leq r(x) < 1$.

Theorem 1. *If* $|e_i| \leq 2^{L-1} - 1$ *for* $i = 2, \ldots, n$, *the robust algorithm reconstructs* I_i *in every iteration correctly, i.e.* $\tilde{I}_i \doteq \tau_i \tilde{R}_i = I_i$. *Especially it holds that* $\tilde{I}_n = \tilde{R}_n = I_n$ *and hence the true radiance map is reconstructed as well as possible.*

Proof Sketch. We proceed by induction. By assumption, the first modulo image has no rollovers, *i.e.* $I_1 = M_1$, and hence $I_1 = \tau_1 \tilde{R}_1$. The induction step proceeds by contradiction and relies on a case distinction on the possible values of Δ_i and whether the true k_i is over- or underestimated. In particular, we show that

$$\tau_i \tilde{R}_i \neq I_i \implies |e_i| > 2^{L-1} - 1. \tag{20}$$

We refer to the supplemental material for details, but note that it is somewhat intuitive that Eq. (17) leads to a correct reconstruction of the rollover maps. Consequently, the robust algorithm leads to the radiance being reconstructed as well as possible even for substantial amounts of noise.

This is in contrast to the original reconstruction approach of [22], for which the robustness depends on the image values itself. For some image values, it tolerates $|e_i| = 2^L - 1$, while for others $|e_i| = 1$ already produces wrong results. As we have seen in the simple example above, even rounding errors can already cause the original approach to fail. Even if rounding errors could be eliminated by carefully choosing exposure times, a small amount of noise leads to similar failures.

5   Robust Capture Protocol

Theorem 1 shows that our reconstruction algorithm recovers the true intensities as long as the compound noise of imaging $\tau_i R$ and $\tau_{i-1} R$ is small enough. Since the noise and rounding error of $\tau_{i-1} R$ enter the definition of e_i with a factor of $\tau_i/\tau_{i-1} > 1$ (Eq. 19), we can control the distribution of e_i by choosing the ratio of exposure times τ_i/τ_{i-1}. For practical applications it is highly desirable to find an explicit exposure time schedule such that the number of exposures is minimized while guaranteeing correctness with high probability. Let us consider that in iteration i we want to reconstruct a pixel correctly with some probability p. Then we aim to find the maximal τ_i given τ_{i-1} such that

$$P\big[|e_i| \leq 2^{L-1} - 1\big] \geq p. \tag{21}$$

We can bound the probability on the left-hand side by the CDF of the absolute value of a Gaussian (for details see supplemental material)

$$P\big[|e_i| \leq 2^{L-1} - 1\big] \geq P\left[|\mathcal{N}(0, \sigma_i^2)| \leq 2^{L-1} - 1 - \frac{\tau_i}{\tau_{i-1}}\right] \tag{22}$$

with

$$\sigma_i^2 = \beta_1 \tau_i R \left(1 + \frac{\tau_i}{\tau_{i-1}}\right) + \beta_2 \left(1 + \frac{\tau_i^2}{\tau_{i-1}^2}\right). \tag{23}$$

This can be used to derive an upper bound on τ_i such that Eq. (21) is satisfied:

$$\tau_i \leq \tau_{i-1} \frac{-b + \sqrt{b^2 - 4ac}}{2a} \tag{24}$$

with

$$a = \beta_1 \tau_{i-1} R + \beta_2 - \left(\Phi^{-1}\left(\tfrac{1}{2} + \tfrac{1}{2}p\right)\right)^{-2} \tag{25}$$

$$b = \beta_1 \tau_{i-1} R + \left(\Phi^{-1}\left(\tfrac{1}{2} + \tfrac{1}{2}p\right)\right)^{-2}(2^L - 2) \tag{26}$$

$$c = \beta_2 - \left(\Phi^{-1}\left(\tfrac{1}{2} + \tfrac{1}{2}p\right)\right)^{-2}(2^{L-1} - 1)^2, \tag{27}$$

where Φ^{-1} is the inverse CDF of a standard normal distribution. We again refer to the supplemental material for details. The noise parameters β_1, β_2 can be estimated for a specific camera, e.g. with the technique of Foi et al. [5]. However, the scene radiance R is needed in the calculation of τ_i. We make a conservative guess and use the maximal value, i.e. 2^K. That way every pixel is reconstructed correctly with probability at least p, while pixels with a lower intensity will be reconstructed with higher probability.

In general, if we always take the upper bound in Eq. (24) the resulting series will converge to a limiting exposure time τ^*. We state an explicit formula for τ^* in the supplementary. Note, that the limiting exposure time can be greater than 1 and that it effectively allows us to characterize the *maximum bit depth* that can be resolved using a modulo camera with bit depth L that, in contrast to [22], assumes realistic noise with parameters β_1, β_2. If β_2 is too large, τ^* will become complex-valued. In contrast, if β_1 is too large, we get $\tau^* < 1$, i.e. we cannot reconstruct R with the required certainty.

6 Evaluation

We now analyze our robust reconstruction algorithm on real HDR data. We use the Cityscapes dataset [3], which provides 16-bit linear HDR images of road scenes. Since the images have already been debayered, we apply a color filter array to remove the interpolated pixels. Given the 16-bit images, we simulate the imaging process of an L-bit modulo camera as well as a conventional L-bit camera that goes into saturation. Note that we need to rely on simulation here, as modulo sensors have not been manufactured yet apart from early prototypes [22]. We choose the base parameters of the noise distribution as $10^{-8} \leq \beta_1 \leq 10^{-2}$ and $\beta_2 = 0.01\beta_1$, which are reasonable for consumer grade cameras [15]. In practice a certain camera has a fixed bit depth. In order to nevertheless compare the results across different bit depths for the same camera, we normalize the noise parameters such that an L-bit camera has $\beta_1^{(L)} = \alpha\beta_1$ and $\beta_2^{(L)} = \alpha^2\beta_2$, where $\alpha = 2^L - 1$. This implies that an L-bit camera collects 2^{K-L} times more photons to increment the intensity by one than the K-bit ground truth camera, thus improving the signal-to-noise ratio. This assumption is reasonable since cameras with a smaller bit depth can afford to integrate bigger capacitors instead.

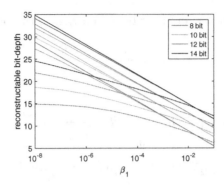

Fig. 2. Maximal bit depth that can be reconstructed from modulo images under realistic image noise using 2 (dot-dashed), 5 (dotted) and infinitely many (solid) images for varying bit depth and noise parameters. We set $\beta_2 = 0.01\beta_1$.

Maximal Bit Depth. We first analyze the maximum bit depth that can be reconstructed and compare the proposed approach against the original reconstruction from [22]. We choose the exposure times according to Eq. (24) such that a pixel is reconstructed correctly with $p > 0.99$ in each iteration. While the effect of having a maximum of 1% of pixels potentially incorrect could be drastic when many iterations need to be made, this is a worst case estimate. In practice, many fewer errors occur, since the image is not bright everywhere. Moreover, we observe that choosing $p > 0.999$ or 0.9999 did not yield significantly better results in practice, but required more images. Figure 2 shows how many bits can be reconstructed accurately from 2 and 5 exposures, respectively, as well as in the hypothetical case of infinitely many exposures, where the last exposure time is given by τ^*. Depending on the bit depth of the camera and the noise characteristics, we achieve very high maximal exposure times and therefore a large dynamic range that can be recovered. For example, roughly 18 bits can be reconstructed with only 2 images, if $\beta_1 = 10^{-5}, \beta_2 = 10^{-7}$ and $L = 12$. Moreover, with just 5 exposures we already achieve a bit depth that is close to the theoretical maximum, meaning that the exposure time schedule given by Eq. (24) quickly converges to its limit. It is important to note that in the presence of realistic amounts of sensor noise, and even with our robust reconstruction algorithm, the modulo camera does not enable HDR images with an unbounded dynamic range, unlike what is claimed in [22]. Nevertheless, our derivation shows that even with realistic camera noise, significant gains in dynamic range can be achieved. Further improvements could potentially be made by considering the modulo images jointly, *c.f.* [8], instead of sequentially. We leave that for future work.

HDR Reconstruction. We now compare the results from the original algorithm, our robust approach, and a simple HDR reconstruction method based on images from a saturating sensor, all with the same number of exposures. For the latter, we average over all images in which a pixel is neither under- nor oversaturated. We measure the quality of the reconstruction using the peak signal-to-noise ratio

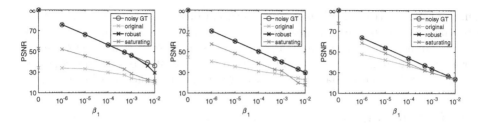

Fig. 3. PSNR of HDR reconstruction on the Cityscapes dataset with various methods for different noise levels ($\beta_2 = 0.01\beta_1$). *(from left to right)* 10, 12, 14 bit cameras. The overall noise increases with the bit depth since fewer photons are needed to increment the intensity value in a pixel site.

Fig. 4. HDR reconstruction of a scene in the Stanford Memorial Church. We use the HDR reconstruction of [4] from 18 exposures as ground truth for simulation. *(from left to right)* ground truth, conventional reconstruction using simulated saturating images, reconstruction from modulo images using the original algorithm, and using the proposed robust reconstruction approach. We simulated 12-bit cameras and added moderate amounts of noise ($\beta_1 = 10^{-3}, \beta_2 = 10^{-5}$).

between the debayered and tone-mapped images: $\text{PSNR} \doteq 10\log_{10}\left(\frac{\text{MAX}_I^2}{\text{MSE}}\right)$, where $\text{MAX}_I = 2^{16} - 1$ is the maximum intensity of the reconstructed image and MSE is the mean squared error. We determined the number of required exposures using the bound from Sect. 5. In the case of $\tau^* < 1$ we padded the first two exposure times to reach $\tau_n = 1$, for $\tau^* \ll 1$, *i.e.* extreme noise, we used 6 predefined exposures. Other schedules did not significantly affect the findings.

As we can see in Fig. 3 for low and moderate noise, the result of our robust algorithm is very close to the noisy ground truth. For strong noise the results become slightly suboptimal, since the calculated exposure times are too small, *i.e.* $\tau^* < 1$. The original modulo reconstruction approach of [22] and a simple HDR pipeline with a saturating sensor do much worse, since we are using as few exposures as possible. Especially for weak noise we often only need 2 images for our approach. Note, that the HDR pipeline with a saturating sensor combines a long-exposure image with a short-exposure image by appropriately upscaling the short-exposure image and subsequently averaging both images. In the upscaled image this effectively leads to an amplification of the noise parameter β_2 that is otherwise independent of the exposure time. This does not occur when reconstruction an HDR image using our approach as in every step only information from a single image is used to add detail to the reconstruction. Figure 4 shows an image from another dataset. We experience the same effects as in Fig. 1.

7 Conclusion

Modulo cameras have promised to be an interesting, practical alternative to conventional sensors that enable HDR reconstruction from a small number of exposures. However, as we have shown in this paper, the original reconstruction algorithm fails even in the noise-free case. Realistic image noise severely limits the attainable image quality. We proposed a novel, robust HDR reconstruction algorithm for images from a modulo camera and established clear criteria for its correctness. It can deal with significant amounts of noise and allows to assert stringent bounds on the probability of a successful reconstruction. We derived an optimal exposure time schedule for images with realistic noise and empirically showed that our robust algorithm performs very close to the ground truth, clearly outperforming the original modulo camera algorithm as well as standard HDR pipelines. Future work should consider extending the multi-image approach to dynamic scenes. Furthermore, an evaluation of a physical modulo camera in terms of the attainable noise level as well as production costs would be useful to determine the practicality of modulo sensors in consumer cameras.

Acknowledgments. The research leading to these results has received funding from the European Research Council under the European Union's Seventh Framework Programme (FP/2007–2013)/ERC Grant agreement No. 307942.

References

1. Böhm, M., Blecher, F., Eckhardt, A., Schneider, B., Benthien, S., Keller, H., Lulé, T., Rieve, P., Sommer, M., Lind, R.C., Humm, L., Daniels, M., Wu, N., Yen, H., Efron, U.: High dynamic range image sensors in thin film on ASIC technology for automotive applications. In: Ricken, D.E., Gessner, W. (eds.) Advanced Microsystems for Automotive Applications, pp. 157–172. Springer, Berlin (1998). (Jan)
2. Chavez, S., Xiang, Q.S., An, L.: Understanding phase maps in MRI: a new cutline phase unwrapping method. IEEE Trans. Med. Imaging **21**, 966–977 (2002)
3. Cordts, M., Omran, M., Ramos, S., Scharwächter, T., Enzweiler, M., Benenson, R., Franke, U., Roth, S., Schiele, B.: The Cityscapes dataset for semantic urban scene understanding. In: IEEE Conference on Computer Vision and Pattern Recognition (CVPR), June 2016
4. Debevec, P.E., Malik, J.: Recovering high dynamic range radiance maps from photographs. In: ACM Transactions Graphics (Proceedings of ACM SIGGRAPH), pp. 369–378, August 1997
5. Foi, A., Trimeche, M., Katkovnik, V., Egiazarian, K.: Practical poissonian-Gaussian noise modeling and fitting for single-image raw-data. IEEE Trans. Image Process. **17**(10), 1737–1754 (2008)

6. Fuji Photo Film Co., Ltd: 4th-generation Super CCD (2003). http://www.fujifilmusa.com/shared/bin/4thGenSUPERCCDBrochure.pdf

7. Gallo, O., Gelfand, N., Chen, W., Tico, M., Pulli, K.: Artifact-free high dynamic range imaging. IEEE International Conference on Computer Photography (ICCP), April 2009

8. Goldstein, R.M., Zebker, H.A., Werner, C.L.: Satellite radar interferometry: two-dimensional phase unwrapping. Radio Sci. **23**(4), 713–720 (1988)

9. Granados, M., Ajdin, B., Wand, M., Theobalt, C., Seidel, H.P., Lensch, H.P.A.: Optimal HDR reconstruction with linear digital cameras. In: IEEE Conference on Computer Vision and Pattern Recogion (CVPR), pp. 215–222, June 2010

10. Grossberg, M.D., Nayar, S.K.: High dynamic range from multiple images: which exposures to combine?. In: ICCV Workshop on Color and Photometric Methods in Computer Vision (CPMCV), October 2003

11. Heo, Y.S., Lee, K.M., Lee, S.U., Moon, Y., Cha, J.: Ghost-free high dynamic range imaging. In: Kimmel, R., Klette, R., Sugimoto, A. (eds.) ACCV 2010. LNCS, vol. 6495, pp. 486–500. Springer, Heidelberg (2011). doi:10.1007/978-3-642-19282-1_39

12. Hoefflinger, B. (ed.): High-Dynamic-Range (HDR) Vision. Springer, Heidelberg (2007)

13. Jacobs, K., Loscos, C., Ward, G.: Automatic high-dynamic range image generation for dynamic scenes. IEEE Comput. Graph. Appl. **28**(2), 84–93 (2008)

14. Loose, M., Meier, K., Schemmel, J.: A self-calibrating single-chip CMOS camera with logarithmic response. IEEE J. Solid-State Circuits **36**(4), 586–596 (2001)

15. Mäkitalo, M., Foi, A.: Noise parameter mismatch in variance stabilization, with an application to Poisson-Gaussian noise estimation. IEEE Trans. Image Process. **23**(12), 5348–5359 (2014)

16. Mann, S., Picard, R.W.: On being 'undigital' with digital cameras: extending dynamic range by combining differently exposed pictures. In: Proceedings of Imaging Science and Technology, pp. 442–448, May 1995

17. Mantiuk, R.K., Myszkowski, K., Seidel, H.P.: High dynamic range imaging. In: Wiley Encyclopedia of Electrical and Electronics Engineering. Wiley (2015)

18. Nayar, S.K., Mitsunaga, T.: High dynamic range imaging: spatially varying pixel exposures. In: IEEE Conference on Computer Vision and Pattern Recogition (CVPR), June 2000

19. Robertson, M.A., Borman, S., Stevenson, R.L.: Estimation-theoretic approach to dynamic range enhancement using multiple exposures. Electron. Imaging **12**(2), 219–228 (2003)

20. Stumpfel, J., Tchou, C., Jones, A., Hawkins, T., Wenger, A., Debevec, P.: Direct HDR capture of the sun and sky. In: Proceedings of the 3rd International Conference on Computer Graphics, Virtual Reality, Visualisation and Interact, in Africa. pp. 145–149. AFRIGRAPH 2004, November 2004

21. Tumblin, J., Agrawal, A., Raskar, R.: Why I want a gradient camera. In: IEEE Conference on Computer Vision and Pattern Recognition (CVPR), pp. 103–110, June 2014

22. Zhao, H., Shi, B., Fernandez-Cull, C., Yeung, S.K., Raskar, R.: Unbounded high dynamic range photography using a modulo camera. In: International Conference on Computational Photography (ICCP), April 2015

Trainable Regularization for Multi-frame Superresolution

Teresa Klatzer[1]([⊠]), Daniel Soukup[2], Erich Kobler[1], Kerstin Hammernik[1], and Thomas Pock[1,2]

[1] Institute of Computer Graphics and Vision, Graz University of Technology, Graz, Austria
klatzer@icg.tugraz.at
[2] Center for Vision, Automation and Control, AIT, Vienna, Austria

Abstract. In this paper, we present a novel method for multi-frame superresolution (SR). Our main goal is to improve the spatial resolution of a multi-line scan camera for an industrial inspection task. High resolution output images are reconstructed using our proposed SR algorithm for multi-channel data, which is based on the trainable reaction-diffusion model. As this is a supervised learning approach, we simulate ground truth data for a real imaging scenario. We show that learning a regularizer for the SR problem improves the reconstruction results compared to an iterative reconstruction algorithm using TV or TGV regularization. We test the learned regularizer, trained on simulated data, on images acquired with the real camera setup and achieve excellent results.

1 Introduction

In this paper, we investigate the problem of multi-frame superresolution (SR) on an exemplary industrial inspection task. To speed up image acquisition, we acquire multiple low resolution (LR) images using the lines of a multi-line scan camera with planar objects being moved under the sensor. To reduce redundancy and to improve the sampling pattern, the sensor is tilted. In such a setup, we can vary the resolution not only in transport direction by controlling the transport speed of the imaged object, but also in lateral direction by varying the tilting angle of the camera. This is visualized in Fig. 1. The acquisition using different lines of the camera can be interpreted as a multi-camera setup, therefore we solve a multi-frame SR problem as a post-processing step. A similar idea has been used for reducing data transfer for a remote sensing application in satellite imaging [10] where several sub-pixel translated cameras were used to acquire images in half the desired resolution.

The multi-line camera setup is reflected in the forward model. Assuming registered images according to the forward model, our problem reduces to estimate a deblurred HR image from blurry but registered measurements. In our

Electronic supplementary material The online version of this chapter (doi:10. 1007/978-3-319-66709-6_8) contains supplementary material, which is available to authorized users.

© Springer International Publishing AG 2017
V. Roth and T. Vetter (Eds.): GCPR 2017, LNCS 10496, pp. 90–100, 2017.
DOI: 10.1007/978-3-319-66709-6_8

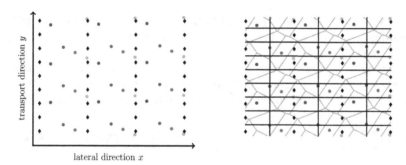

Fig. 1. Left: Black diamonds depict a regular upsampling pattern, the colored dots depict the sampling pattern with the suggested 4 line setup using a tilted multi-line scan camera, projected to HR space. With the proposed setup, the resolution is increased in x and y direction. Right: The corresponding Voronoi tessellation shows better coverage of the HR space with the suggested setup (yellow) vs. the regular (black) setup. (Color figure online)

work, we view the SR problem as a variational image reconstruction problem which is one of the most popular approaches tackling SR according to the recent review article [15]. We propose a trainable regularizer based on the trainable reaction-diffusion model [5] and its extension to color images [8] applied to our multi-frame SR problem. During inference, the trained regularizer does neither require parameter search nor the selection of stopping criteria and has constant run time for the reconstruction which depends on the amount of parameters and processed image data. In this sense, our approach could be seen as learning an optimal SR algorithm tailored for our task. With our approach, we show a successful application example where machine learning can improve image quality in a setup where ground truth is hard to obtain. If the specific camera setup is known the presented SR method is very effective and can recover fine details that are lost with common reconstruction techniques.

2 Multi-frame Superresolution

We introduce the forward model for the multi-frame SR setup

$$f_l = BW_l u_{gt} + \eta_l \tag{1}$$

which describes the degradation of a HR image $u_{gt} \in \mathbb{R}^{MNC}$ through the acquisition process plus some additive Gaussian noise η_l, MN defines the number of pixels and C the number of image channels. The result is a degraded LR image $f_l \in \mathbb{R}^{mnC}, l = 1 \ldots L$, with L being the total number of observations (or readout lines). The degradation is modeled with the matrices $W_l \in \mathbb{R}^{mnC \times MNC}$ and $B \in \mathbb{R}^{mnC \times mnC}$. The matrix W_l encodes the warping from the HR space to the LR space, including downsampling, with possible shear and translation between the observed images, and interpolation to the pixel grid of the respective HR and LR coordinate system. The blur matrix B describes the point spread function (PSF) of the camera.

Based on the forward model (1) *regularization-based SR reconstruction approaches* aim to reconstruct a HR image from a set of L LR images. SR is an ill-posed inverse problem, so we formulate the following minimization problem

$$\underset{u}{\text{argmin}} \sum_{c \in \mathcal{C}} \sum_{l=1}^{L} \psi(B_c W_l \mathcal{I}_c u - f_{l,c}) + \lambda \mathcal{R}(u) := \sum_{c \in \mathcal{C}} \sum_{l=1}^{L} \mathcal{D}(u, f_{l,c}) + \lambda \mathcal{R}(u) \quad (2)$$

where we estimate $u \in \mathbb{R}^{MNC}$ from observations $f_{l,c} \in \mathbb{R}^{mn}$ for each color channel $c \in \mathcal{C} := \{r, g, b\}$. The matrix $\mathcal{I}_c$ selects a single color channel from u. The left part is the data fidelity term $\mathcal{D}(\cdot)$, where $\psi(\cdot)$ is typically $\| \cdot \|_k^k$ with $k \in \{1, 2\}$. We assume that the blur matrix B_c is constant for all observations, but different for each color channel $c \in \mathcal{C}$. The right part defines the regularization term $\mathcal{R}(\cdot)$ which is added to make the reconstruction problem well-posed by imposing some prior knowledge about image structures. There have been many approaches tackling the SR problem based on model (2), also for the related task of video SR [15]. In the following we will describe two standard choices for the regularization term $\mathcal{R}(u)$.

Image Priors. A very popular prior that has been used for regularization in SR [6] is the total variation (TV) prior. The discrete version of the TV image prior can be written as $\mathcal{R}(u) = \text{TV}(u) = \|\nabla u\|_{2,1}$, with $\nabla \in \mathbb{R}^{2MNC \times MNC}$ a finite differences approximation of the image gradient. This prior assumes that an image consists of a finite number of piecewise constant regions. This works very well for certain image types, but for general images this assumption does not hold and leads to the staircasing effect. However, a bilateral version of this prior has been exploited for robust multi-frame SR in [6]; Babacan et al. [1] use the TV prior in a Bayesian framework for multi-frame SR, Liu and Sun [11] for video SR, to name a few. A second-order extension of the TV prior is the Total Generalized Variation (TGV) [2] $\mathcal{R}(u) = \text{TGV}_2(u) = \lambda_1 \|\nabla u - v\|_{2,1} + \lambda_0 \|Dv\|_{2,1}$, with $D \in \mathbb{R}^{4MNC \times 2MNC}$ and $v \in \mathbb{R}^{2MNC}$ which is able to get rid of staircasing effects in affine parts of images.

Learned Regularization. In general, the structure of images is more complex than assumed by the previously described priors. Especially for the SR task, it would be beneficial to have a regularizer that can describe high frequency content, because this is especially hard to reconstruct from the LR images. Recently, Chen et al.proposed the trainable reaction-diffusion model [5] which can be interpreted as a generalization of regularization terms. The SR problem from (2) with these generalized regularization terms is embedded in a learning framework. This consists of unrolling a few steps of a simple projected gradient descent optimization algorithm and learning the whole reconstruction algorithm based on training data. A few advantages of this approach are: fast and efficient reconstruction, no parameter tuning at inference, as well as more expressive image priors. We will use this idea together with its extension to color images [8] to build our trained regularizer for the SR task.

The fundamental differences between image priors and the learned regularization is the dependence of the latter on available training data. This might be a drawback, but we solve this problem by careful design of the imaging setup and data simulation. In some settings, this will not be possible, at the expense of image-per-image optimization using a fixed image prior and manual choice of regularization parameters.

There exist also a number of multi-frame SR approaches based on learned correspondences between LR and HR image pairs, disregarding the forward model (1), mostly based on sparse coding [12–14]. However, these methods are designed to reconstruct images patch by patch, which can cause artifacts when combining patches to form the final image. With our approach, we do not rely on patches, but rather reconstruct the whole image, independent of the input data size. In that sense, inference with our approach is similar to CNN models, which have been successfully applied to video superresolution [7,9].

3   SR Method Description

We define the regularization term for the trained reconstruction algorithm as

$$\mathcal{R}(u;\theta) = \sum_{i=1}^{N_k} \sum_{p=1}^{MNC} \phi_i((K_i u)_p) \tag{3}$$

where the matrices K_i denote convolutions of the C channel image u with kernels $k_i \in \mathbb{R}^{h \times h \times C}$ as defined in [8]. N_k defines the number of activation function-kernel pairs ϕ_i and k_i. As a data term we use the model defined in (2) with different choices for $\psi(\cdot)$. The resulting minimization problem becomes

$$\min_{u \in \mathcal{U}} \mathcal{R}(u;\theta) + \lambda \sum_{c \in \mathcal{C}} \sum_{l=1}^{L} \mathcal{D}(u, f_l) \tag{4}$$

with λ weighting the influence of the data term. To obtain our reconstruction algorithm, we unroll a few projected gradient steps T of Problem (4)

$$u_{t+1} = \text{proj}_{\mathcal{U}}(u_t - \nabla \mathcal{R}(u_t; \theta_t) - \lambda_t \sum_{c \in \mathcal{C}} \sum_{l=1}^{L} \nabla \mathcal{D}(u_t, f_l)) \tag{5}$$

and obtain the superresolved result u_T. Each step of the algorithm is parametrized by parameters θ_t. The projection onto the set $\mathcal{U}$ ensures that the result image lies in an admissible range of values, typically $\mathcal{U} = \{u \in \mathbb{R}^{MNC} : 0 \leq u_p \leq \xi, p = 1, \dots, MNC\}$, with ξ being the maximal image intensity. The trainable activation functions are parametrized using N_w radial basis functions (RBFs) as

$$\phi_i'(z) = \sum_{j=1}^{N_w} w_{i,j} \exp \left(-\frac{(z - \mu_j)^2}{2\sigma^2} \right) \tag{6}$$

with equidistant means μ_j and fixed standard deviation σ for all components.

Parameters of the regularizer from (3) are summarized in the vector $\theta = \{w_{i,j,t}, k_{i,t}, \lambda_t\}_{i,j,t=1}^{N_k, N_w, T}$. These parameters comprise the step dependent weights of the activation functions $w_{i,j,t}$, the convolution kernels $k_{i,t}$, and data term weights λ_t. Because we require that the convolution kernels are zero-mean and have norm one to ensure that the output of the convolution lies in the domain of the activation functions, we add constraints to ensure that the parameters θ lie in an admissible set $\mathcal{Y}$ (see supplemental). We train our algorithm based on a loss function comparing ground truth HR data with the output of (5)

$$\min_{\theta \in \mathcal{Y}} \mathcal{L}(\theta) := \frac{1}{2N_b} \sum_{b=1}^{N_b} \|u_{T,b}(\theta) - u_{gt,b}\|_2^2 \tag{7}$$

evaluated on a mini-batch of training data consisting of N_b samples. Training is performed using standard backpropagation. Optimization of (7) was performed using a stochastic inertial incremental proximal gradient (IIPG) optimization algorithm which accounts for the constraint $\theta \in \mathcal{Y}$ (see supplemental).

Parametrization of the Data Term. As mentioned earlier, the function $\psi(\cdot)$ in the data term can be chosen in various ways. For our experiments, we consider a trained regularizer with following ℓ_2 data term as *type A*

$$\mathcal{D}(u, f_l) = \sum_{c \in \mathcal{C}} \sum_{l=1}^{L} \|B_c W_l \mathcal{I}_c u - f_{l,c}\|_2^2 \tag{8}$$

trained for a single color channel, and trained for 3 color channels as *type C*. Additionally, we use a data term

$$\mathcal{D}(u, f_l) = \sum_{c \in \mathcal{C}} \sum_{l=1}^{L} \sum_{j=1}^{N_d} \rho_j(\bar{K}_j B_c W_l \mathcal{I}_c u - f_{l,c}) \tag{9}$$

with N_d trainable filter-function pairs $\bar{K}_j$ and ρ_j which we refer to as *type B*. The parametrization of ρ_j is analogous to (6).

4   Data Acquisition

We designed our application such that prior knowledge about the geometry of the acquisition setup enables precise determination of the (affine) registration transformations between the individual views. As a result, the warping component W of the transformations' forward model (1) is constant for all acquisitions and can be specified accurately. As registration quality is a crucial part for successful multi-frame SR, reliable knowledge about the warping transformations is an advantage. Furthermore, it makes the comparison of different SR algorithms independent of adverse influences of registration inaccuracies.

Additionally to real acquisitions, a sufficient amount of data for training of the SR algorithm was simulated. In that process, we generated not only simulated acquisitions in the setup's resolution, but also required ground truth data in the targeted SR. For real acquisitions and for simulations, we used banknotes as they comprise fine-textured image structures that allow to point out improvements w.r.t. reconstruction quality.

4.1 Acquisition Setup

The acquisition setup comprises a camera with a multi-line scan sensor. Thereby, a selectable set of individual sensor lines can be read-out separately. While planar objects are transported orthogonal to those sensor lines, read-outs are done at according time instances. In the course of that line-scan procedure, each utilized sensor line yields a separate image of the object, where all those images are slightly translated versions of each other. As we use only one sensor, accurate registration is possible in practice.

To achieve the SR requirement of multiple, possibly equally distributed samples around each object point, the entire sensor is rotated slightly w.r.t. the transport direction. Thus the sensor lines are not exactly perpendicular to the transport direction anymore, while the sensor plane remains parallel to the object

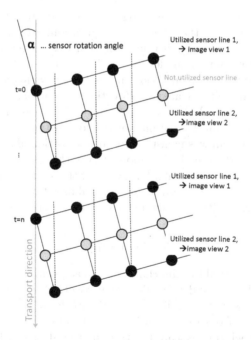

Fig. 2. The multi-line scan sensor is represented as grid of 12 pixels rotated by α w.r.t. the transport direction. Sensor lines with black pixel dots are actually utilized for line-scan acquisition. Those lines are read-out at time instances $t = 0, \ldots, n$, thus each sensor line yields an image of $n + 1$ image lines. Dashed vertical lines indicate that sensor line 2 samples the object space perpendicular to the transport direction at slightly translated positions w.r.t. sensor line 1, only at different time instances.

plane. Depending on the number and mutual distances between the utilized sensor lines, a rotation angle can be derived so that each object line is sampled by the total of pixels of all those sensor lines in an equally distributed manner at a higher sampling rate than a single sensor line could (see Fig. 2) - only distributed over different time instances. As a result of sensor rotation, the resulting images comprise an induced vertical shear, together with a slight scale compression along the sensor line directions, while they mutually are translated versions of each other.

Mere rotation of the sensor enables oversampling perpendicularly to the transport direction. To sample the objects also at a higher rate in transport direction, the transport speed has to be decelerated slightly, depending on the rotation angle, the number of utilized lines, and the mutual distances between the lines. This results in an equally distributed oversampling in transport direction by means of the set of sensor images. The speed reduction induces a further dilation in the individual sensor images which will be considered in the warping model, while they mutually still only differ by constant translations.

4.2   Real Acquisitions

Real acquisitions were conducted utilizing 4 sensor lines, resulting in a targeted SR upsampling factor of 2, although other configurations are possible. One sensor line has 2320 pixel, and the acquisition resolution was set to $100\,\mu m$ per pixel. We used two different sensor angles $\alpha \sim 1.75°$ and $\alpha \sim 1.15°$, respectively, with accordingly reduced transportation speeds to achieve higher sampling rates in and perpendicular to the transport direction. From those acquisitions, the precise mutual image translations and rotation angles were measured and the corresponding warping transformations for the forward model (1) derived. The PSF of the camera system was measured for an acquisition of a calibration sheet to get an estimate for the blurring component B of the forward model (1) which is of size 21×21 in our experiments. By means of the slanted edge approach [3], the line spread functions in horizontal and vertical directions were used to derive a Gaussian PSF kernel with corresponding variances in both directions.

4.3   Simulated Acquisitions for Learning

Simulations were generated by mimicking the real acquisition process on 1200 dpi scans of three banknotes and one calibration sheet. Estimates of the forward warping model W, the corresponding PSF estimate B, and a downsampling factor of 5 were derived from real acquisitions and were applied at 1000 random image positions of each source scan. For training the SR algorithms, 4000 image quadruplets at $100\,\mu m$ per pixel resolution were generated together with a corresponding ground truth image (single-line scan, unrotated) per quadruplet in double resolution, i.e. the SR target resolution.

5   Experiments and Results

We conducted experiments for two setups with angles $\alpha = 1.15°$ and $\alpha = 1.75°$ as described in Sect. 4. For each setup, three different SR algorithms were trained comprising of trained regularizers along with different data terms. The steps T were chosen to balance computation time and reconstruction accuracy. The acquired data was split into distinct training and test sets. For all trained algorithms we used 400 images for training, and tested on 800 images. The resulting run time of the algorithm is 0.5 s per MP on average using a current GPU. Further training details can be found in the supplemental.

Trained Type A. This reconstruction algorithm is trained for a single channel (gray) and is optimized for $T = 10$ projected gradient steps. The convolution kernel size in the regularizer is 7×7, the data term is according to (8).

Trained Type B. The setup of the regularizer is the same as *type A*, the data term is according to (9). The data term functions are initialized to ℓ_2 functions, and the data term convolution kernels are of size 5×5.

Trained Type C. This reconstruction algorithm is trained for three color channels and is optimized for $T = 10$ projected gradient steps. The convolution kernel size in the regularizer is $5 \times 5 \times 3$, the data term is according to (8).

Results for both algorithms *type A* and *B* are shown in Fig. 3, and we observe that fine structures are nicely reconstructed by the trained regularizer where the TV and TGV regularized solutions fail. We also observe some hallucinated image structure in texture-less regions which can be seen both as a strength and limitation of our approach, because this effect is in general very helpful for reconstructing fine details. It is challenging to find an optimal trade-off between smoothing and enhancing fine image structures, which can be controlled by choosing the "right" training data. As the training data contains many oscillating patterns,

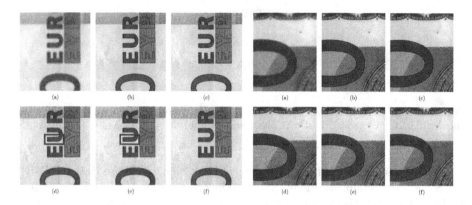

Fig. 3. Left: $\alpha = 1.15°$, Right: $\alpha = 1.75°$. (a) the average solution, (b) the TV reconstruction, (c) the TGV reconstruction, (d) the reconstruction with the trained regularizer *type A*, (e) trained regularizer *type B*, (f) ground truth.

there is a subtle bias towards those in the reconstructions. Comparing Fig. 3(d) and (e) we observe that the trainable data term function and kernel pairs help to reconstruct the fine stripe pattern marked in the images.

Qualitative results for the algorithm *type C* with the regularizer trained on color images are shown in Figs. 4 and 5. Again, fine details and text are nicely recovered. In the color setting hallucinating of structures in homogeneous areas is hardly visible compared to the single-channel case, which is apparent in Fig. 5(b). However, we observe some ringing artifacts which are due to over-enhancing little edges in the image.

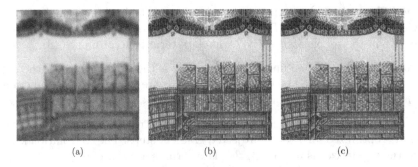

(a)   (b)   (c)

Fig. 4. $\alpha = 1.15°$ (a) average reconstruction, (b) the reconstruction with trained regularizer *type C*, (c) ground truth. (Color figure online)

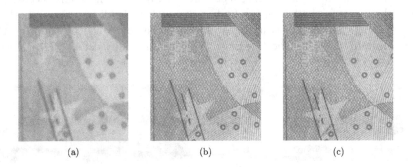

(a)   (b)   (c)

Fig. 5. $\alpha = 1.75°$ (a) average reconstruction, (b) the reconstruction with trained regularizer *type C*, (c) ground truth. (Color figure online)

The SR results are evaluated in terms of Peak Signal to Noise Ratio (PSNR) and Structured Similarity Index (SSIM). The error measures are only evaluated in the image area where all observations overlap, because the reconstruction is not valid outside this area. As a baseline, we compare our algorithms with the solutions of TV and TGV regularized Problem (2) which were solved with a first-order primal-dual algorithm [4].

In Table 1 we summarize the performance of the different algorithms. It is remarkable that by using color data *type C* the SSIM index is much better compared to the results using only single-channel images, which is due to hallucinated structure in texture-less regions. PSNR values are similar in both cases. The regularizer *type A* yields better PSNR than *type B*, but the SSIM results are reversed. We believe this is due to the "invented" checker board patterns which are a little more pronounced for *type B*, as the results in general appear sharper.

Table 1. Results for 800 images from the test set (simulated data)

Angle	$\alpha \approx 1.15°$		$\alpha \approx 1.75°$	
reconstruction	PSNR	SSIM	PSNR	SSIM
Average	22.43	0.4915	22.35	0.4924
TV	25.00	0.5886	25.12	0.5906
TGV	25.63	0.6117	25.78	0.6146
Trained Type A	29.51	0.7900	29.36	0.7856
Trained Type B	29.30	0.8165	29.06	0.8184
Trained Type C	29.61	0.9121	29.56	0.9102

We also tested our trained color image regularizer *type C* on acquired real data, see Fig. 6. Compared to the average solution, the proposed method leads to significant improvement in reconstructing high frequency content visible in the zoomed views. However, we also observe some overly enhanced edges and a few small artifacts, which stem from imperfections in the imaging setup.

(a)   (b)

Fig. 6. Real acquisition data, $\alpha = 1.15°$ (a) average reconstruction, (b) the reconstruction with trained regularizer *type C*. (Color figure online)

6   Conclusion

In this paper, we proposed a fully learned variational model to improve the resolution of data acquired using a multi-line scan camera. We showed that the learned regularizers can successfully recover high frequency content which is especially apparent when inspecting fine textures. We showed that the capabilities of the reconstruction algorithm trained on simulated data also transfer to real data. The imaging setup together with the novel SR reconstruction algorithm enables faster, memory-efficient data acquisition together with increased image quality and near real-time reconstruction time.

Acknowledgements. We acknowledge grant support from the FWF START project BIVISION, No. Y729, the ERC starting grant HOMOVIS, No. 640156 and from the AIT and the Austrian Federal Ministry of Science under the HRSM programme BGBl. II Nr. 292/2012.

References

1. Babacan, S.D., Molina, R., Katsaggelos, A.K.: Variational Bayesian super resolution. IEEE Trans. Image Process. **20**(4), 984–999 (2011)
2. Bredies, K., Kunisch, K., Pock, T.: Total generalized variation. SIAM J. Imaging Sci. **3**(3), 492–526 (2010)
3. Burns, P.D.: Slanted-Edge MTF for digital camera and scanner analysis. In: Proceedings of the PICS Conference, IS&T, pp. 135–138 (2000)
4. Chambolle, A., Pock, T.: A first-order primal-dual algorithm for convex problems with applications to imaging. J. Math. Imaging Vis. **40**(1), 120–145 (2011)
5. Chen, Y., Yu, W., Pock, T.: On learning optimized reaction diffusion processes for effective image restoration. In: Computer Vision and Pattern Recognition, pp. 5261–5269 (2015)
6. Farsiu, S., Robinson, M.D., Elad, M., Milanfar, P.: Fast and robust multiframe super resolution. IEEE Trans. Image Process. **13**(10), 1327–1344 (2004)
7. Kappeler, A., Yoo, S., Dai, Q., Katsaggelos, A.K.: Video super-resolution with convolutional neural networks. IEEE Trans. Comput. Imaging **PP**(99), 1 (2016)
8. Klatzer, T., Hammernik, K., Knöbelreiter, P., Pock, T.: Learning joint demosaicing and denoising based on sequential energy minimization. In: IEEE International Conference on Computational Photography (2016)
9. Liao, R., Tao, X., Li, R., Ma, Z., Jia, J.: Video super-resolution via deep draft-ensemble learning. In: International Conference on Computer Vision (2015)
10. Lim, K.H., Kwoh, L.K.: Super-resolution for SPOT5-Beyond supermode. In: Asian Conference on Remote Sensing (2009)
11. Liu, C.S.: On Bayesian adaptive video super resolution. IEEE Trans. Pattern Anal. Mach. Intell. **36**(2), 346–360 (2014)
12. Song, B.C., Jeong, S.C., Choi, Y.: Video super-resolution algorithm using bi-directional overlapped block motion compensation and on-the-fly dictionary training. IEEE Trans. Circuits Syst. Video Technol. **21**(3), 274–285 (2011)
13. Yang, J., Wang, Z., Lin, Z., Cohen, S., Huang, T.: Coupled dictionary training for image super-resolution. IEEE Trans. Image Process. **21**(8), 3467–3478 (2012)
14. Yang, J., Wright, J., Huang, T.S., Ma, Y.: Image super-resolution via sparse representation. IEEE Trans. Image Process. **19**(11), 2861–2873 (2010)
15. Yue, L., Shen, H., Li, J., Yuan, Q., Zhang, H., Zhang, L.: Image super-resolution: the techniques, applications, and future. Sig. Process. **128**, 389–408 (2016)

Image and Video Processing

A Comparative Study of Local Search Algorithms for Correlation Clustering

Evgeny Levinkov[1], Alexander Kirillov[2], and Bjoern Andres[1(✉)]

[1] Max Planck Institute for Informatics, Saarland Informatics Campus,
Saarbrücken, Germany
andres@mpi-inf.mpg.de
[2] Computer Vision Lab, Technische Universität Dresden, Dresden, Germany

Abstract. This paper empirically compares four local search algorithms for correlation clustering by applying these to a variety of instances of the correlation clustering problem for the tasks of image segmentation, hand-written digit classification and social network analysis. Although the local search algorithms establish neither lower bounds nor approximation certificates, they converge monotonously to a fixpoint, offering a feasible solution at any time. For some algorithms, the time of convergence is affordable for all instances we consider. This finding encourages a broader application of correlation clustering, especially in settings where the number of clusters is not known and needs to be estimated from data.

1 Introduction

Given a finite set and, for any pair of distinct elements, a real-valued cost to be paid if these elements are put in distinct subsets, partitioning the set optimally, so as to minimize the sum of costs, is an NP-hard problem [7,15]. Given a graph and, for any of its edges, a cost to be paid if the incident nodes are put in distinct components, decomposing the graph optimally, so as to minimize the sum of costs, is a generalization that specializes to the former problem for complete graphs [11,13]. The problem is known as *correlation clustering* from [7,13] and is stated in [11,16] in the form of an integer program whose feasible solutions are binary labelings $x \in \{0,1\}^E$ of the edges E of a graph. For any edge $e = \{v, w\}$, the label $x_e = 1$ indicates that this edge e is cut, i.e., that the nodes v and w are in distinct components:

Definition 1. *For any graph $G = (V, E)$ and any $c \in \mathbb{R}^E$, the instance of the correlation clustering problem w.r.t. G and c is the binary linear problem*

$$\min_{x \in \{0,1\}^E} \quad \sum_{e \in E} c_e \, x_e \tag{1}$$

$$\text{subject to} \quad \forall C \in \text{chordless-cycles}(G) \; \forall e \in C : \; x_e \leq \sum_{e' \in C \setminus \{e\}} x_{e'} \tag{2}$$

© Springer International Publishing AG 2017
V. Roth and T. Vetter (Eds.): GCPR 2017, LNCS 10496, pp. 103–114, 2017.
DOI: 10.1007/978-3-319-66709-6_9

Correlation clustering differs from clustering based on non-negative distances such as *multi-terminal cut* [12], *k-cut* [14], and *balanced cut* problems. In correlation clustering, no costs or constraints are put explicitly on the number or sizes of clusters. These properties need not be known when stating an instance of the problem. Instead, they are defined by any feasible solution. This is appealing in applications where the number and size of clusters is to be estimated from data, e.g., image segmentation and social network analysis.

1.1   Contribution

This paper empirically compares some local search algorithms for some instances of the correlation clustering problem. The algorithms we compare are primal feasible heuristics. They output a sequence of feasible solutions that converges strictly to a fixpoint. They do not offer bounds or optimality certificates for these fixpoints. We compute such bounds by polyhedral algorithms where possible. We show that local search algorithms are practical for relatively large instances of the correlation clustering problem, including one for clustering of the MNIST test set of images of hand-written digits [30] and two for clustering social networks [31].

2   Related Work

One principled approach to solving instances of the correlation clustering problem, pursued e.g. in [19,25,26,38,39], is by solving the linear program (LP) obtained by an outer relaxation [11,15,39] of the multicut polytope [11]. In conjunction with suitable rounding, this yields a logarithmic approximation that was established independently in [10,13]. Solving an LP relaxation and rounding the solution can be efficient in general and practical for small instances. For large and complex instances, even the LP relaxation consisting of only the cycle inequalities 2 can be prohibitive.

In an attempt to avoid this separation problem, [4,20] separate only integral points by cycle inequalities (by breadth first search) and resort to general classes of cuts for fractional points. For some instances of the problem, exact solutions are found in less than the time required to solve the canonical LP relaxation. Yet, the absolute running time of both these algorithms is prohibitive for the large instances we study in Sect. 4.

For planar graphs, the minimum cost multicut problem remains NP-hard [5, 37] but admits a polynomial time approximation scheme (PTAS) [27]. Due to a doubly exponential constant factor, this PTAS has mostly been of theoretical interest.

Partial optimality results for the correlation clustering problem, established in [1,2], imply for some instances, a decomposition into independent subproblems that can in principle be exploited by any algorithm.

3   Local Search Algorithms

This section describes four local search algorithms for correlation clustering, defined in [8,9,22,24]. These algorithms take as input an instance of the problem and output a sequence of feasible solutions that converges strictly to a fixpoint. They do not offer bounds or approximation certificates for these feasible solutions.

3.1   Greedy Additive Edge Contraction (GAEC)

Greedy Additive Edge Contraction (GAEC) as defined in [24] starts from an initial clustering where each node is assigned to its own, one-elementary cluster. It proceeds by greedily contracting edges with maximum cost, as long as this cost is positive. Upon contraction of an edge $e = \{v, w\}$, the nodes v and w become one node representing a cluster. For every node in $V \setminus \{v, w\}$ that is connected by edges to both v and w, these edges become one edge that is assigned the sum of costs. If the set of edges with positive cost is empty, the algorithm terminates. In terms of Defenition 1, GAEC start from $x = 1$ and proceeds by setting subsets of variables to zero. Hence, the treatment of joins (0) and cuts (1) is asymmetric.

We examine here the C++ implementation of [24]. To find an edge with the maximum cost efficiently, it employs a priority queue. To keep track of node contractions, it employs a disjoint-set data structure. The time complexity is polynomial and tends to behave linearithmic in practice.

3.2   Greedy Fixation (GF)

Greedy Fixation (GF), a simple algorithm we propose in this paper, is similar in spirit to GAEC. Unlike GAEC, the treatment of joins (0) and cuts (1) is symmetric. GF starts from the partial labeling $x \in \{0, 1, *\}^E$ of edges according to which all edges are undecided ($*$). It proceeds by fixing edge labels x_e to 0 (join) or 1 (cut) in the order of their absolute cost. Whenever an edge is labeled 0, other edges are labeled 0 if this is implied by transitivity.

We examine here our C++ implementation of GF that is analogous to that of GAEC from [24]. The time complexity of GF is equal to that of GAEC. The absolute running time is longer by a constant factor.

3.3   Cut, Glue and Cut (CGC)

Cut, Glue and Cut (CGC), defined in [9], is a local search algorithm that consists of two phases. During the *cut phase*, the graph is recursively bipartitioned. During the *glue and cut phase*, pairs of neighboring clusters are visited and, for any such pair, a two-colorable cut of their union is found by solving a max-cut problem. If the graph is planar, the max-cut problem is solved exactly and efficiently by the Blossom Algorithm [36]. If the graph is non-planar, the max-cut problem is solved approximately by the QPBO-I Algorithm [35].

We examine here the C++ implementation of [9], using the Blossom Algorithm for planar graphs. The implementation is shown in [9] to converge faster than Expand-and-Explore [6] and PlanarCC [39].

3.4 Kernighan-Lin Algorithm with Joins (KLj)

The Kernighan-Lin Algorithm [22] and its slight generalization by [24] start from any initial clustering. They proceed by assessing, for any pair of neighboring clusters, transformations that change the boundary between these clusters, with the goal of lowering the cost of the decomposition. The transformations consist in moving one node from one cluster to the other. Firstly, a sequence of such transformations is constructed greedily. Secondly, the smallest number k is chosen such that the first k moves in the sequence lower the cost optimally. In case of [22], this sequence of transformations is carried out if it effectively descreases the cost. In case of [24], this cost difference is compared to the cost difference that would result from joining the two clusters entirely. If at least one of these two transformations (moving nodes or joining the clusters entirely) effectively lowers the cost, an optimal among the two transformations is carried out.

We examine here two C++ implementations of the Kernighan-Lin Algorithm, [18] and [34], the C++ implementation of the Kernighan-Lin Algorithm with joins [24] as well as our constant-factor improvement of [24] that we have contributed to the source code at https://github.com/bjoern-andres/graph.

4   Empirical Comparison

We apply the four algorithms described in Sect. 3 to instances of the correlation clustering problem from the six data sets characterized in Table 1. Five of these data sets have been used as a benchmark for correlation clustering algorithms in [8,9,18,20]. The sixth (mnist) is our contribution, a correlation clustering problem whose feasible solutions define a partition of the MNIST test set of hand-written digits [30]. As initial clusterings, we consider the output of GAEC,

Table 1. Characteristics of the data sets of instances of the correlation clustering problem we consider. The size of instances varies between hundreds and thousands of nodes, as well as between hundreds and tens of millions of edges.

Data set	Instances	$|V|$	$|E|$	Properties
seg-2d [3]	100	156–3764	439–10970	Planar
seg-3d-300 [4]	8	3846–5896	23763–36221	Non planar
seg-3d-450 [4]	8	15150–17074	94121–107060	Non planar
Slashdot [31]	1	82144	500481	Unit costs
Epinions [31]	1	131828	711210	Unit costs
MNIST (this paper)	1	10000	49995000	Complete

the output and GF, the clustering in which all nodes are in one cluster ($x = 0$), as well as the clustering in which every node forms a separate cluster ($x = 1$).

The data sets of image segmentation ("seg" in Table 1) come with an estimated cut probability $p_e \in (0, 1)$ for every edge $e \in E$. In order to obtain instances of the correlation clustering problem, we define costs w.r.t. these probabilities according to $c_e := \log \frac{1-p_e}{p_e}$ and refer to [21] for a discussion of the probabilistic model. For the clustering of the MNIST test set of hand-written digits, we estimate the cut probabilities as described in Sect. 4.3. For the clustering of social networks, we transform signed directed graphs encoding (dis)trust as described in Sect. 4.4.

We report for each combination of an algorithm and a data set the running time until termination, the objective value of the output feasible solution, and, where available, a distance of the output feasible solution form a known true clustering. This distance is measured by the variation of information (VI) [33], split additively [23] into the contribution due to false cuts (VI_p) and false joins (VI_r), and is measured also by Rand's Index (RI). VI is a metric that is lower-bounded from below by 0. RI is a measure of similarity that is bounded from above by 1. To put the costs in perspective, we report the lower bounds (LB) on the minimum cost obtained from the LP relaxation of [20], and we also report feasible solutions found by the branch-and-cut algorithm of [4] (B&C).

All C++ implementations are compiled with the same parameters and are executed without multi-threading, on the same machine, an Intel® Core™ i3-2100 CPU, operating at 3.10 GHz and equipped with 8 GB of RAM.

4.1 Image Segmentation (seg-2d)

Toward the problem of segmenting each of the 100 test images of the Berkeley Segmentation Data Set [32], we consider the instances of the correlation clustering problem defined in [3]. These instances are publicly available as part of the OpenGM benchmark [20]. Results are shown in Fig. 1 and Table 2.

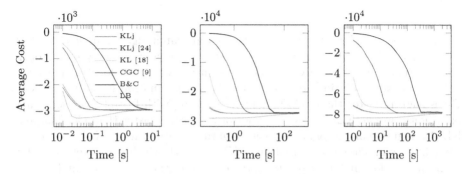

Fig. 1. Convergence of algorithms for seg-2d (left), seg-3d-300 (middle) and seg-3d-450 (right).

Table 2. Empirical comparison of the local search algorithms described Sect. 3 to the problem of segmenting planar images (seg-2d).

Algorithm	T [s]	Value	VI	VI$_p$	VI$_r$	RI
Zeros	0.000	0.00	2.37	0.00	2.37	0.31
Ones	0.000	2201.12	6.10	5.95	0.15	0.74
B& C	1.498	−2966.85	2.50	1.87	0.62	0.80
LB	3.182	−2967.57	−	−	−	−
GAEC [24]	0.019	−2954.40	2.49	1.86	0.63	0.80
GF	**0.013**	−2950.90	2.52	1.90	0.62	0.80
Zeros + KL [18]	0.328	−2771.95	2.72	1.53	1.18	0.68
Zeros + CGC [9]	0.427	−2963.77	2.50	1.86	0.64	0.80
Zeros + KLj [24]	0.062	−2944.14	2.51	1.90	0.61	0.80
Zeros + KLj	0.054	−2944.14	2.51	1.90	0.61	0.80
Ones + KL [18]	0.131	−2808.10	3.18	2.81	0.38	0.78
Ones + CGC [9]	0.990	−2963.94	2.50	1.88	0.62	0.80
Ones + KLj [24]	0.065	−2947.37	2.53	1.91	0.62	0.80
Ones + KLj	0.057	−2947.37	2.53	1.91	0.62	0.80
GAEC + KL [34]	49.948	−2957.84	2.50	1.86	0.63	0.80
GAEC + KL [18]	0.430	−2957.79	2.50	1.86	0.63	0.80
GAEC + CGC [9]	0.393	**−2964.20**	2.50	1.88	0.63	0.80
GAEC + KLj [24]	0.050	−2959.08	2.50	1.87	0.63	0.80
GAEC + KLj	0.046	−2959.08	2.50	1.87	0.63	0.80
GF + KL [34]	49.380	−2955.39	2.52	1.90	0.62	0.80
GF + KL [18]	0.406	−2955.34	2.52	1.90	0.62	0.80
GF + CGC [9]	0.391	−2963.86	2.49	1.87	0.62	0.80
GF + KLj [24]	0.046	−2958.96	2.50	1.88	0.63	0.80
GF + KLj	0.042	−2958.96	2.50	1.88	0.63	0.80

It can be seen form these results that local search algorithms find feasible solutions which are close in terms of objective value and accuracy to the optimal solutions found by B&C for these instances. Moreover, local search algorithms find such solutions one to two orders of magnitude faster than B&C. GF is slightly faster than GAEC [24], terminating with feasible solutions that are slightly worse. KLj [24] is one order of magnitude faster than CGC [9] and KL [18] and is more stable under with regard to initialization. KLj is faster by a small margin. The implementation of KL from [34] which is not optimized for performance does not process the data set within 24 h for "zeros" and "ones" initialization. This shows that attention to constant factors is important at this scale of the problem.

Table 3. Empirical comparison of the local search algorithms described Sect. 3 to the problem of segmenting volume images (seg-3d).

Algorithm	seg-3d-300						seg-3d-450					
	T [s]	Value	VI	VI_p	VI_r	RI	T [s]	Value	VI	VI_p	VI_r	RI
Zeros	0.000	0.00	4.09	0.00	4.09	0.12	0.000	0.00	4.67	0.00	4.67	0.09
Ones	0.000	40478.83	6.77	6.69	0.07	0.88	0.000	186787.03	7.94	7.87	0.07	0.91
B& C	68.088	−27302.76	1.64	0.82	0.82	0.88	4130.273	−78474.69	2.02	0.93	1.09	0.87
LB	631.769	−27304.81	–	–	–	–	10337.771	−78482.98	–	–	–	–
GAEC [24]	0.070	−27162.81	1.76	0.85	0.91	0.87	0.340	−78281.49	2.11	0.94	1.17	0.85
GF	**0.054**	−27142.13	1.75	0.86	0.89	0.87	**0.207**	−78194.01	2.13	0.97	1.16	0.85
Zeros + KL [18]	2.020	−25570.35	3.30	1.13	2.17	0.72	16.007	−72984.82	4.16	1.25	2.91	0.67
Zeros + CGC [9]	5.481	−27253.30	1.80	0.83	0.96	0.86	64.850	−78252.24	2.32	0.96	1.36	0.83
Zeros + KLj [24]	0.906	−27275.89	1.68	0.83	0.85	0.88	13.862	−78390.69	2.09	0.95	1.14	0.86
Zeros + KLj	0.781	−27275.89	1.68	0.83	0.85	0.88	12.687	−78390.69	2.09	0.95	1.14	0.86
Ones + KL [18]	45.608	−25217.20	2.22	1.44	0.77	0.87	628.895	−61755.28	2.95	2.13	0.82	0.89
Ones + CGC [9]	25.144	−27268.02	1.74	0.84	0.91	0.87	375.190	−78369.18	2.17	0.94	1.23	0.85
Ones + KLj [24]	0.766	−27266.11	1.64	0.80	0.84	0.88	13.778	−78388.89	2.08	0.94	1.14	0.86
Ones + KLj	0.647	−27266.11	1.64	0.80	0.84	0.88	12.636	−78388.89	2.08	0.94	1.14	0.86
GAEC + KL [18]	8.543	−27201.47	1.76	0.85	0.91	0.87	122.214	−78358.89	2.11	0.95	1.17	0.85
GAEC + CGC [9]	2.398	−27277.15	1.71	0.84	0.87	0.87	22.815	−78403.27	2.09	0.95	1.14	0.86
GAEC + KLj [24]	0.459	−27258.25	1.69	0.84	0.85	0.88	7.347	−78417.99	2.04	0.94	1.10	0.86
GAEC + KLj	0.406	−27258.25	1.69	0.84	0.85	0.88	6.565	**−78417.99**	2.04	0.94	1.10	0.86
GF + KL [18]	8.628	−27193.11	1.74	0.86	0.88	0.87	127.386	−78345.25	2.12	0.96	1.16	0.85
GF + CGC [9]	2.298	**−27277.64**	1.69	0.83	0.86	0.86	28.497	−78392.97	2.10	0.95	1.15	0.86
GF + KLj [24]	0.495	−27251.91	1.70	0.84	0.85	0.88	7.733	−78412.11	2.08	0.95	1.13	0.86
GF + KLj	0.437	−27251.91	1.70	0.84	0.85	0.88	7.109	−78412.11	2.08	0.95	1.13	0.86

4.2 Volume Image Segmentation (seg-3d-300, Seg-3d-450)

Toward the problem of segmenting volume images of neuronal processes taken by an electron microscope [28] we consider the instances of the correlation clustering problem defined in [4]. These instances are publicly available as part of the OpenGM benchmark [18]. Results are shown in Fig. 1 and Table 3.

These results are comparable to those for image segmentation (Sect. 4.1). Yet, differences between algorithms become more pronounced here, as the instances are larger. For instance, the time until convergence for GAEC [24] divided by the time until convergence of B&C is of the orders 10^{-3} for seg-3d-300 and 10^{-4} for seg-3d-450. KLj converges faster than KL, to better feasible solutions.

4.3 Clustering Images of Hand-Written Digits (MNIST)

Toward the problem of partitioning the MNIST test set of images of hand-written digits [29], we learn from the MNIST training set a Siamese CNN to predict, for any pair of images, whether they depict the same or distinct digits. The learning is described in detail below. The probabilities predicted by this Siamese CNN for the MNIST test set define an instance of the correlation clustering problem for the complete graph whose nodes are the test images.

Results from applying the local search algorithms described in Sect. 3 to this instance are shown in Tables 4 and 5. It can be seen from these results that local search algorithms are practical for this large instance. This is in contrast

Table 4. Empirical comparison of the local search algorithms described Sect. 3 to the problem of clustering the images of hand-written digits in the MNIST test set [29].

Algorithm	Time [s]	Value	VI	VI_p	VI_r	RI	M%
Zeros	0.000	0.0	3.319	0.000	3.319	0.100	90.00
Ones	0.000	−825928042.4	9.968	9.968	0.000	0.900	99.99
GAEC [24]	369.77	−906355440.5	0.220	0.113	0.108	0.995	1.20
GF	148.33	−906355440.5	0.220	0.113	0.108	0.995	1.20
Zeros + KL [18]	1796.64	−906765155.8	0.162	0.083	0.079	0.997	0.82
Zeros + CGC [9]	–	–	–	–	–	–	–
Zeros + KLj [24]	148.97	−906765155.8	0.162	0.083	0.079	0.997	0.82
Zeros + KLj	**120.66**	−906765155.8	0.162	0.083	0.079	0.997	0.82
Ones + KL [18]	50197.41	−906765155.8	0.162	0.083	0.079	0.997	0.82
Ones + CGC [9]	120418.80	−906765155.8	0.162	0.083	0.079	0.997	0.82
Ones + KLj [24]	2310.44	−906765155.8	0.162	0.083	0.079	0.997	0.82
Ones + KLj	1403.22	−906765155.8	0.162	0.083	0.079	0.997	0.82
GAEC + KL [18]	1197.80	−906765155.8	0.162	0.083	0.079	0.997	0.82
GAEC + CGC [9]	1898.33	−906585148.4	0.174	0.089	0.085	0.997	0.91
GAEC + KLj [24]	427.78	−906765155.8	0.162	0.083	0.079	0.997	0.82
GAEC + KLj	415.93	−906765155.8	0.162	0.083	0.079	0.997	0.82
GF + KL [18]	896.51	−906765155.8	0.162	0.083	0.079	0.997	0.82
GF + CGC [9]	1553.41	−906585148.4	0.174	0.089	0.085	0.997	0.91
GF + KLj [24]	206.28	−906765155.8	0.162	0.083	0.079	0.997	0.82
GF + KLj	186.45	−906765155.8	0.162	0.083	0.079	0.997	0.82

Table 5. Confusion matrix related to the clustering of the MNIST test images, with images of one-elementary clusters shown below.

	0	1	2	3	4	5	6	7	8	9	10	11	12	13	Σ
0	976	0	0	0	0	0	1	1	1	0	0	0	1	0	980
1	0	1132	1	2	0	0	0	0	0	0	0	0	0	0	1135
2	1	0	1026	0	1	0	0	3	1	0	0	0	0	0	1032
3	0	0	1	1003	0	4	0	0	1	1	0	0	0	0	1010
4	0	0	0	0	976	0	1	0	0	5	0	0	0	0	982
5	2	0	0	8	0	880	1	0	0	1	0	0	0	0	892
6	4	2	0	0	1	1	946	0	2	0	0	1	0	1	958
7	0	2	5	1	0	0	0	1017	1	1	1	0	0	0	1028
8	2	0	2	1	0	1	0	1	965	2	0	0	0	0	974
9	1	0	0	1	2	4	0	4	0	997	0	0	0	0	1009
Σ	986	1136	1035	1016	980	890	949	1026	971	1007	1	1	1	1	

to the implementations of B&C and LB we have applied, which are impractical for this instance. Secondly, it can be seen from the VI and RI as well as from the confusion matrix in Table 5 that the clustering we obtain as a feasible solution is exceptionally accurate, defining 14 clusters, 4 of which contain only a single image. By relating the ten largest clusters to the ten digits optimally, this clustering can be associated with a misclassification rate of $M = 0.82\%$ (see Table 4) which is lower than the misclassification rate of LeNet trained for classification (1.1%). This result is surprising, given that we solve a clustering problem and do not prescribe the number of clusters. It encourages applications of correlation clustering even in settings where the number of clusters *is* known.

Learning a Siamese CNN for relating images. We train a Siamese CNN from scratch, with a cross entropy loss, built on the architecture of LeNet [29] which has a standard implementation in the Caffe framework [17]. We duplicate the convolution part of LeNet with shared weights to take two images. We feed outputs of these parts to the fully connected layer of the LeNet architecture. The CNN has two outputs, scores for two images depicting the same and distinct digits, respectively. We learn the parameters of this network from the MNIST training set, without any data augmentation. We stick to the solver parameters proposed in the Caffe example[1] in which LeNet is trained for a classification task. Specifically, we use stochastic gradient descent and an inverse decay learning policy with the base learning rate 0.01, $\gamma = 0.0001$, and power 0.75. The batch size is 64. We carry out 150000 iterations.

4.4   Clustering of Social Networks (Epinions, Slashdot)

Toward the clustering of social networks, we consider the directed graphs from [31] called *epinions* and *slashdot*. In these directed graphs $H = (V, A)$ with edge costs $c' : A \to \{-1, 1\}$, each node represents a person and every edge $(v, w) = a \in A$ encodes that a person v either trusts ($c'_a = 1$) or distrusts ($c'_a = -1$) a person w. We define a correlation clustering problem w.r.t. these signed directed graphs by firstly removing self-loops from H and by then defining a cost matrix C w.r.t. the cost matrix C' as $C := \text{sgn}(C' + C'^T)$.

Results for those local search algorithms described in Sect. 3 that are practical for these large instances of the correlation clustering problem are shown in Table 6 and Fig. 2. To make use of the feasible solution with the lowest cost that we find, we report in Fig. 2 the cumulative distribution of cluster sizes, i.e. the number of clusters $N(x)$ of size less than or equal to x. For *epinions*, we observe one large cluster of 93676 people, 6705 clusters of a size between 2 to 1209, and 18905 totally disconnected individuals. This is consistent with the fraction of edges indicating trust, which is 85%. For *slashdot*, we observe one large cluster of 68819 people, 878 clusters of a size between 2 to 851, and 8343 totally disconnected individuals. This is consistent with the fraction of edges indicating trust, which is 77.4%.

---

[1] http://caffe.berkeleyvision.org/gathered/examples/mnist.html.

Table 6. Comparison of performance of different algorithms with different initializations on very large graphs of social networks.

Algorithm	Epinions		Slashdot	
	Time [s]	Value	Time [s]	Value
GAEC [24]	4.35	−70990	2.95	−50057
GF	**2.05**	−71116	**1.39**	−50055
Zeros + KLj [24]	58306.3	−71612	30293.3	−50299
Zeros + KLj	55372.7	−71612	29541.8	−50299
Ones + KLj [24]	47699.7	−72204	33831.6	−50462
Ones + KL	48141.6	−72204	29971.9	−50462
GAEC + KLj [24]	8746.8	−72259	5452.1	−50476
GAEC + KLj	8166.9	**−72259**	4883.2	**−50476**
GF + KLj [24]	8045.8	−72224	7586.3	−50440
GF + KLj	7239.7	−72224	6858.9	−50440

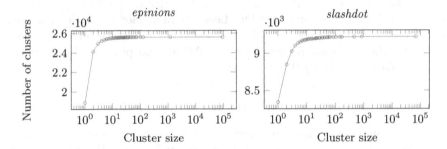

Fig. 2. Cumulative distribution of cluster sizes in social networks, as defined by the best obtained solutions.

5   Conclusion

We have applied four local search algorithms for correlation clustering to a collection of instances of the correlation clustering problem for the tasks of image segmentation, hand-written digit classification and social network analysis. A combination of greedy initialization (by additive edge contraction or fixation) and the Kernihan-Lin Algorithm with joins has proven practical for all instances. It has allowed us to cluster the MNIST test set of hand-written digits into 10 significant clusters with an associated misclassification rate of 0.82%. Moreover, it has allowed us to estimate the distribution of cluster sizes form social network graphs. The practicality of these local search algorithms encourages further applications of correlation clustering, especially in settings where the number of clusters is not known a priori and needs to be estimated from data.

References

1. Alush, A., Goldberger, J.: Ensemble segmentation using efficient integer linear programming. TPAMI **34**(10), 1966–1977 (2012)
2. Alush, A., Goldberger, J.: Hierarchical image segmentation using correlation clustering. IEEE Trans. Neural Netw. Learn. Syst. **PP**(99), 1–10 (2015)
3. Andres, B., Kappes, J.H., Beier, T., Köthe, U., Hamprecht, F.A.: Probabilistic image segmentation with closedness constraints. In: ICCV (2011)
4. Andres, B., Kröger, T., Briggman, K.L., Denk, W., Korogod, N., Knott, G., Köthe, U., Hamprecht, F.A.: Globally optimal closed-surface segmentation for connectomics. In: ECCV (2012)
5. Bachrach, Y., Kohli, P., Kolmogorov, V., Zadimoghaddam, M.: Optimal coalition structure generation in cooperative graph games. In: AAAI (2013). http://www.aaai.org/ocs/index.php/AAAI/AAAI13/paper/view/6407/7071
6. Bagon, S., Galun, M.: Large scale correlation clustering optimization. CoRR abs/1112.2903 (2011). http://arxiv.org/abs/1112.2903
7. Bansal, N., Blum, A., Chawla, S.: Correlation clustering. Mach. Learn. **56**(1–3), 89–113 (2004)
8. Beier, T., Hamprecht, F.A., Kappes, J.H.: Fusion moves for correlation clustering. In: CVPR (2015)
9. Beier, T., Kröger, T., Kappes, J.H., Köthe, U., Hamprecht, F.A.: Cut, Glue & Cut: a fast, approximate solver for multicut partitioning. In: CVPR (2014)
10. Charikar, M., Guruswami, V., Wirth, A.: Clustering with qualitative information. J. Comput. Syst. Sci. **71**(3), 360–383 (2005)
11. Chopra, S., Rao, M.: The partition problem. Math. Program. **59**(1–3), 87–115 (1993)
12. Dahlhaus, E., Johnson, D.S., Papadimitriou, C.H., Seymour, P.D., Yannakakis, M.: The complexity of multiterminal cuts. SIAM J. Comput. **23**, 864–894 (1994)
13. Demaine, E.D., Emanuel, D., Fiat, A., Immorlica, N.: Correlation clustering in general weighted graphs. Theoret. Comput. Sci. **361**(2–3), 172–187 (2006)
14. Goldschmidt, O., Hochbaum, D.S.: A polynomial algorithm for the k-cut problem for fixed k. Math. Oper. Res. **19**(1), 24–37 (1994)
15. Grötschel, M., Wakabayashi, Y.: A cutting plane algorithm for a clustering problem. Math. Program. **45**(1), 59–96 (1989)
16. Horňáková, A., Lange, J.H., Andres, B.: Analysis and optimization of graph decompositions by lifted multicuts. In: ICML (Forthcoming) (2017)
17. Jia, Y., Shelhamer, E., Donahue, J., Karayev, S., Long, J., Girshick, R., Guadarrama, S., Darrell, T.: Caffe: convolutional architecture for fast feature embedding (2014). arXiv preprint arXiv:1408.5093
18. Kappes, J.H., Andres, B., Hamprecht, F.A., Schnörr, C., Nowozin, S., Batra, D., Kim, S., Kausler, B.X., Kröger, T., Lellmann, J., Komodakis, N., Savchynskyy, B., Rother, C.: A comparative study of modern inference techniques for structured discrete energy minimization problems. Int. J. Comput. Vis. **115**(2), 155–184 (2015)
19. Kappes, J.H., Speth, M., Andres, B., Reinelt, G., Schnörr, C.: Globally optimal image partitioning by multicuts. In: EMMCVPR (2011)
20. Kappes, J.H., Speth, M., Reinelt, G., Schnörr, C.: Higher-order segmentation via multicuts. Comput. Vis. Image Underst. **143**, 104–119 (2015)
21. Kappes, J.H., Swoboda, P., Savchynskyy, B., Hazan, T., Schnörr, C.: Probabilistic correlation clustering and image partitioning using perturbed multicuts. In: Scale Space and Variational Methods in Computer Vision (2015)

22. Kernighan, B.W., Lin, S.: An efficient heuristic procedure for partitioning graphs. Bell Syst. Tech. J. **49**, 291–307 (1970)
23. Keuper, M., Andres, B., Brox, T.: Motion trajectory segmentation via minimum cost multicuts. In: ICCV (2015)
24. Keuper, M., Levinkov, E., Bonneel, N., Lavoué, G., Brox, T., Andres, B.: Efficient decomposition of image and mesh graphs by lifted multicuts. In: International Conference on Computer Vision (2015)
25. Kim, S., Nowozin, S., Kohli, P., Yoo, C.: Higher-order correlation clustering for image segmentation. In: NIPS (2011)
26. Kim, S., Yoo, C., Nowozin, S., Kohli, P.: Image segmentation using higher-order correlation clustering. TPAMI **36**, 1761–1774 (2014)
27. Klein, P.N., Mathieu, C., Zhou, H.: Correlation clustering and two-edge-connected augmentation for planar graphs. In: Mayr, E.W., Ollinger, N. (eds.) 32nd International Symposium on Theoretical Aspects of Computer Science (STACS 2015). Leibniz International Proceedings in Informatics, vol. 30, pp. 554–567. Schloss Dagstuhl-Leibniz-Zentrum fuer Informatik, Dagstuhl (2015)
28. Knott, G., Marchman, H., Wall, D., Lich, B.: Serial section scanning electron microscopy of adult brain tissue using focused ion beam milling. J. Neurosci. **28**(12), 2959–2964 (2008)
29. LeCun, Y., Bottou, L., Bengio, Y., Haffner, P.: Gradient-based learning applied to document recognition. Proc. IEEE **86**(11), 2278–2324 (1998)
30. Lecun, Y., Cortes, C.: The MNIST database of handwritten digits. http://yann.lecun.com/exdb/mnist/
31. Leskovec, J., Huttenlocher, D., Kleinberg, J.: Signed networks in social media. In: CHI (2010)
32. Martin, D., Fowlkes, C., Tal, D., Malik, J.: A database of human segmented natural images and its application to evaluating segmentation algorithms and measuring ecological statistics. In: Proceedings of the 8th International Conference on Computer Vision, vol. 2, pp. 416–423, July 2001
33. Meilă, M.: Comparing clusterings–an information based distance. J. Multivar. Anal. **98**(5), 873–895 (2007)
34. Nowozin, S., Jegelka, S.: Solution stability in linear programming relaxations: graph partitioning and unsupervised learning. In: ICML (2009)
35. Rother, C., Kolmogorov, V., Lempitsky, V., Szummer, M.: Optimizing binary MRFs via extended roof duality. In: CVPR (2007)
36. Schraudolph, N.N., Kamenetsky, D.: Efficient exact inference in planar ising models. In: NIPS (2009)
37. Voice, T., Polukarov, M., Jennings, N.R.: Coalition structure generation over graphs. J. Artif. Intell. Res. **45**, 165–196 (2012)
38. Yarkony, J.: Analyzing PlanarCC: demonstrating the equivalence of PlanarCC and the multi-cut LP relaxation. In: NIPS Workshop on Discrete Optimization (2014)
39. Yarkony, J., Ihler, A., Fowlkes, C.C.: Fast planar correlation clustering for image segmentation. In: ECCV (2012)

Combined Precise Extraction and Topology of Points, Lines and Curves in Man-Made Environments

Dominik Wolters[⊠] and Reinhard Koch

Department of Computer Science, Kiel University, Kiel, Germany
dwol@informatik.uni-kiel.de

Abstract. This article presents a novel method for a combined extraction of points, lines and arcs in images. Geometric primitives are fitted into extracted edge pixels. In order to get points, the intersections between the geometric primitives are calculated. The method allows a precise and at the same time robust detection of the image features. By constructing a graph describing the topology between the features, more complex structures can be described over multiple connected primitives.

1 Introduction

The extraction of features in images is relevant for many applications and there are numerous approaches published. The main features that are often used in image processing are points, lines, or even curved structures. The algorithms for the detection are usually specialized on one feature type.

A combined detection of different features and a topology between them can bring many advantages. The neighborhood information can be used to assess the relevance of features, to increase their localization accuracy, or to support the extraction of more complex geometries.

In further processing, e.g. for correspondence search in different images, the topology between the features can be used to make the search more reliable and more robust.

In the extraction of different features, similar image processing methods are used, therefore a combined extraction saves processing time since no redundant calculations have to be carried out.

1.1 Related Work

The detection of elementary geometric objects is one of the fundamental objectives of computer vision, since they are usually the prerequisite for high-level procedures. Many researchers have addressed these issues in recent decades.

In the literature a variety of different corner detectors exist [15]. A set of methods is based on contours in images. Contours are first extracted. Then, the contour is searched for specific features such as a strong curvature. Horaud et al. [9] extract line segments from contours and use intersection of the line segments as interest points.

© Springer International Publishing AG 2017
V. Roth and T. Vetter (Eds.): GCPR 2017, LNCS 10496, pp. 115–125, 2017.
DOI: 10.1007/978-3-319-66709-6_10

Intensity-based methods calculate a measure that indicates whether a feature point is present. Known corner detection methods which belong to this group are the Moravec corner detector [13] and Harris corner detector [8].

Detectors for higher-order geometric primitives, e.g. lines and arcs, can be roughly divided into two classes: Hough-based and edge chain methods.

The Hough-based methods use different versions of the Hough-transform [3, 5, 11]. These methods usually require an accurate adjustment of the parameters depending on the image data and suffer from a high memory consumption and a long execution time.

The edge chain methods use chains of connected edge pixels and fit geometric primitives on the edge chain using least-squares fitting techniques [1, 2, 6, 7] or RANSAC-like approaches [12]. Wenzel und Förstner [18] use an adaption to the Douglas-Peucker algorithm to approximate given pixel chains by a sequence of lines and elliptical arcs.

Recently, a parameterless detector for lines and ellipses was proposed by Patraucean et al. [14]. They use a fitting algorithm for the ellipses that uses both the algebraic distance from the conic equation and the deviation from the gradient direction. For model validation and model selection they use statistical criteria.

1.2 Contribution

In this paper, we propose a method for the combined extraction of points, lines and curved structures from images. Our method allows a precise and at the same time more robust detection of the different feature types than existing approaches.

Furthermore, in our method, by modeling the topological relationships of the individual features in a graph, more complex geometric structures can be described over multiple connected primitives.

2   Characteristics of Different Image Features

The focus of our work is the extraction of image features in urban and man-made environments, which on the one hand are precise and on the other hand describe the relevant geometric primitives.

The different features have advantages and disadvantages for use in urban scenes. Robust point detectors, such as SIFT [10] or SURF [4], enable reliable matching of features across multiple images, but generally do not have high localization accuracy and are usually not located at physical object corners.

Classical precise point features, e.g. Harris-Corners [8] or Good features to track [16], have higher localization accuracy than robust point features but are also often found in non-relevant locations, e.g. on structured surfaces or on trees. They are often missing on geometric primitives which do not have a high cornerness. These may be e.g. windows in the shadow. In addition, the localization accuracy of these points deteriorates in the presence of noise.

Edge and line segments offer a higher level of structure information about the scene and are usually located in relevant places in urban scenes. However, start and end points of line features are often only inaccurately localized.

Corner points generated by the intersecting of line segments have a higher localization accuracy than classical point features and a greater robustness against noise. They are usually located at relevant geometric primitives in urban scenes. However, not always two intersecting line segments are available or detectable.

Combined detection of line segments and points by calculating intersections of lines offer many possibilities. A higher localization accuracy and greater relevance of the point features can be achieved. At the same time, precise endpoints for the lines can be determined in this way. These endpoints can be used to support line triangulation.

The topology between points and lines can be used to support and verify the matching of multiple images in a structure from motion application. Points or lines, which are connected in one image, are probably also connected in other images. Simple contours or polygons can thus be recognized and reconstructed directly.

3 Detection Process

Our approach to extracting image features consists of a multi-step process (Fig. 1). In the first step, edges are detected in the images. Subsequently, geometric primitives, such as line and arc segments are fitted to the extracted edges. The intersections between the geometric primitives are calculated to extract precise point features. At the same time, a graph is constructed which describes the topology of the image features.

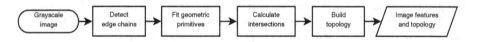

Fig. 1. Flowchart of the detection process

3.1 Extraction of Edges

To extract the edges, we use a customized version of the edge drawing method [17]. Edge drawing is an edge detection algorithm that runs in real-time and produces contiguous pixel chains that are exactly one pixel wide. The edge drawing algorithm consists of 4 steps. In the first step, noise is reduced by using a Gaussian filter, then the gradient magnitude and gradient direction are calculated for each pixel. In the next step anchor points are extracted. These are the peaks in the gradient image. These peaks are linked using smart routing to extract the edges.

For our application, we have adapted the smart routing process in such a way that not only individual contiguous edge chains are extracted, but also the connecting points between the individual edge chains are stored.

The smart routing process is as follows: Beginning with an anchor point, the direction of the gradient is considered. The pixel with the strongest gradient magnitude is then selected orthogonally to the gradient direction and used to iteratively build up a pixel chain. The process is terminated if all neighboring pixels have a gradient magnitude below a threshold value or a previously detected edge pixel is reached. In the latter case, we also store the connection point for the two edges.

Figure 2(b) shows the calculated gradient image with the extracted pixel chains for a simple synthetic example.

3.2   Fitting the Geometrical Primitives

In the next step geometric primitives are fitted into the extracted edges. Our approach is based on a method we presented in [19] that allows a detection of lines with subpixel accuracy.

The process presented by us allows the extraction of different geometric shapes. We limit ourselves to lines and parabolas as these are the predominant forms in our application, which are urban scenes. But an extension which allows the extraction of further geometric forms, e.g. circles or ellipses, is easily possible. Parabolas were chosen as the model for the arcs because they are easy to parameterize and a robust fitting is possible.

The starting point for the detection of the lines and arcs are the edge chains from the first step. The extracted pixel chains are decomposed into one or more geometric primitives. The basic idea is to walk along the pixel chain and to fit geometric primitives.

If the edge has a minimum length, fitting an initial line segment is attempted using a least-squares line fitting method. If an initial line segment has been found, it is tried to extent this line segment. For this purpose, further pixels of the edge chain are added to the line until the deviation exceeds a threshold value.

If a smaller deviation is achieved when fitting a parabola than when fitting a line, the parabola is selected as a model. If the model is changed, the parabolic segment is extended by further pixels from the edge chain until the threshold for the maximum deviation is reached. The extracted element is then stored. Additional models such as ellipses and circles can be considered at this point. When selecting the model, i.e. line or arc, the curvature of the parabola is additionally checked. The parabola is selected only if it has a sufficient curvature.

Similarly, the remaining pixels of the edge chain are processed to extract further geometric primitives. The detected primitives for the simple example are shown in Fig. 2(c).

Refinement. The approach for detection with subpixel accuracy from [19] can also be adapted to parabola segments so that they are also detected with subpixel accuracy.

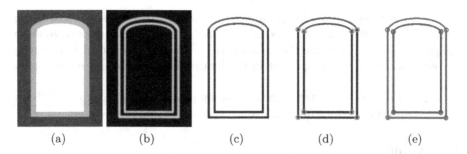

(a)	(b)	(c)	(d)	(e)

Fig. 2. The steps of the detection process: (a) input image, (b) gradient image with extracted edge chains, (c) fitted geometric primitives (red: arcs, blue: line segments), (d) calculated intersections, (e) connected components of the graph (a random color for each component) (Color figure online)

Fusion of Connected Primitives. In case of noise, lines or arcs might fragment into several subsegments which are separately detected. We therefore check for successive line and arc segments whether they have similar parameters and the endpoints are close to each other. If this is the case, the elements are fused.

3.3 Calculation of Intersection Features

In the next step, the intersections of the extracted geometric primitives are calculated (Fig. 2(d)). Only the intersections of successive elements from the same edge chain are calculated. In this way, it is ensured that the elements used for intersecting are connected over a common edge and are thus, with a high probability, part of a contiguous object in the scene.

In addition, intersections are calculated between elements which have been extracted from different edge chains if the edges have a connection and the elements have been extracted in the region of the connection point.

When calculating the intersection, three cases must be distinguished. Intersections between two lines, intersections between parabolas and lines, and intersections between two parabolas.

It is important that arc segments are also extracted from the edges because the approximation of curved contours through line segments would lead to inaccurate intersections.

3.4 Building a Topology

The connections of the intersections and geometrical primitives are stored in a graph, which models the topological relations. The nodes in the graph correspond to the image features, i.e. points, lines and arcs. The relationships between the image features are modeled over the edges of the graph. A point feature that has been created by the intersection of two lines corresponds in the graph to a node with two edges to the two lines, which in turn are also nodes of the graph.

In this way, more complex geometric primitives can be described over the individual elements. The connected components of the graph correspond to more complex geometric shapes in the image. If the connected component has a cycle, a closed contour is usually present in the image. This may be e.g. a window in a facade.

Figure 2(e) shows the topology for the simple example. As expected, both objects are recognized as different connected components of the graph.

4   Evaluation

In the following section, we present qualitative and quantitative results of our detector compared to existing methods. Synthetic computer-generated images as well as natural images are used for the comparisons.

4.1   Detection Accuracy of Intersection Features

The aim of the first experiment is to determine the accuracy of the intersection features compared to classical corner features. For comparison, we use the Good features to track detector [16] with subpixel refinement of the corners.

For the test, 50 synthetic images of simple geometric objects, such as triangles and rectangles, were generated. We add different levels of additive white Gaussian noise. The standard deviation of the noise is varied from 0 to 15. We use 8-bit images, i.e. the pixel values are between 0 and 255.

To evaluate the detection accuracy, we apply both algorithms to the images and determine the residuals from real to the determined corner points of the objects. The results (Fig. 3) show that the intersection features have a significantly higher localization accuracy than classical corner features. In particular, it is shown that the intersection features are more robust against the noise and can still be reliably localized even in the case of strong noise.

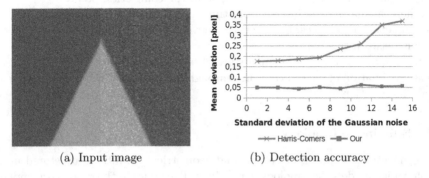

(a) Input image   (b) Detection accuracy

Fig. 3. Detection accuracy of corner features with different levels of Gaussian noise. (a) Cutouts of a corner from two input images. Left half without noise and right half disturbed by noise with standard deviation of 15. (b) Results of the evaluation

4.2   Comparison to ELSDc

To evaluate the results of the line and the arc detection, we compare our results with those of the ELSDc (Ellipse and Line Segment Detector, with Continuous formulation) [14], as this is the state of the art and the source code is available.

Synthetic Data. In a first experiment, we look again at the synthetic data used in the previous section. Since the ELSDc does not calculate intersections between the extracted lines and ellipses and does not build a topology, we use the lines extracted from the images and intersect them in a post-processing step to obtain the corners of the geometric objects and calculate the residuals.

Figure 4(a) shows the results. On clean data, ELSDc achieves a slightly higher detection accuracy. However, the detection accuracy deteriorates significantly with increasing noise, while the detection accuracy with our approach remains stable even with strong noise.

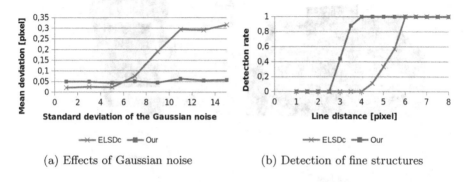

(a) Effects of Gaussian noise   (b) Detection of fine structures

Fig. 4. Comparison between ELSDc and our method

In another experiment the ability to recognize fine details was examined. For this purpose, the minimum distance between two parallel lines is determined, in which they can be detected separately. We have generated synthetic images which contain parallel lines with different distances between 1 and 10 pixels. In the evaluation, we determine how often theses lines are detected as two separate lines for each distance. The results (Fig. 4(b)) show that with our method, two lines can be detected separately with a distance of approximately 3.5 pixels. With the ELSDc, this is possible not until a distance of about 6 pixels.

Natural Images. For a quality evaluation of the detector in real-world applications, we have tested it on numerous natural images that cover common challenges like complex geometric primitives and background clutter. For this purpose, we used the datasets from [14] as well as own images. We describe the typical behavior of the detectors by some examples.

Figure 5 shows the results for detection on a building with arched windows. Both detection algorithms show similar results, but in the detail view of a window typical differences are recognizable. With ELSDc, the upper edge of the arched window is approximated by several line segments and is not detected as an arc. With our approach, all arches of the windows are correctly recognized.

Furthermore, with our approach finer structures can be detected, for example on the window frame. This confirms the quantitative results that have been shown in the analysis with the synthetic images. In addition, the straight lines break down less often into several sub-segments.

The intersections, which are additionally calculated with our approach, are each quite well located at the physical corners of the objects. At the same time, there are hardly any intersection points in non-relevant areas such as the wall surface or the background clutter.

Fig. 5. Detected image features on a natural image. In the upper row are the input images, in the middle the results of ELSDc and in the bottom row our results (red: arcs, blue: line segments, green: intersections). (Color figure online)

Further examples of detection results are given in Fig. 6. Despite the limitation of our detector on parabolas, the circular structures in the left image can be recognized. However, these are approximated by multiple parabolas. The ELSDc correctly recognizes these structures as ellipses.

In the right image, the rounding of the staircase is correctly recognized as a arc with our approach. With ELSDc the arc is again approximated by several line segments.

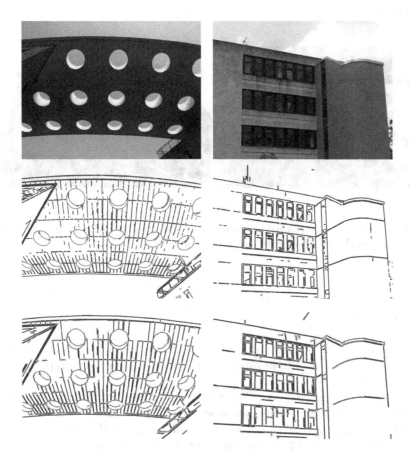

Fig. 6. Detected image features on natural images. In the upper row are the input images, in the middle the results of ELSDc and in the bottom row our results (red: arcs, blue: line segments, green: intersections). Left image is from the dataset from [14] (Color figure online)

On average over the entire data set of 30 natural images, the runtime for the detection per image is 5.1 s for ELSDc and only 1.2 s for our approach on a laptop with a Core i5. The images have different resolutions between 2 MP and 16 MP.

4.3 Detection of Contours

Figure 7(a) shows the result of detection on a synthetic image. The connected components of the graph are each represented with a random color. All corner points and connecting edges of the individual objects were recognized. In addition, the objects are each detected as a connected component.

This can also be confirmed by real world examples. As can be seen in Fig. 7(b), most of the windows are described in the graph by a connected component.

(a)   (b)

Fig. 7. Topology of the detected image features. All nodes of a connected components are drawn with the same color. (Color figure online)

5   Conclusion

In this paper, we have presented a method that enables a combined extraction of points, lines, and arcs from images, and builds a topological graph between these features.

The graph allows the description of complex geometric primitives from multiple individual features. For further processing of the images, e.g. in a structure from motion application, the graph offers numerous possibilities to make the process more robust and to reconstruct more complex primitives.

By comparing to the state of the art methods it can be shown that our approach achieves a precise detection of the image features and, in particular, on noisy data, a significant improvement to the existing approaches. By the reliable detection of structures that are close together, more details can be extracted in the images. At the same time, the runtime for the detection is significantly lower.

References

1. Akinlar, C., Topal, C.: EDCircles: real-time circle detection by Edge Drawing (ED). In: 2012 IEEE International Conference on Acoustics, Speech and Signal Processing (ICASSP), pp. 1309–1312, March 2012
2. Akinlar, C., Topal, C.: EDLines: a real-time line segment detector with a false detection control. Pattern Recognit. Lett. **32**(13), 1633–1642 (2011)
3. Ballard, D.H.: Generalizing the Hough transform to detect arbitrary shapes. Pattern Recognit. **13**(2), 111–122 (1981)
4. Bay, H., Ess, A., Tuytelaars, T., Van Gool, L.: Speeded-Up Robust Features (SURF). Comput. Vis. Image Underst. **110**(3), 346–359 (2008)
5. Bonci, A., Leo, T., Longhi, S.: A Bayesian approach to the Hough transform for line detection. IEEE Trans. Syst. Man Cybern. - Part A: Syst. Hum. **35**(6), 945–955 (2005)
6. Chia, A.Y.S., Rahardja, S., Rajan, D., Leung, M.K.: A split and merge based ellipse detector with self-correcting capability. IEEE Trans. Image Process. **20**(7), 1991–2006 (2011)
7. Fitzgibbon, A., Pilu, M., Fisher, R.B.: Direct least square fitting of ellipses. IEEE Trans. Pattern Anal. Mach. Intell. **21**(5), 476–480 (1999)
8. Harris, C., Stephens, M.: A combined corner and edge detector. In: Alvey Vision Conference. vol. 15, pp. 10–5244. Citeseer (1988)
9. Horaud, R., Veillon, F., Skordas, T.: Finding geometric and relational structures in an image. In: Faugeras, O. (ed.) ECCV 1990. LNCS, vol. 427, pp. 374–384. Springer, Heidelberg (1990). doi:10.1007/BFb0014886
10. Lowe, D.G.: Object recognition from local scale-invariant features. In: The Proceedings of the Seventh IEEE International Conference on Computer Vision, vol. 2, pp. 1150–1157. IEEE (1999)
11. Lu, W., Tan, J.: Detection of incomplete ellipse in images with strong noise by iterative randomized Hough transform (IRHT). Pattern Recognit. **41**(4), 1268–1279 (2008)
12. Mai, F., Hung, Y.S., Zhong, H., Sze, W.F.: A hierarchical approach for fast and robust ellipse extraction. In: 2007 IEEE International Conference on Image Processing, vol. 5, pp. V-345–V-348, September 2007
13. Morevec, H.P.: Towards automatic visual obstacle avoidance. In: Proceedings of the 5th International Joint Conference on Artificial Intelligence, vol. 2, pp. 584–584. IJCAI 1977, Morgan Kaufmann Publishers Inc., San Francisco, CA, USA (1977)
14. Patraucean, V., Gurdjos, P., Grompone von Gioi, R.: Joint a contrario ellipse and line detection. IEEE Trans. Pattern Anal. Mach. Intell. **39**(4), 788–802 (2017)
15. Schmid, C., Mohr, R., Bauckhage, C.: Evaluation of interest point detectors. Int. J. Comput. Vis. **37**(2), 151–172 (2000)
16. Shi, J., Tomasi, C.: Good features to track. In: Proceedings of IEEE Conference on Computer Vision and Pattern Recognition, pp. 593–600, June 1994
17. Topal, C., Akinlar, C.: Edge drawing: a combined real-time edge and segment detector. J. Vis. Commun. Image Represent. **23**(6), 862–872 (2012)
18. Wenzel, S., Förstner, W.: Finding poly-curves of straight line and ellipse segments. Photogrammetrie-Fernerkundung-Geoinformation **2013**(4), 297–308 (2013)
19. Wolters, D., Koch, R.: Precise and robust line detection for highly distorted and noisy images. In: Rosenhahn, B., Andres, B. (eds.) GCPR 2016. LNCS, vol. 9796, pp. 3–13. Springer, Cham (2016). doi:10.1007/978-3-319-45886-1_1

Recurrent Residual Learning for Action Recognition

Ahsan Iqbal$^{(\boxtimes)}$, Alexander Richard, Hilde Kuehne, and Juergen Gall

University of Bonn, Bonn, Germany
{iqbalm,richard,kuehne,gall}@iai.uni-bonn.de

Abstract. Action recognition is a fundamental problem in computer vision with a lot of potential applications such as video surveillance, human computer interaction, and robot learning. Given pre-segmented videos, the task is to recognize actions happening within videos. Historically, hand crafted video features were used to address the task of action recognition. With the success of Deep ConvNets as an image analysis method, a lot of extensions of standard ConvNets were purposed to process variable length video data. In this work, we propose a novel recurrent ConvNet architecture called recurrent residual networks to address the task of action recognition. The approach extends ResNet, a state of the art model for image classification. While the original formulation of ResNet aims at learning spatial residuals in its layers, we extend the approach by introducing recurrent connections that allow to learn a spatio-temporal residual. In contrast to fully recurrent networks, our temporal connections only allow a limited range of preceding frames to contribute to the output for the current frame, enabling efficient training and inference as well as limiting the temporal context to a reasonable local range around each frame. On a large-scale action recognition dataset, we show that our model improves over both, the standard ResNet architecture and a ResNet extended by a fully recurrent layer.

1 Introduction

Action recognition in videos is an important research topic [1,4,18] with many potential applications such as video surveillance, human computer interaction, and robotics. Traditionally, action recognition has been addressed by hand crafted video features in combination with classifiers like SVMs as in [21,22]. With the impressive achievements of deep convolutional networks (ConvNets) for image classification, a lot of research was devoted to extend ConvNets to process video data, however, with unsatisfying results. While ConvNets have shown to perform very well for spatial data, they perform poorly for temporal data since they fail to model temporal dependencies. Heuristics were therefore developed for modeling temporal relations. First attempts, which simply stacked the frames and used a standard ConvNet for image classification [10], performed worse than hand crafted features. More successful have been two stream architectures [18] that use two ConvNets. While the first network is applied to the

© Springer International Publishing AG 2017
V. Roth and T. Vetter (Eds.): GCPR 2017, LNCS 10496, pp. 126–137, 2017.
DOI: 10.1007/978-3-319-66709-6_11

independent frames, the second network processes the optical flow, which needs to be computed beforehand. While two stream architectures achieve lower classification error rates than hand-crafted features, they are very expensive for training and inference since they need two ConvNets and an additional approach to extract the optical flow.

In this work, we propose a more principled way to integrate temporal dependencies within a ConvNet. Our model is based on the state of the art residual learning framework [6] for image classification, which learns a residual function with respect to the layer's input. We extend the approach to a sequence of images by having a residual network for each image and connecting them by recurrent connections that model temporal residuals. In contrast to the two stream architecture [4], which proposes residual connections from the motion to the appearance stream, our approach is a single stream architecture that directly models temporal relations within the spatial stream and does not require the additional computation of the optical flow.

We evaluate our approach on the popular UCF-101 [19] benchmark and show that our approach reduces the error of the baseline [6] by 17%. Although two stream architectures, which require the computation of the optical flow, achieve a lower error rate, the proposed approach of temporal residuals could also be integrated into a two stream architecture.

2 Related Work

Due to the difficulty of modeling temporal context with deep neural networks, traditional methods using hand-crafted features have been state of the art in action recognition much longer than in image classification [12,21,22,24]. The most popular approaches are dense trajectories [21] with a bag-of-words and SVM classification as well as improved dense trajectories [22] with Fisher vector encoding. Due to the success of deep architectures, first attempts in action recognition aimed at combining those traditional features with deep models. In [15], for instance, a combination of hand crafted features and recurrent neural networks have been deployed. Peng et al. [14] proposed Stacked Fisher Vectors, a video representation with multi-layer nested Fisher vector encoding. In the first layer, they densely sample large subvolumes from input videos, extract local features, and encode them using Fisher vectors. The second layer compresses the Fisher vectors of subvolumes obtained in the previous layer, and then encodes them again with Fisher vectors. Compared with standard Fisher vectors, stacked Fisher vectors allow to refine and abstract semantic information in a hierarchical way. Another hierarchical approach has been proposed in [8], who apply HMAX [16] with pre-defined spatio-temporal filters in the first layer. Trajectory pooled deep convolutional descriptors are defined in [23]. CNN features are extracted from a two stream architecture and are combined with improved dense trajectories.

In the past, there have been attempts to address the task of action recognition with deep architectures directly. However, in most of these works, the input to the model is a stack of consecutive video frames and the model is expected to learn spatio-temporal dependent features in the first few layers, which is a difficult task. In [2,13,20], spatio temporal features are learned in unsupervised fashion by using Restricted Boltzmann machines. The approach of [7] combines the information about objects present in the video with the motion in the videos. 3D convolution is used in [9] to extract discriminative spatio temporal features from the stack of video frames. Three different approaches (early fusion, late fusion, and slow fusion) were evaluated to fuse temporal context in [10]. A similar technique as in [9] is used to fuse temporal context early in the network, in late fusion, individual features per frame are extracted and fused in the last convolutional layer. Slow fusion mixes late and early fusion. In contrast to these methods, our method does not rely on temporal convolution but on a recurrent network architecture directly.

More recently, [1] proposed concept of dynamic images. The dynamic image is based on the rank pooling concept [5] and is obtained through the parameters of a ranking machine that encodes the temporal evolution of the frames of the video. Dynamic images are obtained by directly applying rank pooling on the raw image pixels of a video producing a single RGB image per video. And finally, by feeding the dynamic image to any CNN architecture for image analysis, it can be used to classify actions.

The most successful approach to date is the two-stream CNN of [18], where individual frames from the videos are the input to the spatial network, while motion in the form of dense optical flow is the input to the temporal network. The features learned by both networks are concatenated and finally linear SVM is used for classification. Recently, with the success of ResNet [4,6] proposed a model that combines ResNet and the two stream architecture. They replace both spatial and temporal networks in the two stream architecture by a ResNet with 50 layers. They also introduce a temporal or motion residual, i.e. a residual connection from the temporal network to the spatial network to enable learning of spatio temporal features. In contrast to our method, they incorporate temporal information by extending the convolutions over temporal windows. Note that this leads to a largely increased amount of model parameters, whereas our approach shares the weights among all frames, keeping the network size small. [26] proposed the temporal segment networks, which are mainly based on the two stream architecture. However, rather than densely sampling every other frame in the video, they divide the video in segments of equal length, and then randomly sample snippets from these segments as network input. In this way, the two stream network produces segment level classification scores, which are combined to produce video level output.

Deep recurrent CNN architectures are also explored to model dependencies across the frames. In [3], convolutional features are fed into an LSTM network to model temporal dependencies. [28] considered four networks to address action recognition in videos. The first network is similar to spatial network in the two stream architecture. The second network is a CNN with one recurrent layer, it expects a single optical flow image and in recurrent layer, optical flows over a range of frames are combined. In the third network, they feed a stack of consecutive frames, the network is also equipped with a recurrent layer to capture the long term dependencies. Similarly, the fourth network expects a stack of optical flow fields as input. However, the network is equipped with a fully connected recurrent layer. Finally, boosting is used to combine the output of all four networks.

Finally, [27] equip a ResNet with recurrent skip connections that are, contrary to ours, purely temporal skip connections, whereas in our framework, we use spatio-temporal skip connections. Note the significant difference in both approaches: while purely temporal skip connections can be interpreted as usual recurrent connections with unit weights, spatio-temporal skip connections are a novel concept that allow for efficient backpropagation and combine both, changes in the temporal domain and changes in the spation domain at the same time.

3   Recurrent Residual Network

In this section, we describe our approach to address the problem of action recognition in videos. Our approach is an extension of ResNet [6], which reformulates a layer as learning the spatial residual function with respect to the layer's input. State of the art results were achieved in image recognition tasks by learning spatial residual functions. We extend the approach to learn temporal residual functions across the frames to do action recognition in videos. In our formulation, the feature vector at time step t is a residual function with respect to the feature vector at time step $t - 1$. By following the analogy of ResNet, temporal residuals are learned by introducing the temporal skip (recurrent) connections. In the following, we give a brief introduction to ResNet, explain different types of temporal skip connections, and finally describe how to include more temporal context.

3.1   ResNet

ResNet [6] introduces a residual learning framework. In this framework, a stack of convolutional layers fit a residual mapping instead of the desired mapping. Let $H(x)$ denote the desired mapping. The principle of ResNet is to interpret the mapping of the learned function from one layer to another as $H(x) = F(x) + x$, i.e. as the original input x plus a residual function $F(x)$. Introducing the spatial skip connection, the input signal x is directly forwarded and added to the next layer, so it only remains to learn the residual $F(x) = H(x) - x$, see Fig. 1b.

3.2   Type of Temporal Skip Connection

There are multiple possibilities to model the temporal skip connection. The standard spatial skip connections in the classical ResNet architecture are either

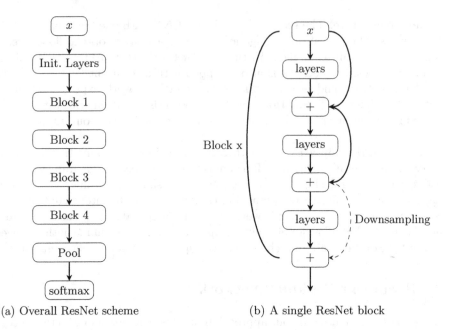

(a) Overall ResNet scheme   (b) A single ResNet block

Fig. 1. ResNet architecture, (a) shows the overall ResNet structure with four building blocks and a final classification layer, (b) is the schema of a single block: each block consists of multiple convolutional layers and skip connections to learn the residuals. At the end, the output feature maps are downsampled.

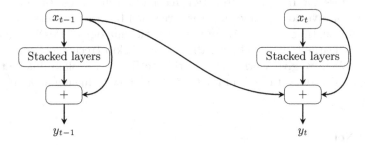

Fig. 2. Building block of our recurrent residual learning, x_{t-1} represents the input to a convolutional layer at time step $t-1$ and x_t represents the input to the same layer at time step t. While the spatial skip connections within a single time frame allow to learn a spatial residual, the spatio-temporal skip connection from time $t-1$ to time t adds temporal information to the learned residual.

an identity mapping, i.e. they just forward the input signal and add it to the destination layer, or they perform a linear transformation in order to establish the downsampling as depicted in Fig. 1. The simplest case for the temporal skip connection is to also use an identity mapping. With the notation of Fig. 2, the layer output y_t at time t is the residual function

$$y_t = \sigma(x_t * W) + x_t, \tag{1}$$

where σ represents the nonlinear operations performed after the linear transformation. Note that for simplicity of notation, we pretend that the residual block contains a single convolutional layer only and W represents weights for the layer. Extending this for the temporal skip connection, we obtain

$$y_t = \sigma(x_t * W) + x_t + x_{t-1}. \tag{2}$$

In order to allow for a weighting of the temporal skip connection with weights W_s, a linear transformation can be applied to x_{t-1} before adding it to y_t,

$$y_t = \sigma(x_t * W) + x_t' + x_{t-1} * W_s. \tag{3}$$

Moreover, in order to learn a nonlinear spatio-temporal mapping, this can be further extended to

$$y_t = \sigma(x_t * W) + x_t + \sigma(x_{t-1} * W_s). \tag{4}$$

3.3   Temporal Context

While recurrent connections in traditional recurrent neural networks feed the output of a layer at time $t-1$ to the same layer as input at time t, our proposed spatio-temporal skip connections are different. For an illustration, see Fig. 3. Here, we unfold a network with two spatio-temporal skip connections over time. Note that the temporal context that influences the output y_t includes x_{t-2}, x_{t-1}, and x_t as there are paths from y_t leading to all these inputs. If we only used one temporal skip connection instead of two, the accessible temporal context for y_t would only be x_{t-1} and x_t, respectively. In general, if a temporal context over T frames is desired, at least $T-1$ temporal skip connections are necessary.

In order to use this approach for action recognition, a video is divided into M small sequences each containing T frames. A recurrent residual network with $T-1$ temporal skip connections is created to capture the dependencies over these T time steps. In training, we optimize the cross-entropy loss of each small video chunk. During inference, for each small sequence $\{x_t^{(i)}\}_{t=1}^T$ within one video, the recurrent residual network computes $P(y = c|\{x_t^{(i)}\}_{t=1}^T)$. In order to obtain an overall classification of a complete video, the individual output probabilities are averaged over the M subsequences of the video. Note that this is similar to existing frame-wise approaches, where an output probability per frame is computed and the overall video action probabilities are obtained by accumulating all single frame probabilities. In our case, instead of frames, we use small subsequences of the original video.

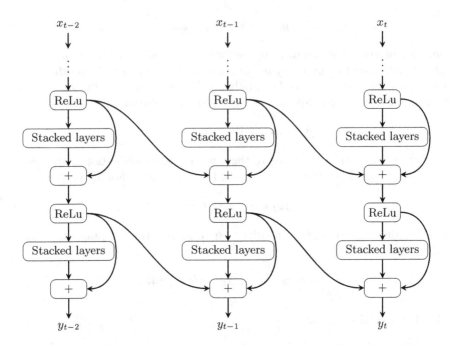

Fig. 3. A network with two temporal skip connections, capable of handling temporal context of three time steps, omitted layers are normal ResNet blocks, i.e. without any temporal skip connections.

4   Experimental Setup

In this section, we describe our experimental setup. We use ADAM [11] as learning algorithm and except for the baseline experiments, we update the model after observing 1% of training data, and every tenth frame from each video is sampled as input to the model. We evaluate our approach on UCF-101 [19], a large-scale action recognition dataset consisting of 13,000 videos from 101 different classes. The dataset comprises about 2.5 million frames in total. All the experimental work was done using our framework squirrel[1]. In the following, we describe the baseline experiments and the experiments with our proposed recurrent residual network.

4.1   Baseline Experiments

As a baseline, we extract imagenet [17] features for individual frames in the video. Averaged individual feature vectors represent the feature vector of the complete video. Feature vectors for individual frames are extracted using a pretrained ResNet model with 50 layers. A batch normalization layer is added after each layer to normalize the input to a layer. This way the network has in total 106 layers.

---

[1] https://github.com/alexanderrichard/squirrel.

Table 1. Results of the baseline experiments.

Features	Method	Error rate (with Z-Norm)	Error rate (without Z-Norm)
Block4	Avg. pool	**0.236**	0.237
Block4	GRU	0.239	0.276
Block3	Avg. pool	0.309	0.313
Block3	GRU	0.403	0.325
Block2	Avg. pool	0.431	0.434
Block2	GRU	0.440	0.493

We extract the imagenet feature vectors for each frame at three different positions of ResNet, i.e. after block4, block3, and block2 respectively, see Fig. 1. We performed two sets of experiments on extracted features for each block. In one set, we average the frame level feature vectors, after Z-normalization and without Z-normalization, and train a linear classifier. We call this model the average pooling model. Similarly, in the other set, we use a recurrent neural network with 128 gated recurrent units (GRUs) in order to evaluate the performance of a classical recurrent network. We call this model the GRU.

Table 1 shows the baseline experiments with imagenet features. The average pooling model outperforms the model with gated recurrent units. Also, it is evident from the experiments that with more depth, features become richer. Hence, the depth plays a significant role in getting good classification accuracy.

4.2   Effect of Type and Position of the Recurrent Connection

In this set of experiments, we evaluate different types of temporal skip connections along with their position in our proposed model. We evaluate temporal skip connections at four different positions, i.e. at the beginning by making the first skip connection in block1 recurrent (referred to as Block1), in the middle by making last skip connection in block2 recurrent (referred to as Block2), by making last convolutional skip connection in block4 recurrent (referred to as Mid Block4), and finally by making last skip connection in block 4 recurrent (referred to as Block4). Also, we evaluate the type of recurrent connections. In these experiments, we evaluate identity mapping temporal skip connections, and temporal skip connections with convolutional weights having kernels of size 1×1. Table 2 shows the deeper we place the temporal skip connection in the network, the better is the classification accuracy.

In another set of experiments, we evaluate the effect of the type of temporal skip connection. We change the configuration of the best working setup, i.e. the one with the skip connection in block4. The connection performs a parametrized linear or non linear transformation and identity mapping.

Table 3 shows the results achieved by different type of connections, placed closer to the output layer as our previous analysis shows that works best. Identity mapping connection with non trainable weights performed best, possibly because introducing more weights in the network causes overfitting.

Table 2. Placing the recurrent connection at different positions in the network.

Position	Type	Error rate
Block1	Convolutional	0.265
Block2	Convolutional	0.234
Mid Block4	Convolutional	0.231
Block4	Convolutional	**0.219**

Table 3. Results achieved by different type of recurrent connections.

Type	Error rate
Identity mapping	**0.197**
Conv. linear	0.219
Conv. non-linear	0.210

4.3 Effect of Temporal Context

In this set of experiments, we explore the effect of temporal context. As discussed earlier, with more recurrent connections, the network is able to include additional temporal dependencies. We already investigated the network with one recurrent connection that is able to include temporal context of two frames. In these experiments, we further explore the temporal context of three frames (by introducing two temporal connections in the network), and the temporal context of five frames (by introducing four temporal skip connections in the network). Figure 3 shows the network architecture to accommodate temporal context of three frames.

As it is evident in Table 4, we do not gain much by including more temporal context. The accuracy improves in case of temporal context three, however it gets worse in case of temporal context five. Hence, considering training time, we consider the model with only one temporal skip connection as the best model. Note that due to the fact that we sample every tenth frame from the video, the overall temporal range is actually ten frames. More precisely, the network learns spatio-temporal residuals between the frames x_t and x_{t-10}, covering a reasonable amount of local temporal progress within the video.

We further evaluate our best model on all three splits of UCF-101. On average our best model achieves **0.198** on UCF-101 [19], which is a relative improvement of 17% over the ResNet baseline which has an error rate of 0.236.

4.4 Comparison with the State of the Art

In this section, our best model (with one temporal skip connection and with sample rate 10) is compared with state of the art action recognition methods. As motion in the frames and appearance in individual frames are two complementary aspects for action recognition, most of the state of the art methods consider

Table 4. Results achieved by including more temporal context. For the best setup (context two), the error is reduced by 17% from 0.236 to 0.194.

Temporal context	Model	Error rate
1	baseline	0.236
2	1 recurrent connection	0.197
3	2 recurrent connections	**0.194**
5	4 recurrent connections	0.209

Table 5. Classification error rates for UCF-101.

Method	Appearance	Motion	App.+Motion
Improved dense trajectories [22]	-	-	0.141
Dynamic image networks [1]	0.231	-	-
Two stream architecture [18]	0.270	0.163	0.120
Two stream architecture (GoogleNet) [25]	0.247	0.142	0.107
Two stream architecture (VGG-Net) [25]	0.216	0.130	0.086
Spatiotemporal ResNets [4]	-	-	0.066
Recurrent residual networks	**0.198**	-	-

two different neural networks, an appearance stream and a motion stream, to extract and use appearance and motion for action recognition. The output of both the networks is fused, and a simple classifier is trained to classify videos. As our model uses the raw video frames only rather than optical flow fields, fair comparison of our model and the state of the art is only possible for the appearance stream. For completeness, we also compare our results with results achieved after the outputs of the appearance and the motion streams are fused, see Table 5. Our model achieves better error rates than the state of the art appearance stream models. Only fused models perform better. Note that the works [4,18,25] are all two-stream architectures. The dynamic image network [1] is a purely appearance base method that reduces that video to a single frame and uses a ConvNet to classify this frame. For a fair comparison, we provide the result of dynamic image network without the combination with dense trajectories as this would include motion features.

5   Conclusion

We extended the ResNet architecture to include temporal skip connections in order to model both, spatial and temporal information in video. Our model performs well already with a single temporal skip connection, enabling to infer context between two frames. Moreover, we showed that fusing temporal information at a late stage in the network is beneficial and that learning a temporal residual is superior to using a classical recurrent layer. Our method is not limited to appearance based models and can easily be extended to motion networks that have shown to further enhance the performance on action recognition datasets. A comparison to both, a ResNet baseline and state of the art methods showed that our approach outperforms other purely appearance based approaches.

Acknowledgement. The authors have been financially supported by the DFG projects KU 3396/2-1 and GA 1927/4-1 and the ERC Starting Grant ARCA (677650). Further, this work was supported by the AWS Cloud Credits for Research program.

References

1. Bilen, H., Fernando, B., Gavves, E., Vedaldi, A., Gould, S.: Dynamic image networks for action recognition. In: IEEE Conference on Computer Vision and Pattern Recognition (2016)
2. Chen, B., Ting, J.A., Marlin, B., de Freitas, N.: Deep learning of invariant spatio-temporal features from video. In: NIPS 2010 Deep Learning and Unsupervised Feature Learning Workshop (2010)
3. Donahue, J., Anne Hendricks, L., Guadarrama, S., Rohrbach, M., Venugopalan, S., Saenko, K., Darrell, T.: Long-term recurrent convolutional networks for visual recognition and description. In: IEEE Conference on Computer Vision and Pattern Recognition (2015)
4. Feichtenhofer, C., Pinz, A., Wildes, R.: Spatiotemporal residual networks for video action recognition. Adv. Neural Inf. Process. Syst. **29**, 3468–3476 (2016)
5. Fernando, B., Gavves, E., Oramas, J., Ghodrati, A., Tuytelaars, T.: Rank pooling for action recognition. IEEE Trans. Pattern Anal. Mach. Intell. **39**(4), 773–787 (2017)
6. He, K., Zhang, X., Ren, S., Sun, J.: Deep residual learning for image recognition. In: IEEE Conference on Computer Vision and Pattern Recognition (2016)
7. Jain, M., van Gemert, J.C., Snoek, C.G.M.: What do 15, 000 object categories tell us about classifying and localizing actions? In: IEEE Conference on Computer Vision and Pattern Recognition (2015)
8. Jhuang, H., Serre, T., Wolf, L., Poggio, T.: A biologically inspired system for action recognition. In: IEEE International Conference on Computer Vision (2007)
9. Ji, S., Xu, W., Yang, M., Yu, K.: 3D convolutional neural networks for human action recognition. IEEE Trans. Pattern Anal. Mach. Intell. **35**(1), 221–231 (2013)
10. Karpathy, A., Toderici, G., Shetty, S., Leung, T., Sukthankar, R., Fei-Fei, L.: Large-scale video classification with convolutional neural networks. In: IEEE Conference on Computer Vision and Pattern Recognition. pp. 1725–1732 (2014)
11. Kingma, D.P., Ba, J.: Adam: a method for stochastic optimization. In: International Conference on Learning Representations (2015)
12. Laptev, I.: On space-time interest points. Int. J. Comput. Vis. **64**, 107–123 (2005)
13. Le, Q.V., Zou, W.Y., Yeung, S.Y., Ng, A.Y.: Learning hierarchical invariant spatio-temporal features for action recognition with independent subspace analysis. In: IEEE Conference on Computer Vision and Pattern Recognition, pp. 3361–3368 (2011)
14. Peng, X., Zou, C., Qiao, Y., Peng, Q.: Action recognition with stacked fisher vectors. In: European Conference on Computer Vision, pp. 581–595 (2014)
15. Richard, A., Gall, J.: A bag-of-words equivalent recurrent neural network for action recognition. Comput. Vis. Image Underst. **156**, 79–91 (2017)

16. Riesenhuber, M., Poggio, T.: Hierarchical models of object recognition in cortex. Nature Neurosci. **2**(11), 1019–1025 (1999)

17. Russakovsky, O., Deng, J., Su, H., Krause, J., Satheesh, S., Ma, S., Huang, Z., Karpathy, A., Khosla, A., Bernstein, M., Berg, A.C., Fei-Fei, L.: Imagenet large scale visual recognition challenge. Int. J. Comput. Vis. **115**(3), 211–252 (2015)

18. Simonyan, K., Zisserman, A.: Two-stream convolutional networks for action recognition in videos. Adv. Neural Inf. Process. Syst. **27**, 568–576 (2014)

19. Soomro, K., Zamir, A.R., Shah, M.: UCF101: A dataset of 101 human actions classes from videos in the wild. CoRR abs/1212.0402 (2012)

20. Taylor, G.W., Fergus, R., LeCun, Y., Bregler, C.: Convolutional learning of spatio-temporal features. In: European Conference on Computer Vision, pp. 140–153 (2010)

21. Wang, H., Klaser, A., Schmid, C., Liu, C.L.: Action recognition by dense trajectories. In: IEEE Conference on Computer Vision and Pattern Recognition, pp. 3169–3176 (2011)

22. Wang, H., Schmid, C.: Action recognition with improved trajectories. In: IEEE International Conference on Computer Vision, pp. 3551–3558 (2013)

23. Wang, L., Qiao, Y., Tang, X.: Action recognition with trajectory-pooled deep-convolutional descriptors. In: IEEE Conference on Computer Vision and Pattern Recognition, pp. 4305–4314 (2015)

24. Wang, L., Qiao, Y., Tang, X.: Mofap: a multi-level representation for action recognition. Int. J. Comput. Vis. **119**(3), 254–271 (2016)

25. Wang, L., Xiong, Y., Wang, Z., Qiao, Y.: Towards good practices for very deep two-stream convnets. CoRR abs/1507.02159 (2015)

26. Wang, L., Xiong, Y., Wang, Z., Qiao, Y., Lin, D., Tang, X., Van Gool, L.: Temporal segment networks: towards good practices for deep action recognition. In: European Conference on Computer Vision (2016)

27. Wang, Y., Tian, F.: Recurrent residual learning for sequence classification. In: Conference on Empirical Methods on Natural Language Processing, pp. 938–943 (2016)

28. Yang, X., Molchanov, P., Kautz, J.: Multilayer and multimodal fusion of deep neural networks for video classification. In: Proceedings of the 2016 ACM on Multimedia Conference, pp. 978–987 (2016)

A Local Spatio-Temporal Approach to Plane Wave Ultrasound Particle Image Velocimetry

Ecaterina Bodnariuc[1], Stefania Petra[1(✉)], Christoph Schnörr[2],
and Jason Voorneveld[3]

[1] Mathematical Imaging Group, Heidelberg University, Heidelberg, Germany
petra@math.uni-heidelberg.de
[2] Image and Pattern Analysis Group, Heidelberg University, Heidelberg, Germany
[3] Department of Biomedical Engineering, Erasmus MC, Thorax Center,
Rotterdam, The Netherlands

Abstract. We present a simple and efficient approach to plane wave ultrasound particle image velocimetry (Echo PIV). Specifically, a carefully designed bank of local motion-sensitive filters is introduced, together with a method for non-linear flow parameter estimation based on time-averaged local flow estimates. The approach is validated and quantitatively assessed using both simulated and in-vitro real data, in scenarios with laminar as well as with turbulent flow.

1 Introduction

We are motivated by the task of estimating the instantaneous velocity of vessel blood flow using *plane wave ultrasound particle image velocimetry* (a.k.a. *Echo PIV*) [5,12,20]. Ultrasound techniques are used to measure blood flow in clinical applications. They enable noninvasive measurements that are applied to opaque flows. Moreover, the use of plane wave ultrasound imaging improves the temporal resolution of the signal by recording sequential ultrasound images at rates of more than 1000 frames per second over a large field of view [19].

Echo PIV is a particle image velocimetry technique developed to improve the in-plane velocity components measurements of the blood flow using clinical ultrasound machines and optical PIV image analysis algorithms [11,15]. A schematic representation of Echo PIV is shown by Fig. 1.

In the presented work we restrict our attention to estimating the velocity field of pipe flows as this approximately resembles the flow in blood vessels. The velocity field of a *laminar and steady* flow (a.k.a. Poiseuille flow) is given by

$$u = u(x) = \big(u_1(x_2), 0\big)^\top, \qquad u_1(x_2) = v_m\Big(1 - \Big(\frac{x_2}{R}\Big)^2\Big), \qquad v_m \geq 0, \quad (1.1)$$

where v_m denotes the peak velocity of the flow in a pipe of size R, assumed to be centered at $x_2 = 0$. Thus, the flow has a parabolic profile, does not depend on x_1, and hence has a single degree of freedom v_m.

V. Roth and T. Vetter (Eds.): GCPR 2017, LNCS 10496, pp. 138–149, 2017.
DOI: 10.1007/978-3-319-66709-6_12

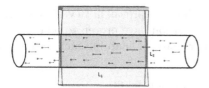 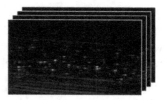

Fig. 1. Schematic representation of the plane wave ultrasound Echo PIV setup (*left*). In a rigid cylindrical tube of inner radius $R = L_2/2$ a liquid flows that is seeded with small bubbles. A linear transducer array is placed along the tube axis and transmits a plane wave acoustic pulse into the inhomogeneous field. The same transducer then records the backscattered acoustic wave that is reflected and scattered by static tube walls and dynamic bubbles. The transmission and recording step is repeated at a rate faster than 1000 Hz. This produces images sequences with high temporal resolution (*right*) that displays speckle patterns driven by the flow.

This smooth and laminar flow occurs at moderate Reynolds numbers. At larger Reynolds numbers the flow becomes *turbulent* and exhibits motion instability. Such flows are unsteady and irregular, yet appear steady and predictable after temporal averaging [21]. There are many empirical formulas describing the velocity profile of turbulent flow in a pipe. In this work we adopt the representation proposed in [18] in terms of the velocity field

$$u = u(x) = \big(u_1(x_2), 0\big)^{\top}, \quad u_1(x_2) = v_m\Big(1 - \Big(\frac{|x_2|}{R}\Big)^{N+1}\Big). \qquad (1.2)$$

For $N = 1$ we recover the parabolic velocity profile of (1.1) and for $N > 1$ a deformed velocity profile is obtained.

A common assumption of experimental fluid dynamics [16] is that the flow has been seeded with a set of randomly located particles, also called tracer particles, that follow the flow dynamics. Motion is estimated via the displacement of these tracer particles. In the present work, we focus on speckle patterns originating from microbubbles that are driven by laminar or turbulent pipe flow (Fig. 1).

Related Work and Contribution. Research on plane wave Echo PIV is concerned with (i) image reconstruction and (ii) motion estimation. We only focus on (ii) motion estimation. For recent work on (i) image reconstruction based on inverse scattering, we refer to [4] and references therein.

We present the *design* of a spatio-temporal filter bank for local motion extraction from plane wave Echo PIV image sequences. The motivation is threefold:

1. The high frame rates of plane wave ultrasound imaging lead to displacements that enable the application of *differential* motion estimation techniques [2].
2. The flow model (1.2) corresponds to a specific geometry of the spectral support of the image sequence in the Fourier domain. This motivates a careful design of a filter bank in order to properly "discretize" the Fourier domain, while forming a partition of unity to achieve uniform motion sensitivity.

3. While correlation technique for motion estimation prevail in PIV applications [16], alternative techniques from computer vision have proven to be useful as well [10]. Our present work constitutes a first step of adapting such techniques to the specific domain of Echo PIV.

The design of orientation- and motion-sensitive local filters has a long tradition in image processing and computer vision [6,7,9], in models of early natural vision [1,14] and in the wavelet community [13,17]. Our goal is a proper discretization of a half-space in the spatio-temporal Fourier domain (only relevant for real-valued signals) in terms of a collection of motion-sensitive filters whose spectral supports form a partition of unity. This requirement rules out Gabor filters in favour of log-Normal filters that behave more conveniently in the spectral domain (cf. [14]), and wavelet filter banks [13] due to the lack of rotational invariance.

Our filter bank is presented in Sect. 2. Section 3 summarizes established techniques for local motion estimation based on the phase-shifts of filter responses. Experimental results using the filter bank are discussed in Sect. 4: computer-generated ground-truth sequences illustrate properties of the filter bank; flow and flow model parameter estimates for real in-vitro data, both in laminar and in turbulent flow scenarios, validate our approach.

The integration of our local approach into a more advanced non-local variational scheme is beyond the scope of this paper and will be reported elsewhere.

2   Spatio-Temporal Filter Bank

We detail the design of a bank of spatio-temporal filters. The representation in spherical coordinates enables to illustrate the radial dependency in 1D and the two angular dependencies in 2D and 3D, respectively.

Design Criteria. The major aspects are:

- Self-similar parametrization in terms of a sequence of center frequencies, such that all filters form a partition of unity of the frequency interval $[\frac{\pi}{16}, \frac{\pi}{4}]$. Structures that generate lower frequencies are not relevant in our scenario, and the dependency on the global mean is removed. Frequencies larger than $\frac{\pi}{2}$ are regarded as noise.
- All filters form a partition of unity of both angular ranges. We thereby ignore an arbitrary half-space due to the symmetry of real signals in the Fourier domain.
- The coordinate system is oriented so that the second angular dependency enables to control the selectivity with respect to the flow velocities parametrized by x_2 in (1.2), including the peak velocity v_m at $x_2 = 0$.

The Log-Normal Filters. The transfer function of the one-dimensional log-normal filter with center frequency $\omega_i \geq 0$ and width $\sigma_i \geq 0$ is given by

$$\hat{g}_i(\omega) = \frac{1}{C(\sigma_i)} \frac{\omega_i}{\omega} \exp\left[-\frac{1}{2}\left(\frac{\log(\frac{\omega}{\omega_i})}{\sigma_i}\right)^2 \right], \quad \omega \geq 0, \tag{2.1}$$

where $C(\sigma_i) = \sqrt{2\pi}\sigma_i$. The norm of each filter is

$$\|\hat{g}_i\|_{L^1(\mathbb{R}_+)} = \omega_i. \tag{2.2}$$

The set of center frequencies and frequency widths

$$\omega_i = c^{(i-1)}\omega_1, \quad \sigma_i^2 = \log\frac{\omega_{i+1}}{\omega_i} = \log c, \quad c > 1, \, i = 1, 2, \ldots \tag{2.3}$$

defines a filter bank $\{\hat{g}_i(\omega)\}_{i\geq1}$, given by (2.1) such that $\hat{g}_{i+1}(\omega) = \frac{\omega}{\sqrt{\omega_i\omega_{i+1}}}\hat{g}_i(\omega)$. These parameters are also used below in the case of 2- and 3-dimensional filter banks.

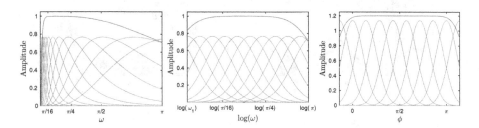

Fig. 2. LEFT: The log-normal bandpass filter bank with $\omega_1 = \pi/50$ and $c = 1.5$ defining the parameter values (2.3). CENTER: Summing up the filter responses enables almost uniform detection of spectral signal support within the interval $\omega \in [\frac{\pi}{16}, \frac{\pi}{4}]$, cf. (2.4). RIGHT: The angular part $\hat{g}_j(\phi)$ defined by (2.5) also provides a partition of unity within the interval $\phi \in [0, \pi]$.

Figure 2 illustrates this filter bank and also shows that it approximately provides a partition of unity of the frequency range of interest,

$$\sum_{i\in[12]} \hat{g}_i(\omega) \approx \text{constant}, \quad \text{for } \omega \in \left[\frac{\pi}{16}, \frac{\pi}{4}\right]. \tag{2.4}$$

In particular, very low frequencies and the global mean value of a signal, to which these filters are applied, are suppressed, as is the high-frequency range $\omega > \frac{\pi}{2}$ which is likely to be dominated by noise under realistic imaging conditions.

Extension to 2D. The extension of (2.1) to 2D reads

$$\hat{g}_{i,j}(\omega) = \frac{\omega_i}{\|\omega\|}\hat{g}_i(\|\omega\|)\hat{g}_j(\phi) \tag{2.5}$$

$$= \frac{1}{C(\sigma_i)\,C(n_\phi)}\left(\frac{\omega_i}{\|\omega\|}\right)^2\exp\left[-\frac{1}{2}\left(\frac{\log(\frac{\|\omega\|}{\omega_i})}{\sigma}\right)^2\right]\cos\left(\frac{\phi - \phi_j}{2}\right)^{2n_\phi}, \tag{2.6}$$

with polar coordinates $\omega = (\omega_1, \omega_2) \mapsto (\|\omega\|, \phi)$ on the right hand side and parameters: center frequency ω_i, frequency width σ, center angle ϕ_j, parameter

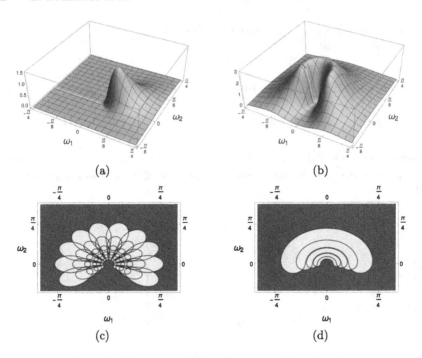

Fig. 3. (a) Two dimensional log-normal filter defined by (2.5) for $i = 6$, $j = 2$. (b) The composed log-normal filter $G_i(\omega)$ given by (2.11) illustrates the contribution of all filters at a single center frequency to the entire angular range. (c) Contours of log-normal filters illustrate the self-similar design and the partition of unity. (d) Contours of the composed log-normal filters used as a filter bank for our application.

$n_\phi \in \mathbb{N}$ and $C(n_\phi) = \frac{2\pi}{2^{2n_\phi}} \binom{2n_\phi}{n_\phi}$. In comparison to the one-dimensional case (2.1), this filter consists of a radial and an angular part. This *separability* is relevant for implementations of the filter in the spatial domain as convolution operators. The angular part yields orientation-selective filters whose selectivity can be tuned by selecting n_ϕ. In connection with the filter parameters (2.3), we fixed $n_\phi = 16$.

Figure 3 (c) illustrates the filters $\{\hat{g}_{i,j}(\omega)\}$ corresponding to the parameters (2.3), with additional center angles ϕ_j given by

$$\phi_j = (j-1)\frac{\pi}{7}, \qquad j \in \{0, 1, \ldots, 9\}. \tag{2.7}$$

Extension to 3D. In spherical coordinates $\omega = (\omega_1, \omega_2, \omega_3) \mapsto (\|\omega\|, \theta, \phi)$, our three-dimensional version of the log-normal filter reads

$$\hat{g}_{i,j,k}(\omega) = \left(\frac{\omega_i}{\|\omega\|}\right)^2 \hat{g}_i(\|\omega\|)\hat{g}_j(\phi)\hat{g}_k(\theta) = \tag{2.8}$$

$$\frac{1}{C}\left(\frac{\omega_i}{\|\omega\|}\right)^3 \exp\left[-\frac{1}{2}\left(\frac{\log(\frac{\|\omega\|}{\omega_i})}{\sigma}\right)^2\right] \cos\left(\frac{\phi - \phi_j}{2}\right)^{2n_\phi} \cos\left(\frac{\theta - \theta_k}{2}\right)^{2n_\theta}, \tag{2.9}$$

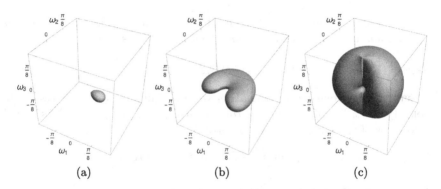

Fig. 4. In figure (a) we illustrate the extension of the 2D filter to 3D defined by (2.8) for the parameters $i = 7$, $j = 1$ and $k = 5$. (b) $\sum_j \hat{g}_{i,j,k}(\omega)$ for fixed $i = 7$ and $k = 5$. (c) $G_i(\omega) = \sum_{j,k} \hat{g}_{i,j,k}(\omega)$ for fixed $i = 7$ (cf. (2.11)).

with the normalizing factor $C = C(\sigma)C(n_\phi)C(n_\theta)$, $C(n_\phi) = C(n_\theta)$ and $n_\phi = n_\theta$. The center values of the additional angular variable are

$$\theta_k = (k-1)\frac{\pi}{7}, \quad k = 1, \ldots, 8. \tag{2.10}$$

Figure 4 illustrates the resulting filters. The proposed filter bank is designed to "see" the flow in all directions (in view of turbulent flow scenarios) and to be independent of the orientation angle. For this reason we sum up several filters along the angular parameters and consider the remaining radial component ω_i as the only filter parameter.

Spatio-Temporal Filter Bank. The filter bank is parametrized by the finite set of center frequency values ω_i and defined by

$$\hat{G}_i(\omega) = \sum_j \hat{g}_{i,j}(\omega) \text{ (in 2D)} \quad \text{and} \quad \hat{G}_i(\omega) = \sum_{j,k} \hat{g}_{i,j,k}(\omega), \text{ (in 3D)} \tag{2.11}$$

where $\hat{g}_{i,j}(\omega)$ and $\hat{g}_{i,j,k}(\omega)$ are given by (2.5) and (2.8), respectively. The parameters are listed in (2.3), (2.7), (2.10).

3   Local Flow Estimation

For an image sequence $f(x,t)$, the response function of a filter G_i (2.11) reads

$$h_i(x,t) = (f * G_i)(x,t) = \mathcal{F}^{-1}(\hat{f} \cdot \hat{G}_i)(x,t) = r_i(x,t)e^{i\psi_i(x,t)}, \tag{3.1}$$

with the amplitude function $r_i(x,t) = |h_i(x,t)|$ and the phase function

$$\psi_i(x,t) = \arg(h_i(x,t)) = \Im(\ln(h_i(x,t))) \in (-\pi, \pi]. \tag{3.2}$$

The basic assumption underlying local motion estimation is that *phase functions* $\psi_i(x, t)$ *are approximately conserved under motion*, that is

$$\frac{d}{dt}\psi_i = \langle \nabla\psi_i(x, t), (\dot{x}, 1)\rangle = \langle \nabla_x\psi_i(x, t), \dot{x}\rangle + \partial_t\psi(x, t) \approx 0, \quad \forall(x, t). \qquad (3.3)$$

As a result, after estimating the partial derivatives of all functions ψ_i, we estimate the velocity $v = \dot{x}$ *for any fixed space-time point* (x, t) by minimizing the squared residual error of the latter equation, namely

$$u(x, t) = \arg\min_v \sum_i \left(\langle \nabla_x\psi_i(x, t), v\rangle + \partial_t\psi(x, t)\right)^2. \qquad (3.4)$$

Estimating the Partial Derivatives of $\psi(x, t)$. We express the partial derivatives $\nabla\psi$ by partial derivatives of a *smooth* signal h, as follows

$$h = re^{i\psi}, \qquad \nabla h = (\nabla r)e^{i\psi} + (re^{i\psi})(i\nabla\psi) = e^{i\psi}\nabla r + ih\nabla\psi \qquad (3.5a)$$

$$\nabla\psi = \frac{1}{|h|^2}\Im(\bar{h}\nabla h), \qquad \bar{h}\nabla h = re^{-i\psi}\nabla h = r\nabla r + i|h|^2\nabla\psi. \qquad (3.5b)$$

We numerically estimate the partial derivatives of ∇h by separable 3D filters whose frequency response are obtained by an orthogonal expansion of the desired behaviour in the Fourier domain (derivative filter at low frequencies, noise suppression at high frequencies) using Krawtchouk polynomials [8,22]. These filters are similar to derivative-of-Gaussian filters but avoid aliasing artefacts in the case of filters with small spatial support, that would result from merely sampling the continuous impulse response.

4   Experimental Results

In Sect. 4.1 we report synthetic experiments for '1D videos' that validate and illustrate the filter bank design, followed by 2D pipe flow scenarios in Sects. 4.2 and 4.3, including real in-vitro data in laminar and turbulent flow scenarios.

4.1   One-Dimensional Synthetic Ground Truth Videos

We illustrate the filter characteristics for the following 1D scenarios:

(a) Harmonic oscillation of a single particle, $x(t) = a\sin(\omega t)$, with oscillation amplitude $a > 0$ and angular frequency $\omega > 0$.
(b) Elastic collision of two point particles that move with constant velocities.
(c) Flow of multiple particles with velocities

$$\dot{x} = v(x) = \begin{cases} -\alpha x^2, & x \leq 0 \\ \alpha x^2, & x > 0 \end{cases}, \qquad \alpha > 0. \qquad (4.1)$$

Figures 5 and 6 illustrate the videos in terms of space-time trajectories of the particles and their velocities, and the phase functions of the aggregated complex filter responses (2.11). Due to the smoothness of these functions, velocity estimates are accurate even though moving particles cause sharp intensity changes in the spatio-temporal domain.

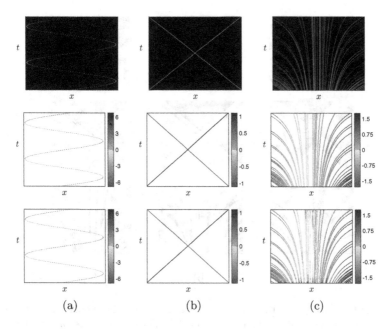

Fig. 5. TOP ROW: Space-time trajectories for the 1D videos of Sect. 4.1. CENTER ROW: Ground truth velocities. BOTTOM ROW: Estimated velocities for the harmonic oscillator (a), the elastic collision of two particles (b) and for the flow of multiple particles (c), using the phase functions displayed by Fig. 6. These estimates are accurate except for small regions close to the boundaries in trajectory direction, that exhibit natural errors caused by overlapping filter supports.

4.2 Laminar Pipe Flow: Ground Truth Data

We validated the proposed method in 2D using synthetic image sequences of uniformly distributed point-particles, driven the laminar pipe flow in (1.1). We generated a spatial-temporal dataset of size $256 \times 256 \times 256$ with peak velocities $v_m \in \{0.5, 1, ..., 4, 4.5\}$ pixels/frame. We estimated the velocity field by minimizing (3.4) using the 3D filter bank in (2.11). The results are shown in Fig. 7.

4.3 Ultrasound Particle Image Velocimetry: In Vitro Data

Figure 8 depicts *real* in vitro *flows* for both a *laminar and* a *turbulent* scenario, along with time-averaged local flow estimates $\hat{u}(x^{(k)}) = \left(\hat{u}_1(x^{(k)}), \hat{u}_2(x^{(k)}) \right)^\top$ based on (3.4) and parameter estimates v_m, N of the flow model (1.2). The in vitro plane wave ultrasound experiments imaging the flow in a pipe of a fluid seeded with air bubbles were performed under controlled conditions [20]. The relevant experimental parameters include: image acquisition rate $f = 6.66$ kHz, fluid density $\rho = 1038$ kg/m^3, viscosity $\mu = 4.1$ mPa·s, radius of the pipe $R = 5$ mm, field of view 21.3×37.8 mm^2, image size 288×384 and number

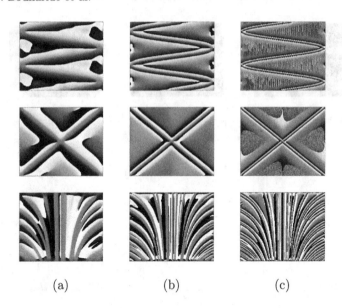

(a)   (b)   (c)

Fig. 6. COLUMNS: Phase output ψ_i due to (3.2) for center frequencies ω_i, $i \in \{5,7,9\}$ given by (2.3). ROWS: The 1D-videos of Sect. 4.1. These plots illustrate that even for the 'very sparse' 1D-videos of moving particles, aggregating multiple filter responses due to (2.11) enables to estimate *locally* motion information at every spatio-temporal point (x,t).

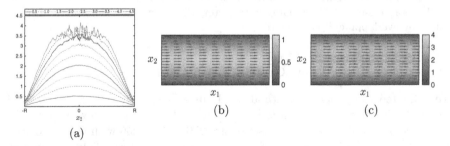

(a)

(b)   (c)

Fig. 7. (a) Estimates of time-averaged velocity profiles for several peak velocities v_m. The parabolic profile is well reconstructed if $v_m < 3$. For $v_m \geq 3$, motion-induced temporal frequencies cause aliasing effects (cf. [2, Sect. 2.2.3]) at the center of the tube, which could be fixed by spatial subsampling. Figure (b) and (c) illustrate the accurately estimated time-averaged velocity fields for $v_m = 1$ and $v_m = 4$, respectively.

of temporal frames 298. We obtained parameter estimates v_m, N by minimizing the objective

$$f(v_m, N) = \sum_k \left\| \hat{u}(x^{(k)}) - R(\vartheta)u(x^{(k)}; v_m, N) \right\|^2, \quad v_m \geq 0, \ N \geq 1, \quad (4.2)$$

Table 1. In vitro ultrasound experiments. Relevant parameters: volume flow rate Q, measured with a flow-meter, and Reynolds number Re. Estimated parameters (cf. (1.2)): v_m, N; relation to the average velocity $v_{(ave)} = v_m(N+1)/(N+3)$; independent reference value for the average velocity: $v_{(ave)}^* = Q/(\pi R^2)$. The velocities are given in pixels/frame.

	$Q\ [\mathrm{m}^3/\mathrm{s}]$	Re	v_m	N	$v_{(ave)}$	$v_{(ave)}^*$
laminar flow	$15 \cdot 10^{-6}$	484	0.356	1.361	0.193	0.295
turbulent flow	$80 \cdot 10^{-6}$	2579	1.557	3.547	1.081	1.577

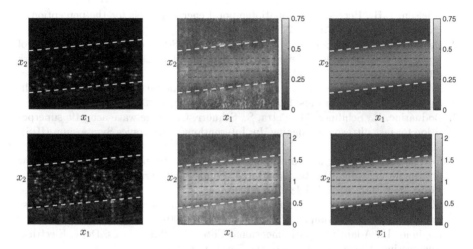

Fig. 8. In vitro data. TOP ROW: laminar steady flow. BOTTOM ROW: turbulent flow. LEFT: image sequence. CENTER: time-averaged local flow estimate. RIGHT: flow model estimate. Table 1 reports quantitative results.

where the rotation matrix $R(\vartheta)$ accounts for the tilted pipe (indicated by the dashed lines in Fig. 8) and $u(x^{(k)}; v_m, N)$ is given by (1.2).

The sum runs over all image points $x^{(k)}$ contained in the interior of the tube. The minimization problem was solved using the spectral projected gradient method [3] using the default parameters specified by the authors and with the non-monotone parameter value $M = 2$. The initial values for v_m and N where randomly chosen in the intervals $(0, 2)$ and $(1, 4)$, respectively. The program was stopped after 10 iterations. The estimated velocity fields depicted by Fig. 8 and the quantitative results in Table 1 show that our method achieves realistic estimates. The reference value $v_{(ave)}^*$ is calculated form the volume flow rate Q that was measured during the experiment.

5   Conclusion

We presented an efficient approach to flow parameter estimation using plane wave ultrasound image sequences. The method achieves realistic estimates in laminar and turbulent scenarios. We consider it as a first step towards adapting techniques from computer vision to Echo PIV, to provide an alternative to the prevailing correlation methods. Future work will reconsider (i) the image reconstruction methods that lead to Echo PIV image sequences, (ii) refine our local spatio-temporal approach based on a more detailed flow representation in Fourier space, and (iii) integrate both lines of research into a variational model.

References

1. Adelson, E.H., Bergen, J.R.: Spatiotemporal energy models for the perception of motion. J. Opt. Soc. Am. A **2**(2), 284–299 (1985)
2. Becker, F., Petra, S., Schnörr, C.: Optical flow. In: Scherzer, O. (ed.) Handbook of Mathematical Methods in Imaging, 2nd edn, pp. 1945–2004. Springer, New York (2015). doi:10.1007/978-1-4939-0790-8_38
3. Birgin, E.G., Martinez, J.M., Raydan, M.: Nonmonotone spectral projected gradient methods on convex sets. SIAM J. Optim. **10**(4), 1196–1211 (2000)
4. Bodnariuc, E., Schiffner, M., Petra, S., Schnörr, C.: Plane wave acoustic superposition for fast ultrasound imaging. In: International Ultrasonics Symposium (IUS). IEEE (2016)
5. Correia, M., Provost, J., Tanter, M., Pernot, M.: 4D ultrafast ultrasound flow imaging in vivo quantification of arterial volumetric flow rate in a single heartbeat. Phys. Med. Biol. **61**(23), L48–L61 (2016)
6. Fleet, D., Jepson, A.: Computation of component image velocity from local phase information. Int. J. Comput. Vis. **5**(1), 77–104 (1990)
7. Haglund, L.: Adaptive Multidimensional Filtering. Ph.D. thesis, Dept. Electrical Engineering, University of Linköping, Sweden (1992)
8. Hashimoto, M., Sklansky, J.: Multiple-order derivatives for detecting local image characteristics. Comput. Vis. Graphics Image Underst. **39**, 28–55 (1987)
9. Heeger, D.: Optical flow using spatiotemporal filters. Int. J. Comput. Vis. **1**(4), 279–302 (1988)
10. Heitz, D., Mémin, E., Schnörr, C.: Variational fluid flow measurements from image sequences: synopsis and perspectives. Exp. Fluids **48**(3), 369–393 (2010)
11. Kim, H., Hertzberg, J., Shandas, R.: Development and validation of echo PIV. Exp. Fluids **36**(3), 455–462 (2004)
12. Leow, C.H., Bazigou, E., Eckersley, R.J., Yu, A.C.H., Weinberg, P.D., Tang, M.X.: Flow velocity mapping using contrast enhanced high-frame-rate plane wave ultrasound and image tracking: methods and initial in vitro and in vivo evaluation. Ultrasound Med. Biol. **41**(11), 2913–2925 (2015)
13. Margarey, J., Kingsbury, N.: Motion estimation using a complex-valued wavelet transform. IEEE Trans. Signal Proc. **46**(4), 1069–1084 (1998)
14. Massot, C., Hérault, J.: Model of frequency analysis in the visual cortex and the shape from texture problem. Int. J. Comput. Vis. **76**(2), 165–182 (2008)
15. Poelma, C.: Ultrasound imaging velocimetry: a review. Exp. Fluids **58**(1), 3–31 (2017)
16. Raffel, M., Willert, C.E., Wereley, S.T., Kompenhans, J.: Particle Image Velocimery - A Practical Guide. Springer, Heidelberg (2007)
17. Simoncelli, E., Freeman, W., Adelson, E., Heeger, D.: Shiftable multiscale transforms. IEEE Trans. Inf. Theory **38**, 587–607 (1992)

18. Stigler, J.: Analytical velocity profile in tube for laminar and turbulent flow. Eng. Mech. **21**(6), 371–379 (2014)
19. Tanter, M., Fink, M.: Ultrafast imaging in biomedical ultrasound. IEEE Trans. Ultrason. Ferroelectr. Freq. Control **61**(1), 102–119 (2014)
20. Voorneveld, J., Kruizinga, P., Vos, H.J., Gijsen, F.J.H., Jebbink, E.G., van der Steen, A.F.W., de Jong, N., Bosch, J.G.: Native blood speckle vs ultrasound contrast agent for particle image velocimetry with ultrafast ultrasound - in vitro experiments. In: International Ultrasonics Symposium. IEEE (2016)
21. White, F.M.: Fluid Mechanics. McGraw-Hill Series in Mechanical Engineering, McGraw Hill (2011)
22. Yap, P.T., Paramesran, R., Ong, S.H.: Image analysis by Krawtchouk moments. IEEE Trans. Image Process. **12**(11), 1367–1377 (2003)

Machine Learning and Pattern Recognition

Object Boundary Detection and Classification with Image-Level Labels

Jing Yu Koh[1], Wojciech Samek[2], Klaus-Robert Müller[3,4], and Alexander Binder[1(✉)]

[1] ISTD Pillar, Singapore University of Technology and Design, Singapore, Singapore
alexander_binder@sutd.edu.sg
[2] Department of Video Coding and Analytics,
Fraunhofer Heinrich Hertz Institute, Berlin, Germany
[3] Department of Computer Science, TU Berlin, Berlin, Germany
[4] Department of Brain and Cognitive Engineering,
Korea University, Seoul, Republic of Korea

Abstract. Semantic boundary and edge detection aims at simultaneously detecting object edge pixels in images and assigning class labels to them. Systematic training of predictors for this task requires the labeling of edges in images which is a particularly tedious task. We propose a novel strategy for solving this task, when pixel-level annotations are not available, performing it in an almost zero-shot manner by relying on conventional whole image neural net classifiers that were trained using large bounding boxes. Our method performs the following two steps at test time. Firstly it predicts the class labels by applying the trained whole image network to the test images. Secondly, it computes pixel-wise scores from the obtained predictions by applying backprop gradients as well as recent visualization algorithms such as deconvolution and layer-wise relevance propagation. We show that high pixel-wise scores are indicative for the location of semantic boundaries, which suggests that the semantic boundary problem can be approached without using edge labels during the training phase.

1 Introduction

Neural net based predictors achieve excellent results in many data-driven tasks, examples among the newer being [6,10,14,15,17], while others such as video detection or machine translation [8,21] are equally impressive. Rather than extending neural networks to a new application, we focus here on the question whether a neural network can solve problems which are *harder* than the one for which the network was trained. In particular, we consider the task of semantic boundary detection which we aim to solve without appropriately fine-grained training labels.

The problem of semantic boundary detection (SBD) [5] can be defined as the simultaneous detection of object edge pixels and assignment of class labels to such edge pixels in images. Recently, the work of [3,16,24,25] showed substantial improvement using neural nets, however, the approach relied on end-to-end

© Springer International Publishing AG 2017
V. Roth and T. Vetter (Eds.): GCPR 2017, LNCS 10496, pp. 153–164, 2017.
DOI: 10.1007/978-3-319-66709-6_13

training with a dataset for which semantic boundary labels were available. When trying to build a predictor for SBD, practitioners face the problem that the classical inductive machine learning paradigm requires to create a dataset with semantic boundary labels, that is, for each image a subset of pixels in images corresponding to object edges is labeled with class indices. Creating such labelling is a particularly tedious task, unlike labelling whole images or drawing bounding boxes, both of which can be done very quickly. The best proof for this difficulty is the fact that we are aware of only one truly semantic boundary dataset [5]. Note that SBD is different from contour detection tasks [23] which aim at finding contours of objects without assigning class labels to them. In that sense the scope of our proposed work is different from unsupervised contour detection as in [13].

The main question in this paper is to what extent it is possible to solve the semantic boundary or edge detection task without having appropriately fine-grained labels, i.e., pixel-level ground truth, which are required for classical training paradigms? We do not intend to replace the usage of pixel-wise boundary labels when they are available. We aim at use cases in which pixel-wise boundary labels are not available during the training phase. One example of using weaker annotations for semantic boundary detection is [9] where bounding box labels are used to learn semantic boundaries. We propose a novel strategy to tackle a problem requiring fine-grained labels, namely semantic boundary detection, with a classifier trained for image classification using only image-wise labels. For that we use neural nets that classify an image, and apply existing visualization methods that are able to assign class-specific-scores to single pixels. These class-specific pixel scores can then be used to define semantic boundary predictions.

The contribution of this paper is as follows. We demonstrate that classifier visualization methods are useful beyond producing nice-to-look-at images, namely for approaching prediction tasks on the pixel-level in the absence of appropriately fine-grained training labels. As an example, we apply and evaluate the performance of classifier visualization methods to the SBD task. We show that these visualization methods can be used for producing quantifiably meaningful predictions at a higher spatial resolution than the labels, which were the basis for training the classifiers. We discuss the shortcomings of such approaches when compared to the proper training paradigm that makes use of pixel-level labels. We do not expect such methods to beat baselines that employ the proper training paradigm and thus use pixel-level labels during training, but rather aim at the practitioner's case in which fine-grained training data is too costly in terms of money or time.

2   Obtaining Pixel-Level Scores from Image-Wise Predictions

In the following we introduce the methods that we will use for producing pixel-level scores without pixel-level labels during training time. It is common to all these methods that they take a classifier prediction $f_c(x)$ on an image x and produce scores $s_c(p)$ for pixels $p \in x$. Suppose we have classifiers $f_c(x)$ for multiple classes c. Then we can tackle the SBD problem by (1) classifying an image, i.e., determine those classes that are present in the image, and (2) computing pixel-wise scores for those classes using one of the following methods.

2.1 Gradient

Probably the most obvious idea to tackle the SBD problem is to run a forward prediction with a classifier, and compute the gradient for each pixel. Let x be an input image, $f_1, \ldots, f_C$ be C outputs of a multi-class classifier and x_p be the p-th pixel. Computing pixel-wise scores for a class c and pixel p can be achieved using

$$s(p) = \left\| \frac{\partial f_c}{\partial x_p}(x) \right\|_2 \tag{1}$$

The norm runs here over the partial derivatives for the (r, g, b)-subpixels of a pixel p. Alternatively one can sum up the subpixel scores in order to have a pixel-score. Using gradients for visualizing sensitivities of neural networks has been shown in [20]. A high score in this sense indicates that the output f_c has high sensitivity under small changes of the input x_p, i.e. there exists a direction in the tangent space located at x for which the slope of the classifier f_c is very high.

In order to see the impact of partial derivatives, consider the case of a simple linear mapping that takes subpixels $x_{p,s}$ of pixel p as input.

$$f(x) = \sum_p \sum_{s \in \{r,g,b\}} w_{p,s} x_{p,s} \tag{2}$$

In this case backpropagation combined with an ℓ_2-norm yields:

$$s(p) = (w_{p,r}^2 + w_{p,g}^2 + w_{p,b}^2)^{1/2} \tag{3}$$

Note that the input $x_{p,s}$, and in particular its sign plays no role in a visualization achieved by backpropagation, although obviously the sign of $x_{p,s}$ does matter for deciding whether to detect an object ($f(x) > 0$) or not ($f(x) < 0$). This is a limiting factor, when one aims to explain what pixels are relevant for the prediction $f(x) > 0$.

2.2 Deconvolution

Deconvolution [26] is an alternative method to compute pixel-wise scores. Starting with scores given at the top of a convolutional layer, it applies the transposed filter weights to compute scores at the bottom of the same layer. Another important feature is used in max-pooling layers, where scores from the top are distributed down to the input that yielded the maximum value in the max pooling. Consider the linear mapping case again. Then deconvolution in the sense of multiplying the transposed weights w (as it is for example implemented in the Caffe package) yields for subpixel s of channel p

$$s(p, s) = f_c(x) w_{p,s} \tag{4}$$

This score can be summed across subpixels, or one can take again an ℓ_p-norm. When using summation across subpixels, then deconvolution is proportional to the prediction $f_c(x)$, in particular it expresses the dominating terms $w_{p,s} x_{p,s} \approx f_c(x)$ correctly which contribute most to the prediction $f(x)$.

2.3   Layer-Wise Relevance Propagation

Layer-wise Relevance Propagation (LRP) [2] is a principled method for explaining neural network predictions in terms of pixel-wise scores. LRP reversely propagates a numerical quantity, named relevance, in a way that preserves the sum of the total relevance at each layer. The relevance is initialized at the output as the prediction score $f_c(x)$ and propagated down to the inputs (i.e., pixels), so that the relevance conservation property holds at each layer

$$f_c(x) = \ldots = \sum_j R_j^{(l+1)} \ldots = \sum_i R_i^{(l)} = \ldots = \sum_p R_p^{(1)} \tag{5}$$

where $\{R_j^{(l+1)}\}$ and $\{R_i^{(l)}\}$ denote the relevance at layer $l+1$ and l, respectively, and $\{R_p^{(1)}\}$ represents the pixel-wise relevance scores.

Let us consider the neural network as an feed-forward graph of elementary computational units (neurons), each of them realizing a simple function of type

$$x_j^{(l+1)} = g\left(0, \sum_i x_i^{(l)} w_{ij}^{(l,l+1)} + b_j^{(l+1)}\right) \quad \text{e.g. } g(z) = \max(0, z) \tag{6}$$

where j denotes a neuron at a particular layer $l+1$, and, where $\sum_i$ runs over all lower-layer neurons connected to neuron j. $w_{ij}^{(l,l+1)}$, $b_j^{(l+1)}$ are parameters of a neuron. The prediction of a deep neural network is obtained by computing these neurons in a feed-forward pass. Conversely, [2] have shown that the same graph structure can be used to redistribute the relevance $f(x)$ at the output of the network onto pixel-wise relevance scores $\{R_p^{(1)}\}$, by using a local redistribution rule

$$R_i^{(l)} = \sum_j \frac{z_{ij}}{\sum_{i'} z_{i'j}} R_j^{(l+1)} \quad \text{with} \quad z_{ij} = x_i^{(1)} w_{ij}^{(1,l+1)} \tag{7}$$

where i indexes a neuron at a particular layer l, and where $\sum_j$ runs over all upper-layer neurons to which neuron i contributes. Application of this rule in a backward pass produces a relevance map (heatmap) that satisfies the desired conservation property.

We consider two other LRP algorithms introduced in [2], namely the ϵ-variant and the β-variant. The first rule is given by:

$$R_i^{(l)} = \sum_j \frac{z_{ij}}{\sum_{i'} z_{i'j} + \epsilon \operatorname{sign}(\sum_{i'} z_{i'j})} R_j^{(l+1)} \qquad (8)$$

Here for $\epsilon > 0$ the conservation idea is relaxated in order to gain better numerical stability. The second formula is given by:

$$R_i^{(l)} = \sum_j \left(\alpha \cdot \frac{z_{ij}^+}{\sum_{i'} z_{i'j}^+} + \beta \cdot \frac{z_{ij}^-}{\sum_{i'} z_{i'j}^-} \right) R_j^{(l+1)}. \qquad (9)$$

Here, z_{ij}^+ and z_{ij}^- denote the positive and negative part of z_{ij} respectively, such that $z_{ij}^+ + z_{ij}^- = z_{ij}$. We enforce $\alpha + \beta = 1$, $\alpha > 0$, $\beta \leq 0$ in order for the relevance propagation equations to be conservative layer-wise. Note that for $\alpha = 1$ this redistribution rule is equivalent (for ReLU nonlinearities g) to the z^+-rule by [18].

In contrast to the gradient, LRP recovers the natural decomposition of a linear mapping

$$f(x) = \sum_{i=1}^{D} w_i x_i \qquad (10)$$

i.e., the pixel-level score

$$R_i = w_i x_i \qquad (11)$$

not only depends on whether the classifier reacts to this input dimension ($w_i > 0$), but also if that feature is actually present ($x_i > 0$). An implementation of LRP can be found in [12].

3   Experiments

We perform the experiments on the SBD dataset with a Pascal VOC multilabel classifier from [11] that is available in the BVLC model zoo of the Caffe [7] package. This classifier was trained using the 4 edge crops and the center crops of the ground truth bounding boxes of the Pascal VOC dataset [4]. We do not use pixel labels at training time, however, for evaluation at test time we use the pixel-wise ground truth, in order to be able to compare all methods quantitatively. Same as [5] we report the maximal F-score and the average precision on the pixel-level of an image. We stick to the same convention regarding counting true positives in a neighborhood, as introduced in [5].

3.1   Performance on the SBD Task

Table 1 shows the average precision (AP) scores for all methods. We can see from the table that the neural-network based method [3] which uses pixel-level ground truth at training time performs best by a large margin. Methods that do not employ pixel-level labels at training time perform far worse. However, we can see a certain surprise: all the methods perform better than the method [5] on Semantic Boundary Detection that was the best baseline before the work of [3] replaced it. Note that [5] as well as [3] relies on pixel-wise labels during training, whereas the proposed methods require only image-wise labels. This result gives a realistic comparison of how good methods on pixel-wise prediction without pixel-labels in the training phase can perform.

Table 1. Average precision (AP) and maximal F-scores (MF) scores of various methods to compute pixel-wise scores from whole image classifiers without pixel-labels at training time, compared against the original method *InverseDetectors* [5] and Boundary detection using Neural nets *HFL* [3]. Only the last two both use pixel-labels at training time. All other use no pixel-level labels during training. Grad denotes Gradient, Deconv denotes [26], ϵ and β refer to LRP variants given in Eqs. 8 and 9 taken from [2].

Training phase	Image-level labels						Pixel-level labels	
Method	Gradient	Deconv	$\beta = 0$	$\beta = -1$	$\epsilon = 1$	$\epsilon = 0.01$	InvDet [5]	HFL [3]
AP	22.5	25.0	28.4	27.3	**31.4**	31.2	19.9	**54.6**
MF	31.0	33.3	35.1	34.1	38.0	**38.1**	28.0	**62.5**

The pixel-wise scores for LRP are computed by summing over subpixels. For Gradient and Deconvolution using the negative sum over subpixels performed better than using the sum or the ℓ_2-norm. For both cases negative pixel scores were set to zero. This follows our experience with Deconvolution and LRP that wave-like low-level image filters, which are typically present in deep neural nets, receive equally wave-like scores with positive and negative half-waves. Removing the negative half waves improves the prediction quality. Table 2 shows the comparison of AP scores for various methods to compute a pixel-wise score from subpixel scores. Note that we do not show the ℓ_2-norm, or the summed negative scores for the LRP methods, as LRP does preserve the sign of the prediction and thus using the sum of negative scores or ℓ_2-norm has no meaningful interpretation for LRP.

Table 2. Comparison of various ways to combine subpixel scores into a pixel-wise score.

Subpixel aggregation method	Sum	Sum of negative scores	ℓ_2-norm
Gradient AP	22.0	22.5	18.8
Deconvolution AP	22.9	25.0	21.9

3.2   Shortcomings of Visualization Methods

Semantic boundaries are not the most relevant regions for the decision of above mentioned classifiers trained on images of natural scenes. This does not devaluate models trained on shapes. It merely says that, given RGB images of natural scenes as input, above object class predictors put considerable weight on internal edges and textures rather than outer boundaries, an effect which can be observed in the heatmaps in Figs. 1 and 2. This is the primary hypothesis why the visualization methods above are partially mismatching the semantic boundaries. We demonstrate this hypothesis quantitatively by an experiment. For this we need to introduce a measure of relevance of a set of pixels which is independent of the computed visualizations.

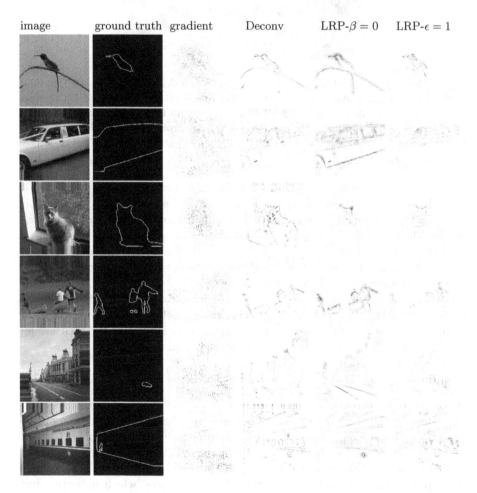

Fig. 1. Heatmaps of pixel-wise scores compared against the groundtruth. From left to right: original image, pixel-level ground truth, gradient (negative scores), deconvolution (negative scores), LRP with $\beta = 0$ and with $\epsilon = 1$.

Fig. 2. Heatmaps of pixel-wise scores computed for the GoogleNet Reference Classifier of the Caffe package show the sparsity of pixel-wise prediction methods. The used classifiers were: Timber wolf, Bernese mountain Dog and Ram. Left column: image as it enters the deep neural net. Middle: pixel-wise scores computed by LRP with $\epsilon = 1$. Right: pixel-wise scores computed by LRP with $\beta = 0$.

Perturbation Analysis. We can measure the relevance of a set of pixels $S \subset x$ of an image x for the prediction of a classifier by replacing the pixels in this set by some values, and comparing the prediction on the modified image $\tilde{x}_S$ against the prediction score $f(x)$ for the original image [19] (similar approach has been applied for text in [1]). This idea follows the intuition that most random perturbations in a region that is important for classification will lead to a decline of the prediction score for the image as a whole: $f(\tilde{x}_S) < f(x)$. It is clear that there exist perturbations of a region yield an increase of the prediction score: for example a change that follows the gradient direction locally. Thus we will draw many perturbations of the set S from a random distribution P and measure an approximation the expected decline of the prediction

$$m = f(x) - \mathbb{E}_{S \sim P}[f(\tilde{x}_S)] \tag{12}$$

We intend to measure the expected decrease for the set S being the ground truth pixels for the SBD task, and compare it against the set of highest scoring pixels. For a fair comparison the set of highest scoring pixels will be limited to have the same size as the number of ground truth pixels. Highest scoring pixels will be defined by the pixel-wise scores from the above methods. We will show that the expected decrease is higher for the pixel-wise scores, which indicates that ground truth pixels representing semantic boundaries are not the most relevant subset for the classifier prediction.

The experiment to demonstrate this will be designed as follows. For each test image and each ground truth class we will take the set of ground truth pixels, and randomly perturb them. For a (r, g, b)-pixel we will draw the values from a uniform distribution in $[0, 1]^3 \subset \mathbb{R}^3$. For each image and present class of semantic boundary task ground truth we repeat 200 random perturbations of the set in order to compute an approximation to Eq. 12. We compute the average over all images to obtain the average decrease on ground truth pixels m_{GT}. m_{GT} is an average measure of relevance of the ground truth pixels. m_{GT} is to be compared against the analogous quantity m_V derived from the top-scoring pixels of a visualization method. For a given visualization method $V \in \{Gradient, Deconv, LRP\text{-}\beta, LRP\text{-}\epsilon\}$, we define the set of pixels to be perturbed as the pixels with the highest pixel-wise scores computed from the visualization method. The set size for this set will be the same as the number of ground truth pixels of the semantic boundary task of the same image and class. Running the same perturbation idea according to Eq. 12 on this set yields a measure m_V of average decrease of classifier prediction that is specific to the most relevant pixels of the given visualization method.

Table 3 shows the results of the comparison. Note that we take the ground truth in the image that has been resized to match the receptive field of the neural net (227×227), and apply one step of classical morphological thickening. This thickened ground truth set will be used. The standard deviation was computed for the 200 random perturbations and averaged over images and classes. We can see from the table that the decrease is stronger for the visualization methods compared to the ground truth pixels. This holds for Deconvolution as well as for LRP. The pixels highlighted by these methods are more relevant for the classifier prediction, even though they disagree with boundary pixel labels. In summary this supports our initially stated hypothesis that boundary pixels are not the most relevant for classification, and our explanation why these methods are partially mismatching the set of boundary ground truth labels.

Table 3. Comparison of the averaged prediction scores. $f(x)$ denotes the average prediction for the unperturbed images for all ground truth classes. m_{GT} denotes the average prediction for images with perturbed ground truth pixels. m_{Deconv} and $m_{LRP, \epsilon=1}$ denotes the average prediction for images with perturbed highest scoring pixels having the same cardinality as the ground truth pixels, using Deconvolution and LRP.

$f_c(x)$	m_{GT}	m_{Deconv}	$m_{LRP, \epsilon=1}$
10.20 ± 0	7.73 ± 0.36	5.68 ± 0.38	1.73 ± 0.34

We can support this numerical observation also by example images. We can observe two error cases. Firstly, the pixel-wise predictions may miss semantic boundaries that are deemed to be less discriminative for the classification task. This adds to false negatives. Secondly, the pixel-wise predictions may assign high scores to pixels that are relevant for the classification of an object and lie inside the object. Figure 1 shows some examples. We can clearly see false negatives and false positives in these examples, for example for the car and LRP-$\epsilon = 1$ where the window regions are deemed to be highly relevant for the classifier decision, but the outer boundary on the car top is considered irrelevant which is a bad result with respect to boundary detection. For the cat most of the methods focus on its face rather than the cat boundaries. The bird is an example where deconvolution gives a good result. For the people with the boats the heatmap is shown for the people class. In this example LRP-$\epsilon = 1$ focuses correctly most selectively on the people, same as for the tiny car example.

We can observe from these figures a common sparsity of the pixel-wise prediction methods. This motivates why we did not aim at solving segmentation tasks with these methods. Finally we remark that this sparsity is not an artefact of the particular deep neural network from [11] tuned for PASCAL VOC. Figure 2 shows the same effect for the GoogleNet Reference Classifier [22] of the Caffe Package [7]. As an example, for the wolf, parts of the body in the right have missing boundaries. Indeed this part is not very discriminative. A similar interpretation can be made for the lower right side of the dog which has a strong image gradient but not much dog-specific evidence.

4   Conclusion

We presented here several methods for zero-shot learning for semantic boundary detection and evaluated them quantitatively. These methods are useful when pixel-level labels are unavailable at training time. These methods perform reasonably against previous state of the art. It would be interesting to evaluate these methods on other datasets with class-specifically labeled edges, if they would become available in the future. Furthermore we have shown that classifier visualization methods [2,20,26] have applications beside pure visualization due to their property of computing predictions at a finer scale.

References

1. Arras, L., Horn, F., Montavon, G., Müller, K.R., Samek, W.: Explaining predictions of non-linear classifiers in NLP. In: Proceedings of the 1st Workshop on Representation Learning for NLP, pp. 1–7. Association for Computational Linguistics (2016)
2. Bach, S., Binder, A., Montavon, G., Klauschen, F., Müller, K.R., Samek, W.: On pixel-wise explanations for non-linear classifier decisions by layer-wise relevance propagation. PloS one **10**(7), e0130140 (2015)
3. Bertasius, G., Shi, J., Torresani, L.: High-for-low and low-for-high: efficient boundary detection from deep object features and its applications to high-level vision. In: IEEE ICCV, pp. 504–512 (2015)
4. Everingham, M., Van Gool, L., Williams, C., Winn, J., Zisserman, A.: The pascal visual object classes (voc) challenge. IJCV **88**(2), 303–338 (2010)
5. Hariharan, B., Arbeláez, P., Bourdev, L.D., Maji, S., Malik, J.: Semantic contours from inverse detectors. In: IEEE ICCV, pp. 991–998 (2011)

6. Hariharan, B., Arbeláez, P., Girshick, R.B., Malik, J.: Hypercolumns for object segmentation and fine-grained localization. In: IEEE CVPR, pp. 447–456 (2015)
7. Jia, Y., Shelhamer, E., Donahue, J., Karayev, S., Long, J., Girshick, R.B., Guadarrama, S., Darrell, T.: Caffe: convolutional architecture for fast feature embedding. In: Proceedings of the ACM International Conference on Multimedia, pp. 675–678 (2014)
8. Karpathy, A., Toderici, G., Shetty, S., Leung, T., Sukthankar, R., Li, F.: Large-scale video classification with convolutional neural networks. In: IEEE CVPR, pp. 1725–1732 (2014)
9. Khoreva, A., Benenson, R., Omran, M., Hein, M., Schiele, B.: Weakly supervised object boundaries. In: The IEEE Conference on Computer Vision and Pattern Recognition (CVPR), June 2016
10. Koutník, J., Cuccu, G., Schmidhuber, J., Gomez, F.J.: Evolving large-scale neural networks for vision-based reinforcement learning. In: GECCO, pp. 1061–1068 (2013)
11. Lapuschkin, S., Binder, A., Montavon, G., Müller, K.R., Samek, W.: Analyzing classifiers: fisher vectors and deep neural networks. In: IEEE CVPR, pp. 2912–2920 (2016)
12. Lapuschkin, S., Binder, A., Montavon, G., Müller, K.R., Samek, W.: The layer-wise relevance propagation toolbox for artificial neural networks. J. Mach. Learn. Res. 17(114), 1–5 (2016)
13. Li, Y., Paluri, M., Rehg, J.M., Dollar, P.: Unsupervised learning of edges. In: The IEEE Conference on Computer Vision and Pattern Recognition (CVPR), June 2016
14. Long, J., Shelhamer, E., Darrell, T.: Fully convolutional networks for semantic segmentation. In: IEEE CVPR, pp. 3431–3440 (2015)
15. Malinowski, M., Rohrbach, M., Fritz, M.: Ask your neurons: a neural-based approach to answering questions about images. In: IEEE ICCV, pp. 1–9 (2015)
16. Maninis, K.K., Pont-Tuset, J., Arbelaez, P., Gool, L.V.: Convolutional oriented boundaries: from image segmentation to high-level tasks. IEEE Trans. Pattern Anal. Mach. Intell. PP(99), 1–1 (2017)
17. Mnih, V., Kavukcuoglu, K., Silver, D., Rusu, A.A., Veness, J., Bellemare, M.G., Graves, A., Riedmiller, M., Fidjeland, A.K., Ostrovski, G., Petersen, S., Beattie, C., Sadik, A., Antonoglou, I., King, H., Kumaran, D., Wierstra, D., Legg, S., Hassabis, D.: Human-level control through deep reinforcement learning. Nature 518(7540), 529–533 (2015)
18. Montavon, G., Bach, S., Binder, A., Samek, W., Müller, K.R.: Explaining nonlinear classification decisions with deep taylor decomposition. Pattern Recognit. 65, 211–222 (2017)
19. Samek, W., Binder, A., Montavon, G., Lapuschkin, S., Müller, K.R.: Evaluating the visualization of what a deep neural network has learned. IEEE Trans. Neural Netw. Learn. Syst. (2016)
20. Simonyan, K., Vedaldi, A., Zisserman, A.: Deep inside convolutional networks: visualising image classification models and saliency maps. CoRR abs/1312.6034 (2013)
21. Sutskever, I., Vinyals, O., Le, Q.V.: Sequence to sequence learning with neural networks. In: Advances in NIPS, pp. 3104–3112 (2014)
22. Szegedy, C., Liu, W., Jia, Y., Sermanet, P., Reed, S., Anguelov, D., Erhan, D., Vanhoucke, V., Rabinovich, A.: Going deeper with convolutions. CoRR abs/1409.4842 (2014)

23. Xie, S., Tu, Z.: Holistically-nested edge detection. Int. J. Comput. Vis. (2017). http://dx.doi.org/10.1007/s11263-017-1004-z
24. Yang, J., Price, B., Cohen, S., Lee, H., Yang, M.H.: Object contour detection with a fully convolutional encoder-decoder network. In: The IEEE Conference on Computer Vision and Pattern Recognition (CVPR), June 2016
25. Yu, Z., Feng, C., Liu, M.Y., Ramalingam, S.: CASENet: Deep Category-Aware Semantic Edge Detection. ArXiv e-prints, May 2017
26. Zeiler, M.D., Fergus, R.: Visualizing and understanding convolutional networks. In: Fleet, D., Pajdla, T., Schiele, B., Tuytelaars, T. (eds.) ECCV 2014. LNCS, vol. 8689, pp. 818–833. Springer, Cham (2014). doi:10.1007/978-3-319-10590-1_53

Semantic Segmentation of Outdoor Areas Using 3D Moment Invariants and Contextual Cues

Sven Sickert[1(✉)] and Joachim Denzler[1,2]

[1] Computer Vision Group, Friedrich Schiller University Jena, Jena, Germany
sven.sickert@uni-jena.de
[2] Michael Stifel Center Jena, Jena, Germany

Abstract. In this paper, we propose an approach for the semantic segmentation of a 3D point cloud using local 3D moment invariants and the integration of contextual information. Specifically, we focus on the task of analyzing forestal and urban areas which were recorded by terrestrial LiDAR scanners. We demonstrate how 3D moment invariants can be leveraged as local features and that they are on a par with established descriptors. Furthermore, we show how an iterative learning scheme can increase the overall quality by taking neighborhood relationships between classes into account. Our experiments show that the approach achieves very good results for a variety of tasks including both binary and multi-class settings.

1 Introduction

In recent years, several new techniques for the creation of 3D point clouds have emerged. Current structure from motion techniques like LSD-SLAM [2] raise each webcam to a powerful 3D scanning device. Furthermore, in companies and research groups the use of laser based devices like LiDAR scanners (*light detection and ranging*) becomes more common. Today, this recording technique is also advanced enough to allow for a fast and easy scanning procedure. Thus, the demand increases for algorithms which are able to process such data with respect to typical pattern recognition tasks like detection, segmentation or classification.

In biological research projects like [6,19] with a focus on the ecological system of forests such scanners are used to create a 3D representation of an area. It opens up the possibility to use computer-assisted systems for their analysis. However, there is often the need for a certain amount of user interaction. While this might be feasible in environmental research, other areas like autonomous driving or robotics in general are in need of real-time and thereby fully-automatic systems.

In this paper, we provide an approach for the fully-automatic semantic segmentation of 3D point cloud data recorded by LiDAR scanning devices. We make use of 3D moment invariants [9] which are a powerful local representation and are invariant to Euclidean and affine transformations. For regular 2D image data semantic segmentation represents the pixel-by-pixel classification of a whole scene leading to a segmentation into meaningful regions [3,11,15,16]. The classification is based on local pixel representations within a certain neighborhood.

V. Roth and T. Vetter (Eds.): GCPR 2017, LNCS 10496, pp. 165–176, 2017.
DOI: 10.1007/978-3-319-66709-6_14

(a)   (b)

Fig. 1. Datasets for the analysis of outdoor areas used in our experiments: (a) 3DForest dataset [19] with labels for *tree, terrain, dead wood* and *miscellaneous* and (b) Oakland 3D Point Cloud Dataset [12] with labels for *facade, ground, vegetation, wire* and *pole*.

While in grid data this neighborhood can easily be retrieved using common faces or corners of pixels the neighborhood in an orderless point cloud is not as trivial.

We show how to create a local feature descriptor based on moment invariants and augmented contextual cues that can represent neighborhood relations of present classes. For the latter we make use of a cascade of classifiers and the concept of *auto-context* [11,16,21]. Our experiments demonstrate the power of our approach for the automatic segmentation of individual trees, as well as the analysis of whole outdoor areas in general.

The outline of this paper is as follows. We first give a short overview of related work in this field of research. In Sect. 3 we describe how local 3D moment invariants as a feature descriptor can be derived. The iterative classification scheme and the use of context information during learning is described in Sect. 4. An evaluation of the proposed framework follows in Sect. 5. A summary in Sect. 6 concludes the paper.

2   Related Work

Segmentation tools provided with [6,19] for the analysis of forestal areas are based on local statistics and heuristics. Especially, the clustering routines of [6] are mainly based on outlier estimation and distance thresholding. These are basic features for tasks like unsupervised segmentation that are not invariant with respect to scaling and change of density in the data. An analysis of a variety of such local statistics and features can be found in [22].

In a more recent approach local concavity is used as an indicator for boundaries to achieve a bottom-up segmentation [14]. Supervoxels have to be generated in a first step. The authors of [5] propose a contour detection method to find regions of interest. In both [5,14] graph-cut techniques are applied to finally segment the point cloud based on the features. In our work, however, we also try to find the meaning of these segmented regions which places additional demands on the features itself.

Many works of the past decade focused on the development of meaningful 3D feature descriptors for classification tasks. In [4,17] neighborhood spheres are defined to create histograms of local features. For the 3D shape context descriptor [4] the distribution of points within individual parts of the sphere are used. The histograms of the SHOT descriptor [17] represent the distribution of normal vectors in these parts. A similar work is based on spinning planes around a point along all three axes in order to get a distribution of the residuals [7,8]. In all cases the main direction of the descriptor has to be computed in order to make them invariant with respect to rotations. We propose to use features that are derived for the purpose of being invariant to Euclidean and affine transformations.

For a task like semantic segmentation the modeling of context information is possible. Relationships between nearby points can be directly modeled using graphical models like *Markov random fields* (MRF) [10,13] or *Markov networks* [12]. In the latter, a functional gradient approach is used to increase the performance of MRFs by learning high-order interactions. Additionally, in [18] it was shown how a classification approach based on *conditional random fields* can be extended to an online learning setting that is able to improve iteratively.

Such a system can also be used to integrate classification outputs of previous predictions. In [23] a sequence of classifiers is trained to iteratively refine the learned model by adding context information. The authors of [3] propose to train *random decision forests* (RDF) in an incremental manner using contextual cues in deeper levels to semantically segment single images and image stacks. We adopt this concept for the processing of 3D point clouds by augmenting our initial set of features with information on the class distributions in a certain neighborhood. This allows for modeling of relationships between both points and classes. We also use RDFs in our framework as they are fast to learn and only have very few setup parameters.

3 Local Features Based on 3D Moment Invariants

In order to classify each individual point, we need a powerful representation for it which is especially robust against scaling as well as rotational and translational transformations in 3D space. A natural choice are statistical moments and their associated invariants. In this section, we describe how local 3D moment invariants can be derived for our purpose. As a prerequisite, we define a set $\mathcal{P} \subset \mathbb{R}^3$ of 3D points $\mathbf{p}^{(i)}$, with $1 \leq i \leq N$ and $N = |\mathcal{P}|$ the amount of points in the cloud.

3.1 3D Surface Moments

Let us assume there is a surface triangulation $\mathcal{S}$ given representing the object or scenery using $\mathcal{P}$. Furthermore, $\mathcal{S}$ consists of triangles $\mathcal{T}^{(j)}$, with $1 \leq j \leq N_{\mathcal{T}}$ and $N_{\mathcal{T}} = |\mathcal{S}|$ being the amount of triangles. Such a surface representation can be efficiently created using a *Delaunay* triangulation.

Each triangle consists of three corner points $\mathbf{c}_1^{(j)}, \mathbf{c}_2^{(j)}, \mathbf{c}_3^{(j)} \in \mathcal{P}$. The 3D surface moments M_{kln} of $(k + l + n)^{\text{th}}$ order for $\mathcal{S}$ are defined as the accumulated surface moments of the associated triangles $\mathcal{T}^{(j)}$: $M_{kln} = \sum_j m_{kln}^{(j)}$. In the following we skip the superscript for easier readability. The surface moment m_{kln} for a triangle $\mathcal{T}$ can be computed using

$$m_{kln} = \int \int_{\mathcal{T}} x^k y^l z^n \rho(x, y, z) \mathrm{d}s, \tag{1}$$

where ρ is a density function, with $\rho(x, y, z) = 1$ in our case.

As was shown in [20,24] the calculation of m_{kln} can be reduced to the computation of the area moments

$$m_{pq} = \int \int_D u^p v^q \mathrm{d}u \mathrm{d}v, \tag{2}$$

where $u, v \in D \subset \mathbb{R}^2$ and $P_{\mathcal{T}}(u, v)(x_{\mathcal{T}}, y_{\mathcal{T}}, z_{\mathcal{T}})$ a suitable parametrization. For details on the parametrization and a derivation on how to exactly compute m_{kln} using m_{pq} we refer to [20].

3.2 Local 3D Moment Invariants

By calculating M_{kln} using the accumulated surface moments $m_{kln}^{(i)}$ we are now able to compute the eleven 3D moment invariants $I_{22}^2, I_{222}^2, \ldots, I_{1113}^3$ which were originally proposed by Lo and Don in [9]. The authors present moment invariants of second and third order surface moments. Details about their derivation can be found in [9].

In general, these 3D moment invariants can be computed using $\mathcal{P}$ to build a descriptor that characterizes it. However, for a task like semantic segmentation we are interested in a powerful feature representation of each individual point. Hence, we need to compute moment invariants *locally*.

While it would be possible to classify complete objects that are part of a scenery using the moment invariant representation, this would require a very good pre-clustering of $\mathcal{P}$ into objects. However, we can not rely on such a method to be given. Therefor, we propose to represent each point by its local surrounding surface shape. We follow [20] by defining a sphere $S_1^{(i)}$ of radius r_1 around each $\mathbf{p}^{(i)}$. For each $S_1^{(i)}$ we compute the 3D surface and consequently the 3D surface moments using only the 3D points within that sphere. The individual local 3D surface moments can be used to compute individual local 3D moment invariants. We will denote these as features which are part of the vector $\mathbf{x}^{(i)}$.

4   Leveraging Context Information Using Random Forests

In this section, we focus on how to augment the features described before with context information using a cascade of classifiers. First, we give a short description of random forests. After that, we explain how intermediate classification outputs can be used to enforce local smoothness and model class relations.

4.1   Random Forests for Semantic Segmentation

Random decision forest (RDF) is a well known machine learning tool that is based on an ensemble of decision trees. Individual decision trees are of limited discriminative power and are also prone to over-fitting during training. Breiman proposed in [1] randomization techniques that can help to overcome several shortcomings of single decision trees. Multiple decision trees are learned using different parts of the whole training data. Additionally, a random sampling of features for the splitting decisions and a subsequent evaluation of these splits increase diversity between the individually learned trees. A final voting among the learned trees yields the final classification result.

In our case each point $\mathbf{p}^{(i)}$ is represented by its local moment invariants in $\mathbf{x}^{(i)} \in \mathbb{R}^{11}$. Accordingly, the splits are based on these feature dimensions only. Local moment invariants are based on a certain neighborhood (see Sect. 3.2) and should thereby be similar for neighboring points. However, in RDFs each example is classified individually without taking classification results of neighboring examples into account. Hence, uncertain areas in the feature space can lead to a partially scattered classification output. In the following we propose an iterative classification scheme that helps to overcome this issue.

4.2   Contextual Cues from Local Neighborhoods

The standard framework of feature extraction and classification provides us with a class decision for each point of the whole point cloud. While this classification result might not be consistent in every detail, it allows to deduce the principal semantics. Otherwise the originally chosen features must have been insufficient for the given task or the classifier was configured poorly. Inspired by [3] we propose to use these results to augment the original feature vector with local class distributions within a certain neighborhood.

Let $\mathbf{p}^{(i)}$ and $S_1^{(i)}$ be a point and its surrounding sphere as described in Sect. 3.2. Furthermore, let $\mathcal{P}^{(i)} \subset \mathcal{P}$ be the set of points within $S_1^{(i)}$. The amount of examples classified as class c is represented by $N_c^{(i)}$, with $1 \leq c \leq C$ and C the amount of classes. Hence, we can retrieve the relative frequencies for class c by $f_c^{(i)} = \frac{N_c^{(i)}}{|\mathcal{P}^{(i)}|}$ and use them as additional features.

In the same manner, we define a second sphere S_2 with radius $r_2 < r_1$ around that point and retrieve the relative class frequencies therein as well. The idea is, to distinguish between the class distribution next to the point from the distribution in an extended neighborhood. While the inner sphere S_2 should enforce *smoothness* among nearby points, the outer sphere S_1 allows for the modeling of *relationships* between occurring classes.

After computing these features we augment the initial feature vector $\mathbf{x}^{(i)}$ with them. In order to avoid concatenation and thereby reallocation of memory we suggest to initialize the $2C$ dimensions as $\frac{1}{C}$. Thus, the dimension $d = 2C+11$ of a feature vector is constant during the whole classification process.

4.3   Cascaded Random Forests

After the feature augmentation step we train a new RDF with the same configuration as before. Hence, the root nodes include all training examples and entirely new trees are built in the process. A continuous learning scheme like in [3] could also be applied to build one entire RDF in a level-wise manner. However, we find it important to have meaningful contextual cues as possible splitting features for all examples early in the training procedure.

In general, the concept of iteratively learning classifiers based on previous outputs is referred to as auto-context [11,16,21]. Such a step-wise learning procedure can be applied multiple times. The additional information input should increase the performance of the classifier. Thus, its output can again be used to refine the features as were described in Sect. 4.2. The performance gain after each iteration is likely to decrease over time. At some point the overall performance might even get worse because of over-fitting. We will show in our experiments that multiple iterations are beneficial in certain scenarios.

5   Experiments

We evaluate our proposed framework using three datasets. First, we apply it to the binary segmentation task *tree* against *background*. After that, we use a public dataset of a LiDAR scanned forestal area to demonstrate the power of 3D moment invariants as features in comparison with other 3D feature descriptors. Furthermore, we analyze the impact of our proposed iterative classification scheme. In the third experiment we show that our method is also applicable to other outdoor scenes like urban areas.

For the evaluation we use the evaluation metrics *precision* and *recall*. These measures account for unbalanced testing datasets. Additionally, we report the *f1 score* which is the harmonic mean of both measures. In multi-class settings we report metrics that are averaged over all classes. In all our experiments we set the radius of the inner sphere as $r_2 = \frac{1}{2}r_1$. The size of r_1 was analyzed during our experiments and is provided in the evaluation sections, respectively. The RDF consists of 20 trees with a minimum amount of 15 examples in each leaf node. All reported performance results are averaged over five runs.

5.1   Segmentation of Individual Trees

Experimental Setup. In this series of experiments we want to show how our proposed framework performs for the task of segmenting an individual tree in a noisy recording. We use a point cloud consisting of 180,304 points showing one tree and its surrounding. A visualization of the point cloud can be found in Fig. 2b. The lower half of the scene is heavily distorted by noise. A ground-truth labeling for the classes *tree* and *background* is available. We split this cloud into two parts in a way that the subsets contain both classes allowing us to report quantitative results. The training set contains 94,488 points and the testing set the remaining 85,816 points.

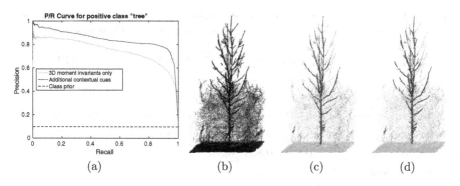

Fig. 2. Results for the segmentation of an individual tree: (a) Precision-recall curve for the testing data. Qualitative results for the whole tree (b) including both training and testing data: (c) only 3D moment invariants and (d) with additional contextual cues.

Evaluation. First, we evaluated how 3D moment invariants alone are suited for the segmentation of trees. As can be seen from the precision-recall curve in Fig. 2a the features work already very well for this task. The visualization of the qualitative result in Fig. 2c amplifies this observation. However, in details the results are scattered as was expected (see Sect. 4.1) given the individual classification of each point. By augmenting the raw features with contextual cues we are able to increase the performance. The modeled influence from nearby points and classes has an effect that is both visible in quality and measurable by performance criteria. Especially, the precision increases considerably given our proposed contextual cues.

5.2   Analysis of Forestal Areas

Experimental Setup. To evaluate our method on a larger area with multiple trees we use the data of the 3DForest project [19]. It consists of 467,211 points which were recorded using a terrestrial LiDAR scanner. The authors provide labels for the classes *tree*, *terrain* and *dead wood*. Additionally, a background class *miscellaneous* is available. For our experiments we split the data into two parts of almost the same size using the center position along the longest dimension. Points lower and equal to $y = 528.0$ are used for training and the remaining points are used for testing. The complete scenery is depicted in Fig. 1a. Examples of the background class ($\approx$10,000 points) are excluded from the evaluation.

Evaluation. In a first series of experiments we want to know how the 3D moment invariants perform in comparison with established feature descriptors like HOR [7] and SHOT [17]. The pure performance of the features can be seen in the upper part of Table 1. For all features the best performing configuration with respect to the neighborhood parameters k and r_1 was used. As can be seen from the results, the SHOT descriptor reaches the best average precision over all classes. In contrast, the average recall using moment invariants is considerably better. In total the averaged f1 score over all classes is best for our proposed descriptor.

Table 1. Comparison of different feature descriptors for 3DForest [19] using our proposed framework. For the context-based features a radius $r_1 = 0.5$ m was used.

	Precision			Recall			F1 Score
	tree	terrain	dead w.	tree	terrain	dead w.	average
Without context (it. 1)							
HOR [7] ($k = 100$)	0.903	0.676	0.523	0.969	0.664	0.090	0.586
SHOT [17] ($r_1 = 1.7$ m)	0.912	0.795	**0.735**	**0.998**	0.721	0.052	0.602
Ours ($r_1 = 0.4$ m)	**0.920**	**0.831**	0.551	0.977	**0.723**	**0.276**	**0.696**
Context-based (it. 2)							
HOR [7] ($k = 100$)	0.950	0.663	**0.818**	0.979	0.812	0.226	0.693
SHOT [17]	0.933	0.746	0.654	0.984	**0.873**	0.174	0.665
Ours	**0.960**	**0.862**	0.660	**0.987**	0.797	**0.531**	**0.796**

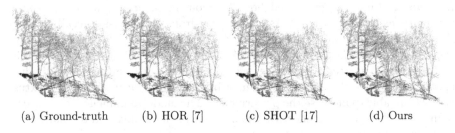

(a) Ground-truth   (b) HOR [7]   (c) SHOT [17]   (d) Ours

Fig. 3. Qualitative results for 3DForest [19] using different descriptors to classify tree, **dead wood** and **terrain**. This figure is best viewed in color (zoom in for details).

Adding the contextual cues improves the performance of all descriptors. However, the advantage of combining moment invariants and context information is obvious. Especially, the class *dead wood* with fewer examples is captured better using our method leading to a higher recall in general. This is also visible from the qualitative results which can be found in Fig. 3. All features can be used to differentiate between *terrain* and *tree*. However, the use of moment invariants performs best on average over all classes.

For a more thorough analysis of our framework we continued with experiments with respect to different parameter settings. The results in Fig. 4a demonstrate how the size of the neighborhood influences the performance of moment invariants in general. Although, the optimal value for parameter r_1 is dependent on the data itself, we observed that a value of 0.5 is very good starting point. A larger value might be necessary for the modeling of class relationships.

In our last series of experiments we look into the iterative classification itself. As can be seen from the plot in Fig. 4b more than two iterations are in most cases not beneficial. However, this is not true for the use of moment invariants as features. The performance improved after the third iteration showing again how well the combination of moment invariants and contextual cues work.

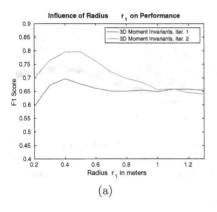 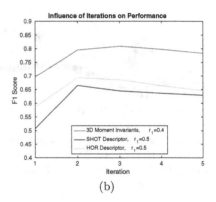

(a)   (b)

Fig. 4. Quantitative analysis of different feature configurations for 3DForest [19]: (a) Influence of radius r_1 on the performance of the 3D moment invariants and (b) performance depending on the amount of iterations of the cascaded RDF.

5.3 Urban Scenes

Experimental Setup. In our last series of experiments we test our method in a different setting to show its wide applicability. We use the *Oakland 3D Point Cloud Dataset* [12] which contains scenes from an urban area (see Fig. 1b). For the experimental setup we follow the training and testing splits provided in [12]. Thus, we train our approach using 36,932 points with labels of the classes *facade, ground, pole/trunk, wire* and *vegetation.*

Evaluation. In contrast to the analysis of forestal areas the task of urban scene understanding contains even more classes with few examples and tiny details. Hence, the modeling of contextual information is even more important. However, the performance of moment invariants as a feature descriptor alone is still interesting. In comparison with other local features without context modeling we are able to outperform the best setup of [22] in terms of precision by almost 7 percentage points. Our performance with respect to recall is only slightly worse. An overview over all results can be found in Table 2. We are also able to compete

Table 2. Quantitative results for the Oakland 3D Point Cloud Dataset [12]: the measures are averaged over all five classes. Misses for the subtle class wire have a negative effect on our overall recall in comparison with MRF-based approaches.

average	Without context		Context-based			
	[22]	Ours	[13]	[10]	[12]	Ours
Precision	0.611	**0.678**	0.566	0.704	0.730	**0.736**
Recall	**0.739**	0.710	0.807	0.866	**0.902**	0.798
F1 Score	0.623	**0.655**	0.587	0.757	**0.778**	0.695

(a) Ground-truth   (b) Ours

Fig. 5. Qualitative result for a partial view of the Oakland 3D Point Cloud Dataset [12] with visible classes facade, vegetation, pole and **ground**. Areas with low spatial density tend to be confused with the class pole because of their structural appearance. (Color figure online)

with state-of-the-art results which include context modeling. The recall for all classes on average is worse than the MRF methods because of false negatives for the class wire. Especially [12], with its highly optimized learning procedure is performing better with repsect to subtle structures. However, in terms of precision and overall performance our proposed method is very well suited for this task. A comparison of our result with the ground-truth can be found in Fig. 5.

6   Conclusions

In this paper, we showed how 3D moment invariants and contextual cues can be combined for the semantic segmentation of outdoor areas. With this approach 3D point clouds created by terrestrial LiDAR scanners can be analyzed in a fully automatic manner. We proposed an iterative classification framework based on powerful local feature descriptors that are invariant to many transformations in 3D space. Furthermore, we were able to overcome the drawback of RDFs for the task of semantic segmentation which often leads to scattered classification results due to its individual classification scheme. Experiments show its power for tasks like the segmentation of individual trees and the analysis of whole forestal or urban areas with multiple classes.

References

1. Breiman, L.: Random forests. Mach. Learn. **45**(1), 5–32 (2001)
2. Engel, J., Schöps, T., Cremers, D.: LSD-SLAM: large-scale direct monocular SLAM. In: Fleet, D., Pajdla, T., Schiele, B., Tuytelaars, T. (eds.) ECCV 2014. LNCS, vol. 8690, pp. 834–849. Springer, Cham (2014). doi:10.1007/978-3-319-10605-2_54
3. Fröhlich, B., Rodner, E., Denzler, J.: Semantic segmentation with millions of features: integrating multiple cues in a combined random forest approach. In: Lee, K.M., Matsushita, Y., Rehg, J.M., Hu, Z. (eds.) ACCV 2012. LNCS, vol. 7724, pp. 218–231. Springer, Heidelberg (2013). doi:10.1007/978-3-642-37331-2_17

4. Frome, A., Huber, D., Kolluri, R., Bülow, T., Malik, J.: Recognizing objects in range data using regional point descriptors. In: Pajdla, T., Matas, J. (eds.) ECCV 2004. LNCS, vol. 3023, pp. 224–237. Springer, Heidelberg (2004). doi:10.1007/ 978-3-540-24672-5_18
5. Hackel, T., Wegner, J.D., Schindler, K.: Contour detection in unstructured 3D point clouds. In: IEEE International Conference on Computer Vision and Pattern Recognition, pp. 1610–1618 (2016)
6. Hackenberg, J., Spiecker, H., Claders, K., Disney, M., Raumonen, P.: Simpletree - an efficient open source tool to build tree models from TLS clouds. Forests **6**(11), 4245–4294 (2015)
7. Krückhans, M.: Ein Detektor für Ornamente auf Gebäudefassaden auf Basis des histogram-of-oriented-gradients- Operators, Master's thesis. Rheinische Friedrich-Wilhelms-Universitt Bonn (2010)
8. Lang, D., Friedmann, S., Paulus, D.: Semantic 3D octree maps based on conditional random fields. In: IAPR International Conference on Machine Vision Applications, pp. 185–188 (2013)
9. Lo, C.H., Don, H.S.: 3-D moment forms: their construction and application to object identification and positioning. IEEE Trans. Pattern Anal. Mach. Intell. **11**(10), 1053–1064 (1989)
10. Lu, Y., Rasmussen, C.: Simplified Markov random fields for efficient semantic labeling of 3D point clouds. In: IEEE/RSJ International Conference on Intelligent Robots and Systems, pp. 2690–2697 (2012)
11. Montillo, A., Shotton, J., Winn, J., Iglesias, J.E., Metaxas, D., Criminisi, A.: Entangled decision forests and their application for semantic segmentation of CT images. In: Székely, G., Hahn, H.K. (eds.) IPMI 2011. LNCS, vol. 6801, pp. 184–196. Springer, Heidelberg (2011). doi:10.1007/978-3-642-22092-0_16
12. Munoz, D., Bagnell, J.A., Vandapel, N., Hebert, M.: Contextual classification with functional max-margin Markov networks. In: IEEE International Conference on Computer Vision and Pattern Recognition, pp. 975–982 (2009)
13. Munoz, D., Vandapel, N., Hebert, M.: Onboard contextual classification of 3-D point clouds with learned high-order Markov random fields. In: IEEE International Conference on Robotics and Automation, pp. 2009–2016 (2009)
14. Schoeler, M., Papon, J., Wörgötter, F.: Constrained planar cuts - object partitioning for point clouds. In: IEEE International Conference on Computer Vision and Pattern Recognition, pp. 5207–5215 (2015)
15. Shelhamer, E., Long, J., Darrell, T.: Fully convolutional networks for semantic segmentation. IEEE Trans. Pattern Anal. Mach. Intell. **39**, 640–651 (2017)
16. Shotton, J., Johnson, M., Cipolla, R.: Semantic texton forests for image categorization and segmentation. In: IEEE Conference on Computer Vision and Pattern Recognition, pp. 1–8 (2008)
17. Tombari, F., Salti, S., Stefano, L.: Unique signatures of histograms for local surface description. In: Daniilidis, K., Maragos, P., Paragios, N. (eds.) ECCV 2010. LNCS, vol. 6313, pp. 356–369. Springer, Heidelberg (2010). doi:10.1007/ 978-3-642-15558-1_26
18. Tombari, F., Stefano, L.D., Giardino, S.: Online learning for automatic segmentaton of 3D data. In: IEEE/RSJ International Conference on Intelligent Robots and Systems, pp. 4857–4864 (2011)
19. Trochta, J., Krůček, M., Král, K.: 3D forest. http://www.3dforest.eu/. Accessed 07 Mar 2017

20. Trummer, M., Süße, H., Denzler, J.: Coarse registration of 3D surface triangulations based on moment invariants with applications to object alignment and identification. In: IEEE International Conference on Computer Vision, pp. 1273–1279 (2009)
21. Tu, Z., Bai, X.: Auto-context and its application to high-level vision tasks and 3d brain image segmentation. IEEE Trans. Pattern Anal. Mach. Intell. **32**(10), 1744–1757 (2010)
22. Weinmann, M., Jutzi, B., Mallet, C.: Feature relevance assessment for the semantic interpretation of 3D point cloud data. In: ISPRS Annals of Photgrammetry, Remote Sensing and Spatial Information Science, vol. II-5/W2, pp. 313–318 (2013)
23. Xiong, X., Munoz, D., Bagnell, J.A., Hebert, M.: 3-D scene analysis via sequenced prediction over points and regions. In: IEEE International Conference on Robotics and Automation, pp. 2609–2616 (2011)
24. Xu, D., Li, H.: 3-D surface moment invariants. In: International Conference on Pattern Recognition, pp. 173–176 (2006)

Neuron Pruning for Compressing Deep Networks Using Maxout Architectures

Fernando Moya Rueda[✉], Rene Grzeszick, and Gernot A. Fink

Department of Computer Science, TU Dortmund University, Dortmund, Germany
fernando.moya@tu-dortmund.de

Abstract. This paper presents an efficient and robust approach for reducing the size of deep neural networks by pruning entire neurons. It exploits maxout units for combining neurons into more complex convex functions and it makes use of a local relevance measurement that ranks neurons according to their activation on the training set for pruning them. Additionally, a parameter reduction comparison between neuron and weight pruning is shown. It will be empirically shown that the proposed neuron pruning reduces the number of parameters dramatically. The evaluation is performed on two tasks, the MNIST handwritten digit recognition and the LFW face verification, using a LeNet-5 and a VGG16 network architecture. The network size is reduced by up to 74% and 61%, respectively, without affecting the network's performance. The main advantage of neuron pruning is its direct influence on the size of the network architecture. Furthermore, it will be shown that neuron pruning can be combined with subsequent weight pruning, reducing the size of the LeNet-5 and VGG16 up to 92% and 80% respectively.

1 Introduction

Having today available a big number of large-scale datasets and powerful GPUs, deep neural networks have become the state-of-the-art in many computer vision, and speech recognition tasks [1,6,10]. They achieve high performance in many applications, e.g., scene and object recognition, object detection, scene parsing, face recognition, and medical imaging. However, they utilize high computational resources coming along with high memory cost [13]. For example, AlexNet and DeepFace have around 60M and 120M parameters, respectively [7]. Furthermore, they consume significant energy making their application on embedded devices difficult [7]. Containing a huge amount of parameters, deep neural networks may also be subject to over-parametrization. Thus, there could exist redundancies, and their generalization is not proper [12]. In general, networks with a small number of parameters generalize better extracting the important information of the data, rather than over-parametrized networks. Nevertheless, smaller networks are harder to train, since they are sensible to initialization [13].

Designing a network, i.e., setting the number of layers, neurons per layer, and parameters is typically still a "trial and error" process. Mostly, it depends on

© Springer International Publishing AG 2017
V. Roth and T. Vetter (Eds.): GCPR 2017, LNCS 10496, pp. 177–188, 2017.
DOI: 10.1007/978-3-319-66709-6_15

experience [1]. Moreover, training does not affect the structure of the network [8]. Several attempts have been developed for reducing the effect of the huge number of parameters, e.g., dropout [10], creating an optimal-sized network by adding additional regularizers, or pruning the network parameters [1,12,17]. The latter ones attempt to either remove edges or complete neurons from a network. However, most of these approaches require an expensive comparison of all neurons in the network or additional and expensive post-processing, e.g., the computation of the network's Hessian.

We propose an efficient and robust method for neuron pruning based on a local decision for reducing the number of parameters in a deep neural network. We will empirically show that pruning neurons rather than weights is essential for reducing the size of a neural network at runtime. The proposed approach for pruning neurons is based on the good performance of maxout units [5], which were developed for boosting the impact of dropout in training, and on their capacity to combine neurons for approximating more complex functions. It is assumed that redundancies typically exist in a neural network, so they also exist in a maxout unit, which combines the output of multiple neurons. Thus, pruning can be performed in a very local approach based on a single maxout unit.

The remainder of the paper is structured as follows: Sect. 2 will discuss the related work in the field of parameter pruning for deep networks. In Sects. 3 and 4, the maxout approach will be reviewed and an approach for pruning neurons will be introduced. Experiments on two datasets, the MNIST digits dataset and the labeled faces in the wild dataset, will be shown in Sect. 5. Face recognition has been chosen as an application that is of special interest for embedded devices such as smartphones. The last section presents a short conclusion.

2   Related Work

Though deep neural networks are very powerful, they are known to be over-parametrized, possessing millions of parameters [13]. This over-parametrization may cause performance deficits, e.g., poor generalization, overfitting, slow testing time, and enormous energy and memory consumption [3,7,8,12]. Therefore, reducing the size of the network by removing unimportant parameters, or designing optimal-sized networks becomes imperative. For those purposes, different attempts have been developed. These attempts can be grouped in constructive and destructive methods.

In constructive methods, neurons or layers are added to a trained shallow neural network. For example, in [17] a very deep convolutional neural network (CNN) is trained by continuously adding convolutional layers to an initial CNN of 11 layers for obtaining a better performance. However, the initial shallow networks must be properly trained, as the network can otherwise get stuck into a local optimum. Moreover, as the idea is to improve the network's performance by adding layers and neurons, the network's size increases, and redundancies could be introduced into the network.

In destructive methods, non-relevant neurons (neuron pruning) and/or parameters (weights pruning) of an initial deep neural network are removed, while maintaining its behaviour. The authors in [12, 14] started the concept of pruning neural networks, both using a sort of relevance measure. In [12], parameters, with the smallest relevance in the network, which is computed by using the Hessian of the loss function, are deleted. In [14], complete neurons are deleted by using a relevance measurement based on the difference of the network's performance with and without the neuron. Nevertheless, especially with today's very deep neural networks with millions of parameters, computing the relevance of each neuron or parameter demands very high computational resources.

Different from the relevance measure methods, the authors in [7, 8] prune weights by thresholding them. Afterwards, the network is re-trained for compensating the lost connections. One of the most prominent destructive methods is Deep Compression [7]. The authors reduced the storage required for a deep CNN by a factor of 35 and 49. They used a combination of three steps: weight pruning, weight quantization and Huffman coding. First, weight pruning is applied by thresholding the weights and thus setting them to zero. The remaining weights are then quantized, which reduces the number of bits for representing weights. Finally, a Huffman coding is applied. However, the networks are currently de-compressed for inference.

Recently, the authors in [1] determined the best number of parameters, by using a regularizer while training the network. The regularizer forces all the weights of single neurons to be zero. For testing, these dead neurons are removed from the network. Nevertheless, additional hyper-parameters must be determined for the regularization. The authors in [3] reduced the number of parameters to be learned by factorizing the weight matrices as a low rank product of two matrices: a static, and a dynamic matrix. First, they trained the static matrices as a general dictionary, obtaining a prior knowledge of the smoothness structures that are expected to be seen. Second, they fine-tuned the dynamic matrix, which are the weights to be learned.

Comparing the approaches, the destructive methods are more popular than the constructive ones as the networks are often easier to train. Good compression results are achieved by the deep compression approach in [7]. However, pruning weights has the disadvantage of rarely removing neurons from the network architecture. To make this clear, we show in Fig. 1 the relation between the proportion of remaining neurons in the network versus the proportion of pruned weights using the LeNet-5 [11] and the VGG16 [16] as examples. It clearly shows that neurons only get pruned at a very high compression ratio, which typically influences the networks performance. Thus, thresholding parameters allows for compressing a network but does not influence the size of the architecture. At runtime a sparse matrix library would be required, which efficiently evaluates the compressed network. Otherwise, the network must be de-compressed for inference. The zeroed weights are again stored in the memory, as in [7], which generates a waste in memory consumption as well as computational power.

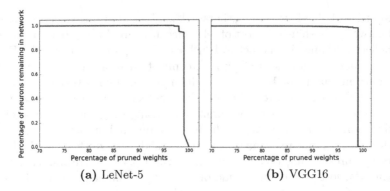

(a) LeNet-5   **(b)** VGG16

Fig. 1. Percentage neurons remaining in network vs percentage of pruned weights for a LeNet-5 trained for digit recognition and for a VGG16 trained for face recognition (for details see Sect. 5).

3   Fundamentals

The proposed approach builds on a maxout architecture [5] for pruning the neural networks in a destructive manner. A maxout layer can be considered as a cross-channel pooling operation, performing a max operation between k adjacent neurons. These layers were designed to boost the model's averaging ability of dropout [10], thought for preventing overfitting, and to improve the optimization. Given an input layer $X = [x_0, x_1, x_2, \ldots, x_N]$ with N neurons, a maxout layer computes:

$$h(X) = \max[x_{jk+0}, x_{jk+1}, x_{jk+2}, \ldots, x_{jk+(k-1)}] \quad \forall j \in [0, N/k - 1], \quad (1)$$

where k is the number of neurons that are combined into a single maxout unit.

As the authors in [5] show, a maxout unit is a universal approximator. It combines k single neurons implementing a piecewiese linear function that can approximate arbitrary convex functions. So, in theory, the maximum of several neurons is able to approximate a more complex neuron. Moreover, the maxout unit becomes a sort of an activation function, replacing other activation functions, but with a factor of k smaller number of parameters. For example, two linear functions can implement a ReLU function, or five different linear functions can implement an approximation of a quadratic one, as shown in [5].

4   Compressing Networks with Maxout Architectures

The idea of the proposed approach is to use the maxout units and their model selection abilities for pruning entire neurons from an architecture without expensive processing. Thus, reducing the size and the memory consumption of a deep network. In some cases, the performance of the network may even increase as redundancies get reduced or eliminated.

Following the assumption that redundancies exist in a deep neural network, it is assumed that if a network contains a maxout layer, redundancies will, also, exist in the maxout units. This is a valid assumption, since dropout and other regularization approaches cause the learn process to create different paths through the deep network, which yield similar outputs [5]. Using this premise, a reduction of the number of neurons in a maxout layer can be done without an expensive relevance measurement.

4.1 Neuron Pruning

For reducing the size of a CNN using maxout units, an iterative process is followed. First, a CNN with a maxout layer is trained. This maxout layer performs a max function among k adjacent neurons, reducing the amount of weights connecting with the next layer by a factor of k. So, placing this maxout layer after the one with the highest number of weights would be advisable. Second, by counting the number of times neurons become the maximal value in each maxout unit when computing a forward pass over the training dataset, the least active neurons of each maxout unit are removed from the network. Their effects are negligible with respect to other neurons. Third, the remaining neurons of the CNN are re-trained. After re-training, the process is repeated; in this case, the maxout layer performs a max function among $k-1$ neurons, and so on. Figure 2 shows an example for $k = 4$.

In comparison with [14], pruning neurons takes place locally, since relevance values are not computed depending on the network's output for each single neuron. The pruning in maxout architectures is therefore more feasible for very large networks with millions of parameters.

4.2 Weight Pruning

Having reduced the number of parameters in the network by pruning neurons from the maxout units of the network, further compression operations can be performed. Following the approach in [7,8], connections (weights) can be pruned in an additional processing step. Based on thresholding, edges with lower value than a threshold are set to zero. Thus, learning which connections are important and deleting the unimportant ones. By this weight pruning, the network

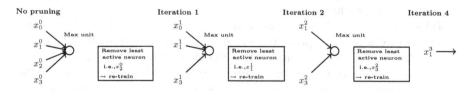

Fig. 2. Neuron pruning process for $k = 4$ inputs per maxout unit. x_a^b represents a neuron with 'a' the neuron index and 'b' the iteration.

becomes a sparse network. For pruning weights, a three-step procedure is followed, as proposed in [7,8]. Given the network that has been compressed by the proposed neuron pruning, the important connections are learned based on a global threshold. The threshold can be set such that as many connections as possible are removed without deteriorating the performance on a validation set. Second, weights below this threshold are deleted; that is, weights are set to zero. Third, the network is re-trained, learning the final weights.

5   Evaluation

An evaluation of both neuron and weight pruning is carried out for two different tasks: handwritten digit recognition, MNIST dataset [11], and face verification, LFW dataset [9]. The later is of special interest for embedded domains, e.g., in mobile phones. In general, the performance of the networks is evaluated with a varying percentage of pruned weights: after applying maxout, when pruning several neurons from the maxout units, and finally after applying additional weight pruning. While in the first task a very small LeNet-5 architecture is compressed, in the second task a large VGG16 architecture is compressed.

For the experiments, we chose $k = 4$ for the size of the maxout units as it allows for a fairly good compression and does not reduce the descriptiveness of the network compared to a network without maxout units. The neurons are then iteratively pruned from the maxout units and the network is re-trained after each pruning step.

5.1   Handwritten Digit Recognition

For the digit-recognition task, two networks, using the LeNet-5 architecture [11] with two convolutional layers, a fully connected layer and a softmax layer as a classificator, were trained. One network contains a maxout layer after the fully connected layer (LeNet-MFC), while the other has a maxout layer after the last convolutional layer (LeNet-MC). An iterative training following the steps in Sect. 4.1 is executed using the MNIST dataset [11]. This dataset consists of 60000 handwritten-digit images (of size $[28 \times 28]$) for training and 10000 images for testing. We used stochastic gradient descent (SGD) with a momentum of 0.9, weight decay of 5×10^{-4} with inverse decay, a base learning rate of 0.01 that is iteratively reduced and a batch size of 64 for training. The networks were trained for 10000 iterations.

Table 1 shows the classification accuracy for both networks with different fully connected layer sizes, with and without maxout (after the fully connected layer or the last convolutional layer). Pruning of one up to three neurons is evaluated. It shows also the percentage of pruned weights which do not remain in the network's architecture, denoted by $p.w.\%$. In general, for both networks when using maxout and pruning neurons, the accuracy is maintained. The slight deviations of the accuracies of both networks with respect to the original networks

Table 1. Accuracies in [%] and pruned weight's proportions (p.w.%) in [%] for LeNet-5 with Maxout layer ($k = 4$) after last fully connected layer (LeNet-MFC) and last convolutional layer (LeNet-MC).

Network		No maxout	No prun		1 neuron prun.		2 neuron prun.		3 neuron prun.	
Type	FC size	Acc%	Acc%	p.w.%	Acc%	p.w.%	Acc%	p.w.%	Acc%	p.w.%
LeNet-MFC	128	98.1	99.1	0.74	99.1	22.6	99.1	40.4	99.1	60.2
	256	98.3	99.2	0.82	99.2	22.8	99.2	44.8	99.0	66.8
	512	99.1	99.2	0.87	99.2	24.1	99.2	47.4	**99.1**	**70.7**
LeNet-MC	128	98.1	99.2	59.4	99.2	64.2	99.2	69.1	99.0	73.9
	256	98.3	99.0	65.9	99.2	68.6	99.3	71.3	99.0	73.9
	512	99.1	99.2	69.7	99.3	71.1	**99.3**	**72.6**	**99.3**	**74.0**

are not significant based on a randomization test [15]. Moreover, the number of weights are considerably reduced with up to 70% for LeNet-MFC and 74% for LeNet-MC. However, this reduction changes with respect to the position of the maxout layer. In LeNet-MFC, each neuron pruning step reduces the number of weights by 19.8%, because the neurons are pruned from the fully connected layer, which has the largest number of weights in the network. Besides, the maxout layer does not provide a considerable reduction, since it reduces the size of the softmax layer that has less number of weights compared with the other layers. In contrast, the weight reduction in LeNet-MC due to neuron pruning is just 1.4% per step, and it comes mostly from the maxout layer. In this case, the maxout layer reduces the fully connected layer instead, and the neurons are pruned from the last convolutional layer. However, in the last convolutional layer the number of weights is negligible.

Following the neuron pruning, additional weight pruning, as discussed in Sect. 4.2, can be applied. As mentioned in [8], neurons could also be pruned from the network if all their input weights are zero; that is, the neuron can be considered as *dead*. So, the number of neurons, and thus the number of weights, could be considerably reduced if a proper threshold is used. Nevertheless, analyzing the proportion of dead neurons versus the proportion of pruned weights, neurons do not become *dead* before pruning more than 98% of the weights, see Fig. 1(b). Consequently, weight pruning rarely prunes neurons. Thus, zeroed weights remain in the network as part of the neurons and the network's architecture does not change so that a sparse representation would be required at runtime [7]. However, assuming the usage of such a representation and for reducing storage size of the network, additional weight pruning is applied to both networks. As a basis, we use the networks after pruning three out of four neurons in the maxout units. The results in Table 2 show that the accuracy will not drop if less than 70% of the weights are thresholded. So, a total compression rate of **91%** for LeNet-MFC and **92%** for LeNet-MC, of pruned and zeroed weights, can be reached.

Table 2. Accuracies in [%] for both networks, after pruning three neurons out of four, under different proportions of pruned weights.

Network		Proportions in [%] of pruned weights								
Type	FC size	0	10	30	50	60	70	80	90	98
LeNet-MFC	128	99.0	99.0	99.0	99.0	99.0	**99.0**	98.9	98.3	82.1
	256	99.3	99.3	99.3	99.3	**99.3**	99.2	99.2	98.9	91.0
	512	99.3	99.3	99.3	99.3	99.3	**99.3**	99.2	99.1	92.2
LeNet-MC	128	99.2	99.2	99.2	99.2	99.1	99.1	98.9	97.8	26.5
	256	99.3	99.3	99.3	99.2	99.2	99.1	98.9	96.3	55.3
	512	99.2	99.2	99.2	99.2	99.2	**99.2**	99.0	97.4	60.8

5.2 Face Verification

The neuron pruning was also carried out for a larger network for the purpose of face verification. The task is to verify whether two face-images portray the same person or not. For that purpose, the VGG16 network [16] was utilized, using The Visual Geometry Group Face Dataset (VGG face-dataset) as a training-dataset. This dataset is a large collection of face-images containing 2.6 million face-images from 2622 identities. It does not contain overlapping identities with standard benchmark datasets (LFW, YFT), so it is suitable for training. The VGG16 network, configuration D in [16], is a deep CNN with 16 layers: 13 convolutional layer, two fully connected layers, and a softmax layer. Analogous to the previous LeNet configurations, two configuration of VGG16 are used, in which a maxout network with $k = 4$ is added after the first fully connected layer ($fc6$), called VGG16-MFC, and after the last convolutional layer ($conv\_5$), called VGG16-MC, see Fig. 3. The positions of the maxout layers are set after the layers with the most quantity of weights. Since, the connections between $conv\_5$ and $fc6$ have 70.1% of the total amount of weights in the network and the connections between $fc6$ and $fc7$ have an additional 11.6% of the network's weights. The last three fully connected layers were fined-tuned for both networks. In the case of VGG16-MC, the $conv\_5$ was also fine-tuned. We used SGD with a momentum of 0.9, weight decay of 5×10^{-4}, three learning rates $[10^{-2}, 10^{-3}, 10^{-4}]$, as [16], and a batch size of 128.

The network was tested following the procedure in [16], but using the restricted configuration of The Labeled Faces in the Wild (LFW) [9]. The LFW dataset is a standard benchmark dataset for face verification. It contains 13233 face-images from 5749 identities extracted from the Internet. Faces in images were detected using the Viola-Jones face detector [9]. Faces are roughly centered, contain lesser noise but larger bounding-box than the ones in the VGG dataset. Besides, the Bray-Curtis distance (BC; [2]) was used instead of the Euclidean distance. Since, the BC distance works better for high-dimensional vectors in comparison with the Euclidean and the L1 distances [18]. The BC distance was measured between the descriptors of two face-images from a set

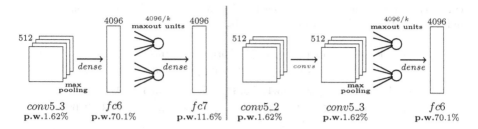

Fig. 3. Comparison of two architectural approaches for placing the maxout units: (left) VGG16-MFC, (right) VGG16-MC. The weight proportions p.w.% per layer are also shown.

Table 3. EER in [%] and pruned weight's proportions for the VGG16 with maxout layer ($k = 4$) after the first fully connected layer (VGG16-MFC) and after the last convolutional layer (VGG16-MC).

Network	No maxout	No prun		1 neuron prun.		2 neuron prun.		3 neuron prun.	
Type	EER%	EER%	p.w.%	EER%	p.w.%	EER%	p.w.%	EER%	p.w.%
VGG16-MFC	3.7	3.33	8.68	**2.83**	26.39	**2.76**	44.11	**2.66**	**61.82**
VGG16-MC	3.7	3.7	53.15	3.36	53.56	3.36	53.96	**3.23**	**54.37**

of 3000 matched and 3000 non-matched pairs of images. Different from [10,16], the feature vectors from the crops of the image's corners were not utilized for computing the final descriptor, but only the crops from the image's centers. If the BC distance is smaller than a threshold, then the two images portray the same identity. The Equal Error Rate (EER) [4,16] was used as the metric, which is defined as the value where the False Acceptance Rate (FAR), and the False Rejection Rate (FRR) are equal.

Table 3 shows the EER for networks without a maxout layer and with a maxout layer with $k = 4$, as well as the results for pruning from one up to three neurons from each maxout unit. Similar to the previous results, neurons are pruned, and consequently weights are reduced, from the networks without affecting their performance negatively. In fact, the EER decreases by 1% and 0.47% for the VGG16-MFC and the VGG16-MC respectively. It is assumed that this improvement is produced by the elimination of redundancies in the maxout units. Based on a randomization test, the improvement in the VGG16-MFC is highly significant with $p = 0.0026$ [15].

The weight reduction changes depending on the position of the maxout layer and on the layer where neurons are pruned in the network. In VGG16-MFC, neurons are pruned from the largest layer in the network $fc6$ reducing the number of weights by 17.7% per each neuron pruning step. Moreover, the maxout layer reduces directly the size of the second largest layer $fc7$. In VGG16-MC on the contrary, neuron pruning does not affect considerably the size of the network, since it reduces a small layer $conv5$ compared to $fc6$. The weight reduction comes precisely from the maxout layer, which reduces the size of $fc6$. There is

Table 4. EER in [%] for both VGG16 networks, after pruning three out of four neurons, under different proportions of pruned weights.

Network	Proportions in [%] of pruned weights								
Type	0	10	30	50	60	70	80	90	98
VGG16-MFC	2.66	2.90	3.4	**3.34**	3.5	4.0	4.53	50.00	50.00
VGG16-MC	3.26	3.77	**3.93**	4.30	5.40	8.3	35.47	47.63	50.00

a difference of 7.45% between the weight reduction for both networks, since the size of the layer $fc7$ is never changed in VGG16-MC.

Additional to neuron pruning, weights from both networks were thresholded after pruning three out of four neurons in the maxout units with the results shown in Table 4. The network's performance will be, deeply, affected if more than 50% for the VGG16-MFC and 30% for the VGG16-MC of the weights are pruned. Nevertheless, a total compression rate of 80.1% for VGG16-MFC and 68% for VGG16-MC without performance deterioration can be reached.

6   Conclusion

We have presented an efficient approach for reducing the size of deep neural networks. This approach prunes entire neurons and thus reduces the number of weights in neural networks. It uses maxout units for combining k single neurons into complex ones. A maxout layer reduces the number of weights between two adjacent layers by k. By using these maxout units, the network's performance is not negatively affected, since they boost the dropout benefits reducing redundancies in the network. Within these maxout units, neurons are pruned based on a local and non-expensive relevance measure. This relevance measure depends on the number of times neurons are maximal for each of the k adjacent input-neurons per maxout unit. It differs from previous relevance measures, because it does not depend on the overall network's performance with and without individual neurons [14]. In general, this approach does not require expensive post-processing, only a single re-training after pruning. The performance of this reduction approach depends strongly on the position of the maxout layer in the network. As inputs from maxout units are the neurons to be pruned, it is advisable to place the maxout units after the largest layer in the network, because neurons in this layer have large numbers of weights compared with neurons in other layers. So, pruning these neurons out of the network is favorable.

By comparing the number of pruned neurons and network's performances between the aforementioned approach and weight pruning, the last one does not delete entire neurons, but rather sets weights to zero. Therefore, the architecture's size is only implicitly reduced, and the memory footprint remains equal without a sparse representation. The proposed approach allows to reduce a network's size by 61–74% on an architectural level and without affecting the network's performance. Assuming a sparse representation, a combination of the proposed neuron pruning with additional weight pruning allows for reducing the size of a network by up to 92%.

Acknowledgment. This work has been supported by the German Research Foundation (DFG) within project Fi799/9-1 ('Partially Supervised Learning of Models for Visual Scene Recognition').

References

1. Alvarez, J.M., Salzmann, M.: Learning the number of neurons in deep networks. In: Advances in Neural Information Processing Systems, pp. 2262–2270 (2016)
2. Bray, J.R., Curtis, J.T.: An ordination of the upland forest communities of southern wisconsin. In: Ecological monographs, vol. 27, pp. 325–349. Wiley Online Library (1957)
3. Denil, M., Shakibi, B., Dinh, L., Ranzato, M., de Freitas, N.: Predicting parameters in deep learning. CoRR abs/1306.0543 (2013). http://arxiv.org/abs/1306.0543
4. Giot, R., El-Abed, M., Rosenberger, C.: Fast computation of the performance evaluation of biometric systems: application to multibiometrics. In: Future Generation Computer Systems, vol. 29, pp. 788–799. Elsevier (2013)
5. Goodfellow, I.J., Warde-Farley, D., Mirza, M., Courville, A.C., Bengio, Y.: Maxout Networks. In: ICML (3), vol. 28, pp. 1319–1327 (2013)
6. Grzeszick, R., Sudholt, S., Fink, G.A.: Optimistic and pessimistic neural networks for scene and object recognition. CoRR abs/1609.07982 (2016). http://arxiv.org/abs/1609.07982
7. Han, S., Mao, H., Dally, W.J.: Deep compression: compressing deep neural network with pruning, trained quantization and huffman coding. CoRR abs/1510.00149 (2015). http://arxiv.org/abs/1510.00149
8. Han, S., Pool, J., Tran, J., Dally, W.J.: Learning both weights and connections for efficient neural networks. CoRR abs/1506.02626 (2015). http://arxiv.org/abs/1506.02626
9. Huang, G.B., Ramesh, M., Berg, T., Learned-Miller, E.: Labeled faces in the wild: a database for studying face recognition in unconstrained environments. Technical Report, pp. 07–49. University of Massachusetts, Amherst, October 2007
10. Krizhevsky, A., Sutskever, I., Hinton, G.E.: Imagenet classification with deep convolutional neural networks. In: Advances in neural information processing systems, pp. 1097–1105 (2012)
11. LeCun, Y., Bottou, L., Bengio, Y., Haffner, P.: Gradient-based learning applied to document recognition. Proc. IEEE **86**(11), 2278–2324 (1998)
12. LeCun, Y., Denker, J.S., Solla, S.A., Howard, R.E., Jackel, L.D.: Optimal brain damage. In: Advances in Neural Information Processing Systems, vol. 2, pp. 598–605. Morgan-Kaufmann (1989). http://papers.nips.cc/paper/250-optimal-brain-damage.pdf
13. Liu, B., Wang, M., Foroosh, H., Tappen, M., Pensky, M.: Sparse convolutional neural networks. In: Proceedings of the IEEE Conference on Computer Vision and Pattern Recognition, pp. 806–814 (2015)
14. Mozer, M.C., Smolensky, P.: Skeletonization: a technique for trimming the fat from a network via relevance assessment. In: Advances in Neural Information Processing Systems, pp. 107–115 (1989)

15. Ojala, M., Garriga, G.C.: Permutation tests for studying classifier performance. J. Mach. Learn. Res. **11**, 1833–1863 (2010)
16. Parkhi, O.M., Vedaldi, A., Zisserman, A.: Deep face recognition. In: British Machine Vision Conference (2015)
17. Simonyan, K., Zisserman, A.: Very Deep Convolutional Networks for Large-Scale Image Recognition. CoRR abs/1409.1 (2014)
18. Sudholt, S., Fink, G.A.: A modified isomap approach to manifold learning in word spotting. In: Gall, J., Gehler, P., Leibe, B. (eds.) GCPR 2015. LNCS, vol. 9358, pp. 529–539. Springer, Cham (2015). doi:10.1007/978-3-319-24947-6_44

A Primal Dual Network for Low-Level Vision Problems

Christoph Vogel[1(✉)] and Thomas Pock[1,2]

[1] Graz University of Technology, Graz, Austria
christoph.vogel@icg.tugraz.at
[2] AIT Austrian Institute of Technology, Vienna, Austria

Abstract. In the past, classic energy optimization techniques were the driving force in many innovations and are a building block for almost any problem in computer vision. Efficient algorithms are mandatory to achieve real-time processing, needed in many applications like autonomous driving. However, energy models - even if designed by human experts - might never be able to fully capture the complexity of natural scenes and images. Similar to optimization techniques, Deep Learning has changed the landscape of computer vision in recent years and has helped to push the performance of many models to never experienced heights. Our idea of a *primal-dual network* is to combine the structure of regular energy optimization techniques, in particular of first order methods, with the flexibility of Deep Learning to adapt to the statistics of the input data.

1 Introduction

Classic energy optimization techniques, like dynamic programming, graph-cut, belief propagation, dual decomposition and first-order methods [8,16,17,25,26] paved the way for several milestones of computer vision. This led to efficient algorithms for stereo [23], optical flow [3] and image editing [38], to name only a few examples. However, there is reason to believe that energy based models like Potts model [48], Total Variation (TV) [39], general Markov-Random-Fields (MRF) [27] or even any expert designed energy formulation will never be able to fully capture the complexity of natural images.

More recently, convolutional neural networks (CNN), omnipresent for classical machine learning problems like object detection and image classification [40], also start to surpass energy based models for more and more low-level vision tasks *e.g.* [14,15].

Our idea is to unify both fields. Relying on the structure of regular energy optimization algorithms we seek to utilize the capability of Deep Learning (DL) to adapt to the statistics of data, to learn a generalized optimization algorithm.

Electronic supplementary material The online version of this chapter (doi:10.1007/978-3-319-66709-6_16) contains supplementary material, which is available to authorized users.

© Springer International Publishing AG 2017
V. Roth and T. Vetter (Eds.): GCPR 2017, LNCS 10496, pp. 189–202, 2017.
DOI: 10.1007/978-3-319-66709-6_16

In other words, we do not predefine the energy but rather provide a specific algorithmic structure to generate an output for a certain task. This paper aims to take a step towards this ambitious goal.

To provide this algorithmic framework we believe that first order (FO)-methods are the most appropriate of the optimization algorithms mentioned. FO-methods possess a structure that can be generalized, are inherently parallel and simple enough to be implemented in neural network. As an example for this class of algorithms, we utilize the algorithm of Chambolle and Pock [8], which is designed for general non-smooth problems and can be applied for many tasks in computer vision.

Not only the high memory consumption of backpropagation limit the number of iterations the network can perform, such that we can only expect an approximate solution. Here, machine learning techniques like DL can be helpful to improve the approximation quality. Our learned algorithm does not need to reserve equal capacity to all possible inputs, but can adapt its local filters to activate on the more likely and w.r.t. the approximation quality, more relevant substructures in the data. On the other hand, given the algorithmic framework to solve a specific problem, DL can potentially generalize the structure to also provide approximate solutions for related problem instances.

In a CNN, the receptive field of a neuron is limited by the size of its filters, such that the number of necessary steps to transport local information between unknowns that are not coupled directly will easily exceed the maximal possible number of iterations of a network. FO methods have essentially the same problems. Here, multigrid methods [2,4,7] can accelerate convergence. In this work we resort to a simpler strategy, which works on the same problem over multiple scales. In the encoding stage, operating from fine to coarse, a feature representation of the input is generated and used later, at the respective resolution in the inference stage. The inference phase proceeds from coarse to fine and executes several optimization steps given the upsampled output of the stage below and the features. To apply the multiscale scheme on arbitrarily sized input data, we introduce the idea of weight sharing across the different resolution levels.

The contributions of this work are threefold. At first, we train and analyze our network on known models from the TV family to obtain high-quality approximate solutions for all these models in only a fraction of time, compared to regular energy optimization. We further exploit that multi-label problems with a linearly ordered label set can be formulated as a ROF problem and solved globally optimal [5,24,35]. Our multi-scale extension allows to overcome the limited receptive field of convolutions and due to our idea of sharing weights across resolution levels we can apply our model on inputs of arbitrary size. Finally, we train our proposed network structure without the requirement to minimize a certain energy model and achieve state-of-the-art results for image denoising and competitive results for stereo estimation.

2   Related Work

Provably optimal convergence rates for different problem classes, and a low memory footprint render first-order methods [1,8,13] attractive for large-scale computer vision problems. Despite optimality, accelerating these methods further is ongoing research. These efforts include pre-conditioning [34], inertia or heavy-ball like acceleration for strongly convex problems [1,8] and lately accelerating the computation of certain proximal operators [9]. In contrast to these methods we voluntarily abandon the idea of optimality and (partially) even that of minimizing an energy. Instead we search for the best solution that can be reached in a limited and very small number of steps. We only specify the algorithmic framework, namely we follow the primal-dual method proposed in [8] that has also been applied to non-convex optimization problems [44].

Multi-grid methods [2] are a general framework to accelerate optimization and have lately been extended to non-smooth optimization problems [4,7]. In this work we resort to a simpler, less sophisticated multiscale scheme. However, apart from a coarse solution, our method also has access to higher dimensional feature maps.

First-order methods have already found their way into neural networks. Possibly the first application was proposed in the context of sparse coding [21]. Here, an unrolled and generalized implementation of the Ista algorithm [13] is shown to require less iterations to achieve a certain approximation quality than its accelerated version [1]. This framework was later extended by [46] and used for image super-resolution in [47]. [11] proposes a more general network structure in which each iteration can be interpreted as one gradient step of a certain (at each step different) energy function. Later a network that essentially implements the same idea was introduced in [50]. More recently, [37] suggest to unroll iterations of a primal-dual method for the same application and learn the step sizes and smoothness weights. In contrast, we propose a general structure that can be applied to multiple problems. We augment our network with features generated from the input that are used to generalize our projection operations and filters. Parameters of the algorithm, like the smoothness weight, are not learned and kept fixed, but treated as additional input, such that our network behaves just like a general algorithm. We provide a principled evaluation of different generalizations and finally, all of these works do not use a multiscale scheme, but always operate on the finest resolution level.

Our coarse-to-fine scheme is realized as a stacked autoencoder [45] with additional lateral connections [36]. Similar architectures have been successfully used for different applications, e.g. for semantic segmentation [29], stereo [31] and optical flow [15].

We focus our investigation on problems from the Total Variation family, and in particular on the model proposed by Rudin et al. [39]. Its relation to graph-cut [26] was analyzed in [5] and exploited in [35] to solve a certain class of multi-label problems following the construction of [24]. This links our work also to approaches that combine deep neural networks and Markov Random Fields (MRF) [28,41,51].

Our design is further inspired by the residual network architecture (Resnet) [22], which introduces skip connections to alleviate the gradient flow of the network.

3   Method

In this work we start by putting our emphasis on the well known Rudin-Osher Fatemi (ROF) [39] model for image restoration. To write the ROF model in its discretized form we partition a subset of $\mathbb{R}^d$ into equally sized and piecewise constant elements $\mathbf{i} \in I$, with $I = \{1, \ldots, N^1\} \times \ldots \times \{1, \ldots, N^d\}, N^i \in \mathbb{N}$, $\forall i \leq d$. ROF can then be written as the following non-smooth convex optimization problem:

$$\min_{\mathbf{x}} \lambda \|Q\mathbf{x}\|_{p,1} + \frac{1}{2}\|\mathbf{x} - \mathbf{f}\|_2^2, \quad \text{with} \quad \|Q\mathbf{x}\|_{p,1} = \sum_{\mathbf{i}} |(Q\mathbf{x})_{\mathbf{i},\cdot}|_p. \quad (1)$$

where $\mathbf{x}, \mathbf{f} \in \mathbb{R}^{N^1 \times \ldots \times N^d}$, with $\mathbf{f}$ being the input and $\mathbf{x}$ the regularized output. The term $\|Q\mathbf{x}\|_{p,1}$ refers to the discrete Total Variation. For $p = 1$ we obtain the anisotropic (ℓ_1) and for $p = 2$ the isotropic (ℓ_2) Total Variation. In this work, we will mainly stick to the anisotropic case $p = 1$. The free parameter $\lambda \geq 0$ controls the amount of smoothness of the solution. The linear operator $Q : \mathbb{R}^{N^1 \times \ldots \times N^d} \rightarrow \mathbb{R}^{N^1 \times \ldots \times N^d \times d}$ approximates the spatial gradient via finite differences and is defined by $(Q\mathbf{x})_{\mathbf{i},k} = \mathbf{x}_{\mathbf{i}+e_k} - \mathbf{x}_{\mathbf{i}}$, if $\mathbf{i}, \mathbf{i}+e_k \in I$ and 0 else. Here, e_k denotes the unit vector in direction k.

There are several reasons why we consider the ROF model in this paper: It is simple enough to render results interpretable for the human observer, but nevertheless has immediate applications, *e.g.* in image denoising [39] or segmentation [10].

Moreover, it defines the archtype model for more advanced TV based models that proved to be effective for other low-level vision problems such as stereo, depth-map–fusion [49] and optical flow [3]. Finally, its strong connections to max-flow/minimum-cut problems [26] make it further attractive. To solve (1), common options are first-order (FO) algorithms, *e.g.* [33] and parametric max-flow [19]. In this paper, we posit that FO-methods are a suitable and convenient representation, to be transformed into a neural network and generalized via learning. To that end, we first write (1) in its primal-dual form [8], *i.e.* we introduce (dual) variables y and replace the ℓ_1-norm by its conjugate:

$$\min_{\mathbf{x}} \max_{\mathbf{y}} \langle Q\mathbf{x}, \mathbf{y} \rangle + \frac{1}{2}\|\mathbf{x} - \mathbf{f}\|_2^2, \quad \text{s.t.} \quad \|\mathbf{y}\|_\infty \leq \lambda. \quad (2)$$

This saddle-point problem can be solved by alternating gradient ascent and descent steps on the primal and dual variables. In particular we select the algorithm proposed in [8], which for problem (2) takes the following form:

$$\begin{aligned} \mathbf{y}^{n+1} &= \text{proj}_\lambda(\mathbf{y}^n + \sigma Q(2\mathbf{x}^n - \mathbf{x}^{n-1})), \\ \mathbf{x}^{n+1} &= (1 + \tau)^{-1}(\mathbf{x}^n - \tau(Q^*\mathbf{y}^{n+1} - \mathbf{f})). \end{aligned} \quad (3)$$

Here, $\text{proj}_\lambda(\cdot) := \max(-\lambda, \min(\cdot, \lambda))$ denotes the projection into the interval $[-\lambda, \lambda]$, which is applied per component in the anisotropic case. The step sizes τ

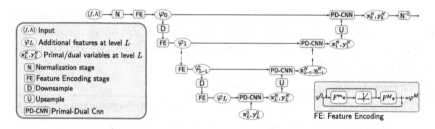

Fig. 1. Our network architecture is known as U-shaped network with lateral links. In our case to enable a multiscale framework. The network is divided in 2 stages: Feature encoding and optimization. Both are applied at each resolution, with variables initialized from the previous level.

and σ are chosen such that $(\tau\sigma) \leq \|Q\|_2^{-2}$ (*cf.* [8] for a more detailed explanation). We picked this particular primal-dual algorithm since it provides a rather flexible and general optimization framework with many applications. Lately, this specific update scheme was extended to the non-convex case [44]. This finding further confirms our choice.

3.1   Network Structure

Our network architecture is depicted in Fig. 1. Its input consists of a discretized version of $\mathbf{f}$ (*e.g.* an image) and in addition a scalar field Λ (8), encoding spatial smoothness weights between adjacent elements of $\mathbf{f}$. Thus, we always model the more general, weighted ROF problem (Sect. 3.2). After normalization (*cf.* supplementary), we identify two main stages: an encoding stage, to generate the feature representation φ and the optimization stage realizing our primal-dual network (PD-CNN). Both stages are embedded into a multiscale framework. The principal idea is to work on a low resolution version of the problem first and reuse the output at the next higher level as initialization. Between levels we use simple fixed up- and downsample operators, mean-pooling (D in Fig. 1) and nearest-neighbor interpolation (U in Fig. 1), and let the encoding and PD-CNN modules compensate potential artifacts. We initialize our variables at the coarsest resolution ($\mathbf{x}_L^0, \mathbf{y}_L^0$ in Fig. 1) with a downsampled version of $\mathbf{f}$ and set $\mathbf{y}$ to zero.

Feature Encoding. In the encoding stage, operating from fine to coarse, a feature representation, φ, of the input is created that is used later, at the respective resolution in the PD-CNN. At each resolution level we apply a small sub-network on the current feature representation to perform this task. In practice, the sub-networks are so called residual functions [22] of depth M; *i.e.* M pairs of conv-relu before a final convolution takes place. The result is then added back to the input feature vector (Fig. 1, lower right). These, so called, identity skip connections should mitigate effects of vanishing gradients and allow to train very deep architectures [22]. The resulting features φ, consist of multiple channels. Before they are used in our PD-CNN, a downsampled version of the input $\mathbf{f}$ is concatenated as an additional channel.

Optimization Network. The mentioned properties, render the primal-dual framework a good candidate to serve as template for the optimization stage of our network. Equations (4)–(7) compare our proposed PD-CNN and the original primal-dual method of (3).

Primal-Dual algorithm	Primal-Dual-CNN
$\mathbf{y}^{n+1} = \mathrm{proj}_\lambda(\mathbf{y}^n + \sigma Q(2\mathbf{x}^n - \mathbf{x}^{n-1}))$ (4)	$\mathbf{y}^{n+1} = \mathrm{proj}_{\rho(T^n*(\mathbf{y}^n, \mathbf{x}^n, \varphi))}(\mathbf{y}^n + s_\sigma^n D^n*(2\mathbf{x}^n - \mathbf{x}^{n-1}))$ (5)
$\mathbf{x}^{n+1} = (1+\tau)^{-1}(\mathbf{x}^n - \tau(Q^*\mathbf{y}^{n+1} - \mathbf{f}))$ (6)	$\mathbf{x}^{n+1} = (1 + s_\tau^n)^{-1}(\mathbf{x}^n - s_\tau^n((D^n)^* * \mathbf{y}^{n+1} - C^n * \varphi))$ (7)

First notice that all utilized operations posses an easy to compute subgradient, which directly enables backpropagation in a CNN. In our PD-CNN all linear operators of (4) and (6) are replaced by iteration dependent convolutions, expressed by the superscript n. For instance, the learned operator D is equivalent to a linear map $\hat{D} : \mathbb{R}^{N^1 \times \dots \times N^d} \to \mathbb{R}^{N^1 \times \dots \times N^d \times d}$, to replace the forward differences encoded by Q. T and C are defined in a similar manner. In the proximal step for the primal variable $\mathbf{x}$ (7), our generated feature maps replace our input $\mathbf{f}$, for which we learn a convolution operator 'C' per iteration. The feature maps also occur in our spatially adaptive projection operator. Here, the thresholds are not constant any more, but a function of the current primal and dual variables and feature encoded by 'T'. Further, we utilize a 'softplus' $\rho(\cdot) := \log(1 + \exp(\cdot))$ and employ the outcome as a direct replacement for λ in (5). Thus, the projection operations are based on local information of all variables and features. We also use different step sizes (s_σ^n, s_τ^n) per iteration, to potentially learn some form of acceleration [1,8]. The last form of generalization is achieved by allowing the network to utilize more channels during the computation than the optimization problem would suggest. In this work we donate multiple dimensions to $\mathbf{y}$ and the feature vector φ, but restrict our primal variable $\mathbf{x}$ to a single dimension. I.e. $\mathbf{y}, \varphi \in \mathbb{R}^c$ for some $c \geq d$. The linear operators are adjusted accordingly. Note that the algorithm described by (7) and (5) can still be interpreted as minimizing a (in every step) different energy. Because the convolutions 'D' are still adjoint linear operators, the saddle-point structure remains intact. Note that the residual structure is already inherent to FO-methods and, thus, also to our PD-CNN.

Parameter Sharing. The primal dual algorithm (3) has no restriction on the size of the input data $\mathbf{f}$. We want our network to have similar characteristics. To apply the network on arbitrarily sized input data, we can rely on the fact that our network is 'fully convolutional' (*e.g.* [29]). Yet, while we have no spatial restriction on the input, the number of iterations in each PD-CNN stage and the depth of our multiscale framework is limited. RNNs [20] address this problem by sharing the parameters of the convolutions in each step. In contrast, the design of our coarse-to-fine network suggests to share parameters across the different levels, not across iterations within one resolution level. This allows to adjust the number of levels to the input size after training. Here, the basic assumption is that similar problems have to be solved at each resolution and not at each step. Compared to weight-sharing across iterations, this treatment provides more freedom to the network, *e.g.*, the step size can still be variable per iteration.

It is not required to share the filter maps at the finest resolution to create this behavior. In fact, we experience better results if we exploit this freedom and only share weights across all lower levels.

Training. Recall that we treat the smoothness parameter as additional input to the network (Fig. 1) and specifically design the training data to contain a large range of values. To guide the training process further, we combine the same **f** with multiple values for λ in the training set. This enables the network to apply the correct regularization for any value in the learned range and even to extrapolate the amount of smoothing up to a certain degree (about 1.5 times the maximal trained value). To further guide the training, we optionally specify a loss at each resolution level, penalizing the difference to the downsampled ground-truth. This treatment can stabilize the training in its early stages. At least, this finding confirms our assumption that per resolution level similar problems are solved and with that our idea of sharing the parameters across resolution levels.

3.2 Extension to Related Problems (from the TV-family)

Our network was designed to be applicable to different vision problems. Here we provide some examples. We start with a more general version of the ROF model. An extension for TV-ℓ_1 can be found in the supplementary.

Weighted ROF. The problem in (1) can be extended, by allowing the smoothness weight λ to be spatially different. Analogous to (2) we directly describe the primal-dual form of the weighted ROF problem (WROF):

$$\min_{\mathbf{x}} \max_{\mathbf{y}} \langle Q\mathbf{x}, \mathbf{y}\rangle + \frac{1}{2}\|\mathbf{x} - \mathbf{f}\|_2^2, \text{ s.t. } |\mathbf{y}_{i,k}| \leq \Lambda(\mathbf{i}, k). \tag{8}$$

Thus, we can encode the weights Λ with d dimensions. The problem is now exactly in a form to be used by our proposed network from Sect. 3.1.

MRF with TV Regularization. Multi-label problems are in general NP-hard and cannot be minimized globally. An exception occurs in the case of a linearly ordered label set. If the pairwise interactions form a convex function on this set, an optimal solution can be obtained by finding a minimum cut in a higher-dimensional graph [24]. The problem can alternatively be formulated in the form of (8) [6,35]. Summarized in (9) the graph construction works by extending the domain of the problem by one dimension, the 'label-direction'. Edge-costs along this dimension are associated with the data costs for a particular label $l \in L$ and spatial position $\mathbf{i}$. All spatial weights are copied along the label-axis. The data cost at the vertices is zero, except for vertices above (below) the first (last) set of edges in label direction. Here, one uses a cost of $-\gamma$ (γ).

$$\Lambda((\mathbf{i}, l), k) := \theta_{\mathbf{i},k} \quad \text{for } k \leq d \quad \text{and} \quad \Lambda((\mathbf{i}, l), d+1) := \vartheta_{\mathbf{i},l} \quad \text{else} \tag{9}$$
$$\mathbf{f}_{(\mathbf{i},0)} := -\gamma, \quad \mathbf{f}_{(\mathbf{i},|L|)} := \gamma \quad \text{and} \quad \mathbf{f}_{(\mathbf{i},l)} := 0 \quad \text{for } 0 < l < |L|.$$

Here, we use θ and ϑ to denote edge and data costs of the original multi-label problem. The solution of the original problem is recovered as the 0-levelset of problem (9) [6].

Fig. 2. Training our stereo network. *Left*: Example scene of out training set. [18] *Right*: Truncated 3D distance function. The disparity is recovered as the 0-levelset of the distance function.

From Energy Optimization to General Models. We have motivated our network design to mimic and generalize a FO-method from convex analysis. Apart from allowing for a detailed analysis and fast approximate solutions, the construction admits to utilize the generalized algorithmic structures for related problems. We argue that a structure that is used to solve related (convex) problems could be a good starting point to generalize to more complex tasks via learning. As a demonstration we train networks for Gaussian denoising and stereo estimation. For the denoising task we use our 2D WROF network, but train it directly with easily available ground truth data. For the stereo problem we use the 3D WROF model from (9). To go beyond TV regularization, we train the model on a truncated 3D distance function, generated by applying a fast marching method [42] on the provided ground-truth (Fig. 2). Note that employing a 3D graph significantly increases the number of variables in the network. Here, sharing weights across levels proves useful. Because of the weight sharing, the network can be trained on data with a small label-space, but still be applied to much larger label-spaces; simply by extending the hierarchy with additional resolution levels, until the whole label-space is covered.

4   Evaluation

Our evaluation is split into two distinct parts. First, we analyze the capability of our network to approximate solutions for optimization problems from the TV-family and investigate different levels of generalization of the algorithm. Second, we test our network on the tasks of denoising and stereo estimation as explained in the previous section.

Data Set and Training Procedure. We train our networks with the Theano package [43] on a machine equipped with a NVIDIA Titan X GPU with 12 GB of RAM. Our standard training sets consist of 1000 images from the KITTI dataset [18] randomly cropped to the size of 256×256 pixels. For our test dataset we use 300 images from the Berkeley segmentation dataset (BSD68) [30]. All images are in the interval $[0, 1]$. To train our models we use 6 different smoothness weights per image, ranging from 0.1 to 3, *cf*. Fig. 3. Thus, our full data sets contains 7800 images. The edges weights for the WROF model are extracted via filtering from random images. We randomly flip and rotate the images for data augmentation. We measure the peak signal-to-noise ratio (PSNR) and the mean absolute difference in percent (MADP) to analyze our network. Our networks are

	$\lambda = 0.093$		$\lambda = 0.19$		$\lambda = 0.38$		$\lambda = 1.5$		$\lambda = 3.0$	
In	GT	Result	GT	Result	GT	Result	GT	Result	GT	Result

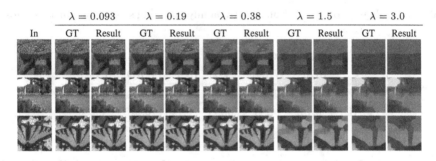

Fig. 3. Test set examples for varying smoothness costs (λ) for our ROF(*top*)/WROF(*middle*)/TV-ℓ_1 models (*bottom*). Displayed are input (*In*), ground truth (*GT*) and prediction (*Result*).

Table 1. Step-by-step generalization of the PD-CNN algorithm for the ROF model.

Step	Algorithm (6 level of 6 iterations)	channels	PSNR
(i)	$\mathbf{y}^{n+1} = \mathrm{proj}_\lambda(\mathbf{y}^n + s_\sigma Q(2\mathbf{x}^n - \mathbf{x}^{n-1}))$ $\mathbf{x}^{n+1} = (1 + s_\tau)^{-1}(\mathbf{x}^n - s_\tau(Q^*\mathbf{y}^{n+1} - \mathbf{f}))$	2	18.57
(ii)	$\mathbf{y}^{n+1} = \mathrm{proj}_\lambda(\mathbf{y}^n + s_\sigma^n Q(2\mathbf{x}^n - \mathbf{x}^{n-1}))$ $\mathbf{x}^{n+1} = (1 + s_\tau^n)^{-1}(\mathbf{x}^n - s_\tau^n(Q^*\mathbf{y}^{n+1} - \mathbf{f}))$	2	30.92
(iii)	$\mathbf{y}^{n+1} = \mathrm{proj}_\lambda(\mathbf{y}^n + D^n*(2\mathbf{x}^n - \mathbf{x}^{n-1}))$ $\mathbf{x}^{n+1} = (1 + s_\tau^n)^{-1}(\mathbf{x}^n - s_\tau^n((D^n)^* * \mathbf{y}^{n+1} - \mathbf{f}))$	2	32.23
(iv)	$\mathbf{y}^{n+1} = \mathrm{proj}_{\rho(T^n*(\mathbf{y}^n;\mathbf{x}^n,\varphi))}(\mathbf{y}^n + s_\sigma^n D^n*(2\mathbf{x}^n - \mathbf{x}^{n-1}))$ $\mathbf{x}^{n+1} = (1 + s_\tau^n)^{-1}(\mathbf{x}^n - s_\tau^n((D^n)^**\mathbf{y}^{n+1} - \mathbf{C^n}*\varphi))$	2	35.34
(v)	$\mathbf{y}^{n+1} = \mathrm{proj}_{\rho(T^n*(\mathbf{y}^n;\mathbf{x}^n,\varphi))}(\mathbf{y}^n + s_\sigma^n D^n*(2\mathbf{x}^n - \mathbf{x}^{n-1}))$ $\mathbf{x}^{n+1} = (1 + s_\tau^n)^{-1}(\mathbf{x}^n - s_\tau^n((D^n)^**\mathbf{y}^{n+1} - \mathbf{C^n}*\varphi))$	8	45.38

fully convolutional and use a filter size of 3×3 everywhere. As training objective we use an ℓ_1-loss. For more details please refer to the supplementary material.

Generalization of Primal-Dual. We start our evaluation by analyzing the effect of different forms of generalization of our PD-CNN and use the ROF model for that purpose. In this experiment we employ 6 resolution levels and 6 iterations of PD-CNN per level. At first, we restrict ourselves to the minimal 2 channels for $\mathbf{y}$ and φ. Table 1 summarizes our procedure, we mark relevant changes for each step in blue. In the first steps (*i,ii*) we use finite differences to implement gradient and divergence and only learn the step-sizes. Interestingly, compared to sharing all values (*i*), *i.e.* learning just 2 scalars, the PSNR increases by 66%, if we allow the step-sizes to vary per iteration (*ii*). Next, we replace the fixed linear operators with convolutions but keep the saddle-point structure per iteration (*iii*). After we utilize our learned features for the primal updates and generalize our projection operator (*iv*) we again observe a significant improvement, which is even more visible after employing additional channels for φ and $\mathbf{y}$ (*v*).

Table 2. Evaluation of models from the TV family including sharing parameters across levels.

	Sharing: ✗			Sharing: ✓		
	ROF	WROF	TV-ℓ_1	ROF	WROF	TV-ℓ_1
PSNR	53.75	49.83	46.45	52.78	49.21	46.12
MADP	0.132	0.211	0.277	0.145	0.228	0.285

Performance Evaluation. The results for all TV problems ROF, WROF and TV-ℓ_1 are summarized in Table 2. We use 16 channels for y and φ, 6 levels, 6 iterations of PD-CNN and 2 in the encoding stage per level. Note that PSNR and the number of iterations of our prototype algorithm are related via the primal dual gap [8]. *E.g.*, to achieve a PSNR of 50 requires about 530 iterations. TV-ℓ_1 appears to be the hardest problem of the three, followed by WROF. Sharing parameters across levels does barely harm our performance. Figure 3 displays examples with the worst MADP score in the test set. An inspection reveals that some edges are not as crisp as in the ground truth, especially, if long range interactions have to be modeled. This finding is confirmed in Table 3. As expected, ROF becomes the harder the stronger we regularize. Note, that our multiscale framework proves effective in reducing the error for stronger regularization (*cf.* supplementary). For WROF we exemplarily trained a deeper model with 10 iterations per level (Table 4). Using a loss function at every resolution level led to consistently better results. With only a single loss the training might get stuck in a bad local minimum.

4.1   From Energy Optimization to Algorithm Learning

For our denoising example we train our ROF network on gray images from the BSD68 dataset. We deviate from our standard settings and use only 2 levels, but 48 channels and 10 iterations. Following the standard protocol, the dataset is split into 432 training image from which we randomly crop one 256×256 block and add random Gaussian noise ranging from 0.02 to 0.21. We use the other 68 images for evaluation. Two examples are shown in Fig. 4 for a noise level of 20%. Table 5 lists the PSNR and the structured similarity index (SSIM) for our and competing work. Our results are very close to the state-of-the-art [50], while we apply the same network to all noise levels.

Table 3. Test set performance, for various smoothness costs.

ROF-model						
λ	0.093	0.19	0.38	0.75	1.5	3.0
PSNR	53.10	53.21	52.71	52.00	51.22	49.89

Table 4. Training a deep network with or without an explicit level-wise loss.

Model	Multi-loss	PSNR	MADP
WROF	✓	51.86	0.168
	✗	41.72	0.586

Fig. 4. *Top:* Denoising at 20% noise level. From left to right: Input; result; original. *Bottom:* Stereo examples from [32]. From left to right [9]; ours, trained via [9]; ours, trained via the truncated 3D distance function. Disparity color code: White - near, blue - far. (Color figure online)

Table 5. Performance of selected Gaussian denoising algorithms on the BSD68 dataset.

Noise level	BM3D [12]		EPLL [52]		TNRD [11]		DnCNN-S [50]		Ours	
	PSNR	SSIM	PSNR	SSIM	PSNR	SSIM	PSNR	SSIM	PSNR	SSIM
$\sigma = 15$	31.08	0.8722	31.21	-	31.42	0.8826	**31.73**	-	31.66	**0.8964**
$\sigma = 25$	28.57	0.8017	28.68	-	28.92	0.8157	**29.23**	-	29.21	**0.8359**
$\sigma = 50$	25.62	0.6869	25.67	-	25.97	0.7029	26.23	-	**26.28**	**0.7275**

Table 6. Results of our stereo network; trained on [18], evaluated on [32]. Given are the average endpoint error (AEP) and the percentage of pixel with >N pixel deviation from the ground truth.

All				Non-occluded			
%> 3pix.	%> 4pix.	%> 5pix.	AEP	%> 3pix.	%> 4pix.	%> 5pix.	AEP
4.9	4.4	4.0	1.3	3.6	3.0	2.7	0.9

To perform stereo estimation we employ the multi-label MRF from Sect. 3.2. We train our network on 64×64 snippets from the KITTI dataset [32] following the described lifting approach, *i.e.* we train the 3D WROF model (9). We use normalized cross correlation (NCC) as data cost (ϑ) and image gradients to define the spatial edge weights (θ). At first, we generate our training data with the model described in [9] (Fig. 4, *left*). Optimization in this 3D graph with [9] is several orders slower than in our network Fig. 4 middle). To allow for larger disparities than what we trained on, we employ our weight sharing technique. Recall, that our trained network allows to use different data costs; the weights, and with that the data costs are input to the network. The model trained on the 3D distance function is shown in Fig. 4, *right*. This model (Table 6) behaves differently, surfaces appear to be more planar and boundaries are tighter, *e.g.* around the cyclist. However, in these challenging conditions, training a data cost network jointly with our inference network might be an interesting path to investigate.

5   Conclusion

We have presented our idea of a primal-dual network as a deep CNN that leverages the algorithmic structure provided by energy optimization techniques into learning a generalized optimization algorithm. To achieve this goal, we integrated a modern and general FO-method into a multiscale framework, in order to overcome a limited receptive field and number of iterations. We further introduced weight sharing across resolution levels to apply our framework on arbitrarily sized input. We have already shown several possible applications that are worthwhile to be investigated further. We also plan to extend the scheme to more advanced Total Variation based models such as optical flow.

Acknowledgements. This work was supported from the ERC grant HOMOVIS No. 640156.

References

1. Beck, A., Teboulle, M.: A fast iterative shrinkage-thresholding algorithm for linear inverse problems. SIAM J. Imaging Sci. **2**, 183–202 (2009)
2. Briggs, W.L., Henson, V.E., McCormick, S.F.: A Multigrid Tutorial. Society for Industrial and Applied Mathematics, Philadelphia (2000)
3. Brox, T., Bruhn, A., Papenberg, N., Weickert, J.: High accuracy optical flow estimation based on a theory for warping. In: Pajdla, T., Matas, J. (eds.) ECCV 2004. LNCS, vol. 3024, pp. 25–36. Springer, Heidelberg (2004). doi:10.1007/978-3-540-24673-2_3
4. Bruhn, A., Weickert, J., Kohlberger, T., Schnörr, C.: A multigrid platform for real-time motion computation with discontinuity-preserving variational methods. Int. J. Comput. Vis. **70**, 257–277 (2006)
5. Chambolle, A.: Total variation minimization and a class of binary MRF models. In: Rangarajan, A., Vemuri, B., Yuille, A.L. (eds.) EMMCVPR 2005. LNCS, vol. 3757, pp. 136–152. Springer, Heidelberg (2005). doi:10.1007/11585978_10
6. Chambolle, A., Darbon, J.: A parametric maximum flow approach for discrete total variation regularization. In: Image Processing and Analysis with Graphs (2012). Chap. 4
7. Chambolle, A., Levine, S.E., Lucier, B.J.: An upwind finite-difference method for total variation-based image smoothing. SIAM J. Imaging Sci. **4**, 277–299 (2011)
8. Chambolle, A., Pock, T.: A first-order primal-dual algorithm for convex problems with applications to imaging. J. Math. Imaging Vis. **40**(1), 120–145 (2011)
9. Chambolle, A., Pock, T.: A remark on accelerated block coordinate descent for computing the proximity operators of a sum of convex functions. SMAI-JCM **1**, 29–54 (2015)
10. Chan, T.F., Esedoglu, S., Nikolova, M.: Algorithms for finding global minimizers of image segmentation and denoising models. SIAM J. Appl. Math. **66**, 1632–1648 (2006)
11. Chen, Y., Yu, W., Pock, T.: On learning optimized reaction diffusion processes for effective image restoration. In: CVPR, June 2015
12. Dabov, K., Foi, A., Katkovnik, V., Egiazarian, K.O.: Image restoration by sparse 3D transform-domain collaborative filtering. In: Transactions on Image Processing (2008)

13. Daubechies, I., Defrise, M., De Mol, C.: An iterative thresholding algorithm for linear inverse problems with a sparsity constraint. Commun. Pure Appl. Math. **57**, 1413–1457 (2004)
14. Dong, C., Loy, C.C., He, K., Tang, X.: Learning a deep convolutional network for image super-resolution. In: Fleet, D., Pajdla, T., Schiele, B., Tuytelaars, T. (eds.) ECCV 2014. LNCS, vol. 8692, pp. 184–199. Springer, Cham (2014). doi:10.1007/978-3-319-10593-2_13
15. Dosovitskiy, A., Fischer, P., Ilg, E., Häusser, P., Hazırbaş, C., Golkov, V., van der Smagt, P., Cremers, D., Brox, T.: Flownet: learning optical flow with convolutional networks. In: ICCV (2015)
16. Felzenszwalb, P.F., Huttenlocher, D.P.: Efficient belief propagation for early vision. Int. J. Comput. Vis. **70**, 41–54 (2006)
17. Felzenszwalb, P.F., Zabih, R.: Dynamic programming and graph algorithms in computer vision. IEEE Trans. Pattern Anal. Mach. Intell. **33**(4), 721–740 (2011). doi:10.1109/TPAMI.2010.135
18. Geiger, A., Lenz, P., Urtasun, R.: Are we ready for autonomous driving? In: CVPR (2012)
19. Goldfarb, D., Yin, W.: Parametric maximum flow algorithms for fast total variation minimization. SIAM J. SCI-COMP **31**, 3712–3743 (2009)
20. Goller, C., Küchler, A.: Learning task-dependent distributed representations by backpropagation through structure. In: IEEE International Conference on Neural Networks, vol. 1, pp. 347–352. IEEE (1996). doi:10.1109/icnn.1996.548916
21. Gregor, K., LeCun, Y.: Learning fast approximations of sparse coding. In: ICML (2010)
22. He, K., Zhang, X., Ren, S., Sun, J.: Deep residual learning for image recognition. In: CVPR (2016)
23. Hirschmüller, H.: Stereo processing by semiglobal matching and mutual information. PAMI **30**(2), 328–341 (2008)
24. Ishikawa, H.: Exact optimization for Markov random fields with convex priors. PAMI **25**, 1333–1336 (2003)
25. Kolmogorov, V., Rother, C.: Minimizing nonsubmodular functions with graph cuts-a review. PAMI **29**(7), 1274–1279 (2007)
26. Kolmogorov, V., Zabih, R.: What energy functions can be minimized via graph cuts? PAMI **26**, 147–159 (2004)
27. Li, S.Z.: Markov Random Field Modeling in Image Analysis. Advances in Pattern Recognition. Springer, Heidelberg (2009). doi:10.1007/978-1-84800-279-1
28. Lin, G., Shen, C., Reid, I.D., van den Hengel, A.: Efficient piecewise training of deep structured models for semantic segmentation. CoRR (2015)
29. Long, J., Shelhamer, E., Darrell, T.: Fully convolutional networks for semantic segmentation. In: CVPR (2015)
30. Martin, D., Fowlkes, C., Tal, D., Malik, J.: A database of human segmented natural images and its application to evaluating segmentation algorithms. In: ICCV (2001)
31. Mayer, N., Ilg, E., Häusser, P., Fischer, P., Cremers, D., Dosovitskiy, A., Brox, T.: A large dataset to train convolutional networks for disparity, optical flow, and scene flow estimation. In: CVPR (2016)
32. Menze, M., Geiger, A.: Object scene flow for autonomous vehicles. In: CVPR (2015)
33. Pock, T., Unger, M., Cremers, D., Bischof, H.: Fast and exact solution of Total Variation models on the GPU. In: CVPR - Workshop (2008)
34. Pock, T., Chambolle, A.: Diagonal preconditioning for first order primal-dual algorithms in convex optimization. In: ICCV (2011)

35. Pock, T., Schoenemann, T., Graber, G., Bischof, H., Cremers, D.: A convex formulation of continuous multi-label problems. In: Forsyth, D., Torr, P., Zisserman, A. (eds.) ECCV 2008. LNCS, vol. 5304, pp. 792–805. Springer, Heidelberg (2008). doi:10.1007/978-3-540-88690-7_59

36. Rasmus, A., Valpola, H., Honkala, M., Berglund, M., Raiko, T.: Semi-supervised learning with ladder networks. In: NIPS (2015)

37. Riegler, G., Ferstl, D., Rüther, M., Bischof, H.: A deep primal-dual network for guided depth super-resolution. CoRR (2016)

38. Rother, C., Kolmogorov, V., Blake, A.: "Grabcut": interactive foreground extraction using iterated graph cuts. ACM Trans. Graph. **23**(3), 309–314 (2004). doi:10.1145/1015706.1015720

39. Rudin, L.I., Osher, S., Fatemi, E.: Nonlinear total variation based noise removal algorithms. Phys. D: Nonlinear Phenom. **60**(1), 259–268 (1992). http://dx.doi.org/10.1016/0167-2789(92)90242-F

40. Russakovsky, O., Deng, J., Su, H., Krause, J., Satheesh, S., Ma, S., Huang, Z., Karpathy, A., Khosla, A., Bernstein, M., Berg, A.C., Fei-Fei, L.: ImageNet Large Scale Visual Recognition Challenge. Int. J. Comput. Vis. **115**, 211–252 (2015)

41. Schwing, A.G., Urtasun, R.: Fully connected deep structured networks. CoRR (2015)

42. Sethian, J.A.: Level set methods and fast marching methods. Cambridge monographs on applied and computational mathematics. Cambridge University Press, Cambridge (1999)

43. Theano Development Team: Theano: a Python framework for fast computation of mathematical expressions. CoRR (2016)

44. Valkonen, T.: A primal-dual hybrid gradient method for nonlinear operators with applications to MRI. In: Inverse Problems (2014)

45. Vincent, P., Larochelle, H., Lajoie, I., Bengio, Y.: Stacked denoising autoencoders: learning useful representations in a deep network with a local denoising criterion. J. Mach. Learn. Res. **11**, 3371–3408 (2010)

46. Wang, Z., Ling, Q., Huang, T.: Learning deep ℓ_0 encoders. In: AAAI (2016)

47. Wang, Z., Liu, D., Yang, J., Han, W., Huang, T.: Deep networks for image super-resolution with sparse prior. In: ICCV, pp. 370–378 (2015)

48. Wu, F.Y.: The potts model. Rev. Mod. Phys. **54**, 235 (1982)

49. Zach, C., Pock, T., Bischof, H.: A globally optimal algorithm for robust TV-L1 range image integration. In: ICCV (2007)

50. Zhang, K., Zuo, W., Chen, Y., Meng, D., Zhang, L.: Beyond a Gaussian denoiser: residual learning of deep CNN for image denoising. CoRR (2016)

51. Zheng, S., Jayasumana, S., Romera-Paredes, B., Vineet, V., Su, Z., Du, D., Huang, C., Torr, P.: Conditional random fields as recurrent neural networks. In: ICCV (2015)

52. Zoran, D., Weiss, Y.: From learning models of natural image patches to whole image restoration. In: ICCV (2011)

End-to-End Learning of Video Super-Resolution with Motion Compensation

Osama Makansi, Eddy Ilg$^{(\boxtimes)}$, and Thomas Brox

Department of Computer Science, University of Freiburg,
Freiburg im Breisgau, Germany
{makansio,ilg,brox}@cs.uni-freiburg.de

Abstract. Learning approaches have shown great success in the task of super-resolving an image given a low resolution input. Video super-resolution aims for exploiting additionally the information from multiple images. Typically, the images are related via optical flow and consecutive image warping. In this paper, we provide an end-to-end video super-resolution network that, in contrast to previous works, includes the estimation of optical flow in the overall network architecture. We analyze the usage of optical flow for video super-resolution and find that common off-the-shelf image warping does not allow video super-resolution to benefit much from optical flow. We rather propose an operation for motion compensation that performs warping from low to high resolution directly. We show that with this network configuration, video super-resolution can benefit from optical flow and we obtain state-of-the-art results on the popular test sets. We also show that the processing of whole images rather than independent patches is responsible for a large increase in accuracy.

1 Introduction

The task of providing a good estimation of a high-resolution (HR) image from low-resolution (LR) input with minimum upsampling effects, such as ringing, noise, and blurring has been studied extensively [4,10,24,25]. In recent years, deep learning approaches have led to a significant increase in performance on the task of image super-resolution [7,13–15]. Potentially, multiple frames of a video provide extra information that allows even higher quality up-sampling than just a single frame. However, the task of simultaneously super-resolving multiple frames is inherently harder and thus has not been investigated as extensively. The key difficulty from a learning perspective is to relate the structures from multiple frames in order to assemble their information to a new image.

Kappeler et al. [12] were the first who proposed a convolutional network (CNN) for video super-resolution. They excluded the frame registration from

Electronic supplementary material The online version of this chapter (doi:10.1007/978-3-319-66709-6_17) contains supplementary material, which is available to authorized users.

© Springer International Publishing AG 2017
V. Roth and T. Vetter (Eds.): GCPR 2017, LNCS 10496, pp. 203–214, 2017.
DOI: 10.1007/978-3-319-66709-6_17

the learning problem and rather applied motion compensation (warping) of the involved frames using precomputed optical flow. Thus, only a small part of the video super-resolution task was learned by the network, whereas large parts of the problem rely on classical techniques.

In this work, we provide for the first time an end-to-end network for video super-resolution that combines motion compensation and super-resolution into a single network with fast processing time. To this end, we make use of the FlowNet2-SD for optical flow estimation [11], integrate it into the approach by Kappeler et al. [12], and train the joint network end-to-end. The integration requires changing the patch-based training [7,12] to an image-based training and we show that this has a positive effect. We analyze the resulting approach and the one from Kappeler et al. [12] on single, multiple, and multiple motion-compensated frames in order to quantify the effect of using multiple frames and the effect of motion estimation. The evaluation reveals that with the original approach from Kappeler et al. both effects are surprisingly small. Contrary, when switching to image-based training we see an improvement if using motion compensated frames and we obtain the best results with the FlowNet2-SD motion compensation.

The approach of Kappeler et al. [12] follows the common practice of first upsampling and then warping images. Both operations involve an interpolation by which high-frequency image information is lost. To avoid this effect, we then implement a motion compensation operation to directly perform upsampling and warping in a single step. We compare to the closely related work of Tao et al. [23] and also perform experiments with their network architecture. Finally, we show that with this configuration, CNNs for video super-resolution clearly benefit from optical flow. We obtain state-of-the-art results.

2   Related Work

2.1   Image Super-Resolution

The pioneering work in super-resolving a LR image dates back to Freeman et al. [10], who used a database of LR/HR patch examples and nearest neighbor search to perform restoration of a HR image. Chang et al. [4] replaced the nearest neighbor search by a manifold embedding, while Yang et al. built upon sparse coding [24,25]. Dong et al. [7] proposed a convolutional neural network (SRCNN) for image super-resolution. They introduced an architecture consisting of the three steps patch encoding, non-linear mapping, and reconstruction, and showed that CNNs outperform previous methods. In Dong et al. [5], the three-layer network was replaced by a convolutional encoder-decoder network with improved speed and accuracy. Shi et al. [19] showed that performance can be increased by computing features in the lower resolution space. Recent work has extended SRCNN to deeper [13] and recursive [14] architectures. Ledig et al. [15] employed generative adversarial networks.

2.2 Video Super-Resolution

Performing super-resolution from multiple frames is a much harder task due to the additional alignment problem. Many approaches impose restrictions, such as the presence of HR keyframes [20] or affine motion [2]. Only few general approaches exist. Liu and Sun [16] provided the most extensive approach by using a Bayesian framework to estimate motion, camera blur kernel, noise level, and HR frames jointly. Ma et al. [17] extended this work to incorporate motion blur. Takeda et al. [22] followed an alternative approach by considering the video as a 3D spatio-temporal volume and by applying multidimensional kernel regression.

A first learning approach to the problem was presented by Cheng et al. [6], who used block matching to find corresponding patches and applied a multi-layer perceptron to map the LR spatio-temporal patch volumes to HR pixels. Kappeler et al. [12] proposed a basic CNN approach for video-super-resolution by extending SRCNN to multiple frames. Given the LR input frames and optical flow (obtained with the method from [9]), they bicubically upsample and warp distant time frames to the current one and then apply a slightly modified SRCNN architecture (called VSR) on this stack. The motion estimation and motion compensation are provided externally and are not part of the training procedure.

Caballero et al. [3] proposed a spatio-temporal network with 3D convolutions and slow fusion to perform video super-resolution. They employ a multi-scale spatial transformer module for motion compensation, which they train jointly with the 3D network. Very recently, Tao et al. [23] used the same motion compensation transformer module. Instead of a 3D network, they proposed a recurrent network with an LSTM unit to process multiple frames. Their work introduces an operation they call SubPixel Motion Compensation (SPMC), which performs forward warping and upsampling jointly. This is strongly related to the operation we propose here, though we use backward warping combined with a confidence instead of forward warping. Moreover, we use a simple feed-forward network instead of a recurrent network with an LSTM unit, which is advantageous for training.

2.3 Motion Estimation

Motion estimation is a longstanding research topic in computer vision, and a survey is given in [21]. In this work, we aim to perform video super-resolution with a CNN-only approach. The pioneering FlowNet of Dosovitskiy et al. [8] showed that motion estimation can be learned end-to-end with a CNN. Later works [11,18] elaborated on this concept and provided multiscale and multistep approaches. The FlowNet2 by Ilg et al. [11] yields state-of-the-art accuracy but is orders of magnitudes faster than traditional methods. We use this network as a building block for end-to-end training of a video super-resolution network.

3 Video Super-Resolution with Patch-Based Training

In this section we revisit the work from Kappeler et al. [12], which applies network-external motion compensation and then extends the single-image SRCNN [7] to operate on multiple frames. This approach is shown in Fig. 1(a).

Kappeler et al. [12] compare different numbers of input frames and investigate early and late fusion by performing the concatenation of features from the different frames after different layers. They conclude that fusion after the first convolution works best. Here, we use this version and furthermore stick to three input frames and an upsampling factor of four throughout the whole paper.

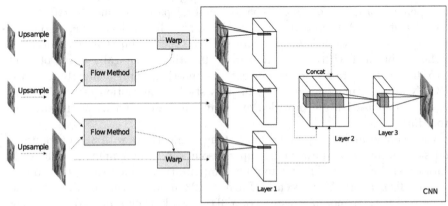

(a) Architecture as proposed by Kappeler et al. [12]

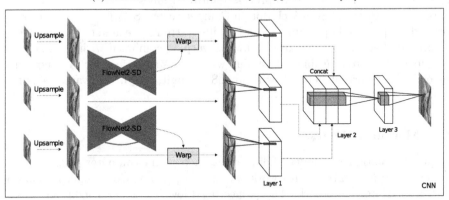

(b) Architecture with integrated FlowNet2-SD from [11]

Fig. 1. Video super-resolution architectures used by the basic models tested in this paper. Optical flow is estimated from the center to the outer frames using either an external method or a CNN. The flow is used to warp all frames to the center frame. The frames are then input into to the VSR network [12]. The complete network in (b) can be trained end-to-end including the motion estimation.

Table 1. Analysis of Kappeler et al. [12] on the different versions of the Myanmar dataset. Numbers show the PSNR in dB. The first row is with the original code and test data from [12], while the second and third row are with our re-implementation and the new test data that was recently downloaded. The third column shows results when the logo area is cropped off. Fourth and fifth columns show the PSNR when motion compensation is disabled during testing, by using only the center frame or the original frames without warping. There is no significant improvement by neither the use of multiple frames nor by the use of optical flow.

Dataset/model	SRCNN [7]	VSR [12]	VSR [12] (cropped)	VSR [12] (only center)	VSR [12] (no warp.)
Myanmar validation from [12]	31.26	**31.81**	32.95	**31.71**	-
Myanmar validation (ours)	31.30	**31.30**	32.88	31.23	31.19
Myanmar validation (ours), retrained		**31.81**	32.76	31.74	31.77

We performed an analysis of their code and model. The results are given in the first row of Table 1. Using their original code, we conducted an experiment, where we replaced the three frames from the image sequence by three times the same center frame (column 4 of Table 1), which corresponds to the information only from single-image super-resolution. We find that on the Myanmar validation set the result is still much better than SRCNN [7] but only marginally worse than VSR [12] on real video information. Since except for a concatenation there is no difference between the VSR [12] and SRCNN [7] architectures, this shows that surprisingly the improvement is mainly due to training settings of VSR [12] rather than the usage of multiple frames.

For training and evaluation, Kappeler et al. [12] used the publicly available Myanmar video [1]. We used the same training/validation split into 53 and 6 scenes and followed the patch sampling from [12]. However, the publicly available data has changed by that the overlaid logo at the bottom right corner from the producing company is now bigger than before. Evaluating on the data with the different logo gives much worse results (row 2 of Table 1), while when the logo is cropped off (column 3 of Table 1), results are comparable. The remaining difference stems from a different implementation of the warping operation[1]. However, when we retrained the approach with our implementation and training data (row 3 of Table 1), we achieved results very close to Kappler et al. [12].

To further investigate the effects of motion compensation, we retrained the approach using only the center frame, the original frames, and frames motion compensated using FlowNet2 [11] and FlowNet2-SD [11] in addition to the method from Drulea [9]. For details we refer to the supplemental material. Again we observed that including or excluding motion compensation with different optical flow methods has no effect on the Myanmar validation set. We additionally evaluated on the commonly used Videoset4 dataset [12,16]. In this case we do see a PSNR increment of 0.1 with Drulea [9] and higher increment of 0.18 with

---

[1] We use the implementation from [11]; it differs from [12] in that it performs bilinear interpolation instead of bicubic.

FlowNet2 [11] when using motion compensation. The Videoset4 dataset includes larger motion and it seems that there is some small improvement when larger motion is involved. However, the effect of motion compensation is still very small when compared to the effect of changing other training settings.

4   Video Super-Resolution with Image-Based Training

In contrast to Kappeler et al., we combine motion compensation and super-resolution in one network. For motion estimation, we used the FlowNet2-SD variant from [11]. We chose this network, because FlowNet2 itself is too large to fit into GPU memory besides the super-resolution network and FlowNet2-SD yields smooth flow predictions and accurate performance for small displacements. Figure 1(b) shows the integrated network. For the warping operation, we use the implementation from [11], which also allows a backward pass while training. The combined network is trained on complete images instead of patches. Thus, we repeated our experiments from the previous section for the case of image-based training. The results are given in Table 2. In general, we find that image-based processing yields much higher PSNRs than patch-based processing. Detailed comparison of the network and training settings for both variants can be found in the supplemental material.

Table 2 shows that motion compensation has no effect on the Myanmar validation set. For Videoset4 there is an increase of 0.12 with motion compensation using Drulea's method [9]. For FlowNet2 the increase of 0.42 is even bigger. Since FlowNet2-SD is completely trainable, it is also possible to refine the optical flow for the task of video super-resolution by training the whole network end-to-end with the super-resolution loss. We do so by using a resolution of 256×256 to enable a batch size of 8 and train for $100\,k$ more iterations. The results from Table 2 again show that for Myanmar there is no significant change. However, for Videoset4 the joint training further improves the result by 0.1 leading to a total PSNR increase of 0.52.

We show a qualitative evaluation in Fig. 2. On the enlarged building, one can see that bicubic upsampling introduces some smearing across the windows.

Table 2. PSNR scores from Myanmar validation (ours) and Videoset4 for image-based training. For each column of the table we trained the architecture of [7,12] by applying convolutions over the complete images. We used different types of motion compensation for training and testing (FN2-SD denotes FlowNet2-SD). For Myanmar, motion compensation still has no significant effect. However, on Videoset4 an effect for motion compensation using Drulea's method [9] is noticeable and is even stronger for FlowNet2-SD [11].

Network	SRCNN [7]	VSR [12]	VSR [12]	VSR [12]	VSR [12]	VSR [12] joint
Motion compensation	-	Only center	No warp.	Drulea [9]	FN2-SD [11]	FN2-SD [11]
Myanmar validation (ours)	32.42	32.41	32.55	32.60	32.62	32.63
Videoset4	24.63	24.66	24.79	24.91	25.12	25.21

This effect is also present in the methods without motion compensation and in the original VSR [12] with motion compensation. When using image-based trained models, the effect is successfully removed. Motion compensation with FlowNet2 [11] seems to be marginally sharper than motion compensation with Drulea [9]. We find that the joint training reduces ringing artifacts; an example is given in the supplemental material.

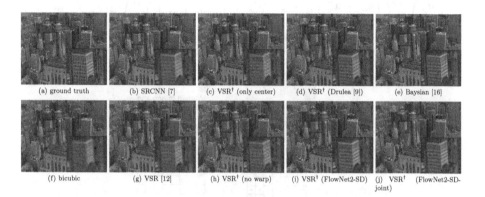

Fig. 2. Comparison of existing super-resolution methods to our trained models. † Indicates models retrained by us using image-based training. Note that (b) and (g) are patch-based, while (c), (d), (e), (h), (i) and (j) are image-based.

5   Combined Warping and Upsampling Operation

The approach of Kappeler et al. [12] and the VSR architecture discussed so far follow the common practice of first upsampling and then warping the images. Both operations involve an interpolation during which image information is lost. Therefore, we propose a joint operation that performs upsampling and backward warping in a single step, which we name Joint Upsampling and Backward Warping ($JUBW$). This operation does not perform any interpolation at all, but additionally outputs sub-pixel distances and leaves finding a meaningful interpolation to the network itself. Let us consider a pixel p and let x_p and y_p denote the coordinates in high resolution space, while x_p^s and y_p^s denote the source coordinates in low resolution space. First, the mapping from low to high resolution space using high resolution flow estimations (u_p, v_p) is computed according to the following equation:

$$\begin{pmatrix} x_p^s \\ y_p^s \end{pmatrix} = \frac{1}{\alpha} \begin{pmatrix} x_p + u_p + 0.5 \\ y_p + v_p + 0.5 \end{pmatrix} - \begin{pmatrix} 0.5 \\ 0.5 \end{pmatrix}, \tag{1}$$

where $\alpha = 4$ denotes the scaling factor and subtraction/addition of 0.5 places the origin at the top left corner of the first pixel. Then the warped image is computed as:

$$I_w(p) = \begin{cases} I(\lfloor x_p^s \rceil, \lfloor y_p^s \rceil) & \text{if } \lceil x_p^s \rfloor, \lceil y_p^s \rfloor \text{ is inside } I, \\ 0 & \text{otherwise,} \end{cases} \tag{2}$$

where $\lfloor \cdot \rceil$ denotes the round to nearest operation. Note, that no interpolation between pixels is performed. The operation then additionally outputs the following distances per pixel (see Fig. 3 for illustration):

$$\begin{pmatrix} d_p^x \\ d_p^y \end{pmatrix} = \begin{pmatrix} \lfloor x_p^s \rceil - x_p^s \\ \lceil y_p^s \rfloor - y_p^s \end{pmatrix} \text{ if } \lceil x_p^s \rfloor, \lceil y_p^s \rfloor \text{ is inside } I \text{ and } \begin{pmatrix} 0 \\ 0 \end{pmatrix} \text{ otherwise.} \tag{3}$$

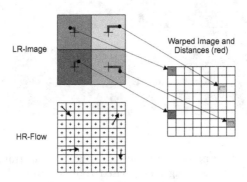

Fig. 3. Illustration of the Joint Upsampling and Backward Warping operation (JUBW). The output is a dense image (left sparse here for illustration purposes) and includes x/y distances of the source locations to the source pixel centers.

We also implemented the joint upsampling and forward warping operation from Tao et al. [23] for comparison and denote it as SPMC-FW. Contrary to our operation, SMPC-FW still involves two types of interpolation: (1) subpixel-interpolation for the target position in the high resolution grid and (2) interpolation between values if multiple flow vectors point to the same target location. For comparison, we replaced the architecture from the previous section by the encoder-/decoder part from Tao et al. [23] (which we denote here as SPMC-ED). We also find that this architecture itself performs better than SRCNN [7]/VSR [12] on the super-resolution only task (see supplementary material for details). The resulting configuration is shown in Fig. 4. Furthermore, we also extended the training set by downloading Youtube videos and downsampling them to create additional training data. The larger dataset comprises 162 k images and we call it MYT.

Results are given in Table 3. First, we note that our feed-forward implementation of FlowNet2-SD with SPMC-ED, which simply stacks frames and does not include an LSTM unit, outperforms the original recurrent implementation from Tao et al. [23]. Second, we see that our proposed JUBW operation generally outperforms SPMC-FW. We again performed experiments where we excluded temporal information, by inputting zero flows and duplicates of the center image.

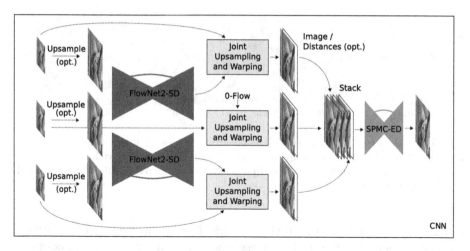

Fig. 4. Network setup with FlowNet2-SD and joint upsampling and warping operation (JUBW or SPMC-FW). Upsampling before feeding into FlowNet2-SD happens only for JUBW. The output of the upsampling and warping operation is stacked and then fed into the SPMC-ED network.

Table 3. PSNR values for different joint upsampling and warping approaches. The first column shows the original results from Tao et al. [23] using the SPMC upsampling, forward warping, and the SPMC-ED architecture with an LSTM unit. Columns two to four show our reimplementation of the SPMC-FW operation [23] without an LSTM unit. Columns five to eight show our joint upsampling and backward warping operation with the same encoder-decoder network on top. With *ours* we denote our implementation according to Fig. 4. In *only center* we input zero-flows and the duplicated center image three times (no temporal information). The entry *joint* includes joint training of FlowNet2-SD and the super-resolution network. For columns two to eight, the networks are retrained on MYT and tested for each setting respectively.

	SPMC	SPMC-FW			JUBW			
	original [23]	Ours	Only center	Joint	Ours	No dist.	Only center	Joint
Myanmar (ours)	-	32.90	32.45	33.05	**33.13**	33.02	32.55	32.69
Videoset4	25.52	25.68	24.94	25.62	**25.85**	25.74	24.96	25.09

We now observe that including temporal information yields large improvements and increases the PSNR by 0.5 to 0.9. In contrast to the previous sections, we see such increase also for the Myanmar dataset. This shows that the proposed motion compensation can also exploit small motion vectors. The qualitative results in Fig. 5 confirm these findings.

Including the sub-pixel distance outputs from JUBW layer to enable better interpolation to the network leads to a smaller improvement than expected. Notably, without these distances the JUBW operation degrades to a simple nearest neighbor upsampling and nearest neighbor warping, but it still outperforms SPMC-FW. We conclude from this that one should generally avoid any kind

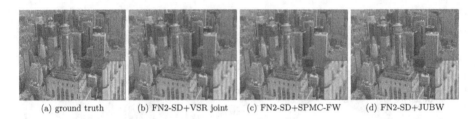

(a) ground truth   (b) FN2-SD+VSR joint   (c) FN2-SD+SPMC-FW   (d) FN2-SD+JUBW

Fig. 5. Examples of a reconstructed image from Videoset4 using different warping methods. FN2-SD stands for FlowNet2-SD. Clearly using JUBW yields sharper and more accurate reconstruction of the estimated frames compared to SPMC-FW [23] and the best VSR [12] result.

of interpolation and leave it to the network. Finally, fine-tuning FlowNet2 on the video super-resolution task decreases the PSNR in some cases and does not provide the best results. We conjecture that this is due to the nature of optimization of the gradient through the warping operation, which is based on the reconstruction error and is prone to local minima.

6   Conclusions

In this paper, we performed an evaluation of different video super-resolution approaches using CNNs including motion compensation. We found that the common practice of patch-based training and upsampling and warping separately yields almost no improvement when comparing the video super-resolution setting against the single-image setting. We obtained a significant improvement over prior work by replacing the patch-based approach by a network that analyzes the whole image. As a remedy for the lacking standard motion compensation, we proposed a joint upsampling and backward warping operation and combined it with FlowNet2-SD [11] and the SPMC-ED [23] architecture. This combination outperforms all previous work on video super-resolution. In conclusion, our results show that: (1) we can achieve the same or better performance with a formulation as a feed-forward instead of a recurrent network; (2) performing joint upsampling and backward warping with no interpolation outperforms joint upsampling and forward warping and the common backward warping with interpolation; (3) including sub-pixel distances yields a small additional improvement; and (4) joint training with FlowNet2-SD so far does not lead to consistent improvements and we leave a more detailed analysis to future work.

Acknowledgements. We acknowledge the DFG Grant BR-3815/7-1.

References

1. Myanmar 60p, Harmonic Inc.: (2014). https://www.harmonicinc.com/resources/videos/4k-video-clip-center

2. Babacan, S.D., Molina, R., Katsaggelos, A.K.: Variational Bayesian super resolution. IEEE Trans. Patt. Anal. Mach. Intell. (TPAMI) **20**(4), 984–999 (2011)
3. Caballero, J., Ledig, C., Aitken, A.P., Acosta, A., Totz, J., Wang, Z., Shi, W.: Real-time video super-resolution with spatio-temporal networks and motion compensation. CoRR abs/1611.05250 (2016). http://arxiv.org/abs/1611.05250
4. Chang, H., Yeung, D.Y., Xiong, Y.: Super-resolution through neighbor embedding. In: IEEE Conference on Computer Vision and Pattern Recognition (CVPR), June 2004
5. Dong, C., Loy, C.C., Tang, X.: Accelerating the super-resolution convolutional neural network. In: Leibe, B., Matas, J., Sebe, N., Welling, M. (eds.) ECCV 2016. LNCS, vol. 9906, pp. 391–407. Springer, Cham (2016). doi:10.1007/978-3-319-46475-6_25
6. Cheng, M.H., Lin, N.W., Hwang, K.S., Jeng, J.H.: Fast video super-resolution using artificial neural networks. In: International Symposium on Communication Systems, Networks Digital Signal Processing (CSNDSP), pp. 1–4, July 2012
7. Dong, C., Loy, C.C., He, K., Tang, X.: Image super-resolution using deep convolutional networks. IEEE Trans. Pattern Anal. Mach. Intell. (TPAMI) **38**(2), 295–307 (2016)
8. Dosovitskiy, A., Fischer, P., Ilg, E., Häusser, P., Hazırbaş, C., Golkov, V., Smagt, P., Cremers, D., Brox, T.: FlowNet: learning optical flow with convolutional networks. In: IEEE International Conference on Computer Vision (ICCV) (2015)
9. Drulea, M., Nedevschi, S.: Total variation regularization of local-global optical flow. In: IEEE Conference on Intelligent Transportation Systems (ITSC), pp. 318–323, October 2011
10. Freeman, W.T., Jones, T.R., Pasztor, E.C.: Example-based super-resolution. IEEE Comput. Graph. Appl. (ICGA) **22**(2), 56–65 (2002)
11. Ilg, E., Mayer, N., Saikia, T., Keuper, M., Dosovitskiy, A., Brox, T.: Flownet 2.0: evolution of optical flow estimation with deep networks. In: IEEE Conference on Computer Vision and Pattern Recognition (CVPR), July 2017
12. Kappeler, A., Yoo, S., Dai, Q., Katsaggelos, A.K.: Video super-resolution with convolutional neural networks. IEEE Trans. Comput. Imaging (TCI) **2**(2), 109–122 (2016)
13. Kim, J., Lee, J.K., Lee, K.M.: Accurate image super-resolution using very deep convolutional networks. In: IEEE Conference on Computer Vision and Pattern Recognition (CVPR), pp. 1646–1654, June 2016
14. Kim, J., Lee, J.K., Lee, K.M.: Deeply-recursive convolutional network for image super-resolution. IEEE Conference on Computer Vision and Pattern Recognition (CVPR) abs/1511.04491 (2016)
15. Ledig, C., Theis, L., Huszar, F., Caballero, J., Aitken, A.P., Tejani, A., Totz, J., Wang, Z., Shi, W.: Photo-realistic single image super-resolution using a generative adversarial network. In: IEEE Conference on Computer Vision and Pattern Recognition (CVPR) (2016)
16. Liu, C., Sun, D.: On Bayesian adaptive video super resolution. IEEE Trans. Pattern Anal. Mach. Intell. (TPAMI) **36**(2), 346–360 (2014)
17. Ma, Z., Liao, R., Tao, X., Xu, L., Jia, J., Wu, E.: Handling motion blur in multi-frame super-resolution. In: IEEE Conference on Computer Vision and Pattern Recognition (CVPR), pp. 5224–5232, June 2015
18. Ranjan, A., Black, M.J.: Optical flow estimation using a spatial pyramid network. CoRR abs/1611.00850 (2016). http://arxiv.org/abs/1611.00850

19. Shi, W., Caballero, J., Huszar, F., Totz, J., Aitken, A.P., Bishop, R., Rueckert, D., Wang, Z.: Real-time single image and video super-resolution using an efficient sub-pixel convolutional neural network. In: IEEE Conference on Computer Vision and Pattern Recognition (CVPR), June 2016
20. Song, B.C., Jeong, S.C., Choi, Y.: Video super-resolution algorithm using bi-directional overlapped block motion compensation and on-the-fly dictionary training. IEEE Trans. Circuits Syst. Video Technol. (TCSVT) 21(3), 274–285 (2011)
21. Sun, D., Roth, S., Black, M.J.: Secrets of optical flow estimation and their principles. In: IEEE Conference on Computer Vision and Pattern Recognition (CVPR), pp. 2432–2439, June 2010
22. Takeda, H., Milanfar, P., Protter, M., Elad, M.: Super-resolution without explicit subpixel motion estimation. IEEE Trans. Pattern Anal. Mach. Intell. (TPAMI) 18(9), 1958–1975 (2009)
23. Tao, X., Gao, H., Liao, R., Wang, J., Jia, J.: Detail-revealing deep video super-resolution. CoRR abs/1704.02738 (2017). http://arxiv.org/abs/1704.02738
24. Yang, J., Wright, J., Huang, T., Ma, Y.: Image super-resolution as sparse representation of raw image patches. In: IEEE Conference on Computer Vision and Pattern Recognition (CVPR), June 2008
25. Yang, J., Wright, J., Huang, T.S., Ma, Y.: Image super-resolution via sparse representation. IEEE Trans. Pattern Anal. Mach. Intell. (TPAMI) 19(11), 2861–2873 (2010)

Convolutional Neural Networks for Movement Prediction in Videos

Alexander Warnecke$^{(\boxtimes)}$, Timo Lüddecke, and Florentin Wörgötter

Georg-August-University, Göttingen, Germany
`alexander.warnecke@stud.uni-goettingen.de`

Abstract. In this work we present a convolutional neural network-based (CNN) model that predicts future movements of a ball given a series of images depicting the ball and its environment. For training and evaluation, we use artificially generated images sequences. Two scenarios are analyzed: Prediction in a simple table tennis environment and a more challenging squash environment. Classical 2D convolution layers are compared with 3D convolution layers that extract the motion information of the ball from contiguous frames. Moreover, we investigate whether networks with stereo visual input perform better than those with monocular vision only. Our experiments suggest that CNNs can indeed predict physical behaviour with small error rates on unseen data but the performance drops for very complex underlying movements.

1 Introduction

Predicting the movement of objects in images is a key capability in human perception and crucial for many tasks in everyday life. Hamrick et al. [3] provided evidence that human intuition for how dynamical systems evolve can be explained by the hypothesis that we use internal models of physics. It seems natural to ask whether a computer system is also able to build such an internal model for itself. This question is not only interesting from a theoretical point of view but also important for many applications in real life environments. In this work, we consider two scenarios in a three-dimensional environment which we call table tennis and squash. The former refers to a flat surface with a bouncing ball while the latter involves a closed, cuboid-like room where multiple interactions with the wall are possible. The input is a fixed number of sequential images showing the movement of the ball. We develop a model that learns the trajectory of a ball from a fixed point in time, i.e. a sequence of (x, y, z) coordinates indicating the position of the ball in the future time steps as depicted in Fig. 1. Since this is trivial in the empty space, in both of our scenarios, we put an emphasis on situations, where the ball changes its movement direction due to collisions with the surrounding walls. Naturally, this problem could also be solved analytically when all parameters are known (ball position, scene geometry, etc.). However, the task we consider here does explicitly require to estimate these parameters from the image. In order to do so, we apply convolutional neural networks, which have proven to be capable of understanding complex images.

© Springer International Publishing AG 2017
V. Roth and T. Vetter (Eds.): GCPR 2017, LNCS 10496, pp. 215–225, 2017.
DOI: 10.1007/978-3-319-66709-6_18

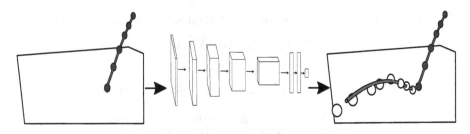

Fig. 1. The movement of a ball is predicted by a convolutional neural network. It is shown the first six input frames and it predicts the trajectory of the future movement.

2   Related Work

Neural networks have already been used to model physical phenomena in different setups. The approaches produce either images or numerical results to describe the movement. Michalski et al. [9] consider a rather abstract model that uses gated autoencoders which are turned into a recurrent neural network. The network takes a sequence of images $I_1, I_2, \ldots, I_t$ as input and learns transformations to create image I_{t+1} from the time series. The authors apply this model successfully to create movements like those of a ball bouncing on the floor. Lerer et al. [8] analyse the capability of convolutional neural networks to predict whether block towers will collapse. Different Convolutional neural networks are trained with rendered images and succeed in both, predicting whether the tower will collapse and creating an image of the final outcome. Walker et al. [13] predict the trajectory of each pixel from a static image for the next second with variational autoencoders using convolutional neural networks for the encoding and decoding part and achieve good results for images from challenging environments.

It is well known that simple movements of bodies are determined by equations of motion from Newtonian mechanics. Therefore, Wu et al. [14], Kyriazis et al. [11] and Bhat et al. [1] propose models to estimate the parameters of these equations from images and videos to compute the dynamics. Mottaghi et al. [10] use a special convolutional neural network that takes a single image as input and predicts the dynamics of an object with two separate streams. One stream predicts in which newtonian scenario the scene is taking place and the other one generates features from the image while using an extra channel indicating the object location. By merging these two information, the network can predict the trajectory of the moving object. However, these approaches have two major drawbacks. Firstly, most humans cannot solve newtonian equations but can still predict the dynamics of a falling object, so these methods are not very natural. Secondly, they require pictures with an additional channel to indicate the position of the moving object.

Fragkiadaki et al. [2] investigate a setup in a 2D billiard environment. At some time t a convolutional neural network similar to the network in [7] receives the picture of the current situation, the last three preceding frames and the forces applied on the ball. The network predicts the movement, i.e. the velocity vector $(\Delta x, \Delta y)$ for each time step up to 20 following instants. The authors show that a model which was trained in a certain environment also performs well in unknown environments (different shape of the table, different length of the table walls). However, it still requires a force information as an additional input to predict the movement which is an unhandy information to give.

Distinction From Related Work. As in [2], we use convolutional neural networks for processing videos that show the movement of an object to predict the further motion. However, our environment is three dimensional which adds "depth" to the images and makes the task harder, moreover, we process videos instead of static images. Another difference to [2,10] is that we use only the images as input without giving any other information about forces, momentum or position of the object. Moreover, the network in [2] looks only one time step into the future since it receives always the latest picture. Our model, in contrast, also predicts positions that are more than one time step away from the input frames. The output of our networks are, in contrast to images being predicted in [8], coordinates in $\mathbb{R}^3$ of the ball's future trajectory, which is a useful information for any system moving and acting in real world environments. To the best of our knowledge, there exists no approach only working on video input data generated from artificial three dimensional scenes predicting numerical information instead of images.

3   Scenarios and Data Acquisition

The video frames for training the convolutional neural network have been created using the open source 3D computer graphics program *blender* [1]. We use blender's physics engine to create rendered frames showing a realistic movement of a ball in different situations. We save the positions of the ball at every frame and train a convolutional neural network to predict the following coordinates after seeing the movement up to some timestep t. The first scenario is a table tennis scenario where a ball bounces on a table from different starting positions and in different directions. The second scenario is a squash environment where a ball is moving inside a box with multiple possible collisions from different starting positions.

3.1   Table Tennis Setup

The table and the ball for the table tennis setup have been created in real life proportions, i.e. the table has size 2.75 m × 1.5 m (length × width) and the ball has a diameter of 4 cm. To increase computational performance and reduce the number of parameters, the frames were created using black-white images with a resolution of 128 × 128 pixels in which the ball has a size of roughly 4 × 4 pixels. The coordinate system is chosen such that the x axis runs along the longer side of the table and the y axis runs along the shorter side of the table. Consequently,

---

[1] https://www.blender.org.

the z axis indicates the height of an object "above" the table. The origin of the coordinate system is the middle point of the table and for computational stability, all axes are scaled by a factor of 10. To create random movements, the starting position of the ball is sampled according to a uniform distribution in the interval $[-5, 5]$ on the y axis and $[1.7, 4.5]$ on the z axis. The movement starts in the middle of the table, i.e. $x = 0$. Afterwards, we sample a random collision point on the table with $x \in [0, 13]$, $y \in [-7.5, 7.5]$ and $z = 0$. The ball flies from the starting point towards the collision point on the table, therefore the velocity and direction of the movement is defined and the physics engine can simulate the trajectory. By this approach we create random movements with random velocities of the balls as the number of frames for the ball to reach the collision point is fixed. The corresponding movement is recorded from two viewpoints, one at each corner of the table, to create a human-like viewpoint and give the network the chance to perceive depth in the frames.

3.2   Squash Setup

The squash setup extends the table tennis setup to a bounded box to create complex movements with multiple collisions. It takes place in a box with 1m height and width and 0.7 m length. The size of the box is chosen to be rather small in order to provoke collisions with the wall easier. The x and y axis run along the width and length of the box and the z axis along its height. Again, the origin is located in the middle of the box. Inside this box, a ball with a diameter of 4 cm is randomly positioned and "shot" into some direction in order to bounce against some walls of the box. The line of sight of the cameras runs along the y axis of the box. As before, the scene is recorded by two cameras, thus one side of the box is open such that the cameras can look into it. The starting positions were created by sampling x, y and z coordinates uniformly from the intervals $[-3.5, -1] \cup [1, 3.5]$, $[-4.5, 1]$ and $[-3.5, 3.5]$ respectively. To create the movement of the ball, we positioned a force field in blender randomly in front of the ball such that it is shot into the box. The coordinates of the force field are determined by adding random numbers Δx, Δy and Δz to the middle point of the sphere, where these numbers have been sampled uniformly from the intervals $[-0.5, 0.5]$, $[-0.3, -0.2]$ and $[-1, 1]$ respectively. Note that the y coordinate is shifted by a negative number in order to make the ball fly into the box and not towards the cameras. Finally, to make the setup harder and test the ability of the network to generalize, we shifted all 5 sides of the box randomly by a number sampled uniformly from the interval $[-1, 1]$ in order to create boxes of different size for every movement. The same way, we shifted the light, which is responsible for the shadow of the ball in the pictures, below the top side of the box by random numbers from the interval $[-1, 1]$ in x and y direction. To take these difficult changes into account, the resolution of the videos is doubled to 256×256 pixels.

4   Trajectory Prediction Model

In this section we explain our CNN-based trajectory prediction model and describe various configurations in detail. In all cases a sequence of images is taken into consideration to predict future positions of the depicted ball in euclidean space.

4.1   Network Architecture

2D vs. 3D Convolution. Firstly, we compare 2D convolutions with 3D convolutions. 2D convolution transforms an input of depth d into a two dimensional output, i.e. a feature map. 3D convolution filters have an additional temporal component and thus work in the spatio-temporal domain. By this construction, their output represents information from several contiguous frames and can thus capture motion information as shown in [5,6,12].

Input Representation. Secondly, we compare different representations of the input to the network. Since we have six frames from each side of the table as input for the networks, we can either concatenate them and process them all at once or make use of the two different perspectives by feeding them separately into a network and merging them at some point. We will call the first model *concatenated input model* and the second one *two-stream model* in the following. Figure 2 shows the difference between the two models. While we can use 2D convolutions and 3D convolutions in the two-stream model, it is problematic to use 3D convolutions with the concatenated input because a 3D convolution filter is processing contiguous frames with the same weights at each position. However, this would treat the transition between the (concatenated) perspectives in the same way as temporal transitions between two subsequent frames which is undesired. Hence 3D convolutions are only applied in the two-stream model.

Mono vs. Stereo. Finally, we investigate the difference between mono- and stereo vision by using input of only one side in the concatenated input model. As shown in Fig. 2(a) the concatenated input network uses four convolution layers

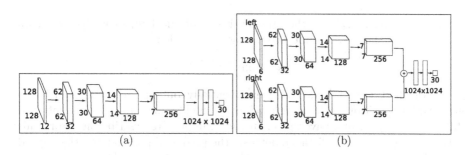

Fig. 2. The different CNN models. (a): The concatenated input model processes all frames from each side at once. (b): The two-stream model processes the frames from the left and right side separately.

where each convolution is followed by batch normalization with $\epsilon = 0.001$, max pooling with a $(2, 2)$ filter and *RELU* (rectified linear unit) where the size of the convolution filters is $(2, 2)$.

Network Head. At the top of the network there are two fully connected layers where the first layer applies the RELU nonlinearity function and the second one a simple linear function, i.e. $f(x) = m \cdot x$ for some $m \in \mathbb{R}$, since we have to be able to predict negative coordinates. Between the two fully connected layers there is a dropout layer which randomly deactivates 50% of the units in the last layer during the learning process to prevent the network from overfitting. In the case of 3D convolutions, we use a network with two convolution layers with 10 and 20 feature maps respectively due to memory restrictions. The first layer uses a filter of size $(2, 2, 1)$ (width×height×time), i.e. the convolution is only performed in space and not in time so that the time axis is not collapsing too fast. The following filter uses a filter of size $(2, 2, 2)$, so that it convolves two contiguous frames in the time domain. As before, we apply batch normalization after convolution, as well as a 3D max-pooling with filter size $(2, 2, 1)$ for the first layer and $(2, 2, 2)$ for the second layer and RELU nonlinearity function. In each case, the streams are fused by using the sum of the feature maps of both streams.

Loss Function. We train the networks to predict the entire trajectory of a ball after some point in time t, i.e. a sequence $(\hat{x}_{t+1}, \hat{y}_{t+1}, \hat{z}_{t+1})$, $(\hat{x}_{t+2}, \hat{y}_{t+2}, \hat{z}_{t+2})$, ..., $(\hat{x}_{t+n}, \hat{y}_{t+n}, \hat{z}_{t+n})$ of 3D coordinates, indicating the position of the ball in the future. For this work, we predict 8 future positions in the table tennis setup and 10 future positions of the ball in the squash setup for an input of 6 frames from each camera. This means, the output of the network is 30 dimensional in the squash setup and 24 dimensional in the table tennis scenario. Since it is very hard to have a good prediction for every point in time, we weighted our loss function as follows. The loss for a prediction sequence is defined by

$$L_\Theta = \sum_{i=1}^{10} w_{i-1}\big((x_{t+i} - \hat{x}_{t+i})^2 + (y_{t+i} - \hat{y}_{t+i})^2 + (z_{t+i} - \hat{z}_{t+i})^2\big), \qquad (1)$$

where $(x_{t+i}, y_{t+i}, z_{t+i})$ are the true positions of the ball, Θ is the set of all parameters of the network and the weights w_k are defined by

$$w_k = \exp(-k^{1/4}). \qquad (2)$$

Thus, the first weight is decaying exponentially but not too fast in order to give the last positions still enough weight in the loss function. If not mentioned differently, we present an average *error radius* in plots to describe the error. This is the average euclidean distance between the predicted position and the ground truth. The network was trained using the rmsprop algorithm [4], i.e.

$$w_{t+1,i} = w_{t,i} - \frac{\lambda}{\sqrt{H_{t,i} + \epsilon}} \cdot g_{t,i} \qquad (3)$$

where $H_{t,i} = \gamma ||g_{t-1,i}||^2 + (1-\gamma)||g_{t,i}||^2$ is a running average over the gradients $g_{t,i} = \frac{\partial C}{\partial w_i}$ of the cost function C with respect to the parameter w_i at timestep t. For training, we used the parameters $\lambda = 1$, $\epsilon = 10^{-6}$ and $\gamma = 0.9$. The computations have been performed on a Geforce GTX TITAN X with batch size of 100 for 2D convolutions and 75 for 3D convolutions.

5   Results

In order to asses the performance of our model, we split the set of $50,000$ movements for both scenarios as follows: In the table tennis scenario, we removed movements from the training set which have their collision point with the table in a random area on the table, where the position of the area is chosen randomly but its size is fixed to contain about 5% of the movements for testing. This way, the test set contains only movements where the ball is moving to a direction the network has not seen before. Similarly, we removed 5% of the movements in the squash setup by choosing movements where the force field, which gives the ball its initial direction, was in a certain box relative to the starting point of the ball.

5.1   Table Tennis Scenario

Figure 3(a) shows the average error radius of the networks (in cm) when predicting the 8 positions of the ball after the last input frame. We compare against the AlexNet architecture which was proposed by Krizhevsky et al. [7] for image classification without using pre-trained weights and replaced the softmax layer in the end with a fully connected layer with the right number of units to produce the trajectory coordinates. In comparison to the AlexNet, our networks use less layers, less feature maps and smaller convolution filters for processing the videos.

We can observe that all network architectures perform well for the first frames and produce error radii around 4cm which is the diameter of the ball and therefore a very good result. In the long term, we can see that the two-stream model with 3D convolutions is clearly the worst one, followed by the AlexNet and the network which has only monocular vision. The two networks with stereo vision show the best performance in the long term and especially the model with concatenated input frames performs well over all frame numbers.

5.2   Squash Scenario

The squash scenario contains more complex movements with multiple collisions and the environment in each trial varies with respect to the size of the box and the position of the light. The quantitative results shown in Fig. 3(b) confirm that the task is harder for all the networks but at the same time we have a greater difference in the performance of the different models. In general, even the best models produce error radii of about 8 cm for the first frame and more than 20 cm for the last frame which is about 2.5 times greater than in the table tennis scenario. AlexNet and the two-stream-model with 3D convolutions

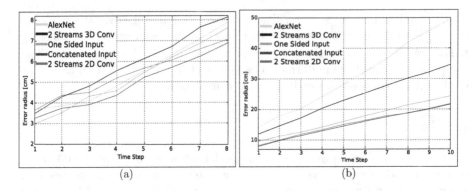

(a)   (b)

Fig. 3. Error radius of the different models for the following frames in the table tennis setting (a) and the squash setting (b). Black: 2-Stream-3D-Convolution, Blue: Concatenated Input, Cyan: AlexNet, Green: One sided Input, Red: Two-Stream-2D-Convolution. (Color figure online)

Table 1. Influence of the dimensions on the average L^2 error.

Network	Δ_{L^2}	$\Delta_{L^2}(x)$	$\Delta_{L^2}(y)$	$\Delta_{L^2}(z)$
Concatenated input	24.66	7.16	10.93	6.57
Two stream 2D Convolution	25.12	6.49	10.92	7.71
One sided Input	31.08	8.21	13.02	9.85

are clearly outperformed by the other models and predict positions with a great error even for early frame numbers. Although the network with monocular vision only performs better than the former two, it is worse than the two networks with stereo image input which is the expected behavior but the difference between them is not too big. The best models are again the two-stream-model with 2D convolutions and the concatenated input model but compared to Fig. 3(a) the two models show an almost identical performance in this task indicating that it makes no difference whether the input is processed concatenated or separated in two streams. Table 1 shows the influence of the different dimensions on the error. We consider the average L^2 error in the blender coordinate system, which is the sum of the average squared error in the x, y and z dimension. We can see that the depth dimension y has clearly the highest error in all models and is roughly 20% higher for the network with monocular vision compared to the stereo vision ones.

5.3   Qualitative Results

Figure 4(a)–(d) show some predictions of the concatenated input model in the table tennis scenario where we can see that the network can predict different movements at different locations on the table. In general, the network performs

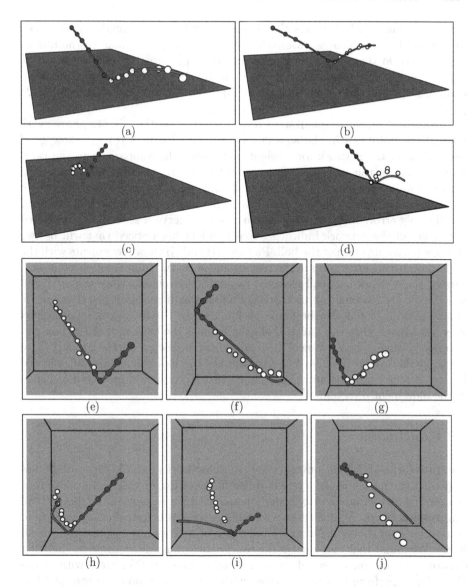

Fig. 4. Qualitative results of the concatenated input model for the table tennis setup. Blue balls correspond to the input frames, white balls are predicted by the network and the red lines indicates the ground truth trajectory. (Color figure online)

best when the ball is flying towards the camera and when there is sufficient distance between two positions of the ball in the trajectory as seen in Fig. 4(a) and (b). Movements that are far away from the camera and have short trajectories like in Fig. 4(c) and (d) are more difficult for the network. Though it is interesting to see that the network is still predicting a trajectory that is meaningful for the movement which shows that it has really learned to predict trajectories during the learning process. Moreover, this result is comparable to the human performance in this task, i.e. the movements in pictures (c) and (d) would be hard to predict also for humans due to their distance to the point of view, especially when taking into account that the input images are only of size 128×128 pixels.

Figure 4(e)–(j) show qualitative results created by the two-stream-network with 2D convolutions in the squash environment. Pictures (e)–(g) show good predictions of the network for straight movements. In comparison to the table tennis scenario, the movements are predicted before or after initial collisions with the walls took place and in boxes of different sizes. In picture (h) we can see a movement where the network has to predict two collisions and produces a rather big error. Interestingly, we can clearly observe a knee in the predicted movement of the network indicating that it might has noticed that will be two changes in the direction of the ball. Pictures (i) and (j) show movements with the highest occurring error rates in the test set and show two important observations. Firstly, the network has really learned to predict movements since the predicted movements are reasonable trajectories of a flying ball. Secondly, the errors made by the network could also be made by humans. In Picture (i) one has to look very hard to see that the ball is bouncing against the back wall of the box and therefore changes its movement instead of just bouncing on the ground. Vice versa, in Picture (j) it is hard to say whether the ball will bounce against the back wall or not and the network assumed that it would and predicted a change in the movement direction.

6   Conclusion

We studied the ability of convolutional neural networks to build physical models to predict the movement of a ball in different scenarios for video input data that contains no further labels or information and with low resolution. To this end, we compared network architectures with different kinds of convolution operation, monocular- and stereo visual input and different ways of processing stereo visual input. We found that these networks can predict many movements in changing environment and on unseen data with small error rates. Networks with stereo visual input perform better than those with monocular vision and can, just like human beings, gain advantage from the additional viewpoint for estimating the depth in images. 3D convolutions, however, are not able to gain advantage by processing contiguous frames of the movement at once and show clearly worse performance than networks with 2D convolutions only. All networks have problems when encountering difficult motions with multiple changes in directions and when the beginning of the movement is hard to see. However, often these falsely predicted movements still appear reasonable to a human.

References

1. Bhat, K.S., Seitz, S.M., Popović, J., Khosla, P.K.: Computing the physical parameters of rigid-body motion from video. In: Heyden, A., Sparr, G., Nielsen, M., Johansen, P. (eds.) ECCV 2002. LNCS, vol. 2350, pp. 551–565. Springer, Heidelberg (2002). doi:10.1007/3-540-47969-4_37

2. Fragkiadaki, K., Agrawal, P., Levine, S., Malik, J.: Learning visual predictive models of physics for playing billiards. CoRR abs/1511.07404 (2015)

3. Hamrick, J.B., Battaglia, P., Tenenbaum, J.B.: Probabilistic internal physics models guide judgments about object dynamics. In: Proceedings of the 33th Annual Meeting of the Cognitive Science Society, CogSci 2011, July 20–23, Boston (2011)

4. Hinton, G.: Neural networks for machine learning, lecture notes. http://www.cs.toronto.edu/~tijmen/csc321

5. Ji, S., Xu, W., Yang, M., Yu, K.: 3D convolutional neural networks for human action recognition. IEEE Trans. Pattern Anal. Mach. Intell. **35**(1), 221–231 (2013)

6. Karpathy, A., Toderici, G., Shetty, S., Leung, T., Sukthankar, R., Fei-Fei, L.: Large-scale video classification with convolutional neural networks. In: Proceedings of the 2014 IEEE Conference on Computer Vision and Pattern Recognition, CVPR 2014, pp. 1725–1732. IEEE Computer Society, Washington (2014)

7. Krizhevsky, A., Sutskever, I., Hinton, G.E.: Imagenet classification with deep convolutional neural networks. In: Pereira, F., Burges, C.J.C., Bottou, L., Weinberger, K.Q. (eds) Advances in Neural Information Processing Systems, vol. 25, pp. 1097–1105. Curran Associates Inc. (2012)

8. Lerer, A., Gross, S., Fergus, R.: Learning physical intuition of block towers by example. In: Proceedings of the 33rd International Conference on Machine Learning, ICML 2016, pp. 430–438, New York City, 19–24 June 2016

9. Michalski, V., Memisevic, R., Konda, K.: Modeling deep temporal dependencies with recurrent grammar cells. In: Advances in Neural Information Processing Systems, vol. 27, pp. 1925–1933. Curran Associates Inc. (2014)

10. Mottaghi, R., Bagherinezhad, H., Rastegari, M., Farhadi, A.: Newtonian image understanding: unfolding the dynamics of objects in static images. CoRR abs/1511.04048 (2015)

11. Kyriazis, N., Oikonomidis, I., Argyros, A.: Binding computer vision to physics based simulation: the case study of a bouncing ball. In: Proceedings of the British Machine Vision Conference, p. 43.1–43.11. BMVA Press (2011)

12. Tran, D., Bourdev, L., Fergus, R., Torresani, L., Paluri, M.: Learning spatiotemporal features with 3D convolutional networks. In: 2015 IEEE International Conference on Computer Vision (ICCV), pp. 4489–4497. IEEE (2015)

13. Walker, J., Doersch, C., Gupta, A., Hebert, M.: An uncertain future: forecasting from static images using variational autoencoders. CoRR abs/1606.07873 (2016)

14. Wu, J., Yildirim, I., Lim, J.J., Freeman, B., Tenenbaum, J.: Galileo: perceiving physical object properties by integrating a physics engine with deep learning. In: Cortes, C., Lawrence, N.D., Lee, D.D., Sugiyama, M., Garnett, R. (eds) Advances in Neural Information Processing Systems, vol. 28, pp. 127–135. Curran Associates Inc. (2015)

Finding the Unknown:
Novelty Detection with Extreme Value
Signatures of Deep Neural Activations

Alexander Schultheiss[1], Christoph Käding[1,2(✉)], Alexander Freytag[3],
and Joachim Denzler[1,2]

[1] Computer Vision Group, Friedrich Schiller University Jena, Jena, Germany
{alexander.schultheiss,christoph.kaeding}@uni-jena.de
[2] Michael Stifel Center Jena, Jena, Germany
[3] Carl Zeiss AG, Jena, Germany

Abstract. Achieving or even surpassing human-level accuracy became
recently possible in a variety of application scenarios due to the rise of
convolutional neural networks (CNNs) trained from large datasets. However, solving supervised visual recognition tasks by discriminating among
known categories is only one side of the coin. In contrast to this, novelty detection is still an unsolved task where instances of yet unknown
categories need to be identified. Therefore, we propose to leverage the
powerful discriminative nature of CNNs to novelty detection tasks by
investigating class-specific activation patterns. More precisely, we assume
that a semantic category can be described by its *extreme value signature*,
that specifies which dimensions of deep neural activations have largest
values. By following this intuition, we show that already a small number
of high-valued dimensions allows to separate known from unknown categories. Our approach is simple, intuitive, and can be easily put on top
of CNNs trained for vanilla classification tasks. We empirically validate
the benefits of our approach in terms of accuracy and speed by comparing it against established methods in a variety of novelty detection
tasks derived from ImageNet. Finally, we show that visualizing extreme
value signatures allows to inspect class-specific patterns learned during
training which may ultimately help to better understand CNN models.

1 Introduction

The availability of large annotated datasets and efficient training algorithms for
supervised deep learning lead the path to a striking increase in performance
of current visual recognition systems [20]. For several applications, however,

This research was supported by grant DE 735/10-1 of the German Research Foundation (DFG).

Electronic supplementary material The online version of this chapter (doi:10.
1007/978-3-319-66709-6_19) contains supplementary material, which is available to
authorized users.

© Springer International Publishing AG 2017
V. Roth and T. Vetter (Eds.): GCPR 2017, LNCS 10496, pp. 226–238, 2017.
DOI: 10.1007/978-3-319-66709-6_19

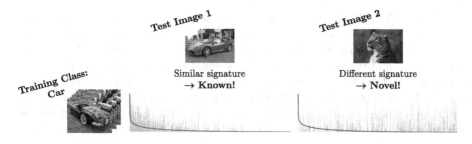

Fig. 1. Shown are neural activation patterns of two test images obtained by a CNN. For the known class, the mean vector of activations which serves as class prototype is sorted by value in descending order and shown in blue. Neural activations of two test images are ordered according to this permutation and are shown in red. For an example of the same category (*left*), the distribution of activation strength follows roughly the same trend as the class prototype. In contrast, the image of a novel category (*right*) has strong activations in a different set of dimensions. (Color figure online)

training discriminative models is not sufficient or even not possible since classes are either not known in advance, or not completely covered by a fixed training dataset. Due to this reason, algorithms are needed that not only discriminate among known categories but which additionally detect instances of yet unknown categories. This important task is known as novelty detection [4,5,14,15,22,27] or open-set recognition [2,3,21] and we present a simple method for this task.

Our approach is based on characterizing known classes with extreme value signatures (EVS) computed for neural activation vectors. Extreme value signatures specify which dimensions of deep neural activations have largest values. Previous work has shown that a surprisingly large fraction of the original image signal can be recovered from the high-scored activations [16]. We go one step further and show that the signatures even capture discriminative information not only with respect to known but also with respect to unknown classes. EVS are therefore suited for novelty detection as visualized in Fig. 1. For an efficient realization, we follow a prototype-based approach, where each known class is encoded by the EVS of the class-mean activation vector. In summary, we found that our extreme value signatures are compact, effective for novelty detection, and a promising representation for further improvements of the terra incognita of open-set recognition.

2   Related Work

In the following, we review related techniques for novelty detection which are most relevant for our approach. For an extensive overview far beyond the current scope, the interested reader is referred to the overview article by Pimentel *et al.* [19].

One-Class Classification. Presumably the most popular approach for novelty detection is the one-class SVM by Schoelkopf *et al.* [22]. Similar to its two-class pendant, a hyperplane is computed which separates all examples of one class from the origin of the feature space with maximal margin. For certain choices of the kernel function, this is identical to the equally popular Support Vector Data Description by Tax and Duin [26], which estimates an enclosing hypersphere of smallest radius. As a third popular technique, the work of Kemmler *et al.* shows how to apply Gaussian processes regression models to one-class classification [14]. Although all techniques are well established, they miss a sound formulation for multi-class scenarios where more than one category is known.

Multi-class Novelty Detection. To overcome the one-class limitation, several approaches have been introduced recently. Vinokurow and Weinshall propose to rely on an ensemble of binary classifiers to detect novel classes [27]. Each binary classifier is trained to discriminate between the raw novelty score of a test sample and the average raw novelty score of a known class. These raw scores involve confidence values which can be obtained from any multi-class classification algorithm. A different approach was proposed by Kenk *et al.* [15] based on calculating a novelty score from the Hellinger distance between color histograms. Jumutc and Suykens [13] proposed three extensions of their earlier work on Supervised Novelty Detection (SND) [12] for multi-class novelty detection. Bodesheim *et al.* introduced the Kernel Null Foley-Sammon Transform (KNFST) for multi-class novelty detection [5]. The learned transformation maps all examples from a single class to a unique point in the null space. Thereby, novelty of unseen instances can be estimated by the minimal distance to all available class points in the null space. The authors extended their approach in [4] using local learning. KNFST models are learned for each test sample separately using only the K most similar training examples which leads to exemplar-specific novelty detection models. Although these approaches come with their own benefits, they require time-consuming training of the novelty detection model. Furthermore, they do not take the nature of underlying representations into account. In contrast, we exploit that CNNs can act as a joint model for representation and classification and leverage this idea to skip additional training of novelty detection models.

Open-Set Recognition. The idea of open-set risk for open set recognition was presented by Scheirer *et al.* [21]. Their formulation results in a special kind of one-class SVM, referred to as 1-vs-set machine. The idea of open set risk was further refined by Bendale and Boult [2]. The authors present the nearest-non-outlier algorithm, which is an extension of the nearest-class-mean algorithm for open-set scenarios. Similar in spirit is the openmax-approach by the same authors [3]. They propose to replace the commonly used `softmax` layer in CNNs with an `openmax` layer which classifies into known categories or "unknown". We follow their approaches by re-using existing classification CNNs as-is, but aim at predicting novelty based on neural activations of arbitrary layers.

Binarizing CNN Activations. A technique which is conceptually similar to EVS was proposed by Li *et al.* [16] for learning with few examples. They propose to binarize CNN activations using the K largest values and conclude that "discriminative information within CNN activation is mostly embedded in the dimension indices of the K largest magnitudes". A similar analysis has been done in [8] with the goal of reconstructing original images from given CNN activations. Finally, a similar transformation of activations was used in [17] for regularizing autoencoders and in [11] for stochastic pooling. We follow their path by using EVS for image encoding and show how to analyze them to predict novelty in multi-class scenarios.

3   Extreme Value Signatures

Neural Activations for Novelty Detection. Many popular approaches in machine vision use activations of pre-trained CNNs as off-the-shelf image representations [7,23]. Our current understanding is that the majority of trainable layers in CNNs (especially convolutional layers) becomes sensitive to the specific characteristics that are common in natural images when fed with millions of training images. In particular, it has been shown that filter masks of convolutional layers become sensitive to visual "elements" that can be commonly found in natural images [28]. Whereas these elements mainly correspond to low-level texture patterns for lower layers, they can be related to semantically meaningful object parts in higher layers [24]. This data-driven approach to representation learning is obviously appealing in several aspects, especially when large amounts of data are available [20]. Although the respective CNNs have originally been trained for discriminating among known categories, we show that their extreme value statistics can also be used to detect instances of novel categories.

Extreme Value Signatures for Individual Images. Let $\mathbf{x} \in \mathbb{R}^D$ be the activation extracted at a chosen layer when applying a given CNN to a single image. Babenko *et al.* showed in [1] that this representation still maintains a large amount of discriminative information after binarization with a fixed threshold τ. Hence, the binary vector $\mathbf{b}$:

$$\mathbf{b}\left(\mathbf{x}, \tau\right) = \left(\delta\left(\mathbf{x}\left[d\right] > \tau\right)\right)_{d=1}^{D} \tag{1}$$

can serve as a substitute for $\mathbf{x}$ when the threshold τ is chosen appropriately since it translates $\mathbf{x}$ into a binary representation. Note that for the ease of readability, $\mathbf{x}\left[d\right]$ denotes the dth dimension of $\mathbf{x}$ and the function $\delta\left(v\right)$ maps to 1 or 0 if v is true or false, respectively.

Despite the successful application of binarized neural activations in [1], relying on a constant threshold might be too restrictive for the complexity of visual recognition tasks. In a more general setting, we can replace this constant threshold by a threshold function $T\left(\cdot\right)$ which returns a threshold specifically tailored to each example $\mathbf{x}$:

$$\mathbf{b}\left(\mathbf{x}, T\left(\mathbf{x}\right)\right) = \left(\delta\left(\mathbf{x}\left[d\right] > T\left(\mathbf{x}\right)\right)\right)_{d=1}^{D}. \tag{2}$$

Our extreme value signature follows this general concept. Let us therefore denote $\pi_{\mathbf{x}}$ the permutation that brings $\mathbf{x}$ into descending order:

$$\mathop{\forall}_{i,j \in \{1,\dots,D\}, i<j} : \mathbf{x}\left[\pi_{\mathbf{x}}\left[i\right]\right] \geq \mathbf{x}\left[\pi_{\mathbf{x}}\left[j\right]\right]. \tag{3}$$

Thereby, we obtain a threshold $T_{\mathrm{rank\_K}}\left(\mathbf{x}\right)$ for each $\mathbf{x}$ using the K-highest activation:

$$T_{\mathrm{rank\_K}}\left(\mathbf{x}\right) = \mathbf{x}\left[\pi_{\mathbf{x}}\left[K\right]\right]. \tag{4}$$

The resulting binary vector $\mathbf{b}\left(\mathbf{x}, T_{\mathrm{rank\_K}}(\mathbf{x})\right)$ can therefore be seen as an indicator for the K highest values of $\mathbf{x}$, which we refer to as the EVS of $\mathbf{x}$. When thinking of visual recognition scenarios, we expect that two images that contain similar visual concepts also lead to a similar set of extreme dimensions in the resulting neural activations. Hence, their binarized codes based on $T_{\mathrm{rank\_K}}$ should be close as well. Therefore, we can apply the inner product

$$\gamma(\mathbf{x}', \mathbf{x}) = 1 - \frac{\mathbf{b}(\mathbf{x}', T_{\mathrm{rank\_K}}\left(\mathbf{x}'\right))^{\mathrm{T}} \, \mathbf{b}(\mathbf{x}, T_{\mathrm{rank\_K}}\left(\mathbf{x}\right))}{K} \tag{5}$$

to estimate the novelty of a test example $\mathbf{x}'$ with respect to a known example $\mathbf{x}$. Note that the normalization $1 - \frac{1}{K}$ is only required to transform the score into $[0,1]$ such that large scores indicate novelty.

Novel Class Detection with Extreme Value Signatures. The previous derivations only focused on the difference of a novel example $\mathbf{x}'$ and a known example $\mathbf{x}$ with respect to their extreme value signatures. In multi-class scenarios, we can additionally exploit the class label which is associated with every training example. To obtain an extreme value signature for an entire known class, we have a variety of options to choose from. We empirically found that computing the mean vector $\boldsymbol{\mu}$ of activations from all examples within a class and determining the K-highest dimensions thereof is simple, easy to implement, and works well in practice. The implicit assumption is that the K-highest dimensions correspond to specific patterns of a known class. Hence, if a test image shows a similar extreme-value signature, it is likely to contain similar visual patterns.

For multiple known classes, we follow [5] and take the minimum over all class distances as measured in Eq. (5) as resulting novelty score. Thereby, a test example will only be considered as novel if it is different from the extreme-value signatures of *all* known categories M. Hence, our final multi-class novelty score $\gamma_{\mathrm{MC}}(\mathbf{x}')$ can be expressed as:

$$\gamma_{\mathrm{MC}}(\mathbf{x}') = \min_{1 \leq m \leq M} \gamma(\mathbf{x}', \boldsymbol{\mu}_m). \tag{6}$$

Novelty Detection Based on Permutation Distances. Comparing the K-highest feature dimensions, as introduced in Eq. (6), does not take the ranking of the K-highest dimensions into account. In consequence, the score can be extremely sensitive to the choice of K. Intuitively, small Ks would not cover all dimensions which are relevant for a category, whereas large Ks would also include irrelevant dimensions. Thereby, already marginal reordering among the highest-valued dimensions could lead to overestimating novelty in the first case. In contrast to this, an underestimation of novelty or a wrong assignment to a known class could happen in the latter case. To overcome these issues, we propose to consider the ranking among the K-highest dimensions by comparing the highest activations based on the Spearman footrule distance [6].

The Spearman footrule distance allows for calculating distances between two D-dimensional permutations $\boldsymbol{\pi_1}$ and $\boldsymbol{\pi_2}$:

$$d_{\text{Spearman}}(\boldsymbol{\pi_1}, \boldsymbol{\pi_2}) = \sum_{k=1}^{D} \sum_{j=1}^{D} \delta_{\boldsymbol{\pi_2}[j], \boldsymbol{\pi_1}[k]} \cdot |k - j|, \tag{7}$$

where the Kronecker delta $\delta_{\boldsymbol{\pi_2}[j], \boldsymbol{\pi_1}[k]}$ filters relevant indices since it has value 1 only if the values of $\boldsymbol{\pi_2}[j]$ and $\boldsymbol{\pi_1}[k]$ are equal, otherwise it has value 0. The difference between j and k measures then the absolute displacement in the two permutations. To estimate the novelty of a test example $\mathbf{x}'$ with respect to a known example $\mathbf{x}$, we can now apply the footrule distance on the permutations $\boldsymbol{\pi_{\mathbf{x}'}}$ and $\boldsymbol{\pi_{\mathbf{x}}}$ as defined in Eq. (3) which re-arranges in descending order the values of $\mathbf{x}'$ and $\mathbf{x}$, respectively. As in Eq. (6), this can finally be transferred to the multi-class scenario by minimizing distance over *all* M class mean vectors:

$$\gamma_{\text{Spearman}}(\mathbf{x}') = \min_{1 \leq m \leq M} \sum_{k=1}^{K} \sum_{j=1}^{D} \delta_{\boldsymbol{\pi_{\mathbf{x}'}}[j], \boldsymbol{\pi_{\mu_m}}[k]} \cdot |k - j|. \tag{8}$$

Note that the Spearman footrule distance originally suggests to compare the ranking of all dimensions. Instead, we propose to only compare the ranking of the K highest activations in $\mathbf{x}'$ with their ranking in each class prototype $\boldsymbol{\mu}_m$.

4   Experiments

We investigated our approach for multi-class novelty detection both quantitatively in comparison with state-of-the-art techniques (Sects. 4.2 to 4.4) and qualitatively (Sect. 4.5). As benchmarking set, we chose the popular ImageNet dataset from ILSVRC'12 [20] and derived novelty detection tasks of varying difficulty. In all experiments, we encode images with neural activations of a AlexNet-Places365-CNN [29] without any fine-tuning. Thereby, none of the involved classes was already observed during model training[1]. We experimented with activations from layers CONV4 to FC8 with and without RELU and feature normalization to unit length. In the following, we only show results for FC6 which lead to highest overall accuracy, but provide evaluations for all layers in the suplementary material (S.1).

---

[1]   We assume that fine-tuning networks for known classes would further improve the overall accuracy since activation patterns are expected to become specific for known classes. However, fine-tuning networks for all evaluated tasks and splits would be too time consuming. Therefore, the used Places-CNN ensures a fair comparison since it was not trained with any involved ImageNet class.

4.1   Baseline Methods

Besides our two introduced approaches based on extreme value signatures (denoted as K-extremes and Spearman), we chose several techniques for comparison as reviewed in Sect. 2. The presumably simplest baseline is to transfer the nearest-class mean approach [18] from classification to novelty detection. In this spirit, the euclidean distance to the closest class mean serves as novelty score (NCM(Euclid)). Modeling each class by a Gaussian distribution is similarly simple [10]. Computing the negative log-likelihood for each class and returning the largest value thereof serves as a simple estimate of novelty (Maximum-likelihood). Alternatively, one-class SVMs [22] can be trained for each class. Distances to all M decision boundaries are maximum-pooled as suggested in [4] (1-SVM). Modeling the entire training data by a Gaussian process regression [14] allows for computing the predictive variance for unseen data (GP-VAR). Exemplar-specific novelty detection models are obtained by local KNFST as introduced in [4] (Local-KNFST). Finally, we compare against K-extremesvalue which is inspired by our extreme value signatures but directly uses the negative sum of the K largest activations as an indicator for novelty instead of their ranking. If not specified otherwise, we follow the setup described in [4] regarding the choice of hyperparameters.

4.2   Multi-class Novelty Detection on ImageNet Subsets

We first put a focus on accuracy rather than scalability. Hence, we start with an evaluation on ILSVRC'12 data with small and medium sized splits.

Setup. We follow Bodesheim *et al.* [4] and use the setup initially described in [5]. Therefore, we randomly select different subsets of the ILSVRC'12 classes and split them into known and novel categories. For now, we consider all split sizes which were used in [4]. This results in scenarios with ratios of 10:10 (*i.e.*, 10 known and 10 novel classes) up to 50:50. For each known class, a random training set of 100 samples is drawn. From the remaining images as well as from all elements of the novel classes, 50 samples per class are randomly drawn to serve as test set. We average results over 20 random splits for each task to allow for statistically valid conclusions. To allow for direct comparison, we use the same class splits and selected samples as in [4]. Accuracy is measured by AUC [9]. The size of the neighborhood for each split for Local-KNFST is set to best performing values according to [4]. For K-extremes, Spearman, and K-extremes-value, we exhaustively tested K over a broad range and report the best results here ($K = D \cdot 0.1$ for K-extremes and Spearman, $K = D \cdot 0.7$ for K-extremes-value). Furthermore, we evaluated neural activations of different layers with or without passing them through RELUs and with or without normalization to unit length. Here, we only report the best results for each combination of method, encoding, and parameter setting. For the sake of completeness and reproducibility, we provide results obtained with all settings in the suplementary material (S.1).

Table 1. Results from different tasks for multi-class novelty detection using FC6 features and best parameter settings per method (averaged over 20 splits per task).

Method	10:10	20:20	30:30	40:40	50:50	500:500
NCM(Euclid)	71.70%	67.17%	65.14%	62.37%	62.45%	53.99%
Maximum-likelihood	63.84%	61.07%	60.13%	58.77%	58.18%	-
Local-KNFST [4]	71.38%	**68.16%**	65.79%	64.16%	61.56%	-
GP-VAR [14]	71.67%	67.19%	65.19%	62.33%	62.51%	-
1-SVM [22]	64.75%	60.72%	59.54%	57.26%	57.52%	-
K-extremes-value	71.60%	68.01%	65.98%	63.77%	62.33%	-
K-extremes (ours)	71.72%	68.04%	66.21%	**64.38%**	63.05%	**54.56%**
Spearman (ours)	**71.87%**	68.14%	**66.25%**	64.24%	**63.06%**	54.44%

Results. In the first columns of Table 1, results for baseline methods in comparison with our approaches are shown[2]. As a general trend, we observe that the accuracy of all methods drops with an increasing number of known and unknown classes. This behavior is not surprising, since random chance for missclassification increases with more available classes. In addition, we find that the difference in the resulting accuracies of the tested methods is only marginal on the 10:10 split. The only notable exceptions are 1-SVM and Maximum-likelihood which are clearly inferior to the remaining methods. This pattern becomes even more dominant for an increasing number of classes. To check for statistical significance of the small but observable differences in accuracy, we performed a Wilcoxon signed rank test. Due to the matter of space, the results can be found in the suplementary (S.4). The analysis can be summarized as follows: there are no significant differences on small splits, but significant differences on large splits slightly in favor of our proposed extreme value signatures.

The results also reveal that summing up values of dimensions with largest values (K-extremes-value) is not superior to simply considering the indices of the dimensions themselves. Therefore, we can conclude that the actual values of neural activations can be ignored when their relative order is known. The results also imply that Spearman is not clearly advantageous in comparison to the vanilla K-extremes method. However, this is not surprising when we consider that the main advantage of Spearman is the robustness towards wrong choices of K. Since Table 1 only shows the configuration of each method which lead to highest accuracy, the proper selection K is neglected. The overview of results from all settings in the suplementary material (S.1) underlines Spearman's robustness regarding the choice of K. As a final note, the suplementary also contains a qualitative result showing most and least novel images (S.3).

---

[2] Note that the reported results for Local-KNFST differ from [4] since we use CNN features instead of dense SIFT features which results in improved performance.

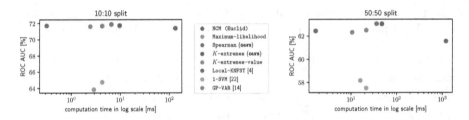

Fig. 2. Comparison of all approaches on the 10:10 split (*left*) and the 50:50 split (*right*) taking accuracy and computation time into account (computation times averaged over all examples in each split).

4.3 Computation Time Analysis

Besides accuracy, computation time is one of the most critical aspects of algorithms. Therefore, we investigate the execution times of testing a single image for each of the evaluated novelty detection methods.

Setup. We conduct a computation time analysis on a desktop computer with an Intel Core 2 Quad CPU with 2.4 GHz and 8 GB of system RAM. For Local-KNFST, GP-VAR and 1-SVM, we use the MATLAB code provided by [4]. All remaining methods are implemented in python. Computation times of each method are evaluated on a 10:10 split and a 50:50 split and averaged over all test examples in each split.

Results. In Fig. 2, we show the relationship between accuracy and computation time. The observable relation is not unexpected: NCM(Euclid) is the fastest baseline since it only requires simple distance calculations. On the other side of the spectrum, LocalKNFST is an order of magnitude slower due to the necessity of training a model specifically for each test sample. The remaining techniques are roughly equally fast with ∼10 ms per evaluation. However, K-extremes and Spearman are slowest wrt. to absolute numbers. We attribute this to the explicit sorting of feature vectors in our non-optimized implementation and assume that an optimized implementation involving bit-level operations could reduce the required computation time.

4.4 Large-Scale Multi-class Novelty Detection on ImageNet

The results presented so far in Sect. 4.2 imply that the accuracy of all methods drops the more classes are involved. Hence, we were interested in conducting a large scale analysis for further investigation.

Setup. We split the available classes of the ILSVRC'12 data randomly in half which results in 500 known and 500 unknown classes. The remaining setup is kept identical to Sect. 4.2 and we present an exhaustive evaluation of all investigated settings in the suplementary material (S.2). Note that Local-KNFST would not be applicable in this scenario in terms of computation time as shown in Sect. 4.3. Additionally, kernel dimensions are also too large for our available implementation of GP-VAR and 1-SVM. Therefore, we only compare the proposed Spearman and K-extremes criterion with the remaining (and best performing) baseline NCM(Euclid).

Results. Results are shown in the last column of Table 1. As expected, the overall accuracy drops in comparison to the setup in Sect. 4.2. The proposed K-extremes performs best closely followed by Spearman. Both methods are able to outperform NCM(Euclid) by a small but significant margin. The suplementary material contains a significance analysis (S.4) as well as further evidence for the robustness of Spearman towards the choice of K (S.2). Although we conclude that our proposed novelty detection methods can be successfully applied in large scale scenarios, our best-performing method improves over random guessing by only less than 5%. Hence, novelty detection in large-scale scenarios still remains an unsolved problem which sorely needs increased attention.

4.5   Visualizing Class-Indicative Image Parts with EVS

In addition to the quantitative estimation of novelty as presented so far, we can further exploit the comparison of EVS to assess which parts of a novel image are indicative for a known category. A visualization is shown in Fig. 3.

Setup. We compute gradient maps as suggested by [25] using the FC6 layer of a Places205-CNN [30][3]. To visually inspect class-indicative image parts, we set all entries to 1 which correspond to the K-highest feature dimension of class m ($K = 0.1 \cdot D$). All remaining values are set to 0 and the derivative of this target vector wrt. the input image is computed using backprop. The generated gradient map is then smoothed for better visualization with a Gaussian kernel (size 20×20 pixels, $\sigma = 5$). After resizing of the smoothed map to the original image size and normalization[4], we threshold all values against $1/3$ and consider all pixels

 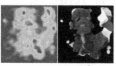 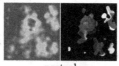 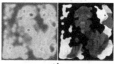

| input image | sussex spaniel | pretzel | tie |

Fig. 3. Which parts of a novel image are characteristic for known classes? Saliency maps obtained from comparing extreme value signatures allow for visual analysis.

---

[3] Due to implementation constraints we applied a different network as in Sects. 4.2 to 4.4.

[4] Gradient maps are normalized individually for better visualization, hence, the scaling can not be compared directly. Results of uniformly normalized maps are similar.

above this value as relevant. Irrelevant pixels are blacked out. Visualizations for different values of K are provided in the suplementary material (S.5).

Results. Using this visualization heuristic, it can be seen that only few image parts would be indicative for the category `pretzel`. On the contrary, the class `tie` is supported by image regions from foreground and background making it a vague indicator as well. Only for the (correct) category `Sussex spaniel`, the indicative image regions are entirely in the foreground and closely align with the object boundary. Hence, we conclude that EVS are indeed indicative for class-specific image parts and allow for visual inspection of classification decisions.

5   Conclusion

In this paper, we proposed to exploit the discriminative nature of CNNs to tackle the challenging task of multi-class novelty detection. Our approach is inspired by the sensitivity of internal nodes of neural networks to class-specific patterns when trained in a supervised manner. We empirically found that simple statistics regarding which nodes are most heavily activated allow for discriminating between known and unknown classes. Since these *extreme value signatures* are intuitive and easy to implement on top of existing models, they allow to "upgrade" arbitrary classification networks to jointly estimate novelty and class membership. An analysis on different subsets of the ILSVRC'12 data shows performance benefits in terms of accuracy, computation time, and scalability of our approach in comparison with established baselines. To gain further insights, we finally investigated class-indicative image parts which can be obtained by visualizing extreme value signatures. Besides the positive aspects, however, our results also underline clearly that multi-class novelty detection is far from being solved when more than a handful of classes are involved.

References

1. Babenko, A., Slesarev, A., Chigorin, A., Lempitsky, V.: Neural codes for image retrieval. In: Fleet, D., Pajdla, T., Schiele, B., Tuytelaars, T. (eds.) ECCV 2014. LNCS, vol. 8689, pp. 584–599. Springer, Cham (2014). doi:10.1007/978-3-319-10590-1_38
2. Bendale, A., Boult, T.: Towards open world recognition. In: Computer Vision and Pattern Recognition (CVPR) (2015)
3. Bendale, A., Boult, T.E.: Towards open set deep networks. In: The IEEE Conference on Computer Vision and Pattern Recognition (CVPR), June 2016
4. Bodesheim, P., Freytag, A., Rodner, E., Denzler, J.: Local novelty detection in multi-class recognition problems. In: Winter Conference on Applications of Computer Vision (WACV) (2015)
5. Bodesheim, P., Freytag, A., Rodner, E., Kemmler, M., Denzler, J.: Kernel null space methods for novelty detection. In: Computer Vision and Pattern Recognition (CVPR) (2013)

6. Brandenburg, F.J., Gleißner, A., Hofmeier, A.: The nearest neighbor spearman footrule distance for bucket, interval, and partial orders. J. Comb. Optim. **26**(2), 310–332 (2013)
7. Donahue, J., Jia, Y., Vinyals, O., Hoffman, J., Zhang, N., Tzeng, E., Darrell, T.: DeCAF: A deep convolutional activation feature for generic visual recognition. In: International Conference on Machine Learning (ICML) (2014)
8. Dosovitskiy, A., Brox, T.: Inverting convolutional networks with convolutional networks. CoRR abs/1506.02753 (2015)
9. Fawcett, T.: An introduction to ROC analysis. Pattern Recogn. Lett. **27**(8), 861–874 (2006)
10. Friedman, J., Hastie, T., Tibshirani, R.: The Elements of Statistical Learning. Springer, Heidelberg (2001). doi:10.1007/978-0-387-21606-5
11. Huang, Y., Sun, X., Lu, M., Xu, M.: Channel-max, channel-drop and stochastic max-pooling. In: Computer Vision and Pattern Recognition Workshop (CVPR-WS) (2015)
12. Jumutc, V., Suykens, J.A.: Supervised novelty detection. In: Computational Intelligence and Data Mining (CIDM) (2013)
13. Jumutc, V., Suykens, J.A.: Multi-class supervised novelty detection. Pattern Anal. Mach. Intell. (PAMI) **36**(12), 2510–2523 (2014)
14. Kemmler, M., Rodner, E., Denzler, J.: One-class classification with Gaussian processes. In: Kimmel, R., Klette, R., Sugimoto, A. (eds.) ACCV 2010. LNCS, vol. 6493, pp. 489–500. Springer, Heidelberg (2011). doi:10.1007/978-3-642-19309-5_38
15. Kenk, V.S., Kovačič, S., Kristan, M., Hajdinjak, M., Perš, J., et al.: Visual re-identification across large, distributed camera networks. Image Vis. Comput. **34**, 11–26 (2015)
16. Li, Y., Liu, L., Shen, C., Van Den Hengel, A.: Mining mid-level visual patterns with deep CNN activations. Int. J. Comput. Vis. **121**(3), 344–364 (2017). http://dx.doi.org/10.1007/s11263-016-0945-y
17. Makhzani, A., Frey, B.J.: Winner-take-all autoencoders. In: Neural Information Processing Systems (NIPS) (2015)
18. Mensink, T., Verbeek, J., Perronnin, F., Csurka, G.: Distance-based image classification: generalizing to new classes at near-zero cost. Pattern Anal. Mach. Intell. (PAMI) **35**(11), 2624–2637 (2013)
19. Pimentel, M.A., Clifton, D.A., Clifton, L., Tarassenko, L.: A review of novelty detection. Signal Process. **99**, 215–249 (2014)
20. Russakovsky, O., Deng, J., Su, H., Krause, J., Satheesh, S., Ma, S., Huang, Z., Karpathy, A., Khosla, A., Bernstein, M., et al.: Imagenet large scale visual recognition challenge. Int. J. Comput. Vis. (IJCV) **115**(3), 211–252 (2015)
21. Scheirer, W.J., de Rezende Rocha, A., Sapkota, A., Boult, T.E.: Toward open set recognition. Pattern Anal. Mach. Intell. (PAMI) **35**(7), 1757–1772 (2013)
22. Schölkopf, B., Platt, J.C., Shawe-Taylor, J., Smola, A.J., Williamson, R.C.: Estimating the support of a high-dimensional distribution. Neural Comput. **13**(7), 1443–1471 (2001)
23. Sharif Razavian, A., Azizpour, H., Sullivan, J., Carlsson, S.: CNN features off-the-shelf: an astounding baseline for recognition. In: Conference on Computer Vision and Pattern Recognition Workshops (CVPR-WS) (2014)
24. Simon, M., Rodner, E., Denzler, J.: Part detector discovery in deep convolutional neural networks. In: Cremers, D., Reid, I., Saito, H., Yang, M.-H. (eds.) ACCV 2014. LNCS, vol. 9004, pp. 162–177. Springer, Cham (2015). doi:10.1007/978-3-319-16808-1_12

25. Simonyan, K., Vedaldi, A., Zisserman, A.: Deep inside convolutional networks: visualising image classification models and saliency maps. In: International Conference on Learning Representations Workshop (ICLR-WS) (2014)
26. Tax, D.M., Duin, R.P.: Support vector data description. Mach. Learn. **54**(1), 45–66 (2004)
27. Vinokurov, N., Weinshall, D.: Novelty detection in multiclass scenarios with incomplete set of class labels. arXiv preprint arXiv:1604.06242 (2016)
28. Zeiler, M.D., Fergus, R.: Visualizing and understanding convolutional networks. In: Fleet, D., Pajdla, T., Schiele, B., Tuytelaars, T. (eds.) ECCV 2014. LNCS, vol. 8689, pp. 818–833. Springer, Cham (2014). doi:10.1007/978-3-319-10590-1_53
29. Zhou, B., Khosla, A., Lapedriza, A., Torralba, A., Oliva, A.: Places: an image database for deep scene understanding. arXiv preprint arXiv:1610.02055 (2016)
30. Zhou, B., Lapedriza, A., Xiao, J., Torralba, A., Oliva, A.: Learning deep features for scene recognition using places database. In: Neural Information Processing Systems (NIPS) (2014)

Improving Facial Landmark Detection via a Super-Resolution Inception Network

Martin Knoche, Daniel Merget$^{(\boxtimes)}$, and Gerhard Rigoll

Institute for Human-Machine Communication, Technical University of Munich,
Munich, Germany
daniel.merget@tum.de

Abstract. Modern convolutional neural networks for facial landmark detection have become increasingly robust against occlusions, lighting conditions and pose variations. With the predictions being close to pixel-accurate in some cases, intuitively, the input resolution should be as high as possible. We verify this intuition by thoroughly analyzing the impact of low image resolution on landmark prediction performance. Indeed, performance degradations are already measurable for faces smaller than 50×50 px. In order to mitigate those degradations, a new super-resolution inception network architecture is developed which outperforms recent super-resolution methods on various data sets. By enhancing low resolution images with our model, we are able to improve upon the state of the art in facial landmark detection.

1 Introduction

In the last couple of years, convolutional neural networks (CNNs) have proven to be very powerful in many applications surrounding image processing, computer vision and pattern recognition. While CNNs already outperform humans in the field of image recognition [7,18] and face recognition [24], they still struggle with facial landmark detection [6]. This is not too surprising given that humans are very experienced and well-trained in detecting and locating human faces. Facial landmark detection is difficult because of the large variety of parameters that need to be considered, for example, shape, pose, gender, age, race, lighting, (self-)occlusion, and many more.

Many facial landmark data sets have acknowledged this variety with "in-the-wild" images [3,9,14]. The train and test images are typically of fairly high resolution. This is sensible since the facial landmarks have to be labeled accurately, which requires some minimum resolution. Real-world data, however, may be captured under far worse conditions. For example, surveillance systems often operate at high compression rates, recording people from relatively far away. In that sense, reality can be "even wilder" than common "in-the-wild" data sets. Wang et al. [27] distinguish two principle approaches of dealing with low resolution: Direct and indirect.

© Springer International Publishing AG 2017
V. Roth and T. Vetter (Eds.): GCPR 2017, LNCS 10496, pp. 239–251, 2017.
DOI: 10.1007/978-3-319-66709-6_20

Direct Methods try to find appropriate feature representations in the low resolution space. For example a *direct* approach is to create low resolution images from the high resolution data sets via post-processing. This requires additional effort during training and is not common practice. State-of-the-art landmark detection methods are therefore optimized for medium to high resolution images.

Indirect Methods try to restore high resolution information, for example, via statistical models or super resolution. The key advantage of *indirect* approaches is that they operate independently of the landmark detection algorithm, simplifying training and preserving maximum flexibility. For example, there is much more available training data for super resolution than for landmark detection.

In this work, we pursue an indirect approach to facial landmark detection on low resolution images. Our main contributions are the following:

– We analyze the impact of low resolution images on CNN landmark detection.
– We present a new super-resolution inception (SRINC) architecture with slight improvements over the state of the art in super resolution.
– We demonstrate that CNN landmark detection performance can be improved by applying super resolution to low quality images.
– We show that additional performance can be gained by training the super-resolution network in the same domain as the landmark detection algorithm (i.e., faces).

2   Related Work

Facial Landmark Detection on Low Resolution Images has not been addressed in many publications. While there is a wide range of research for face recognition in the context of low image resolution, facial landmark detection has not gained nearly as much attention. The few works that exist mostly focus on direct methods.

Biswas et al. [2] provide an in-depth analysis of pose regression in low resolution images, using five different landmarks. They transform "the poor quality probe images and the high-quality gallery images in such a manner that the distances between them approximate the distances had the probe images been captured in the same condition". In other words, they use a direct approach in the taxonomy of Wang et al. [27].

An elaborate analysis considering the impact of low resolution in the context of facial landmark detection is provided by Seshadri [21]. In the taxonomy of Wang et al. [27], Seshadri also uses a direct approach by adopting the training set resolution to the test set, but also investigates some cross-resolution effects. In contrast to our approach, Seshadri does not consider convolutional neural networks. Indirect approaches are not considered, either.

Super Resolution. Since our proposed super-resolution method is based on CNNs, we focus on related work in the field of deep learning. A thorough overview of classical image super resolution methods is given in [4, 29].

Dong et al. were the first to implement image super resolution using a convolutional neural network (SRCNN) [5] and were able to beat the fairly recent methods A+ [25], super-resolution forests [20], and transformed self-exemplars [10] concerning PSNR and structural similarity (SSIM) [28]. In the following, we will discuss a number of improved network architectures that have since been proposed [11–13,26].

Tuzel et al. [26] train a global-local upsampling network specifically suited for super resolution of human faces. They demonstrate superior performance compared to SRCNN and other face-specific methods on face data sets. However, they neither provide their model, nor any comparisons for non-facial images, which makes it overall difficult to compare against their results.

Kim et al. propose a very deep super-resolution (VDSR) architecture [12]. In contrast to SRCNN, VDSR is trained on the residual between the ground truth and the interpolated bicubic result. This residual learning strategy is similar to the recently proposed ResNet approach by He et al. [8] but only affects the very last layer, i.e., there is a shortcut connection from input to output but none in between layers. Since VDSR is still shallow compared to ResNet, the single shortcut is already sufficient to boost the network performance considerably. In another work, Kim et al. use the same residual learning target as in [12], but instead of a linear deep architecture they use a recurrent neural network [13].

Another interesting method was proposed by Johnson et al. [11]. Instead of optimizing their network towards PSNR, they introduce a perceptual loss that accounts for the way the human eye perceives image quality. Although their PSNR is worse than simple bicubic interpolation, the results are optically very appealing and realistic. Apart from the fact that the perceptual quality is hard to compare objectively, using a perceptual loss results in more drastically altered images, especially on small scales. This would likely confuse a landmark detection algorithm relying heavily on small scale features. Therefore, we do not consider perceptual loss for our further analysis.

3   Landmark Detection on Low Resolution Images

In this section we investigate the impact of low resolution images on two state-of-the art landmark detection algorithms: TCDCN [34] and CFSS [35]. We use the iBUG [19] (135 images) and HELEN [15] (330 images) data sets for the evaluation. By empirical analysis we found that there are no significant differences for bounding boxes larger than 100×100 px. The images are thus sampled down such that the bounding boxes (provided by [35]) are 100 px in width. Images with bounding boxes narrower than 100 px are discarded. These new test sets will be referred to as iBUG-Norm (90 images) and HELEN-Norm (330 images).

The landmark detection performance is measured using the detection error as used in [22]:

$$\varepsilon = \frac{1}{N d_0} \sum_{n=1}^{N} \sqrt{(x_n - x'_n)^2 + (y_n - y'_n)^2}, \tag{1}$$

where (x_n, y_n) and (x'_n, y'_n) represent the ground truth and predicted coordinates for the $N = 68$ landmarks, respectively. The error is normalized in relation to the ocular distance d_0.

For the analysis, the images are scaled down and up again by different factors ($\times 2$, $\times 3$, and $\times 4$) via bicubic interpolation. Figure 1 depicts the detection error distributions for TCDCN and CFSS on both test sets. The detection error increases considerably at factors $\times 3$ and $\times 4$, but even for factor $\times 2$ there is a slight degradation. Note that CFSS and TCDCN use an internal resizing to 60×60 px and 250×250 px, respectively, which explains why the effect of $\times 2$ scaling is less significant for CFSS. The results indicate that there is a general margin for improving landmark detection on low resolution images: A super resolution algorithm preceding CFSS could theoretically reduce the error for iBug-Norm at $\times 4$ scaling from 12.0% to under 9.7%, which is a relative improvement of 19.5%.

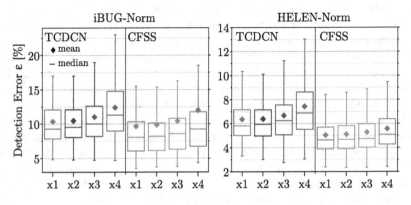

Fig. 1. Landmark detection error (Eq. 1) for TCDCN [34] and CFSS [35] on iBUG-Norm and HELEN-Norm test sets at original scale ($\times 1$) and scaling factors $\times 2$ through $\times 4$. The detection error clearly increases for larger scalings, i.e., for lower image quality.

4   Proposed Super-Resolution Network

In order to improve the landmark detection on low resolution images we implement a novel super resolution network, which is described in more detail in the following sections.

4.1   Network Architecture

We follow the general idea of a deep convolution neural network as described by Kim et al. (VDSR) [12] and combine it with inception modules inspired by Szegedy et al. [23] as illustrated in Fig. 2. As proposed in [12], the network is trained on the residual by adding the input to the output before calculating the loss. This helps the network to converge much faster. The model was implemented using Microsoft's Cognitive Toolkit (CNTK) [32]. We provide the network configurations and trained models at www.mmk.ei.tum.de/srinc/.

The fact that the network is fully convolutional without any fully-connected layers allows for arbitrary input dimensions and therefore arbitrary input scales. Since the patterns on different scales differ, each scale requires a separate set of filters. The core idea behind using inception modules is to allow the network to combine and select among several filter scales in each layer that account for different object scales.

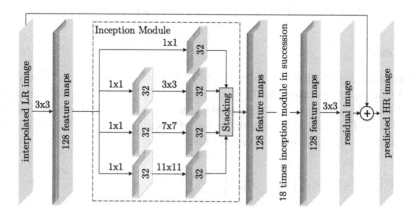

Fig. 2. Proposed super resolution inception (SRINC) architecture: The zero-padded input image is convolved with 128 3×3 filters in the first layer. After 19 successive inception modules, a last convolutional layer shrinks the feature maps down to the number of output channels, i.e., in our case one (grayscale) channel. Rectified linear units are used between layers except after the final convolution and addition.

Another benefit lies in the fact that the receptive field of the network is increased. The maximum receptive field of the network is 195×195 px via the path of consecutive 11×11 convolutions. Nevertheless, we use 51×51 px patches for training to limit memory consumption. The patch size obviously does not exploit the full capacity of the network, but we found that it is sufficient for scaling factors up to $\times 4$. This can be explained by two facts: (1) the output of the network depends mostly on local features and (2) the outer parts of the receptive field are supported by far less paths through the network and therefore contain mostly noise. Further tests (not shown) revealed that the patch size has to be increased for scaling factors larger than $\times 10$ because the local regions affecting the pixels are enlarged.

4.2 Training

Our SRINC model is trained on Set291 which is a composition of 91 natural images by Yang et al. [31] and another 200 natural images from the Berkeley Segmentation Dataset [17].

As in Sect. 3, the training images are sampled down and up, creating a multi-scale training set. Additionally, the data is rotated and flipped, following the same protocol as SRCNN, VDSR and DRCN [5,12,13]. Finally the data set is broken down into approximately 1.2 million 51×51 px patches at a stride of 26 px. As described in [12], deeper networks are more likely to fail to converge. For this reason, adjustable gradient clipping is used for training in order to prevent exploding gradients. The clipping threshold per sample is set to 0.01 at a mini-batch size of 32. All weights are initialized according to He et al. [7]. The learning rate is set to 0.0596 and divided by a factor of 3 every 20 epochs. Training 60 epochs on a GTX1080 takes roughly 10 days.

4.3   Results

We benchmark our SRINC model against the state of the art on four widely used test sets for super resolution: Set5 [1], Set14 [33], BSD100 [30] and Urban100 [10]. Table 1 provides a summary of the quantitative evaluation. With only few exceptions, our SRINC model outperforms recent approaches consistently in both PSNR and structural similarity (SSIM) [28]:

$$\text{PSNR} = 10 \log_{10} \left(N_{\text{px}} \cdot I_{max}^2 \left(\sum_x \sum_y \left(I(x,y) - I'(x,y) \right)^2 \right)^{-1} \right) \tag{2}$$

$$\text{SSIM} = \frac{(2\mu_x\mu_y + C)(2\sigma_{xy} + 9C)}{(\mu_x^2 + \mu_y^2 + C)(\sigma_x^2 + \sigma_y^2 + 9C)} \quad \text{with} \quad C = \left(\frac{I_{max}}{100} \right)^2 \tag{3}$$

I_{max} describes the maximum intensity value (i.e., 255 for 8 bits); I and I' are the ground truth and predicted images, respectively; μ_* and σ_* are the means and (co-)variances, respectively.

In order to get a deeper understanding of these results, we conduct a more fine-grained analysis, comparing against VDSR and DRCN as the closest competitors. Instead of the mean PSNR, we take a look at the error distribution. Therefore, we define the cumulative PSNR, considering only errors up to $\delta_{\text{px}} \in [1, I_{max}]$ pixels:

$$\text{PSNR}_\Sigma = 10 \sum_{n=1}^{\delta_{\text{px}}} \log_{10} \left(N_{\text{px}} \cdot I_{max}^2 \left(\sum_x \sum_y \left(I(x,y) - I'(x,y) \right)^2 \right)^{-1} \right) \tag{4}$$

$$\forall x, y \mid I(x,y) - I'(x,y) = n$$

N_{px} denotes the number of pixel in the image. The differences are emphasized by putting the cumulative PSNR in relation to our SRINC method:

$$\Delta\text{PSNR}_{\Sigma, <\text{method}>} = \text{PSNR}_{\Sigma, <\text{method}>} - \text{PSNR}_{\Sigma, \text{SRINC}} \tag{5}$$

The fine-grained results are illustrated in Fig. 3. Reflected by the slope from upper left to bottom right, the most evident observation is that both VDSR

Table 1. Average PSNR/SSIM on Set5 [1], Set14 [33], BSD100 [30], and Urban100 [10] test sets for scaling factors ×2, ×3 and ×4. The best performance is highlighted in bold.

Method Training Set		Bicubic		SRCNN [5] Set291		VDSR [12] Set291		DRCN [13] Set91		SRINC (ours) Set291	
Data Set	Scale	PSNR	SSIM	PSNR	SSIM	PSNR	SSIM	PSNR	SSIM	PSNR	SSIM
Set5	x2	33.66	0.930	36.66	0.954	37.53	**0.959**	**37.63**	**0.959**	37.58	**0.959**
	x3	30.39	0.868	32.75	0.909	33.66	0.921	33.82	**0.923**	**33.92**	**0.923**
	x4	28.42	0.810	30.48	0.863	31.35	0.884	31.53	0.885	**31.55**	**0.886**
Set14	x2	30.24	0.869	32.42	0.906	33.03	**0.912**	33.04	**0.912**	**33.07**	**0.912**
	x3	27.55	0.774	29.28	0.821	29.77	0.831	29.76	0.831	**29.87**	**0.834**
	x4	26.00	0.703	27.49	0.750	28.01	0.767	28.02	0.767	**28.09**	**0.770**
BSD100	x2	29.56	0.843	31.36	0.888	31.90	0.896	31.85	0.894	**31.97**	**0.897**
	x3	27.21	0.738	28.41	0.786	28.82	0.798	28.80	0.796	**28.88**	**0.800**
	x4	25.96	0.668	26.90	0.710	27.29	0.725	27.23	0.723	**27.34**	**0.728**
Urban100	x2	26.88	0.840	29.50	0.895	30.76	0.914	30.75	0.913	**30.89**	**0.915**
	x3	24.46	0.735	26.24	0.799	27.14	0.828	27.15	0.828	**27.29**	**0.832**
	x4	23.14	0.658	24.52	0.722	25.18	0.752	25.14	0.751	**25.31**	**0.758**

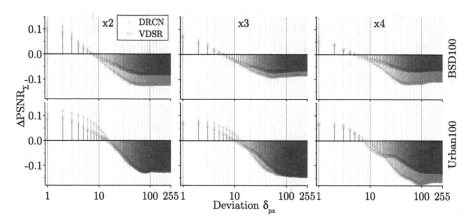

Fig. 3. $\Delta PSNR_{\Sigma}$ for VDSR [12] and DRCN [13] compared to our approach (SRINC) on test sets BSD100 [30] and Urban100 [10]. Since errors are less likely for large deviations, the abscissa is scaled logarithmically. Both VDSR and DRCN perform clearly better for small deviations, but produce more outliers which dominate the overall PSNR.

and DRCN perform better than SRINC for small errors, but worse overall. This behavior persists on all tested data sets and scaling factors. It can be concluded that VDSR and DRCN are more susceptible to generating outlier pixels. In our intuition, outlier robustness is very important for tasks such as facial landmark detection, because those tasks require reliable data down to the pixel level. This should be kept in mind when analyzing the results presented in Sect. 5.1.

5   Super Resolution for Facial Landmark Detection

Putting the theoretical insights from Sect. 3 into practice, the actual impact of super resolution for facial landmark detection remains to be investigated. For optimal results, it is crucial to choose the training set according to the purpose of the model avoiding domain shift. Hence, we train our SRINC model on a different training set, CelebA [16], containing facial images rather than natural images. Only the first 5k images are used. These are cropped and decomposed into 51×51 px patches at a stride of 26 px. Patches with a bicubic PSNR less than 35.12 for $\times 3$ scaling are discarded for being too blurry, for example, because they contain background. This results in approximately 227k patches total. We refer to this newly trained model as SRINC-F. Except for an additional dropout rate of 10% (all 3×3, 7×7, and 11×11 convolutions), the parameterizations for training SRINC and SRINC-F are identical, see Sect. 4.2.

5.1   Results

Following the same protocol as in Sect. 3, we compare VDSR [12] and DRCN [13] with our SRINC and SRINC-F models on the iBUG-Norm and HELEN-Norm data sets, using TCDCN [34] and CFSS [35] for facial landmark detection. In order to highlight the differences between the methods in a more readable fashion, Fig. 4 shows the error reduction ($\varepsilon_{SR} - \varepsilon_{LR}$) rather than the absolute error (ε_{SR}, cf. Eq. 1).

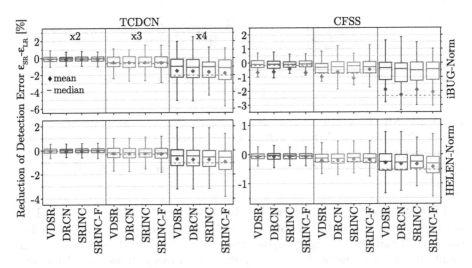

Fig. 4. The landmark detection error reduction (cf. Eq. 1) after applying different super-resolution methods to low resolution images from iBUG-Norm and HELEN-Norm, cf. Sect. 3. As a reference, the red line indicates the theoretical performance limit, i.e., the mean ground-truth resolution performance according to Fig. 1. Best viewed in the digital version. (Color figure online)

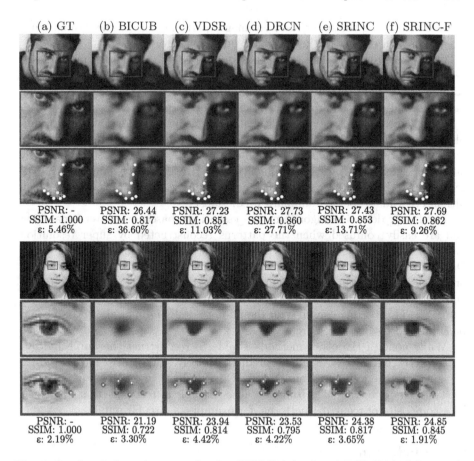

Fig. 5. Landmark detection examples for CFSS [35] (top) and TCDCN [34] (bottom) on super resolved LR images (×4). Third row also shows ground truth (red dots) and predicted landmarks (green crosses). The provided PSNR and SSIM figures refer to the zoomed patches only. Best viewed in the digital version. (Color figure online)

The results clearly indicate that both TCDCN and CFSS profit from super resolution when the original image resolution is low. The variance is relatively high and no method is strictly dominating. For the iBUG-Norm data set, this can be attributed to the relatively small test set (90 images). The small test set also explains why the super-resolution methods are sometimes able to help perform better than the ground-truth resolution (red line).

The margin for improving landmark detection using super resolution is exploited pretty well by our SRINC-F model. Linking the results to the findings from Sect. 3, the landmark detection error can be reduced by up to 17.5% (ground-truth resolution 19.5%) relative to the bicubic error, with an average improvement of 13.2% (ground-truth resolution 15.5%) for ×4 scaling. Even for

×2 and ×3 scaling the super-resolved images perform close to the ground-truth resolution with respect to the landmark detection error.

Compared with the other approaches, our SRINC-F model is the most consistent and performs overall best with a clear advantage over SRINC, although the training set is significantly smaller. This underlines that selecting the training data best suited for the problem is of key importance.

Complementary to the quantitative results in Fig. 4, Fig. 5 depicts two sample images, visualizing the qualitative nature of the different super-resolution methods. Not only do the images look more realistic, but they also explain why landmark detection is positively influenced by SRINC-F. For example, SRINC-F reconstructs the top image with a clearer and more realistic nose contour, which ultimately leads to better landmark predictions.

Landmark detection algorithms are essentially based on pattern matching and are easily confused when the patterns reconstructed by super resolution differ from the expectation. This is most evident in the bottom example of Fig. 5. Despite the higher PSNR and SSIM, the standard super resolution approaches are outperformed by a simple bicubic interpolation. This is a hint that PSNR and SSIM alone are no ideal metrics for evaluating the reliability of landmark detection. This correlates well with the findings of Johnson et al. [11] and could be addressed by future research.

While none of the other methods is able to reconstruct the pupil and eye lid correctly, our SRINC-F model predicts a nicely shaped eye. This is mostly explained by the different training sets. Our SRINC-F model blends well with the landmark detection algorithms because it is able to recognize that eyes must be a composite of recurring patterns, for example, a circular pupil.

6   Conclusion

While there is a wide range of research for face recognition considering low image resolution, facial landmark detection has not been thoroughly addressed, yet. Tackling this problem, we first showed that low image resolution degrades facial landmark detection performance, especially for faces smaller than 50×50 px, leaving a margin for improvement of up to 19.5%. A new super-resolution inception (SRINC) convolutional neural network architecture was thus presented, beating state-of-the-art super-resolution methods in both PSNR and SSIM. By practical experiments, it was verified that super-resolution indeed helps to improve landmark detection considerably.

Subsequently, in order to achieve the best result possible, the SRINC network was trained on faces rather than natural images. This enables the network to identify recurring patterns such as eyes more accurately and thus enhance the landmark prediction performance even further. Applying our super-resolution network before landmark detection, we are able to improve the average landmark prediction error by up to 17.5% (⌀13.2%) which is very close to the ground-truth resolution performance with 19.5% (⌀15.5%).

References

1. Bevilacqua, M., Roumy, A., Guillemot, C., Alberi-Morel, M.L.: Low-complexity single-image super-resolution based on nonnegative neighbor embedding (2012)
2. Biswas, S., Aggarwal, G., Flynn, P.J., Bowyer, K.W.: Pose-robust recognition of low-resolution face images. IEEE Trans. Pattern Anal. Mach. Intell. **35**(12), 3037–3049 (2013)
3. Burgos-Artizzu, X.P., Perona, P., Dollár, P.: Robust face landmark estimation under occlusion. In: Proceedings of the IEEE International Conference on Computer Vision, pp. 1513–1520 (2013)
4. Chaudhuri, S.: Super-Resolution Imaging, vol. 632. Springer Science & Business Media, New York (2001)
5. Dong, C., Loy, C.C., He, K., Tang, X.: Image super-resolution using deep convolutional networks. IEEE Trans. Pattern Anal. Mach. Intell. **38**(2), 295–307 (2016)
6. Fan, H., Zhou, E.: Approaching human level facial landmark localization by deep learning. Image Vis. Comput. **47**, 27–35 (2016)
7. He, K., Zhang, X., Ren, S., Sun, J.: Delving deep into rectifiers: Surpassing human-level performance on imagenet classification. In: Proceedings of the IEEE International Conference on Computer Vision, pp. 1026–1034 (2015)
8. He, K., Zhang, X., Ren, S., Sun, J.: Deep residual learning for image recognition. In: Proceedings of the IEEE Conference on Computer Vision and Pattern Recognition, pp. 770–778 (2016)
9. Huang, G.B., Ramesh, M., Berg, T., Learned-Miller, E.: Labeled faces in the wild: a database for studying face recognition in unconstrained environments. Technical Report 07–49, University of Massachusetts, Amherst (2007)
10. Huang, J.B., Singh, A., Ahuja, N.: Single image super-resolution from transformed self-exemplars. In: Proceedings of the IEEE Conference on Computer Vision and Pattern Recognition, pp. 5197–5206 (2015)
11. Johnson, J., Alahi, A., Fei-Fei, L.: Perceptual losses for real-time style transfer and super-resolution. In: Leibe, B., Matas, J., Sebe, N., Welling, M. (eds.) ECCV 2016. LNCS, vol. 9906, pp. 694–711. Springer, Cham (2016). doi:10.1007/978-3-319-46475-6_43
12. Kim, J., Kwon Lee, J., Mu Lee, K.: Accurate image super-resolution using very deep convolutional networks. In: Proceedings of the IEEE Conference on Computer Vision and Pattern Recognition, pp. 1646–1654 (2016)
13. Kim, J., Kwon Lee, J., Mu Lee, K.: Deeply-recursive convolutional network for image super-resolution. In: Proceedings of the IEEE Conference on Computer Vision and Pattern Recognition, pp. 1637–1645 (2016)
14. Köstinger, M., Wohlhart, P., Roth, P.M., Bischof, H.: Annotated facial landmarks in the wild: a large-scale, real-world database for facial landmark localization. In: IEEE International Conference on Computer Vision Workshops (ICCV Workshops), pp. 2144–2151 (2011)
15. Le, V., Brandt, J., Lin, Z., Bourdev, L., Huang, T.S.: Interactive facial feature localization. In: Fitzgibbon, A., Lazebnik, S., Perona, P., Sato, Y., Schmid, C. (eds.) ECCV 2012. LNCS, vol. 7574, pp. 679–692. Springer, Heidelberg (2012). doi:10.1007/978-3-642-33712-3_49
16. Liu, Z., Luo, P., Wang, X., Tang, X.: Deep learning face attributes in the wild. In: Proceedings of the International Conference on Computer Vision (ICCV) (2015)

17. Martin, D., Fowlkes, C., Tal, D., Malik, J.: A database of human segmented natural images and its application to evaluating segmentation algorithms and measuring ecological statistics. In: Proceedings of the 8th International Conference on Computer Vision, vol. 2, pp. 416–423 (2001)
18. Russakovsky, O., Deng, J., Su, H., Krause, J., Satheesh, S., Ma, S., Huang, Z., Karpathy, A., Khosla, A., Bernstein, M., et al.: Imagenet large scale visual recognition challenge. Int. J. Comput. Vis. 115(3), 211–252 (2015)
19. Sagonas, C., Tzimiropoulos, G., Zafeiriou, S., Pantic, M.: 300 faces in-the-wild challenge: the first facial landmark localization challenge. In: Proceedings of the IEEE International Conference on Computer Vision Workshops, pp. 397–403 (2013)
20. Schulter, S., Leistner, C., Bischof, H.: Fast and accurate image upscaling with super-resolution forests. In: Proceedings of the IEEE Conference on Computer Vision and Pattern Recognition, pp. 3791–3799 (2015)
21. Seshadri, K.T.: Robust Facial Landmark Localization Under Simultaneous Real-World Degradations (2015)
22. Sun, Y., Wang, X., Tang, X.: Deep convolutional network cascade for facial point detection. In: Proceedings of the IEEE Conference on Computer Vision and Pattern Recognition, pp. 3476–3483 (2013)
23. Szegedy, C., Liu, W., Jia, Y., Sermanet, P., Reed, S., Anguelov, D., Erhan, D., Vanhoucke, V., Rabinovich, A.: Going deeper with convolutions. In: Proceedings of the IEEE Conference on Computer Vision and Pattern Recognition, pp. 1–9 (2015)
24. Taigman, Y., Yang, M., Ranzato, M., Wolf, L.: Deepface: closing the gap to human-level performance in face verification. In: Proceedings of the IEEE Conference on Computer Vision and Pattern Recognition, pp. 1701–1708 (2014)
25. Timofte, R., De Smet, V., Van Gool, L.: A+: adjusted anchored neighborhood regression for fast super-resolution. In: Cremers, D., Reid, I., Saito, H., Yang, M.-H. (eds.) ACCV 2014. LNCS, vol. 9006, pp. 111–126. Springer, Cham (2015). doi:10.1007/978-3-319-16817-3_8
26. Tuzel, O., Taguchi, Y., Hershey, J.R.: Global-local face upsampling network. arXiv preprint arXiv:1603.07235 (2016)
27. Wang, Z., Miao, Z., Wu, Q.J., Wan, Y., Tang, Z.: Low-resolution face recognition: a review. Vis. Comput. 30(4), 359–386 (2014)
28. Wang, Z., Bovik, A.C., Sheikh, H.R., Simoncelli, E.P.: Image quality assessment: from error visibility to structural similarity. IEEE Trans. Image Process. 13(4), 600–612 (2004)
29. Yang, C.-Y., Ma, C., Yang, M.-H.: Single-image super-resolution: a benchmark. In: Fleet, D., Pajdla, T., Schiele, B., Tuytelaars, T. (eds.) ECCV 2014. LNCS, vol. 8692, pp. 372–386. Springer, Cham (2014). doi:10.1007/978-3-319-10593-2_25
30. Yang, C.Y., Yang, M.H.: Fast direct super-resolution by simple functions. In: Proceedings of the IEEE International Conference on Computer Vision, pp. 561–568 (2013)
31. Yang, J., Wright, J., Huang, T.S., Ma, Y.: Image super-resolution via sparse representation. IEEE Trans. Image Process. 19(11), 2861–2873 (2010)
32. Yu, D., Eversole, A., Seltzer, M., Yao, K., Kuchaiev, O., Zhang, Y., Seide, F., Huang, Z., Guenter, B., Wang, H., Droppo, J., Zweig, G., Rossbach, C., Gao, J., Stolcke, A., Currey, J., Slaney, M., Chen, G., Agarwal, A., Basoglu, C., Padmilac, M., Kamenev, A., Ivanov, V., Cypher, S., Parthasarathi, H., Mitra, B., Peng, B., Huang, X.: An introduction to computational networks and the computational network toolkit. Technical report (2014)

33. Zeyde, R., Elad, M., Protter, M.: On single image scale-up using sparse-representations. In: Boissonnat, J.-D., Chenin, P., Cohen, A., Gout, C., Lyche, T., Mazure, M.-L., Schumaker, L. (eds.) Curves and Surfaces 2010. LNCS, vol. 6920, pp. 711–730. Springer, Heidelberg (2012). doi:10.1007/978-3-642-27413-8_47

34. Zhang, Z., Luo, P., Loy, C.C., Tang, X.: Learning deep representation for face alignment with auxiliary attributes. IEEE Trans. Pattern Anal. Mach. Intell. **38**(5), 918–930 (2016)

35. Zhu, S., Li, C., Loy, C.C., Tang, X.: Face alignment by coarse-to-fine shape searching. In: Proceedings of the IEEE Conference on Computer Vision and Pattern Recognition, pp. 4998–5006 (2015)

Mathematical Foundations, Statistical Data Analysis and Models

Diverse M-Best Solutions
by Dynamic Programming

Carsten Haubold[1], Virginie Uhlmann[2], Michael Unser[2],
and Fred A. Hamprecht[1(✉)]

[1] IWR/HCI, University of Heidelberg, 69115 Heidelberg, Germany
{carsten.haubold,fred.hamprecht}@iwr.uni-heidelberg.de
[2] BIG, École Polytechnique Fédérale de Lausanne (EPFL),
1015 Lausanne, Switzerland

Abstract. Many computer vision pipelines involve dynamic programming primitives such as finding a shortest path or the minimum energy solution in a tree-shaped probabilistic graphical model. In such cases, extracting not merely the best, but the set of M-best solutions is useful to generate a rich collection of candidate proposals that can be used in downstream processing. In this work, we show how M-best solutions of tree-shaped graphical models can be obtained by dynamic programming on a special graph with M layers. The proposed multi-layer concept is optimal for searching M-best solutions, and so flexible that it can also approximate M-best diverse solutions. We illustrate the usefulness with applications to object detection, panorama stitching and centerline extraction.

1 Introduction

A large number of problems in image analysis and computer vision involve the search for the *shortest path* (*e.g.*, finding seams and contours) or for the *maximum-a-posteriori* (MAP) configuration in a tree structured graphical model, as in hierarchies of segmentation hypotheses or deformable part models. To compute the solution to those problems, one relies on efficient and optimal methods from dynamic programming [4] such as Dijkstra's algorithm [7]. In many of these scenarios, it is of interest to find not merely the single lowest energy (*i.e.*, MAP) solution, but the M solutions of lowest energy (*M-best*) [3,17,19,23,26]. This can *e.g.* be useful for learning [16], tracking-by-detection methods that allow competing hypotheses [13,18,24], or for re-ranking [28] solutions based on higher order features which would be prohibitively complex for the original optimization problem. If these M solutions are required to differ in more than one label, the problem is referred to as *diverse M-best* [2,14,22].

Electronic supplementary material The online version of this chapter (doi:10.1007/978-3-319-66709-6_21) contains supplementary material, which is available to authorized users.

V. Roth and T. Vetter (Eds.): GCPR 2017, LNCS 10496, pp. 255–267, 2017.
DOI: 10.1007/978-3-319-66709-6_21

Contributions: In this work, we show how the optimal second best $(M = 2)$ solution of a tree-shaped graphical model can be found through dynamic programming in a multi-layer graph by using a replica of the original graph as second layer and connecting both layers through edges with special jump potentials (Sect. 3). Using these building blocks, we extend our approach to exactly find the $M > 2$ best solutions sequentially by constructing M-layer graphs (Sect. 4). While the above can be seen as a special case of [29], our multi-layer approach is an intuitive interpretation that allows flexible modeling of the desired result. We thus develop two heuristics using multiple layers to find the approximate diverse M-best solutions for tree-shaped graphical models (Sect. 5). Lastly, we experimentally compare the different diversity approximations to prior work, and show results for a variety of applications, namely: *(i)* panorama stitching, *(ii)* nested segmentation hypotheses selection, and *(iii)* centerline extraction (Sect. 6).

2   Related Work

M-best MAP: An algorithm for sequentially finding the M most probable configurations of general combinatorial problems was first presented in [17]. To find the next best solution, they branch on the state of every single variable, resolve, and finally choose the best of all resulting configurations. While this works for any optimization method and model, it is in practice prohibitively expensive. Several works have extended this to junction trees [19, 26] that work in $O(|\mathcal{V}|(L^2 + M + M \log(|\mathcal{V}|M)))$, while [9, 23] developed a similar bucket elimination scheme $(O(M|\mathcal{V}|L^{|\mathcal{V}|}))$. A similar idea was applied in [8] to find the M shortest paths jointly by building an auxiliary graph with a heap at every node that contains the M-best paths to reach that node. For situations where the optimal or approximative max-marginals can be computed, [29] derived an improvement on [19] such that the max-marginals have to be computed only $2M$ times, yielding the same runtime complexity $(O(M|\mathcal{V}|L^2))$ as the method we present here. A method that finds the M best solutions on trees in only $O(L^2V + \log(L)|\mathcal{V}|(M-1))$ by an algebraic formulation that is similar to sending messages containing M best values as in [9] was presented by [25, Chap. 8]. However, in contrast to [25, 29], our approach provides a lot of modeling flexibility, allowing it to be used to approximate diverse M best solutions as well. A polyhedral optimization view of the sequential M-best MAP problem is given in [10]. There, a linear programming (LP) relaxation is constructed by characterizing the assignment-excluding local polytope through spanning-tree-inequalities. This LP relaxation is tight for trees for $M = 2$, but not for higher M or loopy graphs because the assignment-excluding inequalities could together cut away other integral vertices of the polytope. An efficient message passing algorithm for the same LP relaxation exploiting the structure of the polytope was designed by [3]. A completely orthogonal way to explore solutions around the optimum would be to sample from the modeled distribution, *e.g.* using Perturb-and-MAP [20].

Diverse M-Best: For general graphical models, the first formulation of the *diverse M-best* problem can be found in [2]. Even though their Lagrangian relaxation of the diversity constraint can work with any choice of metric, it is not even tight for Hamming distances of $k > 1$. Different diversity metrics are explored in [22], where a greedy method to find good instances from the (exponentially big) set of possible solutions is designed by setting up a factor graph with higher order potentials, assuming that the diversity metric is submodular. In [14], the authors construct a factor graph that *jointly* finds the diverse M-best solutions by replicating the original model M times and inserting factors for the diversity penalty depending on the structure of the chosen distance. It is shown that maximizing the diversity of the M-best solutions jointly, not only sequentially as in [2], can yield better results. They propose a reformulation that preserves solvability with α-β-*swap*-like methods. Still, when applied to trees, the factors introduced for diversity unfortunately turn the problem into a loopy graph and prevent the application of dynamic programming. All those approaches incorporate the diversity constraint into the original optimization problem by Lagrangian relaxation. In contrast, the constructions we propose in this work yield a solution with the desired diversity in a single shot. A different line of work [5,6] focused on extracting the M-best *modes*, but those methods' computational complexity renders them intractable for large graphs.

3   Optimal Second Best Tree Solutions

We now present how the second best solution of a tree-shaped graphical model can be obtained using dynamic programming on a special graph construction. By second best, we mean a solution that differs from the best configuration in at least one node, *i.e.*, that has a Hamming distance of $k \geq 1$ to the best solution. We begin with an informal motivation based on the search for the second best shortest path.

Motivation: The Dual Dijkstra method from [11] allows finding not only the best, but a collection of M shortest paths from a source σ to a target τ in a graph. To do so, two shortest path trees are constructed, one starting at the source and one at the target. Thus, for every node v, the shortest path from the source $\mathcal{P}_{\sigma,v}$ and to the target $\mathcal{P}_{v,\tau}$ is known. Summing the distances to source and target gives the length of the shortest path from σ to τ via v. An important property is that, for all vertices along the shortest path from σ to τ, this sum is equal to the length of the shortest path.

Now imagine these shortest path trees as two copies of the initial graph stacked as two layers, as seen in Fig. 1(a). The lower layer indicates the lowest cost to reach every vertex v from σ, and the upper layer the cost of the shortest path to reach τ from v. By selecting any vertex v and connecting the paths at v in the lower and upper layer, one can again find the shortest path from σ to τ via v, this time by introducing an auxiliary *jump* edge between the two layers.

The benefit of this two layer setup is that to find the *second* best solution, we simply have to search for the vertex that *does not* lie on the best path, at which jumping between the layers leads to the minimal cost path.

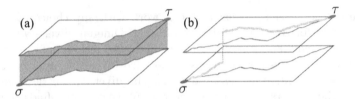

Fig. 1. A schematized two-layer grid-graph construction to find the second best shortest path from the source σ in the lower, to the target τ in the upper layer. A valid path is required to jump between layers, which is allowed everywhere for the best path. (a) Shown in blue is the best solution, which could have jumped to the upper layer at every node along the path with the lowest cost. (b) To find the second best path, layer jumps are forbidden at the nodes used by the best solution. Thus the second path diverges to the jump location leading to the next minimal cost path. (Color figure online)

Dynamic Programming: Let us briefly review the dynamic programming (DP) paradigm on an undirected tree-shaped graph $\bar{G} = (\mathcal{V}, \bar{\mathcal{E}})$. We denote the state of a node $v \in \mathcal{V}$ as $\mathbf{x}_v$, and the full state vector as $\mathbf{x} = \{\mathbf{x}_v : v \in \mathcal{V}\}$. The potentials of node v (*unary* potential) and of the edge connecting nodes u and v (*pairwise* potential) are represented by $\theta_v(\mathbf{x}_v)$ and $\theta_{uv}(\mathbf{x}_u, \mathbf{x}_v)$, respectively. From this, we define the inference problem as an energy minimization task [15] with objective

$$\min_{\mathbf{x}} \sum_{v \in \mathcal{V}} \theta_v(\mathbf{x}_v) + \sum_{(u,v) \in \bar{\mathcal{E}}} \theta_{uv}(\mathbf{x}_u, \mathbf{x}_v). \tag{1}$$

When applying dynamic programming, one successively computes the energy E of optimal solutions of subproblems of increasing size. One node of the graph $\bar{G}$ is arbitrarily selected as the root node r. This results in a directed graph $G = (\mathcal{V}, \mathcal{E})$ where edges point towards the root. Let $\overleftarrow{N}(v)$ denote the neighboring nodes along incoming edges of v in G. Using the tree-imposed ordering of edges, one starts processing at the leaves and sends messages embodying the respective subproblem solutions towards the root. Whenever a node v has received a message from all incoming edges, it can – disregarding its successors in G – compute the lowest energies $E_v(\mathbf{x}_v)$ of the subtree rooted at v for every state $\mathbf{x}_v$, and send a message to its parent [21]. Because leaves have no incoming edges, their energy is equal to their unary potentials. All subsequent nodes combine the incoming messages with their unary potentials to obtain the energy of the subtree rooted at them by

$$E_v(\mathbf{x}_v) := \theta_v(\mathbf{x}_v) + \sum_{u \in \overleftarrow{N}(v)} \min_{\mathbf{x}_u} \left[\theta_{uv}(\mathbf{x}_u, \mathbf{x}_v) + E_u(\mathbf{x}_u) \right]. \tag{2}$$

While sending these messages, each node v stores which state ($\arg\min_{\mathbf{x}_u}$) of the previous node ($u \in \overleftarrow{N}(v), v$) along each incoming edge led to the minimal energy of every state $\mathbf{x}_v$. When the root has been processed, the state that led to the minimal energy is selected and, by backtracking all the recorded $\arg\min$, the best global configuration $\mathbf{x}^*$ can be found. Figure 2 shows a minimal tree example.

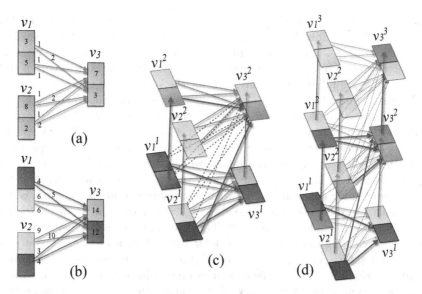

Fig. 2. (a) Minimal tree structured graph of nodes v_1, v_2, and v_3, with two states each, visualized as stacked boxes. v_3 is arbitrarily designated as the root, or target. Unary and pairwise costs are shown as numbers in boxes and along edges, respectively. Its optimal solution is highlighted in red in (b). Green edges correspond to the arg min incoming configurations for each state, and green numbers depict the accumulated min-sum messages. (c) Two-layer tree used to find the second best solution. Blue arcs represent layer-jump-edges with finite potential, which are available at states not occupied by the best solution. Purple dashed edges need to be considered if, at a branching point (such as v_3^2), not all incoming messages are coming from the upper layer. The second best solution is represented in green. (d) Searching for the 3rd-best solution (blue) with a Hamming distance of $k = 1$ to the best (red) and second best solution. The new solution must jump twice to reach the upper layer, by taking a state that was not used in the configuration represented by layers 1 and 2. (Color figure online)

Regarding DP runtime complexity, consider that (2) needs to be evaluated for every state of every node exactly once. In addition, in (2), we consider all states of every incoming edge, of which there are $|\mathcal{E}| = |\mathcal{V}| - 1$ in a tree. If L denotes the maximum number of states, one obtains $O(|\mathcal{V}|L^2)$.

Two-Layer Model: Once the optimal solution is found, we might be interested in the second best solution $\mathbf{x}$, which assigns a different state to at least one node $\exists v \in \mathcal{V} : \mathbf{x}_v \neq \mathbf{x}_v^\star$. Because messages in DP only convey the optimal subtree energies, we cannot immediately extract this second best solution. Hence we are looking for a way to enforce that a different state is attained at least once, but we do not know at which node(s) this should happen to yield the optimal energy. Fortunately, we can apply the same idea as in the second shortest path example: We duplicate the graph to get a second layer and insert edges connecting the two layers such that jumping is only permitted at states not used in the optimal solution $\mathbf{x}^\star$. After propagating messages through both layers, the second best solution can be obtained by backtracking from the minimum energy state of the root in the second layer to leaves in the first layer. This means that messages must have jumped to the second layer at least once at some node v with a state different to $\mathbf{x}_v^\star$, fulfilling our requirement for the second best solution.

We here state the layer setup conceptually and provide the formal construction in the Supplementary. To create the two layers, we duplicate graph G (Fig. 2a) such that we get a layer 1, and a layer 2 replica. We address the instances of every node $v \in V$ by v^1 and v^2 for layer 1 and layer 2, respectively. When duplicating the graph, the unary and pairwise potentials of nodes and edges are copied to layer 2. At every node $v \in V$, we insert a *layer-jump-edge* from v^1 to v^2 (blue edges in Fig. 2c) with a pairwise potential $\theta_{v^1 v^2}$ that is only zero if both variables take the same state $\mathbf{x}_{v^1} = \mathbf{x}_{v^2}$ different from v's state in $\mathbf{x}^\star$, and infinity (forbidden) otherwise. This way, finite valued messages in layer two represent configurations that did differ from $\mathbf{x}^\star$ at least once. These jump edges would suffice for a chain graph, but the branching points in a tree need special consideration. When a layer 2 branching point is not reached by a layer jump, the current construction only allows considering incoming messages from layer 2. However, since we only require *one* variable to take a new state, only one branch is necessary to reach layer 2 on a path with finite cost. To cope with this situation, we insert *layer-crossing* edges from u^1 to v^2 for all edges $(u, v) \in \mathcal{E}$ (dashed purple edges in Fig. 2c) with the same pairwise potential as in the original graph $\theta_{u^1 v^2} = \theta_{uv}$, and alter the DP update equation for nodes in layer 2 to

$$E_{v^2}(\mathbf{x}_{v^2}) := \min \Big(\theta_{v^1 v^2}(\mathbf{x}_{v^1}, \mathbf{x}_{v^2}) + E_{v^1}(\mathbf{x}_{v^1}), \tag{3}$$

$$\theta_{v^2}(\mathbf{x}_{v^2}) + \min_{\substack{L_2 \subseteq \overleftarrow{N}(v) \\ |L_2| \geq 1}} \sum_{u \in L_2} \min_{\mathbf{x}_{u^2}} [\theta_{u^2 v^2}(\mathbf{x}_{u^2}, \mathbf{x}_{v^2}) + E_{u^2}(\mathbf{x}_{u^2})]$$

$$+ \sum_{u \in \overleftarrow{N}(v) \backslash L_2} \min_{\mathbf{x}_{u^1}} [\theta_{u^1 v^2}(\mathbf{x}_{u^1}, \mathbf{x}_{v^2}) + E_{u^1}(\mathbf{x}_{u^1})] \Big). \tag{4}$$

Compared to (2), we now have two options instead of one at every node v in layer 2. Firstly, we can reach v^2 by a layer jump. Note that, in case of a jump (3), we do not account for the unary $\theta_{v^2}(\mathbf{x}_{v^2})$ as $E_{v^1}(\mathbf{x}_{v^1})$ contains the same term already. Alternatively, at least one of the incoming messages must come from a nonenpty set L_2 of predecessors in layer 2 (4), while the remaining messages could *cross* layers. These options are visualized in Fig. 2c.

Optimality and Runtime: By duplicating the directed graph and inserting two sets of new edges which are oriented towards the root in layer two, the topology of the graph remains a directed acyclic graph, and DP hence yields the optimal configuration. As long as the solution has finite energy, no forbidden *layer-jump-edge* is used, giving us the second best solution. In terms of runtime complexity, we have duplicated the number of vertices and have four times as many edges, which are small constant factors that disappear in $O(|\mathcal{V}|L^2)$. For optimal performance, one can reuse the messages in layer 1 because these do not change.

4   Optimal M-Best Tree Solutions

The two-layer setup can easily be extended to multiple layers, which allows us to search for the M-best solutions with a Hamming distance of $k \geq 1$. We use one additional layer per previous best configuration; that is, M layers. Each layer is responsible for one of the previous solutions, hence its *layer-jump-edges* are restricted according to the respective solution. Solutions must be ordered by increasing cost; such that the first layer constrains jumps with respect to the best configuration, the second layer for the second best, and so on. The new update rules from in Sect. 3 can then be applied to every consecutive pair of layers. Figure 2d shows an example.

Optimality and Runtime: When considering more than one previous solution using the multi-layer setup, the jump restrictions encoded in the *layer-jump-edge* potentials are independent at each layer. For any given node and state in a layer, the cost and path to reach it are optimal with respect to all layers below. This straightforwardly holds for the one and two layer cases, and is the reason why layers must be ordered by increasing cost of the represented previous solutions. For the sake of argument, layers could be flattened as they are getting processed, bringing back the problem to a series of $M - 1$ optimal two-layer cases, which yields a computational complexity of $O(M|\mathcal{V}|L^2)$.

5   Approximate Diverse M-Best Solutions

In the classical diverse-M-best setting [2], additional solutions are required to have *e.g.* a Hamming distance of $k > 1$. Here, we look at the straightforward multi-layer extension of Sect. 3 to handle $k > 1$. We argue that this approach is suboptimal, and present a two-layer approximation that trades quality for efficiency. Lastly, we discuss how this could be used to find M diverse solutions.

Multi-layer Model: To ensure that the next solution differs by at least k from the best one, we could construct a $k + 1$-layer graph using the same jumping criteria between all layers. To reach the top layer, a solution must hence jump k times. This raises two challenges: *(a)* a branching point at layer N can be reached by a combination of edges from different layers such that the predecessors *in total* account for a Hamming distance of N, and *(b)* a solution should never jump more than once at a single node, otherwise it will not have the desired diversity. Both can be achieved by adjusting the DP update equation to consider a set of admissible incoming edge combinations. We provide the precise expression in the Supplementary.

Unfortunately, this simple setup does not yield optimal solutions. To forbid two jumps in a row, one needs to introduce a dependence on a previously made decision. These dependencies invalidate the subproblem optimality criterion for DP to yield the correct result. It is thus possible that DP does not reach the root on layer k with finite cost, as shown in the Supplementary. Using the same reasoning, even if a valid solution is found, it is not necessarily optimal. Additionally, the set of admissible combinations of incoming edges grows combinatorially, making this approach unsuited for large k.

Diversity Accumulation: Instead of using k layers, one can also formulate a heuristic on a two-layer graph that ensures that any found solution contains the desired amount of diversity. To do so, we reformulate the Hamming distance constraint (that the new solution must differ from the previous one at k nodes) as a constraint on accumulated diversity, *i.e.*, that $\sum_{v \in \mathcal{V}} \alpha_v(\mathbf{x}_v) > T$, where α is a measure of diversity per node and state, and T a threshold. We change the DP update rules as follows. First, while propagating messages from the leaves of the tree to the root in layer 1, one must also propagate the amount of diversity accumulated by the corresponding configuration of the subtree. Let us denote nodes and edges of the subtree rooted at node v in layer 1 by $\overleftarrow{\mathcal{V}_{v^1}}$ and $\overleftarrow{\mathcal{E}_{v^1}}$, respectively. The accumulated diversity $\mathcal{A}$ is given by

$$\mathcal{A}_{v^1}(\mathbf{x}_{v^1}) := \sum_{i \in \overleftarrow{\mathcal{V}_{i^1}}} \alpha_i(\mathbf{x}_i) + \sum_{(i,j) \in \overleftarrow{\mathcal{E}_{i^1}}} \alpha_{ij}(\mathbf{x}_i, \mathbf{x}_j). \qquad (5)$$

Then, we define the layer jump potential $\tilde{\theta}_{v^1 v^2}(\mathbf{x}_{v^1}, \mathbf{x}_{v^2})$ to be infinity as long as the accumulated diversity is below the desired threshold $\mathcal{A}_{v^1}(\mathbf{x}_{v^1}) < k$. The limitation of this heuristic is that, at each node and state, we find the optimal subtree configuration by minimizing the energy without considering diversity. This can prevent us from finding solutions with large diversity. Yet, as we will see in the experiments, this approach has an attractive runtime because it only requires two layers to find a solution with any Hamming distance k, and thus has the constant runtime complexity of $O(|\mathcal{V}|L^2)$ per solution.

Extension to M Diverse Solutions: Finding M solutions with a Hamming distance of k could be achieved by stacking $M \times (k + 1)$ layers, but then the long range dependency problems depicted above are even more prominent. With diversity accumulation on the other hand, M diverse solutions can be obtained heuristically by using one diversity map α and one accumulator $\mathcal{A}$ per previous solution. The jump criterion must then ensure that enough diversity has been accumulated with respect to each previous solution.

6   Applications and Experiments

We now evaluate the performance of our heuristics to obtain diverse solutions with prior work, and demonstrate its applicability to several problems in Computer Vision[1].

---

[1] See the Supplementary for an application to depth estimation from stereo.

Comparison with Existing Works: [2, 14, 28] search for the diverse-M-best solutions by incorporating the diversity constraint via Lagrangian relaxation. Our heuristics follow a different approach and turn the constraint into a lower bound instead of relaxing it. The resulting advantage is that we guarantee the set of solutions to be as diverse as required, at the possible expense of a higher cost or the inability to find a solution at all. On 50 random trees, with 100 nodes each, all nodes having 3 states with unary and pairwise potentials drawn uniformly from the range $[0, 1]$, we evaluate different Hamming distances in Fig. 3. We let the method of [2] run for 100 iterations with a step size of $1/n$ in iteration n or stop at convergence. In terms of runtime, diversity accumulation stands out as it constantly requires only two layers. Because the distance to the best configuration is not enforced by hard constraints, solutions found by [2] often contain too little diversity, yielding a too low mean Hamming distance. Diversity accumulation gives solutions with more diversity than required, and hence also deviates more from the optimal energy. In terms of returned diversity and energy, the multi-layer dynamic programming solution yields favorable results compared to the other two methods, but is unfortunately slower – it suffers from the combinatorial explosion of admissible edge sets to consider – and fails to find a valid solution on several trees due to the limitations described in Sect. 5.

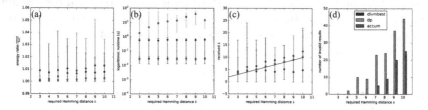

Fig. 3. Comparison of the $k + 1$-layer `dp` and diversity `accumulation` heuristic for obtaining diverse solutions (Sect. 5) against `divmbest` [2]. All results show mean, minimum and maximum over the valid solutions obtained for every setting on 50 random trees, where (d) shows the number of experiments that did not find a valid solution. (a) Energy ratio between the optimal unconstrained solution and the one with Hamming distance k. (b) Runtime. (c) Hamming distance of the resulting solution. Lower is better in all plots but (c), where the returned Hamming distance should be close to, or preferably above the drawn diagonal.

Medial Axis Identification in Biological Objects: Identifying the medial axis of biological objects is a common problem in bioimage analysis, as it serves as a basis for length or growth estimation and tracking-by-assignment. Simple dynamic programming can achieve this task given the end points, although, as biological images tend to get noisy or crowded, designing a robust cost function is difficult. In Fig. 4, we illustrate the usefulness of searching for a collection of possible best solutions instead of only one shortest path in brightfield microscopy images of *C. elegans* nematodes.

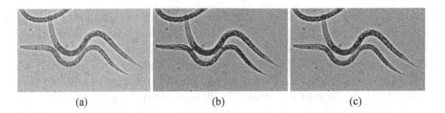

(a)   (b)   (c)

Fig. 4. Diverse shortest path finding in noisy bioimages featuring objects in close contact. (a) Raw brightfield microscope images of *C. elegans*, (b) first best path, and (c) 5th best path between auto-selected end points using an exclusion corridor of 30 pixels and a required accumulated diversity of $k \geq 25$.

Selection of Segmentation Hypotheses: In datasets with cell clumps, it is often hard to select the correct detections from a set of segmentation hypotheses. We illustrate this problem in images from the Mitocheck project dataset[2] [12] using the tree model proposed in [1]. There, the task is to assign a class label to each element of a set of nested maximally stable extremal regions. The labels indicate the number of objects that each particular region represents. In the tree, nodes correspond to regions, and edges between parent and child node model the nestedness properties. In Fig. 5, we show results obtained when constraining dynamic programming with our M-best approach. This is useful to generate segmentation or pose candidates as needed by joint segmentation and tracking procedures, *e.g.* [13,24].

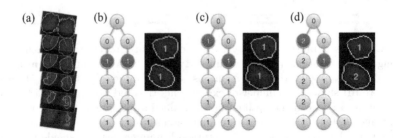

Fig. 5. Finding the M-best configurations of a tree (a) of MSER segmentation hypotheses as in [1]. The best (b), second (c) and third (d) best configuration found by blocking previous solutions in the respective *layer-jump-edge* potentials. The selected label at each node denotes the predicted object count of the first nonzero ancestor in the tree.

Panorama Stitching: In our motivation in Sect. 3, we mentioned that the proposed multi-layer setup can also be used for shortest paths. Here, we apply that in the context of boundary seam computation for panorama stitching [27]. We

---

[2] http://www.mitocheck.org/.

Fig. 6. Finding diverse best paths (seams) for panorama stitching. Once the best solution (a) has been found, layer-jump-edges were blocked in a corridor around it to obtain the diverse second best solution (b).

stitch images taken during the Apollo 11 moon landing (Apollo-Armstrong: 2 images of 2349 × 2366, courtesy of NASA). As observed in Fig. 6, the second diverse shortest path also corresponds to a visually correct stitching, although the resulting path significantly differs from the globally optimal one.

7 Conclusion

We have presented a multi-layer graph construction that allows formulating the M-best problem for tree-shaped graphical models efficiently through dynamic programming. This flexible framework can be used to find M-best solutions for a Hamming distance of $k = 1$ optimally. For $k > 1$, we present two heuristics, one using a multi-layer graph, and one using two-layers where each new configuration must accumulate diversity before it can reach the upper layer. We evaluated both heuristics against diverse-M-best [2], revealing that both perform favourably with certain strengths over the baseline. We demonstrated for several practical applications that the presented methods can reveal interesting alternative solutions.

Acknowledgements. This work was partially supported by the HGS MathComp Graduate School, DFG grant HA 4364/9-1, SFB 1129 for integrative analysis of pathogen replication and spread, and the Swiss National Science Foundation under Grant 200020_162343/1.

References

1. Arteta, C., Lempitsky, V., Noble, J.A., Zisserman, A.: Learning to detect partially overlapping instances. In: Proceedings of the IEEE Conference on Computer Vision And Pattern Recognition (CVPR 2013), Portland, OR, USA, 25–27 June 2013, pp. 3230–3237 (2013)
2. Batra, D., Yadollahpour, P., Guzman-Rivera, A., Shakhnarovich, G.: Diverse M-best solutions in Markov random fields. In: Fitzgibbon, A., Lazebnik, S., Perona, P., Sato, Y., Schmid, C. (eds.) ECCV 2012. LNCS, vol. 7576, pp. 1–16. Springer, Heidelberg (2012). doi:10.1007/978-3-642-33715-4_1

3. Batra, D.: An efficient message-passing algorithm for the M-best map problem. In: Proceedings of the 28th Conference on Uncertainty in Artificial Intelligence (UAI 2012) (2012)

4. Bellman, R.: On the theory of dynamic programming. Proc. Nat. Acad. Sci. **38**(8), 716–719 (1952)

5. Chen, C., Liu, H., Metaxas, D., Zhao, T.: Mode estimation for high dimensional discrete tree graphical models. In: Advances in Neural Information Processing Systems (NIPS 2014), Montréal, Canada, 8–13 December 2014, pp. 1323–1331 (2014)

6. Chen, C., Kolmogorov, V., Zhu, Y., Metaxas, D.N., Lampert, C.H.: Computing the M most probable modes of a graphical model. In: AISTATS, pp. 161–169 (2013)

7. Dijkstra, E.: A note on two problems in connexion with graphs. Numer. Math. **1**(1), 269–271 (1959)

8. Eppstein, D.: Finding the k shortest paths. SIAM J. Comput. **28**(2), 652–673 (1998)

9. Flerova, N., Rollon, E., Dechter, R.: Bucket and mini-bucket schemes for M Best solutions over graphical models. In: Croitoru, M., Rudolph, S., Wilson, N., Howse, J., Corby, O. (eds.) GKR 2011. LNCS, vol. 7205, pp. 91–118. Springer, Heidelberg (2012). doi:10.1007/978-3-642-29449-5_4

10. Fromer, M., Globerson, A.: An LP view of the M-best MAP problem. In: Advances in Neural Information Processing Systems, pp. 567–575 (2009)

11. Fujita, Y., Nakamura, Y., Shiller, Z.: Dual Dijkstra search for paths with different topologies. In: Proceedings of the IEEE International Conference on Robotics and Automation (ICRA 2003), vol. 3, Taipei, Taiwan, 14–19 September 2003, pp. 3359–3364 (2003)

12. Held, M., Schmitz, M., Fischer, B., Walter, T., Neumann, B., Olma, M., Peter, M., Ellenberg, J., Gerlich, D.: Cellcognition: time-resolved phenotype annotation in high-throughput live cell imaging. Nat. Methods **7**(9), 747–754 (2010)

13. Jug, F., Pietzsch, T., Kainmüller, D., Funke, J., Kaiser, M., van Nimwegen, E., Rother, C., Myers, G.: Optimal joint segmentation and tracking of Escherichia coli in the mother machine. In: Proceedings of the First International Workshop on Bayesian and grAphical Models for Biomedical Imaging (BAMBI 2014), Cambridge, MA, USA, 18 September 2014, pp. 25–36 (2014)

14. Kirillov, A., Savchynskyy, B., Schlesinger, D., Vetrov, D., Rother, C.: Inferring M-best diverse labelings in a single one. In: Proceedings of the IEEE International Conference on Computer Vision (ICCV 2015), Santiago, Chile, 13–16 December 2015, pp. 1814–1822 (2015)

15. Koller, D., Friedman, N.: Probabilistic Graphical Models: Principles and Techniques. MIT Press, Cambridge (2009)

16. Lampert, C.H.: Maximum margin multi-label structured prediction. In: Advances in Neural Information Processing Systems, pp. 289–297 (2011)

17. Lawler, E.: A procedure for computing the k best solutions to discrete optimization problems and its application to the shortest path problem. Manag. Sci. **18**(7), 401–405 (1972)

18. Milan, A., Schindler, K., Roth, S.: Detection- and trajectory-level exclusion in multiple object tracking. In: Proceedings of the IEEE Conference on Computer Vision and Pattern Recognition, pp. 3682–3689 (2013)

19. Nilsson, D.: An efficient algorithm for finding the m most probable configurationsin probabilistic expert systems. Stat. Comput. **8**(2), 159–173 (1998)

20. Papandreou, G., Yuille, A.L.: Perturb-and-map random fields: using discrete optimization to learn and sample from energy models. In: 2011 International Conference on Computer Vision, pp. 193–200. IEEE (2011)

21. Pearl, J.: Probabilistic Reasoning in Intelligent Systems: Networks of Plausible Inference. Morgan Kaufmann, Burlington (1988)
22. Prasad, A., Jegelka, S., Batra, D.: Submodular meets structured: finding diverse subsets in exponentially-large structured item sets. In: Advances in Neural Information Processing Systems (NIPS 2014), Montréal, Canada, 8–13 December 2014, pp. 2645–2653 (2014)
23. Rollon, E., Flerova, N., Dechter, R.: Inference schemes for M best solutions for soft CSPs. In: Proceedings of the Seventh International Workshop on Preferences and Soft Constraints, vol. 2. Sitges, Spain, 1 October 2011
24. Schiegg, M., Hanslovsky, P., Haubold, C., Koethe, U., Hufnagel, L., Hamprecht, F.: Graphical model for joint segmentation and tracking of multiple dividing cells. Bioinformatics **31**(6), 948–956 (2015)
25. Schlesinger, M.I., Hlaváč, V.: Ten Lectures on Statistical and Structural Pattern Recognition, vol. 24. Springer Science & Business Media, New York (2013)
26. Seroussi, B., Golmard, J.L.: An algorithm directly finding the k most probable configurations in Bayesian networks. Int. J. Approx. Reason. **11**(3), 205–233 (1994)
27. Summa, B., Tierny, J., Pascucci, V.: Panorama weaving: fast and flexible seam processing. ACM Trans. Graph. **31**(4), 83:1–83:11 (2012)
28. Yadollahpour, P., Batra, D., Shakhnarovich, G.: Discriminative re-ranking of diverse segmentations. In: The IEEE Conference on Computer Vision and Pattern Recognition (CVPR), June 2013
29. Yanover, C., Weiss, Y.: Finding the m most probable configurations using loopy belief propagation. In: Advances in Neural Information Processing Systems, vol. 16, p. 289 (2004)

Adaptive Regularization in Convex Composite Optimization for Variational Imaging Problems

Byung-Woo Hong[1($\boxtimes$)], Ja-Keoung Koo[1], Hendrik Dirks[2], and Martin Burger[2]

[1] Computer Science Department, Chung-Ang University, Seoul, Korea
hong@cau.ac.kr
[2] Institute for Computational and Applied Mathematics, University of Münster, Münster, Germany

Abstract. We propose an adaptive regularization scheme in a variational framework where a convex composite energy functional is optimized. We consider a number of imaging problems including segmentation and motion estimation, which are considered as optimal solutions of the energy functionals that mainly consist of data fidelity, regularization and a control parameter for their trade-off. We presents an algorithm to determine the relative weight between data fidelity and regularization based on the residual that measures how well the observation fits the model. Our adaptive regularization scheme is designed to locally control the regularization at each pixel based on the assumption that the diversity of the residual of a given imaging model spatially varies. The energy optimization is presented in the alternating direction method of multipliers (ADMM) framework where the adaptive regularization is iteratively applied along with mathematical analysis of the proposed algorithm. We demonstrate the robustness and effectiveness of our adaptive regularization through experimental results presenting that the qualitative and quantitative evaluation results of each imaging task are superior to the results with a constant regularization scheme. The desired properties, robustness and effectiveness, of the regularization parameter selection in a variational framework for imaging problems are achieved by merely replacing the static regularization parameter with our adaptive one.

1 Introduction

A variety of computer vision problems can be casted as energy minimization problems in a variational framework where an energy functional is formulated and the minimum energy is attained at the solution to the problem. One fundamental categorization of the energy functional is convex or non-convex. The advantage of convex energy is that a unique global solution can be obtained independent of the initial condition in contrast to non-convex energy that may have several local minima. Although the non-convex formulation often accounts for more realistic imaging models [15,21,25,26], the desirable computational property of convex formulations has led to recent advances in their

© Springer International Publishing AG 2017
V. Roth and T. Vetter (Eds.): GCPR 2017, LNCS 10496, pp. 268–280, 2017.
DOI: 10.1007/978-3-319-66709-6_22

efficient optimization algorithms [4,5,10,22]. Such convex optimization techniques have been applied to various computer vision problems including segmentation [9,11,30] and motion estimation [1,33,35].

The convex optimization of such problems in a variational approach generally has the composite form of a data fidelity term and a regularization term. The data fidelity term measures the discrepancy between the model and measurements, whereas the regularization term incorporates additional a-priori information about the solution. The trade-off between the model fit and the regularity is usually controlled by a static positive weight. This parameter is often critically related to the quality of the solution. One of the common criteria for determining suitable values of the control parameters in a variational framework is the manual selection via extensive visual inspections or the exhaustive search with respect to certain quality measures via a training process. In addition to the difficulty and sensitivity of selecting an optimal control parameter, the static balancing between the data fidelity and the regularization is not suited for considering intermediate solutions that are led to better final solution with an alternative adaptation of the balancing between the two terms in the optimization procedure where the data fidelity and the regularization energies keep changing for a balance. Another aspect of the need for adaptive parameter balancing is that it is desirable to consider local residual that is related to the degree of desired regularity of the solution. For example, a constant global regularization parameter is not effective to cope with multiple objects with different velocities in the motion estimation application. Similarly, a constant global regularity often fails to deal with spatially varying noises in the image denoising or segmentation problem.

In this work, we propose a novel algorithm for adjusting the balancing parameter that is determined by the intermediate solution at each iteration of the optimization procedure. The iterative adaptation of the balancing parameter between the data fidelity and the regularization facilitates the optimization process to obtain more precise results. In addition to the dynamic property of the proposed adaptive balancing, we consider local residual for adaptively determining the degree of regularization in order to deal with statistical discrepancy that may spatially vary between the model and observation.

1.1   Related Work

For image denoising problems, the noise variation has been estimated for choosing the proper value of the regularization parameter in [14] and the stability analysis of the parameter estimate has been performed in [32]. As a selection criterion of the regularization parameter, the generalized cross-validation has been used for image restoration applications in [24]. To infer the value of regularization parameters from the observed data, a number of techniques have been proposed. In the computation of optical flow, the regularization parameter is chosen in such a way that the estimated error is minimized [23], and the joint probability of the gradient field and the velocity field is maximized [18]. Another approach is to apply a smoothing kernel on the approximated flow using bilateral filtering [19] and incorporate noise estimation [13]. A non-local regularization has been applied for the computation of motion in [17,31,36]. The image gradient information has been widely used in the form of edge indicator function as a weighting factor to the regularity in the computation of optical flow [34,37]. Moreover, this technique has also been applied to the image segmentation problem [7,8]. Alternatively, a learning scheme has been used to measure the segmentation quality with AdaBoost where the optimal regularization parameter is selected with respect to the learned measures in [28]. In most computer vision problems only static information from the observation is considered to balance data fidelity and regularization. The static regularity is inadequate for iteratively incorporating into the optimization procedure, which is a motivation to propose an iterative regularity scheme with spatial adaptation.

2   Variational Model with Adaptive Parameter Balancing

Let $\mathcal{U}$ and $\mathcal{W}$ be finite dimensional real vector spaces equipped with inner product $\langle \cdot, \cdot \rangle$ and induced norm $\| \cdot \|$. Let $K : \mathcal{U} \to \mathcal{W}$ be a continuous linear operator with the induced norm:

$$\|K\| = \max\{\|Ku\| : u \in \mathcal{U}, \ \|u\| \le 1\}. \tag{1}$$

Our problem of interest is to solve the following composite convex optimization formulation:

$$\min_{u \in \mathcal{U}} \lambda \, \mathcal{D}(u) + (1 - \lambda) \, \mathcal{R}(Ku), \tag{2}$$

where $\lambda \in [0,1]$ is a control parameter that determines the overall trade-off between the two terms $\mathcal{D} : \mathcal{U} \to \mathbb{R}$ and $\mathcal{R} : \mathcal{W} \to \mathbb{R}$. The functionals $\mathcal{D}$ and $\mathcal{R}$ are assumed to be closed, proper and convex. The control parameter λ determines the relative weight of the two terms in the objective functional in which the functional $\mathcal{D}$ generally corresponds to the data fidelity and the functional $\mathcal{R}$ to the regularization. In most cases, λ takes a constant value over the entire domain of the unknown function u, thus it considers the overall weight between the data fidelity and the regularization. However, the constant control parameter does not take into account the local balance of the two terms, which may occur with spatially varying image degradation. Thus, we propose to apply a spatially adaptive balancing parameter that determines the relative weight based on the local fit of the data to the model. We now consider the objective functional $\mathcal{E}_\lambda$ that consists of the data fidelity ρ and the regularization γ with a spatially adaptive weighting parameter λ:

$$\mathcal{E}_\lambda(u) = \int_\Omega \lambda \, \rho(u) \, \mathrm{d}x + \int_\Omega (1 - \lambda) \, \gamma(Ku) \, \mathrm{d}x, \quad \lambda = \exp\left(-\frac{\rho(u)}{\beta}\right), \tag{3}$$

where Ω denotes the domain of the unknown function u, and the parameter $\beta \in \mathbb{R}$ is related to the distribution of the values in λ that are restricted to the range $(0,1]$. The adaptive weighting parameter λ is designed to use higher weights for the points in the data fidelity where the residual ρ is lower so that the regularization γ is less imposed. On the other hand, lower weights are applied to the points in the data fidelity where the residual ρ is higher so that the regularization γ is more imposed. As we shall see below, the model Eq. (3) has a certain bias towards achieving $\rho(u) = 0$, hence in some applications it will be beneficial to use the following model:

$$\mathcal{E}_\lambda(u) = \int_\Omega (\lambda\,\rho(u) + (1 - \lambda)\,\gamma(Ku))\,\mathrm{d}x, \quad \lambda = (1 - \epsilon)\exp\left(-\frac{G * \rho(u)}{\beta}\right), \quad (4)$$

with some small $\epsilon > 0$ to ensure that $\lambda(u)$ is actually positive, hence there is nonzero regularization and therefore well-posedness holds. The additional convolution with a kernel G, e.g. a Gaussian with small variance, can be applied to promote smoothness in the balancing parameter. Note that the original model Eq. (3) can be understood as the special case of $\epsilon = 0$ and G being the Dirac delta in the model Eq. (4).

2.1   Optimization with ADMM Algorithm

In the computation of optimal u in Eq. (3), we provide an optimization scheme in the framework of the alternating direction method of multipliers (ADMM) algorithm [6]. The optimization problem of the objective functional $\mathcal{E}_\lambda$ in Eq. (3) is represented by the splitting of variables with a new variable $z = Ku$ as follows:

$$\min_{u,z}\langle \lambda, \rho(u)\rangle + \langle 1 - \lambda, \gamma(z)\rangle \ \text{ subject to } \ z = Ku, \quad \lambda = \exp\left(-\frac{\rho(u)}{\beta}\right), \quad (5)$$

where K is a continuous linear operator, and $\beta > 0$ is a scalar parameter. The associated augmented Lagrangian with Eq. (5) in the scaled form [6] is given as:

$$\mathcal{L}_\mu(u, z, y) = \langle \lambda, \rho(u)\rangle + \langle 1 - \lambda, \gamma(z)\rangle + \frac{\mu}{2}\|Ku - z + y\|_2^2, \quad (6)$$

where $\mu > 0$ is a scalar augmentation parameter and y is a Lagrangian multiplier associated with u and z. The ADMM algorithm is an alternative minimization scheme that consists in minimizing the augmented Lagrangian in Eq. (6) with respect to the primal variables u and z, and applying a gradient ascend scheme to the dual variable y. The update of the adaptive balancing parameter λ is followed by the update of the variables u, z and y. The optimization procedure using ADMM algorithm is presented in Algorithm 1 where k is the iteration counter.

The optimality condition of the update for the primal variable u^{k+1} in Eq. (7) can be simplified by the linearization of the quadratic regularization term using the Taylor expansion at u^k in combination with an additional quadratic regularity as follows:

$$u^{k+1} := \operatorname*{argmin}_u \langle \lambda^k, \rho(u)\rangle + \mu K^*(Ku^k - z^k + y^k)u + \frac{\tau}{2}\|u - u^k\|_2^2, \quad (11)$$

Algorithm 1. The ADMM updates for solving the objective in Eq. (5)

$$u^{k+1} := \underset{u}{\operatorname{argmin}} \langle \lambda^k, \rho(u) \rangle + \frac{\mu}{2} \|Ku - z^k + y^k\|_2^2 \tag{7}$$

$$z^{k+1} := \underset{z}{\operatorname{argmin}} \langle 1 - \lambda^k, \gamma(z) \rangle + \frac{\mu}{2} \|Ku^{k+1} - z + y^k\|_2^2 \tag{8}$$

$$y^{k+1} := y^k + Ku^{k+1} - z^{k+1} \tag{9}$$

$$\lambda^{k+1} := \exp \left(-\frac{\rho(u^{k+1})}{\beta} \right) \tag{10}$$

---

where K^* represents the adjoint operator of K and $\tau > 0$ is a scalar regularity parameter. Then, the optimality condition for the update of the primal variables u^{k+1} and z^{k+1} yields:

$$0 \in \lambda^k \, \partial\rho(u) + \mu K^*(Ku^k - z^k + y^k) + \tau(u - u^k), \tag{12}$$

$$0 \in (1 - \lambda^k) \, \partial\gamma(z) - \mu(Ku^{k+1} - z + y^k), \tag{13}$$

where ∂ denotes the subdifferential operator. The solution for updating u in Eq. (12) and z in Eq. (13) is obtained by the proximal operator:

$$u^{k+1} := \operatorname{prox} \left(u^k - (\mu/\tau) \, K^*(Ku^k - z^k + y^k) \, | \, \rho \, \lambda^k / \tau \right) \tag{14}$$

$$z^{k+1} := \operatorname{prox} \left(Ku^{k+1} + y^k \, | \, \gamma \, (1 - \lambda^k)/\mu \right) \tag{15}$$

where the proximal operator is defined by:

$$\operatorname{prox}(v \, | \, \mu f) := \underset{x}{\operatorname{argmin}} \left(\frac{1}{2} \|x - v\|_2^2 + \mu f(x) \right), \tag{16}$$

where $\mu > 0$ is the weighting parameter. The solution for the proximal operator $\operatorname{prox}(v \, | \, \mu f)$ when $f(x) = \|x\|_1$ is obtained by the soft shrinkage operator $S(x \, | \, \mu)$ with threshold μ:

$$S(x \, | \, \mu) = \begin{cases} x - \mu & : x > \mu \\ 0 & : \|x\|_1 \leq \mu \, . \\ x + \mu & : x < -\mu \end{cases} \tag{17}$$

3   Applications

We demonstrate the effectiveness and robustness of the proposed variational model that incorporates the adaptive balancing parameter in the application of image segmentation and motion estimation. We present the variational energy formulations of those problems using the classical models where the constant balancing parameter is replaced with our adaptive one.

3.1   Image Segmentation

We consider an image segmentation problem based on the piecewise constant model [12]. Let $f : \Omega \to \mathbb{R}$ be an input image. A convex energy formulation for a bi-partitioning problem [7] with the proposed adaptive balancing parameter λ leads to:

$$\min_{0 \leq u \leq 1} \int_\Omega \lambda \left\{ (f - c_1)^2 u + (f - c_2)^2 (1 - u) \right\} \, \mathrm{d}x + \int_\Omega (1 - \lambda) \|\nabla u\|_1 \, \mathrm{d}x, \quad (18)$$

where c_1 and c_2 are estimates of the interior and exterior of the segmenting boundary, respectively. A smooth function $u : \Omega \to [0,1]$ represents a partitioning interface that determines regions Ω_1 and Ω_2 by thresholding with a parameter $\theta \in [0,1]$:

$$\Omega_1 = \{ x \in \Omega | u(x) > \theta \}, \ \Omega_2 = \{ x \in \Omega | u(x) \leq \theta \}, \ \Omega_1 \cup \Omega_2 = \Omega. \quad (19)$$

The adaptive balancing parameter λ is determined by the data fidelity term:

$$\lambda = \exp \left(- \frac{(f - c_1)^2 \, u + (f - c_2)^2 \, (1 - u)}{\beta} \right) \quad (20)$$

where $\beta > 0$ is a scalar parameter. The constraint on $u(x) \in [0,1]$ can be imposed by adding an indicator function δ_C on the convex set $C = [0,1]$ to the objective functional:

$$\delta_C(u) = \begin{cases} 0 & \text{if } u \in C \\ \infty & \text{if } u \notin C. \end{cases} \quad (21)$$

Then, the unconstrained objective functional reads:

$$\min_u \int_\Omega \lambda \left\{ (f - c_1)^2 u + (f - c_2)^2 (1 - u) \right\} \, \mathrm{d}x + \int_\Omega (1 - \lambda) \|\nabla u\|_1 \, \mathrm{d}x + \delta_C(u),$$

and it reduces to:

$$\min_u \int_\Omega \lambda(u) \, \rho(u) \, \mathrm{d}x + \int_\Omega (1 - \lambda(u)) \, \gamma(\nabla u) \, \mathrm{d}x + \delta_C(u), \quad (22)$$

where $\rho(u) = \left((f - c_1)^2 - (f - c_2)^2 \right) u$ and $\gamma(\nabla u) = \|\nabla u\|_1$. The balancing parameter λ is designed to adaptively choose regularity depending on the residual ρ. A higher residual would allow more regularity to effectively deal with inhomogeneity. In the same way, a lower residual would impose a higher regularity so that a precise segmentation boundary can be obtained despite its complex shape that is often unnecessarily blurred due to the global constant regularity.

3.2   Motion Estimation

For the motion estimation problem, we let $I_0(x), I_1(x) : \Omega \to \mathbb{R}$ be images taken at two different instances and Ω be the image domain. We consider an optical flow model based on the brightness consistency assumption [16]:

$$I_1(x + v(x)) - I_0(x) = 0.$$

Due to the non-linearity of the formulation above, one can linearize the first term with respect to some a-priori solution v_0 close to v leading to:

$$\rho(v(x)) := \nabla I_1(x + v_0(x)) \cdot (v(x) - v_0(x)) + I_1(x + v_0(x)) - I_0(x). \quad (23)$$

The linearized brightness consistency assumption can then be used as a data fidelity term together with a total variation regularization on both components of the velocity field (see [29,35]) leading to the following convex energy formulation:

$$\int_\Omega \lambda(x) |\rho(v(x))| + \sum_{i=1}^{2} (1 - \lambda(x)) \|\nabla v_i(x)\|_2 \, dx, \quad (24)$$

where $\lambda(x) = \exp(-|\rho(v(x))|/\beta)$ and $\beta > 0$ is a scalar parameter related to the overall distribution of $0 < \lambda \leq 1$. Since the optical flow constraint is valid for small motion, we consider a coarse-to-fine approach including warping on each level of the pyramid. The balancing parameter λ automatically controls the trade-off between the data fidelity and the regularization, imposing a higher regularity on the velocity where mismatch occurs, for example at occlusions. On the other hand, it is not necessary to impose any regularity on the velocity where perfect match is achieved.

4   Numerical Results

In the following experiments, we demonstrate the robustness and effectiveness of our proposed adaptive balancing scheme to image segmentation and motion estimation. The major objective of the following experiments is to present the advantage of using the adaptive balancing scheme over the conventional static one. Thus, we use the classical model for each problem as shown in the previous section and compare the performance of the same algorithm using our adaptive scheme against the static one. In the experiments, we denote by $\lambda \in \mathbb{R}$ the control parameter for the conventional static balancing and by $\beta \in \mathbb{R}$ for our adaptive balancing in Eq. (3). The same values for the common parameters in the ADMM optimization are used $\mu = 1$ and $\tau = 8$.

4.1   Image Segmentation

We solve Eq. (18) for the image segmentation of noisy images with spatially biased Gaussian noises of different levels using Berkeley segmentation dataset [20] where images that are suited for the bi-partitioning segmentation model are selected. We use F-measure for the quantitative evaluation of the segmentation result. In Fig. 1, the input images with different noise standard deviations σ are shown (top) and the segmentation results using the constant regularity parameter (middle) and our adaptive one (bottom) are shown in blue and red, respectively. The ground truth boundary[1] is indicated in yellow. The

---

[1] The ground truth boundary is not uniquely provided in the Berkeley dataset and we have chosen the one suited for our bi-partitioning segmentation model.

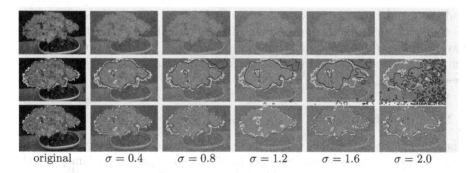

original $\sigma = 0.4$ $\sigma = 0.8$ $\sigma = 1.2$ $\sigma = 1.6$ $\sigma = 2.0$

Fig. 1. [Segmentation] Visual comparison of the segmentation results with the best F-measure. Yellow line indicates the ground truth. (top) input images with spatially biased Gaussian noises with different standard deviations. (middle) optimal solutions using the constant regularity. (bottom) optimal solutions using our adaptive regularity. (Color figure online)

graphically illustration of the segmentation results demonstrate that the constant regularity parameter suffers from the spatially varying noise levels in which large regularity due to the locally present high noise levels excessively blurs the segmenting boundary at the regions with low noise levels, and in the same way small regularity due to the locally present low noise levels unnecessarily captures undesirable insignificant details.

In Fig. 2, the quantitative evaluation for the segmentation is presented based on F-measure with respect to (a) the varying regularity parameters, λ for the constant regularity (bottom x-axis) and β for our adaptive one (top x-axis), and (b) the different noise levels σ using the example images that are suited for bi-partitioning in the dataset. It is shown that our adaptive regularity parameter consistently outperforms the constant one over both the entire range of parameters and all the noise levels. The temporal adjustment of our adaptive regularity to the local property of input data is demonstrated in (c) where the average

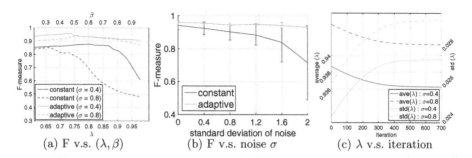

(a) F v.s. (λ, β) (b) F v.s. noise σ (c) λ v.s. iteration

Fig. 2. [Segmentation] (a) F-measures with varying regularization parameters, λ (constant) and β (adaptive). (b) F-measures with respect to varying noise standard deviations. (c) Average (left y-axis) and standard deviation (right y-axis) of our adaptive regularity λ with respect to the optimization iteration.

and the standard deviation of the values in λ for our adaptive parameter are plotted over the optimization iteration. It is shown that the average of adaptive λ decreases and its standard deviation increases gradually over iterations until convergence since the initialization for the solution is made with the input image.

4.2 Motion Estimation

The quantitative evaluation of the algorithm is performed using the angular error (AE) [3] and absolute endpoint error (EE) [27]. A set of gray-valued images with given ground truth flow from the Middlebury optical flow database [2] has been used to quantify the proposed adaptive regularization strategy against the static one. First of all, the robustness of our method is shown in Fig. 3. The angular and absolute endpoint errors for a wide range of static regularization parameters λ and weights β for the adaptive strategy is plotted. The graph indicates the robustness of the adaptive strategy, except for very small values of β. In general, there exist static parameters λ that creates equally good results, but those are unstable with respect to the chosen dataset. Table 1 includes a quantitative performance overview of our method. Angular and endpoint error are listed for static regularization parameters $\lambda = 0.01$ and $\lambda = 0.2$, and for the best static parameter λ that could be found in $[0, 1]$. In addition, we list the errors for the simple choice $\beta = 1$. The results demonstrate that the adaptive strategy may not necessarily generate the overall best result compared to static parameters, but yields nearly equally good results without any tuning of parameters. Finally, a visual comparison of the velocity fields is provided in Fig. 4 where the estimated flows obtained with best parameters and their ground truth are presented.

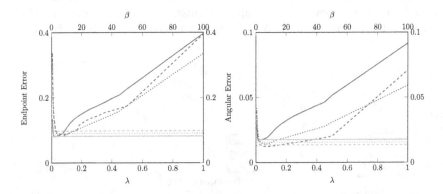

Fig. 3. Left: Endpoint error (left) and angular error (right) with respect to λ (blue) and β (red). The Dimetrodon (solid), Grove2 (dotted) and Hydrangea (dashed) datasets from [2] were used to generate these graphs. (Color figure online)

Table 1. Endpoint error and angular error for static and adaptive regularization parameters. The adaptive case does not necessarily create the best result (compared to static choices), but yields encouraging results along all datasets.

	Static $\lambda = 0.01$		Static $\lambda = 0.2$		Best static		Adaptive $\beta{=}1$	
Dataset	AEE	AE	AEE	AE	AEE	AE	AEE	AE
Dimetrodon	0.09	0.019	0.15	0.032	0.082	0.018	0.082	0.017
Grove2	0.185	0.028	0.108	0.019	0.082	0.014	0.089	0.016
Hydrangea	0.185	0.023	0.122	0.014	0.088	0.012	0.096	0.013
Urban2	0.445	0.027	0.509	0.062	0.21	0.018	0.214	0.018
Venus	0.64	0.051	0.291	0.059	0.214	0.042	0.206	0.044

Fig. 4. Visual illustration of the optical flow. Left to right: image, ground truth flow field, result with adaptive parameter choice, best result with static parameter. The velocity is represented by the conventional color coding scheme.

5   Conclusion and Discussion

We have presented a novel balancing parameter selection scheme in a variational framework where the energy functional consists of data fidelity and regularization. The trade-off between the data fidelity and the regularization is determined based on the data fidelity that measures how well the observed data fits to the designed model. The proposed adaptive scheme has been designed to determine the degree of local regularity based on the residual in such a way that higher residual is to allow more flexible regularity and lower residual is to impose more rigid regularity. We have applied the adaptive parameter balancing scheme to segmentation and motion estimation. Experimental results show that higher accuracy is achieved based on its classical energy functional merely by replacing the constant balancing parameter with our adaptive one. Our adaptive scheme can be naturally integrated into other problems that can be formulated by a composite convex energy.

Acknowledgement. This work was supported by NRF-2014R1A2A1A11051941 and NRF-2017R1A2B4006023.

References

1. Ayvaci, A., Raptis, M., Soatto, S.: Occlusion detection and motion estimation with convex optimization. In: Advances in Neural Information Processing Systems, pp. 100–108 (2010)
2. Baker, S., Scharstein, D., Lewis, J., Roth, S., Black, M.J., Szeliski, R.: A database and evaluation methodology for optical flow. Int. J. Comput. Vis. **92**(1), 1–31 (2011)
3. Barron, J.L., Fleet, D.J., Beauchemin, S.S.: Performance of optical flow techniques. Int. J. Comput. Vis. **12**(1), 43–77 (1994)
4. Beck, A., Teboulle, M.: A fast iterative shrinkage-thresholding algorithm for linear inverse problems. SIAM J. Imaging Sci. **2**(1), 183–202 (2009)
5. Becker, S., Bobin, J., Candès, E.J.: Nesta: a fast and accurate first-order method for sparse recovery. SIAM J. Imaging Sci. **4**(1), 1–39 (2011)
6. Boyd, S., Parikh, N., Chu, E., Peleato, B., Eckstein, J.: Distributed optimization and statistical learning via the alternating direction method of multipliers. Found. Trends Mach. Learn. **3**(1), 1–122 (2010)
7. Bresson, X., Esedoḡlu, S., Vandergheynst, P., Thiran, J.P., Osher, S.: Fast global minimization of the active contour/snake model. J. Math. Imaging Vis. **28**(2), 151–167 (2007)
8. Caselles, V., Kimmel, R., Sapiro, G.: Geodesic active contours. Int. J. Comput. Vis. **22**(1), 61–79 (1997)
9. Chambolle, A., Cremers, D., Pock, T.: A convex approach to minimal partitions. SIAM J. Imaging Sci. **5**(4), 1113–1158 (2012)
10. Chambolle, A., Pock, T.: A first-order primal-dual algorithm for convex problems with applications to imaging. J. Math. Imaging Vis. **40**(1), 120–145 (2011)
11. Chan, T.F., Esedoglu, S., Nikolova, M.: Algorithms for finding global minimizers of image segmentation and denoising models. SIAM J. Appl. Math. **66**(5), 1632–1648 (2006)
12. Chan, T.F., Vese, L.A.: Active contours without edges. IEEE Trans. Image Process. **10**(2), 266–277 (2001)
13. Chantas, G., Gkamas, T., Nikou, C.: Variational-Bayes optical flow. J. Math. Imaging Vis. **50**(3), 199–213 (2014)
14. Galatsanos, N.P., Katsaggelos, A.K.: Methods for choosing the regularization parameter and estimating the noise variance in image restoration and their relation. IEEE Trans. Image Process. **1**(3), 322–336 (1992)
15. Hintermüller, M., Wu, T.: Nonconvex tv $\hat{q}$-models in image restoration: analysis and a trust-region regularization-based superlinearly convergent solver. SIAM J. Imaging Sci. **6**(3), 1385–1415 (2013)

16. Horn, B.K., Schunck, B.G.: Determining optical flow. In: 1981 Technical Symposium East, pp. 319–331. International Society for Optics and Photonics (1981)
17. Krähenbühl, P., Koltun, V.: Efficient nonlocal regularization for optical flow. In: Fitzgibbon, A., Lazebnik, S., Perona, P., Sato, Y., Schmid, C. (eds.) ECCV 2012. LNCS, vol. 7572, pp. 356–369. Springer, Heidelberg (2012). doi:10.1007/978-3-642-33718-5_26
18. Krajsek, K., Mester, R.: A maximum likelihood estimator for choosing the regularization parameters in global optical flow methods. In: 2006 IEEE International Conference on Image Processing, pp. 1081–1084. IEEE (2006)
19. Lee, K.J., Kwon, D., Yun, D., Lee, S.U., et al.: Optical flow estimation with adaptive convolution kernel prior on discrete framework. In: 2010 IEEE Conference on Computer Vision and Pattern Recognition (CVPR), pp. 2504–2511. IEEE (2010)
20. Martin, D., Fowlkes, C., Tal, D., Malik, J.: A database of human segmented natural images and its application to evaluating segmentation algorithms and measuring ecological statistics. In: Proceedings of the 8th International Conference on Computer Vision, vol. 2, pp. 416–423, July 2001
21. Möllenhoff, T., Strekalovskiy, E., Moeller, M., Cremers, D.: The primal-dual hybrid gradient method for semiconvex splittings. SIAM J. Imaging Sci. **8**(2), 827–857 (2015)
22. Nesterov, Y., Nemirovskii, A., Ye, Y.: Interior-Point Polynomial Algorithms in Convex Programming, vol. 13. SIAM, Philadelphia (1994)
23. Ng, L., Solo, V.: A data-driven method for choosing smoothing parameters in optical flow problems. In: Proceedings of the International Conference on Image Processing, 1997, vol. 3, pp. 360–363. IEEE (1997)
24. Nguyen, N., Milanfar, P., Golub, G.: Efficient generalized cross-validation with applications to parametric image restoration and resolution enhancement. IEEE Trans. Image Process. **10**(9), 1299–1308 (2001)
25. Nikolova, M., Ng, M.K., Tam, C.P.: Fast nonconvex nonsmooth minimization methods for image restoration and reconstruction. IEEE Trans. Image Process. **19**(12), 3073–3088 (2010)
26. Ochs, P., Dosovitskiy, A., Brox, T., Pock, T.: An iterated L1 algorithm for nonsmooth non-convex optimization in computer vision. In: Proceedings of the IEEE Conference on Computer Vision and Pattern Recognition, pp. 1759–1766 (2013)
27. Otte, M., Nagel, H.-H.: Optical flow estimation: advances and comparisons. In: Eklundh, J.-O. (ed.) ECCV 1994. LNCS, vol. 800, pp. 49–60. Springer, Heidelberg (1994). doi:10.1007/3-540-57956-7_5
28. Peng, B., Veksler, O.: Parameter selection for graph cut based image segmentation. In: BMVC, vol. 32, pp. 42–44 (2008)
29. Pérez, J.S., Meinhardt-Llopis, E., Facciolo, G.: TV-L1 optical flow estimation. Image Process. On Line **2013**, 137–150 (2013)
30. Pock, T., Chambolle, A.: Diagonal preconditioning for first order primal-dual algorithms in convex optimization. In: 2011 IEEE International Conference on Computer Vision (ICCV), pp. 1762–1769. IEEE (2011)
31. Ranftl, R., Bredies, K., Pock, T.: Non-local total generalized variation for optical flow estimation. In: Fleet, D., Pajdla, T., Schiele, B., Tuytelaars, T. (eds.) ECCV 2014. LNCS, vol. 8689, pp. 439–454. Springer, Cham (2014). doi:10.1007/978-3-319-10590-1_29
32. Thompson, A.M., Brown, J.C., Kay, J.W., Titterington, D.M.: A study of methods of choosing the smoothing parameter in image restoration by regularization. IEEE Trans. Pattern Anal. Mach. Intell. **4**, 326–339 (1991)

33. Unger, M., Werlberger, M., Pock, T., Bischof, H.: Joint motion estimation and segmentation of complex scenes with label costs and occlusion modeling. In: 2012 IEEE Conference on Computer Vision and Pattern Recognition (CVPR), pp. 1878–1885. IEEE (2012)
34. Wedel, A., Cremers, D., Pock, T., Bischof, H.: Structure-and motion-adaptive regularization for high accuracy optic flow. In: ICCV, pp. 1663–1668 (2009)
35. Wedel, A., Pock, T., Zach, C., Bischof, H., Cremers, D.: An improved algorithm for TV-L^1 optical flow. In: Cremers, D., Rosenhahn, B., Yuille, A.L., Schmidt, F.R. (eds.) Statistical and Geometrical Approaches to Visual Motion Analysis. LNCS, vol. 5604, pp. 23–45. Springer, Heidelberg (2009). doi:10.1007/978-3-642-03061-1_2
36. Werlberger, M., Pock, T., Bischof, H.: Motion estimation with non-local total variation regularization. In: 2010 IEEE Conference on Computer Vision and Pattern Recognition (CVPR), pp. 2464–2471. IEEE (2010)
37. Werlberger, M., Trobin, W., Pock, T., Wedel, A., Cremers, D., Bischof, H.: Anisotropic Huber-l1 optical flow. In: BMVC. vol. 1, p. 3 (2009)

Variational Networks: Connecting Variational Methods and Deep Learning

Erich Kobler[1(✉)], Teresa Klatzer[1], Kerstin Hammernik[1], and Thomas Pock[1,2]

[1] Institute of Computer Graphics and Vision, Graz University of Technology,
Graz, Austria
erich.kobler@icg.tugraz.at
[2] Center for Vision, Automation and Control, Austrian Institute of Technology,
Vienna, Austria

Abstract. In this paper, we introduce variational networks (VNs) for image reconstruction. VNs are fully learned models based on the framework of incremental proximal gradient methods. They provide a natural transition between classical variational methods and state-of-the-art residual neural networks. Due to their incremental nature, VNs are very efficient, but only approximately minimize the underlying variational model. Surprisingly, in our numerical experiments on image reconstruction problems it turns out that giving up exact minimization leads to a consistent performance increase, in particular in the case of convex models.

1 Introduction

There has been a long tradition of using variational methods to tackle computer vision problems including denoising [32], deblurring [24,39], segmentation [9,29], tracking [2,14] and optical flow [18] due to their simplicity, performance and profound theoretical foundations. In recent years, these approaches have been outperformed by deep learning methods. Despite the success of deep learning in computer vision [17,26], it is unclear whether there exists a theoretical connection between variational methods and deep learning. In this paper, we try to answer this question by establishing relations between both worlds.

Variational methods are based on minimizing an energy functional. An archetype convex variational model (VM) for image restoration is the Rudin-Osher-Fatemi (ROF) model [32]. In the discrete setting it is defined as

$$x^*(x_0) = \arg\min_x F(x) := \|\nabla x\|_1 + \frac{\alpha}{2} \|x - x_0\|_2^2, \tag{1}$$

where $x \in \mathfrak{R}^n$ represents an image with n pixels, $x_0 \in \mathfrak{R}^n$ the noisy observation and $\nabla \in \mathfrak{R}^{2n \times n}$ is a linear operator that computes the discrete horizontal and vertical derivatives. As a motivational example, we analyze the

Electronic supplementary material The online version of this chapter (doi:10.1007/978-3-319-66709-6_23) contains supplementary material, which is available to authorized users.

V. Roth and T. Vetter (Eds.): GCPR 2017, LNCS 10496, pp. 281–293, 2017.
DOI: 10.1007/978-3-319-66709-6_23

2×2 patch statistics of a set of natural images $\mathcal{G}$ and the set of minimizers $\mathcal{S} = \{\boldsymbol{x}^*(\boldsymbol{x}_0) : \partial F(\boldsymbol{x}^*) \ni 0, \boldsymbol{x}_0 = \boldsymbol{g} + \boldsymbol{n}, \boldsymbol{g} \in \mathcal{G}, \boldsymbol{n} \sim \mathcal{N}(0, \sigma^2 I)\}$. Figure 1 visualizes these statistics along with those of noisy images. The solution set $\mathcal{S}$ shows a significant difference to the true image statistics especially in the polar regions, which suggests that the solution set $\mathcal{S}$ cannot capture the complexity of natural images. This originates either from a too simple model or the optimality condition $\partial F(\boldsymbol{x}^*) \ni 0$ is too restrictive.

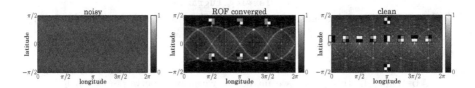

Fig. 1. Estimated log–probability density of 2×2 image patches from the BSDS500 data set [27] on the unit sphere in the zero-mean and contrast-normalized patch space. The projection onto this sphere is performed in analogy to [23] and its surface is parametrized by the longitudinal and the lateral angle.

A natural idea for improving the ROF model is to increase its flexibility by introducing additional terms. Chambolle and Lions [8] increased the model complexity by formulating image reconstruction as a convex infimal convolution problem. Another convex VM is the total generalized variation [7], which extends the ROF model by *modeling* higher order statistics. However, Black and Anandan [4] demonstrated that incorporating non-convex functions improves results because the applied non-convex functions suppress outliers as known from robust statistics. They optimize the non-convex VMs using the graduated non-convexity method [5], which solves a sequence of VMs starting with a convex model that gradually becomes non-convex.

The idea of *learning* higher order statistics to enhance the results of variational methods for image reconstruction was introduced by Roth and Black [31]. They proposed to learn a prior (regularization) consisting of an ensemble of filters together with corresponding non-convex potential functions called Fields of Experts (FoE) using contrastive divergence. Later [21] formulated the learning of regularization parameters of a VM as a bi-level optimization problem, which was extended in [10] to learn analysis operators of (non-)convex VMs including the FoE model. Their results on image denoising indicate that non-convex models perform best, confirming the findings of Zhu and Mumford [43]. Also Domke [13] enhanced the performance of the FoE model by discriminatively learning incomplete energy minimization schemes that consist just of a few iterations inspired by [15]. The combination of (1) unrolling a gradient descent scheme for the FoE model and (2) abandoning energy minimization by parameterizing each step individually led to the optimized reaction-diffusion processes of Chen et al. [11], which improved the state-of-the-art on several reconstruction tasks [16, 19, 40].

The neural network community pursues a completely different approach for increasing the model complexity. Since the early convolutional neural networks [22,33], advances in network training and the use of more complex, deeper networks have led to remarkable results in many areas of computer vision, including classification [17,20] and restoration [26,41]. Increasing the model complexity by stacking more and more layers works just to some extent due to a degradation problem reported by He et al. [17]. To avoid this problem, they introduced residual networks that have a simple computational structure which eases the training of very deep models.

In this work, we introduce variational networks that are developed by minimizing a parametrized energy using proximal incremental methods [3]. The VNs have the same computational structure as residual networks and thus are easy to train. Moreover, the concept of VNs enables us to explore theoretical properties such as the role of convexity in the field of natural image reconstruction. Therefore, we extend the FoE regularization structure by fully parametrized potential functions that can be trained either convex or non-convex.

2   Variational Networks

We propose *variational networks* (VNs) that are motivated by proximal gradient and proximal incremental methods and yield the same computation structure as residual networks. The basic structure of VNs evolves naturally by performing incremental proximal gradient steps [3] to solve problems of the form

$$\min_{\boldsymbol{x}} F(\boldsymbol{x}) := \sum_{c=1}^{C} f_c(\boldsymbol{x}; \boldsymbol{\theta}_c) + h(\boldsymbol{x}), \tag{2}$$

where C defines the number of components, $\boldsymbol{x} \in \mathfrak{R}^n$ represents some data, i. e., an image, $f_c : \mathfrak{R}^n \mapsto \mathfrak{R}$ are smooth component functions parametrized by $\boldsymbol{\theta}_c$ and $h : \mathfrak{R}^n \mapsto \mathfrak{R}$ is a convex, lower semi-continuous (l.s.c.) function. An incremental proximal gradient step is defined as

$$\boldsymbol{x}_{t+1} = \mathrm{prox}_h^{\eta_t} \left(\boldsymbol{x}_t - \eta_t \nabla f_{c(t)}(\boldsymbol{x}_t; \boldsymbol{\theta}_{c(t)}) \right), \tag{3}$$

where η_t is the step size of the t-th step. We fix the component selection function $c(t) = \mathrm{mod}(t, C) + 1$ to obtain a cyclic procedure as depicted in Fig. 2. We call the scheme (3) variational unit (VU) in analogy to residual units. The VU is the

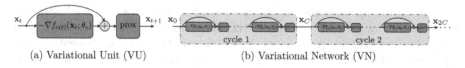

(a) Variational Unit (VU)   (b) Variational Network (VN)

Fig. 2. This figure shows an illustration of (a) our proposed variational units (3) and their combination to a variational network (b) that uses a cyclic scheme.

basic building block of a VN. The output of the C-th unit $\boldsymbol{x}_{t=C}$ ends the first cycle. It is also the output of a corresponding residual network [17]. Moreover, VNs generalize the optimized reaction-diffusion processes [11] as they can be interpreted as a single cycle of a parametrized incremental scheme.

2.1   Relation to Incremental Gradient Methods

The formulation of VNs is based on incremental proximal methods, which were proposed by Nedić and Bertsekas [3,30]. These methods were designed to solve large-scale energy minimization problems consisting of smooth and non-smooth components. Such problems can be cast into the form

$$\min_{\boldsymbol{x}\in\mathcal{X}} F(\boldsymbol{x}) := f(\boldsymbol{x}) + h(\boldsymbol{x}) = \sum_{c=1}^{C} f_c(\boldsymbol{x}) + h(\boldsymbol{x}), \tag{4}$$

where f aggregates the smooth components $f_c : \mathfrak{R}^n \mapsto \mathfrak{R}$ and $h : \mathfrak{R}^n \mapsto \mathfrak{R}$ holds the convex, l.s.c. and non-smooth parts. Problem (4) can be turned into an unconstrained form by including the indicator function of $\mathcal{X}$ in $h(x)$. In analogy to [3] an incremental proximal gradient step is given by

$$\boldsymbol{x}_{t+1} = \text{prox}_h^{\eta_t}\left(\boldsymbol{x}_t - \eta_t \nabla f_{c(t)}(\boldsymbol{x}_t)\right), \tag{5}$$

where $\nabla f_{c(t)}(\boldsymbol{x}_t)$ is the gradient of a single component selected by $c(t)$ and the proximal map is defined by

$$\text{prox}_h^{\eta}(\boldsymbol{z}) := \arg\min_{\boldsymbol{x}}\left(h(\boldsymbol{x}) + \frac{1}{2\eta}\|\boldsymbol{x} - \boldsymbol{z}\|_2^2\right). \tag{6}$$

If f consists only of a single component, i. e., $f(\boldsymbol{x}) = f_1(\boldsymbol{x})$, the scheme (5) simplifies to the proximal gradient method defined as

$$\boldsymbol{x}_{t+1} = \text{prox}_h^{\eta_t}\left(\boldsymbol{x}_t - \eta_t \nabla f(\boldsymbol{x}_t)\right). \tag{7}$$

First assume that all components f_c are *convex*. In this case, Bertsekas [3] showed that the incremental proximal method (5) converges to a stationary point in the limit for a diminishing step size, satisfying $\sum_{t=0}^{\infty} \eta_t = \infty$, $\sum_{t=0}^{\infty} \eta_t^2 < \infty$, for both cyclic and random component selection $c(t)$. Moreover, he proved approximate convergence for a constant step size ($\eta_t = \eta > 0$). The assumptions of the proofs are fulfilled if all components f_c are Lipschitz continuous on $\mathcal{X}$.

If the components f_c are *non-convex*, one can still show approximate convergence of (5) in the limit using the inexact non-convex proximal splitting algorithm of Sra [37]. In addition to the requirements of Sra, i. e., all f_c have a Lipschitz continuous gradient on $\mathcal{X}$, we assume that the components f_c are Lipschitz on $\mathcal{X}$, just as in the convex case. Then (5) approximately converges to a stationary point for a constant step size $\eta_t = \eta > 0$. The proof can be found in the supplemental material.

2.2 Relation to Residual Networks

Deep residual networks were proposed by [17] to alleviate a degradation problem arising in deep neural network training, indicated by increasing training *and* test error despite growing model complexity. Residual networks circumvent this problem by stacking many simple residual units, which are characterized by

$$x_{t+1} = p(x_t + g_t(x_t)), \tag{8}$$

where $x_t, x_{t+1} \in \mathfrak{R}^n$ are the input and output of the t-th layer, $p : \mathfrak{R}^n \mapsto \mathfrak{R}^n$ is a point-wise scalar function (e. g., ReLU) and $g_t : \mathfrak{R}^n \mapsto \mathfrak{R}^n$ are residual functions. Typically, these residual functions are defined as

$$g_t(x_t) = \sum_{i=1}^{N_r} K_{t,i}^2 a(K_{t,i}^1 x_t), \tag{9}$$

where the matrices $K_{t,i}^1, K_{t,i}^2 \in \mathfrak{R}^{n \times n}$ model convolutions and N_r defines the number of convolution kernels. The function $a : \mathfrak{R}^n \mapsto \mathfrak{R}^n$ is often set to the ReLU activation. The resulting networks can be efficiently trained for more than 1000 layers. The combination of the individual residual units forms a powerful ensemble of networks [38], yielding state-of-the-art results on challenging competitions, e. g., ImageNet [20] and MS COCO [25].

By comparing the structure of variational units (3) and residual units (8), we see that the proximal map in (3) corresponds to $p(x) = \text{ReLU}(x)$ in (8) if h is the indicator function of the positive orthant. If we assume $\eta_t = 1$, then g_t corresponds to $-\nabla f_{c(t)}(x_t)$. This is either true for $t \leq C$ or if a residual net shares parameters in a periodic fashion [1]. To emphasize this structural resemblance, Fig. 3 visualizes a residual and a variational unit. The residual function (9) corresponds to a gradient if $K_{t,i}^2 = K_{t,i}^{1\top}$. If this relation is approximate ($K_{t,i}^2 \approx K_{t,i}^{1\top}$), g_t can still be interpreted as a gradient with error. Consequently, this type of networks fits into the VN formulation and both networks have the same computational structure. Hence, VNs combine the practical benefits of residual networks, i. e., avoid the degradation problem, and the rich theory of incremental methods, including convergence and convex optimization theory.

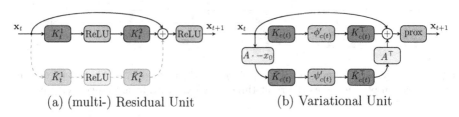

(a) (multi-) Residual Unit   (b) Variational Unit

Fig. 3. Visualization of the structural correspondence between (a) multi-residual units [28] and (b) variational units for image reconstruction (13). Note the data term gradient in (b) can be interpreted as a second residual mapping in the data domain. The multi-residual unit is turned into a residual unit [17] by omitting the dashed path.

3   Variational Networks for Image Reconstruction

We formulate image reconstruction as a variational energy minimization problem with a fully trainable regularization as well as data term and cast this problem into the VN formulation.

3.1   Problem Formulation and Parametrization

A variational model for image reconstruction in the form of (2) is given by

$$\min_{\boldsymbol{x} \in \mathcal{X}^n} F(\boldsymbol{x}) := \sum_{c=1}^{C} f_c(\boldsymbol{x}; \boldsymbol{\theta}_c) = R_c(\boldsymbol{x}; \boldsymbol{\theta}_c) + D_c(\boldsymbol{x}; \boldsymbol{\theta}_c), \tag{10}$$

where $\boldsymbol{x} \in \mathcal{X}^n$ represents an image, constrained on $\mathcal{X} = \{x \in \mathfrak{R} : 0 \le x \le m\}$ with $m > 0$. The vector $\boldsymbol{\theta}_c$ holds the parameters for each component. The regularization term $R_c(\boldsymbol{x}; \boldsymbol{\theta}_c)$ models prior knowledge, whereas, the data term $D_c(\boldsymbol{x}; \boldsymbol{\theta}_c)$ models the data fidelity. The specific form of the FoE regularization term variant is given by

$$R_c(\boldsymbol{x}; \boldsymbol{\theta}_c) = \sum_{i=1}^{N_r} \sum_{j=1}^{n} \phi_i^c \left((K_i^c \boldsymbol{x})_j \right), \tag{11}$$

where $\phi_i^c(x) : \mathcal{Y} \mapsto \mathfrak{R}$ are potential functions defined on $\mathcal{Y} = \{y \in \mathfrak{R} : |y| \le m\}$, their associated matrices $K_i^c \in \mathfrak{R}^{n \times n}$ model convolutions of the image x with kernels k_i^c and N_r defines the number of regularization functions. Some learned kernel-function pairs are depicted in Fig. 4. The convolution of a $s_k \times s_k$ kernel k_i^c can also be expressed as matrix-vector multiplication $X k_i^c$ with the matrix $X \in \mathfrak{R}^{n \times s_k^2}$ and the vector $\boldsymbol{k}_i^c \in \mathfrak{R}^{s_k^2}$.

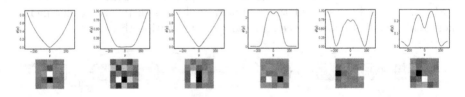

Fig. 4. Sample kernel-function pairs $(k_i^c, \phi_i^c(y))$ of the trained VNs. The left three pairs are convex samples, whereas the right three were extracted from non-convex VNs.

We parametrize the data term also with kernel-function pairs to incorporate higher-order statistics in the data domain, motivated by [36]. It is defined as

$$D_c(\boldsymbol{x}; \boldsymbol{\theta}_c) = \sum_{i=1}^{N_d} \sum_{j=1}^{n} \psi_i^c \left((\bar{K}_i^c(A\boldsymbol{x} - \boldsymbol{x}_0))_j \right), \tag{12}$$

where $x_0 \in \mathcal{X}^n$ describes the degraded observation and $A \in \mathfrak{R}^{n \times n}$ models a linear operator. As before, the matrices $\bar{K}_i^c \in \mathfrak{R}^{n \times n}$ model convolutions with kernels $\bar{k}_i^c$, $\psi_i^c(y) : \mathcal{Y} \mapsto \mathfrak{R}$ are the corresponding potential functions and N_d specifies the number of kernel-function pairs.

We define the VUs for image reconstruction akin to (3) as

$$x_{t+1} = \text{proj}_{\mathcal{X}^n}(x_t - \eta_t \nabla f_{c(t)}(x_t; \boldsymbol{\theta}_{c(t)})) \tag{13}$$

where the proximal operator of (3) simplifies to the projection onto $\mathcal{X}^n$. The gradient for a selected component $f_c(x; \boldsymbol{\theta}_c)$ is given by

$$\nabla f_c(x_t; \boldsymbol{\theta}_c) = \sum_{i=1}^{N_r} K_i^{c\top} \phi_i'^c (K_i^c x_t) + A^\top \sum_{i=1}^{N_d} \bar{K}_i^{c\top} \psi_i'^c (\bar{K}_i^c(Ax_t - x_0)). \tag{14}$$

Since we learn the influence functions $\phi_i'^c(y)$ and $\psi_i'^c(y)$, we can fix the step size $\eta_t = 1$ as it is reflected in the scale of both influence functions. Due to the above parametrization, all the component functions f_c of the according VN are smooth, Lipschitz continuous functions with bounded and Lipschitz continuous gradient as long as the functions $\phi_i'^c(y)$ and $\psi_i'^c(y)$ fulfill these constraints. The proofs are in the supplemental material. Note that the runtime and memory requirements of the VNs resemble those of [11], since the basic operations are identical.

3.2   Training

To train the VNs for image reconstruction we parametrize the influence functions $\phi_i'^c(y)$ and $\psi_i'^c(y)$ in analogy to [11,35] with radial basis functions

$$\phi_i'^c(y) = \sum_{j=1}^{N_w} \exp\left(-\frac{(y - \mu_j)^2}{2\sigma^2}\right) w_{ij}^c, \tag{15}$$

where w_{ij}^c are the individual basis weights that correspond to a single radial basis (μ_j, σ) and N_w defines the number of basis functions. To shorten notation we group the coefficients into $\boldsymbol{w}_i^c = (w_{i1}^c, \ldots, w_{iN_w}^c)^\top$. The functions $\psi_i'^c(x)$ are parametized in the same way by $\bar{\boldsymbol{w}}_i^c$. We group the parameters of a single component c into the vector $\boldsymbol{\theta}_c = (k_1^c, w_1^c, \ldots, k_{N_r}^c, w_{N_r}^c, \bar{k}_1^c, \bar{w}_1^c, \ldots, \bar{k}_{N_d}^c, \bar{w}_{N_d}^c)$. The parameters of all components are gathered into $\boldsymbol{\theta} = (\boldsymbol{\theta}_i, i = 1 \ldots C)$. We define the training cost for N_s input-target pairs (x_0^s, x_{gt}^s) as

$$\min_{\boldsymbol{\theta} \in \mathcal{T}} L(\boldsymbol{\theta}) := \frac{1}{N_s} \sum_{s=1}^{N_s} \|x_T^s(\boldsymbol{\theta}) - x_{gt}^s\|_1, \tag{16}$$

where x_T^s is the output after T steps (13). We use the ℓ_1-norm because of its robustness [42]. In addition, we constrain the parameters $\boldsymbol{\theta}$ to be in an admissible set $\mathcal{T}$. This set ensures that the kernels k_i^c and $\bar{k}_i^c$ have zero-mean and ℓ_2-norm one, to avoid a scaling problem as outlined in [11]. $\mathcal{T}$ also allows us to incorporate constraints on the functions $\phi_i^c(y)$ and $\psi_i^c(x)$ such as convexity by defining suitable conditions for $\boldsymbol{w}_i^c$ and $\bar{\boldsymbol{w}}_i^c$ as shown in the supplemental material. Note if all $\phi_i^c(y)$ and $\psi_i^c(x)$ are convex, the entire energy (10) becomes convex [6].

We optimize the non-convex training problem (16) with the inertial incremental proximal method (IIPG) defined in Algorithm 1 in the supplemental material. It is an incremental proximal method that uses preconditioning for acceleration and is capable of handling the constraints incorporated in the admissible set $\mathcal{T}$.

4   Experiments

We conduct three groups of experiments to show the versatility of VNs and to explore the role of convexity. Table 1 defines all used VN types and outlines their relation to the previously discussed methods. We conduct all experiments for denoising and non-blind delurring. In the case of denoising, the degraded input $\boldsymbol{x}_0$ is a noisy observation and the linear operator A in (12) simplifies to an identity operation. For non-blind deblurring, the input is a blurry and noisy observation and the linear operator A models a convolution with a known blur kernel. The denoising VNs (N-VN) use just a single data term $N_d = 1$ and an identity kernel $\bar{k}_1^1$, while the deblurring VNs (B-VN) apply $N_d = N_r$ kernel-function pairs. To train VNs for both problems, we use 400 training patches of size 180×180 extracted from the BSDS500 train and test sets [27]. We generate the noisy training inputs by adding white Gaussian noise with $\sigma = 25$ to the clean images. To generate the blurry training data, we extract 11×11 motion blur kernels from [34], convolve them with the clean training patches and add 1% white Gaussian noise. The test sets are generated in the same way for denoising and non-blind deblurring. We use 68 images from the BSDS500 [27] validation set and the motion blur kernels from [24] to ensure that neither the images nor the blur kernels are used during training. Finally, it is important to point out that all found schemes are local optima of the non-convex training problem (16).

Table 1. Overview of the VN types. The subscript N defines the number of used kernel-function pairs $N_r = N$. The superscript specifies the number of components C and the step t for which the VN was optimized.

Type	Corresponding scheme
$VN_N^{1,t}$	Proximal gradient method (7) (energy minimization)
$VN_N^{C,t}$	Proximal incremental method (5) (approximate energy minimization)
$VN_N^{t,t}$	Single cycle proximal incremental method (5) (reaction diffusion)

4.1   Energy Minimization with VNs

In the first experiment, we set up VNs to perform energy minimization following the proximal gradient method (7) by fixing the number of components to $C = 1$, i. e., $F(\boldsymbol{x}) = f_1(\boldsymbol{x})$. For both denoising and non-blind deblurring, we train convex and non-convex VNs up to $t = 100$ steps. The resulting PSNR scores and the

ℓ_2-norm of the gradients $\|\nabla F(\boldsymbol{x}_t)\|_2$ are depicted in green color in Figs. 5 and 6. As expected, the decreasing gradient-norm with increasing steps t indicates that the methods actually minimize the underlying energy (10).

The PSNR curves for denoising (Fig. 5) differ for convex and non-convex N-VN$_{24}^{1,t}$. The performance of the non-convex VNs increases initially and slowly declines with increasing t, while the convex N-VN$_{24}^{1,t}$ yield the best results after a single step. This indicates that a convex regularization of the form (11) is not a good prior for natural images because by approaching a minimizer (increasing t) the results become worse. Surprisingly, the highly parametrized convex N-VN$_{24}^{1,t}$ performs marginally better than the ROF model for $t > 10$, consistent with [21]. In the case of non-blind deblurring the PSNR curves (Fig. 6) are similar for convex and non-convex B-VN$_{24}^{1,t}$. Both VNs require more steps to yield satisfactory results since deblurring is a harder problem than denoising. Nevertheless, the non-convex B-VN$_{24}^{1,t}$ outperform the convex ones by a large margin (1 dB).

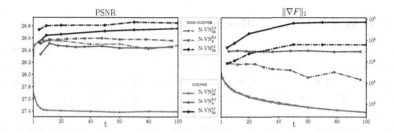

Fig. 5. Average PSNR curves on the test set of the trained VN types for Gaussian image denoising along with the gradient norm of the corresponding energy $F(\boldsymbol{x}_t)$. (Color figure online)

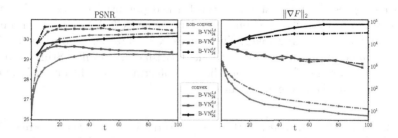

Fig. 6. Average PSNR scores and corresponding gradient norm on the test set of the different VN types for non-blind deblurring. (Color figure online)

4.2 Approximate Incremental Minimization with VNs

In a second experiment, we evaluate the performance of VNs that follow an incremental approximate energy minimization scheme (5). We use $C = 6$ components and $N_r = 4$ kernel-function pairs. Thus, the number of parameters is approximately the same as in the previous experiment. The resulting PSNR scores as well as the gradient norm for the trained convex and non-convex $\text{VN}_4^{6,t}$ are depicted in red color in Fig. 5 for denoising and Fig. 6 for non-blind deblurring.

In contrast to the previous experiment, the PSNR curves for denoising and deblurring are rather flat for both convex and non-convex $\text{VN}_4^{6,t}$. So, they manage to generate good results after just a few steps and maintain the quality with increasing t. However, the results after 100 steps are far from approaching a stationary point, as indicated by the rather slowly decreasing gradient-norm $\|\nabla F\|_2$. This effect is very strong for the convex N-$\text{VN}_4^{6,t}$ because these VNs learn a sequence of components that alternate between strong blurring and detail recovery from the data term, leading to large gradients. In terms of PSNR scores this behavior yields superior results compared to the first experiment. The decreasing PSNR of the convex B-$\text{VN}_4^{6,t}$ with increasing depth may originate from local optima of the learning problem.

4.3   VNs in a Reaction Diffusion Setup

In the final experiment, we investigate the performance of VNs in a residual network or trainable reaction-diffusion setting [11], i. e., each step (13) has its own parameter set θ_t ($C = t$). Hence, the number of parameters increases linearly with the depth of the $\text{VN}_{24}^{t,t}$. These VN types can still be interpreted as an incremental proximal methods that apply each component just once.

The increasing model complexity with increasing t leads to a steady increase of the performance for the $\text{VN}_{24}^{t,t}$ on both reconstruction tasks, depicted in Figs. 5 and 6. The gradient-norm increases also along with the depth t due to the additional components. Consequently, these VNs do not minimize a corresponding energy. However, they yield the best performance on the image reconstruction tasks as shown in Table 2. In contrast to Chen et al. [11], our findings on image denoising suggest that the shape of the learned potential functions (Fig. 4) is of little importance since the convex and non-convex N-$\text{VN}_{24}^{t,t}$ perform almost equally well, as shown in Table 2. The convex N-VNs rather require the flexibility of incremental schemes in order to yield satisfactory results. Still, convexity seems to be a limiting factor for non-blind deblurring since all convex VNs perform worse than the non-convex ones.

Table 2. Average PSNR scores on the test set for the VN types. The reported PSNR scores are computed using the best performing depth t of each VN type.

	ROF [32]	Convex			Non-convex			BM3D [12]	$\text{TRD}_{5\times5}^5$[11]
		$\text{VN}_{24}^{1,t}$	$\text{VN}_4^{6,t}$	$\text{VN}_{24}^{t,t}$	$\text{VN}_{24}^{1,t}$	$\text{VN}_4^{6,t}$	$\text{VN}_{24}^{t,t}$		
Denoising	27.39	27.69	28.51	*28.76*	28.56	28.60	**28.87**	28.56	*28.78*
Non-blind deblurring	28.35	29.26	29.66	30.16	30.31	*30.56*	**30.76**	-	-

5 Conclusion

In this work, we explored links between variational energy minimization methods and deep learning approaches by introducing variational networks (VNs). The VNs consist of stacked parametrized incremental proximal steps that have the same favorable computational structure as residual units. We demonstrated that the versatile VN formulation can be used to learn proximal gradient schemes, incremental proximal schemes as well as residual networks and optimized reaction-diffusion processes. Moreover, our parametrization of the VNs for image reconstruction allows us to learn corresponding *convex* energies.

We used this novel possibility to evaluate the limitations of convexity in the context of natural image reconstruction. Our findings on denoising and non-blind deblurring show that our convex formulations yield inferior results than non-convex formulations. Additionally, the incremental VN types require just a few steps to yield reasonable results even for the challenging task of non-blind deblurring. In the future we would like to further investigate the role of convexity by learning different classes of convex models and analyze the stability of VNs.

Acknowledgements. We acknowledge grant support from the Austrian Science Fund (FWF) under the START project BIVISION, No. Y729 and the European Research Council under the Horizon 2020 program, ERC starting grant HOMOVIS, No. 640156.

References

1. Alexandre, B.: Sharesnet: reducing residual network parameter number by sharing weights. arXiv e-prints 1702.08782 (2017)
2. Bertalmio, M., Sapiro, G., Randall, G.: Morphing active contours. TPAMI **22**(7), 733–737 (2000)
3. Bertsekas, D.P.: Incremental proximal methods for large scale convex optimization. Math. Program. **129**(2), 163 (2011). doi:10.1007/s10107-011-0472-0
4. Black, M.J., Anandan, P.: The robust estimation of multiple motions: parametric and piecewise-smooth flow fields. Comput. Vis. Image Underst. **63**(1), 75–104 (1996)
5. Blake, A., Zisserman, A.: Visual Reconstruction. MIT Press, Cambridge (1987)
6. Boyd, S., Vandenberghe, L.: Convex Optimization. Cambridge University Press, Cambridge (2004)
7. Bredies, K., Kunisch, K., Pock, T.: Total generalized variation. SIIMS **3**(3), 492–526 (2010)
8. Chambolle, A., Lions, P.L.: Image recovery via total variation minimization and related problems. Numer. Math. **76**(2), 167–188 (1997)
9. Chan, T.F., Vese, L.A.: Active contours without edges. IEEE Trans. Image Process. **10**(2), 266–277 (2001)
10. Chen, Y., Ranftl, R., Pock, T.: Insights into analysis operator learning: from patch-based sparse models to higher order MRFs. IEEE Trans. Image Process. **23**(3), 1060–1072 (2014)
11. Chen, Y., Yu, W., Pock, T.: On learning optimized reaction diffusion processes for effective image restoration. In: CVPR (2015)

12. Dabov, K., Foi, A., Katkovnik, V.: Image denoising by sparse 3D transformation-domain collaborative filtering. IEEE Trans. Image Process. **16**(8), 1–16 (2007)
13. Domke, J.: Generic methods for optimization-based modeling. In: AISTATS, pp. 318–326 (2012)
14. Freedman, D., Zhang, T.: Active contours for tracking distributions. IEEE Trans. Image Process. **13**(4), 518–526 (2004)
15. Gregor, K., LeCun, Y.: Learning fast approximations of sparse coding. In: ICML (2010)
16. Hammernik, K., Knoll, F., Sodickson, D., Pock, T.: Learning a variational model for compressed sensing MRI reconstruction. In: ISMRM (2016)
17. He, K., Zhang, X., Ren, S., Sun, J.: Deep residual learning for image recognition (2016)
18. Horn, B., Schunck, B.: Determining optical flow. Artif. Intell. **17**, 185–203 (1981)
19. Klatzer, T., Hammernik, K., Knöbelreiter, P., Pock, T.: Learning joint demosaicing and denoising based on sequential energy minimization. In: ICCP (2016)
20. Krizhevsky, A., Sutskever, I., Hinton, G.E.: Imagenet classification with deep convolutional neural networks. In: NIPS (2012)
21. Kunisch, K., Pock, T.: A bilevel optimization approach for parameter learning in variational models. SIIMS **6**, 938–983 (2013)
22. LeCun, Y., Boser, B., Denker, J.S., Henderson, D., Howard, R.E., Hubbard, W., Jackel, L.D.: Backpropagation applied to handwritten zip code recognition. Neural Comput. **1**(4), 541–551 (1989)
23. Lee, A.B., Pedersen, K.S., Mumford, D.: The nonlinear statistics of high-contrast patches in natural images. IJCV **54**(1–3), 83–103 (2003)
24. Levin, A., Weiss, Y., Durand, F., Freeman, W.T.: Understanding and evaluating blind deconvolution algorithms. In: CVPR (2009)
25. Lin, T.-Y., Maire, M., Belongie, S., Hays, J., Perona, P., Ramanan, D., Dollár, P., Zitnick, C.L.: Microsoft COCO: common objects in context. In: Fleet, D., Pajdla, T., Schiele, B., Tuytelaars, T. (eds.) ECCV 2014. LNCS, vol. 8693, pp. 740–755. Springer, Cham (2014). doi:10.1007/978-3-319-10602-1_48
26. Mao, X.J., Shen, C., Yang, Y.B.: Image restoration using convolutional auto-encoders with symmetric skip connections. arXiv e-prints 1606.08921 (2016)
27. Martin, D., Fowlkes, C., Tal, D., Malik, J.: A database of human segmented natural images and its application to evaluating segmentation algorithms and measuring ecological statistics. In: ICCV (2001)
28. Masoud, A., Saeid, N.: Multi-residual networks. arXiv e-prints 1609.05672 (2016)
29. Mumford, D., Shah, J.: Optimal approximations by piecewise smooth functions and associated variational problems. Commun. Pure Appl. Math. **42**(5), 577–685 (1989)
30. Nedić, A., Bertsekas, D.: Convergence rate of incremental subgradient algorithms. In: Uryasev, S., Pardalos, P.M. (eds.) Stochastic Optimization: Algorithms and Applications. Applied Optimization, vol. 54, pp. 223–264. Springer, Boston (2001)
31. Roth, S., Black, M.J.: Fields of experts. IJCV **82**, 205–229 (2009)
32. Rudin, L.I., Osher, S., Fatemi, E.: Nonlinear total variation based noise removal algorithms. Phys. D: Nonlinear Phenom. **60**(1–4), 259–268 (1992)
33. Rumelhart, D.E., Hinton, G.E., Williams, R.J.: Learning representations by back-propagating errors. Nature **323**(6088), 533–536 (1986)
34. Schelten, K., Nowozin, S., Jancsary, J., Rother, C., Roth, S.: Interleaved regression tree field cascades for blind image deconvolution. In: IEEE Winter Conference on Applications of Computer Vision (2015)

35. Schmidt, U., Roth, S.: Shrinkage fields for effective image restoration. In: CVPR (2014)
36. Shan, Q., Jia, J., Agarwala, A.: High-quality motion deblurring from a single image. In: SIGGRAPH (2008)
37. Sra, S.: Scalable nonconvex inexact proximal splitting. In: NIPS (2012)
38. Veit, A., Wilber, M., Belongie, S.: Residual networks are exponential ensembles of relatively shallow networks. arXiv e-prints 1605.06431 (2016)
39. Xu, L., Zheng, S., Jia, J.: Unnatural L0 sparse representation for natural image deblurring. In: CVPR (2013)
40. Yu, W., Heber, S., Pock, T.: Learning reaction-diffusion models for image inpainting. In: Gall, J., Gehler, P., Leibe, B. (eds.) GCPR 2015. LNCS, vol. 9358, pp. 356–367. Springer, Cham (2015). doi:10.1007/978-3-319-24947-6_29
41. Zhang, K., Zuo, W., Chen, Y., Meng, D., Zhang, L.: Beyond a Gaussian denoiser: residual learning of deep CNN for image denoising. arXiv e-prints 1608.03981 (2016)
42. Zhao, H., Gallo, O., Frosio, I., Kautz, J.: Loss functions for neural networks for image processing. arXiv e-prints 1511.08861 (2015)
43. Zhu, S.C., Mumford, D.: Prior learning and gibbs reaction-diffusion. TPAMI **19**(11), 1236–1250 (1997)

Gradient Flows on a Riemannian Submanifold for Discrete Tomography

Matthias Zisler[1(✉)], Fabrizio Savarino[1], Stefania Petra[2], and Christoph Schnörr[1]

[1] Image and Pattern Analysis Group, Heidelberg University, Heidelberg, Germany
zisler@math.uni-heidelberg.de
[2] Mathematical Imaging Group, Heidelberg University, Heidelberg, Germany

Abstract. We present a smooth geometric approach to discrete tomography that jointly performs tomographic reconstruction and label assignment. The flow evolves on a submanifold equipped with a Hessian Riemannian metric and properly takes into account given projection constraints. The metric naturally extends the Fisher-Rao metric from labeling problems with directly observed data to the inverse problem of discrete tomography where projection data only is available. The flow simultaneously performs reconstruction and label assignment. We show that it can be numerically integrated by an implicit scheme based on a Bregman proximal point iteration. A numerical evaluation on standard testdatasets in the few angles scenario demonstrates an improvement of the reconstruction quality compared to competitive methods.

1 Introduction

Discrete tomography [9] denotes the problem to reconstruct *piecewise constant* functions from projection data, that are taken from few projection angles only. Such extremely ill-posed inverse problems are motivated by industrial applications, like quality inspection. Regularization of such problems essentially rests upon the fact that the functions to be reconstructed only take values in a finite set of labels $\mathcal{L} := \{c_1, \ldots, c_K\} \subset [0, 1]$. This is similar to the common image labeling problem in computer vision, with the essential difference that the function u to be labelled is only *indirectly* observed. Specifically, after a standard problem discretization resulting in the representation $u \in \mathbb{R}^N$, projection data b given by

$$Au = b \quad \text{s.t.} \quad u_i \in \mathcal{L}, \quad \forall i = 1, \ldots, N \tag{1}$$

are observed, where the matrix A is underdetermined but known. The task is to reconstruct u subject to the labeling constraints $u_i \in \mathcal{L}, \forall i$.

Related Work. A natural class of approaches are based on minimizing *convex sparsifying functionals* of u (e.g. total variation) subject to the affine subject constraints (1), but *without* the labeling constraints [7,8,14]. Unless sufficient conditions for unique recovery are met, in terms of the number of projection

© Springer International Publishing AG 2017
V. Roth and T. Vetter (Eds.): GCPR 2017, LNCS 10496, pp. 294–305, 2017.
DOI: 10.1007/978-3-319-66709-6_24

measurements relative to the complexity of the discontinuity set of u [7], the performance of the necessary rounding post-processing step is difficult to control, however. Likewise, a binary discrete graphical model from labeling was adopted by [10], and a sequence of s-t graph-cuts was solved to take into account the affine projection constraints. An extension to the non-binary case (multiple labels) seems to be involved. The authors of [15] minimize the ℓ_0-norm of the gradient directly by a dynamic programming approach, but do not exploit the set $\mathcal{L}$ of feasible labels for regularization.

Approaches that aim to enforce the labeling constraints by *continuous non-convex* optimization include [12,18,20,21]. Unlike our approach proposed below, that limits the degrees of freedom by restricting the feasible set to a Riemannian submanifold, these approach work in the higher-dimensional ambient Euclidean space and hence are more susceptible to poor initializations and local minima. A step towards alleviating these problems was recently done by [19], where a different regularization strategy was proposed based on the Kullback-Leibler (KL) divergence.

Further approaches that define the state of the art include [4,16]. The authors of [16] proposed a heuristic algorithm that adaptively combines an energy formulation with a non-convex polynomial representation, in order to steer the reconstruction towards the feasible label set. Batenburg et al. [4] proposed the *Discrete Algebraic Reconstruction Technique (DART)* algorithm which starts with a continuous reconstruction by a basic algebraic reconstruction method, followed by a thresholding operation. These steps, interleaved with smoothing, are iteratively repeated to refine the locations of the boundaries. This heuristic approach yields good reconstructions in practice, but cannot be characterized by an objective function which is optimized.

We regard [4,16,20] as state-of-the-art approaches in our experimental comparison.

Contribution. We present a novel geometric approach to discrete tomography by optimizing over a Riemannian submanifold of discrete probability measures with full support. Our work is motivated by the recent work [3], where the ordinary labeling problem (with directly observed data) is solved by a Riemannian gradient flow on a manifold of discrete probability measures that represent label assignments. By restricting the feasible set to a submanifold, equipped with a natural extension of the Fisher-Rao metric, we extend this approach to discrete tomography. The resulting gradient flow takes into account the projection constraints and simultaneously performs reconstruction and label assignment. We show that this flow can be numerically integrated by an implicit scheme requires to solve a convex problem at each step. A comprehensive numerical evaluation demonstrates the superior reconstruction performance of our approach compared to related work.

Basic Notation. Functions like log and binary operations (multiplication, subdivision) are applied *component-wise* to vectors and matrices, e.g., $vw = (\dots, v_i w_i, \dots)^T$. The KL-divergence is defined by $\mathrm{KL}(x, y) = \langle x, \log(x/y) \rangle + \langle y - x, \mathbb{1} \rangle$ for both vectors and matrices with non-negative entries, where $\langle \cdot, \cdot \rangle$ denotes the Euclidean scalar product. We set $\mathbb{1} = (1, 1, \ldots, 1)^T$ and $[n] = \{1, 2, \ldots, n\}$ for $n \in \mathbb{N}$. The linear operator $\mathrm{vec}(\cdot)$ maps matrices to vectors by stacking columns. Finally $\otimes$ denotes the Kronecker product.

2   Approach

We briefly summarize the approach [3]. Then we extend this approach in order to additionally take into account the affine subspace constraint: We construct a smooth Riemanian gradient flow, for any smooth objective function, restricted to the relative interior. Finally, we specify an objective function that is used for the experimental evaluation.

Smooth Geometric Label Assignment. Each label $c_k \in \mathcal{L}$ is represented by a vertex of the probability simplex $e_k \in \mathbb{R}^K$, and the set of feasible label assignments to all pixels corresponds to the set of row-stochastic matrices with full support, denoted by $\mathcal{W} \subset \mathbb{R}_{++}^{N \times K}$. In [3] a smooth geometric approach for labeling is proposed, where $\mathcal{W}$ is turned into a Riemannian manifold using the Fisher-Rao (information) metric [5]. For a given image $u \in \mathbb{R}^N$, the distance between each pixel u_i, $i \in [N]$ and each label $c_k \in \mathcal{L}$, $k \in [K]$ is measured and collected by a distance matrix D_{ik}. Next this matrix is projected onto the tangent space $T^N \simeq T_W \mathcal{W} = \{T \in \mathbb{R}^{N \times K} \,|\, T\mathbb{1}_K = 0_N\}$ by subtracting pixelwise the mean of D, i.e. $\Pi(D) = D - \frac{1}{K}D\mathbb{1}_K\mathbb{1}_K^T$. The projection $\Pi(D)$ in turn is mapped to the manifold $\mathcal{W}$ by the so-called lifting map

$$\exp\colon \mathcal{W} \times T^N \to \mathcal{W}, \quad (W, V) \mapsto \exp_W(V) := \frac{We^V}{\langle W, e^V \rangle}, \tag{2}$$

to obtain the likelihood matrix $L = \exp_W(\Pi(D))$. Next, spatial regularization is performed by computing Riemannian means of the row vectors L_i within a spatial neighbourhood $\mathcal{N}(i)$ for each pixel $i \in [N]$. It is shown in [3] that these means admit the closed-form solution

$$S(W)_i = \frac{m_g(\{L(W)_j\}_{j\in\mathcal{N}(i)})}{\langle m_g(\{L(W)_j\}_{j\in\mathcal{N}(i)}), \mathbb{1}_K \rangle}, \quad m_g(\{L(W)_j\}_{j\in\mathcal{N}(i)}) := \prod_{j\in\mathcal{N}(i)} L(W)_j^{\frac{1}{|\mathcal{N}(i)|}}. \tag{3}$$

Finally, a labeling in terms of $W \in \mathcal{W}$ is determined by maximizing the correlation $\langle W, S(W) \rangle$. The optimization is carried out on the manifold $\mathcal{W}$ by an explicit Euler scheme for integrating the Riemannian gradient flow (assignment flow).

Tomographic Assignment Flow. We now consider the situation where the image data are only indirectly observed through the projection constraints (1). To this end, we extend the approach [3] using techniques developed by [2], in order to restrict the smooth Riemannian flow to assignments that respect the projection constraints.

Our starting point is the observation that the Riemannian metric used in [3] is induced by the Hessian of the convex Legendre function

$$h(W) := \langle W, \log(W) - \mathbb{1}_N\mathbb{1}_K^T \rangle, \tag{4}$$

with domain restricted to the relative interior of $\overline{\mathcal{W}} = \{W \in \mathbb{R}_+^{N \times K} : W\mathbb{1}_K = \mathbb{1}_N\}$. In order to take into account the projection constraints (1), we introduce the assignment operator

$$P_{\mathcal{L}} : \mathcal{W} \to \mathbb{R}^N, \quad W \mapsto P_{\mathcal{L}}(W) = (I_N \otimes c^T)\operatorname{vec}(W) = Wc, \tag{5}$$

that makes explicit the reconstructed function $u = Wc$ in terms of the given labels c and the assignment W. Based on this correspondence and (1), we extend the set $\overline{\mathcal{W}}$ to

$$\overline{\mathcal{F}} = \left\{ W : \mathbb{R}_+^{N \times K}, \ B \operatorname{vec}(W) = \left(\begin{smallmatrix} b \\ \mathbb{1}_N \end{smallmatrix}\right) \right\}, \qquad B = \left(\begin{smallmatrix} A(I_N \otimes c^T) \\ I_N \otimes \mathbb{1}_K^T \end{smallmatrix}\right). \tag{6}$$

The following non-degeneracy property is crucial for the smooth geometric construction below. The proof exploits the structure of B and properties of the Kronecker product. We omit details due to the page limit.

Lemma 1 (rank of B). *The matrix B has full row rank by construction, if the measurement matrix A has full row rank.*

Our next step is to extend the manifold $\mathcal{W}$ to a manifold $\mathcal{F}$, based on the extension of $\overline{\mathcal{W}}$ to $\overline{\mathcal{F}}$. We adopt the convex Legendre function $h(W)$ from above and take as its domain the linear manifold $\mathcal{M} = \mathbb{R}_{++}^{N \times K}$. Then the Hessian $\nabla^2 h(W) = \frac{1}{W}$ (*componentwise* inverse) smoothly depends on $W \in \mathcal{M}$ and defines the linear mapping

$$H(W) : \mathbb{R}^{N \times K} \to \mathbb{R}^{N \times K}, \quad U \mapsto H(W)U := \left(U_{ij}/W_{ij}\right)_{i \in [N], j \in [K]}. \tag{7}$$

Based on the canonical identification of the tangent spaces $T_W \mathcal{M} \simeq \mathbb{R}^{N \times K}$ for linear manifolds, the mapping $H(W)$ defines the Riemannian metric

$$(U, V)_W^H := \langle H(W)U, V \rangle, \qquad \forall W \in \mathcal{M}, \ U, V \in \mathbb{R}^{N \times K}. \tag{8}$$

Given some smooth objective $J(W)$, the corresponding Riemannian gradient field restricted to $\mathcal{M}$ is given by

$$\nabla_H J_{|\mathcal{M}}(W) := H(W)^{-1} \nabla J(W). \tag{9}$$

Next we consider the smooth submanifold $\mathcal{F} := \operatorname{rint}(\overline{\mathcal{F}}) = \mathcal{M} \cap \overline{\mathcal{F}}$ of $\mathcal{M}$ with tangent space $T_W \mathcal{F} \simeq \mathcal{N}(B)$. The metric on $\mathcal{M}$ induces a metric on $\mathcal{F}$, and the Riemannian gradient field of $J(W)$ restricted to $\mathcal{F}$ is given by

$$\nabla_H J_{|\mathcal{F}}(W) := P_W^{\mathcal{N}(B)}\big(H(W)^{-1} \nabla J(W)\big), \tag{10}$$

where $P_W^{\mathcal{N}(B)}$ is the $(\cdot, \cdot)_W^H$-orthogonal projection onto the nullspace $\mathcal{N}(B)$. Since the matrix B has full rank due to Lemma 1, this projection reads

$$P_W^{\mathcal{N}(B)}(H(W)^{-1} \nabla J(W)) = \operatorname{vec}^{-1}\big[(I - (BD_W^H B^T)^{-1} BD_W^H)(D_W^H)^{-1} \operatorname{vec}[\nabla J(W)]\big], \tag{11}$$

where $D_W^H = \text{Diag}[\text{vec}(H(W))]$. The vector $-\nabla_H J_{|\mathcal{F}}(W)$ for $W \in \mathcal{F}$ is the steepest descent direction in $\mathcal{N}(B)$. Furthermore, minimization of an objective J on the Riemannian manifold $(\mathcal{F}, (\cdot, \cdot)_W^H)$ amounts to find the solution trajectory $W(t)$ of the dynamical system

$$\dot{W}(t) + \nabla_H J_{|\mathcal{F}}(W(t)) = 0, \quad W(0) = W^0 \in \mathcal{F}, \tag{12}$$

with initial condition $W^0 \in \mathcal{F}$.

Objective Function. We adopt and modify the approach of [3] sketched in Sect. 2, for our purpose. Defining the distance matrix $D(\hat{W}) := \frac{1}{\rho}(\|P_{\mathcal{L}}(\hat{W})_i - c_k\|_2^2)_{i \in [N], k \in [K]}$, with the assignment operator $P_{\mathcal{L}}(\hat{W})$ given by (5) and a scaling parameter $\rho > 0$, we compute a similarity matrix $S(\hat{W})$ as described in connection with (3). Based on $S(\hat{W})$, we define the objective function

$$J(W, \hat{W}) = \text{KL}\left(W, S(\hat{W})^{1+\alpha}\right), \quad \alpha > 0. \tag{13}$$

Minimizing J with respect to W encodes two aspects. Firstly, the discrete assignment distributions comprising W should be consistent with the spatially regularized similarities $S(\hat{W})$, that correspond to the lifted distances $D(\hat{W})$ between the reconstructed function $P_{\mathcal{L}}(\hat{W})$ and the labels c. Secondly, since W appears as first argument of the KL-distance, W matches the prominent *modes* of the discrete distributions comprising $S(\hat{W})$ (cf. [11]), and hence enforces unique labelings. The damping parameter α enables to control this "rounding property".

Since the assignment $\hat{W}$ is not given beforehand, we pursue an iterative strategy and set $\hat{W} = W^k$ to the current iterate, in order to compute W^{k+1} by minimizing (13). In the next section, we formulate this process in a more principled way as a fixed point iteration, that properly discretizes and solves the continuous flow (12).

3   Optimization

In this section we want to find a solution trajectory of the initial value problem (12) associated with the steepest Riemannian gradient descent of the convex objective function J in (13) on the smooth manifold $\mathcal{F}$. Following [2], we reformulate (12) as a differential inclusion for a time interval (T_m, T_M) corresponding to the unique maximal solution of (12) and obtain

$$\frac{d}{dt}\nabla h(W(t)) + \nabla J(W(t)) \in \mathcal{N}(B)^{\perp}, \quad W(t) \in \mathcal{F}, \quad W(0) = W^0 \in \mathcal{F}, \tag{14}$$

with h given by (4). Since J is convex, an implicit discretization yields the iterative scheme: $\nabla h(W^{k+1}) - \nabla h(W^k) + \mu_k \nabla J(W^{k+1}) \in \mathcal{N}(B)^{\perp}$, $B\,\text{vec}(W^{k+1}) = y$ and $W^0 \in \mathcal{F}$, where μ_k is a step-size parameter. These relations are just the optimality conditions of the Bregman proximal point method with the KL-divergence as proximity measure

$$W^{k+1} \in \arg\min_{W \in \mathbb{R}_+^{N \times K}} J(W, \hat{W}) + \frac{1}{\mu_k} \text{KL}(W, W^k) \quad \text{s.t.} \quad B\,\text{vec}(W) = y. \tag{15}$$

Algorithm 1. Iterated Primal Dual Algorithm

Init: choose the barycenter for $W^0 \in \mathcal{G}$, dual variable $Q^0 \in \mathbb{R}^m$ and $\tau, \sigma > 0$
Parameters: selectivity $\rho > 0$, discretization $\alpha > 0$, trust region $\mu_k > 0$

while *not converged* **do**

    Warmstart for PD: $W^0 = W^k$, $\tilde{W} = T_{\mu_k}(W^k)$, $Q^0 = Q^{last}$, $n = 1$
    while *not converged* **do**

$$W^{n+1} = \arg\min_{W \in \overline{W}} \mathrm{KL}(W, \tilde{W}) + \langle W, \mathrm{P}_{\mathcal{L}}^T(A^T Q^n)\rangle + \frac{1}{\tau}\mathrm{KL}(W, W^n) \quad (17)$$

$$Q^{n+1} = \arg\min_{Q} \langle Q, b - A\mathrm{P}_{\mathcal{L}}(2W^{n+1} - W^n)\rangle + \frac{1}{2\sigma}\|Q - Q^n\|_2^2 \quad (18)$$

        $n \leftarrow n + 1$
    $k \leftarrow k + 1$, $W^k \leftarrow W^n$
Output: W^k

We solve (15) for fixed W^k by an iterative algorithm to perform an implicit integration step on the flow (12). In order to update the fixed $\hat{W}$ in $J(W, \hat{W})$ defined by (13), we set $\hat{W} = W^k$. Inserting into (15) and combining the KL-divergences as a multiplicative convex combination with respect to the second argument yields the fixed point iteration

$$W^{k+1} \in \arg\min_{W \in \overline{W}} \mathrm{KL}(W, \underbrace{(W^k)^{\frac{1}{1+\mu_k}}(S(W^k))^{\frac{\mu_k(1+\alpha)}{1+\mu_k}}}_{:=T_{\mu_k}(W^k)}) \quad \text{s.t.} \quad A\mathrm{P}_{\mathcal{L}}(W) = b, \quad (16)$$

where the constraints $W \in \mathbb{R}_+^{N \times K}$ and $B\,\mathrm{vec}(W) = y$ are rewritten as $W \in \overline{W}$ and $A\mathrm{P}_{\mathcal{L}}(W) = b$. Regarding convergence of the fixed point iteration (16), we use a non-summable diminishing step-size parameter $\mu_k = \frac{1}{0.005 \cdot k \cdot \|A\mathrm{P}_{\mathcal{L}}(W^k) - b\|_2}$ with $\lim_{k \to \infty} \mu_k = 0$. Hence the operator T_{μ_k} becomes $T_{\mu_k} \longrightarrow \mathrm{Id}$ for $k \to \infty$ and the influence of the objective function J vanishes. When the iteration converges, then (16) reduces to the KL-projection onto the fixed feasible set $\overline{\mathcal{F}}$. A rigorous mathematical convergence analysis of the iterations (16) is left for future work.

Solving the Fixed Point Iteration. Algorithm 1 solves Eq. (16) iteratively using the generalized primal dual algorithm [6]. The primal update step (17) can be evaluated in closed form

$$W^{n+1} = \arg\min_{W \in \overline{W}} \mathrm{KL}(W, \tilde{W}) + \langle W, \mathrm{P}_{\mathcal{L}}^T(A^T Q^n)\rangle + \frac{1}{\tau}\mathrm{KL}(W, W^n) \quad (19a)$$

$$= \frac{(W^n)^{\frac{1}{1+\tau}}(\tilde{W})^{\frac{\tau}{1+\tau}}\exp(-\frac{\tau}{1+\tau}\mathrm{P}_{\mathcal{L}}^T(A^T Q^n))}{\langle (W^n)^{\frac{1}{1+\tau}}(\tilde{W})^{\frac{\tau}{1+\tau}}, \exp(-\frac{\tau}{1+\tau}\mathrm{P}_{\mathcal{L}}^T(A^T Q^n))\rangle}. \quad (19b)$$

The dual update step (18) admits a closed form as well,

$$Q^{n+1} = \arg\min_Q \langle Q, b - AP_{\mathcal{L}}(2W^{n+1} - W^n)\rangle + \frac{1}{2\sigma}\|Q - Q^n\|_2^2 \qquad (20a)$$

$$= Q^n + \sigma(AP_{\mathcal{L}}(2W^{n+1} - W^n) - b). \qquad (20b)$$

Parameter Selection. For the step-size parameters τ and σ of the iterated primal-dual algorithm, we adopt the parameter values of [6, Example 7.2] and set $\tau = \sqrt{K}/L_{12}^2$ for the primal update and $\sigma = 1/\sqrt{K}$ for the dual update. This choice implies that the condition $\sigma\tau\|AP_{\mathcal{L}}(\cdot)\|^2 \leq 1$ for convergence holds, with the operator norm $\|AP_{\mathcal{L}}(\cdot)\| = \sup_{\|x\|_1 \leq 1}\|A(I_N \otimes c^T)x\|_2 = \max_j \|(A(I_N \otimes c^T))_j\|_2$. This reflects the fact that the negative entropy is 1-strongly convex with respect to the L_1-norm when restricted to the probability simplex.

4   Numerical Experiments

We compared the proposed approach to state-of-the-art approaches for discrete tomography, including the Discrete Algebraic Reconstruction Technique (*DART*) [4], the energy minimization method of Varga et al. [16] (*Varga*), and the layer-wise total variation approach (*LayerTV*) [20].

Setup. We adapted the binary phantoms from [17] to the multi-label case, shown as phantom 1, 2 and 3 in Fig. 1. Phantom 4 is the well-known Shepp-Logan phantom [13]. We simulated noisy scenarios by applying Poisson noise to the measurements b with a signal-to-noise ratio of $SNR = 20\,\mathrm{dB}$. The geometrical setup was created by the ASTRA-toolbox [1], where we used parallel projections along equidistant angles between 0 and $180°$. The width of the sensor-array was set 1.5 times the image size, such that every pixel is intersecting with at least one single projection ray.

Implementation Details. The subproblems of Algorithm 1 were approximately solved by the generalized PD algorithm [6]. For the multiplicative updates (19b), we adopted the renormalization strategy from [3] to avoid numerical issues close to the boundary of the manifold, that correspond to unambigous label assignments. The outer iteration was terminated when $\|AP_{\mathcal{L}}(W^k) - b\|_2 < 0.1$. For the geometric averaging (cf. (3) and (13)), we used a 3×3 neighborhood for the smaller phantom 1 and 5×5 for all others. In order to reconstruct from *noisy* measurements, we modified the proposed approach by using the squared L_2-reprojection error as relaxed dataterm, so that the objective (13) reads

$$J(W, \hat{W}) = \mathrm{KL}\left(W, S(\hat{W})^{1+\alpha}\right) + \frac{1}{2}\|AP_{\mathcal{L}}(W) - b\|_2^2, \quad \alpha > 0, \qquad (21)$$

which is smooth and convex in W as well. In this case, the fixed point iteration (16) is applied to the modified objective (21) and the dual update step (18) of Algorithm 1 is additionally rescaled, i.e. $Q^{n+1} = (Q^n + \sigma(AP_{\mathcal{L}}(2W^{n+1} - W^n) - b))/(1 + \sigma)$ compared to (20b).

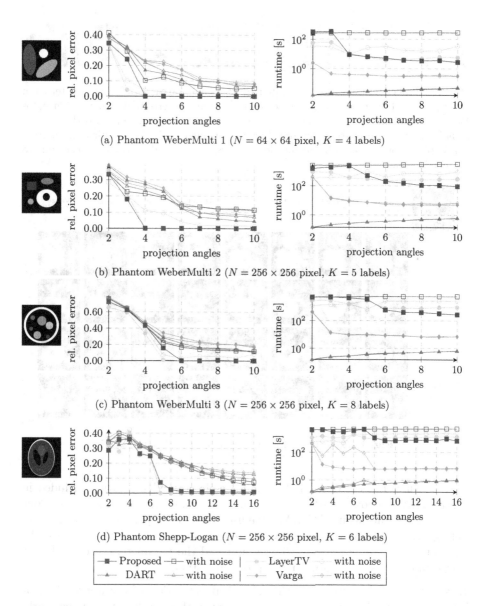

(a) Phantom WeberMulti 1 ($N = 64 \times 64$ pixel, $K = 4$ labels)

(b) Phantom WeberMulti 2 ($N = 256 \times 256$ pixel, $K = 5$ labels)

(c) Phantom WeberMulti 3 ($N = 256 \times 256$ pixel, $K = 8$ labels)

(d) Phantom Shepp-Logan ($N = 256 \times 256$ pixel, $K = 6$ labels)

Fig. 1. Evaluation of the approaches for the different test-datasets and increasing (but small) numbers of projections angles, in the noiseless case (**filled markers**) and in the noisy case (**non-filled markers**), noise level $SNR = 20\,$dB. The relative pixel error and runtime is displayed. The proposed approach gives perfect reconstructions with a small number of projection angles in the noiseless case and also returns good reconstructions in the presence of noise, compared to the other approaches. The single competing approach, LayerTV, uses a special rounding strategy to obtain meaningful solutions (phantom 3 and 4) and a dedicated data term to cope with Poisson noise.

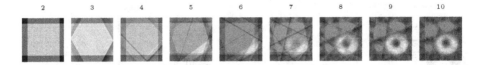

Fig. 2. "Implicit data terms" generated by the tomographic constraints, in terms of the reprojected dual variable $A^T Q$ (scaled to $[0, 1]$ and inverted) after convergence, for WeberMulti 2 and an increasing number of projection angles. The proposed approach achieves a perfect reconstruction from 4 projection angles only. The missing information is effectively compensated by geometric label assignment and spatial coherence due to geometric averaging.

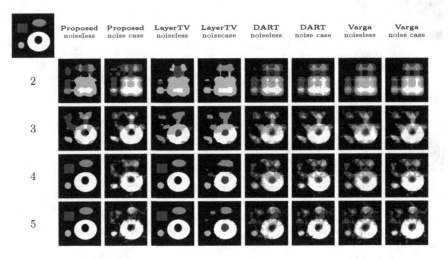

Fig. 3. Experimental results for phantom WeberMulti 2.

Regarding DART we used the public available implementation included in the ASTRA-toolbox [1], whereas for Varga [16] and LayerTV [20] we used our own implementations in MATLAB. We used the default parameters of the competing approaches as proposed by the respective authors. However, since the test-datasets differ in size, we slightly adjusted the parameters in order to get best results for every algorithm and problem instance.

Results. Figure 1 summarizes the numerical evaluation of the approaches for increasing (but small) numbers of projections, in the noiseless case (filled markers) and in the noisy case (non-filled markers), with Poisson noise $SNR = 20$ dB. Each test-dataset is depicted in the leftmost column, followed by the relative pixel error and runtime. The proposed approach achieved perfect reconstructions with a small number of projection angles in the noiseless case. Only LayerTV needed one projection less at phantom 3 and 4. LayerTV however tends to return non-integral solutions when the regularization parameter is large and then requires a special rounding strategy to obtain a meaningful reconstruction. In noisy scenarios, LayerTV performs better due to use of inequality projection

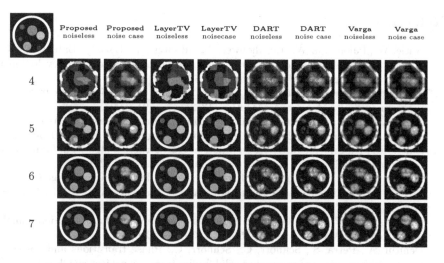

Fig. 4. Experimental results for phantom WeberMulti 3.

constraints, followed by the proposed method that outperforms both DART and Varga. Figure 2 shows the poor "implicit data terms" generated by the tomographic constraints in case of phantom 2, to illustrate the severe ill-posedness of these inverse problems (see the caption for more details).

Considering the runtime (right plots from Fig. 1), DART is the fastest approach followed by Varga. The proposed approach and LayerTV are clearly consuming more runtime to return more accurate solutions. In the noiseless and with a sufficient projection angles, the proposed approach is faster. We point out that the proposed approach could be easily parallelized using graphics cards. In Figs. 3 and 4 the visual results are displayed for the phantoms 2 and 3.

5   Conclusion and Future Work

We presented a novel smooth geometric approach for jointly solving tomographic reconstruction and assignment. We derived a suitable Riemannian structure on the feasible set in order to optimize a smooth objective function on a manifold that respects the projection constraints. The Riemannian gradient flow combines tomographic reconstruction and labeling in a smooth and mathematically sound way.

Our future work will include a rigorous mathematical convergence analysis of the fixed-point iteration (16) and of the stability of the corresponding Riemannian gradient descent flow (12), that entails iterative updates $\hat{W} = W^k$ of the objective function $J(W, \hat{W})$. Such issues are not covered by standard convex programming. A promising extension of the proposed approach concerns the ability to handle inequality constraints, in order to further improve the performance in scenarios with high noise levels.

References

1. Aarle, W., Palenstijn, W., Beenhouwer, J., Altantzis, T., Bals, S., Batenburg, K., Sijbers, J.: The ASTRA toolbox: a platform for advanced algorithm development in electron tomography. Ultramicroscopy **157**, 35–47 (2015)
2. Alvarez, F., Bolte, J., Brahic, O.: Hessian Riemannian gradient flows in convex programming. SIAM J. Control Optim. **43**(2), 477–501 (2004)
3. Åström, F., Petra, S., Schmitzer, B., Schnörr, C.: Image labeling by assignment. J. Math. Imaging Vis. 1–28 (2017). http://dx.doi.org/10.1007/s10851-016-0702-4
4. Batenburg, K., Sijbers, J.: DART: a practical reconstruction algorithm for discrete tomography. IEEE Trans. Image Process. **20**(9), 2542–2553 (2011)
5. Burbea, J., Rao, C.R.: Entropy differential metric, distance and divergence measures in probability spaces: a unified approach. J. Multivar. Anal. **12**(4), 575–596 (1982)
6. Chambolle, A., Pock, T.: On the ergodic convergence rates of a first-order primal-dual algorithm. Math. Program. **159**(1), 253–287 (2016)
7. Denitiu, A., Petra, S., Schnörr, C., Schnörr, C.: Phase transitions and cosparse tomographic recovery of compound solid bodies from few projections. Fundamenta Informaticae **135**, 73–102 (2014)
8. Goris, B., Broek, W., Batenburg, K., Mezerji, H., Bals, S.: Electron tomography based on a total variation minimization reconstruction technique. Ultramicroscopy **113**, 120–130 (2012)
9. Herman, G., Kuba, A.: Discrete Tomography: Foundations, Algorithms and Applications. Birkhäuser, Basel (1999)
10. Kappes, J.H., Petra, S., Schnörr, C., Zisler, M.: TomoGC: binary tomography by constrained GraphCuts. In: Gall, J., Gehler, P., Leibe, B. (eds.) GCPR 2015. LNCS, vol. 9358, pp. 262–273. Springer, Cham (2015). doi:10.1007/978-3-319-24947-6_21
11. Minka, T.: Divergence measures and message passing. Technical report, MSR-TR-2005-173, Microsoft Research Ltd., Cambridge, UK (2005)
12. Schüle, T., Schnörr, C., Weber, S., Hornegger, J.: Discrete tomography by convex-concave regularization and D.C. programming. Discret. Appl. Math. **151**(13), 229–243 (2005)
13. Shepp, L., Logan, B.: The Fourier reconstruction of a head section. IEEE Trans. Nucl. Sci. **21**(3), 21–43 (1974)
14. Sidky, E.Y., Pan, X.: Image reconstruction in circular cone-beam computed tomography by constrained, total-variation minimization. Phys. Med. Biol. **53**(17), 4777 (2008)
15. Storath, M., Weinmann, A., Frikel, J., Unser, M.: Joint image reconstruction and segmentation using the Potts model. Inverse Prob. **31**(2), 025003 (2015)
16. Varga, L., Balázs, P., Nagy, A.: An energy minimization reconstruction algorithm for multivalued discrete tomography. In: 3rd International Symposium on Computational Modeling of Objects Represented in Images, Rome, Italy, Proceedings, pp. 179–185. Taylor & Francis (2012)
17. Weber, S., Nagy, A., Schüle, T., Schnörr, C., Kuba, A.: A benchmark evaluation of large-scale optimization approaches to binary tomography. In: Kuba, A., Nyúl, L.G., Palágyi, K. (eds.) DGCI 2006. LNCS, vol. 4245, pp. 146–156. Springer, Heidelberg (2006). doi:10.1007/11907350_13
18. Weber, S., Schnörr, C., Hornegger, J.: A linear programming relaxation for binary tomography with smoothness priors. Electron. Notes Discret. Math. **12**, 243–254 (2003)

19. Zisler, M., Åström, F., Petra, S., Schnörr, C.: Image reconstruction by multilabel propagation. In: Lauze, F., Dong, Y., Dahl, A.B. (eds.) SSVM 2017. LNCS, vol. 10302, pp. 247–259. Springer, Cham (2017). doi:10.1007/978-3-319-58771-4_20

20. Zisler, M., Petra, S., Schnörr, C., Schnörr, C.: Discrete tomography by continuous multilabeling subject to projection constraints. In: Rosenhahn, B., Andres, B. (eds.) GCPR 2016. LNCS, vol. 9796, pp. 261–272. Springer, Cham (2016). doi:10.1007/978-3-319-45886-1_21

21. Zisler, M., Kappes, J.H., Schnörr, C., Petra, S., Schnörr, C.: Non-binary discrete tomography by continuous non-convex optimization. IEEE Trans. Comput. Imaging **2**(3), 335–347 (2016)

Model Selection for Gaussian Process Regression

Nico S. Gorbach, Andrew An Bian, Benjamin Fischer, Stefan Bauer$^{(\boxtimes)}$, and Joachim M. Buhmann

Department of Computer Science, ETH Zurich, Zürich, Switzerland
{stefan.bauer,jbuhmann}@inf.ethz.ch

Abstract. Gaussian processes are powerful tools since they can model non-linear dependencies between inputs, while remaining analytically tractable. A Gaussian process is characterized by a mean function and a covariance function (kernel), which are determined by a model selection criterion. The functions to be compared do not just differ in their parametrization but in their fundamental structure. It is often not clear which function structure to choose, for instance to decide between a squared exponential and a rational quadratic kernel. Based on the principle of *posterior agreement*, we develop a general framework for model selection to rank kernels for Gaussian process regression and compare it with maximum evidence (also called marginal likelihood) and leave-one-out cross-validation. Given the disagreement between current state-of-the-art methods in our experiments, we show the difficulty of model selection and the need for an information-theoretic approach.

1 Introduction

A Gaussian process generalizes the multivariate Gaussian distribution to a distribution over functions [17]. Model selection aims to adapt this distribution to a given set of data points, finding a trade-off between underfitting and overfitting. For Gaussian processes, we wish to select a mean function and a covariance function (also known as a kernel). Selecting a function is a difficult problem because the possibilities are virtually unlimited. Typically, one considers a handful of function structures parametrized by hyperparameters, which are determined during model selection. Table 1 gives examples of kernels. In domains such as systems biology [21], there is often no prior knowledge for selecting a certain function structure. A model selection criterion that is good at both hyperparameter optimization and function structure selection is thus extremely desirable.

1.1 Existing Model Selection Criteria for Gaussian Processes

Two well-known model selection criteria for Gaussian processes exist, namely maximum evidence and cross validation. Maximum evidence (also called marginal likelihood) maximizes the probability of the data under the model assumptions. Given a regression data set of inputs X with corresponding outputs y, the

N.S. Gorbach and A.A. Bian—These two authors contributed equally.

© Springer International Publishing AG 2017
V. Roth and T. Vetter (Eds.): GCPR 2017, LNCS 10496, pp. 306–318, 2017.
DOI: 10.1007/978-3-319-66709-6_25

Table 1. Examples of kernel structures with their hyperparameters [17].

Name	$k\left(\boldsymbol{x}, \boldsymbol{x}'\right)$	Hyperparameters
Squared exponential	$\sigma_f^2 \exp\left(-\frac{1}{2\ell^2}\left\|\boldsymbol{x}-\boldsymbol{x}'\right\|_2^2\right)$	ℓ, σ_f
Rational quadratic	$\sigma_f^2 \left(1 + \frac{1}{2\alpha\ell^2}\left\|\boldsymbol{x}-\boldsymbol{x}'\right\|_2^2\right)^{-\alpha}$	ℓ, σ_f, α
Exponential	$\sigma_f^2 \exp\left(-\frac{1}{\ell}\left\|\boldsymbol{x}-\boldsymbol{x}'\right\|_2\right)$	ℓ, σ_f
Periodic	$\sigma_f^2 \exp\left(-\frac{2}{\ell^2}\sin^2\left(\frac{\pi}{T}\left\|\boldsymbol{x}-\boldsymbol{x}'\right\|_2\right)\right)$	ℓ, T, σ_f

objective of maximum evidence is to maximize the evidence $p_{\boldsymbol{\theta}}\left(\boldsymbol{y} \mid \boldsymbol{X}\right)$ w.r.t. the hyperparameter vector $\boldsymbol{\theta}$. We write $p_{\boldsymbol{\theta}}\left(\cdot\right)$ to make clear that this probability density function depends on $\boldsymbol{\theta}$. Cross-validation, on the other hand, minimizes an estimated generalization error of the model. In case of K-fold cross-validation, the objective is $-\frac{1}{K}\sum_{k=1}^{K}\log p_{\boldsymbol{\theta}}\left(\boldsymbol{y}_k \mid \boldsymbol{X}, \boldsymbol{y}_{-k}\right)$, where the outputs $\boldsymbol{y}_k$ of the kth fold are used to validate the model trained on the remaining outputs $\boldsymbol{y}_{-k}$. A lesser-known criterion is to minimize a bound on the generalization error from the framework of probably approximately correct (PAC) learning. However, while the concerned PAC-Bayesian theorem holds for Gaussian process classification, it seems unclear whether it can be applied to Gaussian process regression [18]. Maximum evidence is generally preferred "if you really trust your prior," [7, p. 19] for instance, if one is sure about the choice of the kernel structure, so that only its hyperparameters need to be optimized. Under certain circumstances, cross-validation is more resistant to model misspecification. However, it may suffer from a higher variance [1] which is a potential risk for model selection [6]. These criteria (including ours, derived in Sect. 2) can be used for model evaluation in automatic model construction [15].

1.2 Our Contributions

Originally the posterior agreement was applied to a discrete setting (i.e. clustering [4,8]). However for GP regression we extend it to the continuous domain, similar in spirit to [10]. Thus a first contribution of our work is to apply posterior agreement to any model that defines a parameter prior and a likelihood, as it is the case for Bayesian linear regression. This gives birth to a family of model selection methods. The developed framework is applied in two variants to Gaussian process regression, which naturally comes with a prior and a likelihood. Furthermore the resulting model selection criteria are then compared to state-of-the-art methods such as maximum evidence and leave-one-out (LOO) cross-validation on the two distinct subproblems of hyperparameter optimization and function structure selection. In an experiment for kernel structure selection based on real-world data, it is interesting to see how maximum evidence and leave-one-out cross-validation disagree on which kernel structure should model the data best. This demonstrates the difficulty of model selection and highlights the shortcoming (i.e. bias) of current state-of-the-art methods.

2   Posterior Agreement Applied to Model Selection for Gaussian Process Regression

In this section we first introduce the general model selection framework based on posterior agreement, then explain how to apply it to model selection for Gaussian process regression. The posterior agreement determines an optimal trade-off between the expressiveness of a model and robustness [4,5] by measuring the overlap between posteriors of the model parameter conditioned on the two partitioned datasets (as illustrated in Fig. 1). The model selection principle is also termed "approximation set coding" because the same tool used to bound the error probability in communication theory can be used to quantify the trade-off between expressiveness and robustness. The posterior agreement has been used for a variety of applications, for example, selecting the number of clusters in K-means clustering [8], selecting the rank for a truncated singular value decomposition [10], and determining the optimal early stopping time in the algorithmic regularization framework [2,3,11].

2.1   General Model Selection Framework Using Posterior Agreement

Specifically, the algorithm for model selection randomly partitions a given data set $\mathcal{D}$ into two subsets $\mathcal{D}_1$ and $\mathcal{D}_2$. Let $\alpha \in \mathbb{R}^M$ denote a parameter vector in the model, it would be the hidden function values in a Gaussian process. Assuming that we have a likelihood $p_\theta(\mathcal{D} \mid \alpha)$ and a prior $p_\theta(\alpha)$, the principle of posterior agreement optimizes the hyperparameters by

$$\theta^\star \in \arg\max_\theta \eta_\theta \quad \text{where} \quad \eta_\theta := \int_{\mathbb{R}^M} p_\theta(\alpha \mid \mathcal{D}_1) \, p_\theta(\alpha \mid \mathcal{D}_2) \, p_\theta(\alpha) \, \mathrm{d}^M \alpha. \quad (1)$$

The term η_θ is called *posterior agreement* [2] since it measures how much the posteriors $p_\theta(\alpha \mid \mathcal{D}_1)$ and $p_\theta(\alpha \mid \mathcal{D}_2)$ overlap. The prior $p_\theta(\alpha)$ gives more weight to the agreement corresponding to parameters that are a priori more plausible. An example is illustrated by Fig. 1. One can consider J partitions of the data into subsets $\mathcal{D}_i$, averaging their η_θ to improve the estimate for the error bound. In this paper we consider two variants of posterior agreement. The first one is the Natural PA which infers the posterior by Bayes's rule using the naturally given prior (i.e. GP). The second one chooses the posterior that has maximum entropy [13,14], thus is abbreviated as max ent PA. Specifically, using the negative log-likelihood $-\log p_\theta(\mathcal{D} \mid \alpha)$ as the cost function, and let β be the inverse temperature of the Gibbs distribution, the maximum entropy posterior is,

$$p_\theta(\alpha \mid \mathcal{D}) \propto \exp[-\beta(-\log p_\theta(\mathcal{D} \mid \alpha))] = p_\theta(\mathcal{D} \mid \alpha)^\beta,$$

where β controls the width of the distribution. The maximum entropy principle introduces the variable β that determines with how much precision we can distinguish parameters α with statistical significance. The precision β is to be optimized alongside the hyperparameters θ. Since β controls the noise level alongside parameters of the likelihood σ_n, we fix $\beta = 1$, thereby assigning σ_n the (inverse) role of β.

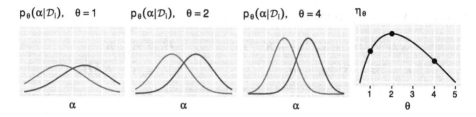

Fig. 1. Posteriors $p_\theta\left(\alpha \mid \mathcal{D}_1\right)$ and $p_\theta\left(\alpha \mid \mathcal{D}_2\right)$ over the parameters α for various hyperparameters θ. Our method basically maximizes the posterior agreement η_θ of (1), so that in this example it would select a model with $\theta = 2$.

2.2   Application to Gaussian Process Regression

Given N inputs arranged as columns of a matrix $\boldsymbol{X} \in \mathbb{R}^{D \times N}$, a Gaussian process defines a joint distribution over the corresponding N function values arranged as a vector $\boldsymbol{f} \in \mathbb{R}^N$. The distribution over $\boldsymbol{f}$ is an N-dimensional Gaussian $\boldsymbol{f} \mid \boldsymbol{X} \sim \mathcal{N}\left(m\left(\boldsymbol{X}\right), k\left(\boldsymbol{X}, \boldsymbol{X}\right)\right)$, where the mean function $m\left(\cdot\right)$ and the kernel $k\left(\cdot, \cdot\right)$ characterize the Gaussian process. In Gaussian process regression, the outputs $\boldsymbol{y} \in \mathbb{R}^N$ are modeled by the latent $\boldsymbol{f}$ affected by noise: the likelihood is $\boldsymbol{y} \mid \boldsymbol{f} \sim \mathcal{N}\left(\boldsymbol{f}, \sigma_n^2 \boldsymbol{I}\right)$ for the noise level σ_n.

To apply the posterior agreement principle, the parameters $\boldsymbol{\alpha}$ are given by random subvectors of $\boldsymbol{f}$ with $M \leq N$ entries. The hyperparameters $\boldsymbol{\theta}$ are those of the mean function and the kernel as well as σ_n. The resulting η_θ for Natural and Max ent PAs can be calculated analytically. The time complexity to all the criteria is $\Theta\left(N^3\right)$, asymptotically on a par with the objectives of maximum evidence and leave-one-out cross-validation.

For an M-dimensional posterior agreement, let $\widetilde{\boldsymbol{X}} \in \mathbb{R}^{D \times M}$ be made of M distinct columns of $\boldsymbol{X}$, with the corresponding latent function values being $\widetilde{\boldsymbol{f}} \in \mathbb{R}^M$. The data is randomly partitioned into two subsets denoted by $\left(\boldsymbol{X}_1, \boldsymbol{y}_1\right)$ and $\left(\boldsymbol{X}_2, \boldsymbol{y}_2\right)$. For notational convenience we further define

$$\widetilde{\boldsymbol{m}} = m\left(\widetilde{\boldsymbol{X}}\right), \qquad\qquad \widetilde{\boldsymbol{K}} = k\left(\widetilde{\boldsymbol{X}}, \widetilde{\boldsymbol{X}}\right),$$
$$\boldsymbol{m}_i = m\left(\boldsymbol{X}_i\right), \qquad\qquad \boldsymbol{K}_i = k\left(\boldsymbol{X}_i, \boldsymbol{X}_i\right) + \sigma_n^2 \boldsymbol{I},$$
$$\widetilde{\boldsymbol{K}}_i = k\left(\boldsymbol{X}_i, \widetilde{\boldsymbol{X}}\right),$$

for $i = 1, 2$. The predictive distribution is given by

$$\begin{bmatrix} \widetilde{\boldsymbol{f}} \\ \boldsymbol{y}_i \end{bmatrix} \sim \mathcal{N}\left(\begin{bmatrix} \widetilde{\boldsymbol{m}} \\ \boldsymbol{m}_i \end{bmatrix}, \begin{bmatrix} \widetilde{\boldsymbol{K}} & \widetilde{\boldsymbol{K}}_i^\mathsf{T} \\ \widetilde{\boldsymbol{K}}_i & \boldsymbol{K}_i \end{bmatrix} \right). \tag{2}$$

For this Gaussian distribution to be non-degenerate, $\widetilde{\boldsymbol{K}}$ needs to be symmetric positive-definite. Hence, we constrain the choice of $\widetilde{\boldsymbol{X}}$ such that $\widetilde{\boldsymbol{K}}$ is invertible. The derivations for the variants of the posterior agreement η_θ will need some propositions about Gaussian distributions, which are deferred to Appendix A.

Natural posterior agreement. To derive the formula, let

$$
\begin{aligned}
s &= V_1^{-1} s_1 + V_2^{-1} s_2 + \widetilde{K}^{-1} \widetilde{m}, \qquad & B_i &= K_i^{-1} \widetilde{K}_i, \\
s_i &= \widetilde{m} + B_i^{\mathsf{T}} (y_i - m_i), \qquad & V_i &= \widetilde{K} - \widetilde{K}_i^{\mathsf{T}} B_i, \\
P &= V_1^{-1} + V_2^{-1} + \widetilde{K}^{-1}.
\end{aligned}
$$

Applying Proposition 1 to Eq. (2), the posterior evaluated at $\boldsymbol{X}$ is

$$
\widetilde{f} \mid X_i, y_i, \overline{X} \sim \mathcal{N}(s_i, V_i).
$$

Since $\widetilde{f} \sim \mathcal{N}\left(\widetilde{m}, \widetilde{K}\right)$, and according to (1), the objective is thus

$$
\eta_\theta^{\text{natural}} = \int_{\mathbb{R}^M} \mathcal{N}\left(\widetilde{f} \mid s_1, V_1\right) \mathcal{N}\left(\widetilde{f} \mid s_2, V_2\right) \mathcal{N}\left(\widetilde{f} \mid \widetilde{m}, \widetilde{K}\right) \mathrm{d}^M \widetilde{f}.
$$

Using Proposition 3, it amounts to

$$
\eta_\theta^{\text{natural}} = \frac{\mathcal{N}(s_1 \mid 0, V_1) \mathcal{N}(s_2 \mid 0, V_2)}{|P| \mathcal{N}(s \mid 0, P)} \mathcal{N}\left(\widetilde{m} \mid 0, \widetilde{K}\right). \tag{3}
$$

Maximum entropy posterior agreement

Let

$$
\begin{aligned}
r &= r_1 + r_2 + \widetilde{K}^{-1} \widetilde{m}, \qquad & \Lambda &= \Lambda_1 + \Lambda_2 + \widetilde{K}^{-1}, \\
r_i &= A_i \Sigma_i^{-1} \mu_i, \qquad & \Lambda_i &= A_i \Sigma_i^{-1} A_i^{\mathsf{T}}, \\
\mu_i &= y_i - m_i + A_i^{\mathsf{T}} \widetilde{m}, \qquad & \Sigma_i &= K_i - \widetilde{K}_i A_i, \\
A_i &= \widetilde{K}^{-1} \widetilde{K}_i^{\mathsf{T}}.
\end{aligned}
$$

Again applying Proposition 1 to Eq. (2),

$$
y_i \mid \overline{X}, \widetilde{f}, X_i \sim \mathcal{N}\left(m_i + A_i^{\mathsf{T}}\left(\widetilde{f} - \widetilde{m}\right), \Sigma_i\right).
$$

The corresponding density can be rewritten as

$$
p\left(y_i \mid \overline{X}, \widetilde{f}, X_i\right) = \mathcal{N}\left(A_i^{\mathsf{T}} \widetilde{f} \mid \mu_i, \Sigma_i\right).
$$

We now to derive a maximum entropy density over $\widetilde{f}$ which yields a new posterior distribution

$$
\frac{\mathcal{N}\left(A_i^{\mathsf{T}} \widetilde{f} \mid \mu_i, \Sigma_i\right)^\beta}{\int_{\mathbb{R}^M} \mathcal{N}\left(A_i^{\mathsf{T}} \widetilde{f} \mid \mu_i, \Sigma_i\right)^\beta \mathrm{d}^M \widetilde{f}} = \mathcal{N}\left(\widetilde{f} \mid \Lambda_i^{-1} r_i, \Lambda_i^{-1}\right),
$$

where we use Proposition 6 to normalize the distribution. We further assume that $\boldsymbol{A}_i$ has full row rank and we set $\beta = 1$. Substituting the maximum entropy density into Eq. (1) yields

$$\eta_\theta^{\text{max ent}} = \int_{\mathbb{R}^M} \mathcal{N}\left(\widetilde{\boldsymbol{f}} \mid \boldsymbol{\Lambda}_1^{-1}\boldsymbol{r}_1, \boldsymbol{\Lambda}_1^{-1}\right)\mathcal{N}\left(\widetilde{\boldsymbol{f}} \mid \boldsymbol{\Lambda}_2^{-1}\boldsymbol{r}_2, \boldsymbol{\Lambda}_2^{-1}\right)\mathcal{N}\left(\widetilde{\boldsymbol{f}} \mid \widetilde{\boldsymbol{m}}, \widetilde{\boldsymbol{K}}\right) \mathrm{d}^M\widetilde{\boldsymbol{f}},$$

which by Proposition 3 is

$$\eta_\theta^{\text{max ent}} = \frac{\mathcal{N}\left(\boldsymbol{\Lambda}_1^{-1}\boldsymbol{r}_1 \mid \boldsymbol{0}, \boldsymbol{\Lambda}_1^{-1}\right)\mathcal{N}\left(\boldsymbol{\Lambda}_2^{-1}\boldsymbol{r}_2 \mid \boldsymbol{0}, \boldsymbol{\Lambda}_2^{-1}\right)}{|\boldsymbol{\Lambda}|\mathcal{N}\left(\boldsymbol{r} \mid \boldsymbol{0}, \boldsymbol{\Lambda}\right)}\mathcal{N}\left(\widetilde{\boldsymbol{m}} \mid \boldsymbol{0}, \widetilde{\boldsymbol{K}}\right). \quad (4)$$

Note that even though e.g. the Natural PA in (3) is in closed form, it is like all objectives (Maximum evidence or max ent PA) generally non-convex such that there is no global optimization guarantee using state-of-the-art optimization solvers.

3   Experimental Results

In all our experiments, we use $J = 256$ data partitions with dimensionality $M = 2$ for the objective in Eq. (1). Any Gaussian process uses the zero mean function for simplicity. The error measure is the mean standardized log loss according to [17], which considers both the predictive mean and covariance. To numerically optimize objective functions, the algorithm of limited-memory BFGS [16] is applied.

3.1   Experiments for Hyperparameter Optimization on Synthetic Data

We start by comparing the model selection criteria on hyperparameter optimization for a fixed kernel structure. From a one-dimensional Gaussian process, we randomly draw 128 data sets, each with $N = 64$ training and 2048 test points. Every criterion is then applied to the training set to optimize the hyperparameters of a Gaussian process with the same kernel structure. Figure 2 shows the test errors for the popular squared exponential kernel structure with various noise levels σ_n (definition in Table 1). Maximum evidence generally has the best test

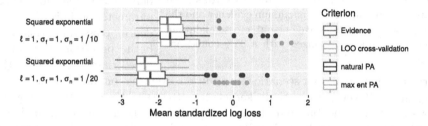

Fig. 2. Test errors for hyperparameter optimization.

312   N.S. Gorbach et al.

error, which is to be expected since the kernel structure is known. It is closely followed by leave-one-out cross-validation. Both variants of posterior agreement have a slightly worse median and a wider spread. Given the extended and generalized framework of *posterior agreement* compared to e.g. cross-validation or maximum evidence, which is indicated e.g. by allowing to determine the optimal early stopping time in the algorithmic regularization framework [3,11], it is a positive sign that it is able to compete at times with the classic criteria for the simpler task of finding the correct hyper-parameters for a fixed kernel structure. In the following we will therefore investigate the performance of *posterior agreement* for the more difficult tasks of kernel ranking.

3.2 Experiment for Kernel Ranking on Synthetic Data

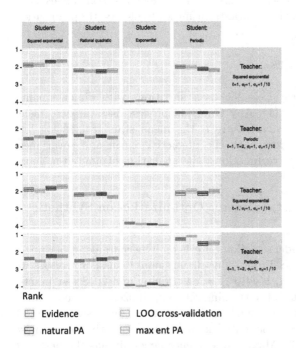

Fig. 3. Ranking of kernels for synthetic data with rank 1 being the best. The top two rows estimate hyperparameters by maximum evidence and the bottom two rows by leave-one-out cross-validation. The mean rank is visualized with a 95% confidence interval.

The model selection criteria rank kernels consistently for synthetic data as shown in Fig. 3. Hyperparameters in the top two rows were estimated by maximum evidence whereas for the bottom two rows they were estimated by leave-one-out cross-validation. The kernel to generate the data is depicted on the right (teacher) and we fitted the squared exponential, the rational quadratic, the exponential and the periodic kernels to the data (students). In most cases the criteria selected the correct kernel that was used to generate the data. The mean rank is visualized with a 95% confidence interval. Independent of the choice for hyperparameter optimization, evidence, cross-validation and both posterior agreement based methods select the

correct kernels in all four scenarios. In addition, even the confidence intervals are very similar. Overall, the periodic kernel seems to be slightly easier to learn, while the squared exponential and the rational quadratic kernel are often assigned equal ranks by all methods. Finally, all methods clearly separate the exponential kernel as a student from both the periodic and the squared exponential as teachers. Thus for kernel selection the posterior agreement based methods seem to be consistent and equally good as both evidence and cross-validation for kernel selection. It is a sign of robustness of the underlying theoretic framework that both versions of *posterior agreement* consistently vote for the same kernel.

3.3 Experiments for Kernel Ranking on Real-World Data

Next, we compare the criteria on kernel structure selection on two public datasets for different applications.

Berkeley Earth. As a first real-world data set, we use Earth's land temperature averaged per day of the year from 1880 until 2014[1]. It has 365 data points, which we randomly partition 256 times into $N = 64$ training and 301 test points. Given a training set, the hyperparameters are optimized by leave-one-out cross-validation for each kernel structure of Table 1. The resulting Gaussian process models are then ranked by the various criteria objectives. An additional ranking according to the test error serves as a guide for the assessment.

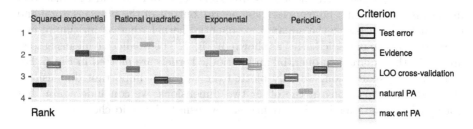

Fig. 4. Kernel structure selection for Berkeley Earth's land temperature. The mean rank is visualized with a 95% confidence interval, rank 1 is the best.

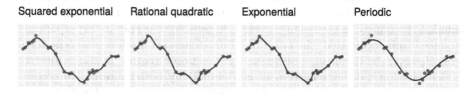

Fig. 5. Predictive means (lines) for a real-world data example points from the Berkeley Earth's land temperature data.

Figure 4 shows the rankings averaged over the data partitions. According to the average test error, the exponential kernel structure seems the most suitable, followed by the rational quadratic kernel structure. Maximum evidence would

---

[1] http://berkeleyearth.org/data/.

select an exponential, leave-one-out cross-validation a rational quadratic, and both variants of posterior agreement a squared exponential kernel structure. It is interesting to see this clear disagreement between the criteria. An example for the learned Gaussian processes is visualized in Fig. 5. The test set of this example is representative in the sense that the rankings according to the criteria and the test error are the same as on average. The exponential kernel fits a lot to the data, similar to a linear interpolation, which raises doubts about maximum evidence. Despite its unfavorable test error, the squared exponential kernel appears to be a valid choice based on this manual assessment. We conclude visually that posterior agreement selects a good trade-off between overfitting (exponential) and underfitting (periodic). While such a manual inspection is possible for the *Berkeley Earth* dataset, it is rather difficult in higher dimensions as detailed in the next section. This shows the need for additional criterions like *posterior agreement*, in order to allow data to vote on its own model.

Combined Cycle Power Plant. The dataset contains 9568 data points collected from a Combined Cycle Power Plant over 6 years (2006–2011), when the power plant was set to work with full load[2]. Features consist of hourly average ambient variables Temperature, Ambient Pressure, Relative Humidity and Exhaust Vacuum to predict the net hourly electrical energy output of the plant. Natural and max ent PA both prefer the squared exponential kernel whereas maximum evidence prefers the periodic kernel as shown in Fig. 7. The predictive means associated with the squared exponential and periodic kernels are plotted in Fig. 6. For a simplified visualization, we only plotted the two most important dimensions. Given smaller variations in the other two dimensions, we conclude again that both choices, from maximum evidence or PA seem to be valid choices.

4   Discussion and Conclusion

In this work we developed a framework to rank kernels for Gaussian process regression and compared it to state-of-the-art methods such as maximum evidence and leave-one-out cross-validation. In the most simplistic case, i.e. if the function structure of a Gaussian process is known, so that only its hyperparameters need to be optimized, the criterion of maximum evidence seems to perform best. However, in the usual case where the function structure is also subject to model selection, posterior agreement is a potentially better alternative according to manual examinations. For the example of the *Berkeley Earth* dataset, where a visual inspection is feasible, we conclude that the investigated versions of posterior agreement consistently select a good trade-off between overfitting and underfitting. Unfortunately for higher dimensions without the possibility of visual inspections, we are unable to formally define what function structure should be recovered since this may possibly solve the model selection problem itself. The disagreement between current state-of-the-art methods (maximum evidence and cross-validation) shows the difficulty of model selection and the

---

[2] http://archive.ics.uci.edu/ml/datasets/Combined+Cycle+Power+Plant.

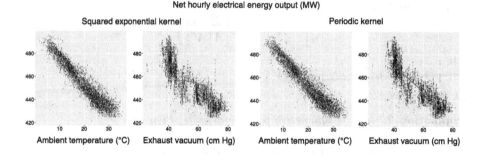

Fig. 6. Test data for the net hourly electrical energy output is plotted against the ambient temperature and the exhaust vacuum. The other two dimensions, namely the ambient pressure and relative humidity are less decisive and were omitted for a simplified visualization. Natural and max ent PAs both prefer the squared exponential kernel whose predictive means (red lines) is shown in the top two plots. Maximum evidence on the other hand selects the periodic kernel whose predictive means (red line) is shown in the bottom two plots. (Color figure online)

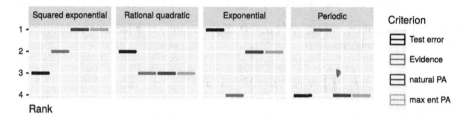

Fig. 7. Ranking of kernels for the power plant data set. As before, Natural and max ent PAs consistently rank the kernels and choose the squared exponential kernel as the optimum whereas maximum evidence prefers the periodic kernel. The test error prefers the exponential kernel.

need for additional measures like posterior agreement, which as a a novel concept already shows promising results in various domains (e.g. [8,10]). In future work, the outlined framework can easily be extended for general model selection problems, e.g., in GP classification or deep GP [9].

Acknowledgments. This research was partially supported by the Max Planck ETH Center for Learning Systems and the SystemsX.ch project SignalX.

Appendix

A   Propositions of Gaussian distribution

This is a collection of properties related to Gaussian distributions for the derivations in Sect. 2.2.

Proposition 1. *If*

$$\begin{bmatrix} t \\ u \end{bmatrix} \sim \mathcal{N} \left(\begin{bmatrix} \mu \\ r \end{bmatrix}, \begin{bmatrix} \Sigma & A \\ A^\mathsf{T} & V \end{bmatrix} \right)$$

then

$$t \mid u \sim \mathcal{N} \left(\mu + AV^{-1} (u - r), \Sigma - AV^{-1}A^\mathsf{T} \right)$$

[19, Theorem 3.3.4].

Proposition 2. *If Λ is symmetric positive-definite, then*

$$\int_{\mathbb{R}^D} \exp \left(x^\mathsf{T} \left(\mu - \frac{1}{2} \Lambda x \right) \right) \, \mathrm{d}^D x = \frac{1}{|\Lambda| \, \mathcal{N} (\mu \mid 0, \Lambda)}$$

[20, 14].

Proposition 3. *It holds that,*

$$\int_{\mathbb{R}^D} \prod_{k=1}^K \mathcal{N} (x \mid \mu_k, \Sigma_k) \, \mathrm{d}^D x = \frac{\prod_{k=1}^K \mathcal{N} (\mu_k \mid 0, \Sigma_k)}{|\Lambda| \, \mathcal{N} (r \mid 0, \Lambda)},$$

where $r = \sum_{k=1}^K \Sigma_k^{-1} \mu_k$ and $\Lambda = \sum_{k=1}^K \Sigma_k^{-1}$.

Proof. We shorten $\gamma = \prod_{k=1}^K \mathcal{N} (\mu_k \mid 0, \Sigma_k)$ to move this factor γ independent of x out of the integral as in

$$\int_{\mathbb{R}^D} \prod_{k=1}^K \mathcal{N} (x \mid \mu_k, \Sigma_k) \, \mathrm{d}^D x$$

$$= \gamma \int_{\mathbb{R}^D} \prod_{k=1}^K \exp \left(x^\mathsf{T} \Sigma_k^{-1} \left(\mu_k - \frac{1}{2} x \right) \right) \, \mathrm{d}^D x$$

$$= \gamma \int_{\mathbb{R}^D} \exp \left(\sum_{k=1}^K x^\mathsf{T} \Sigma_k^{-1} \left(\mu_k - \frac{1}{2} x \right) \right) \, \mathrm{d}^D x$$

$$= \gamma \int_{\mathbb{R}^D} \exp \left(x^\mathsf{T} \left(r - \frac{1}{2} \Lambda x \right) \right) \, \mathrm{d}^D x.$$

The remaining integral can be calculated by Proposition 2.

Proposition 4. *If Σ is symmetric positive-definite, then Σ is invertible and Σ^{-1} is symmetric positive-definite [12, 430].*

Proposition 5. *If Σ is symmetric positive-definite and A has full row rank, then $A\Sigma A^\mathsf{T}$ is symmetric positive-definite [12, Observation 7.1.8.(b)].*

Proposition 6. *For $A \in \mathbb{R}^{D \times N}$ of full row rank, the density*

$$p(x) = \frac{\mathcal{N} (A^\mathsf{T} x \mid \mu, \Sigma)}{\int_{\mathbb{R}^D} \mathcal{N} (A^\mathsf{T} x \mid \mu, \Sigma) \, \mathrm{d}^D x}$$

has the equivalent form as $p(x) = \mathcal{N} (x \mid \Lambda^{-1} r, \Lambda^{-1})$, where $r = A\Sigma^{-1}\mu$ and $\Lambda = A\Sigma^{-1}A^\mathsf{T}$.

Proof. First, we separate a factor independent of x in

$$\mathcal{N}\left(A^\mathsf{T}x \mid \mu, \Sigma\right) = \mathcal{N}\left(\mu \mid 0, \Sigma\right)\exp\left(x^\mathsf{T}\left(r - \frac{1}{2}\Lambda x\right)\right).$$

Therefore,

$$p\left(x\right) = \frac{\exp\left(x^\mathsf{T}\left(r - \frac{1}{2}\Lambda x\right)\right)}{\int_{\mathbb{R}^D}\exp\left(x^\mathsf{T}\left(r - \frac{1}{2}\Lambda x\right)\right)\,\mathrm{d}^D x}.$$

We now calculate the integral. From Proposition 4 and Proposition 5, one can see that Λ is symmetric positive-definite, so that Proposition 2 can be applied to find

$$\int_{\mathbb{R}^D}\exp\left(x^\mathsf{T}\left(r - \frac{1}{2}\Lambda x\right)\right)\,\mathrm{d}^D x = \frac{1}{|\Lambda|\mathcal{N}\left(r \mid 0, \Lambda\right)}.$$

Finally, one gets

$$p\left(x\right) = |\Lambda|\mathcal{N}\left(r \mid 0, \Lambda\right)\exp\left(x^\mathsf{T}\left(r - \frac{1}{2}\Lambda x\right)\right)$$

$$= \mathcal{N}\left(x \mid \Lambda^{-1}r, \Lambda^{-1}\right).$$

References

1. Bachoc, F.: Cross validation and maximum likelihood estimations of hyper-parameters of Gaussian processes with model misspecification. Comput. Stat. Data Anal. **66**, 55–69 (2013)
2. Bian, A.A., Gronskiy, A., Buhmann, J.M.: Information-theoretic analysis of max-cut algorithms. Technical report, Department of Computer Science, ETH Zurich (2016). http://people.inf.ethz.ch/ybian/docs/pa.pdf
3. Bian, Y., Gronskiy, A., Buhmann, J.M.: Greedy maxcut algorithms and their information content. In: IEEE Information Theory Workshop (ITW), pp. 1–5 (2015)
4. Buhmann, J.M.: Information theoretic model validation for clustering. In: IEEE International Symposium on Information Theory (ISIT), pp. 1398–1402 (2010)
5. Buhmann, J.M.: SIMBAD: emergence of pattern similarity. In: Pelillo, M. (ed.) Similarity-Based Pattern Analysis and Recognition. ACVPR, pp. 45–64. Springer, London (2013). doi:10.1007/978-1-4471-5628-4_3
6. Cawley, G.C., Talbot, N.L.C.: On over-fitting in model selection and subsequent selection bias in performance evaluation. J. Mach. Learn. Res. **11**, 2079–2107 (2010)
7. Chapelle, O.: Some thoughts about Gaussian processes (2005). http://is.tuebingen.mpg.de/fileadmin/user_upload/files/publications/gp_[0].pdf
8. Chehreghani, M.H., Busetto, A.G., Buhmann, J.M.: Information theoretic model validation for spectral clustering. In: International Conference on Artificial Intelligence and Statistics (AISTATS), pp. 495–503 (2012)
9. Damianou, A.C., Lawrence, N.D.: Deep Gaussian processes. In: International Conference on Artificial Intelligence and Statistics (AISTATS), pp. 207–215 (2013)
10. Frank, M., Buhmann, J.M.: Selecting the rank of truncated SVD by maximum approximation capacity. In: IEEE International Symposium on Information Theory (ISIT), pp. 1036–1040 (2011)

11. Gronskiy, A., Buhmann, J.: How informative are minimum spanning tree algorithms? In: IEEE International Symposium on Information Theory (ISIT), pp. 2277–2281 (2014)
12. Horn, R.A., Johnson, C.R.: Matrix Analysis, 2nd edn. Cambridge University Press, Cambridge (2012)
13. Jaynes, E.T.: Information theory and statistical mechanics. Phys. Rev. **106**, 620–630 (1957)
14. Jaynes, E.T.: Information theory and statistical mechanics. ii. Phys. Rev. **108**, 171–190 (1957)
15. Lloyd, J.R., Duvenaud, D., Grosse, R., Tenenbaum, J.B., Ghahramani, Z.: Automatic construction and natural-language description of nonparametric regression models. In: AAAI Conference on Artificial Intelligence (AAAI) pp. 1242–1250 (2014)
16. Nocedal, J.: Updating quasi-Newton matrices with limited storage. Math. Comput. **35**, 773–782 (1980)
17. Rasmussen, C.E., Williams, C.K.I.: Gaussian Processes for Machine Learning. The MIT Press, Cambridge (2006)
18. Seeger, M.W.: PAC-Bayesian generalisation error bounds for Gaussian process classification. J. Mach. Learn. Res. **3**, 233–269 (2002)
19. Tong, Y.L.: The Multivariate Normal Distribution. Springer Science & Business Media, New York (2012)
20. Zee, A.: Quantum Field Theory in a Nutshell. Princeton University Press, Princeton (2003)
21. Zhu, X., Welling, M., Jin, F., Lowengrub, J.S.: Predicting simulation parameters of biological systems using a Gaussian process model. Stat. Anal. Data Min. **5**, 509–522 (2012)

Motion and Segmentation

Scalable Full Flow with Learned Binary Descriptors

Gottfried Munda[1]([envelope]), Alexander Shekhovtsov[2], Patrick Knöbelreiter[1], and Thomas Pock[1,3]

[1] Institute of Computer Graphics and Vision, Graz University of Technology, Graz, Austria
gottfried.munda@icg.tugraz.at
[2] Czech Technical University in Prague, Prague 6, Czech Republic
[3] Center for Vision, Automation and Control, Austrian Institute of Technology, Vienna, Austria

Abstract. We propose a method for large displacement optical flow in which local matching costs are learned by a convolutional neural network (CNN) and a smoothness prior is imposed by a conditional random field (CRF). We tackle the computation- and memory-intensive operations on the 4D cost volume by a *min-projection* which reduces memory complexity from quadratic to linear and *binary descriptors* for efficient matching. This enables evaluation of the cost on the fly and allows to perform learning and CRF inference on high resolution images without ever storing the 4D cost volume. To address the problem of learning binary descriptors we propose a new hybrid learning scheme. In contrast to current state of the art approaches for learning binary CNNs we can compute the exact non-zero gradient within our model. We compare several methods for training binary descriptors and show results on public available benchmarks.

1 Introduction

Optical flow can be seen as an instance of the dense image matching problem, where the goal is to find for each pixel its corresponding match in the other image. One fundamental question in the dense matching problem is how to choose good *descriptors* or *features*. Data mining with convolutional neural networks (CNNs) has recently shown excellent results for learning task-specific image features, outperforming previous methods based on hand-crafted descriptors. One of the major difficulties in learning features for optical flow is the high dimensionality of the cost function: Whereas in stereo, the full cost function can be represented as a 3D volume, the matching cost in optical flow is a 4D volume. Especially at high image resolutions, operations on the flow matching cost are expensive both in terms of memory requirements and computation time.

Our method avoids explicit storage of the full cost volume, both in the learning phase and during inference. This is achieved by a *splitting* (or *min-projection*) of the 4D cost into two quasi-independent 3D volumes, corresponding to the u

© Springer International Publishing AG 2017
V. Roth and T. Vetter (Eds.): GCPR 2017, LNCS 10496, pp. 321–332, 2017.
DOI: 10.1007/978-3-319-66709-6_26

and v component of the flow. We then formulate CNN learning and CRF inference in this reduced setting. This achieves a space complexity linear in the size of the search range, similar to recent stereo methods, which is a significant reduction compared to the quadratic complexity of the full 4D cost function.

Nevertheless, we still have to compute all entries of the 4D cost. This computational bottleneck can be optimized by using binary descriptors, which give a theoretical speed-up factor of 32. In practice, even larger speed-up factors are attained, since binary descriptors need less memory bandwidth and also yield a better cache efficiency. Consequently, we aim to incorporate a binarization step into the learning. We propose a novel hybrid learning scheme, where we circumvent the problem of hard nonlinearities having zero gradient. We show that our hybrid learning performs almost as well as a network without hard nonlinearities, and much better than the previous state of the art in learning binary CNNs.

2   Related Work

In the past hand-crafted descriptors like SIFT, NCC, FAST etc. have been used extensively with very good results, but recently CNN-based approaches [13,23] marked a paradigm shift in the field of image matching. To date all top performing methods in the major stereo benchmarks rely heavily on features learned by CNNs. For optical flow, many recent works still use engineered features [1,5], presumably due to the difficulties the high dimensional optical flow cost function poses for learning. Only very recently we see a shift towards CNNs for learning descriptors [9,10,22]. Our work is most related to [22], who construct the full 4D cost volume and run an adapted version of SGM on it. They perform learning and cost volume optimization on $\frac{1}{3}$ of the original resolution and compress the cost function in order to cope with the high memory consumption. Our method is memory-efficient thanks to the dimensionality-reduction by the min-projection, and we outperform the reported runtime of [22] by a factor of 10.

Full flow with CRF [5] is a related inference method using TRW-S [12] with efficient distance transform [8]. Its iterations have quadratic time and space complexity. In practice, this takes $20\,\mathrm{GB}^1$ of memory, and 10–30 s per iteration with a parallel CPU implementation. We use the decomposed model [19] with a better memory complexity and a faster parallel inference scheme based on [18].

Hand-crafted Binary Descriptors like Census have been shown to work well in a number of applications, including image matching for stereo and flow [4,14,15,20]. However, direct learning of binary descriptors is a difficult task, since the hard thresholding function, $\mathrm{sign}(x)$, has gradient zero almost everywhere. In the context of Binary CNNs there are several approaches to train networks with binary activations [2] and even binary weights [7,16]. This is known to give a considerable compression and speed-up at the price of a tolerable loss of accuracy. To circumvent the problem of $\mathrm{sign}(x)$ having zero gradient a.e., surrogate gradients are used. The simplest method, called *straight-through*

---

[1] Estimated for the cost volume size $341{\times}145{\times}160{\times}160$ based on numbers in [5] corresponding to $\frac{1}{3}$ resolution of Sintel images.

estimator [2] is to assume the derivative of $\text{sign}(x)$ is 1, *i.e.*,, simply omit the sign function in the gradient computation. This approach can be considered as the state of the art, as it gives best results in [2,7,16]. We show that in the context of learning binary descriptors for the purpose of matching, alternative strategies are possible which give better results.

3   Method

We define two models for optical flow: a local model, known as Winner-Takes-All (WTA) and a joint model, which uses CRF inference. Both models use CNN descriptors, learned in Sect. 3.1. The joint model has only few extra parameters that are fit separately and the inference is solved with a parallel method, see Sect. 3.2. For CNN learning, we optimize the performance of the local model. While learning by optimizing the performance of the joint model is possible [11], the resulting procedures are significantly more difficult.

We assume color images $I^1, I^2 \ : \ \Omega \to \mathbb{R}^3$, where $\Omega = \{1, \ldots H\} \times \{1, \ldots W\}$ is a set of pixels. Let $\mathcal{W} = \mathcal{S} \times \mathcal{S}$ be a window of discrete 2D displacements, with $\mathcal{S} = \{-D/2, -D/2+1, \ldots, D/2-1\}$ given by the search window size D, an even number. The flow $x \ : \ \Omega \to \mathcal{W}$ associates a displacement to each pixel $i \in \Omega$ so that the displaced position of i is given by $i + x_i \in \mathbb{Z}^2$. For convenience, we denote by $x = (u, v)$, where u and v are mappings $\Omega \to \mathcal{S}$, the components of the flow in horizontal and vertical directions, respectively. The per-pixel *descriptors* $\phi(I; \theta) \ : \ \Omega \to \mathbb{R}^m$ are computed by a CNN with parameters θ. Let ϕ^1, ϕ^2 be descriptors of images I^1, I^2, respectively. The *local matching cost* for a pixel $i \in \Omega$ and displacement $x_i \in \mathcal{W}$ is given by

$$
c_i(x_i) = \begin{cases} d(\phi_i^1, \phi_{i+x_i}^2) & \text{if } i + x_i \in \Omega, \\ c_{\text{outside}} & \text{otherwise,} \end{cases} \tag{1}
$$

where $d \ : \ \mathbb{R}^m \times \mathbb{R}^m \to \mathbb{R}$ is a distance function in $\mathbb{R}^m$. "Distance" is used in a loose sense here, we will consider the negative[2] scalar product $d(\phi^1, \phi^2) = -\langle \phi^1, \phi^2 \rangle$. We call

$$
\hat{x}_i \in \arg \min_{x_i \in \mathcal{W}} c_i(x_i) \tag{2}
$$

the *local optical flow model*, which finds independently for each pixel i a displacement x_i that optimizes the local matching cost. The *joint optical flow model* finds the full flow field x optimizing the coupled CRF energy cost:

$$
\hat{x} \in \arg \min_{u,v: \, \Omega \to \mathcal{S}} \left[\sum_{i \in \Omega} c_i(u_i, v_i) + \sum_{i \sim j} w_{ij}(\rho(u_i - u_j) + \rho(v_i - v_j)) \right], \tag{3}
$$

where $i \sim j$ denotes a 4-connected pixel neighborhood, w_{ij} are contrast-sensitive weights, given by $w_{ij} = \exp(-\frac{\alpha}{3} \sum_{c \in \{R,G,B\}} |I_{i,c}^1 - I_{j,c}^1|)$ and $\rho \colon \mathbb{R} \to \mathbb{R}$ is a robust penalty function shown in Fig. 2(a).

---

[2] Since we want to pose matching as a minimization problem.

3.1   Learning Descriptors

A common difficulty of models (2) and (3) is that they need to process the 4D cost (1), which involves computing distances in $\mathbb{R}^m$ per entry. Storing such cost volume takes $\mathcal{O}(|\Omega|D^2)$ space and evaluating it $\mathcal{O}(|\Omega|D^2m)$ time. We can reduce space complexity to $\mathcal{O}(|\Omega|D)$ by avoiding explicit storage of the 4D cost function. This facilitates memory-efficient end-to-end training on high resolution images, without a patch sampling step [13,22]. Towards this end we write the local optical flow model (2) in the following way

$$\hat{u}_i \in \arg\min_{u_i} c_i^{\mathrm{U}}(u_i), \quad \text{where} \quad c_i^{\mathrm{U}}(u_i) = \min_{v_i} c_i(u_i, v_i); \tag{4a}$$

$$\hat{v}_i \in \arg\min_{v_i} c_i^{\mathrm{V}}(v_i), \quad \text{where} \quad c_i^{\mathrm{V}}(v_i) = \min_{u_i} c_i(u_i, v_i). \tag{4b}$$

The inner step in (4a) and (4b), called *min-projection*, minimizes out one component of the flow vector. This can be interpreted as a decoupling of the full 4D flow problem into two simpler quasi-independent 3D problems on the reduced cost volumes $c^{\mathrm{U}}, c^{\mathrm{V}}$. Assuming the minimizer of (2) is unique, (4a) and (4b) find the same solution as the original problem (2). Using this representation, CNN learning can be implemented within existing frameworks. We point out that this approach has the same space complexity as recent methods for learning stereo matching, since we only need to store the 3D cost volumes c^{U} and c^{V}. As an illustrative example consider an image with size 1024×436 and a search range of 256. In this setting the full 4D cost function takes roughly 108 GB whereas our splitting consumes only 0.8 GB.

Network. Figure 1 shows the network diagram of the local flow model Eq. (2). The structure is similar to the recent methods proposed for learning stereo matching [6,11,13,23]. It is a siamese network consisting of two convolutional branches with shared parameters, followed by a correlation layer. The filter size of the convolutions is 3×3 for the first layer and 2×2 for all other layers. The tanh nonlinearity keeps feature values in a defined range, which works well with the scalar product as distance function. We do not use striding or pooling. The last convolutional layer uses 64 filter channels, all other layers have 96 channels. This fixes the dimensionality of the distance space to $m = 64$.

Loss. Given the groundtruth flow field (u^*, v^*), we pose the learning objective as follows: we define a probabilistic softmax model of the local prediction u_i (resp. v_i) as $p(u_i) \propto \exp(-c_i^{\mathrm{U}}(u_i))$, then we consider a naive model $p(u,v) = \prod_i p(u_i)p(v_i)$ and apply the maximum likelihood criterion. The negative log likelihood is given by

$$L(u, v) = -\sum_{i \in \Omega} \left[\log p(u_i^*) + \log p(v_i^*) \right]. \tag{5}$$

This is equivalent to cross-entropy loss with the target distribution concentrated at the single point (u_i^*, v_i^*) for each i. Variants of the cross-entropy loss, where the target distribution is spread around the ground truth point (u_i^*, v_i^*) are also used in the literature [13] and can be easily incorporated.

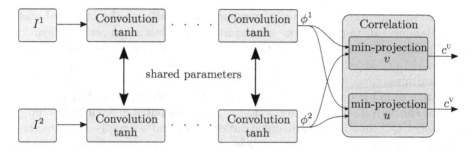

Fig. 1. Network architecture: a number of convolutional layers with shared parameters computes feature vectors ϕ^1, ϕ^2 for every pixel. These feature vectors are cross-fed into a correlation layer, that computes local matching costs in u and v direction by minimizing out the other direction. The result are two quasi-independent cost volumes for the u and v component of the flow.

Learning Quantized Descriptors. The computational bottleneck in scheme (4) is computing the min-projections, with time complexity $\mathcal{O}(|\Omega|D^2 m)$. This operation arises during the learning as well as in the CRF inference step, where it corresponds to the message exchange in the dual decomposition. It is therefore desirable to accelerate this step. We achieve a significant speed-up by quantizing the descriptors and evaluating the Hamming distance of binary descriptors.

Let us define the quantization: we call $\bar{\phi} = \mathrm{sign}(\phi)$ the *quantized descriptor field*. The distance between quantized descriptors is given by $d(\bar{\phi}^1, \bar{\phi}^2) = -\langle \bar{\phi}^1, \bar{\phi}^2 \rangle = 2\mathcal{H}(\bar{\phi}^1, \bar{\phi}^2) - m$, equivalent to the Hamming distance $\mathcal{H}(\cdot, \cdot)$ up to a scaling and an offset. Let the quantized cost function be denoted $\bar{c}_i(x_i)$, defined similar to (1). We can then compute quantized min-projections $\bar{c}^U, \bar{c}^V$.

However, learning model (2) with quantized descriptors is difficult due to the gradient of the sign function being zero almost everywhere. We introduce a new technique specific to the matching problem and compare it to the baseline method that uses the straight-through estimator of the gradient [2]. Consider the following variants of the model (4a)

$$\hat{u}_i \in \arg\min_{u_i} c_i(u_i, \hat{v}_i(u_i)), \quad \text{where} \quad \hat{v}_i(u_i) \in \arg\min_{v_i} \bar{c}_i(u_i, v_i); \qquad \text{(FQ)}$$

$$\hat{u}_i \in \arg\min_{u_i} \bar{c}_i(u_i, \hat{v}_i(u_i)), \quad \text{where} \quad \hat{v}_i(u_i) \in \arg\min_{v_i} \bar{c}_i(u_i, v_i). \qquad \text{(QQ)}$$

The respective variants of (4b) are symmetric. The second letter in the naming scheme indicates whether the inner problem, *i.e.*, the min-projection step, is performed on (Q)uantized or (F)ull cost, whereas the first letter refers to the outer problem on the smaller 3D cost volume. The initial model (4a) is thus also denoted as FF model. While models FF and QQ correspond, up to non-uniqueness of solutions, to the joint minimum in (u_i, v_i) of the cost c and $\bar{c}$ respectively, the model FQ is a mixed one. This hybrid model is interesting because minimization in v_i can be computed efficiently on the binarized cost with Hamming distance, and the minimization in u_i has a non-zero gradient in c^U. We thus consider the model FQ as an efficient variant of the local optical flow model (2). In addition, it is a good learning proxy for the model QQ: Let $\hat{u}_i = \arg\min_{u_i} c_i(u_i, \hat{v}_i(u_i))$ be a minimizer of the outer problem FQ. Then the derivative of FQ is defined by the indicator of the pair $(\hat{u}_i, \hat{v}_i(u_i))$. This is the same as the derivative of FF, except that $\hat{v}_i(u_i)$ is computed differently. Learning the model QQ involves a hard quantization step, and we apply the straight-through estimator to compute a gradient. Note that the exact gradient for the model FQ can be computed at approximately the same reduced computational cost as the straight-through gradient in the model QQ.

3.2   CRF

The baseline model, which we call *product* model, has $|\Omega|$ variables x_i with the state space $S \times S$. It has been observed in [8] that max-product message passing in the CRF (3) can be computed in time $\mathcal{O}(D^2)$ per variable for separable interactions using a fast distance transform. However, storing the messages for a 4-connected graph requires $\mathcal{O}(|\Omega|D^2)$ memory. Although such an approach was shown feasible even for large displacement optical flow [5], we argue that a more compact *decomposed* model [19] gives comparable results and is much faster in practice. The decomposed model is constructed by observing that the regularization in (3) is separable over u and v. Then the energy (3) can be represented as a CRF with $2|\Omega|$ variables u_i, v_i with the following pairwise terms: The in-plane term $w_{ij}\rho(u_i - u_j)$ and the cross-plane term $c(u_i, v_i)$, forming the graph shown in Fig. 2(b). In this formulation there are no unary terms, since costs c_i are interpreted as pairwise terms. The resulting linear programming (LP) dual is more economical, because it has only $\mathcal{O}(|\Omega|D)$ variables. The message passing for edges inside planes and across planes has complexity $\mathcal{O}(|\Omega|D)$ and $O(|\Omega|D^2)$, respectively.

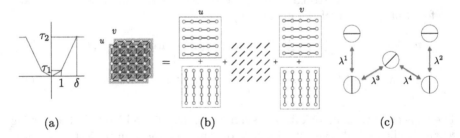

(a)   (b)   (c)

Fig. 2. Building blocks of the CRF. (a) Robust pairwise function ρ. (b) Decomposition of the pairwise CRF into 5 subproblems. (c) Lagrange multipliers in the dual corresponding to equality constraints between the subproblems. They act as offsets of unary costs between subproblems, increasing on one side of the arrow and decreasing on the other.

We apply the parallel inference method [18] to the dual of the decomposed model [19] (see Fig. 2(b)). Although different dual decompositions reach different objective values in a fixed number of iterations, it is known that all decompositions with trees covering the graph are equivalent in the optimal value [21]. The decomposition in Fig. 2(b) is into horizontal and vertical chains in each of the u- and v- planes plus a subproblem containing all cross-layer edges. We introduce Lagrange multipliers $\lambda = (\lambda^k \in \mathbb{R}^{\Omega \times S} \mid k = 1, 2, 3, 4)$ enforcing equality constraints between the subproblems as shown in Fig. 2(c). The Lagrange multipliers λ^k are identified with modular functions $\lambda^k \colon S^\Omega \to \mathbb{R} \colon u \mapsto \sum_i \lambda_i^k(u_i)$. Let us also introduce shorthands for the sum of pairwise terms over horizontal chains $f^h \colon S^\Omega \to \mathbb{R} \colon u \mapsto \sum_{ij \in \mathcal{E}^h} w_{ij} \rho(u_i - u_j)$, and a symmetric definition f^v for the sum over the vertical chains. The lower bound $\Psi(\lambda)$ corresponding to the decomposition in Fig. 2(c) is given by:

$$\Psi(\lambda) = \Psi^1(\lambda) + \Psi^2(\lambda) + \Psi^3(\lambda), \text{ where} \tag{6a}$$

$$\Psi^1(\lambda) = \min_u \left[(\lambda^1 + \lambda^3)(u) + f^h(u) \right] + \min_u \left[-\lambda^1(u) + f^v(u) \right]; \tag{6b}$$

$$\Psi^2(\lambda) = \min_v \left[(\lambda^2 + \lambda^4)(v) + f^h(v) \right] + \min_v \left[-\lambda^2(v) + f^v(v) \right]; \tag{6c}$$

$$\Psi^3(\lambda) = \sum_i \min_{u_i, v_i} \left[c_i(u_i, v_i) - \lambda_i^3(u_i) - \lambda_i^4(v_i) \right]. \tag{6d}$$

Our Lagrangian dual to (3) is to maximize $\Psi(\lambda)$ in λ, which enforces consistency between minimizers of the subproblems. The general theory [21] applies, in particular, when the minimizers of all subproblems are consistent they form a global minimizer. In (6b), there is a sum of horizontal and vertical chain subproblems in the u-plane. When λ^3 is fixed, $\Psi^1(\lambda)$ is the lower bound corresponding to the relaxation of the energy in u with the unary terms given by λ^3. It can be interpreted as a stereo-like problem with 1D labels u. Similarly, $\Psi^2(\lambda)$ is a lower bound for the v-plane with unary terms λ^4. Subproblem $\Psi^3(\lambda)$ is simple, it contains both variables u, v but the minimization decouples over individual pairs (u_i, v_i). It connects the two stereo-like problems through the 4D cost volume c.

Updating messages inside planes can be done at a different rate than across planes. The optimal rate for fast convergence depends on the time complexity of the message updates. [19] reported an optimal rate of updating in-plane messages 5 times as often using the TRW-S solver [12]. The decomposition (6a) facilitates this kind of strategy and allows to use the implementation [18] designed for stereo-like problems. We therefore use the dual solver [18], denoted Dual Minorize-Maximize (DMM) to perform in-plane updates. When applied to the problem of maximizing $\Psi^1(\lambda)$ in λ^1, it has the following properties: (a) the bound $\Psi^1(\lambda)$ does not decrease and (b) it computes a modular minorant s such that $s(u) \le \lambda^3(u) + f^h(u) + f^v(u)$ for all u and $\Psi^1(\lambda) = \sum_i \min_{u_i} s_i(u_i)$. The modular minorant s is an excess of costs, called *slacks*, which can be subtracted from λ^3 while keeping $\Psi^1(\lambda)$ non-negative. The associated update of the u-plane can be denoted as

---

Algorithm 1. Flow CRF Optimization

   Input: Cost volume c;
   Output: Dual point λ optimizing $\Psi(\lambda)$;
1   Initialize $\lambda := 0$;
2   **for** $t = 1, \ldots, \texttt{it\_outer}$ **do**
3   Perform the following updates:
4         $v \to u$: pass slacks to u-plane by (9), changes λ^3;
5   u-plane: DMM with $\texttt{it\_inner}$ iterations for u-plane (7a), changes λ^1, λ^3;
6         $u \to v$: pass slacks to v-plane by (8), changes λ^4;
7   v-plane: DMM with $\texttt{it\_inner}$ iterations for v-plane, changes λ^2, λ^4;

$$(\lambda^1, s) := \mathrm{DMM}(\lambda^1, \lambda^3, f^{\mathrm{h}}, f^{\mathrm{v}}), \tag{7a}$$
$$\lambda^3 := \lambda^3 - s. \tag{7b}$$

The slack s is then passed to the v plane by the following updates, *i.e.,*, message passing $u \to v$:

$$\lambda_i^4(v_i) := \lambda_i^4(v_i) + \min_{u_i} \left[c_i(u_i, v_i) - \lambda_i^3(u_i) \right]. \tag{8}$$

The minimization (8) has time complexity $\mathcal{O}(|\Omega| D^2)$, assuming the 4D costs c_i are available in memory. As discussed above, we can compute the costs c_i efficiently on the fly and avoid $\mathcal{O}(|\Omega| D^2)$ storage. The update $v \to u$ is symmetric to (7a):

$$\lambda_i^3(u_i) := \lambda_i^3(u_i) + \min_{v_i} \left[c_i(u_i, v_i) - \lambda_i^4(v_i) \right]. \tag{9}$$

The complete method is summarized in Algorithm 1. It starts from collecting the slacks in the u-plane. When initialized with $\lambda = 0$, the update (9) simplifies to $\lambda_i^3(u_i) = \min_{v_u} c_i(u_i, v_i)$, *i.e.,*, it is exactly matching to the min-projection c^{U} (4). The problem solved with DMM in Line 5 in the first iteration is a stereo-like problem with cost c^{U}. The dual solution redistributes the costs and determines which values of u are worse than others, and expresses this cost offset in λ^3 as specified in (7a). The optimization of the v-plane then continues with some information of good solutions for u propagated via the cost offsets using (8).

4   Evaluation

We compare different variants of our own model on the Sintel optical flow dataset [3]. In total the benchmark consists of 1064 training images and 564 test images. For CNN learning we use a subset of 20% of the training images, sampled evenly from all available scenes. For evaluation, we use a subset of 40% of the training images.

Comparison of Our Models. To investigate the performance of our model, we conduct the following experiments: First, we investigate the influence of the

Table 1. Comparison of our models on a representative validation set at scale $\frac{1}{2}$. We present the end-point-error (EPE) for non-occluded (noc) and all pixels on Sintel clean.

		Local flow model (WTA)		CRF	
Train	#Layers	As trained	QQ	F	Q
		noc (all)	noc (all)	noc (all)	noc (all)
FF	5	5.25 (10.38)	10.45 (15.67)	1.58 (4.48)	1.64 (4.87)
	7	4.72 (10.04)	9.43 (14.93)	1.53 (4.32)	1.61 (4.70)
	9	–[a]	–[a]	–[a]	–[a]
FQ	5	6.15 (11.36)	11.43 (16.78)	–[b]	1.63 (4.62)
	7	5.62 (10.98)	10.15 (15.70)	–[b]	1.65 (4.62)
	9	5.62 (11.13)	9.87 (15.52)	–[b]	1.64 (4.69)
QQ	5	same as QQ	9.63 (14.80)	–[b]	1.72 (4.91)
	7	same as QQ	9.75 (15.23)	–[b]	1.66 (4.78)
	9	same as QQ	9.72 (15.31)	–[b]	1.72 (4.85)

[a]Omitted due to very long training time.
[b]Not applicable.

size of the CNN, and second we investigate the effect of quantizing the learned features. Additionally, we evaluate both the WTA solution (2), and the CRF model (3). To assess the effect of quantization, we evaluate the local flow model (a) as it was trained, and (b) QQ, *i.e.*,, with quantized descriptors both in the min-projection step as well as in the outer problem on c^U, c^V respectively. In CRF inference the updates (8) and (9) amount to solving a min-projection step with additional cost offsets. F and Q indicate how this min-projection step is computed. CRF parameters are fixed at $\alpha = 8.5$, (3), $\tau_1 = 0.25$, $\tau_2 = 25$ (Fig. 2) for all experiments and we run 8 inner and 5 outer iterations. Table 1 summarizes the comparison of different variants of our model. We see that the WTA solution of model FQ performs similarly to FF, while being much faster to train and evaluate. In particular, model FQ performs better than QQ, which was trained with the straight through estimator of the gradient. If we switch to QQ for evaluation, we see a drop in performance for models FF and FQ. This is to be expected, because we now evaluate costs differently than during training. Interestingly, our joint model yields similar performance regardless whether we use F or Q for computing the costs.

Runtime. The main reason for quantizing the descriptors is speed. In CRF inference, we need to compute the min-projection on the 4D cost function twice per outer iteration, see Algorithm 1. We show an exact breakdown of the timings for $D = 128$ on full resolution images in Table 2, computed on a Intel i7 6700K and a Nvidia Titan X. The column WTA refers to computing the solution of the local model on the cost volumes c^U, c^V, see Eq. (4). Full model is the CRF inference, see Sect. 3.2. We see that we can reach a significant speed-up by using binary descriptors and Hamming distance for computing intensive calculations.

Table 2. Timings of the building blocks (seconds).

Method	Feature extraction	WTA	Full model
FF	0.04–0.08	4.25	24.8
FQ	0.04–0.08	1.82	-
QQ	0.04–0.08	0.07	3.2
[22] ($\frac{1}{3}$ res.)	0.02	0.06	3.4
QQ ($\frac{1}{3}$ res.)	0.004–0.008	0.007	0.32

Table 3. Comparison on the Sintel clean test set.

Method	noc	all
EpicFlow [17]	1.360	4.115
FullFlow [5]	1.296	3.601
FlowFields [1]	1.056	3.748
DCFlow [22]	1.103	3.537
Ours QQ	2.470	8.972

For comparison, we also report the runtime of [22], who, at the time of writing, report the fastest execution time on Sintel. We point out that our CRF inference on full resolution images takes about the same time as their method, which constructs and optimizes the cost function at $\frac{1}{3}$ resolution (Table 2).

Test Performance. We compare our method on the Sintel clean images. In contrast to the other methods we do not use a sophisticated post-processing pipeline, because the main focus of this work is to show that learning and inference on high resolution images is feasible. Therefore we cannot compete with the highly tuned methods. Figure 3 shows that we are able to recover fine details, but since we do not employ a forward-backward check and local planar inpainting we make large errors in occluded regions.

Fig. 3. Sample output of our method. Left figure, top row shows the WTA solution of a 7-layer network for *FF, FQ, QQ* training. The bottom row shows results of the same network with CRF inference. The right part shows the highlighted region enlarged. (Color figure online)

5 Conclusion

We showed that both learning and CRF inference of the optical flow cost function on high resolution images is tractable. We circumvent the excessive memory requirements of the full 4D cost volume by a min-projection. This reduces the space complexity from quadratic to linear in the search range. To efficiently compute the cost function, we learn binary descriptors with a new hybrid learning scheme, that outperforms the previous state-of-the-art straight-through estimator of the gradient.

Acknowledgements. We acknowledge grant support from Toyota Motor Europe HS, the ERC starting grant HOMOVIS No. 640156 and the research initiative Intelligent Vision Austria with funding from the AIT and the Austrian Federal Ministry of Science, Research and Economy HRSM programme (BGBl. II Nr. 292/2012).

References

1. Bailer, C., Taetz, B., Stricker, D.: Flow Fields: dense correspondence fields for highly accurate large displacement optical flow estimation. In: International Conference on Computer Vision (ICCV) (2015)
2. Bengio, Y., Léonard, N., Courville, A.C.: Estimating or propagating gradients through stochastic neurons for conditional computation. CoRR abs/1308.3432 (2013). http://arxiv.org/abs/1308.3432
3. Butler, D.J., Wulff, J., Stanley, G.B., Black, M.J.: A naturalistic open source movie for optical flow evaluation. In: Fitzgibbon, A., Lazebnik, S., Perona, P., Sato, Y., Schmid, C. (eds.) ECCV 2012. LNCS, vol. 7577, pp. 611–625. Springer, Heidelberg (2012). doi:10.1007/978-3-642-33783-3_44
4. Calonder, M., Lepetit, V., Strecha, C., Fua, P.: BRIEF: binary robust independent elementary features. In: Daniilidis, K., Maragos, P., Paragios, N. (eds.) ECCV 2010. LNCS, vol. 6314, pp. 778–792. Springer, Heidelberg (2010). doi:10.1007/978-3-642-15561-1_56
5. Chen, Q., Koltun, V.: Full Flow: optical flow estimation by global optimization over regular grids. In: Conference on Computer Vision and Pattern Recognition (CVPR) (2016)
6. Chen, Z., Sun, X., Wang, L., Yu, Y., Huang, C.: A deep visual correspondence embedding model for stereo matching costs. In: International Conference on Computer Vision (ICCV) (2015)
7. Courbariaux, M., Bengio, Y.: BinaryNet: training deep neural networks with weights and activations constrained to +1 or −1. CoRR abs/1602.02830 (2016). http://arxiv.org/abs/1602.02830
8. Felzenszwalb, P.F., Huttenlocher, D.P.: Efficient belief propagation for early vision. Int. J. Comput. Vis. **70**(1), 41–54 (2006)
9. Gadot, D., Wolf, L.: PatchBatch: a batch augmented loss for optical flow. In: Conference on Computer Vision and Pattern Recognition, (CVPR) (2016)
10. Güney, F., Geiger, A.: Deep discrete flow. In: Lai, S.-H., Lepetit, V., Nishino, K., Sato, Y. (eds.) ACCV 2016. LNCS, vol. 10114, pp. 207–224. Springer, Cham (2017). doi:10.1007/978-3-319-54190-7_13
11. Knöbelreiter, P., Reinbacher, C., Shekhovtsov, A., Pock, T.: End-to-end training of hybrid CNN-CRF models for stereo. In: Conference on Computer Vision and Pattern Recognition, (CVPR) (2017). http://arxiv.org/abs/1611.10229
12. Kolmogorov, V.: Convergent tree-reweighted message passing for energy minimization. Trans. Pattern Anal. Mach. Intell. **28**(10), 1568–1583 (2006)
13. Luo, W., Schwing, A., Urtasun, R.: Efficient deep learning for stereo matching. In: International Conference on Computer Vision and Pattern Recognition (ICCV) (2016)
14. Ranftl, R., Bredies, K., Pock, T.: Non-local total generalized variation for optical flow estimation. In: Fleet, D., Pajdla, T., Schiele, B., Tuytelaars, T. (eds.) ECCV 2014. LNCS, vol. 8689, pp. 439–454. Springer, Cham (2014). doi:10.1007/978-3-319-10590-1_29

15. Ranftl, R., Gehrig, S., Pock, T., Bischof, H.: Pushing the limits of stereo using variational stereo estimation. In: IEEE Intelligent Vehicles Symposium (IV) (2012)
16. Rastegari, M., Ordonez, V., Redmon, J., Farhadi, A.: XNOR-Net: ImageNet classification using binary convolutional neural networks. In: Leibe, B., Matas, J., Sebe, N., Welling, M. (eds.) ECCV 2016. LNCS, vol. 9908, pp. 525–542. Springer, Cham (2016). doi:10.1007/978-3-319-46493-0_32
17. Revaud, J., Weinzaepfel, P., Harchaoui, Z., Schmid, C.: EpicFlow: edge-preserving interpolation of correspondences for optical flow. In: Computer Vision and Pattern Recognition (CVPR) (2015)
18. Shekhovtsov, A., Reinbacher, C., Graber, G., Pock, T.: Solving dense image matching in real-time using discrete-continuous optimization. ArXiv e-prints, January 2016
19. Shekhovtsov, A., Kovtun, I., Hlaváč, V.: Efficient MRF deformation model for non-rigid image matching. CVIU **112**, 91–99 (2008)
20. Trzcinski, T., Christoudias, M., Fua, P., Lepetit, V.: Boosting binary keypoint descriptors. In: Conference on Computer Vision and Pattern Recognition (CVPR) (2013)
21. Wainwright, M., Jaakkola, T., Willsky, A.: MAP estimation via agreement on (hyper)trees: message-passing and linear-programming approaches. IT **51**(11), 3697–3717 (2005)
22. Xu, J., Ranftl, R., Koltun, V.: Accurate optical flow via direct cost volume processing. In: Conference on Computer Vision and Pattern Recognition (CVPR) (2017)
23. Žbontar, J., LeCun, Y.: Computing the stereo matching cost with a convolutional neural network. In: Conference on Computer Vision and Pattern Recognition (CVPR) (2015)

Edge Adaptive Seeding for Superpixel Segmentation

Christian Wilms$^{(\boxtimes)}$ and Simone Frintrop

University of Hamburg, Hamburg, Germany
`wilms@informatik.uni-hamburg.de`

Abstract. Finding a suitable seeding resolution when using superpixel segmentation methods is usually challenging. Different parts of the image contain different levels of clutter, resulting in an either too dense or too coarse segmentation. Since both possible solutions cause problems with respect to subsequent processing, we propose an edge adaptive seeding for superpixel segmentation methods, generating more seeds in areas with more edges and vise versa. This follows the assumption that edges distinguish objects and thus are a good indicator of the level of clutter in an image region. We show in our evaluation on five datasets by using three popular superpixel segmentation methods that using edge adaptive seeding leads to improved results compared to other priors as well as to uniform seeding.

1 Introduction

Superpixels, defined by [19] as local and coherent sets of pixels capturing the relevant structures of an image, have become a popular pre-processing stage for different computer vision tasks over the last 15 years, like tracking [28,31], recognition tasks [4,27], or object proposal detection [15,18,25]. Integrating a number of neighboring pixels into one superpixel does not only decrease the number of basic entities of an image, but also the shape of these entities becomes arbitrary and can better fit to the image content as it is not defined by the layout of the imaging sensor. The decreased number of basic entities allows for more complex processing of the superpixels and possibly faster execution time.

An important aspect when using superpixels is the property that superpixels capture the relevant structure of an image. Missing boundaries of objects can lead to drastic degradation of the results of subsequent methods: objects that are segmented into the same superpixel can not be distinguished at later stages. Therefore, a good adherence to boundaries as well as minimizing the "leakage" of superpixels across boundaries is crucial for the success of the entire system. The size of the relevant structures varies not only between images but also within images. One area of an image might only feature few or no objects at all such

Electronic supplementary material The online version of this chapter (doi:10. 1007/978-3-319-66709-6_27) contains supplementary material, which is available to authorized users.

V. Roth and T. Vetter (Eds.): GCPR 2017, LNCS 10496, pp. 333–344, 2017.
DOI: 10.1007/978-3-319-66709-6_27

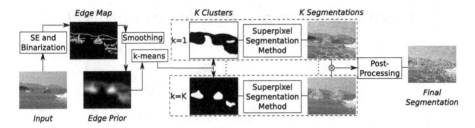

Fig. 1. Overview of the edge adaptive seeding mechanism. First, edges are generated using SE [6,7] and the result is binarized. After smoothing, the result is used as a prior (edge density) to cluster the image into different parts. Each cluster is segmented with a segmentation method using a different number of superpixels depending on the average edge density. Finally, the results are combined and post-processed to form the final segmentation.

as walls or skies, while other areas of the same image are highly cluttered with shelves or a crowd. The major difference between non-cluttered and cluttered regions is the number of edges as they separate objects from each other.

Most state-of-the-art superpixel segmentation algorithms [1,5,13,32] are initially based on a uniform grid of seeds. A common problem with this approach is that all image regions are treated with the identical seed resolution while the level of clutter between image regions might vary substantially. One solution is to highly oversegment the image by generating a large amount of superpixels, which reduces the speed-up effect described above. The second solution does the opposite by only generating a relatively small number of superpixels that will reduce the complexity of subsequent analysis at the expense of missing small objects that are not segmented as individual superpixels. A third option is to use multiple superpixel resolutions [33], which again reduces the speed-up effect.

In this paper, we propose an edge adaptive seeding method to overcome this problem. The seeding can be combined with different segmentation algorithms. In contrast to [10,12], which change the seeding of 3D point cloud segmentations based on saliency or colorfulness, we adapt the number of seeds in different image regions by measuring the edge density in an area around each pixel. We are to the best of our knowledge the first to apply adaptive seeding purely on 2D image data. As outlined in Fig. 1, a state-of-the-art edge detector [6,7] is used to generate edge responses. The edge responses are smoothed and clustered using k-means clustering to generate areas in the image with different levels of clutter. The seeding resolution for each cluster is then adapted to the average edge density, leading to more dense segmentation in more cluttered areas and vise versa. Our results show that our edge adaptive seeding mechanism improves segmentation results in terms of boundary recall and undersegmentation error using multiple segmentation methods. Furthermore, we also released the source code of our implementation[1].

---

[1] https://www.inf.uni-hamburg.de/easpxs.

The rest of the paper is organized as follows. Section 2 discusses related work in segmentation and adaptive seeding. In Sect. 3, we describe the edge adaptive seeding approach. An evaluation of our method on five datasets is presented in Sect. 4. The paper closes with concluding remarks in Sect. 5.

2   Related Work

Since the definition of superpixels by [19], a variety of superpixel segmentation methods have been proposed [1,5,8,13,21,32]. A state-of-the-art overview can be found in [24]. One of the most popular and successful methods in recent years [24] is SLIC [1]. The main principle of SLIC is to start from a regular grid of seeds and cluster the pixels in a combined LABXY-space that allows for a weighting of the influence of spatial and color difference. Second, the clustering is only done in a local region around each seed, significantly improving the runtime and restricting the area of each superpixel. Another popular method is SEEDS [5], which uses an energy function to generate homogeneous superpixels with regular boundaries. Other methods starting from a regular grid include [13,32]. Despite the success of these methods on various datasets [24] and in numerous applications [4,18,27,28,31], none of them is able to adapt the number of seeds to the image content and segment different parts of the image with different resolutions. Other methods that are able to segment some parts of an image more densely than other parts like [8] and [26] produce inferior results compared to the above mentioned methods [24]. However, more recent approaches like SMURFS [14], based on iterative splitting and merging of superpixels, are able to keep up with the uniform seeding methods.

Three different adaptive seeding approaches exist in the literature all using 3D data. The first approach to apply adaptive seeding is DASP [29]. As a prior they use depth information and seed areas more densely if they are further away from the camera. This follows the principle that objects further away from the camera appear smaller on the image plane. [12] propose an approach that uses color information to adapt the seeding of a supervoxel clustering. Despite improving on the uniform seeding, this approach is generally not well-suited as neighboring objects do not necessarily have different colors.

Another approach to adapt the number of supervoxels to the image content is presented in [10]. As a prior for adapting the seeding resolution, a saliency map is used. The saliency system [9] highlights parts of the image that attract human visual attention and thereby give a prior for more dense segmentation. In contrast to [10], our method works on the 2D image plane and uses edge detection results as a prior. This seems more favorable since saliency highlights things in the image that stand out, which does not necessarily imply they should be segmented more densely. For example, in a scene with five blue balls and one red ball on the grass, the red ball is more salient. A more dense segmentation of the red ball in contrast to the blue balls however, is not useful. The positive effect of the edge based seeding with respect to the quality of the superpixels can be seen in our results.

3   Edge Adaptive Seeding

This section describes the edge adaptive seeding mechanism for superpixel segmentation methods (overview in Fig. 1). Given a desired number of superpixels and a number of clusters, it generates a prior about cluttered parts in the scene. This prior is used in a variation of the adaptive seeding approach of [10] to segment cluttered parts of the image more densely. As a superpixel segmentation method, any method that generates a predetermined number of superpixels can be used. First, the Structured Edges detector (SE) [6,7] is applied to the input image, generating sharp edges with different strengths. To determine regions of different edge densities, binarization as well as smoothing is applied and the result is clustered using k-means. The seeding resolution of each cluster is determined using the average edge density within the cluster and a desired number of output superpixels. Thereby, a dense segmentation of regions with a high edge density is guaranteed, while regions with a low edge density are segmented more coarsely. After segmenting the image with a segmentation algorithm given the respective seeding resolutions of the clusters, the results of the different segmentations are cut and combined. Finally, we apply post-processing to eliminate disconnected and too small superpixels. The following subsections describe the steps of the approach in detail.

3.1   Edge Detection

To measure the edge density for each pixel in a given input image, we choose the detector SE [6,7]. SE gives competitive results on relevant benchmarks like BSD [2] as well as NYUV2 [22] and shows good performance in many applications [3, 20,34]. According to [6,7], the detector can run at a rate of up to 30 Hz, while still achieving state-of-the-art results. SE detects edges in an image based on a random forest classifier, which makes it easily adaptable to different domains.

The result of SE is a sharp mask of edges with varying strengths. To transform this result into a prior representing the edge density, we first binarize the results given a lower bound τ for the strength of an edge to be detected. This binarization is necessary to become independent of the edge strength, which improved the results in our experiments and follows the assumption that stronger edges are found more easily anyway. Therefore, an overly dense segmentation is not necessary. The binarization is followed by a smoothing step with a Gaussian kernel to determine the edge density as the weighted average number of edge responses above τ within a certain area around each pixel. This leads to a prior that represents the edge density and highlights regions with many detected edges. The two steps are visualized in the second and third image of Fig. 2.

3.2   Adaptive Seeding

Given the prior from the processed edge detection result, a k-means clustering similar to [10] is done on the prior resulting in K clusters. The clusters are sorted in ascending order with respect to their average edge density. Each pixel of the

Fig. 2. Intermediate steps of the proposed method. From left to right: input image with ground truth, binarized edges (dilated for better visualization), smoothed prior, clustering for $K = 3$, and final segmentation.

image is assigned to one of the K clusters according to the edge density value of the prior. As we request superpixel algorithms used in this approach to generate a desired number of superpixels, we are in contrast to [10] able to determine the seeding resolution of each cluster.

For each of the K clusters, we apply a segmentation with a seeding resolution adapted to the average edge density e_k with $k = 1, \ldots, K$. Based on the assumptions of Sect. 1, a higher average edge density leads to a more dense seeding resolution and more superpixels. The exact number of superpixels of the k-th cluster n_k is defined based on the average edge density of a cluster, the desired number of superpixels in the final segmentation n, the number of superpixels of either the minimal or maximal resolution n_1 and n_K and a weight w_k determining the number of superpixels of the k-th cluster n_k in relation to n_1 and n_K. First, the number n of superpixels of the final segmentation generated by K different resolutions on K distinct clusters of the image is defined as

$$n = \sum_{k=1}^{K} a_k (n_1 + (n_K - n_1) \frac{w_k}{w_K}), \tag{1}$$

with a_k being the relative size of the k-th cluster. The weight factor w_k, which is normalized to the maximum of the weights, determines the number of superpixels relative to n_1 and n_K. w_k is chosen exponentially based on e_k as well as the minimum and maximum edge density e_1 and e_K. This weighting leads to a number of superpixels that is adaptive to the edge density in the clusters. The weight w_k is therefore defined as

$$w_k = \begin{cases} 1 - b^{\frac{e_k - e_1}{e_K - e_1}} & \text{if } b < 1 \\ b^{\frac{e_k - e_1}{e_K - e_1}} - 1 & \text{else} \end{cases} \tag{2}$$

with b being a parameter to adapt the weighting. As all variables of Eq. (1) are known with the exception n_1 and n_K, one of those has to be fixed as a parameter. While fixing n_K could lead to a negative number of superpixels for n_1, given an unfavorable choice of n, fixing n_1 and then determining n_K and with that all intermediate numbers of superpixels n_k is easily possible. Therefore, Eq. (1) can be transformed into

Fig. 3. Comparison of clipping the segmentations. To avoid artificial edges at cluster borders as in image 3 (red lines), coarser segmentations are overlayed with finer ones (image 4). Left: original image (part of Figs. 1 and 2), second image: clustering. (Color figure online)

$$n_K = \frac{n_1 \sum_{k=1}^{K} a_k \left(1 - \frac{w_k}{w_K}\right) - n}{-\sum_{k=1}^{K} a_k \frac{w_k}{w_K}}, \tag{3}$$

giving the number of superpixels n_K for the densest cluster. The intermediate number of superpixels n_k for the respective clusters can now be calculated as

$$n_k = n_1 + (n_K - n_1)\frac{w_k}{w_K}. \tag{4}$$

3.3 Superpixel Segmentation

After calculating the number of superpixels for all clusters, a superpixel segmentation algorithm that is able to generate a predetermined number of superpixels, can be applied to the whole image K times with the different number of superpixels n_k. Exemplary we use SLIC, SEEDS and SMURFS in Sect. 4. The parallelized application of the algorithm only on the relevant parts of the image for speed-up is also possible, if the algorithm supports masks or can be adapted in such way. This step results in K segmentations or partial segmentations of the image that need to be combined for the final segmentation.

While directly clipping the clusters in the respective segmentations and combining them would lead to a correct oversegmentation, it would introduce the continuous, artificial edges of the clusters into the segmentation result as marked red in the third image of Fig. 3 and visible in the results of [10]. This can be a drawback, e.g., if the continuation of edges is a cue for later merging steps. Therefore, we propose to sequentially combine the different segmentations starting with the coarsest. From the next finest segmentation, all superpixels that contain pixels from the respective cluster will be selected. The part of the image covered by those superpixels will be replaced in the combined result with this new, finer segmentation. This procedure continues until all segmentations are processed. As visible in the last image in Fig. 3, an edge adaptive segmentation without the artificial, continuous edges of the clusters is generated.

3.4 Post-processing

One problem introduced by the previously described combination technique is that superpixels might be cut into multiple components by overlaying a finer segmentation. Furthermore, due to the imperfect estimation of the number of superpixels a method produces, the overall number of superpixels might not fit the desired number. Therefore, we propose a two-step post-processing with first relabeling all unconnected superpixels and second merging small superpixels into one of their neighbors, similar to the post-processing done in [1]. To prevent merging only in the finest superpixel resolution, the size of a superpixel is normalized by the seeding resolution of the cluster the superpixel results from. This merging is done until the desired number of superpixels n is reached, resulting in a final edge adaptive segmentation as shown in the last image in Fig. 2.

4   Results and Evaluation

The evaluation is done based on the superpixel evaluation framework presented in [24]. Therefore, the datasets used are BSD [2], NYUV2 [22], SUNRGBD [23], SBD [11] and Fashionista [30]. They cover a wide variety of images containing different indoor and outdoor scenes with various levels of clutter. The number of images per dataset and splits are the same as in [24] resulting in around 200 images for training and 400 images for testing per dataset. Image sizes vary between 658×486 and 316×240 depending on the dataset. The metrics used for comparison are standard boundary recall (REC) [16] and undersegmentation error (UE) defined by [17] and recommended in [24]. For parameter optimization the same combination as in [24] is used ($\epsilon = (1 - \text{REC}) + \text{UE}$).

As superpixel segmentation methods we chose the widely used SLIC [1] and SEEDS [5] as both approaches satisfy our requirement of generating a specified number of superpixels. To compare our approach with an adaptive superpixel segmentation method, we also chose SMURFS [14]. We compare our method to SLIC, SEEDS and SMURFS with uniform seeding as well as with the saliency based seeding method of [10] adapted to the 2D-domain by using the saliency map instead of the edge prior. Furthermore, on the datasets NYUV2 and SUN-RGBD a comparison to DASP is made as depth data is available. A comparison with [12] is not possible as their changes in seeding rely on the specifics of the used supervoxel segmentation method. To show that our general approach is beneficial, we also present the results of our system using the ground truth (GT) edges instead of the SE results as a perfect prior. This prior leads to results that are independent of the edge detection quality and therefore define an upper bound for our approach.

To make the results comparable, the parameters were optimized on the training sets for each dataset and each superpixel resolution independently as outlined in [24]. The parameters optimized were the parameters of the segmentations, n_1 and K in Eq. (1), b in Eq. (2) as well as τ and σ from pre-processing the edge detection result. n_1 was optimized in the range of $\frac{1}{10}n, \ldots, \frac{6}{10}n, K$ in the range of $3, \ldots, 6, b$ in the range of $0.75, 2, 5, 10, \tau$ in the range of $0.05, \ldots, 0.25$, and σ in the range of $5, \ldots, 30$. The models for the SE detector were also learned on the training datasets.

The results using SMURFS, described in the supplementary material, indicate that our method can also improve adaptive segmentations, given edge detection results that are superior to current state-of-the-art results. For DASP, the lower performances on NYUV2 and SUNRGBD, described in the supplementary material, confirm the findings of [24] that depth does not always lead to improved results.

4.1 Results Using SLIC

In our first experimental set-up, we use SLIC as the segmentation method. Qualitative results are shown in Fig. 4. The results in row 1 and 2 clearly show the coarse segmentation in areas of the image covered with sky or sea, while areas around objects are segmented more densely. The results of our experiments in terms of REC and UE over the test sets of BSD and SBD as a function of the number of superpixels are shown in Fig. 5. The results on the other datasets can be found in the supplementary material. It is clearly visible that our approach of using edge detection results is beneficial for the segmentation result. Our approach consistently outperforms SLIC in REC over both datasets and the rest of the datasets, as the results in the supplementary material show. For instance, on SBD with 250 superpixels the edge adaptive seeding improves the REC form around 77% to almost 82%. Therefore, the edge prior leads to a less densely segmented image in parts like backgrounds and a more densely segmented image in interesting parts with many objects. This is useful, as given the same number of superpixels the more complex parts can be analyzed in much more detail.

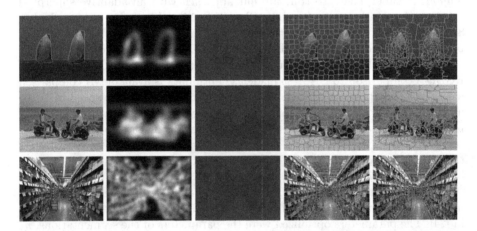

Fig. 4. Qualitative results of the edge adaptive seeding with SLIC on images from SBD (1st & 2nd row) and NYUV2 (3rd row). From left to right: input image with ground truth, edge density, clusters, uniform SLIC segmentation, result of proposed seeding with SLIC. For qualitative results using SEEDS and SMURFS see the supplementary material.

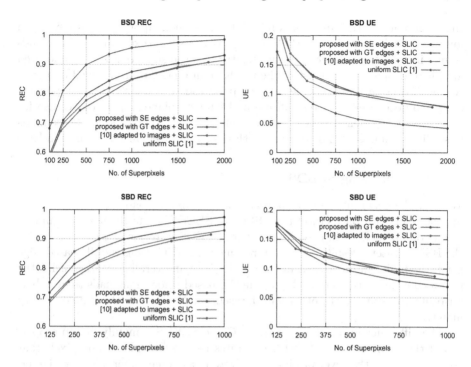

Fig. 5. Boundary recall (REC) and undersegmentation error (UE) on the BSD (top) and SBD (bottom) datasets using SLIC. For results on the other datasets see the supplementary material.

These findings can be confirmed if the GT edges of the images are used instead of the SE results. Those perfect priors improve the results even more, leading to 86% in REC on SBD using 250 superpixels (82% with SE based prior). The large improvement when using the GT prior compared to the SE prior on some images can be explained by many different entities of the same class in an image, like books in the library that generate many edge results. As the distinction between the individual entities is not always made in the GT data, the ability to segment individual entities much better is not reflected in positive performance (cf. Fig. 4, 3rd row). Similar effects arise on high textured images.

The relatively constant performance in terms of UE when using the edge detection prior across all datasets can be explained by GT segments in areas that are classified as background given the prior. In that case, the superpixels covering those background areas are much larger than before, leading to a large UE in those areas and neglecting the improvements in the finer segmented areas. This can also be validated when using the GT edges as input to the system. With those GT edges such cases are not possible, thus only the advantage of the finer segmentation of relevant parts remains.

We outperform [10] across all datasets and resolutions in REC and are on a similar level in terms of UE. The explanation of the lower performance of their approach is the different kind of data, as their approach was developed for supervoxel clustering of RGBD data. Using supervoxels and point clouds results in a different general seeding strategy, as the supervoxels can be located anywhere in space in contrast to the pixels of an image, that are fixed to a grid. As the clustering based on the saliency prior usually leads to thin components around objects, the seed resolution on the image plane can be too coarse for those thin components, which leads to components without a seed. These kinds of seeding artifacts are not possible with the supervoxel clustering used in [10].

4.2   Results Using SEEDS

To show the generality of our approach, we set up a second experiment changing the segmentation method from SLIC to SEEDS. Figure 6 shows exemplary results of our method in combination with SEEDS in terms of REC and UE on the BSD dataset. Despite minor improvement in REC using the SE based edge prior, the major improvement in UE still leads to an overall advantage using the proposed edge based seeding. Using the GT based prior again leads to even better results. Results on the other four datasets can be found in the supplementary material.

The difference in results between SLIC and SEEDS is mainly due to properties of the segmentations. SEEDS generates less equally sized superpixels that adapt better to the level of clutter. However, as some superpixels are larger, the edges missed by SEEDS lead to more leakage than for SLIC, where the size of the superpixels is more evenly distributed. Using the edge adaptive seeding balances this size variation by identifying more edges and forcing a more dense segmentation around them. This is supported by the results using the GT edges.

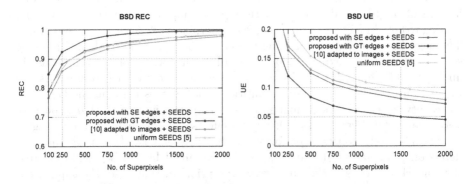

Fig. 6. Boundary recall (REC) and undersegmentation error (UE) on the BSD dataset using SEEDS. As for the results using SLIC, the usage of the edge based prior leads to improved results, here especially in terms of UE. For results on the other datasets see the supplementary material.

5   Conclusion

Finding one superpixel resolution that fits all the different parts of an image is impossible. However, segmenting as many objects correctly with as few superpixels as possible in images with different levels of clutter is important, since wrongly segmented objects or heavily oversegmented scenes hamper subsequent processing steps.

To tackle that problem, we have proposed an approach to adapt the seeding for superpixel segmentations based on the edge density. Edges are a good indicator for the level of clutter, as objects can be discriminated by an edge. Therefore, we segment parts of an image with many edges more densely and vise versa.

Our results show the improved segmentations using the edge adaptive seeding for different superpixel segmentation methods across five datasets in comparison to other adaptive seedings as well as the uniform seeding. In the future, we plan to use the edge detection result to further improve superpixel segmentations.

References

1. Achanta, R., Shaji, A., Smith, K., Lucchi, A., Fua, P., Süsstrunk, S.: SLIC superpixels compared to state-of-the-art superpixel methods. IEEE TPAMI **34**(11), 2274–2282 (2012)
2. Arbelaez, P., Maire, M., Fowlkes, C., Malik, J.: Contour detection and hierarchical image segmentation. IEEE TPAMI **33**(5), 898–916 (2011)
3. Arbelaez, P., Pont-Tuset, J., Barron, J.T., Marques, F., Malik, J.: Multiscale combinatorial grouping. In: CVPR (2014)
4. Baraldi, L., Paci, F., Serra, G., Benini, L., Cucchiara, R.: Gesture recognition in ego-centric videos using dense trajectories and hand segmentation. In: CVPR Workshops (2014)
5. Bergh, M., Boix, X., Roig, G., Capitani, B., Gool, L.: SEEDS: superpixels extracted via energy-driven sampling. In: Fitzgibbon, A., Lazebnik, S., Perona, P., Sato, Y., Schmid, C. (eds.) ECCV 2012. LNCS, vol. 7578, pp. 13–26. Springer, Heidelberg (2012). doi:10.1007/978-3-642-33786-4_2
6. Dollár, P., Zitnick, C.L.: Structured forests for fast edge detection. In: ICCV (2013)
7. Dollár, P., Zitnick, C.L.: Fast edge detection using structured forests. IEEE TPAMI **37**(8), 1558–1570 (2015)
8. Felzenszwalb, P.F., Huttenlocher, D.P.: Efficient graph-based image segmentation. IJCV **59**(2), 167–181 (2004)
9. Frintrop, S., Werner, T., Martín García, G.: Traditional saliency reloaded: a good old model in new shape. In: CVPR (2015)
10. Gao, G., Lauri, M., Zhang, J., Frintrop, S.: Saliency-guided adaptive seeding for supervoxel segmentation. In: IROS (2017)
11. Gould, S., Fulton, R., Koller, D.: Decomposing a scene into geometric and semantically consistent regions. In: ICCV (2009)
12. Kanezaki, A., Harada, T.: 3D selective search for obtaining object candidates. In: IROS (2015)
13. Levinshtein, A., Stere, A., Kutulakos, K., Fleet, D., Dickinson, S., Siddiqi, K.: TurboPixels: fast superpixels using geometric flows. IEEE TPAMI **31**(12), 2290–2297 (2009)

14. Luengo, I., Basham, M., French, A.: SMURFS: superpixels from multi-scale refinement of super-regions. In: BMVC (2016)
15. Manen, S., Guillaumin, M., Van Gool, L.: Prime object proposals with randomized prim's algorithm. In: ICCV (2013)
16. Martin, D., Fowlkes, C., Malik, J.: Learning to detect natural image boundaries using local brightness, color, and texture cues. IEEE TPAMI **26**(5), 530–549 (2004)
17. Neubert, P., Protzel, P.: Superpixel benchmark and comparison. In: Proceedings of the Forum Bildverarbeitung (2012)
18. Rantalankila, P., Kannala, J., Rahtu, E.: Generating object segmentation proposals using global and local search. In: CVPR (2014)
19. Ren, X., Malik, J.: Learning a classification model for segmentation. In: ICCV (2003)
20. Revaud, J., Weinzaepfel, P., Harchaoui, Z., Schmid, C.: EpicFlow: edge-preserving interpolation of correspondences for optical flow. In: CVPR (2015)
21. Shi, J., Malik, J.: Normalized cuts and image segmentation. IEEE TPAMI **22**(8), 888–905 (2000)
22. Silberman, N., Hoiem, D., Kohli, P., Fergus, R.: Indoor segmentation and support inference from RGBD images. In: Fitzgibbon, A., Lazebnik, S., Perona, P., Sato, Y., Schmid, C. (eds.) ECCV 2012. LNCS, vol. 7576, pp. 746–760. Springer, Heidelberg (2012). doi:10.1007/978-3-642-33715-4_54
23. Song, S., Lichtenberg, S.P., Xiao, J.: SUN RGB-D: A RGB-D scene understanding benchmark suite. In: CVPR (2015)
24. Stutz, D., Hermans, A., Leibe, B.: Superpixels: an evaluation of the state-of-the-art. CVIU (2017, in press)
25. Uijlings, J.R.R., van de Sande, K.E.A., Gevers, T., Smeulders, A.W.M.: Selective search for object recognition. IJCV **104**(2), 154–171 (2013)
26. Vincent, L., Soille, P.: Watersheds in digital spaces: an efficient algorithm based on immersion simulations. IEEE TPAMI **13**(6), 583–598 (1991)
27. Wang, C., Liu, Z., Chan, S.C.: Superpixel-based hand gesture recognition with kinect depth camera. IEEE Trans. Multimed. **17**(1), 29–39 (2015)
28. Wang, S., Lu, H., Yang, F., Yang, M.H.: Superpixel tracking. In: ICCV (2011)
29. Weikersdorfer, D., Gossow, D., Beetz, M.: Depth-adaptive superpixels. In: ICPR (2012)
30. Yamaguchi, K., Kiapour, M.H., Ortiz, L.E., Berg, T.L.: Parsing clothing in fashion photographs. In: CVPR (2012)
31. Yang, F., Lu, H., Yang, M.H.: Robust superpixel tracking. IEEE TIP **23**(4), 1639–1651 (2014)
32. Yao, J., Boben, M., Fidler, S., Urtasun, R.: Real-time coarse-to-fine topologically preserving segmentation. In: CVPR (2015)
33. Zhu, L., Klein, D.A., Frintrop, S., Cao, Z., Cremers, A.B.: A multisize superpixel approach for salient object detection based on multivariate normal distribution estimation. IEEE TIP **23**(12), 5094–5107 (2014)
34. Zitnick, C.L., Dollár, P.: Edge boxes: locating object proposals from edges. In: Fleet, D., Pajdla, T., Schiele, B., Tuytelaars, T. (eds.) ECCV 2014. LNCS, vol. 8693, pp. 391–405. Springer, Cham (2014). doi:10.1007/978-3-319-10602-1_26

Pose, Face and Gesture

Optical Flow-Based 3D Human Motion Estimation from Monocular Video

Thiemo Alldieck[1(✉)], Marc Kassubeck[1], Bastian Wandt[2], Bodo Rosenhahn[2],
and Marcus Magnor[1]

[1] Computer Graphics Lab, TU Braunschweig, Braunschweig, Germany
alldieck@cg.cs.tu-bs.de
[2] Institut für Informationsverarbeitung,
Leibniz Universität Hannover, Hannover, Germany

Abstract. This paper presents a method to estimate 3D human pose and body shape from monocular videos. While recent approaches infer the 3D pose from silhouettes and landmarks, we exploit properties of optical flow to temporally constrain the reconstructed motion. We estimate human motion by minimizing the difference between computed flow fields and the output of our novel flow renderer. By just using a single semi-automatic initialization step, we are able to reconstruct monocular sequences without joint annotation. Our test scenarios demonstrate that optical flow effectively regularizes the under-constrained problem of human shape and motion estimation from monocular video.

1 Introduction

Human pose estimation from video sequences has been an active field of research over the past decades with various applications such as surveillance, medical diagnostics or human-computer interfaces [22]. One branch of human pose estimation is referred to as *articulated motion parsing* [41], which defines the combination of monocular pose estimation and motion tracking in uncontrolled environments. We present a new approach to temporally coherent human shape and motion estimation in uncontrolled monocular video sequences. Our work follows the *generative* strategy, where both pose and shape parameters of a 3D body model are found to match the input image through analysis-by-synthesis [21].

The 3D pose of a human figure is highly ambiguous when inferred from only a 2D image. Common generative approaches [8,14,15] try to find human poses that are a good match to given silhouettes. However, human silhouettes can often be explained by multiple poses [14]. Existing methods for landmark-based 3D human motion estimation from monocular images [1,25,33,39,40] can find a pose per frame independently. Although 3D reconstructions from both approaches look very convincing on single images, they can result in significant jumps in position and joint angles between two successive frames. This creates highly unrealistic 3D reconstructions in the temporal domain. Temporal consistency of tracked landmarks is only considered by few researchers [26,35,36].

© Springer International Publishing AG 2017
V. Roth and T. Vetter (Eds.): GCPR 2017, LNCS 10496, pp. 347–360, 2017.
DOI: 10.1007/978-3-319-66709-6_28

In our work we exploit the properties of the optical flow in the sequence to not only enforce temporal coherence but also resolve the pose ambiguities of purely silhouette-based or landmark-based approaches. We develop a motion tracker based on our novel optical flow renderer. Optical flow has proven to improve 2D tracking while also sharing much of the properties of range data [29]. By exploiting properties of the optical flow we construct a robust and stable 3D human motion tracker working on monocular image sequences.

The main idea behind our work is that the optical flow between two consecutive frames largely depends on the change of the human pose between them. Following this idea, we propose an energy minimization problem that infers those model parameters that minimize the distance between observed and rendered flow for two input frames (Fig. 1). Additional energy terms are derived based on typical constraints of the human body, namely joint angle limits, limb interpenetration and continuous motion. For stable tracking, silhouette coverage is enforced.

Fig. 1. Following our main idea we compute the optical flow between two consecutive frames and match it to an optical flow field estimated by our proposed optical flow renderer. From left to right: input frame, color-coded observed flow, estimated flow, resulting pose. (Color figure online)

We evaluate the proposed method using two well known datasets. We analyze the performance of our approach qualitatively and evaluate its 3D and 2D precision quantitatively. In the first experiment, 3D joint positions are compared against ground truth of the HumanEva-I dataset [32] and results of two recently published methods [5,36]. The second evaluation compares projected 2D joint positions against ground truth of the VideoPose 2.0 dataset [30] featuring camera movement and rapid gesticulation. We compare our results against a recent deep-learning-based method for joint localization [24]. Results demonstrate the strengths and potential of the proposed method.

Summarizing, our contributions are:

- We develop a novel optical flow renderer for analysis-by-synthesis.
- We propose a complete pipeline for 3D reconstruction of human poses from monocular image sequences, that is independent of previous annotations of joints. It only uses a single semi-automatic initialisation step.
- Optical flow is exploited to retrieve 3D information and achieve temporal coherence, instead of solely relying on silhouette information.

2   Related Work

Human pose estimation is a broad and active field of research. Here, we focus on model-based approaches and work that exploits optical flow during pose estimation.

Human Pose from Images. 3D human pose estimation is often based on the use of a body model. Human body representations exist in 2D and 3D. Many of the following methods utilize the 3D human body model SCAPE [2]. SCAPE is a deformable mesh model learned from body scans. Pose and shape of the model are parametrized by a set of body part rotations and low dimensional shape deformations. In recent work the SMPL model, a more accurate blend shape model compatible with existing rendering engines, has been presented by Loper et al. [20].

A variety of approaches to 3D pose estimation have been presented using various cues including shape from shading, silhouettes and edges. Due to the highly ill-posed and under-constrained nature of the problem these methods often require user interaction e.g. through manual annotation of body joints on the image. Guan et al. [14] have been the first to present a detailed method to recover human pose together with an accurate shape estimate from single images. Based on manual initialization, parameters of the SCAPE model are optimized exploiting edge overlap and shading. The work is based on [4], a method that recovers the 3D pose from silhouettes from 3–4 calibrated cameras. Similar methods requiring multi-view input have been presented, e.g. [3,10,27,31]. Hasler et al. [15] fit their own statistical body model [16] into monocular image silhouettes with the help of sparse annotations. Chen et al. [8] infer 3D poses based on learned shape priors. In recent work, Bogo et al. [5] present the first method to extract both pose and shape from a single image fully automatically. 2D joint locations are found using the CNN-based approach DeepCut [24], then projected joints of the SMPL model are fitted against the 2D locations. In contrast to our work no consistency with the image silhouette or temporal coherency is taken into consideration.

Pose Reconstruction for Image Based Rendering. 3D human pose estimation can serve as a preliminary step for image based rendering techniques. In early work Carranza et al. [7] have been the first to present free-viewpoint video using model-based reconstruction of human motion using the subject's silhouette in multiple camera views. Zhou et al. [38] and Jain et al. [18] present updates to model-based pose estimation for subsequent reshaping of humans in images and videos respectively. Rogge et al. [28] fit a 3D model for automatic cloth exchange in videos. All methods utilize various cues, none of them uses optical flow for motion estimation.

Optical Flow Based Methods. Previous work has exploited optical flow for different purposes. Sapp et al. [30] and Fragkiadaki et al. [12] use optical flow for segmentation as a preliminary step for pose estimation. Both exploit the rigid structure revealing property of optical flow, rather than information about motion. Fablet and Black [11] use optical flow to learn motion models for automatic detection of human motion. Efros et al. [9] categorize human motion viewed from a distance by building an optical flow-based motion descriptor. Both methods label motion without revealing the underlying movement pattern. In recent work, Romero et al. [29] present a method for 2D human pose estimation using optical flow only. They detect body parts by porting the random forest approach used by the Microsoft Kinect to use optical flow. Brox et al. [6] have shown that optical flow can be used for 3D pose tracking of rigid objects. They propose the use for objects *modeled as kinematic chains*. They argue that optical flow provides point correspondences inside the object contour which can help to identify a pose where silhouettes are ambiguous. Inspired by the above mentioned characteristics, we investigate the extent to which optical flow can be used for 3D human motion estimation from monocular video.

3   Method

Optical flow [13] is the perception of motion by our visual sense. For two successive video frames, it is described as a 2D vector field that matches a point in the first frame to the displaced point in the following frame [17]. Although calculated in the image plane, optical flow contains 3D information, as it can be interpreted as the projection of 3D scene flow [34]. Assuming the presence of optical flow in the sequence (i.e. all observed surfaces are diffuse, opaque and textured), the entire observed optical flow is caused by relative movement between object and camera. Besides the motion of individual body parts, optical flow contains information about boundaries of rigid structures and is an abstraction layer to the input images. Unique appearance effects such as texture and shading are removed [11,29]. We argue that these features make optical flow highly suitable for generative optimization problems.

The presented method estimates pose parameters (i.e. joint angles), global position, and rotation of a human model (Sect. 3.1) frame by frame. The procedure only requires a single semi-automatic initialization step (Sect. 3.6) and then runs automatically. The parameters for each frame are inferred by minimizing the difference between the observed and rendered flow (Sect. 3.3) from our flow renderer (Sect. 3.2). A set of energy functions based on pose constraints (Sect. 3.4) and silhouettes (Sect. 3.5) is defined to regularize the solution to meaningful poses and to make the method more robust.

3.1   Scene Model

In this work, we use the human body model SMPL [20]. The model can be reshaped using 10 shape parameters β. For different poses, 72 pose parameters

θ can be set, including global orientation. β and θ produce realistic vertex transformations and cover a large range of body shapes and poses. We define $(\gamma, \beta, \theta_i, \sigma_i)$ as the model state at time step i, with global translation vector σ and gender γ. Here, for simplicity we assume that the camera positions and rotations as well as its focal lengths are known and static. It is however not required that the cameras of the actual scene are fixed, as the body model can rotate and move around the camera (cf. Sect. 4).

3.2 Flow Renderer

The core of the presented method is our differential flow renderer built upon OpenDR [19], a powerful open source framework for analysis-by-synthesis. The rendered flow image depends on the vertex locations determined by the virtual human model's pose parameters θ and its translation σ. To be able to render the flow *in situ*, we calculate the flow from frame i to $i-1$, referred to as backward flow. With this approach each pixel, and more importantly, each vertex location contains the information where it came from rather than were it went and can be rendered in place. The calculation of the flow is achieved as follows: The first step calculates the displacement of all vertices between two frames i and j in the image plane. Then the flow per pixel is calculated through barycentric interpolation of the neighboring vertices. Visibility and barycentric coordinates are calculated through the standard OpenGL rendering pipeline.

The core feature of the utilized rendering framework OpenDR is the differentiability of the rendering pipeline. To benefit from that property, our renderer estimates the partial derivatives of each flow vector with respect to each projected vertex position.

3.3 Flow Matching

Having a flow renderer available, we can formulate the pose estimation as an optimization problem. The cost function E_f over all pixels p is defined as follows:

$$E_f = \sum_p ||F_o(i, i-1, p) - F_r(i, i-1, p)||^2 \tag{1}$$

where F_r refers to the *rendered* and F_o to the *observed* flow field calculated on the input frames i and $i-1$. The objective drives the optimization in such way that the rendered flow is similar to the observed flow (Fig. 1). As proposed in [19], we evaluate E_f not over the flow field but over its Gaussian pyramid in order to perform a more global search.

For this work we use the method by Xu et al. [37] to calculate the observed optical flow field. The method has its strength in the ability to calculate large displacements while at the same time preserving motion details and handling occlusions. The definition of the objective shows that the performance of the optical flow estimation is crucial to the overall performance of the presented method. To compensate for inaccuracies of the flow estimation and to lower the accumulated error over time, we do not rely exclusively on the flow for pose estimation, but employ additional constraints as well (Sects. 3.4 and 3.5).

3.4   Pose Constraints

SMPL does not define bounds for deformation. We introduce soft boundaries to constrain the joint angles in form of a cost function for pose estimation:

$$E_b = || \max(e^{\theta_{\min} - \theta_i} - 1, 0) + \max(e^{\theta_i - \theta_{\max}} - 1, 0)||^2 \qquad (2)$$

where $\theta_{\min}$ and $\theta_{\max}$ are empirical lower and upper boundaries and e and max are applied component-wise.

Furthermore, we introduce extended Kalman filtering per joint and linear Kalman filtering for translation. In addition to temporal smoothness, the Kalman filters are used to predict an *a priori* pose for the next frame before optimization, which significantly speeds up computation time.

During optimization the extremities of the model may intersect with other body parts. To prevent this, we integrate the interpenetration error term E_{sp} from [5]. The error term is defined over a capsule approximation of the body model. By using an error term interpenetration is not strictly prohibited but penalized.

3.5   Silhouette Coverage

Pose estimation based on flow similarity requires that the rendered human model accurately covers the subject in the input image. Only body parts that cover the correct counterpart in the image can be moved correctly based on flow. To address inaccuracies caused by flow calculation, we introduce boundary matching.

We use the method presented by Bălan et al. [4] and adapt it to make it differentiable (cf. Sect. 3.7). A cost function measures how well the model fits the image silhouette S_I by penalizing non-overlapping pixels by the shortest distance to the model silhouette S_M. For this purpose Chamfer distance maps C_I for the image silhouette and C_M for the model are calculated. The cost function is defined as:

$$E_c = \sum_p ||aS_{M_i}(p)C_I(p) + (1 - a)S_I(p)C_{M_i}(p)||^2 \qquad (3)$$

where a weighs $S_{M_i}C_I$ stronger as image silhouettes are wider to enforce the model to reside within in the image silhouette than to completely cover it. To be able to compute derivatives, we approximate C_M by calculating the shortest distance of each pixel to the model capsule approximation used for E_{sp}. The distance at p is the shortest distance among all distances to each capsule. To lower computation time, we calculate only a grid of values and interpolate in between.

3.6   Initialization

For the initialization of the presented method two manual steps are required. First the user sets the joints of the body model to a pose that roughly matches the observed pose. It is sufficient that only the main joints such as shoulder, elbow, hip and knee are manipulated. In a second step the user marks joint locations of hips, knees, ankles, shoulders, elbows and wrists in the first frame. If the position of a joint cannot be seen or estimated it may be skipped. From this point no further user input is needed.

The initialization is then performed in three steps (Fig. 2). The first step minimizes the distance between the marked joints and their model counterparts projected to the image plane, while keeping E_{sp} and E_b low. We optimize over translation σ, pose θ and shape β. To guide the process we regularize both θ and β with objectives that penalize high differences to the manually set pose and the mean shape. In the second step we include the silhouette coverage objective E_c. Finally, we optimize the estimated pose for temporal consistency. We initialize the second frame with the intermediate initialization result and optimize on the flow field afterwards. While optimizing E_f we still allow updates for θ_0 and σ_0.

Fig. 2. Method initialization. Observed image, manual pose initialization, first optimization based on joint positions (red: model joints; blue: manually marked joints), final result including silhouette coverage and optical flow based correction. (Color figure online)

3.7 Optimization

After initialization we now iteratively find each pose using the defined objectives. The final objective function is a weighted sum of the energy terms of the previous sections:

$$\min_{\sigma,\theta}(\lambda_f E_f + \lambda_c E_c + \lambda_b E_b + \lambda_{sp} E_{sp} + \lambda_M E_M) \qquad (4)$$

with scalar weights λ. E_M regularizes the current state with respect to the last state

$$E_M = ||\theta_i - \theta_{i-1}||^2 + ||\sigma_i - \sigma_{i-1}||^2. \qquad (5)$$

Each frame is initialized with the Kalman prediction as described in Sect. 3.4.

For the optimization we use the OpenDR toolbox [19]. It allows for automatic differentiation of most partially differentiable functions. Therefore we can avoid the laborious and inaccurate task of calculating finite differences. All our energy terms are designed to be fully or partially differentiable. Using this auto-differentiation we are able to optimize Eq. (4) efficiently.

4   Evaluation

We evaluate the 3D and 2D pose accuracy of the presented method using two publicly available datasets: HumanEva-I [32] and VideoPose2.0 [30]. Ground truth is available for both datasets. We compare our results in both tests, 3D and 2D, against state-of-the-art methods [5,24,36]. Foreground masks needed for our method have been hand-annotated using an open-source tool for image annotation[1].

HumanEva-I. The HumanEva-I datasets features different actions performed by 4 subjects filmed under laboratory conditions. We reconstruct 130 frames of the sets *Walking C1* by subject 1 and *Jog C2* by subject 2 without reinitialization. The camera focal length is known. We do not adjust our method for the dataset except setting the λ weights. Figure 3 shows a qualitative analysis. The green plots show the history of the joints used for evaluation. The traces demonstrate clearly the temporal coherence of the presented method. The low visual error in the last frames demonstrates that the presented method is robust over time.

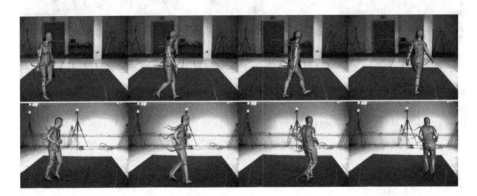

Fig. 3. Resultant poses of frames 30 to 120 of the HumanEva-I test sets. Green traces show the history of evaluated joints. (Color figure online)

We compare our method against the state-of-the-art methods of Bogo et al. [5] and Wandt et al. [36]. We use [5] without the linear pose regressor learned for the HumanEva sequences, which is missing in the publicly available source code. Frames that could not be reconstructed because of undetected joints have been excluded for evaluation. The 3D reconstruction of [36] is initialized with the same DeepCut [24] results as used for [5]. We measure the precision of the methods by calculating the *3D positioning error* as introduced by [33]. It calculates the mean euclidean distance of 13 reconstructed 3D joint locations to ground truth locations from MoCap data. Beforehand, optimal linear alignment of the results of all methods is achieved by Procrustes analysis. In order

---

[1] https://bitbucket.org/aauvap/multimodal-pixel-annotator.

to demonstrate the global approach of our method, we follow two strategies here: First we measure the joint error after performing Procrustes alignment per frame. Afterwards we calculate a per sequence alignment over all joint locations in all frames and measure the resulting mean error. Table 1 shows the result of all tests.

Table 1. Mean 3D joint error in cm for local per frame Procrustes alignment and global per sequence alignment.

	Walking C1		Jog C2	
	Local	Global	Local	Global
Bogo et al. [5]	6.6	17.4	7.5	10.4
Wandt et al. [36]	5.7	34.0	**6.3**	38.0
Our method	**5.5**	**7.6**	7.9	**9.9**

The results show that our method performs best in three of four test scenarios. In contrast to [5,36], our method does not require prior knowledge about the performed motion or training of plausible poses. The better performance of our method can be explained by the temporal coherent formulation using optical flow. This strength is especially noticeable in the global analysis. The method of [5] takes no temporal consistency into consideration, which results in jumps of joint locations between two frames and unresolved pose ambiguities (cf. Fig. 4). Note that some frames cannot be reconstructed due to the joint detector failing to find a feasible skeleton. The algorithm of [36] also estimates the camera trajectory. A slightly wrongly estimated person size results in a global offset of the camera path and causes a larger global error. In order to demonstrate, that our method resolves ambiguities successfully, we conduct the experiment again with E_f set to zero. The resultant motion does no longer resemble the performed action (Fig. 5) and the positioning error raises significantly to 9.8 and 15.9 for local and global analysis of *Walking C1* and 14.5 and 22.3 for *Jog C2* respectively.

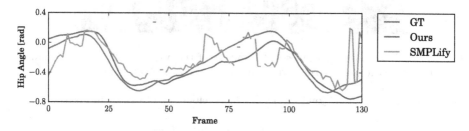

Fig. 4. Temporal behavior of the left hip angle of our method for *Walking C1* in comparison against ground truth (GT) and Bogo et al. (SMPLify) [5].

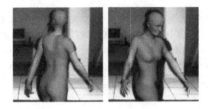

Fig. 5. Frame 120 of *Walking C1* in comparison to reconstruction with E_f set to zero.

VideoPose2.0. After evaluation with fixed camera and under laboratory conditions, we test our method under a more challenging setting. The second evaluation consists of three clips of the VideoPose2.0 dataset. We choose the "fullframe, every frame" (720×540 px) variant in order to face camera movement. Ground truth is given in form of projected 2D location of shoulders, elbows, and wrists for every other frame. The camera focal length has been estimated.

We evaluate our method in 2D by comparison against DeepCut [24], the same method that has been used before as input for the 3D reconstruction methods.

Fig. 6. Resultant poses of frames 1, 21 and 41 of the VideoPose2.0 sets (Chandler, Ross, Rachel) with ground truth arm locations (green and blue). (Color figure online)

Table 2. Mean 2D joint error (shoulders, elbows, and wrists) in pixels.

	Chandler	Ross	Rachel
DeepCut [24]	25.3	**10.5**	32.8
Our method	**23.3**	21.9	**15.9**

Table 2 shows the mean euclidean distance to ground truth 2D joint locations. We use the first detected person by DeepCut and exclude several undetected joints from its evaluation. For our method, we project the reconstructed 3D joint locations to the image plane (Fig. 6). The mixed performance of [24] is due to problems of the CNN with background objects. In order to enable fair comparison, we hand filter the results of [24] to foreground detections only and exclude several undetected joints. The comparison shows that our method produces similar precision while providing much more information. However, the increasing performance of CNN-based methods suggests that our method can benefit from semantic scene information for reinitialization in future work.

5   Conclusions

We have presented a new method for estimating 3D human motion from monocular video footage. The approach utilizes optical flow to recover human motion over time from a single initialization frame. For this purpose a novel flow renderer has been developed that enables direct interpretation of optical flow. The rich human body model SMPL provides the description of estimated human motion. Different test cases have shown applicability and robustness of the approach.

The presented method is dependent on realistic flow fields and good segmentation. It finds its natural limitations in the typical limits of optical flow estimation. Improvements in optical flow estimation, especially multi-frame optical flow, can help to further improve our method. Although our temporal coherent formulation allows for a good occlusion handling, large occlusions and reappearances can still lead to tracking errors.

Our work is focused on automatic estimation of human motion from monocular video. In future work we plan to further automatize our method. The method might benefit from recent developments in semantic segmentation [23] and joint angle priors [1]. Building upon the presented framework, the next steps are texturing of the model and geometry refinement, enabling new video editing and virtual reality applications.

Acknowledgments. The authors gratefully acknowledge funding by the German Science Foundation from project DFG MA2555/12-1.

References

1. Akhter, I., Black, M.J.: Pose-conditioned joint angle limits for 3D human pose reconstruction. In: IEEE Conference on Computer Vision and Pattern Recognition, vol. 2, pp. 1446–1455 (2015)
2. Anguelov, D., Srinivasan, P., Koller, D., Thrun, S., Rodgers, J., Davis, J.: SCAPE: shape completion and animation of people. In: ACM Transactions on Graphics (TOG), vol. 24, pp. 408–416. ACM (2005)
3. Bălan, A.O., Black, M.J., Haussecker, H., Sigal, L.: Shining a light on human pose: on shadows, shading and the estimation of pose and shape. In: IEEE International Conference on Computer Vision, pp. 1–8. IEEE (2007)

4. Bălan, A.O., Sigal, L., Black, M.J., Davis, J.E., Haussecker, H.W.: Detailed human shape and pose from images. In: IEEE Conference on Computer Vision and Pattern Recognition, pp. 1–8. IEEE (2007)

5. Bogo, F., Kanazawa, A., Lassner, C., Gehler, P., Romero, J., Black, M.J.: Keep it SMPL: automatic estimation of 3D human pose and shape from a single image. In: Leibe, B., Matas, J., Sebe, N., Welling, M. (eds.) ECCV 2016. LNCS, vol. 9909, pp. 561–578. Springer, Cham (2016). doi:10.1007/978-3-319-46454-1_34

6. Brox, T., Rosenhahn, B., Cremers, D., Seidel, H.-P.: High accuracy optical flow serves 3-D pose tracking: exploiting contour and flow based constraints. In: Leonardis, A., Bischof, H., Pinz, A. (eds.) ECCV 2006. LNCS, vol. 3952, pp. 98–111. Springer, Heidelberg (2006). doi:10.1007/11744047_8

7. Carranza, J., Theobalt, C., Magnor, M.A., Seidel, H.P.: Free-viewpoint video of human actors. In: ACM transactions on graphics (TOG), vol. 22, pp. 569–577. ACM (2003)

8. Chen, Y., Kim, T.-K., Cipolla, R.: Inferring 3D shapes and deformations from single views. In: Daniilidis, K., Maragos, P., Paragios, N. (eds.) ECCV 2010. LNCS, vol. 6313, pp. 300–313. Springer, Heidelberg (2010). doi:10.1007/978-3-642-15558-1_22

9. Efros, A.A., Berg, A.C., Mori, G., Malik, J.: Recognizing action at a distance. In: IEEE International Conference on Computer Vision, pp. 726–733. IEEE (2003)

10. Elhayek, A., de Aguiar, E., Jain, A., Thompson, J., Pishchulin, L., Andriluka, M., Bregler, C., Schiele, B., Theobalt, C.: MARCOnI—ConvNet-based marker-less motion capture in outdoor and indoor scenes. IEEE Trans. Pattern Anal. Mach. Intell. **39**(3), 501–514 (2017)

11. Fablet, R., Black, M.J.: Automatic detection and tracking of human motion with a view-based representation. In: Heyden, A., Sparr, G., Nielsen, M., Johansen, P. (eds.) ECCV 2002. LNCS, vol. 2350, pp. 476–491. Springer, Heidelberg (2002). doi:10.1007/3-540-47969-4_32

12. Fragkiadaki, K., Hu, H., Shi, J.: Pose from flow and flow from pose. In: IEEE Conference on Computer Vision and Pattern Recognition, pp. 2059–2066 (2013)

13. Gibson, J.J.: The Perception of the Visual World. Houghton Mifflin, Boston (1950)

14. Guan, P., Weiss, A., Bălan, A.O., Black, M.J.: Estimating human shape and pose from a single image. In: International Conference on Computer Vision, pp. 1381–1388. IEEE (2009)

15. Hasler, N., Ackermann, H., Rosenhahn, B., Thormahlen, T., Seidel, H.P.: Multilinear pose and body shape estimation of dressed subjects from image sets. In: IEEE Conference on Computer Vision and Pattern Recognition, pp. 1823–1830. IEEE (2010)

16. Hasler, N., Stoll, C., Sunkel, M., Rosenhahn, B., Seidel, H.P.: A statistical model of human pose and body shape. Comput. Graph. Forum. **28**, 337–346 (2009)

17. Horn, B.K., Schunck, B.G.: Determining optical flow. Artif. Intell. **17**(1–3), 185–203 (1981)

18. Jain, A., Thormählen, T., Seidel, H.P., Theobalt, C.: MovieReshape: tracking and reshaping of humans in videos. ACM Trans. Graph. (TOG) **29**(6), 148 (2010)

19. Loper, M.M., Black, M.J.: OpenDR: an approximate differentiable renderer. In: Fleet, D., Pajdla, T., Schiele, B., Tuytelaars, T. (eds.) ECCV 2014. LNCS, vol. 8695, pp. 154–169. Springer, Cham (2014). doi:10.1007/978-3-319-10584-0_11

20. Loper, M.M., Mahmood, N., Romero, J., Pons-Moll, G., Black, M.J.: SMPL: a skinned multi-person linear model. ACM Trans. Graph. **34**(6), 248:1–248:16 (2015)

21. Magnor, M.A., Grau, O., Sorkine-Hornung, O., Theobalt, C. (eds.): Digital Representations of the Real World: How to Capture, Model, and Render Visual Reality. CRC Press, Boca Raton (2015)
22. Moeslund, T.B., Hilton, A., Krüger, V.: A survey of advances in vision-based human motion capture and analysis. Comput. Vis. Image Underst. **104**(2), 90–126 (2006)
23. Oliveira, G.L., Valada, A., Bollen, C., Burgard, W., Brox, T.: Deep learning for human part discovery in images. In: IEEE International Conference on Robotics and Automation (2016)
24. Pishchulin, L., Insafutdinov, E., Tang, S., Andres, B., Andriluka, M., Gehler, P., Schiele, B.: Deepcut: Joint subset partition and labeling for multi person pose estimation. In: IEEE Conference on Computer Vision and Pattern Recognition (CVPR), June 2016
25. Ramakrishna, V., Kanade, T., Sheikh, Y.: Reconstructing 3D human pose from 2D image landmarks. In: Fitzgibbon, A., Lazebnik, S., Perona, P., Sato, Y., Schmid, C. (eds.) ECCV 2012. LNCS, vol. 7575, pp. 573–586. Springer, Heidelberg (2012). doi:10.1007/978-3-642-33765-9_41
26. Rehan, A., Zaheer, A., Akhter, I., Saeed, A., Mahmood, B., Usmani, M., Khan, S.: NRSfM using local rigidity. In: Winter Conference on Applications of Computer Vision, pp. 69–74. IEEE, Steamboat Springs, March 2014
27. Rhodin, H., Robertini, N., Casas, D., Richardt, C., Seidel, H.-P., Theobalt, C.: General automatic human shape and motion capture using volumetric contour cues. In: Leibe, B., Matas, J., Sebe, N., Welling, M. (eds.) ECCV 2016. LNCS, vol. 9909, pp. 509–526. Springer, Cham (2016). doi:10.1007/978-3-319-46454-1_31
28. Rogge, L., Klose, F., Stengel, M., Eisemann, M., Magnor, M.: Garment replacement in monocular video sequences. ACM Trans. Graph. **34**(1), 6:1–6:10 (2014)
29. Romero, J., Loper, M., Black, M.J.: FlowCap: 2D human pose from optical flow. In: Gall, J., Gehler, P., Leibe, B. (eds.) GCPR 2015. LNCS, vol. 9358, pp. 412–423. Springer, Cham (2015). doi:10.1007/978-3-319-24947-6_34
30. Sapp, B., Weiss, D., Taskar, B.: Parsing human motion with stretchable models. In: IEEE Conference on Computer Vision and Pattern Recognition, pp. 1281–1288. IEEE (2011)
31. Sigal, L., Balan, A., Black, M.J.: Combined discriminative and generative articulated pose and non-rigid shape estimation. In: Advances in Neural Information Processing Systems, pp. 1337–1344 (2007)
32. Sigal, L., Balan, A.O., Black, M.J.: HUMANEVA: synchronized video and motion capture dataset and baseline algorithm for evaluation of articulated human motion. Int. J. Comput. Vis. **87**(1–2), 4–27 (2010)
33. Simo-Serra, E., Ramisa, A., Aleny, G., Torras, C., Moreno-Noguer, F.: Single image 3D human pose estimation from noisy observations. In: Conference on Computer Vision and Pattern Recognition, pp. 2673–2680. IEEE (2012)
34. Vedula, S., Baker, S., Rander, P., Collins, R., Kanade, T.: Three-dimensional scene flow. In: IEEE International Conference on Computer Vision, vol. 2, pp. 722–729. IEEE (1999)
35. Wandt, B., Ackermann, H., Rosenhahn, B.: 3D human motion capture from monocular image sequences. In: IEEE Conference on Computer Vision and Pattern Recognition Workshops, June 2015
36. Wandt, B., Ackermann, H., Rosenhahn, B.: 3D reconstruction of human motion from monocular image sequences. Trans. Pattern Anal. Mach. Intell. **38**, 1505–1516 (2016)

37. Xu, L., Jia, J., Matsushita, Y.: Motion detail preserving optical flow estimation. IEEE Trans. Pattern Anal. Mach. Intell. **34**(9), 1744–1757 (2012)
38. Zhou, S., Fu, H., Liu, L., Cohen-Or, D., Han, X.: Parametric reshaping of human bodies in images. In: ACM Transactions on Graphics (TOG), vol. 29, p. 126. ACM (2010)
39. Zhou, X., Leonardos, S., Hu, X., Daniilidis, K.: 3D shape estimation from 2D landmarks: a convex relaxation approach. In: CVPR, pp. 4447–4455. IEEE Computer Society (2015)
40. Zhou, X., Zhu, M., Leonardos, S., Derpanis, K.G., Daniilidis, K.: Sparseness meets deepness: 3D human pose estimation from monocular video. In: Conference on Computer Vision and Pattern Recognition, June 2016
41. Zuffi, S., Romero, J., Schmid, C., Black, M.J.: Estimating human pose with flowing puppets. IEEE International Conference on Computer Vision, pp. 3312–3319 (2013)

On the Diffusion Process for Heart Rate Estimation from Face Videos Under Realistic Conditions

Christian S. Pilz[1]([✉]), Jarek Krajewski[2], and Vladimir Blazek[3]

[1] CanControls GmbH, Aachen, Germany
pilz@cancontrols.com
[2] Institute of Safety Technology, University of Wuppertal, Wuppertal, Germany
[3] Philips Chair for Medical Information Technology,
Helmholtz-Institute for Biomedical Engineering, RWTH Aachen University,
Aachen, Germany

Abstract. This work addresses the problem of estimating heart rate from face videos under real conditions using a model based on the recursive inference problem that leverages the local invariance of the heart rate. The proposed solution is based on the canonical state space representation of an Itō process and a Wiener velocity model. Empirical results yield to excellent real-time and estimation performance of heart rate in presence of disturbing factors, like rigid head motion, talking and facial expressions under natural illumination conditions making the process of heart rate estimation from face videos applicable in a much broader sense. To facilitate comparisons and to support research we made the code and data for reproducing the results public available.

1 Introduction

In general, the role of physiological states has a large impact on human state computing in computer vision, since it tells something about the affective nature of the human interacting with a machine or being monitored by optical sensors solely. During the last years, the task of measuring skin blood perfusion and heart rate measurements from facial images became part of top computer vision conferences [23,25,34,41]. Interestingly, all these contributions focus on how to cope with motion like head pose variations and facial expressions since any kind of motion on a specific skin region of interest will destroy the underlying blood perfusion signal in a way that no reliable information can be extracted anymore. Apart from being able to estimate vitality parameters like heart rate and respiration, monitoring functional survey of wounds as well as quantification of allergic skin reaction [4] are further topics of discovered employment scenarios of skin blood perfusion analysis. Recently, prediction of emotional states [28,36] and stress [6] became an interesting new achievement in this area, pushing the focus of this technology further towards human-machine interaction. The technical term of skin blood perfusion analysis by image sensors is known as Photoplethysmography Imaging, short PPGI. Although the PPGI measurement is accurate,

© Springer International Publishing AG 2017
V. Roth and T. Vetter (Eds.): GCPR 2017, LNCS 10496, pp. 361–373, 2017.
DOI: 10.1007/978-3-319-66709-6_29

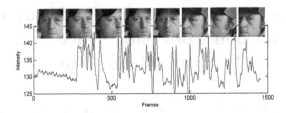

Fig. 1. The average green channel on a face region during rigid head motions. In the first 250 frames the user is in a resting state and the fine pulsation of blood volume is visible. After 300 frames the user started to move his head and the pulse signal gets lost. (Color figure online)

it is bound to specific environmental conditions in order to operate accurately yet. The most significant factors influencing the operational performance are the sensors spectral response, user movements like rigid head motions and facial expressions as well as fast varying illumination conditions. Figure 1 illustrates the disturbing influence of head motions on the raw PPGI blood volume pulse signal. During head motion the pixel intensity distribution varies significantly, much more than the expectation which can be attributed to blood pulsation. This problem can be solved by a feature invariant under local intensity variations larger than blood pulsation and a process model that leverages the local invariance of the heart rate. The main contributions of this work are

- a novel formulation for the problem of estimating heart rate using low-cost camera sensor technology, and
- a spatio-independent feature representation invariant under large varying pixel intensity distribution induced by facial motions.

Initially, from the historical genuine up to the development of the current state of the art in computer vision, the methodology of PPGI will be reviewed. Followed by theoretical aspects, the model will be described in detail. Based upon conducted empirical field data collection the results will be presented and finally discussed.

2   Related Work

The term Photoplethysmography, short PPG, dates back to the late first half of the 20th century, when Molitor and Kniazak [31] recorded peripheral circulatory changes in animals. One year later, Hertzman [16] introduced the term Photo-electric Plethysmograph as "the amplitude of volume pulse as a measure of the blood supply of the skin". Hertzman's instrumentation comprised mainly of a tungsten arc lamp and a photomultiplier tube. An advancement to the classical PPG is the camera based PPGI method introduced by the pioneering work of Blazek [5]. The basic principle behind the measurement of blood volume changes in the skin by means of PPG is the fact that hemoglobin in the blood absorbs specific frequency bands of light many times more strongly than the remaining skin tissues. Since the first published visualisation of pulsatile skin perfusion patterns in the time and frequency domain by Blazek [5], classical signal processing methods are applied commonly to extract reasonable information out of the perfusion signals [17,35,42]. Since it is realized that motion of the skin area of interest [17] and later micro motion of the head due to cardiac activity [3,29] inherently induces artifacts into the extracted signal, especially when lighting is neither uniform nor orthogonal, canceling motion artifacts during signal processing became an important aspect for reliable skin blood perfusion measurements [30]. From the basic early idea of compensating the motion of the skin area of interest by optical flow methods directly in the image plane [17], Poh *et al.* [35] regarded the problem solution for facial videos as a blind source separation task using Independent Component Analysis (ICA) over the different color channels, whereby Lewandowska *et al.* [24] compared ICA against Principal Component Analysis additionally. However, in case the underlying signal basis is majoritarian Gaussian, ICA will not be able to determine a proper de-mixing matrix [8]. This happens exactly when the skin blood perfusion signals contain harmonics beside their fundamental frequency. De Haan and Jeanne [14] and De Haan and Van Leest [15] proposed to map the PPGI-signals by linear combination of RGB data to a direction that is orthogonal to motion induced artifacts. A recent alternative, which does not require skin-tone or pulse-related priors in contrast to the channel mapping algorithms, determines the spatial subspace of skin-pixels and measure its temporal rotation for signal extraction [44]. Tulyakov *et al.* [41] proposed matrix completion to jointly estimate reliable regions and heart rate estimates whereby Li *et al.* [25] applied an adaptive least square approach to extract robust pulse frequencies. Both reported performance gains similar to De Haan and Jeanne [14]. Only Wang *et al.* [44] reports significantly more accurate results especially under head motion and talking.

3 Methodology

The underlying system of measuring heart rate from face regions using conventional camera technology is based upon a diffusion process. The entire process itself consists of independent single processes; the heart frequency, the illumination and the users head movement and facial motion. The periodic event of heart frequency appears in form of a stochastic resonator. The illumination as well as the head movement and facial motion is represented as a Wiener process [45], whereby a violation of the smoothness criterion yields to a generalized Poisson process [9]. The general solution of the corresponding stochastic differential equations is given by Itō's lemma [18]. If the resonator's fundamental frequency is known, the solution yields to a general time-discrete linear dynamic system [21]. However, in case the resonator's fundamental frequency is unknown, the problem is given as latent state of the frequency. This results in a Markov process, whereby the latent states are time-discrete linear dynamic systems. The closed form solution to this problem is described by Bloom and Bar-Shalom [7]. The advantage of this kind of formulation is that the case of non-uniform sampling as well as missing observations is naturally included in the model [20]. The basic idea of methodology is inspired by the work of Särrkä [37] and Särrkä *et al.* [38].

3.1   The Diffusion Process

In mathematics and physics any kind of process producing the same output from a given starting condition or initial state is called a deterministic system. This means in the development of future states of the system there's no randomness involved. Like physical laws they are described by differential equations. Unfortunately, in nature when studying biological systems this is often a rarely case. Here, this can be expressed as a sequence of random variables. The random variables which correspond to various times may be completely different. The only assumption is that these different quantities take values in the same space. In probability theory this phenomena is known as stochastic process. Recalling the ordinary differential equation [1] of the form

$$\frac{d\boldsymbol{x}(t)}{dt} = F\boldsymbol{x}(t) \tag{1}$$

Adding a noise term as function yields to a stochastic differential equation

$$\frac{d\boldsymbol{x}(t)}{dt} = F\boldsymbol{x}(t) + L\boldsymbol{w}(t) \tag{2}$$

where the Itô process [18] defines the solution to the equation.

The discrete-time approximation of a linear stochastic differential equation yields to [32,37]

$$\begin{aligned}
\boldsymbol{x}(t_i + 1) &= e^{\Delta t F} \boldsymbol{x}(t_i) \\
&+ \int_{t_i}^{t_{i+1}} e^{(t-s)F} L\boldsymbol{w}(s) ds,
\end{aligned} \tag{3}$$

with $\Delta t = t_{i+1} - t_i$, the Wiener process $w(t)$ with spectral density W and the covariance of the stochastic integral

$$Q_i = \int_0^{\Delta t} A_i L W L^T A_i^T d\tau, \tag{4}$$

with $A_i = e^{\Delta t F}$, which results to the discrete-time model [10,13,19,21,47]

$$\boldsymbol{x}(t_{i+1}) = A_i \boldsymbol{x}(t_i) + \boldsymbol{q}(t_i) \tag{5}$$

$$\boldsymbol{y}(t_i) = H_i \boldsymbol{x}(t_i) + \boldsymbol{e}(t_i) \tag{6}$$

with process noise

$$\boldsymbol{q}(t_i) = N(0, Q_i) \tag{7}$$

and measurement noise

$$\boldsymbol{e}(t_i) = N(0, \Sigma_i). \tag{8}$$

A_i and H_i corresponds to the state transition and the measurement model respectively. Although, the dynamic of the model is continuous, the measurements are at discrete time steps of a linear Gaussian process.

3.2 The Feature Space

Under natural conditions, illumination is not static as well as not uniform distributed over facial skin regions. The intensity distribution of skin pixels varies significantly when an user starts to move the head as illustrated in Fig. 1. Assuming that the image source S produces random variables X with an associated probability density function $p(x)$, a suitable feature representation for the skin blood perfusion, invariant with respect to the location and large magnitude differences of pixel intensities can be expressed as the average quantization error d of an uniform quantizer and an associated set of decision intervals $\{I_k\}_{k=1}^{M}$, such that $I_k = \{b_{k-1}, b_k)$ for $k = 1, 2, ..., M$, where b_{k-1} and b_k represent the upper and lower limits of the pixels values at each region. Each interval I_k is represented by a quantized value y_k, the mean value of the each region, which implements the mapping $x \in I_k \Rightarrow y = y_k$ [12,33]

$$D = \sum_{k=1}^{M} \int_{b_{k-1}}^{b_k} (x - y_k)p(x)\mathrm{d}x. \tag{9}$$

The quantizers amount of bits has to be chosen smaller than the bits used for the sensors capacitor discharge voltage being read as pixel intensity. Since the contribution of the perfusion signals magnitude inside each code word interval is assumed to be not equal, each average interval distortion is normalized by standard deviation

$$F = \sum_{k=1}^{M} \frac{\int_{b_{k-1}}^{b_k} (x - y_k)p(x)\mathrm{d}x}{\sqrt{\int_{d_k} (d_k - \mu_{d_k})^2 p(d_k)\mathrm{d}d_k}} \tag{10}$$

with

$$u_{d_k} = \int_{d_k} d_k p(d_k)\mathrm{d}d_k. \tag{11}$$

A strategy of normalizing the local intensities is given by a suitable surrounding potential. This can be either realized as the ratio of the green channel and the total amount of RGB information on a given pixel, $G/(R + G + B)$ or for any monochrome intensity by its neighboring values, for example using the Moore neighborhood. As general pre-processing step skin segmentation can be performed by thresholding the chroma components Cr and Cb in the YCrCB color space.

The described feature is a spatio-independent representation under the assumption of a phase synchronized perfusion phenomena, although in detail this is not the case [40].

3.3 The Periodicity

Any band-limited zero-mean periodic signal with stationary frequency f can be approximated to an arbitrary precision with a truncated Fourier series

$$c(t) = \sum_{n=1}^{N} a_n cos(2\pi nft) + b_n sin(2\pi nft) \tag{12}$$

with a_n and b_n the Fourier coefficients. The fundamental frequency f and the harmonic components with frequencies as multiples of their base, nf [22,46].

Physiological signals like the perfusion phenomena are not stationary and they are of quasi-periodic nature. The major source of non-stationary in the perfusion signal is caused by the varying fundamental frequency resulting in a function of time $f(t)$. Another source of aperiodicity of the signal are small changes in amplitudes and phases in the harmonics. This can be modeled by an additional white noise component $e_n(t)$ with spectral density q_n to each harmonic component

$$c(t) = \sum_{n=1}^{N} a_n cos(2\pi n f(t)t) \qquad (13)$$
$$+ b_n sin(2\pi n f(t)t) + e_n(t).$$

However, this representation is sensitive to changes in frequency. When t is large, any change in the frequency causes a large change in signal $c(t)$. Discontinuities in the frequency will also cause the signal $c(t)$ to be discontinuous.

Recalling the classical mechanics of circular motion, the system of a single harmonic oscillator yields to a 2nd order differential equations [11]

$$\frac{d^2 c_n(t)}{dt^2} = -(2\pi n f)^2 c_n(t) \qquad (14)$$

with the solution

$$c_n(t) = a_n cos(2\pi n f t) + b_n sin(2\pi n f t) \qquad (15)$$

where the constants a_n and b_n are set by the initial conditions of the differential equation. Accounting for non-stationary frequency as a function of time and changes in amplitude and phase leads to the differential equation

$$\frac{d^2 c_n(t)}{dt^2} = -(2\pi n f(t))^2 c_n(t) + e_n(t) \qquad (16)$$

for each harmonic component. The major advantage of such a stochastic representation of a resonator is, even when the frequency is discontinuous the signal remains continuous. Figure 2 shows a single stochastic oscillator with time-varying frequency and amplitude. The stochastic state space for the resonator signal yields to

$$\frac{dx(t)}{dt} = F_0(f(t))x(t) + Le(t), \qquad (17)$$

$$c(t) = Hx(t). \qquad (18)$$

Since the frequency is unknown, the state space depends on an additional latent variable

$$\frac{dx(t)}{dt} = F_0(\theta)x(t) + Le(t), \qquad (19)$$

$$c(t) = H(\theta)x(t). \qquad (20)$$

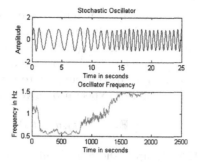

Fig. 2. A simulated trajectory of a stochastic oscillator with frequency trace in a range typical for a human in resting state.

such that

$$\theta \in \Omega = \{\theta^1, \dots, \theta^S\} \tag{21}$$

forming a Markov chain with transition matrix Π with transition probabilities

$$P(\theta_t^i | \theta_{t-1}^j) = \Pi_{ij}. \tag{22}$$

The solution is given by computing the Gaussian mixture approximation to the joint posterior distribution of the latent variables and states [7].

3.4   The Drift

Despite the underlying pure perfusion signal, remote sensing signals of human skin encapsulates further components which can be described as time varying bias and jumps. The bias function $x(t)$ is assumed to be smooth and slow varying and can be assigned to general changes of natural illumination conditions as well as slow head movements and facial motion. Since there's no further distinct knowledge about the drift process it is modeled as Wiener process

$$\frac{\mathrm{d}^2 x(t)}{\mathrm{d}t^2} = w(t), \tag{23}$$

where $w(t)$ corresponds to a white noise process with spectral density q_w and has continuous sample path [45]. However, sudden strong changes in illumination, fast head movements and facial motion causing discontinuities and therefore violating the smoothness criterion of the drift. This yields to a general Markov process that modulates the intensity function of an inhomogeneous Poisson counting process

$$X(t) = X_0 + \sum_{i:s_i \leq t} \xi_i \tag{24}$$

where $X(t)$ is a real-valued stochastic process and (s_i, ξ_i) are the events of a two dimensional Poisson process on $[0, T] \times \mathbb{R}$. The intensity of this process is given by $\lambda(s, y) = \lambda h(y)$, where $\lambda > 0$ describing how frequently the jumps of X occur and $h_\theta(y)$ is the jump density describing magnitudes of jumps ξ_i of process X. Here $\theta \in \Theta$ is an unknown parameter defining the distribution of jumps. The parameters θ and λ have a prior density $\pi(\theta, \lambda)$. As well the initial condition X_0 is assumed to have a prior density π_0. λ will have a time varying intensity $\lambda = \lambda(t)$. The Bayesian approach leads conveniently to the combined parameter and state estimation via the posterior expectation given the observation Y

$$\left(\widehat{X(t), \theta, \lambda(t)} \right) := \mathbb{E}_{\pi, \pi_0}[X(t), \theta, \lambda(t)|Y_1, ...Y_k] \tag{25}$$

for $\tau k \le t < \tau(k+1)$ [27]. Figure 3 shows a simulated trajectory of a Wiener process and its realization modulated by a Poisson process.

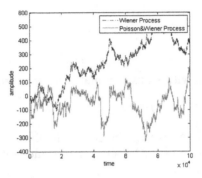

Fig. 3. A simulated trajectory of a Wiener process and its realization modulated by a Poisson process with $\lambda = 1.95$ and $\theta = 35$.

4   Experiments

In order to evaluate the proposed model, empirical data is collected under natural environmental conditions with a typical 24 bit low-cost webcam, a Logitech HD C270, as well as reference ground truth measurements using a common finger pulseoximeter, a CMS50E PPG device. 25 users were asked to perform video recordings in two sessions resulting in a total amount of 50 videos. The first session is selected to be even-tempered without any kind of larger head or body movements and facial expressions. During the second session, participants were free to move their head naturally while remaining seated. Typical movements included tilting the head sideways, nodding the head, looking up/down and leaning forward/backward. Some participants also made facial expressions, or started to talk. The recording illumination environment was chosen as daylight office scenario without any additional lighting. The duration of each session is approximately one minute. The frame rate was fixed to 15 fps in average and the corresponding time stamps for each frame were captured too. The finger pulseoximeter data for each session and participant was stored for later comparison. Bland-Altman [2] and correlation plots were used for combined graphical and statistical interpretation of the two measurement techniques. For every

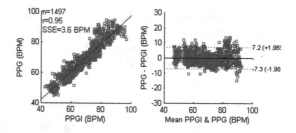

Fig. 4. Correlation and Bland-Altman [2] plots of PPGI diffusion process estimated heart rate against CMS50E PPG finger-pulseoximeter reference of 25 users in resting state.

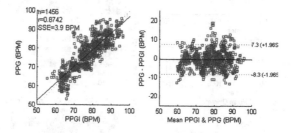

Fig. 5. Correlation and Bland-Altman [2] plots of PPGI diffusion process estimated heart rate against CMS50E PPG finger-pulseoximeter reference of 25 users performing head rotations.

video recording a standard Viola-Jones [43] face finder was used to determine the analysis region of interest. The extracted feature, 6 bit quantized green channel, was feed into the vector valued representation of the diffusion process on a frame by frame basis. On every estimated pulse trace a spectral peak is determined by the Lomb periodogram [26,39]. The frame duration was set to 10 s with an overlap of 90%. The correlation and Bland-Altman plots for the resting and head motion condition are reported in the following Figs. 4 and 5 respectively.

To obtain further insides about the potential strength of the diffusion process model, the approach is compared against the recently published Spatial Subspace Rotation (SSR) [44] and the baseline ICA approach [35][1]. Figure 6 compares an users estimated pulse signal under rigid head motions and the corresponding spectrogram for the three methods. The hear rate frequency for the ICA methods nearly gets lost completely. For the SSR method the frequency trace of heart rate is better visible but cannot compete against the diffusion process model where the heart rate is very clear over the entire sequence of head movements. Interestingly, the heart rate gets slightly increased during the head rotation phases. The detailed correlation coefficients and squared errors of prediction for all approaches are provided for the two data sessions in Table 1. The primary

---

[1] We also reimplemented other methods [14,25,41], since their code is not available. Unfortunately, we obtained worse results.

signal processing and frequency estimation is the same used during the diffusion process experiments. ICA performs worst and is not able to provide reliable heart rate information during head motion. Although SSR performs better it cannot compete against the robustness of the diffusion process.

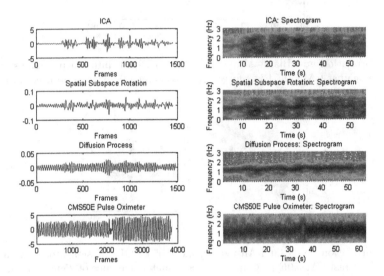

Fig. 6. Comparison of an users estimated blood volume pulse signal. Under rigid head motions and the corresponding spectrogram for the ICA [35], the SSR [44], the diffusion process model and the reference finger pulseoximeter. These estimates are based upon the video illustrated in Fig. 1.

Table 1. Pearson's correlation coefficient and squared errors of prediction of ICA [35], the SSR [44] and the diffusion process (DP).

Type	ICA	SSR	DP
Resting	0.61/7.8	0.78/4.8	0.95/3.6
Head rotation	0.21/14.6	0.47/7.6	0.87/3.9

5   Conclusions

In this work, we have derived a holistic signal interpretation of heart rate estimation from face videos under realistic conditions. The closed form solution of the corresponding stochastic differential equations yields to a diffusion process where the exact estimate of the source separated heart rate signal is obtained via the posterior distribution of the process. The recursive nature of the underlying Bayesian inference scales the processing to a very fast approach. Further, we considered a spatio independent intensity feature. We compared the model against two approaches on face videos under resting as well as head and facial motion scenarios under natural illumination conditions. Measurements on a 25 user experiment showed clearly superior robustness of the diffusion process modelling, although the uncertainty of prediction still gets slightly increased during natural head motion. We conclude that an entirely invariant process model still depends on a more robust feature representation.

References

1. Arnold, I.: Ordinary Differential Equations. MIT Press, Cambridge (1973)
2. Bland, J., Altman, D.: Statistical methods for assessing agreement between two methods of clinical measurement. Lancet **327**(8476), 307–310 (1986)
3. Blanik, N., Blazek, C., Pereira, C., Blazek, V., Leonhardt, S.: Wearable photoplethysmographic sensors: past and present. In: Proceedings of the SPIE 9034, Medical Imaging: Image Processing (2014)
4. Blazek, C., Hülsbusch, M.: Assessment of allergic skin reactions and their hemodynamical quantification using photoplethysmography imaging. In: Proceedings of 11th International Symposium CNVD, Computer-Aided Noninvasive Vascular Diagnostics, vol. 3, 85–90 (2005)
5. Blazek, V.: Optoelektronische Erfassung und rechnerunterstützte Analyse der Mikrozirkulations-Rhythmik. Biomed. Techn. **30**(1), 121–122 (1985)
6. Blazek, V., Blanik, N., Blazek, C., Paul, M., Pereira, C., Koeny, M., Venema, B., Leonhardt, S.: Active and passive optical imaging modality for unobtrusive cardiorespiratory monitoring and facial expressions assessment. Assessment. Anesth Analg. **124**, 104–119 (2017)
7. Bloom, H., Bar-Shalom, Y.: The interacting multiple model algorithm for systems with markovian switching coefficients. IEEE Trans. Autom. Control **33**(8), 780–783 (1988)
8. Cardoso, J.: High-order contrasts for independent component analysis. Neural Comput. **11**(1), 157–192 (1999)
9. Cox, D.: Some statistical methods connected with series of events. J. Roy. Stat. Soc. **17**(2), 129–164 (1950)
10. Durbin, J., Koopman, S.: Time Series Analysis by State Space Methods. Oxford University Press, Oxford (2001)
11. Feynman, R., Leighton, R., Sands, M.: The Feynman Lectures on Physics, vol. 1. Addison-Wesley, Boston (1963). Chap. 21
12. Gray, R., Neuhoff, D.: Quantization. IEEE Trans. Inf. Theory **44**(6), 2325–2383 (1998)
13. Grewal, M., Andrews, A.: Kalman Filtering Theory and Practice Using Matlab. Wiley Interscience, Hoboken (2001)
14. de Haan, G., Jeanne, V.: Robust pulse-rate from chrominance-based rppg. IEEE Trans. Biomed. Eng. **60**(10), 2878–2886 (2014)
15. de Haan, G., van Leest, A.: Improved motion robustness of remote-ppg by using the blood volume pulse signature. Physiol. Meas. **3**(9), 1913–1926 (2014)
16. Hertzman, A.: Photoelectric plethysmography of the fingers and toes in man. Exp. Biol. Med. **37**(3), 529–534 (1937)
17. Hülsbusch, M.: A functional imaging technique for opto-electronic assessment of skin perfusion. Ph.D. thesis, RWTH Aachen University (2008)

18. Itô, K.: On Stochastic Differential Equations, vol. 4. Memoris of The American Mathematical Society (1951)
19. Jazwinski, A.: Stochastic Processes and Filtering Theory. Academic Press, New York (1970)
20. Jones, R.H.: Fitting multivariate models to unequally spaced data. In: Parzen, E. (ed.) Time Series Analysis of Irregularly Observed Data. LNS, vol. 25, pp. 158–188. Springer, New York (1984). doi:10.1007/978-1-4684-9403-7_8
21. Kalman, R., Bucy, R.: New results in linear filtering and prediction theory. Trans. ASME-J. Basic Eng. **83**, 95–108 (1961)
22. Khintchine, A.: Korrelationstheorie der stationären stochastischen Prozesse. Springer-Mathematische Annalen **109**, 604–615 (1934)
23. Lam, A., Kuno, Y.: Robust heart rate measurement from video using select random patches. In: IEEE International Conference on Computer Vision, pp. 3640–3648 (2015)
24. Lewandowska, M., Ruminski, J., Kocejko, T., Nowak, J.: Measuring pulse rate with a webcam - a non-contact method for evaluating cardiac activity. In: Proceedings of the FedCSIS, Szczecin, Poland, pp. 405–410 (2011)
25. Li, X., Chen, J., Zhao, G., Pietikinen, M.: Remote heart rate measurement from face videos under realistic situations. In: IEEE Conference on Computer Vision and Pattern Recognition, Columbus, OH (2014)
26. Lomb, N.: Least-squares frequency analysis of unequally spaced data. Astrophys. Space Sci. **39**(2), 447–462 (1976)
27. Makhnin, O.: Filtering for some stochastic processes with discrete observations. Ph.D. thesis, Department of Statistics and Probability, Michigan State University (2002)
28. McDuff, D., Gontarek, S., Picard, R.: Remote measurement of cognitive stress via heart rate variability. In: 36th Annual International Conference of the IEEE Engineering in Medicine and Biology Society, pp. 2957–2960 (2014)
29. Moço, A., Stuijk, S., de Haan, G.: Ballistocardiographic artifacts in PPG imaging. IEEE Trans. Biomed. Eng. **63**(9), 1804–1811 (2015)
30. Moço, A., Stuijk, S., de Haan, G.: Motion robust PPG-imaging through color channel mapping. Biomed. Opt. Express **7**, 1737–1754 (2016)
31. Molitor, H., Knaizuk, M.: A new bloodless method for continuous recording of peripheral change. J. Pharmacol. Exp. Theret. **27**, 5–16 (1936)
32. Øksendal, B.: Stochastic Differential Equations. Springer, Heidelberg (2003)
33. Oliver, B., Pierce, J., Shannon, C.: The philosophy of PCM. Proc. IRE **36**, 1324–1331 (1948)
34. Osman, A., Turcot, J., Kaliouby, R.E.: Supervised learning approach to remote heart rate estimation from facial videos. In: 11th IEEE International Conference and Workshops on Automatic Face and Gesture Recognition, pp. 1–6 (2015)
35. Poh, M., McDuff, J., Picard, R.: Non-contact, automated cardiac pulse measurements using video imaging and blind source separation. Opt. Express **18**(10), 10762–10774 (2010)
36. Ramirez, G., Fuentes, O., Crites, S., Jimenez, M., Ordonez, J.: Color analysis of facial skin: detection of emotional state. In: IEEE Conference on Computer Vision and Pattern Recognition Workshops, pp. 474–479 (2014)
37. Särkkä, S.: Recursive Bayesian inference on stochastic differential equations. Ph.D. thesis, Helsinki University of Technology (2006)
38. Särkkä, S., Solin, A., Nummenmaa, A., Vehtari, T., Vanni, F.L.: Dynamic retrospective filtering of physiological noise in BOLD fMRI. NeuroImage **60**(2), 1517–1527 (2012)

39. Scargle, J.: Studies in astronomical time series analysis. II - statistical aspects of spectral analysis of unevenly spaced data. Astrophys. J. **263**(1), 835–853 (1982)

40. Teplov, V.: Blood pulsation imaging. Ph.D. thesis, Department of Applied Physics, University of Eastern Finland (2014)

41. Tulyakov, S., Pineda, X.A., Ricci, E., Yin, L., Cohn, J., Sebe, N.: Self-adaptive matrix completion for heart rate estimation from face videos under realistic conditions. In: Computer Vision and Pattern Recognition (2016)

42. Verkruysse, W., Svaasand, L., Nelson, J.: Remote plethysmographic imaging using ambient light. Opt. Express **16**(26), 21434–21445 (2008)

43. Viola, P., Jones, M.: Robust real-time object detection. Int. J. Comput. Vis. **57**, 137–154 (2001)

44. Wang, W., Stuijk, S., de Haan, G.: A novel algorithm for remote photoplethysmography: spatial subspace rotation. IEEE Trans. Biomed. Eng. **63**(9), 1974–1984 (2015)

45. Wiener, N.: The average of an analytical functional and the brownian movement. Proc. Nat. Acad. Sci. USA **7**(1), 294–298 (1921)

46. Wiener, N.: Generalized harmonic analysis. Acta Mathematica **55**, 117–258 (1930)

47. Zakai, M.: On the optimal filtering of diffusion processes. Zeitschrift für Wahrscheinlichkeitstheorie und Verwandte Gebiete **11**(3), 230–243 (1969)

Reconstruction and Depth

Multi-view Continuous Structured Light Scanning

Fabian Groh[✉], Benjamin Resch, and Hendrik P.A. Lensch

University of Tübingen, Tübingen, Germany
`fabian.groh@uni-tuebingen.de`

Abstract. We introduce a highly accurate and precise multi-view, multi-projector, and multi-pattern phase scanning method for shape acquisition that is able to handle occlusions and optically challenging materials. The 3D reconstruction is formulated as a two-step process which first estimates reliable measurement samples and then simultaneously optimizes over all cameras, projectors, and patterns. This holistic approach results in significant quality improvements. Furthermore, the acquisition time is drastically reduced by relying on just six high-frequency sinusoidal captures without the need of phase unwrapping, which is implicitly provided by the multi-view geometry.

1 Introduction

In order to capture a complete model and to provide a good coverage of the visible surface area of any real-world object, a multi-view approach is necessary. In particular, these multi-view recordings are relevant in the context of object recognition, industrial inspection and material acquisition where also the illumination is varied. In all applications, it is beneficial to acquire a detailed geometry model to establish precise correspondences between the different views. In this paper, we propose an active multi-view, multi-projector shape acquisition system.

Multi-view acquisition systems typically consist of multiple cameras that are either distributed at fixed positions [21], or are movable [1] around an object, or get extended with projectors to perform active structured light (SL) scanning alongside reflection measurements [24]. While our proposed method is developed to be used inside such an illumination system for material acquisition, it purely focuses on achieving high-quality active SL geometry reconstruction in the general case of multiple viewpoints. In this case, each projector-pattern produces a continuous SL signal that is captured by every camera as a two-dimensional projection. The main idea is that a surface point is located exactly where all SL signals from different viewpoints align, provided that the surface is visible from the respective camera-projector pair and the signal is not corrupted by material properties like specular- or inter-reflections.

To surpass the projector resolution, which is the most limiting factor of SL scanning, continuous coding methods [20] are suggested. We use traditional phase

© Springer International Publishing AG 2017
V. Roth and T. Vetter (Eds.): GCPR 2017, LNCS 10496, pp. 377–388, 2017.
DOI: 10.1007/978-3-319-66709-6_30

shifting methods (PS), where phases are recovered from projecting at least three shifted sinusoidal patterns [23]. Phase shifting methods have been proven to deliver high-quality results with sub-pixel accuracy, even in optically difficult areas [5,6,14,17]. We fully integrate phase shifting into our multi-view reconstruction pipeline with two benefits. The multi-view approach further improves the accuracy, and we can eliminate the need for explicit phase unwrapping by a multi-view consistency validation. Thus, our method just needs to capture the highest frequency patterns. Real world objects are often composed out of different materials with varying illumination profiles, which make it necessary to capture the phase shifting patterns in high dynamic range (HDR) sequences to achieve precise results in all areas.

Since our optimization requires correct camera and projector poses, a very accurate calibration is required. We perform a precise online bundle adjustment (BA) on actively marked corresponding points. Therefore, we propose to combine the HDR phase shifting results with a fast LDR projector pixel identification scheme to get highly accurate sub-pixel correspondences for a structure from motion reconstruction.

The presented results feature a geometry accuracy far beyond the pixel resolution of both the involved cameras and projectors.

2   Related Work

3D Reconstruction: Three-dimensional shape estimation from real world objects is still a very challenging task and an active field of research. In general, methods can be classified into two major categories: namely passive and active. In passive approaches, the scene is just captured from at least two viewpoints. The most prominent representatives are multi-view stereo systems. However, most of these techniques depend heavily on finding good salient point correspondences between the views. Thus, they have problems in optically challenging and textureless areas that often results in sparse reconstructions. A comparison and evaluation can be found in [22].

Active techniques overcome this issue by establishing correspondences between camera and projector pixels for each scene point with active illumination patterns. Besides laser scanning [4], projector-based structured light pattern are a well-studied technique [7,20]. The projected patterns establish correspondences on the object, in the way that every point has a corresponding code-word, which can be recovered by analyzing the differences in the captured images with the projected patterns. Salvi et al. [20] compare state of the art structured light patterns.

Structured light scanning in the appearance of global illumination, interreflections or challenging materials, e.g. specular reflections, can still be an issue. High frequency patterns can cope with that kind of problems [5,6,17]. Gupta et al. [14] propose to combine different Gray code patterns logically in an ensemble. This method achieves remarkable results. Nevertheless, the used patterns just provide a discrete coding, and in consequence are not able to surpass the projector resolution on their own. Hence, they applied the same technique to a phase shifting method as Micro PS [15].

In traditional approaches, structured light patterns need to be temporally unwrapped by projecting coarse-to-fine patterns consecutively to get a unique correspondence for each point. The disadvantage is the number of additional patterns that are dependent on the projector resolution. In the context of phase shifting methods, this is referred to as phase unwrapping [20], where each frequency band needs to be captured by at least three shifts. Multiple methods are addressing this issue by reducing the amount of necessary patterns [20], e.g. Embedded PS [16], and Micro PS [15]. Our approach replaces phase-unwrapping by exploiting the multi-view setup.

Multi-view Structured Light Scanning: For the purpose of phase unwrapping in a stereo camera plus projector system, Garcia and Zakhor [11] present a method that performs a correspondence labeling in the projector domain via loopy belief propagation. Afterwards, missing absolute phases are estimated in the camera domain from neighboring pixels.

Binary structured light scanning from uncalibrated viewpoints has been proposed by several approaches: with a laser pointer [8], for multiple viewpoints [9,13], and for multiple projectors in a one-shot setting [10]. In a setting with multiple cameras Young et al. [25] suggest using viewpoint-coded structured light to mimic the temporal encoding. In recent years, using multiple cameras and multiple projectors to capture geometry alongside photometric data in self-calibrating systems has been demonstrated by the work of Aliaga et al. [2,3] and Weinmann et al. [24]. Aliaga et al. utilize the projectors as additional virtual cameras. While this is beneficial in settings with few cameras, it makes their approach even more dependent on the projector resolution. For a denser surface, they perform an up-sampling scheme by warping the photometric captures onto the geometrical model [2,3]. Weinmann et al. [24] suggest utilizing overlapping areas of the projected binary codes from multiple projectors to overcome low projector resolutions. The final resolution of the surface area is directly dependent on the overlapping alignment of the projector pixel on the scene.

In contrast, our method utilizes traditional single phase shifting to achieve continuous signals in the scene [23]. Thus, it is possible to optimize directly on the continuous signals from multiple camera-projector pairs to estimate the surface. Further, we introduce a novel multi-view consistency validation that substitutes phase unwrapping, relies solely on high-frequencies patterns at no additional cost, and reliably handles occlusions. All calculations can be done for each 3D point separately without neighboring information. Additionally, we propose to enhance active sparse bundle adjustment with the continuous signal for better multi-view precision.

3   Multi-view Depth Optimization

Our reconstruction pipeline makes use of phase shifting patterns for two steps: Once, to establish active correspondence to perform a highly accurate bundle

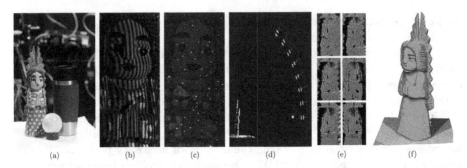

Fig. 1. For objects (a) with optically challenging properties, shifted sinusoidal patterns (b) are captured from multiple cameras and projectors. On top of the phase information, highly accurate features (c) are generated to perform a precise bundle adjustment (d). With the multi-view continuous phase signals (e) the reliable camera-projector pairs for every surface point are estimated by validating multi-view consistency (f). Finally, we optimize the depth over all available information.

adjustment to estimate the camera and projector locations, and, second, for optimizing the 3D geometry.

For the actual depth estimation, at first, a viewpoint consistency validation is completed by coarsely sampling potential depth values. This step performs an explicit multi-view phase unwrapping by utilizing geometrical constraints. The step identifies for each pixel which camera-projector pairs provide valid samples. Subsequently, all points are further optimized solely on the reliable phase signal to achieve highly precise and accurate depth information. Figure 1 shows examples of the specific steps.

3.1   Multi-view HDR Continuous SL Calibration

This section describes our combination of the HDR phase scanning with an active sparse bundle adjustment (SBA). Initially, we calculate the phase responses for a horizontal and vertical projector pattern direction. Afterwards, sub-pixel accurate feature points are generated by utilizing phase responses. These precisely positioned feature points establish exact correspondences between all cameras and all projectors suitable for a high-precision SBA.

We perform this calibration online during the capturing process to estimate all extrinsic and also intrinsic parameters for a moving camera setup. In a fixed system the same calibration could also be performed as a pre-processing step.

HDR Phase Scanning: We use traditional phase shifting [5,20] for the x and y directions of the projectors respectively. Given a linearized projector, a set of N shifted sine patterns $L_{n,x}$ in direction x, period T is generated:

$$L_{n,x}(x,y) = 0.5\,\cos\left(x\,\omega + \theta_n\right) + 0.5, \tag{1}$$

with $\omega = 1/T$ and $\theta_n = n2\pi/N$.

Once successively projected and captured by the camera the phase vector $u = [o, c, s]$ (offset, cosine, sine) can be recovered for a single frequency given the captured intensity responses $r = [r_0, r_1, \ldots, r_n]$ (see [16]):

$$u = \operatorname*{argmin}_u \|r - Au\|_2, \quad \text{with } A := \begin{bmatrix} 1 & \cos(\theta_0) & -\sin(\theta_0) \\ 1 & \cos(\theta_1) & -\sin(\theta_1) \\ \vdots & \vdots & \vdots \\ 1 & \cos(\theta_n) & -\sin(\theta_n) \end{bmatrix}. \qquad (2)$$

The phase ϕ is obtained by $\phi = \tan^{-1}(s/c)$.

Since our goal is to recover the shape of objects with optically challenging materials, the acquisition with a HDR sequence is essential, for which we use the algorithm provided by Granados et al. [12].

Representing Phase Information: All phase differences and interpolations in this work are computed on the respective sine and cosine part, not on the angle. Consequently, for two phase responses a and b, we represent the norm as:

$$\|a - b\|_\Phi := \sqrt{(\cos(a) - \cos(b))^2 + (\sin(a) - \sin(b))^2}, \qquad (3)$$

and for linear interpolation:

$$lerp(a, b; \lambda)_\Phi := \begin{bmatrix} (1 - \lambda) * \cos(a) + \lambda \cdot \cos(b) \\ (1 - \lambda) * \sin(a) + \lambda \cdot \sin(b) \end{bmatrix}. \qquad (4)$$

While this approximation introduces errors on larger intervals, on small scale they perform close to the optimum. This is sufficient, since higher differences are thresholded and interpolation is most likely performed on very small scale. Especially on GPUs, this not only avoids unnecessary branching when dealing with phase values, but also enables the utilization of the texture hardware.

Active Sparse Bundle Adjustment: After capturing the phases patterns for each viewpoint, a sparse set of randomly sampled projector pixels are projected temporally onto the scene using a binary encoding to enumerate these pixels. This is very robust and done in LDR with high gain to be much faster than a single capture of a HDR sequence.

For the selected projector pixels the analytic phase is known. An initial camera pixel position for these feature points is obtained as the center of mass of the detected spots. Afterwards the sub-pixel location is refined by the Nelder-Mead procedure [18] to match the analytically given phase to the measured phase in the camera image. This optimization procedure yields very accurate correspondences and subsequently more precise results in the SBA. For the SBA we use the work from [19].

3.2   Multi-view Depth Optimization

The general concept of our shape reconstruction is to recover the depth of a surface point by a multi-view optimization, i.e. combining the information of all

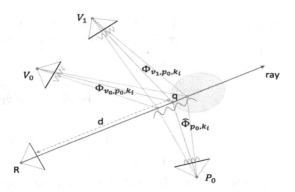

Fig. 2. General concept: points along a ray are projected into all view-projector pairs. Each point is evaluated based on the phase differences between the obtained and the expected phase values for all patterns.

cameras, projectors and patterns. Tracing a ray into the scene from an arbitrarily chosen reference camera system R, we are able to project any point q of depth d along the ray into all camera-views V and projectors P to get the respective phase responses $\Phi_{v,p,k}$ as well as the expected projector phases $\hat{\Phi}_{p,k}$ for all patterns K. This procedure is illustrated in Fig. 2. For an actual surface point the phase differences $\|\Phi_{v,p,k}(d) - \hat{\Phi}_{p,k}(d)\|_{\Phi}$ are required to be minimal. However, we need to ensure to only operate on correct phase signals, since occlusion and optical properties could induce corrupted phase information. Hence, the depth reconstruction can be formulated as an optimization problem over all views, projectors and patterns:

$$d = \operatorname*{argmin}_{d} \sum_{p \in P} \sum_{v \in V} \sum_{k \in K} \Omega_{v,p,k}(d) \, \|\Phi_{v,p,k}(d) - \hat{\Phi}_{p,k}(d)\|_{\Phi}, \tag{5}$$

where $\Omega_{v,p,k}(d)$ is our multi-view consistency validation that evaluates to 1 if the phase information is estimated to be reliable and 0 otherwise.

Multi-view Consistency Validation: This step identifies which phase responses are reliable. For that reason, correct phase responses need to be distinguished from false positives. These wrongly predicted phase signals occur very often in a system that only relies on high frequency patterns. On the other side, phase responses can also be truly wrong or corrupted by optical influences such as inter-reflections (false negatives). As neither of those signals should be used for the optimization, it is necessary to keep track of such events to not falsely exclude cameras or projectors.

We utilize the geometrical setup to perform a consistency check. The acceptance measure of a single pattern is defined as:

$$\hat{\Omega}_{v,p,k}(d) := \begin{cases} 1, & \text{if } \|\Phi_{v,p,k}(d) - \hat{\Phi}_{p,k}(d)\|_{\Phi} < \theta \\ 0, & \text{otherwise} \end{cases}, \tag{6}$$

where θ is the allowed threshold difference for a phase value to still be acceptable.

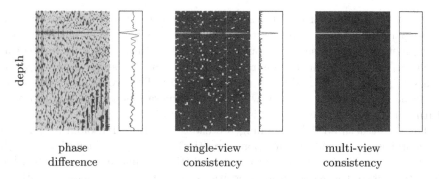

depth

| phase | single-view | multi-view |
| difference | consistency | consistency |

Fig. 3. Evaluation for an example point along a ray (depth) with the error/consistency for all camera-projector-pattern phase signals (horizontal) and the sum of each depth. Our multi-view consistency scheme is able to determine the contributing camera-projector pairs reliably and eliminates all false candidates.

Further, for the correct depth all patterns from the same view-projector pair need to be consistent as well: $\hat{\Omega}_{v,p,k_0}(d) \wedge \cdots \wedge \hat{\Omega}_{v,p,k_{K-1}}(d)$ (single-view consistency).

Finally, we consider the fact that for any point in the scene it is not possible to have disjunctive subsets of valid view-projector pairs: If a projector is valid in one view it cannot be occluded in the other views; and vice versa. If a view is able to receive the signal from one projector this view cannot be occluded for the other projectors. Firstly, the contributing projectors are determined by evaluating the overlap of valid views. Subsequently, a view is accepted if it is valid for at least half of the contributing projectors. In that way, we allow for some optical disturbances. Nonetheless, corrupted phase responses are still excluded from the final optimization. The validation for a single point at different depth is demonstrated in Fig. 3.

Coarse Approximation and Multi-view-Based Phase Unwrapping: For the purpose of finding points close to a surface, the number of consistent phases correlates to a good alignment. Thus, performing multi-view consistency validation along the depth substitutes phase unwrapping.

With relaxing the consistency threshold θ, it is possible to coarsely sample the depth along the ray to approximate a good initial alignment.

Fine Depth Estimation: Our fine depth estimation takes the result of the coarse approximation as seed and performs a simple binary search on Eq. 5. We compute the variance σ of the phase differences for the final depth as an additional measure of fitness.

4   Experimental Hardware Setup

All experiments in this paper have been captured in a light stage setting, with two Point Grey Grasshopper3 (GS3-U3-120S6C-C) 12 MP cameras and three View-sonic Pro9000 1080p LED projectors. The two cameras are moved along an arc at about 1 m distance around the scene to different positions. They are treated as independent cameras in our system. The projectors have to be placed outside the light stage. Otherwise, they would occlude lightpaths for the reflectance measurement. Thus, their distance is roughly 1.40 m, and the scene is only covered by a subset of the projected area for each projector. The projector resolution on the scene is only about 500 μm, whereas the camera has a resolution of about 80 μm on the object. The setting is shown in Fig. 5.

For the structured light scanning, we use two shifted sinusoidal patterns in horizontal as well as vertical direction respectively with a period length of 8 pixels and three shifts. Hence, we need to capture 6 HDR sequences per projector. We chose to capture the scenes from 8 positions along the two-camera-arc with an angle of about 10° apart (vertical) and with the three projectors to the side (horizontal). Altogether, we optimize on 48 camera-projector pairs with two patterns each which result in 96 phases signals. For the demonstration of the results, we always choose the lowest camera viewpoint as the reference view. The global threshold for acceptable points is 8 camera-projector pairs and only phase differences below $\theta = \pi/6$ are considered acceptable. The coarse estimation is calculated in 100 μm steps.

Since all work is done on a per point basis, the problem is highly parallelizable. The optimization is carried out on the GPU requiring just a few seconds of computation time for a whole scene.

5   Results

In this section, we demonstrate our results on three objects that are shown in Fig. 5. The angel is carved out of wood and painted in different colors. The small gold plates are a specular alloy. The mug consists of a plastic top and a rubber middle part with embossed details. In between and at the ground it consists of brushed metal. The ball is a good target since it features specular reflection as well as subsurface scattering; Furthermore, the diameter is known for ground truth evaluation.

Firstly, we demonstrate that our coarse depth estimation finds correct regions and respective visibilities. The colored point clouds are shown in Fig. 4. Bright green areas display that all camera-projector pairs are reliable, whereas the darker regions indicate a drop of supported pairs. Keep in mind that the color does not signal a change in the geometry. Most of the differences are due to occlusion of different projectors, or cameras (blue). The small, isolated areas on the ball as well as on the body of the angel are due to highly specular reflections in some of the camera-projector patterns (red). At the lower mirroring part of the mug, we have inter-reflection with the ground. Nonetheless, most of the shape up front and on the ground is recovered at high precision. Especially on the ground of the mug, many phase signals are dropped due to inconsistency introduced by the interreflections. This shape would definitely benefit from a more azimuthal camera setting. There are also some inaccuracies in the very dark top area due to high gain used to accelerate the capturing.

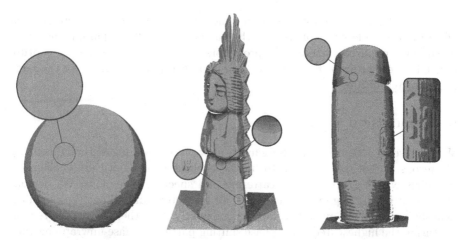

Fig. 4. Pointclouds of the estimated depth with respect to a reference camera. The color encodes the number of contributing camera-projector pairs: green (all) to purple (few). Changes are due to excluding unreliable phase information. Examples are given for specular reflections (red) and occlusions (blue). (Color figure online)

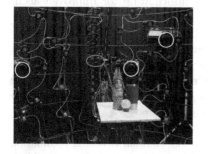

Fig. 5. The test objects in our ex-perimental hardware setup. (Blue: cameras on the arc. Red: projectors) (Color figure online)

Table 1. Results of the cue ball evaluation (RMSE values in μm).

σ^2	Cam/Proj-Pairs			
	8	15	30	45
$\pi/12$	25.2	22.1	18.0	15.0
$\pi/18$	24.9	21.9	17.7	15.0
$\pi/24$	21.9	20.3	17.2	14.9
$\pi/36$	16.1	15.2	14.1	13.9

For the evaluation of our fine optimization step, we follow the work of Weinmann et al. [24]. The reconstructed point cloud of the cue ball is mapped against a sphere and normalized with respect to the specified diameter of 6.02 cm. We need to stress that we do not perform any removal of outliers, except defining an ROI to crop out the mounting device of the ball. We vary the set of used points dependent on the number of at least visible camera-projector pairs and accepted variance in the result of the fine optimization step. The numbers are reported in Table 1 as RMSE values in μm. These numbers indicate that the number of pairs is an important factor for achieving high accuracy.

Comparing the numbers with Weinmann et al., they achieved an RMSE of 23.3 μm with 51 cameras and 10 projectors. We achieve an RMSE error of down to 13.9 μm for the points visible from almost all cameras and projectors. Even when we include less reliable points, the numbers are still comparable, but with much fewer required cameras and projectors. Furthermore, we need to capture only 6 images per projector, whereas their approach would be on 44 for the same projector resolution.

6   Conclusion

We propose an accurate and precise multi-view phase scanning method for robust 3D reconstruction that is able to handle occlusions and optically challenging materials with e.g. subsurface scattering and specular reflections. We demonstrate that optimizing over all cameras, all projectors and all patterns simultaneously improves the overall accuracy significantly. Nonetheless, we only rely on capturing the highest frequency phase shifting patterns. Phase unwrapping with lower frequencies is substituted by a multi-view consistency validation. The final optimization considers the phase of all available SL responses which have been judged to be reliable. The quality of the reconstructed results clearly depends on the number of reliable camera-projector pairs, which strongly indicates that the method fully exploits the available multi-view information for improved accuracy.

While we demonstrate that our combined multi-view and multi-projector approach is able to cope with subsurface scattering and specular reflections, areas of very strong inter-reflections that affect almost all projectors still pose a challenge. The proposed framework is easily extendable with other continuous structured light patterns or even a mixture of different patterns for potentially more reliable detection of correct camera-projector pairs.

Acknowledgement. This work was supported by the German Research Foundation (DFG): SFB 1233, Robust Vision: Inference Principles and Neural Mechanisms, TP 2.

References

1. Ajdin, B., Finckh, M., Fuchs, C., Hanika, J., Lensch, H.: Compressive higher-order sparse and low-rank acquisition with a hyperspectral light stage. Citeseer (2012)
2. Aliaga, D.G., Xu, Y.: Photogeometric structured light: a self-calibrating and multi-viewpoint framework for accurate 3D modeling. In: IEEE Conference on Computer Vision and Pattern Recognition, CVPR 2008, pp. 1–8. IEEE (2008)
3. Aliaga, D.G., Xu, Y.: A self-calibrating method for photogeometric acquisition of 3d objects. IEEE Trans. Pattern Anal. Mach. Intell. **32**(4), 747–754 (2010)
4. Blais, F.: Review of 20 years of range sensor development. J. Electron. Imaging **13**(1), 231–243 (2004)
5. Chen, T., Lensch, H.P., Fuchs, C., Seidel, H.P.: Polarization and phase-shifting for 3D scanning of translucent objects. In: 2007 IEEE Conference on Computer Vision and Pattern Recognition, pp. 1–8. IEEE (2007)
6. Chen, T., Seidel, H.P., Lensch, H.P.: Modulated phase-shifting for 3D scanning. In: IEEE Conference on Computer Vision and Pattern Recognition, CVPR 2008, pp. 1–8. IEEE (2008)

7. Davis, J., Ramamoorthi, R., Rusinkiewicz, S.: Spacetime stereo: a unifying framework for depth from triangulation. In: Proceedigns of the 2003 IEEE Computer Society Conference on Computer Vision and Pattern Recognition, vol. 2, p. II-359. IEEE (2003)

8. Furukawa, R., Kawasaki, H.: Dense 3D reconstruction with an uncalibrated stereo system using coded structured light. In: IEEE Computer Society Conference on Computer Vision and Pattern Recognition-Workshops, CVPR Workshops, p. 107. IEEE (2005)

9. Furukawa, R., Kawasaki, H.: Uncalibrated multiple image stereo system with arbitrarily movable camera and projector for wide range scanning. In: Fifth International Conference on 3-D Digital Imaging and Modeling, 3DIM 2005, pp. 302–309. IEEE (2005)

10. Furukawa, R., Sagawa, R., Kawasaki, H., Sakashita, K., Yagi, Y., Asada, N.: One-shot entire shape acquisition method using multiple projectors and cameras. In: 2010 Fourth Pacific-Rim Symposium on Image and Video Technology (PSIVT), pp. 107–114. IEEE (2010)

11. Garcia, R.R., Zakhor, A.: Consistent stereo-assisted absolute phase unwrapping methods for structured light systems. IEEE J. Sel. Top. Sig. Process. 6(5), 411–424 (2012)

12. Granados, M., Ajdin, B., Wand, M., Theobalt, C., Seidel, H.P., Lensch, H.P.: Optimal HDR reconstruction with linear digital cameras. In: 2010 IEEE Conference on Computer Vision and Pattern Recognition (CVPR), pp. 215–222. IEEE (2010)

13. Gühring, J.: Dense 3D surface acquisition by structured light using off-the-shelf components. In: Photonics West 2001-Electronic Imaging, pp. 220–231. International Society for Optics and Photonics (2000)

14. Gupta, M., Agrawal, A., Veeraraghavan, A., Narasimhan, S.G.: Structured light 3D scanning in the presence of global illumination. In: 2011 IEEE Conference on Computer Vision and Pattern Recognition (CVPR), pp. 713–720. IEEE (2011)

15. Gupta, M., Nayar, S.K.: Micro phase shifting. In: 2012 IEEE Conference on Computer Vision and Pattern Recognition (CVPR), pp. 813–820. IEEE (2012)

16. Moreno, D., Son, K., Taubin, G.: Embedded phase shifting: robust phase shifting with embedded signals. In: 2015 IEEE Conference on Computer Vision and Pattern Recognition (CVPR), pp. 2301–2309. IEEE (2015)

17. Nayar, S.K., Krishnan, G., Grossberg, M.D., Raskar, R.: Fast separation of direct and global components of a scene using high frequency illumination. In: ACM Transactions on Graphics (TOG), vol. 25, pp. 935–944. ACM (2006)

18. Nelder, J.A., Mead, R.: A simplex method for function minimization. Comput. J. 7(4), 308–313 (1965)

19. Resch, B., Lensch, H.P., Wang, O., Pollefeys, M., Hornung, A.S.: Scalable structure from motion for densely sampled videos. In: CVPR (2015)

20. Salvi, J., Fernandez, S., Pribanic, T., Llado, X.: A state of the art in structured light patterns for surface profilometry. Pattern Recogn. 43(8), 2666–2680 (2010)

21. Schwartz, C., Sarlette, R., Weinmann, M., Klein, R.: Dome II: a parallelized BTF acquisition system. In: Rushmeier, H., Klein, R. (eds.) Eurographics Workshop on Material Appearance Modeling: Issues and Acquisition, pp. 25–31. Eurographics Association, June 2013. http://diglib.eg.org/EG/DL/WS/MAM/MAM2013/025-031.pdf

22. Seitz, S.M., Curless, B., Diebel, J., Scharstein, D., Szeliski, R.: A comparison and evaluation of multi-view stereo reconstruction algorithms. In: 2006 IEEE Computer Society Conference on Computer Vision and Pattern Recognition (CVPR 2006), vol. 1, pp. 519–528. IEEE (2006)

23. Srinivasan, V., Liu, H.C., Halioua, M.: Automated phase-measuring profilometry: a phase mapping approach. Appl. Opt. **24**(2), 185–188 (1985). http://ao.osa.org/abstract.cfm?URI=ao-24-2-185
24. Weinmann, M., Schwartz, C., Ruiters, R., Klein, R.: A multi-camera, multi-projector super-resolution framework for structured light. In: 2011 International Conference on 3D Imaging, Modeling, Processing, Visualization and Transmission (3DIMPVT), pp. 397–404. IEEE (2011)
25. Young, M., Beeson, E., Davis, J., Rusinkiewicz, S., Ramamoorthi, R.: Viewpoint-coded structured light. In: IEEE Conference on Computer Vision and Pattern Recognition, CVPR 2007, pp. 1–8. IEEE (2007)

Down to Earth: Using Semantics for Robust Hypothesis Selection for the Five-Point Algorithm

Andreas Kuhn[1,2(✉)], True Price[2], Jan-Michael Frahm[2], and Helmut Mayer[1]

[1] Bundeswehr University Munich, Neubiberg, Germany
andreas.kuhn@unibw.de
[2] The University of North Carolina at Chapel Hill, Chapel Hill, USA

Abstract. The computation of the essential matrix using the five-point algorithm is a staple task usually considered as being solved. However, we show that the algorithm frequently selects erroneous solutions in the presence of noise and outliers. These errors arise when the supporting point correspondences supplied to the algorithm do not adequately cover all essential planes in the scene, leading to ambiguous essential matrix solutions. This is not merely a theoretical problem: such scene conditions often occur in 3D reconstruction of real-world data when fronto-parallel point correspondences, such as points on building facades, are captured but correspondences on obliquely observed planes, such as the ground plane, are missed. To solve this problem, we propose to leverage semantic labelings of image features to guide hypothesis selection in the five-point algorithm. More specifically, we propose a two-stage RANSAC procedure in which, in the first step, only features classified as ground points are processed. These inlier ground features are subsequently used to score two-view geometry hypotheses generated by the five-point algorithm using samples of non-ground points. Results for scenes with prominent ground regions demonstrate the ability of our approach to recover epipolar geometries that describe the entire scene, rather than only well-sampled scene planes.

1 Introduction

Large-scale Structure from Motion (SfM) has tremendously progressed in the last decade [1,7,13,18,23,24]. The key approach in SfM-type methods, and especially in incremental SfM, involves building up scene geometry from initial two-view relationships. To accomplish this, virtually all systems estimate epipolar geometry to establish the overlap between image pairs. When Exchangeable Image File Format (EXIF) information is available for the images, such geometry is typically obtained via essential matrix estimation using the five-point algorithm [21]; alternatively, the eight-point algorithm [11] can be used to estimate a fundamental

Electronic supplementary material The online version of this chapter (doi:10.1007/978-3-319-66709-6_31) contains supplementary material, which is available to authorized users.

V. Roth and T. Vetter (Eds.): GCPR 2017, LNCS 10496, pp. 389–400, 2017.
DOI: 10.1007/978-3-319-66709-6_31

matrix for image pairs with unknown calibration. To provide robustness against incorrect point correspondences, this estimation is usually placed in a RANSAC framework, where a minimal number of correspondences are iteratively sampled to provide statistical guarantees on the computed transformation. The estimated epipolar geometries are vital for recovering relative pose between the two images, which enables the triangulation of scene geometry and other subsequent steps in the SfM pipeline.

In this work, we address a key problem of RANSAC-based essential matrix estimation that arises when the available point correspondences in two images are heavily biased toward a single plane in the scene. We show that while the existing methods work reliably for noise-free data, essential matrix estimation often achieves only a local optimum on real-world data given noisy point detection and, importantly, an uneven 3D spatial distribution of the available point correspondences. We find that such errors often manifest themselves in 3D urban reconstructions, with computed essential matrices largely over-fitting to fronto-parallel structures, such as building facades, and mis-characterizing undersampled planes, in particular the ground. Indeed, for the vast majority of scenes, the popular large-scale reconstruction systems (e.g., [23,28]) almost always fail to capture the ground structure, especially for reconstructions from uncontrolled photo-collections. To account for this apparent limitation in essential matrix estimation, we propose a new approach for scoring proposals for two-view geometries, taking into account semantic labeling of the detected image features. Focusing on ground/non-ground labelings, we demonstrate that our method is able to correctly characterize the epipolar geometry in a variety of image pairs that were only partly correctly treated in a traditional RANSAC framework.

2   Background and Related Work

Solving for relative geometry from five point correspondences does not *per se* provide a globally optimal solution [10]. In general, there exist ten discrete solutions [5], which can be reduced only in special configurations by means of the five-point algorithm [21] itself. Even though global optimally algorithms have been presented [12] for solving for the essential matrix, they are unproven and no practical evidence for an efficient implementation is given [25].

It has long been recognized [3,21,26] that the validity of estimated epipolar geometry (calibrated or uncalibrated) is inherently tied to both the 3D spatial distribution and 2D accuracy of the 2D correspondences shared between a given image pair. As Nistér notes in his seminal five-point algorithm paper [21], however, calibrated two-view geometry estimation (*i.e.*, essential matrix estimation) enjoys substantially less ambiguity than its uncalibrated counterpart. Given perfect correspondences, the geometry provided by the five-point algorithm is unique, except in the case of a planar point set, where possibly a single ambiguity could arise. This is much more manageable than the case for fundamental matrix estimation, wherein a planar point set causes degeneracy

[3,15,31]. Given its significant advantages and superiority in practice [22], calibrated two-view geometry estimation has largely been thought to be a solved problem.

The specific issue we aim to address is the case where essential matrix estimation in a RANSAC framework fails to find a correct solution due to a sub-optimal 3D spatial sampling of feature points in the image, which in the limiting case lie on a single scene plane. In our experience, noise and outliers in the sampled point sets can drive RANSAC to select geometry that overfits to the dominant scene plane(s) if not enough points on less-sampled planes, namely the ground, are available. We briefly explain our observations in the following, before introducing our proposed method.

3 Error Behavior for Oversampled Planes in the RANSAC-Based Five-Point Algorithm

In this section, we provide a high-level overview of the error behavior associated with epipolar geometry estimation in a RANSAC framework for image pairs having planar-biased point sets. Our goal is to emphasize the importance of taking into account all essential scene planes when choosing the best solution from the hypotheses generated by this algorithm.

3.1 The Five-Point Algorithm

Consider a pair of calibrated cameras observing a scene, and let K and $\bar{K}$ represent their intrinsic matrices. The essential matrix E describes the epipolar geometry of the cameras: $\bar{p}^T \bar{K}^{-T} E K^{-1} p = 0$, where p and $\bar{p}$ are corresponding 2D points in each image, respectively. Geometrically speaking, $\bar{K}^{-T} E K^{-1} p$ maps point p in the first image into an epipolar line in the second image, and the equality to zero constrains $\bar{p}$ to lie along this line. Relative camera pose (3-DOF rotation and 2-DOF translation) can be recovered, in part, by decomposing the essential matrix, which makes its estimation vital to tasks such as SfM [9].

Using Nistér's five-point algorithm [21], we can solve for E using just five point correspondences. The algorithm is formed from ten cubic constraints that are well-known properties of the essential matrix [9]:

$$\det(E) = 0, \ 2EE^T E - \mathrm{tr}(EE^T)E = 0. \tag{1}$$

When the constraints in Eq. (1) are used in conjunction with five point correspondences, the problem of solving for E can be reduced to finding the roots of a tenth-degree polynomial [16,21]. This results in up to 10 possible essential matrices, all of which constitute a valid epipolar geometry for the original five correspondences. To select the correct solution for E, traditional methods leverage additional point correspondences and choose the solution with the largest support. Accordingly, the selection of the prevailing hypothesis from the up-to-ten possible essential matrices hinges on the remaining available correspondences.

3.2   Error Behavior in Epipolar Geometry Estimation

In real-world applications, image correspondences are typically obtained using feature matching, which often results in a large number of putative correspondences that are affected by noise and outliers. To robustly recover relative camera pose from such data in a calibrated setting, the five-point algorithm is usually embedded in a RANSAC [6] framework [21]. Here, a minimal number of random correspondences are sampled from the set of potential matches, the geometry estimation algorithm is run, and some subset of the complete set of correspondences is used to select the best of the ten resulting hypotheses. This sampling is repeated for a sufficient number of RANSAC iterations, and the solution with the strongest support, determined by the number of correspondences or a robust metric such as MSAC [27], is chosen as the optimal epipolar geometry.

In RANSAC, the distribution of valid point correspondences plays a strong role in determining the finally estimated two-view transformation. Take, for example, Fig. 1, which shows epipolar error maps for three different correspondence set scenarios. Here, we have added a small amount of noise and outliers to the point correspondence sets and have limited the available points to lie on five, two, and one scene plane. We run five-point RANSAC on these point sets to obtain a best-fitting epipolar geometry based on the criterion of maximal inlier support. It is clear that when all planes in the scene are equally sampled, the epipolar error is low throughout the image. When only one or two scene planes are available, however, the estimated pair-wise geometries have good support on the sampled scene planes, but they completely fail to accurately characterize unsampled scene planes – and the underlying relative pose is necessarily wrong. This short experiment serves to demonstrate that, even if the inlier support for an estimated calibrated two-view geometry "looks" correct in highly sampled regions, the underlying transformation that is estimated may actually very poorly fit unsampled scene planes. The motivation for our approach is to leverage point correspondences on other scene planes, when at least a small number are available, to solve this problem.

Fig. 1. Left three images: 100 sampled 2D points (white dots) drawn from different combinations of scene planes. Right three images: associated epipolar error for the left images given corresponding points in a second (not shown) view. Here, epipolar error is calculated using the pair-wise geometry obtained via five-point RANSAC. Blue pixels indicate no epipolar error for the point in the image, while red pixels indicate a distance from the estimated epipolar line of 10 or more pixels. Even though the general camera pose is incorrect for the two- and one-plane examples, epipolar error is low within the sampled planes. However, large error (>10 pixels) exists on the unsampled planes, especially in the single-plane case. (Color figure online)

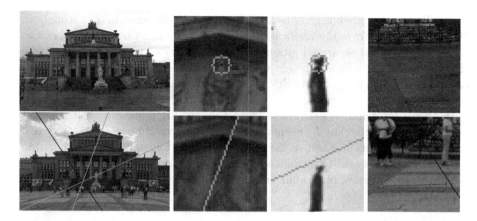

Fig. 2. Epipolar geometry estimated using a state-of-the-art SfM pipeline [23] for an example image pair. The upper left image illustrates a point on the ground area (red circle) and two non-ground points (green circles). On the lower left, the three corresponding epipolar lines (red and green) are illustrated on the second image. The zoomed images for the three points (right three columns) show that the epipolar line has low error for the two green points. The epipolar line for the point on the ground plane (right column), however, is inaccurate by more than 30 pixels (blue line). (Color figure online)

Figure 2 demonstrates the plane-sampling problem for a real-world image pair. Especially for community photo-collections, it is common that points on buildings (which have more favorable views) are extremely well-matched using common feature descriptors like SIFT. Point correspondences on the ground, however, are often embarrassingly underrepresented. Accordingly, RANSAC very often fails to correctly find inlier point pairs on the ground surface, and the estimated epipolar geometry is globally inaccurate. For the interested reader, we provide in the supplementary material a systematic evaluation of the error behavior of the five-point algorithm in a RANSAC framework.

4   Proposed Method

Given our analysis, it is clear that the preservation of ground points during feature verification is a necessary prerequisite for an accurate estimation of the camera geometry from image pairs. In principle, a verification within the RANSAC procedure is possible without initial correspondence determination. To do so, for all solutions the complete image could be used for verification, *e.g.*, by dense matching or extended correspondence search for multiple pixels. Unfortunately, in a RANSAC procedure this would tremendously increase the runtime.

To efficiently obtain correct solutions for the two-view geometry, we propose to employ two distinct matching pipelines, one for the stably detected features of an image and one for features on the non-dominant planes, chiefly the ground plane. The second pipeline gives us a way to maintain efficiency in the estimation. We propose to perform the verification embedded in a RANSAC framework two times: Once for the separated ground areas and a second time for the complete images. This results in a sufficient number of matched ground points, which is essential for achieving accurate SfM including ground scene parts.

We start with a calibrated pair of images and detect SIFT features for both images. Matching is performed using standard SIFT matching with nearest neighbor search under the L_2 norm and a final ratio-based filtering [17]. Successfully matched points are then verified by means of the five-point algorithm within a RANSAC framework. This can lead to missing ground points and, hence, to an inaccurate registration of ground areas. Figure 3 shows an example image pair with verified feature points.

Fig. 3. Left two images: example image pair marked with feature points. Right two images: semantic labels, including ground (purple) and building (grey). The purple points on the image pairs represent the feature points verified by the five-point algorithm in a standard RANSAC framework. On the ground plane, no (correct) verified point correspondences were found. The green and red points are the inliers from the first stage of our pipeline, which employs a homography for ground points. Turquoise and green points are the final features verified by the second RANSAC procedure. (Color figure online)

To avoid behavior where the verification optimizes only specific areas, we propose to match the features for separate classes. To this end, one needs to identify specific semantic regions, such as the ground, in an image. Fortunately, the availability of plenty of labeled data for urban scenes [4] and the recent progress in classification by trained deep CNNs allows for a stable classification of multiple classes including building and ground [30]. We use the latter method to initially label our input images semantically (Fig. 3).

In our matching pipeline, we separate features from the image pairs into two classes: (1) road and sidewalk, and (2) building and wall [4,30]. For our experiments, we ignore other labels, and we ignore correspondences if their classes do

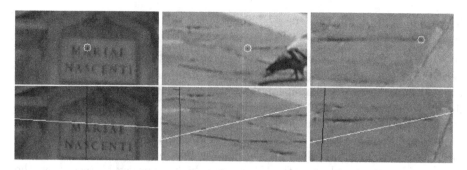

Fig. 4. Top row: three example points from the image pair shown in Fig. 3. Bottom row: corresponding epipolar lines. The red line represents the epipolar line from standard five-point verification of SIFT feature matching by means of RANSAC, and the green line the epipolar line from our method. While both methods are highly accurate on the building (left column), only our method produces accurate epipolar geometry for the ground. The epipolar error for the standard verification is up to 100 pixels. (Color figure online)

not agree. Our first matching and verification stage only makes use of the feature points assigned to the ground. Unfortunately, the matching of ground features usually leads to a high outlier rate. In typical image sets from, *e.g.*, community photo collections, the ground is only captured at an oblique angle. This is typical when using images acquired with a hand-held camera. In addition to perspective deformations, the ground is challenging to match because of many repetitions and a lack of unique structures. Thus, to increase the inlier ratio of ground point correspondences, we process the ground separately first by a ground-to-ground homography assuming a mostly planar ground.

To detect and match features on obliquely viewed surfaces, methods exist based on post-processing of descriptors [14] or a preceding affine transformation of the areas. For the reconstruction of highly slanted areas, complex pipelines allow for the generation of a small number of highly stable matches [19,20]. Unfortunately, the methods from [19,20] are not runtime-efficient. On the other hand, the matching has to be performed on a fraction of the complete image. We empirically found that also using standard SIFT allows ground matching for image pairs with small baselines. If the configuration needs complex matching methods, we use the implementation of [20]. Figure 3 shows the resulting SIFT features after homography-based verification (green and red points).

For a joint representation of the point sets for road and sidewalk as well as building and wall, we use a second verification procedure. The input is the two sets of feature points: (1) The set of unverified SIFT features labeled as building or wall, and (2) the verified ground matches from the first procedure. For every RANSAC iteration, five points are randomly chosen from the first set. The up-to-ten solutions for the essential matrices are evaluated against all other points from this set. In our pipeline, the solution is additionally evaluated against the second set containing the stable ground points. Hence, we have two sets of inliers: ground inliers $\#I_g$ and building inliers $\#I_b$. To estimate the optimal solution from the set of hypotheses, we compare them against the current best solution with inlier sets $\{I_g^*, I_b^*\}$ by defining the quality as: $q_i = \frac{\#I_g^i}{\#I_g^*} \frac{\#I_b^i}{\#I_b^*}$. Hence, the relative ratio of verified ground and building points has to be maximal. The maximum quality over all hypotheses i is chosen for the optimal essential matrix. In Fig. 3, the finally verified points from the second procedure are presented in the form of green ground points and turquoise building points. Figure 4 demonstrates the improvement achieved with our method. It is immediately apparent that for the ground area, the epipolar lines for the first verification have an error of tens of pixels, while our complete method achieves a high accuracy. Moreover, on the building, our method yields a similar quality as the essential matrix derived by the first verification.

5   Experiments

We have evaluated our method on challenging real-world image pairs from community photo-collections to demonstrate the improvement for the accurate estimation of the relative geometry. For the calibration (camera intrinsics), we make use of the EXIF information in the images.

First, the choice of feature detection can be crucial. We use SIFT features for the initial estimation of the matching points for ground and building, but as previously mentioned, these features sometimes have poor performance when matching ground points from wide-baseline pairs. Using SIFT, ground points are typically well-matched for similar small-baseline images (see Fig. 5). However, when even mild changes in appearance or perspective occur, or if the ground is weakly textured, the ground can prove challenging to match. In such cases, we use MODS [19,20] for ground-point matching (Fig. 6). While other feature

Fig. 5. Results of our method on an image pair using SIFT features. Left: images with original inlier points shown in purple. The green and red points are the inliers from the first stage of our pipeline. Turquoise and green points are the final features verified by the second RANSAC procedure. Right: The zoomed images show a ground and a non-ground match. While the non-ground matches are correct for both methods, the ground points were only aligned correctly with our method (green epipolar line). The red epipolar line, representing the five-point essential matrix, shows an error of tens of pixels for the ground. (Color figure online)

Fig. 6. Four examples for optimized essential matrices from image pairs. Because of challenging texture, perspective, resolution and lighting conditions in these examples MODS is used for ground-point matching. Verified features are color-coded as in Fig. 5. The zoomed images show examples for ground and non-ground matches. While the non-ground matches are correct for both methods, the ground points were only related correctly with our method (green epipolar line). The red epipolar line, representing the five-point essential matrix, shows an error of tens of pixels for ground images. (Color figure online)

detection methods have been published recently [8,29], we empirically found that none of them surpasses SIFT in producing reliable matches on obliquely viewed surfaces on our test images.

We use our proposed two-stage RANSAC procedure to solve for the epipolar geometry of the image pairs. More precisely, we use the extension LO-RANSAC [2], as our experience shows it generates better results for both the original verification and our method. RANSAC is parameterized as follows: (1) a maximum error of 2 pixels, (2) a confidence value of 99.99%, and (3) a minimum inlier ration of 20%. Because the matching of the ground produces a higher outlier ratio, in the homography-based procedure a maximum error of 4 pixels is used. The higher maximum error takes into account that, often, the ground cannot be exactly described by a plane. Also, in the second procedure, the ground points are verified with double the pixel accuracy threshold of the building points; this accounts for the fact that the perspective transformation of ground points usually results in lower-quality feature localization and description.

Figures 5 and 6 show several results for our method in comparison to the standard five-point-based estimation employing the complete set of SIFT features. Furthermore, in the supplementary material more results are provided. Our method allows the matching of ground points and the derivation of a highly accurate essential matrix. In situations where the traditional method only produces a sufficient accuracy for areas representing nearly fronto-parallel surface planes, our method produces an accuracy within a few pixels for the entire image. We assume a view without excessive perspective deformation of the building, which is given for typical images showing building and ground in similar proportion as in this case the building is generally captured from a larger distance or with a camera facing the facade in a fronto parallel manner. Because the camera calibration is not optimal, for some examples our verified correspondences do not cover the complete scene. The upper row in Fig. 6 gives two examples with several missing correspondences. Nonetheless, it is apparent that the distance to the epipolar line is within a couple of pixels, whereas insufficient consideration of ground features can lead to pixel errors of up to 100 pixels (Fig. 6). The latter would lead to a completely false estimation of the relative camera pose, prohibiting the image pair from contributing to an accurate 3D reconstruction (see Fig. 2).

6 Conclusion

In this paper, we revisited the five-point algorithm and provided evidence of its potential shortcomings for scene configurations frequently arising in image-based 3D reconstruction. In these configurations, point correspondences on obliquely viewed surfaces — particularly the ground — are largely missed, and even though the resulting essential matrices describe parts of the image well, the representation of the entire scene is strongly distorted in regions with low support. In a RANSAC framework, the five-point algorithm offers a multitude of hypotheses that are verified using the available correspondences. Correspondences situated only on a single fronto-parallel plane, in particular, lead to a poorly estimated essential matrix; this is common in 3D urban modeling, where correspondences are mostly captured on facades, but missing on the ground plane.

Our solution allows the preservation of ground correspondences in addition to those on buildings in urban scenes. To this end, we leverage an existing classification method to semantically segment source images into ground and non-ground regions. Our semantic-based hypothesis scoring approach makes use of these labelings to ensure that the undersampled ground correspondences are still accurately captured during RANSAC-based two-view geometry estimation. Results on a large variety of scenes demonstrate the ability of our approach to successfully maintain dominant-plane correspondences while additionally recovering ground correspondences. In the future, we look to expand the use of semantic labels to other aspects of two-view geometry estimation, including fundamental matrix estimation and related robust statistical measures.

References

1. Agarwal, S., Furukawa, Y., Snavely, N., Simon, I., Curless, B., Seitz, S.M., Szeliski, R.: Building Rome in a day. Commun. ACM **54**(10), 105–112 (2011)
2. Chum, O., Matas, J., Kittler, J.: Locally optimized RANSAC. In: Michaelis, B., Krell, G. (eds.) DAGM 2003. LNCS, vol. 2781, pp. 236–243. Springer, Heidelberg (2003). doi:10.1007/978-3-540-45243-0_31
3. Chum, O., Werner, T., Matas, J.: Two-view geometry estimation unaffected by a dominant plane. In: CVPR, vol. 1, pp. 772–779 (2005)
4. Cordts, M., Omran, M., Ramos, S., Rehfeld, T., Enzweiler, M., Benenson, R., Franke, U., Roth, S., Schiele, B.: The cityscapes dataset for semantic urban scene understanding. In: CVPR (2016)
5. Faugeras, O.D., Maybank, S.J.: Motion from point matches: multiplicity of solutions. IJCV **4**(3), 225–246 (1990). http://dx.doi.org/10.1007/BF00054997
6. Fischler, M.A., Bolles, R.C.: Random sample consensus: a paradigm for model fitting with applications to image analysis and automated cartography. Commun. ACM **24**(6), 381–395 (1981)
7. Frahm, J.-M., et al.: Building Rome on a cloudless day. In: Daniilidis, K., Maragos, P., Paragios, N. (eds.) ECCV 2010. LNCS, vol. 6314, pp. 368–381. Springer, Heidelberg (2010). doi:10.1007/978-3-642-15561-1_27
8. Han, X., Leung, T., Jia, Y., Sukthankar, R., Berg, A.C.: Matchnet: unifying feature and metric learning for patch-based matching. In: CVPR (2015)
9. Hartley, R.I., Zisserman, A.: Multiple View Geometry in Computer Vision. Cambridge University Press, Cambridge (2004). ISBN 0521540518
10. Hartley, R., Kahl, F.: Optimal algorithms in multiview geometry. In: Yagi, Y., Kang, S.B., Kweon, I.S., Zha, H. (eds.) ACCV 2007. LNCS, vol. 4843, pp. 13–34. Springer, Heidelberg (2007). doi:10.1007/978-3-540-76386-4_2
11. Hartley, R.I.: In defense of the eight-point algorithm. PAMI **19**(6), 580–593 (1997)
12. Hartley, R.I., Kahl, F.: Global optimization through searching rotation space and optimal estimation of the essential matrix. In: ICCV (2007)
13. Heinly, J., Schönberger, J.L., Dunn, E., Frahm, J.M.: Reconstructing the world* in six days *(as captured by the Yahoo 100 million image dataset). In: CVPR (2015)
14. Ke, Y., Sukthankar, R.: PCA-SIFT: a more distinctive representation for local image descriptors. In: CVPR (2004)
15. Kushnir, M., Shimshoni, I.: Epipolar geometry estimation for urban scenes with repetitive structures. PAMI **36**(12), 2381–2395 (2014)
16. Li, H., Hartley, R.: Five-point motion estimation made easy. In: ICPR (2006)
17. Lowe, D.G.: Distinctive image features from scale-invariant keypoints. IJCV **60**(2), 91–110 (2004)
18. Mayer, H., Bartelsen, J., Hirschmüller, H., Kuhn, A.: Dense 3D reconstruction from wide baseline image sets. In: 15th International Workshop on Theoretical Foundations of Computer Vision (2011)

19. Mishkin, D., Matas, J., Perdoch, M.: MODS: fast and robust method for two-view matching. CoRR abs/1503.02619 (2015). http://arxiv.org/abs/1503.02619
20. Mishkin, D., Matas, J., Perdoch, M., Lenc, K.: Wxbs: wide baseline stereo generalizations. CoRR abs/1504.06603 (2015). http://arxiv.org/abs/1504.06603
21. Nistér, D.: An efficient solution to the five-point relative pose problem. PAMI **26**(6), 756–777 (2004)
22. Rodehorst, V., Heinrichs, M., Hellwich, O.: Evaluation of relative pose estimation methods for multi-camera setups. International Archives of Photogrammetry and Remote Sensing (ISPRS), pp. 135–140 (2008)
23. Schönberger, J.L., Frahm, J.M.: Structure-from-motion revisited. In: CVPR (2016)
24. Snavely, N., Seitz, S.M., Szeliski, R.: Modeling the world from internet photo collections. IJCV **80**(2), 189–210 (2008)
25. Stewénius, H., Engels, C., Nistér, D.: Recent developments on direct relative orientation. ISPRS J. Photogramm. Remote Sens. **60**, 284–294 (2006). http://dx.doi.org/10.1016/j.isprsjprs.2006.03.005
26. Torr, P.H.: An assessment of information criteria for motion model selection. In: Computer Vision and Pattern Recognition (CVPR), pp. 47–52 (1997)
27. Torr, P.H., Zisserman, A.: MLESAC: a new robust estimator with application to estimating image geometry. Comput. Vis. Image Underst. **78**(1), 138–156 (2000)
28. Wu, C.: Towards linear-time incremental structure from motion. In: 3DV, pp. 127–134 (2013)
29. Yi, K.M., Trulls, E., Lepetit, V., Fua, P.: LIFT: learned invariant feature transform. In: Leibe, B., Matas, J., Sebe, N., Welling, M. (eds.) ECCV 2016. LNCS, vol. 9910, pp. 467–483. Springer, Cham (2016). doi:10.1007/978-3-319-46466-4_28
30. Yu, F., Koltun, V.: Multi-scale context aggregation by dilated convolutions. In: ICLR (2016)
31. Zach, C., Klopschitz, M., Pollefeys, M.: Disambiguating visual relations using loop constraints. In: Computer Vision and Pattern Recognition (CVPR), pp. 1426–1433 (2010)

An Efficient Octree Design for Local Variational Range Image Fusion

Nico Marniok[(⊠)], Ole Johannsen, and Bastian Goldluecke

University of Konstanz, Konstanz, Germany
nico.marniok@uni-kostanz.de

Abstract. We present a reconstruction pipeline for a large-scale 3D environment viewed by a single moving RGB-D camera. Our approach combines advantages of fast and direct, regularization-free depth fusion and accurate, but costly variational schemes. The scene's depth geometry is extracted from each camera view and efficiently integrated into a large, dense grid as a truncated signed distance function, which is organized in an octree. To account for noisy real-world input data, variational range image integration is performed in local regions of the volume directly on this octree structure. We focus on algorithms which are easily parallelizable on GPUs, allowing the pipeline to be used in real-time scenarios where the user can interactively view the reconstruction and adapt camera motion as required.

1 Introduction

One of the fundamental problems of computer vision is the 3D reconstruction of geometry data recorded by a single moving RGB-D camera. Well known as Simultaneous Localization And Mapping (SLAM), this task denotes the problem of simultaneously determining the current view's camera pose and updating the scene geometry from the same view. It has gained a lot of recent interest, particularly with the availability of real-time consumer depth cameras and drones streaming video. Achieving real-time performance on large datasets without sacrificing quality is one of the currently active research goals. It is especially challenging to accomplish both simultaneously if the input data is noisy, and spatial regularization on the reconstruction is needed.

Within this field, volumetric approaches have proven themselves to be very effective at integrating and regularizing the data from many range images [7,20]. However, they suffer from huge memory requirements and associated run-times, and are thus typically limited to relatively small resolutions. In contrast, simple merging schemes on octrees based on averaging distance functions are fast [4,22], but skip explicit regularization and thus require many well calibrated overlapping depth maps with a small amount of noise.

In this paper, we integrate variational models into an octree data structure to jointly enjoy the advantages of variational modeling while retaining the high resolution of octrees. We present a pipeline which builds up a dynamic

© Springer International Publishing AG 2017
V. Roth and T. Vetter (Eds.): GCPR 2017, LNCS 10496, pp. 401–412, 2017.
DOI: 10.1007/978-3-319-66709-6_32

octree from a stream of RGB-D images with the corresponding estimated camera poses, incorporates new views, regularizes the reconstruction directly on the octree using variational methods, and visualizes the data using state-of-the-art rendering techniques.

2   Related Work

Over the last decades, a lot of 3D range image integration algorithms have been proposed. In this section, we give a rough overview of the relevant systems that focus on online reconstruction with active sensors, i.e. the incremental fusion of new views with already computed data. The main task of range image integration is to combine multiple RGB-D images from different views into a global 3D model. Usually, multiple steps are taken independently. First the cameras are registered in relation to each other, i.e. the sequential depth maps are aligned, and afterwards the object is reconstructed. As we assume alignment to be computed by other means in this paper, we focus on the object reconstruction part.

Methods can roughly be classified by the type of surface representation. Working with parametric or mesh based models that assume local surface topology is efficient in terms of memory usage but potentially difficult to regularize, prone to outliers, and it requires complex adjustments if topology changes [5, 24]. On the other end of the spectrum, point or surfel-based methods skip connection and topology reconstruction entirely [19], using point-based rendering techniques to display the illusion of a solid object [9].

Quite popular are approaches utilizing a volumetric data structure, which, for example, sample a truncated signed distance function (TSDF) for a surface on a voxel grid. In the basic framework, the TSDF is simply averaged between the individual TSDFs of the views [6]. This straight-forward averaging scheme can be improved by applying variational regularization techniques that minimize over the reconstructed surfaces [7, 20, 26]. However, a substantial drawback of volumetric reconstruction are the large memory requirement for storing a dense volume and the associated runtime for operations on it. Thus, a lot of effort has been put into optimizing volumetric fusion.

One possibility are moving volumes, which focus solely on the currently visible part and ignore already reconstructed parts, e.g. by storing them offline as meshes [18, 25]. One can also limit storage of the volume to the area around the surface. This can e.g. be performed using hash functions [8] or hierarchical structures like octrees [10, 22]. In [8], the authors thus achieve frame rates up to 1000 per second on state-of-the-art hardware using a hashing function that only stores data in regions where surfaces are present. However, they can not regularize the surface at all. In contrast, [10] proposes an octree-based approach for efficient variational range data fusion. In their paper, the authors formulate an energy which is similar to the energy we employ in our approach and based on ideas in [7, 26]. To make it differentiable this energy is smoothed and a PDE on the octree is solved while the shape of the octree is updated in each step. This allows for regularization of the surfaces, but it needs around 100 iterations to converge and a lot of expensive updates of the octree. In contrast, our approach for local variational fusion works on a fixed octree without the need of approximation of the problem, and it converges within about five iterations. In addition, our approach works on the GPU and only requires around one second to regularize a partial volume within the octree, while theirs needs around 3–4 min.

3 System Overview

In this section, we present an overview of our system for octree-based 3D reconstruction with incremental variational updates. Individual design decisions in our implementation were made carefully to put as few limits as possible upon size and resolution of the reconstruction area as well as the amount of input range image data. Furthermore, we want all steps to be fully parallelizable on the GPU.

Geometry Representation. For this, we represent the scene geometry to be reconstructed by a signed distance function (SDF) $u : \mathbb{R}^3 \to (-\infty, \infty)$, which measures for any $x \in \mathbb{R}^3$ the signed distance of that point to the nearest geometry surface. A negative value means the point lies inside the scene geometry and a positive value indicates the point lies outside of the geometry. In particular, the surface is represented implicitly by the zero-level isosurface of the SDF.

To be able to store large volumes at high resolution, the SDF is densely sampled and represented in an octree structure. An octree is a spatial representation of an axis-aligned cuboid. The root node spans this space completely. A non-leaf node has exactly eight children, each one representing exactly one octant of their parent's space (see Fig. 1). In Sect. 4, we give a detailed overview of our specific implementation.

Input Data and Representation. To reconstruct the scene's surface, we require an RGB-D image stream with the camera's pose for each image. Sophisticated tracking algorithms which can provide camera pose from RGB or RGB-D videos in real-time using only the CPU do already exist [11,21]. By combining one of these with an RGB-D video stream from a camera like, for example, Microsoft Kinect or a depth-less RGB video stream from a flying drone, we are able to reconstruct and visualize the captured scene in real-time with consumer-affordable hardware. We can handle noise and errors in the depth images due to

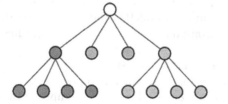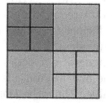

Fig. 1. Example of a 2D octree (quadtree) structure and space divided accordingly.

our global optimization performed by the variational updates. For experiments in this paper, we make use of the RGB-D SLAM Dataset and Benchmark [23].

To facilitate a large amount of input data, we need to implement a method to integrate the large amount of information into simple data structures for each individual voxel. Our method is based on the data term of the variational range image integration framework [7], which adapts [27] to make it scale better with the number of input images. To integrate all images measured so far into the octree, we remark that a depth measurement in an individual pixel is equivalent to observing a truncated signed distance function (TSDF) [6] which measures the distance to the surface on all voxels along the pixel's viewing ray. Thus, we can associate each node of the octree with a discretized histogram $h(x, i)$ over a set of truncated signed distance values d_i spaced evenly within the interval $[-1, 1]$. The histogram counts the number of measurements of an individual distance. In effect, the amount of required memory scales with the number of nodes in the octree, and is otherwise independent of the number of input range maps - once a range map is integrated, we can discard it. The final implicit surface function is obtained as the result of a variational model with a data term defined using the histograms and a surface area regularizer, see Sect. 5.

Reconstruction Pipeline. Our pipeline consists of five basic steps. The first is the estimation of the current view's camera pose and depth map, as described above. In the second step, the generated depth values are propagated into an unbounded octree structure. This octree is optimized in the third step by iterating over every node which changed in the last step. Essentially, if its children share the same information, they are removed and their data is transferred to their parent node. The implementation of the octree and these two update steps are described in detail in the following Sect. 4. After the integration of a specific amount of data, a local variational optimization is performed on the changed region of the octree by minimizing a convex energy function. This step integrates all measurements into a coherent smooth surface and is described in Sect. 5. We designed the system from the ground up with efficient visualization in mind even if the scene becomes very large. Thus, the fifth and final part of the system generates a visualization of the octree by extracting the zero-level isosurface from the locally optimized data, see Sect. 6.

4   Octree Design and Implementation

In this section, we describe our octree implementation. The data structure and all important required operations can be completely implemented on the GPU to allow efficient updating using variational models while avoiding unnecessary memory transfers.

Each node of our octree implementation consists of the following data, see Fig. 3. The first attribute is the node's level l, which is represented by a signed integer value. Thus, the length L of a node's edge can be computed by $L = 2^l$. We also define l_0 as the minimum level that can occur. This can be adjusted and has a great impact on the runtime performance as well as the required

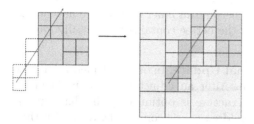 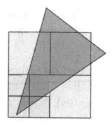

Fig. 2. *Left:* the depth value for each pixel is propagated to all voxels which are hit by its corresponding half ray. Gray voxels are not changed, yellow ones are created as empty voxels, blue ones are created and updated immediately, and green ones are just updated. *Right:* LOD-system used in visualization. The blue triangle depicts the virtual camera's frustum. Each of the blocks has the same volume resolution, while their spatial sizes differ. (Color figure online)

memory space. The minimum world coordinates of the node's bounding box represented by three floats are the second attribute. The histogram of measured signed distance function values per node is discretized as n unsigned integer values, where n can be adjusted to either increase reconstruction quality or save memory. The last value of f calculated by the local optimization algorithm is saved as a floating point number. To allow easy navigation in both directions of the octree, each node has pointers to its parent and eight children saved in the final attribute. A summary of all attributes can be seen in Fig. 3.

OctreeNode
level : int
minWorldCoords : float3
pHistogram : short[n]
value : float
pParent : HistogramOctreeNode*
ppChildren : HistogramOctreeNode*[8]

Fig. 3. Data stored for each of the nodes of the octree.

Local Range Image Integration. A new depth image is integrated into the current octree by executing a ray marching algorithm for each pixel. First, the half ray that originates in the focal position and passes through the center of the pixel is determined. Next, we iterate over all virtual nodes of level l_0 which are intersected by this half ray and create them if they do not exist yet. Finally, for each voxel, the signed distance function is evaluated and the value of the corresponding histogram bin is incremented (see Fig. 2, left). After a leaf node becomes an inner node, the histogram bins are equally distributed across its eight children. When creating a new voxel, it may happen that it is not contained in the octree. In such case, the octree must be extended by creating a new root node. The previous root node will then become an inner node of the new octree. This procedure must be repeated until the octree contains the initially created node.

Octree Optimization and Variational Update. In our implementation each node has either eight or zero children. After an adjustable amount of newly integrated depth images, the octree structure is optimized. This happens by iterating over each node. If a node's children consist only of leaves and if their normalized histograms are the same, they can be deleted, and the histogram values are summed up into the parent node's histogram.

After readjusting the octree structure, we also trigger a variational update of the region which has undergone changes since the last update pass. This allows us to incrementally update the signed distance function using a sophisticated variational model, without actually requiring a full optimization over the complete volume, which might be very large. We describe this optimization step in the next section.

5   Incremental Variational Updates

To locally build a new TSDF from updates observations, we rely on the general framework in [7] - indeed, the histogram representation of the input data already paved the way for its application. However, their method needs to be implemented efficiently on the octree data structure, which we explain in this section.

General Variational Model. The energy is based on the observation that for each histogram bin i with corresponding distance d_i to the surface, the value $h(x, i)$ gives the likelihood for u to have the value d_i. Thus, we penalize the L^1-deviation of u from d_i at locations $x \in \mathbb{R}^3$ where $h(i, x)$ is large. The SDF is regularized with total variation, which favors level sets having smaller area [3]. Thus, we minimize the energy

$$E(u) = \int_{\Omega} \left\{ \lambda |\nabla u(x)| + \sum_{i=1}^{N} h(x, i) |u(x) - d_i| \right\} \, \mathrm{d}x \tag{1}$$

in a local region of the octree, imposing boundary conditions such that it connects smoothly to the neighbouring regions. Note that the histograms need to be normalized per voxel for the formulation to make sense.

The functional is convex, so for optimization, we would like to apply the first-order primal dual algorithm [2]. This requires discretization of the differential operators, in particular the gradient of u and divergence of the dual variables $\boldsymbol{p}$, on the octree data structure.

Dual Variables and Differential Operators on Octrees. We employ a staggered grid discretization popular in computational fluid dynamics [15]. Where dual variables $\boldsymbol{p}$ live on the transitions between voxels instead of inside the voxel regions. For now, this leads primarily to an easier adaption of primal-dual methods to the irregular octree grid, but can also help with anosotropic regularization in future work. The divergence is defined in accordance with the Gaussian divergence theorem, from which it follows that the gradient needs to be adjoint to the negative divergence operator, $\nabla = -\text{div}^T$, under the assumption of Dirichlet boundary conditions $\boldsymbol{p}|_{\partial\Omega} = 0$ on the dual variables [1]. According to the Gaussian divergence theorem, for a voxel V with surface ∂V and outward pointing unit normal field $\boldsymbol{n}$,

$$\int_V \text{div}(\boldsymbol{p}) \ \mathrm{d}x = \oint_{\partial V} \boldsymbol{p} \cdot \boldsymbol{n} \, \mathrm{d}s. \tag{2}$$

Assuming $\boldsymbol{p}$ is locally linearized, this discretizes to

$$|V|\text{div}(\boldsymbol{p}) = \sum_{i=1}^{K} a_i(\boldsymbol{p}_i \cdot \boldsymbol{n}),$$

where the right sum is over the forward neighbors of the voxel in questions, a_i is the area of the shared surface, $\boldsymbol{n}$ the normal, and $\boldsymbol{p}_i$ value of the dual variable $\boldsymbol{p}$ on the shared surface.

We represent the values of u on the voxels of the octree and the dual variables $\boldsymbol{p}$ on the shared voxel surfaces as a linearised list of float values of length M and N, respectively. Note that the number of connectors is usually much larger than the number of nodes in the octree. Thus, computing the divergence comes down to multiplying $\boldsymbol{p}$ with a sparse matrix of size $M \times N$, while the gradient can be computed using the negative transpose of this sparse matrix. For the implementation of the operators, we use the nVidia CUDA Sparse Matrix library (cuSPARSE) [14].

Final Optimization Algorithm. The primal-dual form of energy (1) reads as

$$\min_u \max_{\|\boldsymbol{p}\|_{2,\infty} \leq 1} \left\{ \lambda(u, -\text{div}(\boldsymbol{p})) + \sum_{i=1}^{N} \int_\Omega h(x, i)|u(x) - d_i| \, \mathrm{d}x \right\}, \tag{3}$$

with the dual variable $\boldsymbol{p} \colon \Omega \mapsto \mathbb{R}^3$ and discrete differential operators defined as in the previous section. It can be minimized with the algorithm [17], which essentially consists of alternating gradient descent (and ascend) steps for the primal and dual variables according to

$$u^{n+1} = \text{prox}_{\text{hist}}(u^n + T\text{div}(\boldsymbol{p}^n))$$
$$p^{n+1} = \text{proj}_{\|p\|_\infty \leq \lambda}(p^n + \Sigma\nabla(2u^{n+1} - u^n)),$$

where the *prox* operator for the dual variable is a simple reprojection on the sphere of radius λ and T, Σ are pre-conditioning matrices chosen based on the row and column norms of the gradient operator according to [17]. As the octree is dynamic and we do not know about the neighbourhood system of voxels in advance, they need to be computed individually for each octree volume.

The *prox* operator for the primal variable is defined as

$$\text{prox}_{\text{hist}}(v(x)) := \underset{u \in \mathbb{R}}{\text{argmin}} \left\{ \frac{\|u - v(x)\|^2}{2\tau} + \sum_{i=1}^{N} h(x,i)|u - d_i| \right\}. \quad (4)$$

It was shown by Li and Osher [12] that the global minimizer for the problem above can be obtained by a simple median calculation. It is given by

$$\text{prox}_{\text{hist}}(v) = \text{median}\{d_1, \ldots, d_N, p_0, \ldots, p_N\}, \quad (5)$$

where the $p_i, i = 0, \ldots, N$ can be computed as

$$p_i = v + \tau W_i \quad \text{with} \quad W_i = -\sum_{j=1}^{i} h(x,i) + \sum_{j=i+1}^{N} h(x,i).$$

As the values d_i are already sorted, computing the median comes down to a simple insertion sort.

6   Visualization of the Reconstruction

For a sophisticated visualization of the reconstructed geometry, we choose a raytracing approach. We compress the octree into a large chunk of memory. Each entry represents a node, which now consists of a single floating-point value representing the result of the optimization, its minimum bounding box coordinates and eight offsets into the chunk of memory for its children. This structure needs much less space than the original octree and is well suited for GPU memory access.

Experiments show that directly raytracing this octree representation is very inefficient. Sampling the viewing rays tends to scatter read commands over the whole chunk of memory, for which current graphics hardware is not equipped. Instead, we create a temporary dense 3D texture, where for each texel the octree must be traversed once. Afterwards, a simple ray marching algorithm can easily display this texture.

The visualization system is integrated into a custom high-performance interactive graphics engine, inspired by [13] that supports state-of-the-art rendering techniques building upon deferred rendering [16]. Integrated support for normal mapping and physically based lighting can be used directly to create an appealing preview of the ongoing reconstruction.

For visualization, a virtual camera can be controlled freely during the reconstruction process. To facilitate this, each pixel's viewing ray is sampled multiple times with a step width of the volume's texel size. If a negative value is encountered, the previous and current sample positions are interpolated linearly with respect to the previous and current sampling value. This position and the gradient at this location as a surface normal are then given to the graphics engine.

To display a large section of the reconstruction volume, we use a level-of-detail system. The aforementioned volume visualization algorithm is executed multiple times per frame, each with a different section of the reconstruction volume. Near the camera, the volume's values are sampled from the octree's deepest level, while blocks further away use samples from a higher level (see Fig. 2, right). This technique allows for interactive framerates of about 40 to 50 Hz on a GTX 980 Ti.

7   Experiments

We implement depth image fusion and octree optimization in C++ on a single CPU thread, as parallelization or even implementation on the GPU is not trivial, although theoretically possible. Because every pixel can have a high influence on the overall octree structure, care must be taken when creating or deleting nodes. Thus, we defer a GPU implementation to future work for now. Variational fusion and visualization are performed solely on the GPU.

For our experiments, we chose three datasets from the RGB-D SLAM Dataset and Benchmark [23]. Those are accompanied by predetermined camera poses. For comparison with the already mentioned dense-grid approach, we chose the fr3/teddy scene. It is well suited because its spatial dimension of reconstruction is limited, such that the large memory footprint of the algorithm we compare against is no problem. We constrained the reconstruction volume to a dense 256^3 grid for the full-resolution algorithm.

In the second scene fr3/long_office_household, the camera moves in a complete circle around two desk workspaces. We select this scene to show the reconstruction of a scene with high geometric detail on our octree grid. However, it is too big for the dense grid to be reconstructed with a reasonable amount of memory, we do not provide a comparison for this scene.

As the third scene, we choose fr/pioneer_slam. It is recorded by a mobile robot and demonstrates a large-scale reconstruction. Just like the previous benchmark, this scene is too large to fit into memory when reconstructed with a dense grid.

We set the voxel size for all scenes to 7.8 mm and use 60 frames for the reconstruction. The grid resolution represented by our octree structure starts at 1^3 and can grow with no limits as the camera moves. We provide the resolution reached after the final frame in Fig. 5, and online reconstruction results in Fig. 4.

Our reconstruction pipeline can integrate one frame of size 640×480 roughly every two seconds. This is enough to get an interactive high-quality reconstruction while the camera moves at normal speed. The optimization step is executed every $n = 10$ frames or until the scene's size exceeds a predefined limit. While the optimization executes, which currently still takes roughly 40 s, no additional frames can be integrated. Most of the time is taken by neighbourhood lookup to initialize the derivative operators, which we intend to also move to the GPU in the future. During the whole integration and reconstruction process, an interactive preview of the scene is available, which can be inspected freely by controlling a virtual camera.

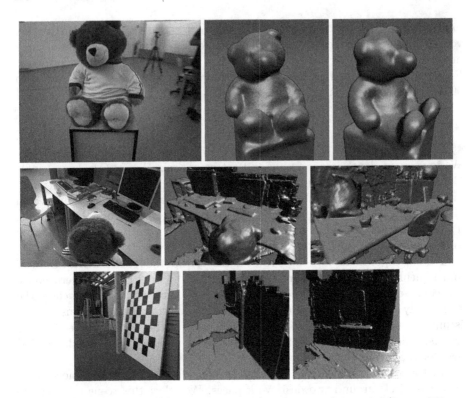

Fig. 4. Reconstruction results. First row: `fr3/teddy`, second row: `fr3/long_office_household`, third row: `fr/pioneer_slam`.

	Dense	Octree			Dense	Octree
fr3/teddy	288.0	401.4	fr3/teddy		256^3	2048^3
fr3/long_office_household	-	953.8	fr3/long_office_household		-	4096^3
fr2/pioneer_slam	-	1347.5	fr2/pioneer_slam		-	4096^3

Fig. 5. Memory requirements in MiB (left table) and resulting reconstruction volume (right table) for each benchmark.

8   Conclusion

We have presented a system for regularized online 3D reconstruction using adaptive octree grids, which can scale to large resolutions and scenes. Our approach combines the advantages of variational regularization methods with the memory efficiency of octrees, and thus allows us to use variational methods on volumes that are much larger than usual. The system is parallelizable and partially already implemented on the GPU, which allows for achieving efficient variational depth image fusion directly on the octree structure. Part of the octree updates are currently still performed on the CPU, we plan to lift the implementation to the GPU in future work. The flexible nature of octrees allows us to grow the reconstruction volume in arbitrary directions and respond to unforeseen camera movements. As we performing variational regularization only in regions where updates have occurred, our method does not suffer from problems with growing amount of integrated views and increasing scene complexity.

Acknowledgements. This work was supported by the ERC Starting Grant "Light Field Imaging and Analysis" (LIA 336978, FP7-2014) and the SFB Transregio 161 "Quantitative Methods for Visual Computing".

References

1. Chambolle, A.: An algorithm for total variation minimization and applications. J. Math. Imaging Vis. **20**(1–2), 89–97 (2004)
2. Chambolle, A., Pock, T.: A first-order primal-dual algorithm for convex problems with applications to imaging. J. Math. Imaging Vis. **40**(1), 120–145 (2011)
3. Chan, T., Esedoglu, S., Nikolova, M.: Algorithms for finding global minimizers of image segmentation and denoising models. SIAM J. Appl. Math. **66**(5), 1632–1648 (2006)
4. Chen, J., Bautembach, D., Izadi, S.: Scalable real-time volumetric surface reconstruction. ACM Trans. Graph. (Proc. SIGGRAPH) **32**(4), 113 (2013)
5. Chen, Y., Medioni, G.: Object modelling by registration of multiple range images. Image Vis. Comput. **10**(3), 145–155 (1992)
6. Curless, B., Levoy, M.: A volumetric method for building complex models from range images. In: Proceedings of the 23rd Annual Conference on Computer Graphics and Interactive Techniques, pp. 303–312. ACM (1996)
7. Graber, G., Pock, T., Bischof, H.: Online 3D reconstruction using convex optimization. In: Proceedings of the International Conference on Computer Vision Workshops (2011)
8. Kahler, O., Adrian Prisacariu, V., Yuheng Ren, C., Sun, X., Torr, P., Murray, D.: Very high frame rate volumetric integration of depth images on mobile devices. IEEE Trans. Vis. Comput. Graph. **21**(11), 1241–1250 (2015)
9. Katz, S., Tal, A.: On the visibility of point clouds. In: The IEEE International Conference on Computer Vision (ICCV), December 2015
10. Kehl, W., Holl, T., Tombari, F., Ilic, S., Navab, N.: An octree-based approach towards efficient variational range data fusion (2016)
11. Klein, G., Murray, D.: Parallel tracking and mapping for small ar workspaces. In: 6th IEEE and ACM International Symposium on Mixed and Augmented Reality (ISMAR), pp. 225–234 (2007). http://ewokrampage.wordpress.com/
12. Li, Y., Osher, S., et al.: A new median formula with applications to pde based denoising. Commun. Math. Sci. **7**(3), 741–753 (2009)
13. McShaffry, M., Graham, D.: Game Coding Complete, 4th edn. Delmar Learning, Clifton Park (2012)
14. NVIDIA CUDA Sparse Matrix library. https://developer.nvidia.com/cusparse
15. Olshanskii, M., Terekhov, K., Vassilevski, Y.: An octree-based solver for the incompressible Navier-Stokes equations with enhanced stability and low dissipation. Comput. Fluids **84**, 231–246 (2013)
16. Pharr, M., Jakob, W., Humphreys, G.: Physically based rendering: From theory to implementation. Morgan Kaufmann, Burlington (2016)

17. Pock, T., Chambolle, A.: Diagonal preconditioning for first order primal-dual algorithms in convex optimization. In: Proceedings of the International Conference on Computer Vision (2011)
18. Roth, H., Vona, M.: Moving volume kinectfusion (2012)
19. Rusinkiewicz, S., Hall-Holt, O., Levoy, M.: Real-time 3D model acquisition. ACM Trans. Graph. (TOG) **21**(3), 438–446 (2002)
20. Schroers, C., Zimmer, H., Valgaerts, L., Bruhn, A., Demetz, O., Weickert, J.: Anisotropic range image integration. In: Pinz, A., Pock, T., Bischof, H., Leberl, F. (eds.) DAGM/OAGM 2012. LNCS, vol. 7476, pp. 73–82. Springer, Heidelberg (2012). doi:10.1007/978-3-642-32717-9_8
21. Slavcheva, M., Kehl, W., Navab, N., Ilic, S.: SDF-2-SDF: highly accurate 3D object reconstruction. In: Leibe, B., Matas, J., Sebe, N., Welling, M. (eds.) ECCV 2016. LNCS, vol. 9905, pp. 680–696. Springer, Cham (2016). doi:10.1007/978-3-319-46448-0_41
22. Steinbruecker, F., Kerl, C., Sturm, J., Cremers, D.: Large-scale multi-resolution surface reconstruction from RGB-D sequences. In: Proceedings of the International Conference on Computer Vision, Sydney, Australia (2013)
23. Sturm, J., Engelhard, N., Endres, F., Burgard, W., Cremers, D.: A benchmark for the evaluation of RGB-D slam systems. In: Proceedings of the International Conference on Intelligent Robot Systems (IROS), October 2012
24. Turk, G., Levoy, M.: Zippered polygon meshes from range images. In: Proceedings of the 21st Annual Conference on Computer Graphics and Interactive Techniques, pp. 311–318. ACM (1994)
25. Whelan, T., Johannsson, H., Kaess, M., Leonard, J.J., McDonald, J.: Robust tracking for real-time dense RGB-D mapping with kintinuous (2012)
26. Zach, C., Pock, T., Bischof, H.: A globally optimal algorithm for robust TV-L1 range image integration. In: Proceedings of the International Conference on Computer Vision (2007)
27. Zach, C.: Fast and high quality fusion of depth maps. In: Proceedings of the International Symposium on 3D Data Processing, Visualization and Transmission (3DPVT) (2008)

Tracking

Measuring the Accuracy of Object Detectors and Trackers

Tobias Böttger$^{(\boxtimes)}$, Patrick Follmann, and Michael Fauser

MVTec Software GmbH, Munich, Germany
{boettger,follmann,fauser}@mvtec.com

Abstract. The accuracy of object detectors and trackers is most commonly evaluated by the Intersection over Union (IoU) criterion. To date, most approaches are restricted to axis-aligned or oriented boxes and, as a consequence, many datasets are only labeled with boxes. Nevertheless, axis-aligned or oriented boxes cannot accurately capture an object's shape. To address this, a number of densely segmented datasets has started to emerge in both the object detection and the object tracking communities. However, evaluating the accuracy of object detectors and trackers that are restricted to boxes on densely segmented data is not straightforward. To close this gap, we introduce the relative Intersection over Union (rIoU) accuracy measure. The measure normalizes the IoU with the optimal box for the segmentation to generate an accuracy measure that ranges between 0 and 1 and allows a more precise measurement of accuracies. Furthermore, it enables an efficient and easy way to understand scenes and the strengths and weaknesses of an object detection or tracking approach. We display how the new measure can be efficiently calculated and present an easy-to-use evaluation framework. The framework is tested on the DAVIS and the VOT2016 segmentations and has been made available to the community.

1 Introduction

Visual object detection and tracking are two rapidly evolving research areas with dozens of new algorithms being published each year. To compare the performance of the many different approaches, a vast amount of evaluation datasets and schemes are available. They include large detection datasets with multiple object categories, such as PASCAL VOC [8], smaller, more specific detection datasets with a single category, such as cars [10], and sequences with multiple frames that are commonly used to evaluate trackers such as VOT2016 [11], OTB-2015 [24], or MOT16 [14]. Although very different in their nature, all of the benchmarks use axis-aligned or oriented boxes as ground truth and estimate the accuracy with the Intersection over Union (IoU) criterion.

Nevertheless, boxes are very crude approximations of many objects and may introduce an unwanted bias in the evaluation process, as is displayed in Fig. 1. Furthermore, approaches that are not restricted to oriented or axis-aligned boxes

© Springer International Publishing AG 2017
V. Roth and T. Vetter (Eds.): GCPR 2017, LNCS 10496, pp. 415–426, 2017.
DOI: 10.1007/978-3-319-66709-6_33

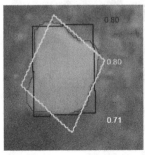  

(a) bag from VOT2016 [11]   (b)   blackswan   from   (c) boat from DAVIS [16]
                            DAVIS [16]

Fig. 1. In image (a), both oriented boxes have an identical IoU with the ground truth segmentation. Nevertheless, their common IoU is only 0.71. Restricting the ground truth to boxes may introduce an undesired bias in the evaluation. In image (b), the best possible IoU of an axis-aligned box is only 0.66. Hence, for segmented data, it is difficult to use the absolute value of the IoU as an accuracy measure since it generally does not range from 0 to 1. Furthermore, although the object detection (green) in image (c) has an overlap of 0.62 with the ground truth segmentation, its IoU with the ground truth axis-aligned bounding box is only 0.45 and would be considered a false detection in the standard procedure. The proposed rIoU is the same for both boxes in (a) and 1.0 for the green boxes in (b) and (c). (Color figure online)

will not necessarily have higher accuracy scores in the benchmarks [3–5]. To address these problems, a number of densely segmented ground truth datasets has started to emerge [13, 16, 23].

Unfortunately, evaluating the accuracy of object detectors and trackers that are restricted to boxes on densely segmented data is not straightforward. For example, the VOT2016 Benchmark [11] generates plausible oriented boxes from densely segmented objects and the COCO 2014 Detection challenge [13] uses axis-aligned bounding boxes of the segmentations to simplify the evaluation protocol. Hence, approaches may have a relatively low IoU with the ground truth, although their IoU with the actual object segmentation is the same (or even better) than that of the ground truth box (see Fig. 1(c)).

To enable a fair evaluation of algorithms restricted to axis-aligned or oriented boxes on densely segmented data we introduce the relative Intersection over Union accuracy (rIoU) measure. The rIoU uses the best possible axis-aligned or oriented box of the segmentation to normalize the IoU score. The normalized IoU ranges from 0 to 1 for an arbitrary segmentation and allows to determine the true accuracy of a scheme. For tracking scenarios, the optimal boxes have further advantages. By determining three different optimal boxes for each sequence, the optimal oriented box, the optimal axis-aligned box and, the optimal axis-aligned box for a fixed scale, it is possible to identify scale changes, rotations, and occlusion in a sequence without the need of by-frame labels.

The optimal boxes are obtained in a fast and efficient optimization process. We validate the quality of the boxes in the experiments section by comparing them to a number of exhaustively determined best boxes for various scenes.

The three main contributions of this paper are:

1. The introduction of the relative Intersection over Union accuracy (rIoU) measure, which allows an accurate measurement of object detector and tracker accuracies on densely segmented data.
2. The proposed evaluation removes the bias introduced by restricting the ground truth to boxes for densely segmented data (such as COCO 2014 Detection Challenge [13] or VOT2016 [11]).
3. A compact, easy-to-use, and efficient evaluation scheme for evaluating object trackers that allows a good interpretability of a trackers strengths and weaknesses.

The proposed measure and evaluation scheme is evaluated on a handful of state-of-the-art trackers for the DAVIS [16] and VOT2016 [11] datasets and made available to the community[1].

2   Related Work

In the object detection community, the most commonly used accuracy measure is the Intersection over Union (IoU), also called Pascal overlap or bounding box overlap [8]. It is commonly used as the standard requirement for a correct detection, when the IoU between the predicted detection and the ground truth is at least 0.5 [13].

In the tracking community, many different accuracy measures have been proposed, most of them center-based and overlap-based measures [11,12,15,18, 22,24]. To unify the evaluation of trackers, Čehovin *et al.* [20,22] provide a highly detailed theoretical and experimental analysis of the most popular performance measures and show that many of the accuracy measures are highly correlated. Nevertheless, the appealing property of the IoU measure is that it accounts for both position and size of the prediction and ground truth simultaneously. This has lead to the fact that, in recent years, it has been the most commonly used accuracy measure in the tracking community [11,24]. For example, the VOT2016 [11] evaluation framework uses the IoU as the sole accuracy measure and identifies tracker failures when the IoU between the predicted detection and the ground truth is 0.0 [12].

Since bounding boxes are very crude approximations of objects [13] and cannot accurately capture an object's shape, location, or characteristics, numerous datasets with densely segmented ground truth have emerged. For example, the COCO 2014 dataset [13] includes more than 886,000 densely annotated instances of 80 categories of objects. Nevertheless, on the COCO detection challenge the segmentations are approximated by axis-aligned bounding boxes to simplify the

---

[1] http://www.mvtec.com/company/research/.

evaluation. As stated earlier, this introduces an unwanted bias in the evaluation. A further dataset with excellent pixel accurate segmentations is the DAVIS dataset [16], which was released in 2017. It consists of 50 short sequences of manually segmented objects which, although originally for video object segmentation, can also be used for the evaluation of object trackers. Furthermore, the segmentations used to generate the VOT2016 ground truths have very recently been released [23].

In our work, we enable the evaluation of object detection and tracking algorithms that are restricted to output boxes on densely segmented ground truth data. The proposed approach is easy to add to existing evaluations and improves the precision of the standard IoU accuracy measure.

3   Relative Intersection over Union (rIoU)

Using segmentations for evaluating the accuracy of detectors or trackers removes the bias a bounding-box abstraction induces. Nevertheless, the IoU of a box and an arbitrary segmentation generally does not range from 0 to 1, where the maximum value depends strongly on the objects' shape. For example, in Fig. 1(b) the best possible axis-aligned box only has an IoU of 0.66 with the segmentation.

To enable a more precise measurement of the accuracy, we introduce the relative Intersection over Union (rIoU) of a box $\mathcal{B}$ and a dense segmentation $\mathcal{S}$ as

$$\Phi_{rIoU}(\mathcal{S}, \mathcal{B}) = \frac{\Phi_{IoU}(\mathcal{S}, \mathcal{B})}{\Phi_{opt}(\mathcal{S})}, \qquad (1)$$

where Φ_{IoU} is the Intersection over Union (IoU),

$$\Phi_{IoU}(\mathcal{S}, \mathcal{B}) = \frac{|\mathcal{S} \cap \mathcal{B}|}{|\mathcal{S} \cup \mathcal{B}|}, \qquad (2)$$

and Φ_{opt} is the best possible IoU a box can achieve for the segmentation $\mathcal{S}$. In comparison to the usual IoU (Φ_{IoU}), the rIoU measure (Φ_{rIoU}) truly ranges from 0 to 1 for all possible segmentations. Furthermore, the measure makes it possible to interpret ground truth attributes such as scale change or occlusion, as is displayed later in Sect. 4.

The calculation of Φ_{opt}, required to obtain Φ_{rIoU}, is described in the following section.

3.1   Optimization

An oriented box $\mathcal{B}$ can be parameterized with 5 parameters

$$b = (r_c, c_c, w, h, \phi), \qquad (3)$$

where r_c and c_c denote the row and column of the center, w and h denote the width and height, and ϕ the orientation of the box with respect to the

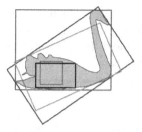

Fig. 2. `blackswan` from DAVIS [16]. The initial values of the optimization process of (4) are displayed. We use the axis-aligned bounding box (green), the oriented bounding box (blue), the inner square of the largest inner circle (magenta), the largest inner axis-aligned box (black) and the oriented box with the same second order moments as the segmentation (orange). (Color figure online)

column-axis. An axis-aligned box can equally be parameterized with the above parameters by fixing the orientation to $0°$.

For a given segmentation $\mathcal{S}$, the box with the best possible IoU is

$$\Phi_{opt}(\mathcal{S}) = \max_b \ \Phi_{IoU}(\mathcal{S}, \mathcal{B}(b)) \qquad s.t. \ b \in \mathbb{R}^4_{>0} \times [0°, 90°). \qquad (4)$$

For a convex segmentation, the above problem can efficiently be optimized with the method of steepest descent. To handle arbitrary, possibly unconnected, segmentations, we optimize (4) with a multi-start gradient descent with a back-tracking line search. The gradient is approximated numerically by the symmetric difference quotient. We use the diverse set of initial values for the optimization process displayed in Fig. 2. The largest axis-aligned inner box (black) and the inner box of the largest inner circle (magenta) are completely within the segmentation. Hence, in the optimization process, they will gradually grow and include background if it improves Φ_{IoU}. On the other hand, the bounding boxes (green and blue) include the complete segmentation and will gradually shrink in the optimization to include less of the segmentation. The oriented box with the same second order moments as the segmentation (orange) serves as an intermediate starting point [17]. Hence, only if the initial values converge to different optima do we need to expend more effort. In these cases, we randomly sample further initial values from the interval spanned by the obtained optima with an added perturbation. In our experiements we used 50 random samples. Although this may lead to many different optimizations, the approach is still very efficient. A single evaluation of $\Phi_{IoU}(\mathcal{S}, \mathcal{B})$ only requires an average of 0.04 ms for the segmentations within the DAVIS [16] dataset in HALCON[2] on an IntelCore i7-4810 CPU @2.8 GHz with 16 GB of RAM with Windows 7 (x64). As a consequence, the optimization of Φ_{opt} requires an average of 1.3 s for the DAVIS [16] and 0.7 s for the VOT2016 [11] segmentations.

The optimization of the IoU for axis-aligned rectangles bears some similarity to the 2D maximum subarray problem [1]. This might make an alternative

---

[2] MVTec Software GmbH, https://www.mvtec.com/.

algorithmic approach to the optimization possible. However, a straightforward adaptation of methods is difficult, since these methods rely on the additive nature of the maximum subarray problem. In contrast, the IoU is inherently non-linear due to the quotient in its definition.

3.2   Validation

To validate the optimization process, we exhaustively searched for the best boxes in a collection of exemplary frames from each of the 50 sequences in the DAVIS dataset [16]. The validation set consists of frames that were challenging for the optimization process. In a first step, we validated the optimization for axis-aligned boxes. The results in Fig. 3 indicate that the optimization is generally very close or identical to the exhaustively determined boxes.

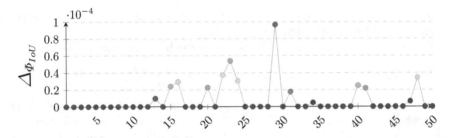

Fig. 3. The absolute difference $\Delta_{\Phi_{IoU}}$ of the exhaustively determined best axis-aligned box and the optimized axis-aligned box for a selected frame in each of the 50 DAVIS [16] sequences. Most boxes are identical, only a handful of boxes are marginally different (<0.0001).

For the oriented boxes, one of the restrictions we can make is that the area must at least be as large as the smallest inner box of the segmentation and may not be larger than the bounding oriented box. Nevertheless, even with further heuristics, the number of candidates to test is in the number of billions for the sequences in the DAVIS dataset. Given a pixel-precise discretization for r_c, c_c, w, h and a 0.5° discretization of ϕ, it was impossible to find boxes with a better IoU than the optimized oriented boxes in the validation set. This is mostly due to the fact that the sub-pixel precision of the parameterization (especially in the angle ϕ) is of paramount importance for the IoU of oriented boxes.

4   Theoretical Trackers

The concept of theoretical trackers was first introduced by Čehovin et al. [22] as an *"excellent interpretation guide in the graphical representation of results"*. In their paper, they use perfectly robust or accurate theoretical trackers to create bounds for the comparison of the performance of different trackers. In our case, we use the boxes with an optimal IoU to create upper bounds for the accuracy

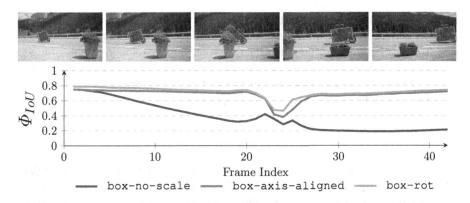

Fig. 4. `motorbike` from DAVIS [16]. The increasing gap between the `box-no-scale` and the other two theoretical trackers indicates a scale change of the motorbike. The drop in all three theoretical trackers around frame 25 indicates that the object is being occluded. The best possible IoU is never above 0.80 for the complete sequence.

of trackers that underlie the box-world assumption. We introduce three theoretical trackers that are obtained by optimizing (4) for a complete sequence. Given the segmentation S, the first tracker returns the best possible axis-aligned box (`box-axis-aligned`), the second tracker returns the optimal oriented box (`box-rot`) and the third tracker returns the optimal axis-aligned box with a fixed scale (`box-no-scale`). The scale is initialized in the first frame with the scale of the box determined by `box-axis-aligned`.

The theoretical tracker can be used to normalize a tracker's IoU for a complete sequence, which enables a fair interpretation of a tracker's accuracy and removes the bias from the box-world assumption. Furthermore, the three different theoretical trackers make it possible to interpret a tracking scene without the need of by-frame labels. As is displayed in Fig. 4, the difference between

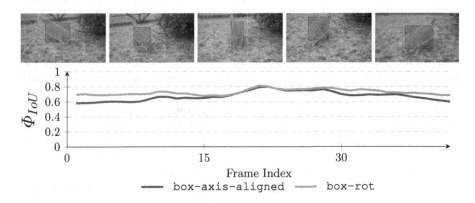

Fig. 5. `dog` from DAVIS [16]. The gaps between the `box-axis-aligned` and `box-rot` tracker indicate a rotation of the otherwise relatively compact segmentation of the dog. The best possible IoU is never above 0.80 for the complete sequence.

the `box-no-scale`, `box-axis-aligned`, and `box-rot` trackers indicates that the object is undergoing a scale change. Furthermore, the decreasing IoUs of all theoretical trackers indicate that the object is either being occluded or deforming to a shape that can be approximated less well by a box. For compact objects, the difference of the `box-rot` tracker and the `box-axis-aligned` tracker indicates a rotation or change of perspective, as displayed in Fig. 5.

5   Experiments

We evaluate the accuracy of a handful of state-of-the art trackers on the DAVIS [16] and VOT2016 [11] datasets with the new rIoU measure. We initialize the trackers with the best possible axis-aligned box for the given segmentation. Since we are primarily interested in the accuracy and not in the trackers robustness, we do not reinitialize the trackers when they move off target. Please note that the accuracy of the robustness measure is also improved when using segmentations; The failure cases (hence $\Phi_{IoU} = 0$) are identified earlier since Φ_{IoU} is zero when the tracker has no overlap with the segmentation and not with a bounding box abstraction of the object (which may contain a large amount of background, see, e.g., Fig. 1).

We restrict our evaluation to the handful of (open source) state-of-the-art trackers displayed in Table 1. A thorough evaluation and comparison of all top ranking trackers is beyond the scope of this paper. The evaluation framework is made available and constructed such that it is easy to add new trackers from MATLAB[3], Python[4] or HALCON.

We include the Kernelized Correlation Filter (KCF) [9] tracker since it was a top ranked tracker in the VOT2014 challenge even though it assumes the scale of the object to stay constant. The Discriminative Scale Space Tracker (DSST) [6] tracker is essentially an extension of KCF that can handle scale changes and outperformed the KCF by a small margin in the VOT2014 challenge. As further axis-aligned trackers, we include ANT [21], L1APG [2], and the best performing tracker from the VOT2016 challenge, the continuous convolution filters (CCOT) from Danelljan *et al.* [7]. We include the LGT [19] as one of the few open source trackers that estimates the object position as an oriented box.

In Table 1, we compare the average IoU with the average rIoU for the DAVIS and the VOT2016 datasets. Please note that we normalize each tracker with the IoU of the theoretical tracker that has the same abilities. Hence, the KCF tracker is normalized with the `box-no-scale` tracker, the LGT tracker with `box-rot`, and the others with `box-axis-aligned`. By these means, it is possible to observe how well each tracker is doing with respect to its abilities. For the DAVIS dataset, the KCF, ANT, L1APG, and LGT trackers all have the same absolute IoU, but when normalized by Φ_{opt}, differences are visible. Hence, it is evident that the KCF is performing very well, given the fact that it does not estimate the scale. On the other hand, the LGT tracker, which has three more

---

[3] The MathWorks, Inc., https://www.mathworks.com/.
[4] Python Software Foundation, https://www.python.org/.

Table 1. Comparison of different tracking approaches and their average absolute (Φ_{IoU}) and relative IoU (Φ_{rIoU}) for the DAVIS [16] and the VOT2016 [11] segmentations

	DAVIS		VOT2016	
	Φ_{IoU}	Φ_{rIoU}	Φ_{IoU}	Φ_{rIoU}
Axis-aligned boxes (fixed scale)				
KCF [9]	0.40	**0.78**	0.23	0.45
Axis-aligned boxes				
DSST [6]	0.43	0.67	0.24	0.32
CCOT [7]	**0.47**	0.73	**0.41**	**0.56**
ANT [21]	0.40	0.64	0.26	0.37
L1APG [2]	0.40	0.63	0.18	0.25
Oriented boxes				
LGT [19]	0.40	0.60	0.25	0.34

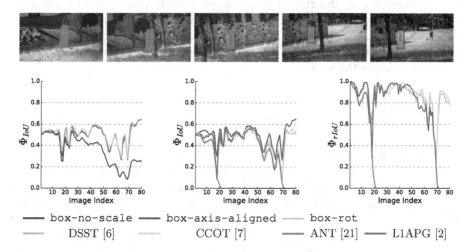

Fig. 6. `bmx-trees` from DAVIS [16]. On the left, differences between `box-no-scale` and `box-axis-aligned` indicate that the object is changing scale and is occluded at frame 18 and around frames 60–70. In the middle plot, we compare the IoU of the axis-aligned box trackers and `box-axis-aligned`. The corresponding rIoU plot is shown on the right. It becomes evident that the ANT tracker fails when the object is occluded for the first time and the L1APG tracker at the second occlusion. The rIoU shows that DSST and CCOT perform well, while the IoU would imply they are weak.

degrees of freedom, is relatively weak. A more detailed example analysis of the `bmx-trees` sequence from DAVIS [16] is displayed in Fig. 6. Please note, the significantly higher difference between the IoU and the rIoU for KCF compared to the other trackers is due to the different normalization factors used in the rIoU measure. The optimal IoU value for a box with fixed size is usually considerably lower than for a general axis-aligned box.

(a) car1   (b) hand   (c) singer2   (d) fish3

Fig. 7. Examples from VOT2016 [11] where the segmentations are degenerated. Sometimes due to motion blur (e.g., (a) and (b)) or a weak contrast of the object and its background (c). (Color figure online)

For the VOT2016 dataset, the overall accuracies are significantly worse than for DAVIS. On the one hand, this is due to the longer, more difficult sequences, and, on the other hand, due to the less accurate and noisier segmentations (see Fig. 7). Nevertheless, the rIoU allows a more reliable comparison of different trackers. For example, ANT, LGT and DSST have almost equal average IoU value, while ANT clearly outperforms LGT and DSST with respect to rIoU. Again, we can see that the KCF tracker is quite strong regarding the fact that it cannot estimate the scale.

6   Conclusion

In this paper, we have proposed a new accuracy measure that closes the gap between densely segmented ground truths and box detectors and trackers. We have presented an efficient optimization scheme to obtain the best possible detection boxes for arbitrary segmentations that are required for the new measure. The optimization was validated on a diverse set of segmentations from the DAVIS dataset [16]. The new accuracy measure can be used to generate three very expressive theoretical trackers, which can be used to obtain meaningful accuracies and help to interpret scenes without requiring by-frame labels. We have evaluated state-of-the-art trackers with the new accuracy measure on all segmentations within the DAVIS [16] and VOT2016 [11] datasets to display its advantages. The complete code and evaluation system will be made available to the community to encourage its use and make it easy to reproduce our results.

References

1. An, S., Peursum, P., Liu, W., Venkatesh, S.: Efficient algorithms for subwindow search in object detection and localization. In: 2009 IEEE Conference on Computer Vision and Pattern Recognition, pp. 264–271, June 2009
2. Bao, C., Yi, W., Ling, H., Ji, H.: Real time robust L1 tracker using accelerated proximal gradient approach. In: IEEE Conference on Computer Vision and Pattern Recognition, pp. 1830–1837 (2012)

3. Böttger, T., Eisenhofer, C.: Efficiently tracking extremal regions in multichannel images. In: International Conference on Pattern Recognition Systems (ICPRS) (2017)

4. Böttger, T., Ulrich, M., Steger, C.: Subpixel-precise tracking of rigid objects in real-time. In: Sharma, P., Bianchi, F.M. (eds.) SCIA 2017. LNCS, vol. 10269, pp. 54–65. Springer, Cham (2017). doi:10.1007/978-3-319-59126-1_5

5. Caelles, S., Maninis, K.-K., Pont-Tuset, J., Leal-Taixé, L., Cremers, D., Van Gool, L.: One-shot video object segmentation. In: IEEE Conference on Computer Vision and Pattern Recognition (2017)

6. Danelljan, M., Häger, G., Khan, F.S., Felsberg, M.: Accurate scale estimation for robust visual tracking. In: British Machine Vision Conference (2014)

7. Danelljan, M., Robinson, A., Shahbaz Khan, F., Felsberg, M.: Beyond correlation filters: learning continuous convolution operators for visual tracking. In: Leibe, B., Matas, J., Sebe, N., Welling, M. (eds.) ECCV 2016. LNCS, vol. 9909, pp. 472–488. Springer, Cham (2016). doi:10.1007/978-3-319-46454-1_29

8. Everingham, M., Ali Eslami, S.M., Van Gool, L.J., Williams, C.K.I., Winn, J.M., Zisserman, A.: The pascal visual object classes challenge: a retrospective. Int. J. Comput. Vis. 111(1), 98–136 (2015)

9. Henriques, J.F., Caseiro, R., Martins, P., Batista, J.: High-speed tracking with kernelized correlation filters. IEEE Trans. Pattern Anal. Mach. Intell. 37(3), 583–596 (2015)

10. Juránek, R., Herout, A., Dubská, M., Zemcík, P.: Real-time pose estimation piggybacked on object detection. In: IEEE International Conference on Computer Vision, pp. 2381–2389 (2015)

11. Kristan, M., et al.: The visual object tracking VOT2016 challenge results. In: Hua, G., Jégou, H. (eds.) ECCV 2016. LNCS, vol. 9914, pp. 777–823. Springer, Cham (2016). doi:10.1007/978-3-319-48881-3_54

12. Kristan, M., Matas, J., Leonardis, A., Vojír, T., Pflugfelder, R.P., Fernández, G., Nebehay, G., Porikli, F., Čehovin, L.: A novel performance evaluation methodology for single-target trackers. IEEE Trans. Pattern Anal. Mach. Intell. 38(11), 2137–2155 (2016)

13. Lin, T.-Y., Maire, M., Belongie, S., Hays, J., Perona, P., Ramanan, D., Dollár, P., Zitnick, C.L.: Microsoft COCO: common objects in context. In: Fleet, D., Pajdla, T., Schiele, B., Tuytelaars, T. (eds.) ECCV 2014. LNCS, vol. 8693, pp. 740–755. Springer, Cham (2014). doi:10.1007/978-3-319-10602-1_48

14. Milan, A., Leal-Taixé, L., Reid, I., Roth, S., Schindler, K.: MOT16: a benchmark for multi-object tracking. arXiv:1603.00831 [cs], March 2016

15. Nawaz, T., Cavallaro, A.: A protocol for evaluating video trackers under real-world conditions. IEEE Trans. Image Process. 22(4), 1354–1361 (2013)

16. Perazzi, F., Jordi Pont-Tuset, B., McWilliams, L.J., Gool, V., Gross, M.H., Sorkine-Hornung, A.: A benchmark dataset and evaluation methodology for video object segmentation. In: IEEE Conference on Computer Vision and Pattern Recognition, pp. 724–732 (2016)

17. Rosin, P.L.: Measuring rectangularity. Mach. Vis. Appl. 11(4), 191–196 (1999)

18. Smeulders, A.W.M., Chu, D.M., Cucchiara, R., Calderara, S., Dehghan, A., Shah, M.: Visual tracking: an experimental survey. IEEE Trans. Pattern Anal. Mach. Intell. 36(7), 1442–1468 (2014)

19. Čehovin, L., Kristan, M., Leonardis, A.: Robust visual tracking using an adaptive coupled-layer visual model. IEEE Trans. Pattern Anal. Mach. Intell. 35(4), 941–953 (2013)

20. Čehovin, L., Kristan, M., Leonardis, A.: Is my new tracker really better than yours? In: IEEE Winter Conference on Applications of Computer Vision, pp. 540–547 (2014)
21. Čehovin, L., Leonardis, A., Kristan, M.: Robust visual tracking using template anchors. In: IEEE Winter Conference on Applications of Computer Vision, pp. 1–8 (2016)
22. Čehovin, L., Leonardis, A., Kristan, M.: Visual object tracking performance measures revisited. IEEE Trans. Image Process. **25**(3), 1261–1274 (2016)
23. Vojir, T., Matas, J.: Pixel-wise object segmentations for the VOT 2016 dataset. Research report CTU-CMP-2017-01, Center for Machine Perception, Czech Technical University, Prague, Czech Republic, January 2017
24. Yi, W., Lim, J., Yang, M.-H.: Object tracking benchmark. IEEE Trans. Pattern Anal. Mach. Intell. **37**(9), 1834–1848 (2015)

Author Index

Printed in the United States
By Bookmasters